The Paradoxical Brain

The Paradoxical Brain

Edited by
Narinder Kapur

with

Alvaro Pascual-Leone
Vilayanur Ramachandran
Jonathan Cole
Sergio Della Sala
Tom Manly
Andrew Mayes

CAMBRIDGE
UNIVERSITY PRESS

CAMBRIDGE UNIVERSITY PRESS
Cambridge, New York, Melbourne, Madrid, Cape Town,
Singapore, São Paulo, Delhi, Tokyo, Mexico City

Cambridge University Press
The Edinburgh Building, Cambridge CB2 8RU, UK

Published in the United States of America by
Cambridge University Press, New York

www.cambridge.org
Information on this title: www.cambridge.org/9780521115575

First published 2011

Printed in the United Kingdom at the University Press, Cambridge

A catalogue record for this publication is available from the British Library

Library of Congress Cataloging-in-Publication Data
The paradoxical brain / edited by Narinder Kapur ; with Alvaro
Pascual-Leone, Vilayanur Ramachandran, Jonathan Cole, Sergio Della Sala,
Tom Manly, Andrew Mayes.
    p. ; cm.
Includes bibliographical references and index.
ISBN 978-0-521-11557-5 (hbk.)
1. Brain. 2. Neurophysiology. 3. Brain–Diseases.
4. Paradox. I. Kapur, Narinder, editor.
[DNLM: 1. Brain–physiology. 2. Brain Diseases.
3. Cognition. 4. Mental Disorders. 5. Neurosciences–methods.
WL 300]
    QP376.P345 2011
    612.8′2–dc22

                                                                    2010050211

ISBN 978-0-521-11557-5 Hardback

In the spirit of the later writings of the only neuropsychologist to win the Nobel Prize, Roger Sperry (1913–1994), this book is dedicated to the memory of Mahatma Gandhi (1869–1948), who viewed his life as one of a scientist, carrying out experiments in Truth, Love and Self-Denial.

Contents

Contents

Acknowledgements

I am grateful to a number of individuals for their support in producing this book. Firstly, and most importantly, I am grateful to the contributors of the chapters who agreed to write such excellent articles in the context of what for most of them must have been very busy schedules, with many competing demands. They were asked to provide a novel perspective on research findings in their field, and they all showed an admirable commitment in taking up this challenge.

My editorial support team (Alvaro Pascual-Leone, Vilayanur Ramachandran, Jonathan Cole, Sergio Della Sala, Tom Manly, Andrew Mayes) is listed on the front cover of the book, and I could not have managed without them.

I am particularly grateful to Jonathan Cole for his priceless and timely comments over many months on the drafts of every chapter. I am indebted to Tom Manly for the weekly sessions we had together, where his advice was illuminating and indispensable. Jonathan and Tom contributed many hours of their time on the book, and their input helped to shape both the chapters and the book itself in innumerable ways.

Alvaro Pascual-Leone provided advice and encouragement in the early stages of the project. I am also grateful to the original anonymous book proposal reviewers, who made helpful comments at the early stages of conception and planning of the project. Itiel Dror, one of the contributors to the book, kindly introduced me to the work of Escher, whose drawing forms part of the front cover to the book, and Cai Wingfield also helped with this cover.

I was fortunate to have general and specific comments on individual chapters from expert referees. I would like to thank Alan Baddeley, Roger Barker, German Berrios, Richard Bond, Carol Brayne, Tim Bussey, John Duncan, James Fawcett, Katerina Fotopoulou, Karl Friston, Chris Frith, Uta Frith, Fernand Gobet, Usha Goswami, Jordan Grafman, Rik Henson, Joe Herbert, Lee Illis, Gerd Kempermann, Franco Lepore, Paresh Malhotra, Roz McCarthy, Pat Rabbitt, Edwin Robertson, Allan Scott, Julie Snowden, Ed Wasserman, Roy Weller, Barbara Wilson, Andy Young and Adam Zeman.

I am grateful to Oliver Sacks for kindly writing a Foreword to the book.

I thank Richard Marley of Cambridge University Press for his advice and support throughout the various stages of this book, and also Katie James of Cambridge University Press for her input during the production phase of the book.

I thank those organizations and individuals who gave permission to reproduce items in question. If there are any individuals or organizations whom I have left out, my apologies and please let me know, so that any errors can be corrected in a future printing of the book.

Cambridge in England is an ideal environment in which to generate academic ideas and dreams, and in which to turn them into reality. The resources available to me in my particular neurosciences setting were only made possible by the dedicated, outstanding endeavours over the years of a number of key individuals in Cambridge, in particular Alastair Compston and John Pickard. It is also impossible to produce a book of this type without having good computing support at hand, and I am grateful to Simon Jones and Tulasi Marrapu for providing this support. My assistant, Kayleigh Kew, helped in a variety of ways, too many to mention. I also thank the other members of my department for their assistance – Fiona Aschmann, Georgina Browne and Mariella Gregori. I have also been fortunate to retain my chair in Neuropsychology at the University of Southampton, and I thank both that university and my colleagues in the Department of Psychology for providing facilities that enabled me to carry out background research for the book and to support my funding of elements of the book.

My apologies to anyone I may have left out in the above listing.

When producing a major piece of work, it is right and customary to thank past colleagues who have directly or indirectly influenced the paths and destinations of professional and scientific journeys – I would like to thank, in memory, Nelson Butters, Laird Cermak, Harold Goodglass, Derek Gordon, John Graham-White, Alan Parkin and George Seth.

Compared to the original caveman, we live in an interdependent world, whereby practically everything that touches our daily existence is only made possible by the efforts of thousands of other people, past or present. I would like to acknowledge the resourcefulness and the kindness of the United States government and people, in making PubMed and similar academic resources freely available to citizens throughout the world. I would also like to acknowledge the genius and generosity of Sir Tim Berners-Lee and his colleague Robert Cailliau in developing the tools that allowed the internet to become a reality and a *modus operandi* through which resources such as PubMed could freely and easily operate.

I am grateful to Dr B. K. Sharma for arranging for my share of royalties from sales of this book to go to the Gwalior Children's Hospital near Delhi, India.

Finally, I thank my wife Ritu and my children Sarina, Soniya and Shashi for their love and support, and for putting up with my absences.

Narinder Kapur

Preface

The study of the human brain has been variously referred to as 'the last great frontier', or a challenge equivalent to that of understanding the universe. Cosmology and neuroscience, in fact, probably have some things in common. Our galaxy, the Milky Way, has thousands of millions of stars, and some commentators have conjectured that the number of stars in the Milky Way may be similar to the number of cells in the human brain. In the past two decades, imaging and sensing technologies have transformed both the field of neuroscience and the field of cosmology. Perhaps a more interesting analogy is in the realm of awareness and human consciousness. With our current awareness mechanisms, we are usually only aware of a tiny amount of cognitive activity that mediates human behaviour – many cognitive and perceptual inferences take place at an unconscious level, we often fail to realize how our perceptions and beliefs may not be completely based on reality, and we often fool ourselves into believing that we have free will and full responsibility for all our thoughts and actions (Frith, 2007). Similarly, in the case of cosmology, with our eyes alone we are only aware of a tiny part of our galaxy, and if we were to take our perceptions literally, we would fall for the simple delusion that the sun moves round the earth.

The human brain, in its present form, seems to have evolved over the past few hundred thousand years, and it is open to debate whether it is still evolving or will remain in its current state, either after a further few hundred thousand years, or towards the end of the existence of the planet (Renfrew *et al.*, 2009). To date, the great achievements of mankind, and many of the great disasters of mankind, are probably directly or indirectly attributable in large measure to the workings of the human brain. It is likely that future achievements and calamities will also be largely due to activities of human beings that emanate from either the brilliance or the frailties of the human brain. To the extent that we can reach a better understanding of how the brain operates, its strengths and its limitations (Rees, 2008a), and how its operations may be modified for the benefit of the individual and of mankind, then it lies within the grasp of experimental and clinical neuroscientists to contribute to the welfare of humanity, and to help meet many of the daunting challenges that face human civilization (Rees, 2008b). From the perspective of the psychological sciences, here too there are major endeavours which can potentially bring about 'greater good' across a range of global issues (Miller, 1969; McKay, 2008). The only neuropsychologist to win the Nobel Prize, Roger Sperry, explored such topics in some of his last writings:

> The outlines of a value-belief system emerge that include an ultimate respect for nature and the evolving quality of the biosphere, which, if implemented, would set in motion the kind of social change needed to lead us out of the vicious spirals of increasing population, pollution, poverty, energy demands, etc. The strategic importance of neuroscience and the central role of prevailing concepts of the mind–brain relation to all of the foregoing remain evident throughout, as does also the direct relevance of efforts to bring added insight and substantiation of these mind--brain concepts through further advances in brain research. (Sperry, 1981, p. 15)

This book aims to contribute to an understanding of the human brain from a novel perspective. The book is based on the premise that studying anomalies, the counterintuitive and the paradoxical may shed light on the workings of the human brain (cf. Ramachandran, 2006). Therefore, I have put together, for the first time in one volume, contributions from a range of researchers who have focused on paradoxical phenomena associated with the human brain. From the perspective of experimental neuroscience, Karl Pribram (1971) helped to set the scene by pointing out a number of paradoxes in more basic neuropsychological studies. From the perspective of clinical neurology, Oliver Sacks has also set the stage for this book by his own innovative and stimulating works and titles (Sacks, 1985, 1995, 2007), including one title (*An Anthropologist on Mars*) with a 'paradoxical' subheading (Sacks, 1995). Sacks has eloquently noted

> nature's richness is to be studied in the phenomena of health and disease, in the endless forms of individual adaptation by which human organisms, people, adapt and reconstruct themselves, faced with the challenges and vicissitudes of life. Defects, disorders, diseases, in this sense, can play a paradoxical role, by bringing out latent powers, developments, evolutions, forms of life, that might never be seen, or even be imaginable, in their absence. It is the paradox of disease, in this sense, its 'creative' potential, that forms the central theme of this book. (Sacks, 1995, p. xii)

I fully accept that some of the content of this book is speculative, and may throw up more questions than answers. One of the primary purposes of this book is to raise questions, rather than to offer answers, and I will have achieved my goal if new questions and new methodologies have been brought to the minds of readers, both in the realm of a theoretical understanding of the human brain and in the realm of therapy for the human brain. In an emerging field, it is sometimes difficult to know when best to take stock and marshal evidence and viewpoints, but I feel that this is a timely opportunity in the light of recent findings and advances, both in neuroscience and in psychology. In addition to drawing attention to new or somewhat neglected experimental and clinical observations, I hope that the book will encourage new ways of thinking of established findings. 'The important thing in science is not so much to obtain new facts as to discover new ways of thinking about them', once remarked the British scientist William L. Bragg, who was awarded the 1915 Nobel Laureate in Physics.

The two main aims in writing this book are first, to provide evidence and to suggest questions and methodologies that clinical and experimental neuroscientists may wish to consider in their journeys to understanding the workings of the human brain, while at the same time disseminating to a wider audience of clinicians and students the evidence and ideas that are the substance of this volume; second, to point to avenues by which the human condition may be improved – whether this be in the healthy population or in those with brain disorders.

I hope that the book will lead to a change in how we view the brain, and that the brain will now be seen as a dynamic, nonlinear and highly plastic device, rather than as a static, linear and rigid entity. I hope that this book will encourage more 'out-of-the-box', lateral thinking as to how the brain operates and how it can be repaired. I also hope that the book will encourage a more enlightened view of people whose brains, in one form or other, fall outside the norm, whether it be due to acquired brain pathology or due to developmental or genetic factors. Many of the findings in this book suggest that we should view such individuals as 'brain different', rather than 'brain damaged', that we should look at their positive coping strategies rather than their deficits and disabilities, and that we should focus on their achievements rather than their handicaps.

In his essay, *The Habit of Truth*, Jacob Bronowski (1961) alludes to three stages in 'the discovery of things' – assembling data, putting the data into order, and producing a conceptual framework around the ordered data. I hope that in this scientific endeavour

I have been successful in the first two stages, and I appreciate that I have only made a humble beginning to the third stage.

This book marks the end of a 20-year journey in which I have viewed the beautiful and inspiring landscapes of paradoxes in brain and behaviour. The duration of this journey is possibly similar to one that might involve human exploration of the far reaches of the Milky Way Galaxy – perhaps this analogy is not too far-fetched if one accepts the folklore that there are a similar number of stars in the galaxy as there are cells in the human brain! Such a journey would not of course have been possible without the dedicated efforts of those researchers who cultivated the findings which adorned the landscapes along my journey, and I thank them for their dedication. 'I have attempted to blaze a track through the jungle, but make no pretence at having reached the end of the journey. I can only hope that some ardent and adventurous spirit may follow my path', wrote Sir Henry Head, the eminent British neurologist in the preface to his treatise on aphasia (Head, 1926, p. x). I hope that 'some ardent and adventurous spirits' may take up the reins and pursue some of the paradoxes highlighted in this book.

Narinder Kapur

References

Bronowski, J. (1961). *Science and Human Values*. London: Hutchinson Press.

Frith, C. (2007). *Making up the Mind*. Oxford: Blackwell Publishing.

Head, H. (1926). *Aphasia and Kindred Disorders of Speech. Volume 1*. Cambridge: Cambridge University Press.

McKay, T. (2008). Can Psychology change the world? *The Psychologist*, **21**: 928–31.

Miller, G. (1969). Psychology as a means of promoting human welfare. *American Psychologist*, **24**: 1063–75.

Pribram, K. H. (1971). *Languages of the Brain: Experimental Paradoxes and Principles in Neuropsychology*. New York, NY: Prentice-Hall.

Ramachandran, V. S. (2006). Creativity versus skepticism within science. *Skeptical Inquirer*, **30**: 48–51.

Rees, M. (2008a). Interview with BBC Religious Affairs Programme on topic of Belief. April 13, 2008. www.bbc.co.uk/religion/programmes/belief

Rees, M. (2008b). Ditchley Foundation Annual Lecture, XLVI, July 12, 2008. www.ditchley.co.uk/page/331/ditchley-lecture-xliv.htm

Renfrew C et al. (2009). *The Sapient Mind: Archaeology meets Neuroscience*. London: The Royal Society.

Sacks, O. (1985). *The Man Who Mistook His Wife for a Hat*. London: Duckworth.

Sacks, O. (1995). *An Anthropologist on Mars. Seven Paradoxical Tales*. London: Picador.

Sacks, O. (2007). *Musicophilia. Tales of Music and the Brain*. London: Picador.

Sperry, R. (1981). Changing priorities. *Annual Review of Neuroscience*, **4**: 1–15.

Foreword

Damage to any part of the body, if severe enough, can cause a corresponding loss of function: cardiac failure, liver failure, renal failure, etc. That this could also occur with specific areas of the brain was supported, in the 1860s, by Broca's demonstration that damage to a particular area of the left frontal lobe led to expressive aphasia – an indication, he felt, that this area constituted a 'centre' for speech. Classical neurology was founded on this deficit/lesion model, and the clinico-pathological method remains the foundation of neurology today. Indeed, in the last few decades, it has flourished, with the added power of brain imaging, which makes it possible to visualize brain lesions and their effects in living patients.

But there have been dissenting voices from the start – in particular, that of Hughlings Jackson, who also studied aphasic patients, but came to think that Broca's view of aphasia – as no more than a loss of function – was inadequate. The loss of speech, Hughlings Jackson emphasized, was never the sole symptom in aphasia; there were always 'positive' ones as well, which were unmasked or released as a consequence of the lesion; one of his papers, for example, was entitled 'Singing by Speechless (Aphasic) Children' (Jackson, 1871). In his 1884 Croonian Lectures on 'Evolution and Dissolution of the Nervous System', Jackson wrote, 'The symptomatology of nervous diseases is a double condition; there is a negative and there is a positive element in every case' (1884, p. 591).

He saw the brain as having many functional levels, developed in the course of evolution and hierarchically arranged, with activity at higher levels making use of, but also restraining, the activities of lower levels. For Jackson (and for Freud, an ardent Jacksonian, a few years later), the brain was not a static mosaic of fixed representations or points, but incessantly active, with certain potentials being actively suppressed or inhibited in a dynamic balance – potentials that could be 'released' if this inhibition was lifted. Among such release phenomena, Jackson included epilepsy and chorea (and Freud the violent affects and impulses of the 'id', if it was uncapped by psychosis).

Hughlings Jackson's views were largely ignored in his own time, as were attempts to reintroduce them (as when Henry Head published a collection of Jackson's articles soon after his death).

In the 1960s and 1970s, the notion of release phenomena was resurrected in regard to hallucinations, especially the visual hallucinations of those who had lost their sight, or had grossly impaired vision. It became clear that visual perception itself was necessary to keep the brain's visual mechanisms in order, and that in the absence of perception, there might be an eruption of images and patterns generated by unbridled, autonomous activity in the visual cortex. While visual hallucinations occur in only a minority of visually impaired people, there is, in almost all of them, a widespread activation of the visual cortex which may lead to exceptional powers of visualization or visual imagery, or to visual areas becoming available for nonvisual processing (reading Braille, for instance, or enhanced auditory sensitivity). These 'paradoxical' heightenings may be maladaptive, or they may be highly adaptive and useful to the individual, and it is especially in relation to these that Kapur speaks of 'paradoxical functional facilitation' (although the term has many other connotations too).

There has long been a tendency to see neurological damage or disease as 'incurable', or treatable only to the extent that there is spontaneous recovery (as from a stroke), removal of a pathology (such as a tumour), or replenishment of something that is deficient (as with giving dopamine precursors to patients with Parkinsonism). However, it is equally important to see what is preserved and even heightened in neurological syndromes – the 'positive' elements that Hughlings Jackson spoke of – and to see these as allowing unexpected compensations and therapeutic powers. Thus, for example, the ability or propensity of aphasic patients to sing can be channelled and used therapeutically (as in music therapy or melodic intonation therapy for aphasic patients).

The great Soviet neuropsychologist Lev Vygotsky, almost a century ago (Vygotsky, 1929), emphasized the importance of positive abilities – what Kapur calls 'paradoxical functional facilitation' – in those who had no vision:

> Blindness is not merely the absence of sight . . . [it] causes a total restructuring of all the strengths of both organism and personality. Blindness, in creating a new, unique cast of personality, brings to life new forces . . . It creatively and organically remakes and forms a person's mind. Consequently, blindness is not merely a defect, a minus, a weakness, but in some sense also the source of manifestations of abilities, a plus, a strength (however strange or paradoxical this may seem!).

In *The Paradoxical Brain*, Narinder Kapur has expanded this concept to cover many areas in neurology, neuroscience and neurorehabilitation, assembling a diverse and comprehensive group of world-class experts to explore the concept of paradox in many different disciplines. Their experience and ideas are of fundamental importance and deserve close attention from all who deal with disorders of brain function, so that we may focus on the uniqueness of the individual and their positive potentials, rather than thinking solely in terms of disorder.

Oliver Sacks

References

Jackson, H. (1871). Singing by speechless (aphasic) children. *The Lancet*, **98**: 430–1.

Jackson, H. (1884). The Croonian lectures on evolution and dissolution of the nervous system. *British Medical Journal*, **1**: 591–3.

Vygotsky, L. S., Rieber, R. W., & Carton, A. S. (Eds). (1993). *The Collected Works of L.S. Vygotsky, Volume 2, The Fundamentals of Defectology*. New York, NY: Springer, p. 97 [1929, republished in 1993].

Author affiliations

Aarts, Esther
Center for Cognitive Neuroimaging,
Donders Institute for Brain, Cognition and
Behaviour, Radboud University, Nijmegen,
The Netherlands
*Chapter 23 – Paradoxical effects of drugs on
cognitive function* pp. 397–417

Ashwin, Chris
Autism Research Centre, University of
Cambridge, Cambridge, UK
Chapter 15 – The paradox of autism
pp. 274–288

Ashwin, Emma
Autism Research Centre, University of
Cambridge, Cambridge, UK
Chapter 15 – The paradox of autism
pp. 274–288

Bajbouj, Malek
Head of the Affective Neuroscience and
Emotion Modulation Research Group,
Charité, University Medicine, Berlin,
Germany
*Chapter 18 – The paradox of
electroconvulsive therapy* pp. 321–331

Baron-Cohen, Simon
Professor, Director of Autism Research
Centre, University of Cambridge,
Cambridge, UK
Chapter 15 – The paradox of autism
pp. 274–288

Brown, Peter
Sobell Department of Motor Neuroscience
and Movement, Institute of Neurology,
London, UK
*Chapter 10 – Paradoxes in Parkinson's
disease and other movement disorders*
pp. 189–203

Butler, Andrew C.
Research Associate, Duke University,
Durham, NC, USA
*Chapter 8 – Paradoxes of learning and
memory* pp. 151–176

Chakrabarti, Bhismadev
Senior Researcher, Autism Research
Centre, University of Cambridge,
Cambridge, UK
Chapter 15 – The paradox of autism
pp. 274–288

Cole, Jonathan
Honorary Senior Lecturer in Clinical
Neurosciences, University of Southampton,
Professor, University of Bournemouth and
Consultant in Clinical Neurophysiology,
Poole and Salisbury Hospitals, Poole
Hospital, UK
*Chapter 1 – The paradoxical nature of
nature* pp. 1–13
*Chapter 24 – The paradoxical brain – so
what?* pp. 418–434

Cools, Roshan
Center for Cognitive Neuroimaging,
Donders Institute for Brain, Cognition and
Behaviour, Radboud University, Nijmegen,
The Netherlands
*Chapter 23 – Paradoxical effects of drugs on
cognitive function* pp. 397–417

Dror, Itiel E.
Institute of Cognitive Neuroscience,
University College London, London, UK
Chapter 9 – The paradox of human expertise
pp. 177–188

Eichenbaum, Howard
Professor, Boston University, Center for
Memory and Brain, Boston, MA, USA

Chapter 22 – The paradoxical hippocampus pp. 379–396

Fisher, James L.
Research Scientist, Ohio State University, Ohio, USA
Chapter 14 – Unexpected benefits of allergies and cigarette smoking pp. 261–273

Ghazanfar, Asif A.
Assistant Professor, Neuroscience Institute and Department of Psychology, Princeton University, Princeton, NJ, USA
Chapter 6 – Paradoxical psychological functioning in early child development pp. 110–129

Goldstein, David
Professor of Psychology, University of Toronto, ON, Canada
Chapter 7 – Cognitive ageing pp. 130–150

Hasher, Lynn
Professor, Department of Psychology, University of Toronto, ON, Canada
Chapter 7 – Cognitive ageing pp. 130–150

Hirstein, William
Professor of Philosophy, Elmhurst College, Elmhurst, IL, USA
Chapter 5 – The paradoxical self pp. 94–109

Hughes, Howard C.
Professor, Department of Psychological and Brain Sciences, Dartmouth College, Hanover, NH, USA
Chapter 19 – Paradoxes of comparative cognition pp. 332–349

Hurlow, Jonathan
Institute of Psychiatry, Kings College, London, UK
Chapter 16 – Paradoxes in creativity and psychiatric conditions pp. 289–300

Jha, Ashwani
Sobell Department of Motor Neuroscience and Movement, Institute of Neurology, London, UK

Chapter 10 – Paradoxes in Parkinson's disease and other movement disorders pp. 189–203

Kapur, Narinder
Visiting Professor of Neuropsychology, University College London;
Honorary Professor of Neuropsychology, University of Southampton; formerly Head of the Neuropsychology Department, Addenbrooke's Hospital, Cambridge, UK
Chapter 1 – The paradoxical nature of nature pp. 1–13
Chapter 3 – Paradoxical functional facilitation and recovery. . . pp. 40–73
Chapter 4 – Paradoxes in neurorehabilitation pp. 74–93
Chapter 14 – Unexpected benefits of allergies and cigarette smoking pp. 261–273
Chapter 24 – The paradoxical brain – so what? pp. 418–434

Karavodin, Linda
Principal Consultant at Karavodin Preclinical Consulting
Chapter 14 – Unexpected benefits of allergies and cigarette smoking pp. 261–273

Kolb, Bryan
Canadian Centre for Behavioural Neuroscience, University of Lethbridge, Alberta, Canada
Chapter 20 – Paradoxical phenomena in brain plasticity pp. 350–364

Lewkowicz, David J.
Professor, Florida Atlantic University, Boca Raton, FL, USA
Chapter 6 – Paradoxical psychological functioning in early child development pp. 110–129

MacCabe, James H.
Senior Lecturer and Honorary Consultant Psychiatrist, National Psychosis Unit, Section of General Psychiatry, Institute of Psychiatry, London, UK

Chapter 16 – Paradoxes in creativity and psychiatric conditions pp. 289–300

Manly, Tom
Research Scientist, MRC Cognition and Brain Sciences Unit, Cambridge, UK
Chapter 1 – The paradoxical nature of nature pp. 1–13
Chapter 4 – Paradoxes in neurorehabilitation pp. 74–93
Chapter 24 – The paradoxical brain – so what? pp. 418–434

Mehta, Mitul A.
PET Psychiatry Group, MRC Clinical Sciences Centre, Institute of Psychiatry, Kings College, London, UK
Chapter 23 – Paradoxical effects of drugs on cognitive function pp. 397–417

Merabet, Lotfi B.
Berenson-Allen Center for Noninvasive Brain Stimulation, Beth Israel Deaconess Medical Center, Harvard Medical School, Boston, MA, USA
Chapter 2 – Paradoxical effects of sensory loss pp. 14–39

Merkl, Angela
Charité, University Medicine, Berlin, Germany
Chapter 18 – The paradox of electroconvulsive therapy pp. 321–331

Miller, Bruce L.
A. W. Clausen Distinguished Professor of Neurology, University of California, San Francisco, CA, USA
Chapter 12 – Paradoxical creativity and adjustment in neurological conditions pp. 221–233

Najib, Umer
Clinical Research Fellow, Department of Medicine, Division of Allergy and Inflammation, Beth Israel Deaconess Medical Center, Harvard Medical School, Boston, MA, USA
Chapter 13 – Paradoxical functional

facilitation with noninvasive brain stimulation pp. 234–260

Obretenova, Souzana
Research Assistant, Berenson-Allen Center for Noninvasive Brain Stimulation, Beth Israel Medical Center, Boston, MA, USA
Chapter 2 – Paradoxical effects of sensory loss pp. 14–39

Pascual-Leone, Alvaro
Berenson-Allen Center for Noninvasive Brain Stimulation, Beth Israel Deaconess Medical Center, Harvard Medical School, Boston, MA, USA
Chapter 1 – The paradoxical nature of nature pp. 1–13
Chapter 2 – Paradoxical effects of sensory loss pp. 14–39
Chapter 13 – Paradoxical functional facilitation with noninvasive brain stimulation pp. 234–260
Chapter 24 – The paradoxical brain – so what? pp. 418–434

Ramachandran, Vilayanur
Professor, Center for Brain and Cognition, University of California, San Diego, CA, USA
Chapter 5 – The paradoxical self pp. 94–109

Robertson, Ian H.
Professor, School of Psychology, Trinity College, Dublin, Ireland
Chapter 4 – Paradoxes in neurorehabilitation pp. 74–93

Roediger, Henry L., III
Washington University, St. Louis, MO, USA
Chapter 8 – Paradoxes of learning and memory pp. 151–176

Sachdev, Perminder S.
Professor, The Neuropsychiatric Institute, Prince of Wales Hospital, University of

New South Wales, Sydney, Australia
*Chapter 17 – The paradox of psychosurgery
to treat mental disorders* pp. 301–320

Schachter, Steven C.
Professor, Department of Neurology,
Harvard Medical School, Boston, MA, USA
*Chapter 11 – Paradoxical phenomena in
epilepsy* pp. 204–220

Schwartzbaum, Judith
Associate Professor, Ohio State University,
Columbus, OH, USA
*Chapter 14 – Unexpected benefits of
allergies and cigarette smoking* pp. 261–273

Tavassoli, Teresa
Autism Research Centre, University of
Cambridge, Cambridge, UK
Chapter 15 – The paradox of autism
pp. 274–288

Teskey, G. Campbell
Professor, Department of Cell Biology and
Anatomy and Psychology, University of

Calgary, Alberta, Canada
*Chapter 20 – Paradoxical phenomena in
brain plasticity* pp. 350–364

Viskontas, Indre V.
Research Fellow, University of California,
San Francisco, CA, USA
*Chapter 12 – Paradoxical creativity and
adjustment in neurological conditions*
pp. 221–233

Wojtowicz, J. Martin
Professor, Department of Physiology,
University of Toronto, ON, Canada
*Chapter 21 – Immature neurons
in the adult brain*
pp. 365–378

Zimerman, Shira
Visiting Graduate Student, Rotman
Research Institute, Baycrest Center,
Toronto, Canada
Chapter 7 – Cognitive ageing
pp. 130–150

Abbreviations

AD	antidepressant drug	MNS	mirror neuron system
ADHD	attention deficit hyperactivity disorder	mPFC	median prefrontal cortex
		MRI	magnetic resonance imaging
AED	antiepileptic drug	MST	magnetic seizure therapy
AS	Asperger's syndrome	NAcc	nucleus accumbens
ASC	autism spectrum conditions	NHL	non-Hodgkin's lymphoma
ASD	autism spectrum disorder	OCD	obsessive–compulsive disorder
AV	audio-visual	OFC	orbital frontal cortex
BDNF	brain-derived neurotrophic factor	ORE	other race effect
BrdU	bromodeoxyuridine	PET	positron emission tomography
CIAT	constraint-induced aphasia therapy	PFC	prefrontal cortex
COMT	catechol-O-methyltransferase	PFF	paradoxical functional facilitation
CRPS	chronic regional pain syndrome	PNFA	progressive non-fluent aphasia
CSF	cerebrospinal fluid	PPC	posterior parietal cortex
CT	computerized tomography	PTSD	post-traumatic stress disorder
CVS	caloric vestibular stimulation	RBD	REM sleep behavioural disorder
DA	dopamine	REM	rapid eye movement
DAT	dopamine transporter	ROC	receiver operating characteristics
DBS	deep brain stimulation	ROI	region of interest
DG	dentate gyrus	RSD	reflex sympathetic dystrophy
DLPFC	dorsolateral prefrontal cortex	rTMS	repetitive transcranial magnetic stimulation
DNA	deoxyribonucleic acid (hereditary material in living organisms)	SCR	skin conductance response
DPSD	dual process signal detection	SEM	standard error of the mean
DRM	Deese–Roediger–McDermott	SGZ	subgranular zone
ECS	electroconvulsive shock	SMA	supplementary motor cortex
ECT	electroconvulsive therapy	SNP	single nucleotide polymorphisms
ED	Executive Dysfunction	SPL	superior parietal lobule
EEG	electro-encephalography	SQ	systemizing quotient
EPF	enhanced perceptual functioning	SRTT	serial reaction time task
FEF	frontal eye fields	SSRI	selective serotonin reuptake inhibitor
FFA	fusiform face area	STS	superior temporal sulcus
GCL	granule cell layer	SUDEP	sudden and unexplained death in epilepsy
GOT	gratings orientation task	SVZ	subventricular zone
GP	globus pallidus	TBI	traumatic brain injury
GPe	globus pallidus externa	tDCS	transcranial direct current stimulation
GPi	globus pallidus interna		
HD	Huntington's disease	TENS	transcutaneous electrical nerve stimulation
HVA	homovanillic acid		
IPL	inferior parietal lobule	TIA	transient ischaemic attack
LTD	long-term depression	TLE	temporal lobe epilepsy
LTP	long-term potentiation	TMS	transcranial magnetic stimulation
MAO	monoamine oxidase	VBM	voxel-based morphometry
MCI	mild cognitive impairment	VNS	vagus nerve stimulation
MEG	magnetoencephalography	VR	virtual reality
MEP	motor-evoked potential	WCC	weak central coherence
MNI	Montreal Neurological Institute		

"I said, one of us is in trouble!"

HUTCH

The paradoxical nature of nature

Narinder Kapur, Alvaro Pascual-Leone, Tom Manly
and Jonathan Cole

Summary

Paradoxes abound in nature and in the realm of the human condition. Paradoxes have been evident in fields of science – from plant biology to human biology to physics – and in areas of human endeavour, ranging through political, literary and social activities. Paradoxes often represent instances where current knowledge may be deficient, and thus predictions based on such knowledge may be inconsistent with actual events or findings. At the level of scientific methodology, paradoxical phenomena offer powerful opportunities to test models and conceptual frameworks, and to enable true 'paradigm shifts' in certain areas of scientific inquiry. Insights from paradoxical phenomena in clinical sciences not only help us to understand mechanisms of function and dysfunction, they also provide clues as to therapeutic strategies, which may alleviate impairment and disability resulting from disease and injury. In addition, they may contribute towards a more positive, humanistic view of diverse states of the human condition.

Introduction

The word paradox is derived from the Greek: the prefix *para* means contrary or opposed, and *doxos* means opinion. The *Shorter Oxford English Dictionary* (2002) includes amongst its definitions of paradox 'a seemingly absurd or self-contradictory statement or proposition which, when investigated or explained, may prove to be well-founded or true'. In his philosophical treatise on paradoxes, Sainsbury (2009) has highlighted the paradoxical nature of paradoxes themselves: 'Paradoxes are fun. In most cases, they are easy to state and immediately provoke one into trying to "solve" them . . . Paradoxes are serious . . . To grapple with them is not merely to engage in an intellectual game, but to come to grips with key issues' (Sainsbury, 2009, p. 1). There are now a number of converging channels of scientific inquiry, across disciplines including the social, biological and physical sciences, that indicate the importance of harnessing paradoxical phenomena to advance our understanding of nature.

Pribram (quoted by Prigatano, 1999, p. 21) has remarked that when science resolves paradox, true knowledge emerges. The Nobel Laureate and former Director of the US National Institutes of Health, Harold Varmus (2009), has commented on the paradoxical nature of the scientific process itself: 'Science is inherently a paradoxical activity. Nearly all great ideas come from individual minds, and they are often first tested experimentally by a

The Paradoxical Brain, ed. Narinder Kapur. Published by Cambridge University Press. © Cambridge University Press 2011.

single person. But validation and acceptance of new information requires communication, convening and consensus building – activities that involve a community' (Varmus, 2009, p. 270).

Social and behavioural sciences

From the perspective of social and behavioural sciences – covering diverse fields such as management, cognition and politics – several authors have pointed to a number of paradoxes (e.g. Handy, 1995; Lewis, 2000; Farson and Keyes, 2002; Ofori-Danwa and Julan, 2004; Medawar and Pyke, 2001; Ariely, 2010). Thus, Lewis (2000) has commented 'Increasing technological change, global competition, and workplace diversity reveal and intensify paradox. Managers, for example, are asked to increase efficiency and foster creativity, build individualistic teams, and think globally while acting locally' (p. 760). Richards (2008) has discussed the paradoxes inherent in empires, such as that of the British Empire, where firm government and encouragement of self-government often went hand-in-hand. The political paradox of atomic science, with its inherent opportunities for good and for evil, has been highlighted by Alario and Freudenburg (2007).

Maurice Allais, who won the 1988 Nobel Prize in Economics, pointed to a paradox in economic behaviour that has become known as the Allais Paradox. Allais referred to the inconsistency of choices made when people make gambles, and how this contradicted the standard economic formulation at the time, 'Expected Utility Theory' (Munier, 1991). This would predict that individuals will make choices according to simple weighted probabilities of risk, whereas in fact they change their attitude towards risk in the direction of certainty when large costs are at stake (i.e. being influenced by 'loss aversion'). Thaler (1992) has also discussed paradoxes in economic life, for example why someone will not pay more than a 100 dollars for a ticket to an event, but will not sell for less than 200 dollars a ticket that they themselves own. More recent studies have highlighted how high rewards can lead to paradoxical decrements in performance (Ariely *et al.*, 2009; Mobbs *et al.*, 2009). Many of the observations of Kahneman (2003), for which he gained the 2002 Nobel Prize in Economics, were based around paradoxes in human reasoning. Droit-Volet and Gil (2009) have also observed the unfortunate paradox that, rather than speeding up when one is miserable, and enhancing pleasurable experiences by moving as slowly as possible, our subjective sense of time shows quite the reverse pattern.

Natural and physical sciences

Renfrew (2008) has referred to the 'sapient paradox' in evolutionary archaeology: why is it that the cultural and cognitive explosion in human development appears to have taken place only over the last 10,000 years, when the biological features necessary to support it seem to date back 60,000–100,000 years? Donald (2009) has discussed the nature of this paradox, and possible ways in which it may be explained – climactic factors such as the Ice Age may have impeded the development of human activities, peculiarities of the interaction between material culture and the brain which led to achievements such as symbolic communication, and a simple failure to detect key developments in the delay period (thus suggesting that there is in fact no delay and thus no paradox). McKay and Dennett (2009) have referred to another evolutionary paradox, where in some instances illusions and misbeliefs may have adaptive value.

In physical sciences such as meteorology, paradoxical phenomena have also been noted, such as types of rainfall normally associated with middle latitudes occurring in the tropics, or the observation that 'rain dries the air' as a result of using up water vapour (Humphreys, 1919; Houze, 1997). In the case of astrophysics, the Nobel Prize-winning Italian physicist, Enrico Fermi, calculated that our galaxy should be teeming with intelligent life, and that the absence of evidence for extra-terrestrial life was a major paradox – this observation came to be known as 'Fermi's paradox', and has generated much discussion (Landis, 1998; see also www.en.wikipedia.org/wiki/Fermi_paradox). Rees (1980) has also referred to a paradox in astrophysics as to how the different parts of the universe managed to start expanding in such a well-coordinated way, if there was at the time of the expansion no causal contact between them. Chandrasekhar's Physics Nobel Prize Lecture (1984) referred to a resolution of the 'Eddington Paradox', named after the famous English astrophysicist, whereby a star which had cooled to absolute zero somehow found the energy to undergo major expansion. Twenty years later, in 2004, the Nobel Prize for Physics was won by Frank Wilczek. His prize lecture was entitled *Asymptotic Freedom: from Paradox to Paradigm* (Wilczek, 2005). Wilczek referred to two paradoxical findings in physics that gave rise to the discovery of a new dynamical principle, 'asymptotic freedom'. The first paradox referred to the fact that one of the hidden building blocks of nature, quarks, are 'born free but everywhere they are in chains'. The second paradox related to the fact that two major theories in physics, Special Relativity Theory and Quantum Mechanics Theory, both seemed to be viable, even though they treated the concepts of space and time differently. Aharonov and Rohrlich (2005) show how errors and gaps in our understanding of phenomena in physics, together with contradictory findings, may result in paradoxes in quantum physics.

Clinical sciences

Entering the term 'paradox' into the online medical search engine PubMed yielded 7715 articles (August, 2010). Particularly in the realm of clinical science, paradoxes may be evident when what normally hinders may help, and what normally helps may hinder. While many medical advances are the result of slow, painstaking increments in knowledge (Sanghavi, 2010), the history of advances in medicine is one where paradoxical phenomena often have major prominence (cf. Ovsiew, 1997). One now-resolved paradox is vaccination, where the administration of a toxic agent results in long-term immunological benefits. Although forms of vaccination appear to have been part of folk medicine in countries such as India and China before 1700 (McNeill, 2000), vaccination gained prominence in the west as a result of a discovery in the late eighteenth century, when Benjamin Jesty and Edward Jenner noted that dairymaids who were infected by cowpox seldom developed smallpox, and reasoned that their exposure to cowpox may have been a factor in their non-infection (Horton, 1995; Pead, 2003, 2006). This led him to the development of vaccination against smallpox. Immunological paradoxes were at the heart of the observations made by Peter Medawar (1953) on the survival of the foetus within an alien female host – he posed the question, 'How does the pregnant mother contrive to nourish within itself, for many weeks or months, a foetus that is an antigenically foreign body?' Medawar gained the Nobel Prize in 1960 for his research into the immune system, and the immunological paradox about which he remarked has remained an active area of research (Billington, 2003; Moffett and Loke, 2004).

The Austrian psychiatrist, Julius Wagner-Jauregg, received the Nobel Prize in 1927 for his use of fever, by malaria inoculation, to cure mental disorders (Wagner-Jauregg, 1927). In recent years, there has been renewed interest in the possibility that, at least in some circumstances, fever may have clinical benefits (Matthews, 2010). An enlightened paradoxical observation that led to a major advance in clinical medicine was made by Philip Hench, who was awarded the Nobel Prize in 1950. On 1 April 1929, when Hench was in clinical practice, a 65-year-old lady with rheumatoid arthritis told him an unusual story, of how a recent occurrence of jaundice had resulted in a remission of her arthritis (cf. Crocker et al., 2002). Hench (1950) built on this observation, and additional observations he made with regards to the remission of rheumatoid arthritis in pregnancy (cf. Straub et al., 2005), to discover the beneficial effects of cortisone and adrenocorticotropic hormone in rheumatic and non-rheumatic conditions.

The concept that 'what normally hinders may help' is evident in a number of other clinical settings (see Stiehm, 2006), and while some issues remain a subject of debate, relevant phenomena include the following.

- Ischaemic preconditioning, whereby an initial transient reduction of blood flow/oxygen will somehow reduce the impact of a subsequent major ischaemic event (Dirnagl et al., 2009; Kharbanda et al., 2009).
- The reduction of certain forms of cancer in Down's syndrome (Baker and Kramer, 2007; Threadgill, 2008; Baek et al., 2009).
- The obesity paradox in cardiac disease, which is controversial, but where it is claimed that some obese people with cardiac disease may have a better prognosis than non-obese individuals (LaVie et al., 2007, 2009; Strandberg et al., 2009; Bray, 2009; Frankenstein et al., 2009).
- The beneficial effects early in life of genetic risk factors that may be harmful late in life, such as the APOE ε4 allele that has been implicated in Alzheimer's disease (Zetterberg et al., 2009); similarly, insulin/IGF-1 signalling enhances growth process during development, but later in life can potentiate the ageing process. This has been called the insulin/IGF-1 paradox (Cohen and Dillin, 2008). The idea that some genes may be beneficial in some contexts but harmful in others, thus having multiple competing effects, has been termed 'antagonistic pleiotropy'; in this context, genes that enhance early survival and function may nevertheless be disadvantageous later in life.
- The protective effects of an inherited blood disorder (alpha+thalassemia) against malaria and other infections (Allen et al., 1997; Enevold et al., 2007).
- The role of infections and immune responses in the treatment of cancer (McCarthy, 2006; Gray et al., 2006; Camus et al., 2009).
- The reduced incidence of melanoma in those with vitiligo (Jin et al., 2010), and of some cancers in those with Parkinson's disease (Fois et al., 2010) and multiple sclerosis (Handel et al., 2010).
- Instances where immune-cell infiltration in the central nervous system may be beneficial as well as detrimental (Wekerle and Hohlfeld, 2010).
- Better adjustment after irreversible compared to reversible colostomies (Smith et al., 2009).
- The dramatic, beneficial effects of propranolol – normally used for hypertension – in resolving lesions associated with severe infantile hemangiomas (Léauté-Labrèze et al., 2008; Sans et al., 2009).
- Paradoxes in the realm of human emotion – for example, the occasional beneficial effects of low mood (Forgas, 2007); the negative hedonic consequences of instigating revenge (Carlsmith et al., 2008); and the pleasure that may sometimes be associated with uncertainty following a positive event (Wilson et al., 2005).

The reverse side of this form of paradox is situations where what normally helps may hinder. Apart from well-established observations such as the side-effects/unintended consequences of medical treatments or the occasional harmful consequences of modern transportation systems (either directly as in the case of accidents, or indirectly by the transmission of infectious diseases), a number of relevant phenomena have emerged, some of which are discussed in more detail in subsequent chapters. These include the following.

- The possible effects of exercise as a contributory factor to the origins of motor neurone disease (Chiò et al., 2005).
- Situations where there may be detrimental effects from power and privilege, or from expertise (Sternberg, 2002; Castel et al., 2007).
- Increase in size or number of lesions after initiation of chemotherapy in neurotuberculosis (Kumar et al., 2006).
- Lack of strict correspondence between wealth and happiness, sometimes known as the Easterlin Paradox, after the economist Richard Easterlin (Easterlin, 1974; Graham, 2008), and the occasional adverse effects of wealth on happiness and efficiency (Kahneman et al., 2006; Quoidbach et al., 2010).
- The possible evolutionary influence of language on the development of psychiatric conditions such as schizophrenia (Crow, 2000).

Paradoxes in public health medicine have also been pointed out (Worthman and Kohrt, 2005; Christakis, 2009; Partridge, 2009). These include increased longevity unmasking diseases associated with ageing, indirect side-effects of the treatment of infectious diseases, coupled with misuse of anti-infectious agents (antibiotics/antifungals/antivirals) where short-term use may alleviate symptoms, but may promote the survival of multi-resistant strains if the drugs are not taken for long enough to eradicate the entire population of the infectious organism. Perceived failures in health care delivery have been attributed to a basic paradox of training of staff to a high degree of excellence, but so stigmatizing errors that institutional learning from mistakes is impeded (Reason, 2008), with the result that excellence and incompetence may often go hand-in-hand (Kapur, 2009). Others have pointed to an 'information paradox', where the explosion of health-related information, and the concentration on evidence-based medicine, has detracted from the personal and social context of the individual patient, leading indirectly to limitations in patient care (Sweeney, 1998).

In recent years, the field of 'paradoxical pharmacology' has emerged (Bond, 2001), where counter-intuitive effects of drugs have encouraged new ways of thinking about pharmacological intervention. For example, drugs that traditionally would be considered to inflict stress on biological systems in the short term may in fact yield benefits in the long term ('short-term pain for long-term gain'). Bond points to a number of such paradoxes in the area of pharmacology, including the use of beta blockers in heart disease and also their possible use in treating asthma (Lipworth and Williamson, 2009). Venkatsubramanian (2010) has also noted instances where a drug may benefit one disease, while at the same time promoting another. Although the formalization and testing of the hypothesis that there may be a difference between the acute and chronic response of drugs may be a novel concept in pharmacology, there are numerous examples of it occurring not only in the treatment of disease, but even in nature itself. Indeed, as mentioned above, it could be argued that even bacteria, fungi and viruses become more resistant as a result of exposure to drugs used to kill them (an example of natural selection). In the case of plant biology, commentators have remarked on the paradoxical presence of plant biodiversity in situations where one would not logically expect it to occur (e.g. Shoresh et al., 2008; Silvertown, 2008), while others have pointed to unusually long life-spans of normally short-living tree species in certain circumstances (Larson, 2001).

Lower doses of drugs may have contrasting effects on function, as in the case of stimulating effects of a sleeping tablet, Zolpiden (Brefel-Courbon et al., 2007) and the calming effects of low doses of a stimulant in Attention Deficit Hyperactivity Disorder (Arnsten, 2006) – see Chapter 23 in this book. As Bond (2001) has argued, acute and chronic effects of interventions such as drug treatment, exercise, etc., may have opposite effects on a key outcome variable – e.g. exercise increases blood pressure in the short term but decreases it in the long term. One of the lessons from paradoxical pharmacology, argues Bond, is that incremental, chronic, intermittent exposure to a drug should be considered as a therapeutic option, especially in cases where the acute effects may be deleterious. Some of these observations have been subsumed in the emerging field of 'hormesis', where nonlinear dose–response curves for particular agents may sometimes result in paradoxical facilitation effects on human biological function (Ricci and MacDonald, 2007; Mattson, 2008; Calabrese, 2008; Jolly and Meyer, 2009). At the level of individual molecules, biological paradoxes have also been observed, as in the effects of acetylcholine on blood vessels, which sometimes produced relaxations and sometimes resulted in contractions of vessels. This paradox was both noted and resolved by Robert Furchgott, for which he subsequently gained the Nobel Prize, when he showed that the response of blood vessels depended critically on the innermost layer of cells lining the vessel, the endothelium – when the endothelium was present, acetylcholine relaxed blood vessels, but when it was removed, they contracted (Furchgott and Zawadski, 1980).

Neurosciences

In the case of the human brain, we are traditionally taught to assume that the brain optimizes behaviour, and that superior brains result in better behavioural capacities. To many people, this traditional view implies that a lesion to the brain will invariably lead to a loss of function, that a second lesion will inevitably exacerbate the adverse effects of an initial lesion, that it is generally not possible to lose function by enhancing brain activity, and that mentally or developmentally delayed individuals or non-human species cannot outperform normally intelligent humans. However, all these assumptions appear to be incorrect. This has implications for how we understand brain–behaviour relations, and – critically – how we implement therapies in clinical settings.

'Neurology's favourite word is deficit, denoting an impairment or incapacity of neurological function', writes Oliver Sacks, in his widely read The Man Who Mistook His Wife for a Hat (1985, p. 1). In his sequel, published 10 years later, An Anthropologist on Mars, Sacks also wrote, 'Defects, disorders, diseases, in this sense, can play a paradoxical role, by bringing out latent powers, developments, evolutions, forms of life, that might never be seen, or even be imaginable, in their absence' (1995, p. xii). In 1929, Vygotsky made a similar point in his treatise 'The Fundamental Problems of Defectology', in which he commented on the importance of considering compensatory strategies and mechanisms in cases such as blindness (Vygotsky *et al.*, 1993). Vygotsky noted 'The doctrine of overcompensation has an important significance and serves as a psychological basis for the theory and practice of educating a child with a loss of hearing, sight and so forth. What horizons will open up to the pedagogue, when he recognizes that a defect is not only a minus, a deficit, or a weakness but also a plus, a source of strength and that it has some positive implications!' (1993, p. 29).

The study of brain–behaviour relationships from cases of cerebral pathology has traditionally been embedded in the lesion-deficit model. While this model has provided valuable insights into our understanding of the organization of function in the human brain, it suffers from a number of drawbacks. First, in focusing on negative changes, it potentially ignores gains in other domains, for example, that may result from plastic reorganization or from the release of another brain region from inhibition. Second, nature is not always so obliging as to provide clear-cut contrasts between what is impaired and what is spared after a brain insult. Third, the lesion-deficit model can lead us to misinterpret findings – we may attribute dysfunction to a single locus when the dysfunction is in fact the result of a general perturbation to the system, or disruption to several interconnected areas/ networks. Fourth, it may discourage thinking about positive compensatory and adaptive strategies that could be employed in rehabilitation.

There is an exciting appeal to maverick theories than can lead to greater attention and indeed high-impact publication than theories lying squarely within accepted thought. Often, of course, there are solid statistical reasons why such outliers and the observations on which they are based are wrong, and why science is generally better advanced by convergence. However, entertaining different ideas about how we think about a topic, such as the effects of brain injury, by embracing paradoxes that do not fit within the prevailing deficit model could prove a fruitful method for illuminating underlying processes. To do so is not to decry other perspectives, or to suggest that, for example, most effects of an injury are not deleterious. However, thinking about exceptions may provide insights into how this highly complex organ functions, and how people who experience neurological, psychiatric or developmental difficulties may best be helped.

Recent years have seen a number of studies, which have begun to challenge the lesion-deficit model. There are instances where there may be limited correspondence between lesion load and dysfunction or disability (Rovaris and Filippi, 2005; Strasser-Fuchs *et al.*, 2008; Savva *et al.*, 2009), or where lesions may be 'silent' for a number of years without any clinical manifestation (Krampla *et al.*, 2008; Kuratsu *et al.*, 2000; Hakiki *et al.*, 2008). The paper by Kapur (1996) provided an earlier review of some paradoxical phenomena in brain research and offered a framework, such as competitive interaction between excitatory and inhibitory systems, that might explain some paradoxical findings. In human lesion studies (reviewed in Chapter 3), the major sets of paradoxical cognitive phenomena generally take one of two forms – enhanced cognitive performance of neurological patients vis-à-vis neurologically intact individuals, and alleviation or restoration to normal of a particular cognitive deficit following the occurrence of a brain lesion. A third set of paradoxical cognitive phenomena represents what may be termed 'inverse effects', where a variable that produces facilitation or detriment of performance in normal subjects results in opposite effects in neurological patients. A fourth set of similar paradoxical effects, sometimes seen in animal lesion studies and very occasionally evident in human studies, arises when there is an inverse relationship between lesion size and functional deficit, with larger lesions leading to less marked functional impairment. Other developments in recent years have included emphasis on the positive features of conditions such as autism (Hermelin, 2001; Frith and Happé, 2009), and the large number of studies that have reported facilitation of function following transient disturbance induced by transcranial magnetic stimulation (Fecteau et al., 2006). The modulation or improvement of cognitive and psychological functions by ablative or blocking influences has hitherto been largely ignored in classical texts in neuropsychology and behavioural neurology.

Almost 40 years ago, Pribram (1971) alluded to more general indications of paradoxical phenomena in the study of brain–behaviour relationships that were evident at that time, including the co-existence of seemingly contradictory facts or observations about the brain, and the unexpected absence of predicted outcomes after brain lesions. For example, Pribram pointed to the ostensive contradiction between greater interconnectivity of the human brain compared to other species and the apparently greater regional specialization of function, to the surprising absence of effects resulting from frontal lobe lesions, to the dissociation between physiological and behavioural indices of a response, and to the unexpectedly close harmony between sensory and motor cortex. Although some of these findings might not now be seen as particularly paradoxical, Pribram's observations and intuitions at that time provide an important historical context to current brain–behaviour paradoxes.

Conclusions

'A prevailing paradigm is likely to be more strongly affected by a new concept than by a new discovery', noted the evolutionary biologist Ernst Mayr (2004, p. 168). To the extent that embracing paradoxical phenomena entails a major change of paradigm in scientific methodology, it may fall under the rubric of Kuhn's criteria for a paradigmatic shift in scientific thinking (Kuhn, 1996).

Weatherall (1999) has alluded to the importance of applying fundamental approaches in biology to the clinical sciences. In particular, he notes the key questions – What, How and Why? This book is very much tentatively in the What mode – it is intended to give as fair and as comprehensive a picture as possible of paradoxes as they relate directly or indirectly to the human brain. Some authors have rightly and courageously offered to answer the How question, and to offer hints as to responses to the Why question, but these two questions will need to await replication of many of the observations that have been reported, and also documentation of the parameters/boundary conditions of particular findings.

The chapters in this book examine paradoxical phenomena from the perspective of clinical and cognitive neuroscience. From a general therapeutic perspective, a number of the chapters highlight the strengths that may accompany functional deficits, either directly or indirectly, and lend weight to the concept of 'neurodiversity' (Armstrong, 2010). This emphasis on strengths rather than weaknesses in neurological conditions has parallels in the field of positive psychology, which is now well established with books, journals, organizations and government reports devoted to the topic (Baumgardner and Crothers, 2009). There is also concordance with some approaches in clinical psychology, where there has been an increasing focus on phenomena such as 'post-traumatic growth', whereby a major physical or mental illness may sometimes result in enhanced adjustment and well-being (Joseph and Linley, 2008). The field of positive neurology appears to be less well defined. To our knowledge, the term 'positive neurology' has only been briefly used on a couple of occasions (Eide and Eide, 2006; Chatterjee, 2004), and the term 'positive neuropsychology' has only briefly been used once in a conference presentation (Eslinger, 2005). This book is intended to set the foundation for the field of positive neurology, and to demonstrate how it may have far-reaching theoretical and therapeutic implications. Such an approach in turn encourages a positive, more humanistic, view of differing or 'impaired' states of the human condition, a form of 'humanistic neuroscience'.

Acknowledgements

We are grateful to a number of referees for their comments on this chapter.

References

Aharonov, Y., & Rohrlich, D. (2005). *Quantum Paradoxes: Quantum Theory for the Perplexed*. Weinheim: Wiley-VCH.

Alario, M., & Freudenburg, W. (2007). Atoms for peace, atoms for war: probing the paradoxes of modernity. *Sociological Inquiry*, 77: 219–40.

Allen, S. J., O'Donnell, A., Alexander, N. D., *et al.* (1997). Alpha+Thalassemia protects children against disease caused by other infections as well as malaria. *Proceedings of the National Academy of Sciences*, 94: 14,736–41.

Ariely, D. (2010). *The Upside of Irrationality*. New York, NY: Harper Collins.

Ariely, D., Gneezy, U., Loewenstein, G., & Mazar, N. (2009). Large stakes and big mistakes. *Review of Economic Studies*, 75: 1–19.

Armstrong, T. (2010). *Neurodiversity*. Cambridge, MA: Da Capo Press.

Arnsten, A. F. (2006). Stimulants: therapeutic actions in ADHD. *Neuropsychopharmacology*, 31: 2376–83.

Baek, K. H., Zaslavsky, A., Lynch, R. C., *et al.* (2009). Down's syndrome suppression of tumour growth and the role of the calcineurin inhibitor DSCR1. *Nature*, 459: 1126–30.

Baker, S. G., & Kramer, B. S. (2007). Paradoxes in carcinogenesis: new opportunities for research directions. *BMC Cancer*, 7: 151.

Baumgardner, S., & Crothers, M. (2009). *Positive Psychology*. New York, NY: Prentice Hall.

Billington, W. (2003). The immunological problem of pregnancy: 50 years with the hope of progress. A tribute to Peter Medawar. Invited Editorial. *Journal of Reproductive Immunology*, 60: 1–11.

Bond, R. A. (2001). Is paradoxical pharmacology a strategy worth pursuing? *Trends in Pharmacological Sciences*, 22: 273–6.

Bray, G. (2009). Risk factors: the obesity paradox – an artifact of small sample size? *Nature Reviews Cardiology*, 6: 561–2.

Brefel-Courbon, C., Payoux, P., Ory, F., *et al.* (2007). Clinical and imaging evidence of zolpidem effect in hypoxic encephalopathy. *Annals of Neurology*, 62: 102–5.

Calabrese, E. J. (2008). Hormesis and medicine. *British Journal of Clinical Pharmacology*, 66: 594–617.

Camus, M. Tosolini, M., Mlecnik, B., *et al.* (2009). Coordination of intratumoral immune reaction and human colorectal cancer recurrence. *Cancer Research*, 69: 2685–93.

Carlsmith, K., Wilson, T., & Gilbert, D. (2008). The paradoxical consequences of revenge. *Journal of Personality and Social Psychology*, 95: 1316–24.

Castel, A., McCabe, D., Roediger, H. L., & Heitman, J. (2007). The dark side of expertise. *Psychological Science*, 18: 3–5.

Chandrasekhar, S. (1984). On stars, their evolution and their stability (Nobel Lecture). *Angewandte Chemie International Edition in English*, 23: 679–89.

Chatterjee, A. (2004). The controversy over enhancing movement, mentation, and mood. *Neurology*, 63: 968–74.

Chiò, A., Benzi, G., Dossena, M., Mutani, R., & Mora, G. (2005). Severely increased risk of amyotrophic lateral sclerosis among Italian professional football players *Brain*, 128: 472–6.

Christakis, N. (2009). Indirectly doing harm. *British Medical Journal*, **339**: 782.

Cohen, E., & Dillin, A. (2008). The insulin paradox: aging, proteotoxicity and neurodegeneration. *Nature Review Neuroscience*, **9**: 759–69.

Crocker, I., Lawson, N., & Fletcher, J. (2002). Effect of pregnancy and obstructive jaundice on inflammatory diseases: the work of P S Hench revisited. *Annals of the Rheumatic Diseases*, **61**: 307–10.

Crow, T. J. (2000). Schizophrenia as the price that *Homo sapiens* pays for language: a resolution of the central paradox in the origin of the species. *Brain Research Reviews*, **31**: 118–29.

Dirnagl, U., Becker, K., & Meisel, A. (2009). Preconditioning and tolerance against cerebral ischaemia: from experimental strategies to clinical use. *Lancet Neurology*, **8**: 398–412.

Donald, M. (2009). The sapient paradox: can cognitive neuroscience solve it? *Brain*, **132**: 820–4.

Droit-Volet, S., & Gil, S. (2009). The time–emotion paradox. *Philosophical Transactions of the Royal Society B*, **364**: 1943–53.

Easterlin, R. (1974). Does economic growth improve the human lot? In: David, P. & Reder, M. (Eds). *Nations and Households in Economic Growth: Essays in Honor of Moses Abramovitz*. New York, NY: Academic Press, pp. 89–125.

Eide, B., & Eide, F. (2006). The mislabelled child. *The New Atlantis*, Spring, pp. 46–57.

Enevold, A., Alifrangis, M., Sanchez, J. J., *et al.* (2007). Associations between alpha+ thalassemia and *Plasmodium falciparum* malarial infection in northeastern Tanzania. *Journal of Infectious Diseases*, **196**: 451–9.

Eslinger, P. (2005). Practising positive Neuropsychology. *Meeting of International Neuropsychological Society, July 2005*. Dublin.

Farson, R., & Keyes, R. (2002). *The Innovation Paradox*. New York, NY: The Free Press.

Fecteau, S. Pascual-Leone, A., & Théoret, H. (2006). Paradoxical facilitation of attention in healthy humans. *Behavioral Neurology*, **17**: 159–62.

Fois, A., Wotton, C., Yeates, D., Turner, M., & Goldacre, M. (2010). Cancer in patients with motor neuron disease, multiple sclerosis and Parkinson's Disease: record linkage studies. *Journal of Neurology, Neurosurgery and Psychiatry*, **81**: 215–21.

Forgas, J. P. (2007). When sad is better than happy: negative affect can improve the quality and effectiveness of persuasive messages and social influence strategies. *Journal of Experimental Social Psychology*, **43**: 513–28.

Frankenstein, L., Zugck, C., Nelles, M., Schellberg, D., Katus, H. A., & Remppis, B. A. (2009). The obesity paradox in stable chronic heart failure does not persist after matching for indicators of disease severity and confounders. *European Journal of Heart Failure*, **11**: 1189–94.

Frith, U., & Happé, F. (Eds). (2009). Autism and talent. *Philosophical Transactions of the Royal Society, B*, **364**: Issue Number 1522.

Furchgott, R., & Zawadski, J. (1980). The obligatory role of endothelial cells in the relaxation of arterial smooth muscle by ACh. *Nature*, **288**: 373–6.

Graham, C. (2008). Happiness and health: lessons and questions for public policy. *Health Affairs*, **27**: 72–87.

Gray, J., Johnson, P. W., & Glennie, M. (2006). Therapeutic potential of immunostimulatory monocolonal antibodies. *Clinical Science (London)*, **111**: 93–106.

Hakiki, B., Goretti, B., Portaccio, E., Zipoli, V., & Amato, M. P. (2008). 'Subclinical MS': follow-up of four cases. *European Journal of Neurology*, **15**: 858–61.

Handel, A., Joseph, A., & Ramagopalan, S. (2010). Multiple sclerosis and lung cancer: an unexpected inverse association. *Quarterly Journal of Medicine*, **103**: 625–6.

Handy, C. (1995). *The Age of Paradox*. Cambridge, MA: Harvard Business School Press.

Hench, P. (1950). The reversibility of certain rheumatic and non-rheumatic conditions by the use of cortisone or of the pituitary adrenocorticotropic hormone. In: Nobel Foundation. *Nobel Lectures, Physiology or Medicine, 1942–62*. Amsterdam: Elsevier.

Hermelin, B. (2001). *Bright Splinters of the Mind*. London: Jessica Kingsley.

Horton, R. (1995). Myths in medicine. Jenner did not discover vaccination. *British Medical Journal*, **310**: 62.

Houze, R. (1997). Stratiform precipitation in regions of convection: a meteorological paradox? *Bulletin of the American Meteorological Society*, **78**: 2179–96.

Humphreys, W. (1919). A bundle of meteorological paradoxes. *Monthly Weather Review*, **47**: 876.

Jin, Y., Birlea, S., Fain, P., *et al.* (2010). Variant of *TYR* and autoimmunity susceptibility loci in generalized vitiligo. *New England Journal of Medicine*, **362**: 1686–97.

Jolly, D., & Meyer, J. (2009). A brief review of radiation hormesis. *Australasian Physical & Engineering Sciences in Medicine*, **32**: 180–7.

Joseph, S., & Linley, P. (Eds). (2008). *Trauma, Recovery and Growth*. Hoboken, NJ: Wiley.

Kahneman, D. (2003). Maps of Bounded Rationality: Psychology for Behavioral Economics. *The American Economic Review*, **93**: 1449–75.

Kahneman, D., Krueger, A. B., Schkade, D., Schwarz, N., & Stone, A. A. (2006). Would you be happier if you were richer? A focusing illusion. *Science*, **312**: 1908–10.

Kapur, N. (1996). Paradoxical functional facilitation in brain–behaviour research: a critical review. *Brain*, **119**: 1775–90.

Kapur, N. (2009). On the pursuit of clinical excellence. *Clinical Governance*, **14**: 24–37.

Kharbanda, R., Nielsen, T., & Redington, A. (2009). Translation of remote ischaemic preconditioning into clinical practice. *The Lancet*, **374**: 1557–65.

Krampla, W. W., Newrkla, S., Pfisterer, W., *et al.* (2008). Tumor growth of suspected meningiomas in clinically healthy 80-year-olds: a follow up five years later. *Zentralblatt für Neurochirurgie*, **69**: 182–6.

Kuhn, T. (1996). *The Structure of Scientific Revolutions. Third Edition*. Chicago, IL: University of Chicago Press.

Kumar, R., Prakash, M., & Jha, S. (2006). Paradoxical response to chemotherapy in neurotuberculosis. *Pediatric Neurosurgery*, **42**: 214–22.

Kuratsu, J., Kochi, M., & Ushio, Y. (2000). Incidence and clinical features of asymptomatic meningiomas. *Journal of Neurosurgery*, **92**: 766–70.

Landis, G. (1998). The Fermi Paradox: an approach based on percolation theory. *Journal of the British Interplanetary Society*, **51**: 163–6.

Larson, D. (2001). The paradox of great longevity in a short-lived tree species. *Experimental Gerontology*, **36**: 651–73.

LaVie, C., Milani, R., & Ventura, H. (2007). Obesity, heart disease, and favourable prognosis – truth or paradox? *American Journal of Medicine*, **120**: 825–6.

LaVie, C., Milani, R., & Ventura, H. (2009). Obesity and cardiovascular disease. Risk factor, paradox and impact of weight loss. *Journal of the American College of Cardiology*, **53**: 1925–32.

Léauté-Labrèze, C., Dumas de la Roque, E., Hubiche, T., Boralevi, F., Thambo, J-B., & Taïeb, A. (2008). Propranolol for severe hemangiomas of infancy. *New England Journal of Medicine*, **358**: 2649–51.

Lewis, M. (2000). Exploring paradox: toward a more comprehensive guide. *The Academy of Management Review*, **25**: 760–76.

Lipworth, B. J., & Williamson, P. A. (2009). Beta blockers for asthma: a double-edged sword. *Lancet*, **373**: 104–05.

Matthews, R. (2010). The heat is on. *New Scientist*, **207** (31 July issue): 43–5.

Mattson, M. P. (2008). Awareness of hormesis will enhance future research in basic and applied neuroscience. *Critical Reviews in Toxicology*, **38**: 633–9.

Mayr, E. (2004). *What Makes Biology Unique? Considerations on the Autonomy of a Scientific Discipline*. Cambridge: Cambridge University Press.

McCarthy, E. (2006). The toxins of William B Coley and the treatment of bone and soft-tissue sarcomas. *The Iowa Orthopaedic Journal*, **26**: 154–8.

McKay, R., & Dennett, D. (2009). The evolution of misbelief. *Behavioural and Brain Sciences*, **32**: 493–561.

McNeill, M. (2000). *Plagues and Peoples*. New York, NY: Anchor Books.

Medawar, J., & Pyke, D. (2001). *Hitler's Gift: The True Story of the Scientists Expelled by the Nazi Regime*. New York, NY: Arcade Publishing.

Medawar, P. (1953). Some immunological and endocrinological problems raised by the evolution of viviparity in vertebrates. *Symposium of the Society for Experimental Biology*, 7: 320–38.

Mobbs, D., Hassabis, D., Seymour, B., *et al.* (2009). Choking on the money: reward-based performance decrements are associated with midbrain activity. *Psychological Science*, 20: 955–62.

Moffett, A., & Loke, Y. (2004). The immunological paradox of pregnancy. A reappraisal. *Placenta*, 25: 1–8.

Munier, B. (1991). The many other Allais paradoxes. *The Journal of Economic Perspectives*, 5: 179–99.

Ofori-Danwa, J., & Julan, S. (2004). Conceptualizing social science paradoxes using the diversity and similarity curves model: illustrations from work/play and theory novelty/continuity paradoxes. *Human Relations*, 57: 1449–77.

Ovsiew, F. (1997). Paradoxical functional facilitation in brain–behaviour research: a critical review [Letter]. *Brain*, 120: 1261–4.

Partridge, L. (2009). The new biology of ageing. *Philosophical Transactions of the Royal Society B*, 365: 147–54.

Pead, P. J. (2003). Benjamin Jesty: new light in the dawn of vaccination. *Lancet*, 362: 2104–09.

Pead, P. J. (2006). *Vaccination Rediscovered: New Light in the Dawn of Man's Quest for Immunity*. London: Timefile Books.

Pribram, K. H. (1971). *Languages of the Brain: Experimental Paradoxes and Principles in Neuropsychology*. New York, NY: Prentice-Hall.

Prigatano, G. (1999). *Principles of Neuropsychological Rehabilitation*. Oxford: Oxford University Press.

Quoidbach, J., Dunn, E., Petrides, K., & Mikolajczak, M. (2010). Money giveth, money taketh away: the dual effect of wealth on happiness. *Psychological Science*, 21: 759–63.

Reason, J. (2008). Foreward. In: Crocksberry, P., Cosby, K., Schenkel, S., & Wears, R. (Eds). *Patient Safety in Emergency Medicine*. Philadelphia, PA: Wolters Kluwer.

Rees, M. (1980). The inhomogeneity and entropy of the universe: some puzzles. *Physica Scripta*, 2: 614–18.

Renfrew, C. (2008). Neuroscience, evolution and the sapient paradox: the factuality of value and of the sacred. *Philosophical Transactions of the Royal Society B*, 363: 2041–7.

Ricci, P. F., & MacDonald, T. R. (2007). Hormesis and precaution: the twain shall meet. *Human and Experimental Toxicology*, 26: 877–89.

Richards, J. (2008). Bastions of Britishness – review of *Decline and Fall of the British Empire* by Piers Brendon. *Times Higher Education Supplement*, 24 January, p. 52.

Rovaris, M., & Filippi, M. (2005). 'Importance sampling': a strategy to overcome the clinical/MRI paradox in MS. *Journal of the Neurological Sciences*, 237: 1–3.

Sacks, O. (1985). *The Man Who Mistook His Wife for a Hat*. London: Duckworth.

Sacks, O. (1995). *An Anthropologist on Mars*. London: Picador.

Sainsbury, R. (2009). *Paradoxes. Third Edition.* Cambridge: Cambridge University Press.

Sanghavi, D. (2010). How should we tell the stories of our medical miracles? *The Lancet*, 375: 2068–9.

Sans, V., Dumas de la Roque, E., Berge, J., *et al.* (2009). Propranolol for severe infantile hemiangiomas: follow-up report. *Pediatrics*, 124: e423–31.

Savva, G. M., Wharton, S. B., Ince, P. G., Forster, G., Matthews, F. E., & Brayne, C.; Medical Research Council Cognitive Function and Ageing Study. (2009). Age, neuropathology, and dementia. *New England Journal of Medicine*, 360: 2302–09.

Shoresh, H., Hegreness, M., & Kishony, R. (2008). Evolution exacerbates the paradox of plankton. *Proceedings of the National Academy of Sciences*, 105: 12,365–9.

Shorter Oxford English Dictionary (2002). *Fifth Edition*. Oxford: Oxford University Press.

Silvertown, J. (2008). *Demons in Eden: The Paradox of Plant Diversity*. Chicago, IL: University of Chicago Press.

Smith, D., Loewenstein, G., Jankovic, A., & Ubel, P. (2009). Happily hopeless: adaptation to a permanent, but not to a temporary, disability. *Health Psychology*, **28**: 787–91.

Sternberg, R. J. (Ed.) (2002). *Why Smart People Can Be So Stupid*. New Haven, CT: Yale University Press.

Stiehm, E. R. (2006). Disease versus disease: how one disease may ameliorate another. *Pediatrics*, **117**: 184–91.

Strandberg, T., Strandberg, A., Salomaa, V., *et al.* (2009). Explaining the obesity paradox: cardiovascular risk, weight change, and mortality during long-term follow-up in men. *European Heart Journal*, **30**: 1720–7.

Straub, R., Buttgereit, F., & Cutolo, M. (2005). Benefit of pregnancy in inflammatory arthritis. *Annals of Rheumatic Diseases*, **64**: 801–03.

Strasser-Fuchs, S., Enzinger, C., Ropele, S., Wallner, M., & Fazekas, F. (2008). Clinically benign multiple sclerosis despite large T2 lesion load: can we explain this paradox? *Multiple Sclerosis*, **14**: 205–11.

Sweeney, K. (1998). The information paradox. *Occasional Papers of the Royal College of General Practitioners*, **76**: 17–25.

Thaler, R. (1992). *The Winner's Curse. Paradoxes and Anomalies of Economic Life*. Princeton, NJ: Princeton University Press.

Threadgill, D. (2008). Paradox of a tumour repressor. *Nature*, **451**: 21–2.

Varmus, H. (2009). *The Art and Politics of Science*. New York, NY: W.W. Norton & Company.

Venkatsubramanian, G. (2010). Pharmacological pleiotropy and antagonistic co-evolutionary processes: a useful hypothetical model for applied evolutionary medicine [Letter]. *Acta Belgica Clinica*, **65**: 62–3.

Vygotsky, L. S., Rieber, R. W., & Carton, A. S. (Eds). (1993). *The Collected Works of LS Vygotsky, Volume 2, The Fundamentals of Defectology*. New York, NY: Springer. [1929, republished in 1993].

Wagner-Jauregg, J. (1927). The treatment of dementia paralytica by Malaria Inoculation. Nobel Prize Lecture. In: *Nobel Lectures, Physiology or Medicine, 1922–1941*. Amsterdam: Elsevier (1965).

Weatherall, D. (1999). The conflict between the science and the art of clinical practice in the next millennium. In: Grossman D, Valtin H (Eds), *Great Issues for Medicine in the Twenty-First Century*. New York, NY: New York Academy of Sciences, pp. 240–6.

Wekerle, H., & Hohlfeld, R. (2010). Beneficial autoimmunity? *Brain*, **133**: 2182–4.

Wilczek, F. (2005). Asymptotic freedom: from paradox to paradigm. *Proceedings of the National Academy of Sciences*, **102**: 8403–13.

Wilson, T., Centerbar, D., Kermer, D., & Gilbert, D. (2005). The pleasures of uncertainty: prolonging positive moods in ways people do not anticipate. *Journal of Personality and Social Psychology*, **88**: 5–21.

Worthman, C. M., & Kohrt, B. (2005). Receding horizons of health: biocultural approaches to public health paradoxes. *Social Science and Medicine*, **61**: 861–78.

Zetterberg, H., Alexander, D., Spandidos, D., & Blennow, K. (2009). Additional evidence for antagonistic pleiotropic effects of APOE. *Alzheimer's & Dementia*, **5**: 75.

Chapter 2

Paradoxical effects of sensory loss

Alvaro Pascual-Leone, Souzana Obretenova
and Lotfi B. Merabet

Summary

We perceive the world by means of an elaborate set of distinct, modality-specific receptor systems. It is hardly conceivable that losing or lacking a sensory modality would not, in some fashion, alter the capacities of processing, understanding or interacting with the world. Therefore, if lack or loss of a sensory modality leads to a compensatory enhancement of other senses, ultimately resulting in minimal functional loss or even functional gains, these would represent instances of paradoxical functional facilitation. In fact, enhancement of functioning in people with chronic or recent sensory loss has been one of the more widely studied and reliable forms of paradoxical functional facilitation. Individuals with visual loss have been found to show enhanced auditory function, tactile function and even verbal memory performance. Analogously, long-term auditory loss has been associated with enhanced cognitive performance, evident on tactile and visual tasks. Functional brain imaging and transcranial magnetic stimulation studies have pointed to a major reorganization of cerebral function in blind or deaf individuals, and these plastic changes are associated with functional adaptations and gains.

Introduction

In his novel *Blindness*, Jose Saramago (1998) uses blindness as a metaphor for both personal misfortune and social catastrophe. A man suddenly loses his vision. Within a few days, people who had contact with him also go blind, and blindness spreads like an epidemic. In the context of practically universal blindness, society breaks down, nothing functions, food and resources become scarce, and lives are threatened. Ultimately, only one character in the novel miraculously avoids blindness. However, despite her attempts to assist the blind and to help control the situation, society continues to deteriorate until vision miraculously begins to return.

In his short story, *The Country of the Blind*, H. G. Wells (1911) also uses blindness to represent restrictions on society and the struggle of the individual against social conformity. However, in Wells' case, a single, sighted individual struggles to cope with the challenges of a society developed and evolved to the needs and capacities of a universally blind population. While attempting to summit a fictitious mountain in Ecuador, the protagonist, Nunez, slips and falls into a secluded valley where congenital blindness has become endemic over time. While the community has fully adapted to life without sight, Nunez finds himself unable to adjust, and eventually escapes from the valley.

The Paradoxical Brain, ed. Narinder Kapur. Published by Cambridge University Press. © Cambridge University Press 2011.

As humans, we rely heavily on vision, and a very large portion of our brain is devoted to processing visual information. Saramago and Wells use blindness in distinct ways, but which metaphor better reflects the reality of the human condition when faced with blindness? Both perspectives may not necessarily be mutually exclusive. Saramago's society becomes blind late in life while Wells' villagers are born blind. Adjusting to a reality without vision becomes much more challenging later in life, when much of one's concept of the world has become heavily grounded in visual experiences. In turn, these metaphors may reflect the distinct realities and challenges experienced by early versus late blind individuals. However, both perspectives illustrate the disconnect between the world of the sighted and that of the blind, and hence the challenge of adjusting to a life without sight. Such portrayals of blindness, therefore, necessitate a better understanding of potentially advantageous changes that may occur in the absence or following the loss of a sensory modality.

Humans are endowed with specialized receptors capable of capturing different types of electromagnetic waves, temperature, pressure, chemical inputs, etc. Thus, we perceive the world by means of an elaborate set of distinct modality-specific receptor systems that feed into specialized brain networks. It is the distinctness of these sensory channels that enables us to experience sensations that are uniquely unimodal. Colour, for example, can only be experienced through vision; pitch can normally only be experienced through audition. However, the acquisition of information in separate modalities also allows us to process the different elements of sensation in parallel in order to form a unitary multimodal percept. The unified and salient nature of our multimodal sensory experiences is the product of extensive and dynamic neural interactions and connections, which in turn are highly influenced by our own experiences and developmental constraints. Current evidence supports the notion that multisensory integration serves to enhance overall perceptual accuracy and saliency through cooperative advantages and provides for a redundancy of cues necessary to fully characterize objects in our environment (Calvert and Thesen, 2004; Duhamel, 2002; Wallace and Stein, 1997). Information garnered by means of one sense impinges upon, enhances, and alters information acquired via others. Well-known perceptual phenomena (e.g. the ventriloquism effect) demonstrate that we are constantly integrating information from different modalities to form richer multisensory experiences. What, then, are the consequences of losing or even growing up without one of the senses?

It would be reasonable to expect, given our specialized senses and our multisensory representation of reality, that the loss of any one of our senses must lead to a functional loss, impairing cognitive abilities and perhaps even rendering the individual mentally handicapped. Certainly, blindness introduces, at least initially, significant challenges in activities of daily living (e.g. way finding), occupational tasks and social interactions (e.g. due to an inability to perceive facial expressions). However, despite the difficulties that blind individuals face, it is the sighted world that seems not to have truly adapted to those without sight, and still retains certain biases and preconceived notions regarding the abilities of the blind.

It is hardly conceivable that losing or lacking a sensory modality would not, in some fashion, alter the capacities of processing, understanding, or interacting with the world, and effectively lead to functional and perhaps structural changes in the plastic brain. If the lost sense plays a preferential role in 'instructing' other senses, the loss of that sensory modality might lead to a particularly widespread cognitive and perceptual breakdown. On the other hand, if lack or loss of a sensory modality can lead to a compensatory enhancement of other senses, ultimately resulting in minimal functional loss or even functional gains, these would represent instances of paradoxical functional facilitation.

In fact, there are many such instances. Enhancement of functioning in people with chronic or recent sensory loss has been one of the more widely studied and reliable forms of paradoxical functional facilitation. Individuals with visual loss have been found to show enhanced auditory function, tactile function and even verbal memory performance (Collignon *et al.*, 2006; Forster *et al.*, 2007; Amedi *et al.*, 2003). Analogously, long-term auditory loss has been associated with enhanced cognitive performance, evident on tactile and visual tasks. More recent studies employing techniques such as functional brain imaging and transcranial magnetic stimulation (TMS) have revealed major reorganization of cerebral function in blind or deaf* individuals (Merabet and Pascual-Leone, 2009), which appear to be associated with functional adaptations and gains. However, not all abilities with the remaining senses are enhanced or even maintained upon the loss of a sensory modality (Amedi *et al.*, 2005a; Dye and Bavelier, 2010; Sathian and Stilla, 2010). Therefore, a careful analysis of the instances of paradoxical facilitation in the context of sensory loss can provide valuable insights into fundamental aspects of brain function and development.

Blindness

As noted previously, various enhancements in the preserved senses have been demonstrated in blind individuals. Rosenbluth *et al.* (2000) and, more recently, Cuevas *et al.* (2009) found that children with early-onset or congenital blindness perform better than sighted children at labelling common odours. Hugdahl *et al.* (2004) found that blind subjects are better than sighted subjects at identifying syllables. Gougoux *et al.* (2004) also reported better pitch discrimination in early-blind, but not late-blind, subjects. Along with many others, Fieger *et al.* (2006) reported that blind individuals are also better than sighted in the localization of sounds, particularly those coming from the periphery. Collignon *et al.* (2006) reported shorter reaction times in auditory as well as tactile spatial attention tasks in the early blind, who also show better divided attention in tests where both tactile and auditory modalities are used. Additionally, using an auditory temporal judgement task, Stevens and Weaver (2005) found that early-blind subjects have lower temporal order judgement thresholds than sighted subjects. Recent evidence further suggests that enhanced auditory capabilities appear to facilitate faster emotional discrimination in blind individuals (Klinge *et al.*, 2010).

In relation to haptic sensitivity, Van Boven *et al.* (2000) as well as Goldreich and Kanics (2003) found that early-blind subjects show enhanced tactile discrimination in a gratings orientation task. Blind subjects also demonstrated lower thresholds on an angle discrimination task compared to sighted subjects, providing further evidence of a heightened sensitivity to tactile inputs (Alary *et al.*, 2008). Forster *et al.* (2007) found that the blind respond faster and are more accurate than sighted subjects in a difficult tactile spatial selection task, and that these behavioural advantages are associated with changes in early somatosensory event-related brain potentials. Röder *et al.* (2004) noted better tactile temporal order judgements in the congenitally blind (Occelli *et al.*, 2008; Wan *et al.*, 2009). Enhanced performance by blind subjects in detecting Braille characters has been noted in a number of studies – for example, Bliss *et al.* (2004) reported that in a tactile n-back task (in which people are asked to judge whether a current stimulus differs from that

---

* Subsequently, we will often refer to 'the blind' and 'the deaf'. This is not to imply that these characteristics are fundamental to a person's identity, but simply convenient shorthand.

presented 1, 2 . . . n trials previously), blind subjects outperformed their sighted counterparts. Blind individuals also show greater accuracy than sighted individuals in bimanual tactile estimations of object size with familiar objects (Smith *et al.*, 2005). Interestingly, enhanced tactile abilities do not appear to be limited to the fingers used for Braille. Some reports have also found greater tactile discrimination ability in the tongue in blind individuals (Chebat *et al.*, 2007). However, not all aspects of haptic processing are enhanced in the blind (Sathian and Stilla, 2010).

Additionally, there is evidence of enhanced memory functioning in blind subjects. For example, Röder *et al.* (2001) found the blind to have better auditory–verbal recognition memory than sighted subjects, and Amedi *et al.* (2003) found enhanced auditory–verbal memory in blind subjects. Raz *et al.* (2007) noted that blind subjects also demonstrate enhanced serial memory. In all domains, however, the specifics of the task appear to determine whether functional gains will be observed (Alary *et al.*, 2009). Recent data suggest that the advantage in blind individuals stems from better stimulus encoding rather than enhancements in later stages of processing (Rokem and Ahissar, 2009).

Deafness

Complementary evidence has accumulated for paradoxical phenomena associated with auditory loss. Levanen and Hamdorf (2001) reported that congenitally deaf subjects show enhanced tactile sensitivity, in terms of tactile change detection, compared to normal control subjects. Recently, Bottari *et al.* (2010) have reported enhanced reactivity to visual stimuli in deaf individuals. Bavelier *et al.* (2006) reviewed an extended body of research and pointed to the selectivity of enhancements in visual processing in the deaf. Deaf signers are better at distributing attention towards the visual periphery during certain visual perception tasks than both sighted-hearing controls and hearing signers (Bavelier *et al.*, 2000; Bosworth and Dobkins, 2002; Neville and Lawson, 1987; Proksch and Bavelier, 2002; Rettenbach *et al.*, 1999). Further studies have shown enhancements, particularly lateralized to the right visual field, in visual motion detection thresholds in deaf signers as compared to hearing subjects (Finney *et al.*, 2003). Dye *et al.* (2007) reported enhancement of peripheral attention mechanisms in deaf subjects (as manifest in greater interference from peripheral flankers), and Dye *et al.* (2009) also demonstrated enhanced visual selective attention within the peripheral visual field. Additionally, Stevens and Neville (2006) found enhanced peripheral attention to visual stimuli in a group of deaf subjects. In a systematic study of the effects of long-term hearing loss, and also the ability to use sign language, Cattani *et al.* (2007) reported that experience in sign language use was a key mechanism underlying the enhancement of visual abilities found in deaf subjects. In fact, different neural substrates may support the perception of American Sign Language compared to other actions (Corina *et al.*, 2007). Additionally, Rouger *et al.* (2007) found better lip-reading performance in deaf subjects, and also the enhanced ability to integrate visual and degraded speech cues during lip-reading. Finally, deaf subjects demonstrate superior performance in detecting emotional expression and local facial features and discriminating between different faces (Arnold and Murray, 1998; McCullough and Emmorey, 1997; Bettger *et al.*, 1997). Deaf individuals also show preserved or even enhanced ability for temporal processing and temporal order judgements (Nava *et al.*, 2008). However, as in the case of blindness, not all aspects of non-hearing sensory processing are enhanced or even maintained in deaf individuals (Dye and Bavelier, 2010).

We shall focus on the case of blindness to further explore the question of paradoxical phenomena associated with sensory loss. Life without vision was viewed as 'incomplete' or 'impoverished' for many centuries, and most early theories postulated that deprivation of any one sensory modality would have devastating effects on development, learning and cognitive behavioural performance. This 'deficiency' theory purports that a lack of perceptual sensory experience leads to an overall impairment in cognitive task performance, given that proper multisensory integration of information can only result from normal development of each individual sense. These notions have remained particularly influential and powerful in the context of vision, guided by the belief that cognitive abilities in humans require a proper understanding of the visual world and that other senses require vision to 'instruct' them. Many scholars have argued that blind individuals have perceptual and learning disabilities because, without vision, a sense of space is not possible, nor a real knowledge of shape and gestalt. So, for example, many have argued that auditory or tactile space per se does not exist, but has to be shaped and calibrated by vision. Similarly, many have argued that understanding shape requires vision and that visualization is needed to develop auditory- or tactile-form perception. Nonetheless, it is clear that despite facing formidable challenges, blind individuals make striking adjustments to their sensory loss in order to interact effectively within their environment. These changes may translate into behavioural skills and task performance levels that are equal, and in certain cases superior, to those of individuals with intact sensory function. Growing evidence from both human and animal research strongly suggests that these adaptations are inextricably linked to modifications occurring at multiple levels of the brain (Sathian and Stilla, 2010; Amedi et al., 2003, 2005a; Wallace and Stein, 1997). In particular, it appears that these changes implicate not only areas of the brain responsible for the processing of the senses that remain intact, but also areas normally associated with the processing of visual information.

A historical perspective from the education of the blind

The medieval model of the mind contained within it the concept of a *sensus communis*, a place in the brain where information from all sensory modalities was summed into an integrated whole that could be utilized by the higher cognitive faculties of reason and memory. This is linked to the idea of 'common sense', and an obvious implication is that lack or loss of one of the body's sensory inputs must be associated with a loss or lack of intelligence, common sense, and perhaps even moral rectitude. It is thus not surprising that the dominating view for many centuries has been that blind or deaf individuals, for example, must be unworthy of attempts to educate or integrate them into society.

Consistent with the notion of a *sensus communis* that required input from all senses to truly form a sound conceptualization of the world and empower normal cognitive abilities, no attempt was made in ancient times to instruct the blind, or in any way to cultivate their intelligence. Blindness was thought to be associated with impaired mental capacities across the board. Of course, such attitudes became self-fulfilling prophecies, and lack of instruction condemned blind individuals to an uneducated, simple existence.

There were some early attempts to provide for the corporal needs of the blind and teach them various handicrafts – for instance, Saint Basil's hospice in Cesarea (fourth century), Limneus' cottages for blind people in Syria (fifth century), the refuge for the blind in Jerusalem (founded in 630 AD), or the hospices for the blind founded in the eleventh century by William the Conqueror in expiation of his sins. Towards 1260, St. Louis, King of

France, established in Paris the 'Hospice des Quinze-Vingts', which housed and instructed 300 blind persons. Thereafter, similar institutions were established and endowed throughout Europe in the 1300s. Instruction was focused on training individuals to behave in a discrete manner in the presence of others, teaching religious education, and singing. No attempts were made to teach the blind to read and write, and they were broadly considered unable to learn from such instruction.

Nonetheless, some began to wonder whether the challenges of educating the blind might not be the consequence of the lack of a reliable system of instruction for reading and writing communication. Eventually, Girolamo Cardano (1501–1576), an Italian mathematician, introduced a way of teaching the blind to read and write by the sense of touch. Blind subjects were to trace with a steel stylus the outline of each of the letters of the alphabet, engraved on metal. With some practice they became able to distinguish the letters by the sense of touch and reproduce them on paper. In the late 1500s, Rampazetto in Rome (Italy) and Lucas in Madrid (Spain) engraved letters in wood for the instruction of the blind. George Harsdörffer, in his book '*Deliciae mathematicae et physicae*' published in 1651, describes how the blind can recognize and be taught to reproduce letters engraved in wax. Harsdörffer (1651) and Lucas both point out that the blind can learn their systems of tactile reading and writing better than sighted individuals, even when instructed while deprived of sight, and thus both emphasize that the blind appear to possess abilities that the sighted seem to lack.

Building on such notions, Valentin Haüy (1745–1822) opened a day-school for blind children in 1784 and two years later he exhibited the achievements of 24 of his best pupils at Versailles. Louis XVI and his court were impressed by the curiosity of children without sight who were reading, writing, ciphering, doing handicraft work and playing music. So great was the interest aroused by this and similar exhibitions that generous patronage by the king and the public followed, and Haüy soon had sufficient means to board his pupils, intensify the educational curriculum and establish a school that has served as the model for educational institutions for the blind around the world. Over the past two centuries, institutions for education for the blind from around the world have provided accumulating evidence that blind individuals are certainly capable of being educated and achieving remarkable accomplishments. Consider Nicholas Saunderson, who had become blind when he was one year old, and who constructed around 1711 the first known tactile ciphering-tablet to perform and record arithmetic operations. Saunderson went on to become such a distinguished mathematician that despite his blindness he was eventually appointed Lucasian Professor of Mathematics at the University of Cambridge.

In his famous '*Lettre sur les aveugles*' (1749) published in London, Denis Diderot provides support that the blind can become as accomplished as the sighted and potentially have abilities that go beyond those of the sighted, provided that they received proper instruction. For example, Diderot relates how the blind man Lenôtre, among other remarkable things, was able to teach his own sighted son to read by means of raised letters, although reportedly this required more effort and dedication from the sighted son than it would have required from a blind person. In his letter, Diderot argues that the fact that 'our blind man judges symmetries quite well' represented a particularly critical example of a normal ability to comprehend shapes and objects. Diderot also argues that the person born blind is 'endowed with an exceptional sensitivity in his fingertips' and that the sense of touch 'weak in us [the seeing], is strong in those born blind and thus compensates for the loss of sight'. This is, in fact, a leading idea of the '*Lettre*': that the blind person is different from the seeing, but not inferior to him; that in the blind, the sense of touch can compensate for the absence of sight; and that the blind have such a highly developed sense of touch that it confers abilities which the seeing do not have and which enrich their experience beyond what sighted individuals can understand. Consistent with this, Diderot reports that when asked if he would be pleased to have his eyes, Lenôtre replies: 'I would like nothing so much as having long arms'. In other words, the value of sight is that one can perceive things at a distance, and long enough arms would overcome that limitation of touch while maintaining its superiority in extracting other details. Society was certainly not ready to embrace such notions. Denis Diderot was imprisoned in the fortress of Vincennes for calling special attention to the condition and needs of the blind in his letter, and accused of distributing writings 'contrary to religion, the state, or morals'.

Nevertheless, the history of the education of the blind is filled with remarkable examples in support of the idea that the blind can not only be educated, but may in fact develop abilities that the sighted lack. For example, in his book '*Biography of the Blind*', James Wilson (1835), himself blind since the age of four, relates the life of Blind Macguire, 'the family tailor of Mr. McDonald of Clanronald in Ivernshire, who lost his sight at fifteen years'. Supposedly his remarkable tactile sensitivity enabled him to distinguish the various Tartan patterns and colours by the feel of the cloth, and he was thus able to make a Tartan dress better and faster than any sighted tailor, since he was able to fit the patterns 'with a mathematical exactness that no tailor who enjoys his sight is capable of'. There are indeed many examples of individuals who have developed rather unique abilities, which they related to their loss of sight. For example, one of the world's most notable experts in marine molluscs, Prof. Geerat Vermeij, has been blind since the age of three, and in his biography '*Privileged Hands*' (1997), he has written eloquently on how blindness empowered and enabled him to explore seashells with such a heightened tactile sensitivity that he became able to distinguish differences between molluscs that had gone undetected by sighted experts.

Despite the anecdotal nature of many of the pertinent reports, educators of the blind recognized long ago the notion that losing sight might enable abilities otherwise not easily accessible. In fact, some went as far as to argue that removing residual sight might be advantageous in the instruction of the blind. One notable example is Reverend Thomas Carroll, former executive director of the Catholic Guild of All the Blind, founder of a number of Rehabilitation Centers for the Blind in the 1950s. He was the author of an influential book on rehabilitation and education of the blind, first published in 1953: '*Blindness: What it is, what it does, and how to live with it*' (Carroll, 1961). Father Carroll argued that, particularly in individuals who lose sight progressively and late in life, and those who have some residual light perception, rehabilitation training should employ 'optical occluders' during 'the greater part of the day', particularly during all skill courses. Complete visual deprivation thanks to the 'occluders' will avoid situations where the blind 'try hard to make use of the modicum sight remaining to him' and thus 'not be able to develop the use of his other senses'. Father Carroll believed that residual light perception can 'become a barrier' to the rehabilitation and education of the blind, as it prevents the full acquisition of non-visual abilities.

In summary, the history of education of the blind illustrates growing evidence that led to the realization that blind people may be different, but not necessarily inferior, to sighted individuals, and that in the absence of vision, certain abilities mediated by non-visual senses can become better than in the sighted. For a long time, this insight remained supported by anecdotal evidence, unsubstantiated by careful experimental testing, and detached from any neurobiological mechanistic explanation.

Reading and writing in the blind: lessons about paradoxical tactile abilities

Haüy not only established the first school for the blind, but also introduced the first reliable and practical system for tactile printing. However, Haüy, and most educators of the blind for many subsequent decades, believed that in the education of the blind, everything should be done to establish a bond of vital unity between the blind and the sighted. This included the writing system, which had to be legible by both the sighted and the blind, and thus systems for the blind to read and write had to be 'pleasing to the eye' and had to follow the principles derived from visual alphabets. As was carefully studied and demonstrated by Susana Millar's work on tactile reading (1997), such systems remained difficult for the blind to learn despite the many improvements and modified systems. Millar's careful study of the functions and limitations of the sense of touch shows that the writing systems for the blind grounded on Roman symbols may have been 'pleasing to the eye', but lacked tangibility.

In 1821, Louis Braille introduced his point-print system. The chief advantages of 'Braille' are its simplicity and easy acquisition; its 'tangibility' or efficiency in impressing the sense of touch; and its adaptability to writing and printing of text, numbers, as well as musical notation. However, in spite of its evident advantages, and the clear preference of this system of notation by the blind themselves, adoption of Braille was slow, in many cases due to obstinate attachment to theories regarding the requirements of the human brain devoid of vision. Perhaps most interesting in this context is that the Braille system, while clearly powerful and superior to the various embossed Roman script systems for the blind, was found to be extremely hard to acquire for the sighted. Blind individuals learned it well, but the sighted and even those visually impaired but with some residual vision found substantial difficulties. Sighted instructors for the blind generally become proficient readers of Braille by sight, not by touch, despite the fact that they need to learn to tilt the pages at the correct angle to the light to be able to see shadows made by the dots, so as to tell when a dot belongs to one side of the page or another. Father Caroll, whom we spoke about earlier, suggested the use of occluders or blindfolds during the instruction of Braille in order to make it easier for blind individuals with some residual vision to acquire the tactile Braille reading skill.

Braille reading requires the discrimination of subtle patterns of raised dots and the transformation of this spatial code into meaningful information. However, early reports did not show differences in sensory thresholds between blind and sighted subjects. Pascual-Leone and Torres (1993) confirmed there were no differences in sensory thresholds between 15 proficient blind Braille readers and 15 sighted volunteers with no Braille reading ability in response to electrical, touch (von Frey hairs) and two-point stimulation. No differences in sensory thresholds between the blind and sighted were also reported for grating ridge width using active scanning and grating discrimination using passive touch (Grant et al., 2000). In a Braille-like discrimination task, blind subjects were shown to have lower thresholds than sighted volunteers (Grant et al., 2000). However, this behavioural advantage receded by the third or fourth session, indicating that blind people might not possess increased tactile sensitivity, but rather use the available information in a more efficient way in great part due to practice (Grant et al., 2000). In addition, blind subjects who use several

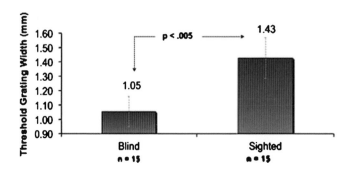

fingers to read Braille frequently misidentify which fingertip is being stimulated by a von Frey hair, suggesting maladaptive compensation in visually deprived individuals (Sterr *et al.*, 1998). While such findings are compelling, much of this work is confounded by the fact that variables such as the age of onset of blindness, the speed of loss of sight and the presence of residual vision were often not carefully controlled for.

Van Boven and collaborators (2000) compared the performance of early-blind subjects with that of sighted volunteers on a gratings orientation task (GOT). This task was chosen because comparing Braille discrimination performance can lead to confounds resulting from differential practice and familiarity effects as was reported by Grant *et al.* (2000). Furthermore, the GOT provides a quantitative measure of spatial acuity, as subjects must discriminate between two orthogonal directions of varying groove widths. Van Boven *et al.* (2000) found that the GOT threshold was significantly lower in blind individuals compared to sighted subjects, and that within the blind group sensory thresholds were lower for the Braille-reading finger compared to the other fingers tested (Figure 2.1).

The demonstration of heightened tactile acuity in the blind suggests that increased practice in the blind, perhaps also mediated by visual deafferentation, results in plastic brain reorganizations that are functionally relevant (Pascual-Leone *et al.*, 2005). Furthermore, it appears that the Braille reading skill can be generalized to some tactile tasks (e.g. grating orientation discrimination) but not to all, as evidenced by the lack of tactile superiority in other paradigms. Thus, different tasks and populations (e.g. early blind vs. late blind) can yield quite different accounts of behavioural compensation in response to blindness.

An interesting question relating to these issues is whether instances of behavioural compensation in the blind are dependent upon irreversible sensory deprivation occurring during a specific developmental period or if, under certain experimental conditions, these changes can be experimentally induced in normal, adult subjects. Kauffman *et al.* (2002) wondered whether prolonged blindfolding in sighted individuals would lead to increased tactile performance on a Braille reading task. They compared the performance of sighted subjects on a Braille character discrimination task to that of normal participants blindfolded for a period of five days. Twenty-four subjects (mean age of approximately 25 years) were recruited and randomized into four groups: blindfolded and stimulated, blindfolded and not stimulated, sighted and stimulated, sighted and not stimulated. The stimulated groups were enrolled in an intensive tactile stimulation programme lasting for more than 6 hours a day including 4 hours of formal Braille instruction. To supplement their tactile stimulation, subjects also engaged in tactile games for at least two additional hours a day. For the Braille instruction, all subjects were taught to read using only their right index finger. Participants in the blindfolded/non-stimulated group were encouraged to use their sense of touch in their daily activities, despite not receiving formal Braille training. Braille recognition ability was tested in all subjects at days one (baseline), three and five, and participants remained blindfolded throughout the testing sessions. Using a specially designed computer-driven Braille stimulator (pins arranged according to a typical Braille cell design and letter standard), testing of both the right and left index finger was carried out. Braille characters were presented to the pad of the index finger using six plastic rods (measuring 1 mm each in diameter and rising to 1.5 mm high). When a Braille character was generated, the corresponding rods would push up and indent the skin of the resting finger pad. Pairs of Braille characters were presented and a forced-choice paradigm was used in which subjects were required to indicate whether a pair of characters were the same or different. The authors found that through five days of complete visual deprivation, blindfolded subjects performed significantly better than sighted subjects in the Braille discrimination task (Figure 2.2).

Indeed, of the blindfolded subjects, those that did not undergo intensive Braille training performed significantly better than the sighted and stimulated group. Thus, the superior performance of blindfolded individuals occurred despite equivalent practice between the two groups, suggesting that tactile differences between blind and sighted subjects do not entirely depend on prior experience and the learning of perceptual skills. Rather, the loss of vision itself paradoxically enhances tactile Braille reading abilities. In the blindfold group, serial fMRI scans revealed an increase in BOLD signal within the occipital cortex in response to tactile stimulation after five days of complete visual deprivation (Merabet et al., 2008) – see Figure 2.3. This increase in signal was no longer present 24 hours after blindfold removal. Reversible disruption of occipital cortex function on the fifth day (by repetitive transcranial magnetic stimulation – rTMS) impaired Braille character recognition ability in the blindfold group but not in non-blindfolded controls (Figure 2.3). This disruptive effect was no longer evident once the blindfold had been removed for 24 hours. Therefore, it appears that superior tactile abilities can develop quickly with visual deprivation and are sustained by rapid plastic changes.

Music in the blind: lessons from paradoxical auditory abilities

Since ancient times, the blind have been taught to sing, and anecdotes abound about the blind being particularly gifted musicians. The common idea that the blind learn music by ear is frequently erroneous, arising partly from the assumption that those who are sightless must of course possess an abnormally acute sense of hearing, and partly from the fact that so many persons are unaware that a tactile musical notation exists. Louis Braille, himself an accomplished musician, adapted his punctographic system to musical notation. Thus, musical instruction is needed for the blind, as it is for the sighted to become proficient musicians, but Valentine Haüy (who is known as the 'father and apostle of the blind') and many subsequent educators of the blind recognized the apparent superior ability that blind children had in learning music. Piano-tuning became a common profession for the blind and thus it is not surprising that, years later, careful epidemiologic and experimental studies confirmed that absolute pitch is many fold more common in early and congenitally blind than among sighted controls (Hamilton et al., 2004).

Absolute pitch is defined as the ability to identify or produce the pitch of a sound on the Western musical scale without any external reference tone. Absolute pitch is exceptionally rare among the musically inexperienced, and is present in a minority of trained Western

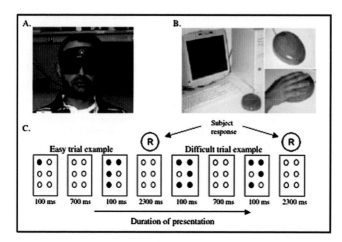

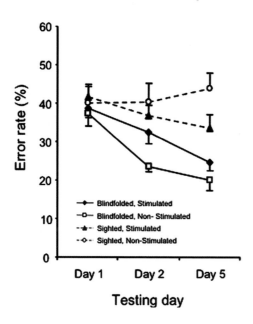

Figure 2.2 TOP: (A) Photograph of the blindfold used in the study. (B) Photograph of the computer-driven Braille stimulator. (C) A schematic summary that exemplifies two trials of varying difficulties of Braille character discrimination. BOTTOM: Results shown for each group's performance on the Braille character discrimination task over the course of the study. Note that blindfolded subjects learn significantly better than sighted controls.

musicians. A number of influences, both genetic and environmental, are thought to contribute to the development of absolute pitch. One critical factor for the acquisition of absolute pitch is early commencement of musical training, and a number of studies (reviewed below) demonstrate that almost all musicians who have absolute pitch begin musical training before the age of 7, and that the development of absolute pitch in musicians who begin training after the age of 11 is highly unlikely.

Hamilton *et al.* (2004) surveyed a group of blind musicians and found the prevalence of absolute pitch to be much higher among blind musicians than among the sighted. In the sample, 57.1% of the blind musicians were found to have absolute pitch, while the highest reported prevalence of absolute pitch among Caucasian musicians is

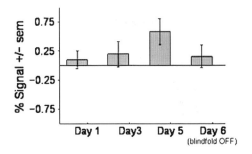

Figure 2.3 Differential tactile activation contrasting the blindfolded and non-blindfolded groups. A region of interest (ROI) was defined by the area of occipital activation found on day 5 in the group maps. The average differential tactile activity between groups in this ROI is plotted here in z-score units across days of the study. The difference between groups was significant on day 5, as expected from the definition of the ROI, but did not reach significance on any other day.

approximately 18%. (For reasons that are yet to be fully explained, the prevalence of absolute pitch among Asians is higher.) All of the blind musicians in the study were rendered blind by peripheral causes that occurred after birth, and thus the high prevalence of absolute pitch in these subjects indicates that an environmental stimulus such as the loss of sight can heavily influence the development of absolute pitch, even in persons who may not have been otherwise genetically predisposed to manifest this ability. In fact, two findings suggest that the mechanisms underlying development of absolute pitch in the blind and the sighted might differ. First, the age of initial music exposure among the blind (average = 8.45 years; range = 3–24 years) was significantly later than that which had been observed among sighted, absolute pitch musicians (average = 5.06 years; range = 3–7 years). Second, blind musicians with absolute pitch did not demonstrate the same exaggerated *planum temporale* asymmetry previously observed in sighted musicians with absolute pitch. In contrast, blind musicians with absolute pitch showed a much greater degree of variability in *planum temporale* than had been previously demonstrated in sighted musicians with or without absolute pitch, in sighted non-musicians, or in blind individuals without absolute pitch regardless of musical training. These findings suggest that in blind subjects, even a late onset of musical training serves to induce neural changes conducive to the development of absolute pitch, and that these neural changes must have a different substrate than those responsible for absolute pitch in the sighted. It is tempting to hypothesize that the plastic changes induced in the brain by blindness must contribute to this fact.

Neural substrate for paradoxical phenomena in the blind: plastic change in non-visual brain areas

Blind individuals need to extract crucial information from available sensory modalities to function in their surroundings. The development of Braille as a written language is an excellent example of how the blind exploit their remaining sensory abilities to read and communicate effectively. In Braille reading, blind individuals learn to explore patterns haptically by sweeping their index finger over raised dots to extract meaningful language (proficient Braille readers often learn to scan with multiple fingers and both hands). Thus, it would be intuitive to think that sensorimotor systems would be a likely locus of neural reorganization in an individual learning to read Braille. Indeed, evidence from both animal and human studies has shown that tactile experience can modify the somatosensory representation of a body part such as the hand and its repeated use can lead to the enlargement of its cortical representation (Jenkins *et al.*, 1990; Merzenich *et al.*, 1984).

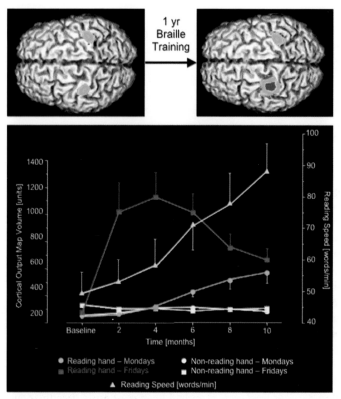

Figure 2.4 TOP: Enlarged cortical representation of the Braille-reading finger following a year of Braille training. BOTTOM: Changes in cortical representation appear to be characterized by two periods: an initial, transient phase (approximately 6 months) followed by a more stable period. Initially, rapid and prominent enlargement of cortical representation occurs, reflecting the recruitment of unmasked connections. Subsequently, cortical representation stabilizes, reflecting enduring structural changes.

Animal evidence also strongly suggests that changes in cortical representation may directly reflect perceptual ability (Recanzone *et al.*, 1990). Similarly, in humans, several lines of evidence suggest that Braille reading is associated with plastic changes within the somatosensory cortex. Pascual-Leone and Torres (1993) recorded somatosensory evoked potentials from proficient Braille readers and demonstrated that the cortical representation of the index finger was larger than that of sighted controls and blind non-Braille readers. In addition, the cortical representation of the Braille-reading finger was enlarged compared to the homologous finger of the opposite hand (Figure 2.4).

Consistent with these findings, transcranial magnetic stimulation (TMS)-induced suppression of tactile stimulus perception could be obtained through the stimulation of a larger number of sites over the sensorimotor cortex representation of the Braille-reading finger of blind individuals compared to non-reading fingers or index fingers of control subjects (Pascual-Leone and Torres, 1993). At a behavioural level, these findings are consistent with the fact that blind individuals must quickly extract highly detailed spatial information for effective Braille reading. This expanded cortical representation may allow blind readers to carry out the complex task of Braille reading. The enlarged representation of the Braille reading finger in proficient Braille readers was further supported by a TMS mapping study in which motor-evoked potentials in the first dorsal interosseus muscle (involved lateral movements of the index finger) of proficient blind Braille readers could be elicited through the stimulation of a larger area of motor cortex than that of the non-reading hand and both hands of control subjects (Pascual-Leone and Torres, 1993). These changes might be due to the fact that Braille reading creates new motor demands on the reading finger, resulting in cortical over-representations. It must be noted that longitudinal studies (over the course of one year) during the learning of Braille have shown cortical enlargements proceeding along two timescales: an initial, transient phase (lasting roughly six months), followed by a more stable period. The initial phase is characterized by a rapid and dramatic enlargement of cortical representation, likely due to the unmasking of existing connections and changes in synaptic efficacy, while the second phase is characterized by a more stable cortical representation of the reading finger, reflecting enduring structural changes at multiple neuronal levels (Pascual-Leone *et al.*, 1999) – see Figure 2.4.

Proficient Braille readers often use more than one finger to read faster. As such, Sterr *et al.* (1998) investigated the effects of three-finger reading on somatotopic representations in Braille readers. They noticed that multiple-finger readers made frequent mistakes in identifying which of their fingers was touched during a sensory threshold task. This behaviour was not observed in single-finger readers or in sighted controls. Using magnetic source imaging, Sterr *et al.* were able to demonstrate that the cortical representation of the reading fingers of blind individuals who are multiple-finger readers is much more complex and appears less simply topographic compared to Braille readers who use one finger. This brain reorganization pattern may correspond to the fusion of the cortical representation of the reading fingers caused by an increased level of simultaneous stimulation. This representational 'smearing' of digital topography may explain the mislocalization of tactile stimuli. The fusing of digital input in multiple finger readers may allow the incoming information to be processed more holistically, likely correlating with enhanced perceptual abilities and increased reading speed.

Parallel plastic changes can also be observed in the auditory brain system related to the enhanced auditory abilities of the blind. For example, responses to tone bursts and tonotopic mapping studies (using magnetoencephalography (MEG)) have revealed an expansion in auditory cortical areas responsive to auditory stimuli (Elbert *et al.*, 2002), and shorter signal response latencies (specifically the N1 potential, associated with acuity in central auditory areas) in blind compared to sighted controls (Elbert *et al.*, 2002). Using fMRI, Stevens and Weaver (2009) recently found that blindness acquired early in life results in more efficient processing of simple auditory stimuli in early stages of the auditory pathway. This further suggests that auditory-related plastic changes may differ in early-blind and late-blind individuals (Stevens *et al.*, 2007). For instance, Voss *et al.* (2008) found that early-blind individuals activated in different areas of the occipital cortex and performed significantly better than late-blind subjects on a monaural task. In addition, Wan *et al.* (2010) found that early-blind subjects performed better than sighted and late-blind subjects on a range of auditory perception tasks, suggesting that only early blindness facilitates heightened auditory perception.

More recently, structural changes outside of somatosensory and auditory cortical areas have also been reported. For example, superior spatial navigation performance in the blind has been correlated with a larger volume of the hippocampus (assessed by morphometric MRI; Fortin *et al.*, 2008; Lepore *et al.*, 2009), a structure whose role in navigation and spatial memory is well-established.

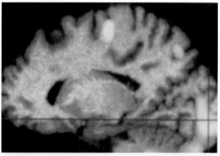

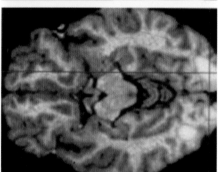

Figure 2.5 PET evidence of activation in visually deprived occipital cortex in early-blind subjects during a Braille reading task. TOP: Sagittal view revealing striate and extrastriate cortical activation. BOTTOM: Axial view confirming bilateral activation.

Neural substrate for paradoxical phenomena in the blind: plastic change in the deprived visual cortex

Studies using positron emission tomography (PET) provided early evidence that the visually deprived occipital cortex was active during processing of tactile information in the blind (Veraart *et al.*, 1990; Wanet-Defalque *et al.*, 1988; De Volder *et al.*, 1997; Sadato *et al.*, 1996), confirming bilateral activation within primary visual (striate) cortex and extrastriate occipital visual areas in early-blind subjects during a Braille reading task (Figure 2.5).

In fact, activation of the visually deprived occipital cortex was also evident during non-Braille tactile discrimination tasks such as angle discrimination. However, passive sweeping over a homogeneous pattern of Braille dots did not lead to such activation. Subsequent investigators have further refined and extended these early findings, addressing the role of imagery, the differences between early and late blind, and the role of tactile versus verbal/linguistic aspects of the task (Burton *et al.*, 2003; Pascual-Leone *et al.*, 2005; Röder and Neville, 2003). Cross-modal occipital cortex activation has also been reported in conjunction with the auditory domain, for example for auditory source localization (e.g. Gougoux *et al.*, 2005; Röder and Neville, 2003), auditory perception, pitch discrimination and speech processing (Röder *et al.*, 2002; Stevens *et al.*, 2007). Furthermore, recent neuroimaging studies have demonstrated occipital cortex activation during tasks requiring auditory verb-generation, semantic judgement tasks and speech processing (see Burton *et al.*, 2003; Amedi *et al.*, 2003; Pascual-Leone *et al.*, 2005; Röder *et al.*, 2002).

Importantly, it appears that behavioural measures of tactile and auditory performance in the blind correlate with the amount of activation in visually deprived occipital cortex. For example, blind subjects show superior verbal memory capabilities when compared to age-matched sighted controls, and in the blind group only, a strong positive correlation was

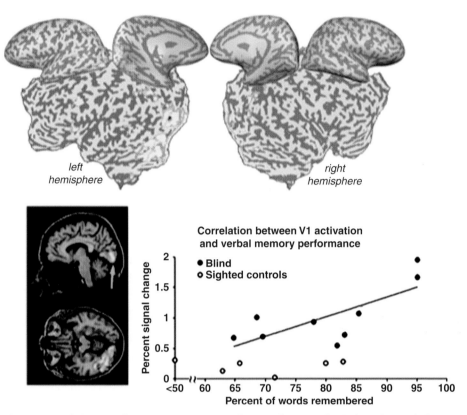

left
hemisphere

right
hemisphere

**Correlation between V1 activation
and verbal memory performance**

● Blind
○ Sighted controls

Percent signal change

Percent of words remembered

Figure 2.6 Verbal memory fMRI activation in early 'visual' cortex of congenitally blind correlates with their superior verbal memory abilities. Top panel shows Talairach normalized brain of both inflated and flattened representations of the cortex. The group results of the congenitally blind group showed robust activation in the left visual cortex during a verbal memory task of abstract words retrieval, which involves no sensory stimulation. The left lateralized activity stretched from V1 via extrastriate retinotopic areas to non-retinotopic areas such as LOC (top panel). This activation was correlated with the subjects' verbal memory abilities (lower panel). The figure shows the percentage of words they remembered six months after the scan. In general, blind subjects remembered more words and showed greater V1 activation than the sighted controls. Blind subjects also showed a significant correlation between brain activity and performance.

found between the magnitude of striate cortex activation and the verbal memory capabilities of individual subjects – see Figure 2.6 (Amedi *et al.*, 2003; Hertrich *et al.*, 2009). These results suggest that tactile, auditory, language and memory processing in the blind incorporates a widespread network that encompasses 'visual' brain areas, and that cross-modal recruitment of the visually deprived occipital cortex plays a critical role in the development of better-than-sighted abilities in the blind.

Such cross-modal plastic changes appear not to be limited to the primary occipital cortex, and may also occur in other brain areas normally considered visual in sighted individuals. For instance, Garg *et al.* (2007) demonstrated that 'visual' frontal eye fields (FEF) are involved in auditory attention in the blind. Amedi *et al.* (2010) found that the lateral occipital cortex is involved in tactile object exploration in blind subjects. Additionally, Saenz *et al.* (2008) showed that the visual motion area MT+/V5 activates in response to auditory motion in two blind subjects who partially recovered their vision. Recent evidence

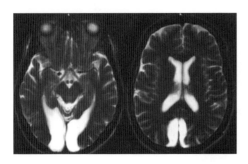

Figure 2.7 A T2-weighted MR image of a bilateral occipital stroke in a highly proficient Braille reader, following which, she lost the ability to read Braille.

further suggests early blindness can lead to neuroplastic changes in the dorsal stream (Fiehler and Rosler, 2010). Using fMRI, Fiehler and Rosler (2010) demonstrated that both congenitally blind and sighted subjects reveal similar activation patterns within the dorsal stream during guided hand movements.

However, patterns of activation revealed by functional neuroimaging establish an *association* between activity in a given region or network with task performance, rather than proving a *causal* link. To establish a casual link, one might rely on serendipity of nature and look for patients with localized brain damage. Indeed, the case of an early-blind woman (once a highly proficient Braille reader) who became unable to read Braille following a bilateral occipital stroke supports the notion of a causal link between the ability to read Braille and occipital function (Hamilton *et al.*, 2000) – see Figure 2.7.

An experimental alternative to naturally occurring lesions is offered by TMS that can be used to induce 'virtual lesions' and recreate the behavioural deficits observed following focal cortical lesions. Cohen *et al.* (1997) were the first to show that tactile identification of Braille letters becomes impaired after TMS delivery to the occipital cortex of early blind subjects. The causal role of visual cortex in Braille reading was also demonstrated by applying rTMS to the occipital cortex (Kupers *et al.*, 2007). In contrast, TMS of the occipital cortex in sighted controls does not impair their ability to identify embossed Roman letters by touch. In a follow-up study, single TMS pulses were applied at varying time intervals following the presentation of a Braille symbol to the subject's index finger (Hamilton and Pascual-Leone, 1998). In sighted and blind subjects, TMS delivered to the somatosensory cortex interfered with the detection of a tactile stimulus presented 20–40 ms earlier to the index finger pad (Figure 2.8), while occipital stimulation had no effect on detection. However, TMS to occipital cortex disrupted processing of Braille symbols only in congenitally blind subjects and at interstimulus intervals of 50–80 ms (Figure 2.8).

Contrary to the findings after sensorimotor TMS, following occipital TMS, blind subjects generally knew that a tactile Braille stimulus had been presented, but they were unable to discriminate what Braille symbol it was. More recently, Amedi and colleagues found similar results for the activation of the occipital cortex during auditory–verb generation in early-blind individuals: TMS of the left occipital or occipito-temporal cortex led to a disruption in verb-generation in the blind, but not in the sighed (Amedi *et al.*, 2004). These and further results by other investigators (for review, see Amedi *et al.*, 2005b) establish a causal link between activity in the visually deprived occipital cortex and processing of non-visual information in the blind, and suggest that the paradoxical, better-than-sighted performance of early and congenitally blind in certain tasks might be linked to the cross-modal recruitment of the visually deprived visual cortex.

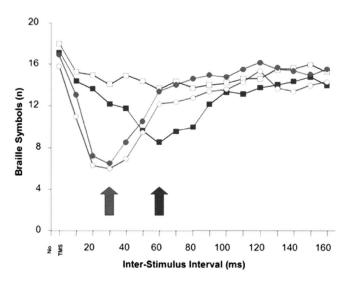

TMS in Somatosensory cortex:
● Braille symbol identification
○ Braille symbol detection

TMS in 'Visual' occipital cortex:
● Braille symbol identification
○ Braille symbol detection

Figure 2.8 Single TMS pulses were applied at varying time intervals following the presentation of a Braille symbol to the subject's index finger. In sighted and blind subjects, TMS delivered to the somatosensory cortex interfered with the detection of a tactile stimulus presented 20–40 ms earlier to the index finger pad, while occipital stimulation had no effect on detection. However, TMS to occipital cortex disrupted processing of Braille symbols only in congenitally blind subjects and at interstimulus intervals of 50–80 ms.

Cross-modal recruitment of occipital cortex appears, however, to be dependent on the timing of visual loss (Sadato et al., 2002). For example, Cohen et al. (1999) found greater activation in congenitally and early-blind individuals than in late-blind and sighted subjects using $H_2{}^{15}O$ PET scanning, suggesting a critical period for cross-modal plasticity. This period of susceptibility may be linked to structural changes and shifts in functional connectivity, such as increased connectivity between occipital and frontal language areas, in early-blind but not late-blind individuals (Lepore et al., 2010; Liu et al., 2007).

Remarkably, complete, but transient, visual deprivation in sighted subjects (i.e. five days of blindfolding) seems to be sufficient to lead to recruitment of the primary visual cortex for tactile and auditory processing (see Pascual-Leone et al., 2005 for review). Sudden visual loss can lead to rapid changes in auditory-evoked visual awareness (Rao et al., 2007). The speed of these functional changes in sighted individuals is such that it is highly improbable that new cortical connections are established. Therefore, somatosensory and auditory connections to the occipital cortex must already be present and are presumably 'unmasked' under these experimental conditions. Nevertheless, these findings in sighted blindfolded subjects do not demonstrate that the mechanisms of recruitment in tactile processing in the blind and under blindfolded conditions are identical. More studies are needed to address this important issue. The substrates recruited in the visually deprived occipital cortex may be mediated by shifts in connectivity across entire brain areas (Liu et al., 2007). However, glial cells may play an important role, such that functional changes become associated with structural changes (Bernabeu *et al.*, 2009; Jiang *et al.*, 2009) in occipital cortex.

Conceptual framework

We have focused on the blind, but there are many parallels (albeit with some differences) between findings in blind and deaf individuals (for review and discussion, see Merabet and Pascual-Leone, 2009). It seems reasonable to presume that in the setting of any sensory deprivation, the brain reorganizes to exploit the sensory inputs at its disposal. We have provided supporting evidence for this in the blind, but similar data are accumulating in the deaf (Lambertz *et al.*, 2005; Bavelier *et al.*, 2000; Neville and Lawson, 1987; Merabet and Pascual-Leone, 2009). In this context, neural processing of the preserved, residual sensory information may change. Some of the changes may prove maladaptive, but others may render the blind individual better than the sighted in processing certain non-visual information, or the deaf better than the hearing in processing certain non-auditory information. In addition, the functional and structural identity of the deprived visual or auditory cortex may switch to the processing of information via other sensory modalities. Alternatively, it is possible that the given cortical brain region inherently possesses the computational machinery necessary for the processing of information from multiple senses. According to this hypothesis, the occipital, 'visual' cortex or the temporal, 'auditory' cortex might be viewed as 'operators' of a given function based on the best-suited input available. When sight is present, visual input may be deemed as ideal for the operation of the occipital cortex, to the point of suppressing or masking inputs from other sensory modalities. Similarly, when hearing is present, auditory input may be ideal for the operation of the superior temporal cortex, to the point of suppressing or masking inputs from other sensory modalities. In the absence of its 'preferred' sensory input, a given cortical area may employ other sensory inputs for its operation (Pascual-Leone and Hamilton, 2001). Such a change may lead to behavioural changes, but the result may paradoxically prove adaptive and result in better-than-normal performance for certain tasks.

In essence, loss of vision or hearing can lead to the paradoxical enhancement of certain abilities in the blind or the deaf by different underlying neural mechanisms. The first mechanism represents 'expression of normal physiology', where normally inhibited or masked functions in the sighted or the deaf are revealed by visual or hearing loss. A second mechanism represents '*de novo* cross-modal plasticity', where in response to visual or auditory deprivation new sensory associations and connectivity patterns are created (Burton *et al.*, 2003). In fact, these two mechanisms may well be inextricably linked. The unmasking of pre-existing connections and shifts in connectivity likely represent rapid, early plastic changes, which can lead, if sustained and reinforced, to slower developing but more permanent structural changes, such as the establishment of new neural connections. This may account for the rapid recruitment of occipital cortex function observed in blindfolded subjects and the difference in the magnitude of the reorganization between early-blind and late-blind. This hypothesis also leads to the prediction that careful task choice and experimental design will reveal non-visual roles of the occipital cortex in sighted subjects. Indeed, such non-visual roles can be demonstrated for object recognition (Amedi *et al.*, 2001), processing of orientation (Zangaladze *et al.*, 1999), and judging distance between Braille dots (Merabet *et al.*, 2004); for review see Amedi *et al.* (2005a). Therefore, the occipital cortex is not 'simply' visual, but rather participates in tactile, auditory and perhaps even linguistic tasks. In parallel to this argument, the superior temporal cortex may be considered to be not 'simply' auditory, but rather participates in tactile, visual and higher-cognitive tasks.

Future challenges and questions

It seems clear that loss of a sensory modality does not lead to a global cognitive decline and is in fact associated with definite and striking advantages for processing of some, but not all, information via the remaining senses. The mechanisms accounting for such instances of paradoxical functional facilitation, and determining which functions are enhanced beyond normal following sensory loss and which are not, remains an important challenge. Similarly, the question of possible critical periods remains unresolved and requires attention. Are there specific developmental time windows for certain instances of paradoxical functional facilitation after sensory loss? If so, is the critical period different for different functions or senses? The effort to further elucidate the mechanisms and clarify the potential functional benefits of such facilitations will help identify the broader implications of current findings for potential therapeutic interventions and a better understanding of recovery and rehabilitation mechanisms.

While TMS and other forms of non-invasive brain stimulation are currently used to measure neuroplastic changes, they may potentially serve as therapeutic agents as well. For instance, transcranial Direct Current Stimulation (tDCS) may promote neuroplastic changes following sensory loss. In combination with rehabilitation therapy, tDCS has been demonstrated to improve motor function following stroke-induced limb paralysis (Bolognini *et al.*, 2009). Although tDCS promotes direct functional recovery of the affected limb, plasticity may be promoted through strengthening existing but non-dominant connections (Bolognini *et al.*, 2009). In turn, application of non-invasive brain stimulation to the visual cortex increases excitability, and in combination with an auditory task may serve to facilitate the unmasking of alternative connections and thereby facilitate cross-modal plastic changes.

In addition to neuromodulation, behavioural interventions or biofeedback might offer valuable strategies to harness brain plasticity and guide the brain changes following sensory loss to maximize functional outcomes. In this context, technology-based interventions, for example computer games, might offer particularly powerful approaches that might be adaptable to blind, deaf and other individuals with sensory impairments.

Another direction for future research is whether paradoxical functional facilitation can be generalized to cases of tactile sensory loss. Werhahn and colleagues (2002) demonstrated that deafferentation within the tactile modality alone can lead to paradoxical functional facilitation. The authors observed enhanced tactile spatial acuity in the left hands of subjects upon cutaneous anaesthesia to the right hand, suggesting that such rapid neuroplastic changes implicate existing neural substrates rather than practice effects (Werhahn *et al.*, 2002).

Moore and colleagues (1999) further suggest that spatial acuity improvements can be observed on the amputated stump. Perhaps, a better understanding of cortical processing mechanisms following deafferentation and sensory loss will elucidate what type of plastic changes will likely occur. In addition, while enhancement in spatial acuity and other perception measures are improvements in the remaining senses, further investigation is needed to determine whether these findings extend to overall functionality in activities of daily living. For instance, does improved tactile discrimination enable faster access to information through increased Braille reading speed? Do improvements in auditory pitch perception also allow blind individuals to navigate more safely within their environment? Are such changes only functionally relevant for individuals who lose a sensory modality early in life?

Ultimately, a major challenge and future hope is whether the insights obtained from the study of paradoxical facilitations in individuals with sensory loss might be applicable to all humans. Potentially, proper multisensory strategies might lead to faster skill acquisition, stronger and more stable knowledge formation, and enhanced abilities.

References

Alary, F., Duquette, M., Goldstein, R., *et al.* (2009). Tactile acuity in the blind: a closer look reveals superiority over the sighted in some but not all cutaneous tasks. *Neuropsychologia*, **47**: 2037–43.

Alary, F., Goldstein, R., Duquette, M., Chapman, C. E., Voss, P., & Lepore, F. (2008). Tactile acuity in the blind: a psychophysical study using a two-dimensional angle discrimination task. *Experimental Brain Research*, **187**: 587–94.

Amedi, A., Floel, A., Knecht, S., Zohary, E., & Cohen, L. G. (2004). Transcranial magnetic stimulation of the occipital pole interferes with verbal processing in blind subjects. *Nature Neuroscience*, 7: 1266–70.

Amedi, A., Malach, R., Hendler, T., Peled, S., & Zohary, E. (2001). Visuo-haptic object-related activation in the ventral visual pathway. *Nature Neuroscience*, 4: 324–30.

Amedi, A., Merabet, L. B., Bermpohl, F., & Pascual-Leone, A. (2005a). The occipital cortex in the blind: lessons about plasticity and vision. *Current Directions in Psychological Science*, 14: 306–11.

Amedi, A., Raz, N., Azulay, H., Malach, R., & Zohary, E. (2010). Cortical activity during tactile exploration of objects in blind and sighted humans. *Restorative Neurology and Neuroscience*, **28**: 143–56.

Amedi, A., Raz, N., Pianka, P., Malach, R., & Zohary, E. (2003). Early 'visual' cortex activation correlates with superior verbal memory performance in the blind. *Nature Neuroscience*, 6: 758–66.

Amedi, A., Von Kriegstein, K., Van Atteveldt, N. M., Beauchamp, M. S., & Naumer, M. J. (2005b). Functional imaging of human crossmodal identification and object recognition. *Experimental Brain Research*, **166**: 559–71.

Arnold, P., & Murray, C. (1998). Memory for faces and objects by deaf and hearing signers and hearing nonsigners. *Journal of Psycholinguistic Research*, **27**: 481–97.

Bavelier, D., Tomann, A., Hutton, C., *et al.* (2000). Visual attention to the periphery is enhanced in congenitally deaf individuals. *Journal of Neuroscience*, **20**: RC93 (1–6).

Bavelier, D., Dye, M. W., & Hauser, P. C. (2006). Do deaf individuals see better? *Trends in Cognitive Science*, **10**: 512–18.

Bernabeu, A., Alfaro, A., Garcia, M., & Fernandez, E. (2009). Proton magnetic resonance spectroscopy (1H-MRS) reveals the presence of elevated myo-inositol in the occipital cortex of blind subjects. *Neuroimage*, **47**: 1172–6.

Bettger, J., Emmorey, K., McCullough, S., & Bellugi, U. (1997). Enhanced facial discrimination: effects of experience with American sign language. *Journal of Deaf Studies and Deaf Education*, 2: 223–33.

Bliss, I., Kujala, T., & Hamalainen, H. (2004). Comparison of blind and sighted participants' performance in a letter recognition working memory task. *Brain Research. Cognitive Brain Research*, 18: 273–7.

Bolognini, N., Pascual-Leone, A., & Fregni, F. (2009). Using non-invasive brain stimulation to augment motor training-induced plasticity. *Journal of Neuroengineering and Rehabilitation*, 6: 8.

Bosworth, R. G., & Dobkins, K. R. (2002). Visual field asymmetries for motion processing in deaf and hearing signers. *Brain and Cognition*, **49**: 170–81.

Bottari, D., Nava, E., Ley, P., & Pavani, F. (2010). Enhanced reactivity to visual stimuli in deaf individuals. *Restorative Neurology and Neuroscience*, **28**: 167–79.

Burton, H., Diamond, J. B., & McDermott, K. B. (2003). Dissociating cortical regions activated by semantic and phonological tasks: a FMRI study in blind and sighted people. *Journal of Neurophysiology*, **90**: 1965–82.

Calvert, G. A., & Thesen, T. (2004). Multisensory integration: methodological approaches and emerging principles in the human brain. *Journal of Physiology Paris*, **98**: 191–205.

Carroll, T. J. (1961). *Blindness: What It Is, What It Does, and How to Live With It*. Boston, MA: Little, Brown & Co.

Cattani, A., Clibbens, J., & Perfect, T. J. (2007). Visual memory for shapes in deaf signers and nonsigners and in hearing signers and nonsigners: atypical lateralization and enhancement. *Neuropsychology*, **21**: 114–21.

Chebat, D. R., Rainville, C., Kupers, R., & Ptito, M. (2007). Tactile-'visual' acuity of the tongue in early blind individuals. *Neuroreport*, **18**: 1901–04.

Cohen, L. G., Celnik, P., Pascual-Leone, A., *et al.* (1997). Functional relevance of cross-modal plasticity in blind humans. *Nature*, **389**: 180–3.

Cohen, L. G., Weeks, R. A., Sadato, N., Celnik, P., Ishii, K., & Hallett, M. (1999). Period of susceptibility for cross-modal plasticity in the blind. *Annals of Neurology*, **45**: 451–60.

Collignon, O., Renier, L., Bruyer, R., Tranduy, D., & Veraart, C. (2006). Improved selective and divided spatial attention in early blind subjects. *Brain Research*, **1075**: 175–82.

Corina, D., Chiu, Y. S., Knapp, H., Greenwald, R., San Jose-Robertson, L., & Braun, A. (2007). Neural correlates of human action observation in hearing and deaf subjects. *Brain Research*, **1152**: 111–29.

Cuevas, I., Plaza, P., Rombaux, P., De Volder, A. G., & Renier, L. (2009). Odour discrimination and identification are improved in early blindness. *Neuropsychologia*, **47**: 3079–83.

De Volder, A. G., Bol, A., Blin, J., *et al.* (1997). Brain energy metabolism in early blind subjects: neural activity in the visual cortex. *Brain Reearchs*, **750**: 235–44.

Diderot, D. (1749). *Lettre Sur Les Aveugles: A L'usage de Ceux qui Voyent*. London [electronic resource].

Duhamel, J. R. (2002). Multisensory integration in cortex: shedding light on prickly issues. *Neuron*, **34**: 493–5.

Dye, M., & Bavelier, D. (2010). Attentional enhancements and deficits in deaf populations; an integrative review. *Restorative Neurology and Neuroscience*, **28**: 181–92.

Dye, M. W., Baril, D. E., & Bavelier, D. (2007). Which aspects of visual attention are changed by deafness? The case of the Attentional Network Test. *Neuropsychologia*, **45**: 1801–11.

Dye, M. W., Hauser, P. C., & Bavelier, D. (2009). Is visual selective attention in deaf individuals enhanced or deficient? The case of the useful field of view. *PLoS One*, **4**: e5640.

Elbert, T., Sterr, A., Rockstroh, B., Pantev, C., Muller, M. M., & Taub, E. (2002). Expansion of the tonotopic area in the auditory cortex of the blind. *Journal of Neuroscience*, **22**: 9941–4.

Fieger, A., Roder, B., Teder-Salejarvi, W., Hillyard, S. A., & Neville, H. J. (2006). Auditory spatial tuning in late-onset blindness in humans. *Journal of Cognitive Neuroscience*, **18**: 149–57.

Fiehler, K., & Rosler, F. (2010). Plasticity of multisensory dorsal stream functions: evidence from congenitally blind and sighted adults. *Restorative Neurology and Neuroscience*, **28**: 193–205.

Finney, E. M., Clementz, B. A., Hickok, G., & Dobkins, K. R. (2003). Visual stimuli activate auditory cortex in deaf subjects: evidence from MEG. *Neuroreport*, **14**: 1425–7.

Forster, B., Eardley, A. F., & Eimer, M. (2007). Altered tactile spatial attention in the early blind. *Brain Research*, **1131**: 149–54.

Fortin, M., Voss, P., Lord, C., *et al.* (2008). Wayfinding in the blind: larger hippocampal volume and supranormal spatial navigation. *Brain*, **131**: 2995–3005.

Garg, A., Schwartz, D., & Stevens, A. A. (2007). Orienting auditory spatial attention engages frontal eye fields and medial occipital cortex in congenitally blind humans. *Neuropsychologia*, **45**: 2307–21.

Goldreich, D., & Kanics, I. M. (2003). Tactile acuity is enhanced in blindness. *Journal of Neuroscience*, **23**: 3439–45.

Gougoux, F., Lepore, F., Lassonde, M., Voss, P., Zatorre, R. J., & Belin, P. (2004). Neuropsychology: pitch discrimination in the early blind. *Nature*, **430**: 309.

Gougoux, F., Zatorre, R. J., Lassonde, M., Voss, P., & Lepore, F. (2005). A functional neuroimaging study of sound localization: visual cortex activity predicts performance in early-blind individuals. *PLoS Biology*, **3**: e27.

Grant, A. C., Thiagarajah, M. C., & Sathian, K. (2000). Tactile perception in blind Braille readers: a psychophysical study of acuity and hyperacuity using gratings and dot patterns. *Perception and Psychophysics*, **62**: 301–12.

Hamilton, R., Keenan, J. P., Catala, M., & Pascual-Leone, A. (2000). Alexia for Braille following bilateral occipital stroke in an early blind woman. *Neuroreport*, **11**: 237–40.

Hamilton, R. H., & Pascual-Leone, A. (1998). Cortical plasticity associated with Braille learning. *Trends in Cognitive Neuroscience*, **2**: 168–74.

Hamilton, R. H., Pascual-Leone, A., & Schlaug, G. (2004). Absolute pitch in blind musicians. *Neuroreport*, **15**: 803–6.

Harsdörffer, G. (1651). *Deliciae Mathematicae et Physicae*. Nuremberg.

Hertrich, I., Dietrich, S., Moos, A., Trouvain, J., & Ackermann, H. (2009). Enhanced speech perception capabilities in a blind listener are associated with activation of fusiform gyrus and primary visual cortex. *Neurocase*, **15**: 163–70.

Hugdahl, K., Ek, M., Takio, F., *et al.* (2004). Blind individuals show enhanced perceptual and attentional sensitivity for identification of speech sounds. *Brain Research. Cognitive Brain Research*, **19**: 28–32.

Jenkins, W. M., Merzenich, M. M., Ochs, M. T., Allard, T., & Guic-Robles, E. (1990). Functional reorganization of primary somatosensory cortex in adult owl monkeys after behaviorally controlled tactile stimulation. *Journal of Neurophysiology*, **63**: 82–104.

Jiang, J., Zhu, W., Shi, F., *et al.* (2009). Thick visual cortex in the early blind. *Journal of Neuroscience*, **29**: 2205–11.

Kauffman, T., Theoret, H., & Pascual-Leone, A. (2002). Braille character discrimination in blindfolded human subjects. *Neuroreport*, **13**: 571–4.

Klinge, C., Roder, B., & Buchel, C. (2010). Increased amygdala activation to emotional auditory stimuli in the blind. *Brain*, **133**: 1729–36.

Kupers, R., Pappens, M., de Noordhout, A. M., Schoenen, J., Ptito, M., & Fumal, A. (2007). rTMS of the occipital cortex abolishes Braille reading and repetition priming in blind subjects. *Neurology*, **68**: 691–3.

Lambertz, N., Gizewski, E. R., de Greiff, A., & Forsting, M. (2005). Cross-modal plasticity in deaf subjects dependent on the extent of hearing loss. *Brain Research. Cognitive Brain Research*, **25**: 884–90.

Lepore, N., Shi, Y., Lepore, F., *et al.* (2009). Pattern of hippocampal shape and volume differences in blind subjects. *Neuroimage*, **46**: 949–57.

Lepore, N., Voss, P., Lepore, F., *et al.* (2010). Brain structure changes visualized in early- and late-onset blind subjects. *Neuroimage*, **49**: 134–40.

Levanen, S., & Hamdorf, D. (2001). Feeling vibrations: enhanced tactile sensitivity in congenitally deaf humans. *Neuroscience Letters*, **301**: 75–7.

Liu, Y., Yu, C., Liang, M., *et al.* (2007). Whole brain functional connectivity in the early blind. *Brain*, **130**: 2085–96.

McCullough, S., & Emmorey, K. (1997). Face processing by deaf ASL signers: evidence for expertise in distinguishing local features.

Journal of Deaf Studies and Deaf Education, **2**: 212–22.

Merabet, L., Thut, G., Murray, B., Andrews, J., Hsiao, S., & Pascual-Leone, A. (2004). Feeling by sight or seeing by touch? *Neuron*, **42**: 173–9.

Merabet, L. B., & Pascual-Leone, A. (2009). Neural reorganization following sensory loss: the opportunity of change. *Nature Reviews Neuroscience*, **11**: 44–52.

Merabet, L. B., Hamilton, R., Schlaug, G., *et al.* (2008). Rapid and reversible recruitment of early visual cortex for touch. *PLoS One*, **3**: e3046.

Merzenich, M. M., Nelson, R. J., Stryker, M. P., Cynader, M. S., Schoppmann, A., & Zook, J. M. (1984). Somatosensory cortical map changes following digit amputation in adult monkeys. *Journal of Comparative Neurology*, **224**: 591–605.

Millar, S. (1997). *Reading by Touch*. Florence, KY: Taylor & Frances/Routledge.

Moore, C. E., Partner, A., & Sedgwick, E. M. (1999). Cortical focusing is an alternative explanation for improved sensory acuity on an amputation stump. *Neuroscience Letters*, **270**: 185–7.

Nava, E., Bottari, D., Zampini, M., & Pavani, F. (2008). Visual temporal order judgment in profoundly deaf individuals. *Experimental Brain Research*, **190**: 179–88.

Neville, H. J., & Lawson, D. (1987). Attention to central and peripheral visual space in a movement detection task: an event-related potential and behavioral study. II. Congenitally deaf adults. *Brain Research*, **405**: 268–83.

Occelli, V., Spence, C., & Zampini, M. (2008). Audiotactile temporal order judgments in sighted and blind individuals. *Neuropsychologia*, **46**: 2845–50.

Pascual-Leone, A., & Hamilton, R. (2001). The metamodal organization of the brain. *Progress in Brain Research*, **134**: 427–45.

Pascual-Leone, A., & Torres, F. (1993). Plasticity of the sensorimotor cortex representation of the reading finger in Braille readers. *Brain*, **116**: 39–52.

Pascual-Leone, A., Amedi, A., Fregni, F., & Merabet, L. B. (2005). The plastic human brain cortex. *Annual Review of Neuroscience*, **28**: 377–401.

Pascual-Leone, A., Tarazona, F., Keenan, J., Tormos, J. M., Hamilton, R., & Catala, M. D. (1999). Transcranial magnetic stimulation and neuroplasticity. *Neuropsychologia*, **37**: 207–17.

Proksch, J., & Bavelier, D. (2002). Changes in the spatial distribution of visual attention after early deafness. *Journal of Cognitive Neuroscience*, **14**: 687–701.

Rao, A., Nobre, A. C., Alexander, I., & Cowey, A. (2007). Auditory evoked visual awareness following sudden ocular blindness: an EEG and TMS investigation. *Experimental Brain Research*, **176**: 288–98.

Raz, N., Striem, E., Pundak, G., Orlov, T., & Zohary, E. (2007). Superior serial memory in the blind: a case of cognitive compensatory adjustment. *Current Biology*, **17**: 1129–33.

Recanzone, G. H., Allard, T. T., Jenkins, W. M., & Merzenich, M. M. (1990). Receptive-field changes induced by peripheral nerve stimulation in SI of adult cats. *Journal of Neurophysiology*, **63**: 1213–25.

Rettenbach, R., Diller, G., & Sireteanu, R. (1999). Do deaf people see better? Texture segmentation and visual search compensate in adult but not in juvenile subjects. *Journal of Cognitive Neuroscience*, **11**: 560–83.

Röder, B., & Neville, H. (2003). Developmental functional plasticity. In: Grafman S, Robertson IH, editors. *Handbook of Neuropsychology. 2nd ed.* Amsterdam: Elsevier, pp. 231–70.

Röder, B., Rosler, F., & Neville, H. J. (2001). Auditory memory in congenitally blind adults: a behavioral–electrophysiological investigation. *Brain Research. Cognitive Brain Research*, **11**: 289–303.

Röder, B., Rosler, F., & Spence, C. (2004). Early vision impairs tactile perception in the blind. *Current Biology*, **14**: 121–4.

Röder, B., Stock, O., Bien, S., Neville, H., & Rosler, F. (2002). Speech processing activates visual cortex in congenitally blind humans. *European Journal of Neuroscience*, **16**: 930–6.

Rokem, A., & Ahissar, M. (2009). Interactions of cognitive and auditory abilities in congenitally blind individuals. *Neuropsychologia*, 47: 843–8.

Rosenbluth, R., Grossman, E. S., & Kaitz, M. (2000). Performance of early-blind and sighted children on olfactory tasks. *Perception*, 29: 101–10.

Rouger, J., Lagleyre, S., Fraysse, B., Deneve, S., Deguine, O., & Barone, P. (2007). Evidence that cochlear-implanted deaf patients are better multisensory integrators. *Proceeding of the National Academy of Sciences USA*, 104: 7295–300.

Sadato, N., Okada, T., Honda, M., & Yonekura, Y. (2002). Critical period for cross-modal plasticity in blind humans: a functional MRI study. *Neuroimage*, 16: 389–400.

Sadato, N., Pascual-Leone, A., Grafman, J., *et al.* (1996). Activation of the primary visual cortex by Braille reading in blind subjects. *Nature*, 380: 526–8.

Saenz, M., Lewis, L. B., Huth, A. G., Fine, I., & Koch, C. (2008). Visual motion area MT+/V5 responds to auditory motion in human sight-recovery subjects. *Journal of Neuroscience*, 28: 5141–8.

Saramago, J. (1998). *Blindness*. New York, NY: Harcourt Brace & Company.

Sathian, K., & Stilla, R. (2010). Cross-modal plasticity of tactile perception in blindness. *Restorative Neurology and Neuroscience*, 28: 271–81.

Smith, M., Franz, E. A., Joy, S. M., & Whitehead, K. (2005). Superior performance of blind compared with sighted individuals on bimanual estimations of object size. *Psychological Science*, 16: 11–14.

Sterr, A., Muller, M. M., Elbert, T., Rockstroh, B., Pantev, C., & Taub, E. (1998). Perceptual correlates of changes in cortical representation of fingers in blind multifinger Braille readers. *Journal of Neuroscience*, 18: 4417–23.

Stevens, A. A., & Weaver, K. (2005). Auditory perceptual consolidation in early-onset blindness. *Neuropsychologia*, 43: 1901–10.

Stevens, A. A., & Weaver, K. E. (2009). Functional characteristics of auditory cortex in the blind. *Behavioural Brain Research*, 196: 134–8.

Stevens, A. A., Snodgrass, M., Schwartz, D., & Weaver, K. (2007). Preparatory activity in occipital cortex in early blind humans predicts auditory perceptual performance. *Journal of Neuroscience*, 27: 10,734–41.

Stevens, C., & Neville, H. (2006). Neuroplasticity as a double-edged sword: deaf enhancements and dyslexic deficits in motion processing. *Journal of Cognitive Neuroscience*, 18: 701–14.

Van Boven, R. W., Hamilton, R. H., Kauffman, T., Keenan, J. P., & Pascual-Leone, A. (2000). Tactile spatial resolution in blind braille readers. *Neurology*, 54: 2230–6.

Veraart, C., De Volder, A. G., Wanet-Defalque, M. C., Bol, A., Michel, C., & Goffinet, A. M. (1990). Glucose utilization in human visual cortex is abnormally elevated in blindness of early onset but decreased in blindness of late onset. *Brain Research*, 510: 115–21.

Vermeij, G. J. (1997). *Privileged Hands: A Scientific Life*. New York, NY: W.H. Freeman.

Voss, P., Gougoux, F., Zatorre, R. J., Lassonde, M., & Lepore, F. (2008). Differential occipital responses in early- and late-blind individuals during a sound-source discrimination task. *Neuroimage*, 40: 746–58.

Wallace, M. T., & Stein, B. E. (1997). Development of multisensory neurons and multisensory integration in cat superior colliculus. *Journal of Neuroscience*, 17: 2429–44.

Wan, C. Y., Wood, A. G., Reutens, D. C., & Wilson, S. J. (2009). Congenital blindness leads to enhanced vibrotactile perception. *Neuropsychologia*, 48: 631–5.

Wan, C. Y., Wood, A. G., Reutens, D. C., & Wilson, S. J. (2010). Early but not late-blindness leads to enhanced auditory perception. *Neuropsychologia*, 48: 344–8.

Wanet-Defalque, M. C., Veraart, C., De Volder, A., *et al.* (1988). High metabolic activity in the visual cortex of early blind human subjects. *Brain Research*, 446: 369–73.

Wells, H. G. (1911). *The Country of the Blind. The Country of the Blind, and Other Stories.* London: T. Nelson and Sons.

Werhahn, K. J., Mortensen, J., Van Boven, R. W., Zeuner, K. E., & Cohen, L. G. (2002). Enhanced tactile spatial acuity and cortical processing during acute hand deafferentation. *Nature Neuroscience,* **5**: 936–8.

Wilson, J. (1835). *Biography of the Blind: Lives of Such as Have Distinguished Themselves as Poets, Philosophers, Artists, etc. 4th ed.* Birmingham: J. W. Showell.

Zangaladze, A., Epstein, C. M., Grafton, S. T., & Sathian, K. (1999). Involvement of visual cortex in tactile discrimination of orientation. *Nature,* **401**: 587–90.

Chapter 3

Paradoxical functional facilitation and recovery in neurological and psychiatric conditions

Narinder Kapur

Summary

In neurological conditions, the major sets of paradoxical cognitive phenomena generally take one of five forms: (1) enhanced cognitive performance of neurological patients vis-à-vis neurologically intact individuals ('lesion facilitation'), and (2) alleviation or restoration to normal of a particular cognitive deficit following the occurrence of a second brain lesion ('double-hit recovery'). (3) A third set of paradoxical cognitive phenomena represents what may be termed 'hinder–help effects', where a variable that produces facilitation or detriment of performance in healthy participants results in opposite effects in neurological patients. (4) A fourth form of paradox relates to anomalies in the usual relationship between the presence/size of a brain lesion and the degree of cognitive deficit ('lesion–load paradox'). (5) A fifth paradox is where there may appear to be direct or indirect benefits for long-term neurological outcome as the result of specific cognitive deficits being present ('paradoxical positive outcome'). Discussion of neurological conditions will mainly be concerned with the first two sets of paradoxical phenomena, although the remaining three sets will also be reviewed briefly. In psychiatric disorders, analogous paradoxical phenomena have mainly been found in instances of enhanced cognitive performance in conditions such as depression and schizophrenia vis-à-vis healthy control participants, and also in reports of 'post-traumatic growth' after a major psychiatric illness or negative life events.

Introduction

As outlined in Chapter 1, the study of brain–behaviour relationships from cases of cerebral pathology has traditionally been embedded in the lesion-deficit model. This model essentially focuses on the presence of deficits following a brain lesion, and the implications that this observation has for understanding the function of the brain tissue which has been damaged. While this has provided important insights into our understanding of the organization of function in the human brain, and will remain a valuable tool for neuropsychologists and neurologists in the years to come, it suffers from a number of limitations.

(1) It concentrates on negative effects of changes to a system, potentially ignoring significant positive changes that have taken place.

(2) It focuses attention away from plasticity-related phenomena – such as involvement of connected remote neural systems, increased activity in homologous areas in the contralateral hemisphere with concomitant reduction in hemispheric specialization of

---

function, and topographical reorganization in areas immediately adjacent to the zone of pathology.

(3) It allows for potential confounds that may be caused by non-specific lesion effects, such as general perturbation of a neural system, making it problematical in linking behavioural deficit to locus of lesion or disease state.

(4) It tends to discourage consideration of positive compensatory and adaptive strategies that the brain can use and which could be employed in rehabilitation approaches to help overcome the effects of impairment.

Taking into account apparently paradoxical findings in brain illness and injury may therefore broaden the perspective of viewing brain–behaviour relationships in useful ways that are helpful in thinking about underlying processes, it may offer new approaches to management and rehabilitation, and it may help patients, families and health workers to think differently about their situation.

Where models of cognitive or brain systems address neurological conditions, most of them predict deficits in performance; some models may predict a double-dissociation between tasks or between patient groups. If a theory or model in science can predict empirical outcomes that are either counter-intuitive, or which go against the grain of established findings or established rules/laws, then they often carry greater weight and provide greater strength to the model or theory than observations that may be obvious or readily predicted to occur. Of course, other perspectives are not to be decried – it is likely that a diverse range of approaches will be required to achieve a full understanding of how the brain works in its normal state and in its diseased state, and how abnormalities in its working can best be rectified.

The general theme of this chapter is that the functions of the brain are based on an interactive network of systems which operates in both competitive and facilitatory modes. This form of interaction means that there is often a delicate balance and harmony between such systems for normal brain operations to successfully occur. It may also mean that damage to one system may sometimes have beneficial effects for particular operations of other systems in the brain. In this chapter, we will mainly focus on cognitive operations, but the same principles may apply to motor, sensory and other brain functions. The chapter will mainly be concerned with human lesion studies, but brief reference will also be made to relevant non-human lesion findings. The focus of this chapter will be on experimental studies in cases of acquired brain injury. Developmental disorders such as autism are discussed in Chapter 15. Studies that have reported enhanced creativity and artistic skills in conditions such as frontotemporal dementia are discussed in Chapter 12. In the case of the 'acquired savant syndrome', the reader is referred to chapter 20 in Treffert's recent book, *Islands of Genius* (Treffert, 2010) and to related articles (e.g. Hughes, 2010).

Lesion facilitation

(a)   Enhanced perceptual recognition

Moscovitch *et al.* (1997) reported that a patient, CK, with visual object agnosia (failure to know the meaning of seen objects) and acquired dyslexia following a closed head injury was able to identify faces embedded in a complex scene more successfully than control participants (Figure 3.1 and Table 3.1). The authors argued that competition from the

Table 3.1 Mean number of faces identified in forest after 1 and 5 min, and initial time elapsed before the first face was identified. (Moscovitch *et al.*, 1997. Reproduced with permission.)

	1 min			5 min			Initial time elapsed (s)		
	Mean	SD	Range	Mean	SD	Range	Mean	SD	Range
Controls (n = 12)	1.4	1.2	0–4	4.6	2.6	0–9	64	83.8	6–241
CK	4			9			1		

Figure 3.1 *The Forest Has Eyes,* © Bev Doolittle, reproduced with permission, courtesy of The Greenwich Workshop®, Inc. www.greenwichworkshop.com The faces are composed of trees, rocks and streams.

object-recognition system prevented normal people from detecting the hidden faces. In the case of the patient, CK, his object-recognition system was damaged. This resulted in reduced competition with the faces processing system, which could then operate more easily '. . . because CK lacked an intact object recognition system, the objects were less likely to capture his perceptual awareness than that of control subjects. As a result, the "faces" in the forest were likely to be detected more easily by CK, who was not prone to interference from the output of a competing object-recognition system' (Moscovitch *et al.*, 1997, p. 590).

Etcoff *et al.* (2000) demonstrated more successful use by aphasic (language-impaired) patients of facial cues to detect the presence of deception in video clips of people displaying or concealing powerful emotions. It is uncertain whether this represented improvement due to repeated practice at using facial expression in social settings, or whether it was due to a more fundamental neural reorganization of non-linguistic social processing mechanisms. This study helped to provide a scientific foundation to some of the 'bedside', clinical observations reported by Oliver Sacks in his book, *The Man Who Mistook His Wife for a Hat* (1985). In that book, Sacks eloquently describes aphasic patients (chapter 9, 'The President's Speech') who were bemused when President Ronald Reagan appeared on television, as they appeared to see through his words and gauge from nonverbal aspects of his communication that there was an element of reduced verisimilitude in his communication:

> Thus, the feeling I sometimes have – which all of us who work closely with aphasics have – that one cannot lie to an aphasic. He cannot grasp your words, and so cannot be deceived by them; but what he grasps he grasps with infallible precision, namely the *expression* that goes with the words, that total, spontaneous, involuntary expressiveness which can never be simulated or faked, as words alone can, all too easily . . . 'One can lie with the mouth', Nietzsche writes, 'but with the accompanying grimace, one nevertheless tells the truth' . . . Thus, it was the grimaces, the histrionisms, the false gestures and, above all, the false tones and cadences of the voice, which rang false for these wordless but immensely sensitive patients. It was to these (for them) most glaring, even grotesque, incongruities and improprieties that my aphasic patients responded, undeceived and undeceivable by words. That is why they laughed at the President's speech. (Sacks, 1985, pp. 78–9)

In the same chapter of his book, Sacks (1985) also refers to a patient, Emily D, with 'tonal agnosia' resulting from a right temporal lobe tumour, who lost the ability to appreciate the nonverbal qualities of speech – tone, timbre, feeling and character. This patient had been a poetess of some repute, and so was well-versed in the intricacies of language. She could no longer tell if a voice was angry or sad or cheerful. This patient too questioned the logic and veracity of what the President was saying. Sacks noted the patient's observations, 'He is not cogent', she said. 'He does not speak good prose. His word-use is improper. Either he is brain-damaged, or he has something to conceal'. 'Thus', Sacks concludes, 'the President's speech did not work for Emily D either, due to her enhanced sense of formal language use, propriety as prose, any more than it worked for our aphasics, with their word-deafness, but enhanced sense of tone' (1985, p. 80).

A few studies have pointed to alterations in processing of facial emotion following brain damage, such that negative affect is more likely to be categorized as positive. Thus, Sato *et al.* (2002) provided a patient with bilateral amygdala lesions who morphed fearful and angry expressions that were blended with some happy content. Compared to healthy people, the patient more frequently categorized these negative faces as having happy facial expressions. A related, but somewhat puzzling, finding was reported by Adolphs *et al.* (2001a), who found that patients with left or right hemisphere focal lesions were better than control participants at discriminating happy faces that were shown in the left half of their visual space. Adolphs *et al.* argued that in healthy participants there may be an active process that somehow impairs the discrimination of happy faces that are shown in the left visual field. Thus, when healthy participants see a happy face to the left of a neutral face, they actively perceive the two faces as being more similar, either because the neutral face is given a more positive valence, or because the happy face is seen more negatively. This active process may be impaired in brain-damaged individuals, and this then leads to positive valence accorded to faces in the left visual field.

(b)   Other lesion facilitation effects in visual perception

The fibre tract that connects the two hemispheres, the corpus callosum, is sometimes sectioned as a form of treatment for intractable epilepsy, to help prevent the spread of seizure activity from one half of the brain to the other. These patients are often referred to as 'split-brain' patients. Glickstein (Glickstein and Sperry, 1960; Glickstein, 2009) has noted that monkeys with split-brain lesions may perform better than monkeys without brain damage on a tactile reversal learning task. In such a task, the monkey may first be rewarded for feeling for and selecting the larger of two presented objects. After a while, the contingencies will change such that the small object is now rewarded. If the first part of the task is completed with the right hand, and the switch in the target object coincides with a change to the left hand, monkeys with intact brains are slow to learn the new relationship – their left hands learned from their right hand. In monkeys with a split brain, however, the system controlling the left hand has not learned from the right hand, and it is as if they are beginning the task anew. Paradoxically, therefore, the monkeys with brain damage outperform those without brain damage after the switch.

Split-brain patients have generally been found to have deficits in performance, and this is evident in clinical tasks such as left-handed tactile anomia – inability to name objects placed in the left hand, with eyes closed. However, in a few instances it would appear that these patients may be able to process information faster than individuals with an intact corpus callosum. Thus, Luck *et al.* (1989) found that bilateral stimulus arrays in a visual search task were scanned at a faster rate by split-brain patients than by control participants. Corballis *et al.* (2002) showed that split-brain patients are helped more than control participants by bilateral duplication of stimuli in a reaction time task. These authors, and others (e.g. Iacoboni, 2005), have speculated that the enhancement effect by bilateral duplication of stimuli may be due to cortical projection to a subcortical arousal system, and that this may be normally inhibited by an intact corpus callosum. Similar facilitation effects were observed by Pollman and Zaidel (1999) in a split-brain patient, and the role of trans-callosal inhibition in seizure-related paradoxical cognitive improvement was highlighted by Regard *et al.* (1994).

An unusual form of paradoxical functional facilitation in a patient with visual field loss has been reported by Trevethan *et al.* (2007). In a well-studied patient, DB, who suffered left-sided visual field loss following right occipital ablation of a vascular malformation, Trevethan *et al.* presented Gabor patches (parallel white gratings that are partially merged in a grey background) in DB's blind field or sighted field. He had to indicate in which of two time intervals the patch was shown. DB performed better in his blind field than in his sighted field, even though his performance in the sighted field was similar to that of control participants. DB reported no awareness when the patch was presented to his sighted field, but some subjective awareness when it was presented to his blind field. It is notable that DB's awareness of the patch vanished when it was randomly presented to the blind or sighted field, suggesting that the effect appeared to depend on his ability to predict its appearance in the blind field, and on the expectation that he might not be able to see it.

(c) Lesion facilitation in memory

(i) When forgetting the gist may help

The precise nature of the neural representation of knowledge remains to be elucidated, but many would agree that associative mechanisms probably play a major role in such representation – e.g. words that have a close semantic relationship with each other seem to form part of a neural network that follows certain principles and rules. A paradigm in memory research that took advantage of the role played by associative mechanisms is the Deese–Roediger–McDermott (DRM) paradigm, derived in part from an early paper by James Deese in the 1950s (Deese, 1959). In this paradigm, people are typically shown a list or words, pictures, etc., then later shown a new list, and are asked to judge whether each item was in the previous list. This new list may include items which were closely related to items in the previous list, but which were not presented – 'lures'. Thus, the word 'sleep' may be a lure for the words bed, pillow, night, tired, mattress, sheet, yawn, blanket.

The main focus of this section will be to consider the effects of brain pathology on performance in the DRM paradigm, and in particular the paradoxical effect that results in patients showing fewer false-alarm responses than controls; that is, they are less likely to state that 'lures' were present in the original list. It is important to note that such 'facilitation' is therefore only partial, since there is inevitably lower-than-normal performance on other components of a memory task, such as the number of correctly recognized items. To my knowledge, the observation of reduced false-positive errors (saying 'Yes' to lures in a recognition memory test) in neurological patients was first reported by Schacter (1996), who found that amnesic patients made fewer false-positive responses to lures than controls on recognition memory testing. Verfaellie et al. (2002) replicated this observation, and also showed that the effect was not dependent on retrieval features of the retention test, suggesting a locus of the effect at the level of initial encoding of the information or storage. In the case of Alzheimer's disease patients, Hudon et al. (2006) also reported fewer false-positive responses to lures compared to those diagnosed as having Mild Cognitive Impairment (MCI), a condition where there is evidence of everyday memory difficulties and some memory impairment, which sometimes represents the very early stages of Alzheimer's disease, but not severe enough to make a confident diagnosis. However, Budson et al. (2000) considered that this effect was dependent on stage of learning, with a greater false recognition effect on later trials when Alzheimer patients were made familiar with stimuli. While most clinical studies of the DRM effect have focused on patients with relatively pure amnesia or patients with dementia, Beversdorf et al. (2000) observed a similar reduction in false-positive responses to lure items in individuals with autism spectrum disorder. These various sets of findings using the DRM paradigm have been interpreted as demonstrating that some memory-disordered patients have a reduced 'gist' memory for material that has been presented earlier, with the implication that this impairment is mediated by limbic–diencephalic pathology.

Related to the DRM false recognition effect, where prior familiarity is based on established knowledge, is the 'illusory truth' effect, whereby prior familiarity based on earlier exposure to an item will result in the item being more likely to be judged 'true' in a subsequent verification task (e.g. 'a swan can stay in the air for four hours'). Mitchell et al. (2006) found that patients with Alzheimer's disease showed fewer illusory truth errors than healthy participants in conditions where there was greater reliance on familiarity judgements. Marsh et al. (2005) found that patients with probable Alzheimer's disease were less likely to be misled into believing the truth of fictional statements that had earlier been embedded in stories.

(ii) Freedom from interference

The phenomenon of proactive interference is a robust one in cognitive psychology – previous learning may interfere with new learning, especially where there are similarities in stimuli and task demands between the old and the new memory testing paradigm. Being adversely influenced by past retention trials depends on being able to retain such information, and several studies have exploited this fact to show that memory-disordered individuals' impaired retention of the past may result in a paradoxical reduction in various forms of proactive interference.

Figure 3.2 Screen appearance at: (A) start of trial and (B) after subject responds correctly. (Myers *et al.*, 2003. Reproduced with permission.)

A form of reduced proactive interference has been described by Myers *et al.* (2000, 2003), using a paradigm that originally derived from animal studies. It builds on observations where two stimuli just happen to be presented together, with no logical reason for their joint occurrence: 'uncorrelated exposure' or 'learned irrelevance'. This juxtaposition of the two stimuli will later interfere with the association of one of these stimuli in a novel pairing. In the case of human studies, this paradigm was instantiated using a cartoon via which participants were told that a magician on a computer screen would try and make a rabbit appear under his hat (Figure 3.2).

In Phase 1, the appearance of the rabbit was conditional on a particular 'magic word' appearing next to the magician, drawn in a balloon as if he was uttering the word. For participants in one group (the Exposed Group), the cartoon balloon was red or green, and was not correlated with the appearance of the rabbit. In Phase 2, the balloon colour did predict the appearance of the rabbit. Participants who were previously exposed to the uncorrelated balloon colour and appearance of the rabbit were slower at learning the association in Phase 2 than those who had not been pre-exposed. More importantly from the perspective of this book, this difference did not occur in amnesic patients, and they in fact learned the new pairings faster than control participants, who were encumbered by their memory of the previous (irrelevant) pairings (Figure 3.3). Clearly for the most part, when we learn rules about the world and apply them to our subsequent experience, this is adaptive. However, there may be conditions, and not simply those that pertain in Psychology experiments, where previous experience leads us astray.

The reverse effect, with exposed trials being easier than non-exposed trials, was found in patients with basal ganglia pathology (Parkinson's disease patients), thus leading Myers

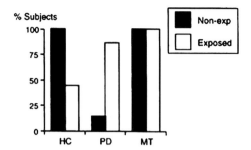

Figure 3.3 Percentage of participants reaching criterion on a test where they had to predict the appearance of a rabbit in the magician's hat. See text for description. HC, Healthy Controls; PD, Parkinson's disease; MT, Medial Temporal Lobe lesioned patients. (Myers *et al.*, 2003. Reproduced with permission.)

et al. to point to the competitive nature of 'declarative' memory systems (impaired in medial temporal lobe amnesia) and 'procedural' memory system (impaired in basal ganglia pathology) in this type of memory setting where there may be at least two routes to performing a task (cf. Wingard and Packard, 2008; Packard, 2009). Competition between more implicit, basal-ganglia based systems, and more explicit, cortically based systems, has also been invoked to account for paradoxes in the retrieval of learned information. For example, it is usually the case that one's first language is best preserved, but there are cases of paradoxically good recovery of second versus first language in some cases of bilingual aphasia, where a subcortical lesion may produce aphasia that particularly compromises an over-learned language system (Aglioti and Fabbro, 1993; Aglioti *et al.*, 1996; Lorenzen and Murray, 2008).

Where there is failure to recognize an item as familiar, and thus generate associations, this can be exploited in selected neurological patients to produce paradoxical functional facilitation effects in a paradigm where interference effects would be found in healthy participants. One such paradigm is a 'contrasting veridicality' paradigm, where familiar stimuli are paired with incongruous responses, as in a paired-associate learning paradigm. Thus, a face of Elvis Presley that was paired with the name 'Peter Williams' would be difficult to learn for healthy participants, but would be easier for someone who did not recognize the face as familiar due to a neurological condition. (The same argument could of course apply to situations where the face and name were unfamiliar for cultural or educational reasons.) Kapur *et al.* (1986) reported a patient with remote memory loss, where he was unable to recognize as familiar some famous personalities. This memory loss was related to a condition known as transient epileptic amnesia. He was better able to learn incongruous pairs (in this case, a name–name paired associate learning task) than control participants. However, McNeil and Warrington (1991) documented robust implicit learning effects in two prosopagnosic patients, such that their re-learning of correct face–name pairs was better than their learning of the wrong combinations. The third patient showed comparable levels of performance for true, false and novel pairings and no implicit memory effects. A further case of prosopagnosia who did not show implicit learning was reported by Riddoch *et al.* (2008).

Reduced interference effects in neurological patients compared to healthy participants have also been found in other studies. Wilson *et al.* (2000) found that over repeated testing on a verbal recognition memory test, people with brain injury did not show a decrease in performance over repeated testing, something that was found in control participants, and which was attributed to the build up in healthy individuals of proactive interference over successive test sessions; on later trials, performance might be affected by items that were intruded from earlier trials.

Bowles *et al.* (2007) reported on a patient with selective ablation of the left perirhinal region, but with relative sparing of the hippocampus. She was asked to view a series of words, and later report whether a given word had been in that series. When her response was positive, she was then asked to judge whether she recollected the specific experience of having encountered the word, or was simply basing her response on a more general sense of familiarity. Whilst overall her performance was in the average range, compared to control participants she rated a much larger number of these words as specific recollections. One possibility is that this may have represented a 'freedom from interference' effect, with hippocampal-mediated recollective processes normally competing with perirhinal-based familiarity processes. Release from such competition may reduce the effects of such familiarity processes, and thus result in enhanced recollective memory performance.

Explicit recollection of events or facts is often referred to as 'declarative memory', and contrasts with 'non-declarative' forms of memory, such as procedural memory. The latter form of memory typically operates in a very automatic way, and includes perceptual-motor skills such as riding a bike or writing. Freedom from the interfering effects of declarative memory was an explanation offered by Cavaco *et al.* (2004) to account for better procedural memory, in the form of a weaving task, in patients with larger medial temporal lobe lesions, compared to those with more selective lesions.

(iii) Does loss of meaning help detect repetition of words?

Exposure to the same items at different times naturally results in faster processing of the items the second time round. In one variation of an experimental paradigm used to study this phenomenon, participants are asked to judge if a word is a real word (e.g. table), amongst a collection of non-words (e.g. trom). Where identical words are used a short time apart, there is a faster response the second time around. If the words are semantically related (e.g. tiger – lion), there is also a faster response the second time round, but the decrease in reaction time is not as great as when the words were identical. However, in patients with loss of meaning of words, such as those with semantic dementia, the words 'tiger' and 'lion' may no longer have the specific connotations that they once had, and may now both be represented in the brain as the concept 'wild animal'. Thus, the argument goes, when the words 'tiger' and 'lion' are repeated in a word-decision task, patients with loss of word meaning due to semantic dementia or Alzheimer's disease, may actually show enhanced priming, 'hyperpriming'. This is in fact what has been found by a number of authors (e.g. Chertkow *et al.*, 1994; Giffard *et al.*, 2001). However, Cumming *et al.* (2006), while replicating the effect, also pointed out that the effect disappeared when allowance was made for slower reaction times at baseline (the occurrence of the first word), and that the effect may be due to reduced processing speed rather than degradation of semantic feature representation of the words. One situation where apparent semantic feature degradation resulted in arguably better-than-normal performance was noted by Kapur (1980). He asked a patient who had suffered a left hemisphere stroke, and was left with semantic paralexia (misreading words by substituting semantically associated words), to judge whether a spoken word reminded him of a given written word in any way. The patient was more likely to take into account high-level semantic categories (e.g. birds), and judge 'ostrich' to be related to 'peacock' than age-matched controls. It was argued that healthy controls were more focused on fine semantic distinctions, and could miss the superordinate connections in this task.

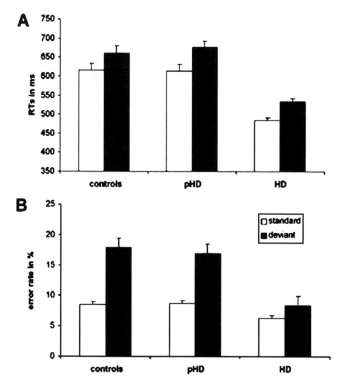

Figure 3.4 A, Mean reaction time (error bars indicate SEM) of the control, the pre-symptomatic (pHD), and the symptomatic (HD) group for the standard and deviant stimuli. B, Mean error rates (error bars indicate SEM) of the control, the pre-symptomatic (pHD), and the symptomatic (HD) group for the standard and deviant stimuli. (Beste *et al.*, 2008. Reproduced with permission.)

(iv) Other examples of paradoxical functional facilitation in human memory

Cools *et al.* (2010) found that patients with Parkinson's disease who were off medication were more resistant to the deleterious effects of a distractor item during a delayed response task where they had to memorize a face or a scene, and ignore a face/scene that was showing in the intervening period of a few seconds before free-choice retention testing. The authors suggested that modulation of prefrontal cortical activity by dopamine levels may have contributed to the effect that they found. Beste *et al.* (2008) reported that patients with Huntington's disease (HD) performed faster and more accurately than control participants or pre-symptomatic HD patients in an auditory signal detection task, where they had to differentially respond to the occurrence of long or short tones (Figure 3.4). At the neuro-physiological level, the authors also found that a neural marker of performance – mismatch negativity – was larger and occurred earlier for the HD group. The authors argued that increased activity of the NMDA-receptor system in HD that occurred as a result of the disease process facilitated signal propagation at the level of the striatum, which is damaged in HD, and that this mediated more efficient task performance. As the authors commented, 'As shown in the present study, a pathogenic increase in responsiveness of a transmitter system can increase cognitive functions if these functions selectively depend on this neural system, whereas other cognitive functions are deteriorated. Thus, highly circumscribed elevations of cognitive functions can be embedded within a pattern of more general decline' (Beste *et al.*, 2008, p. 11700).

Brain structures such as the amygdala have long been associated with the processing of emotion, both negative and positive. In the case of negative emotions, one might predict that damage to the amygdala or related structures could result in fewer negative memories being retrieved, producing a form of paradoxical functional facilitation effect. This particular scenario has in fact been described by Buchanan *et al.* (2005, 2006). In particular, the two sets of studies showed that damage to the right amygdala resulted in fewer negative autobiographical memories being retrieved in a task where participants had to retrieve emotional events from their lives. By contrast, damage either to the left medial temporal lobe, or bilaterally to the hippocampus itself, did not result in such emotional selectivity of memory retrieval. In an earlier study from the same group (Adolphs *et al.*, 2001b), there was also evidence from a single-case study that bilateral damage to the amygdala may result in enhanced memory for visual detail when patients had to remember aversive scenes, although the fact that two separate tasks were used to assess memory for gist and for detail renders the findings somewhat equivocal. However, in a subsequent study (Adolphs *et al.*, 2005) examined proportional gist memory, defined as memory essential to the meaning of picture items, under neutral encoding conditions, where emotionally neutral pictures were shown in the context of other emotionally neutral pictures. They found that gist memory was enhanced after amygdala damage compared to healthy individuals, suggesting a more complex picture than one simply of facilitation of memory for details.

Memory researchers often distinguish between explicit memory tasks, where there is usually deliberate, conscious recollection of events or facts, with implicit memory tasks where one's performance is influenced by prior experience without necessarily recalling the specific episode (e.g. reading unfamiliar words more accurately or faster on a second occasion). There may be instances where the use of explicit strategies interferes with performance on an implicit memory task, and where memory-disordered patients are therefore more likely to perform better than healthy control participants. One such study was reported by Musen *et al.* (1990), where they found that patients showed faster reading of a short story over successive trials on a speeded reading test, presumably because control participants' recollection of the content from earlier trials caused them to reflect and to slow down their reading speed. Where explicit memory for a past event works in opposition to current task performance, due to the fact that amnesic patients may have explicitly but not implicitly forgotten that past event, such patients may appear to show stronger 'memory for the past' than control participants; this was neatly exemplified by Squire and McKee (1993). They found that amnesic patients were less susceptible to a form of illusion seen in the healthy population, whereby prior exposure to non-famous names increases the likelihood that they will subsequently be rated as 'famous'. Similarly, Cermak *et al.* (1997) reported that amnesic patients were more likely than control participants to offer target words that they had previously seen when they were simply asked to guess the first word that came to mind when shown the first three letters of the word, confirming earlier observations in a verbal fluency paradigm (Gardner *et al.*, 1973). This followed elegant earlier examples of enhanced priming performance in amnesic patients which have been noted by other researchers (Warrington and Weiskrantz, 1978; Jacoby and Witherspoon, 1982; Cermak *et al.*, 1988, 1992; Heindel *et al.*, 1990; Randolph, 1991) – see Kapur (1996) for a discussion of these studies.

Klimkowicz-Mrowiec *et al.* (2008) reported that Alzheimer patients with moderate explicit memory impairment performed better than healthy participants on an implicit

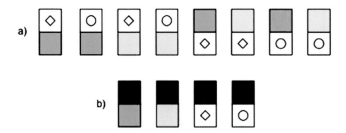

Figure 3.5 The Four Card Task. The top set of eight cards (a) are initially reviewed with participants to indicate all possible shape–colour combinations, and these cards are then put out of sight. Next, the bottom set of four half-masked cards (b) are shown. Instructions to participants are 'Whenever there is a circle on one half of the card, there is a yellow on the other half of the card. Your task is to name those cards and only those cards you would need to unmask in order to find out whether the sentence is true or false for those four cards. You do not need to unmask all of the cards' (Golding, 1981, p. 33).

probabilistic learning task. This used a weather prediction paradigm, where on each trial, participants were required to decide which of two weather outcomes (rain or sunshine) would occur on the basis of a set of cards displayed. The two outcomes of rain or sunshine occurred with equal frequency across the 100 trials.

(d) Lesion facilitation in executive function

(i) Problem-solving ability

One of the first studies to report paradoxical functional facilitation effects in a problem-solving task was by Golding (1981). She found that patients with right hemisphere lesions, in particular those with perceptual classification deficits (difficulty in identifying objects photographed from unconventional angles), performed better than healthy controls on a variation of the Four Card Task (see Figure 3.5). They argued that in basing their judgements more on the verbal descriptions of the cards, the patients with right hemisphere lesions gained greater insight into the underlying structure of the puzzle. However, Evans and Dennis (1982) subsequently noted that the design of the procedure was such that unilateral visual neglect (a condition described in more detail below) may have contributed towards a simpler explanation of the effect that was found, with some right-hemisphere damaged patients being biased to choose a card from the far right of the array due to neglect of a card from the far left of the display.

Reverberi *et al.* (2005) found that patients with dorsolateral frontal lobe lesions were better than controls on a particular part of a matchstick problem-solving task (Figures 3.6). They administered three types of problems:

Type A – This type of problem is solved by moving a matchstick that is part of a numeral, to another numeral. For example, the problem 'II = III + I' is solved by moving one of the matchsticks of the 'III' to the 'II' in head position.

Type B – In this case it is necessary to move a matchstick from the equal sign to the minus sign, in order to change it into an equal sign. Thus, e.g. the false equation 'IV = III – I', should be transformed in the true 'IV – III = I'.

Type C – In this last problem type, a plus sign has to be changed, by rotating its vertical matchstick through 90°, into an equal sign. Crucially, this action transforms the starting equation into a tautology; e.g. 'VI = VI + VI' becomes 'VI = VI = VI'.

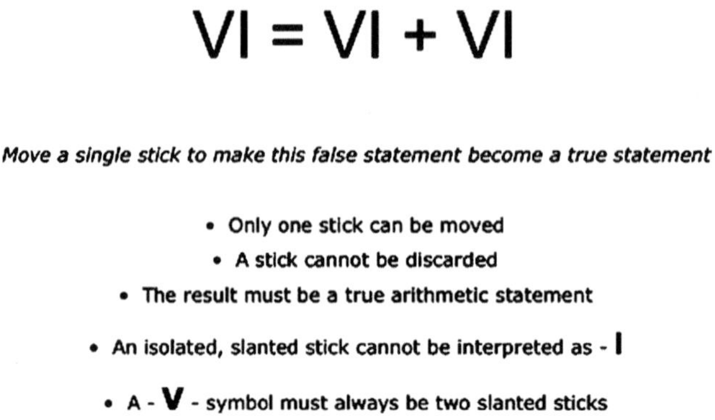

VI = VI + VI

Figure 3.6 Match-Stick Task used by Reverberi *et al.* (2005). Answer – VI = VI = VI.

Move a single stick to make this false statement become a true statement

- Only one stick can be moved
- A stick cannot be discarded
- The result must be a true arithmetic statement
- An isolated, slanted stick cannot be interpreted as - **I**
- A - **V** - symbol must always be two slanted sticks

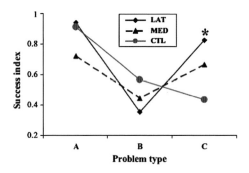

Figure 3.7 Success scores of patient and control groups on the Match-Stick arithmetic task for each problem type. LAT, lateral frontal; MED, medial frontal; CTL, control group. *$P < 0.05$, **$P < 0.01$ for the control group versus patient subgroups comparisons. (Reverberi *et al.*, 2005. Reproduced with permission.)

As can be seen from Figure 3.7, Reverberi *et al.* found that patients with dorsolateral frontal lesions were better than control participants on Task C. They entertained possible explanations including one that invoked the notion of the frontal lobes being critical for 'sculpting response space' (Nathaniel-James and Frith, 2002), and that lateral frontal lesion patients cannot generate/implement constraints to their 'response space' as well as controls, or that they are less aware of/less controlled by contextual cues (e.g. Algebraic solutions) as control participants. Of course, in other circumstances the very constraints from which these patients were freed would be beneficial.

(ii) Inhibition

Although inhibitory processes may be considered to have played a part in some of the paradoxical functional facilitation effects outlined above, there appears to have been only one direct study of inhibitory function that has reported enhanced performance in neurological patients. Pujol *et al.* (2001) used the classic Stroop interference paradigm (naming the ink colour of printed names of colours) with a group of patients having white matter lesions associated with the presence of multiple sclerosis. Those patients with lesions in the left posterior parietal region actually performed faster than control participants in the relevant interference condition. Shiv *et al.* (2005) reported that patients with lesions that primarily involved the amygdala or orbitofrontal cortex performed better than control participants or patients with lesions outside this area on a risk-taking problem-solving task, adopting a less conservative and thus more successful strategy than controls, who appeared to be more affected by the outcomes of decisions made in previous rounds. In a study of more selective, bilateral amygdala pathology, De Martino *et al.* (2010) examined the tendency to avoid risks associated with losses, a tendency that may in healthy individuals be irrationally increased against the benefits of gains in settings such as gambling. In their two cases of amygdala damage, they found that there was a much reduced tendency to show 'loss aversion' compared to healthy controls.

Double-hit recovery

Recovery of function after damage to the human brain is a complex affair, and encompasses a number of phenomena that could be seen to be paradoxical – Cramer (2008) has noted the paradoxical re-emergence of neurological disability, long after good recovery from an initial brain insult, in response to particular drugs, and also notes the 'Uhthoff phenomenon' in multiple sclerosis, whereby dormant symptoms may re-emerge in response to heat or exercise. While two sequential lesions are usually detrimental to function (e.g. Kim, 1999), in this section, I will deal with a particular paradox in recovery where it seems that two brain insults are better than one. Analogous findings in the area of human movement disorder are discussed in Chapter 10. In the area of pain, there are a number of well-documented cases of relief of pain, whether it be classical pain or phantom-limb pain, following cerebral infarction (Daniele *et al.*, 2003; Helmchen *et al.*, 2002; Canavero *et al.*, 2001; Soria and Fine, 1991; Yarnitsky *et al.*, 1988; Appenzeller and Bicknell, 1969; Bornstein, 1949; Head and Holmes, 1911) – see Ovsiew (1997) for a discussion of some of these cases.

In media such as films and cartoons (cf. Baxendale, 2004), it is not uncommon for somebody to appear to become densely amnesic following a bang to the head, only to miraculously recover that memory with a second bump. While these phenomena may be in the realm of fiction, there are, however, a few well-documented cases where a subsequent lesion may ameliorate deficits caused by an initial lesion. A number of relevant studies are described in other chapters in this book, such as those relating to movement disorders and to epilepsy, and this section will primarily focus on cognitive manifestations of this phenomenon.

(a)   'Double-hit recovery' in visual neglect

In the area of animal lesion studies, one of the first PFF effects reported was that by James Sprague (Figure 3.8), Professor of Cell and Developmental Biology at the University of Pennsylvania (see biographical memoir by Rosenquist and Sherman, 2007). In the journal *Science*, he reported (Sprague, 1966) an effect which achieved such distinction that it subsequently became known as the 'Sprague Effect'.

With cats as his subjects, Sprague produced inattention to the left side of space, 'left-sided visual neglect', following ablation of the right posterior neocortex. However, when this lesion was followed by a further lesion, this time to the left superior colliculus, much of this neglect and related visual deficits disappeared. Subsequent studies (summarized in Sprague, 1996 and Ogourtsova *et al.*, 2010) have confirmed the effect, and have also extended it to the field of auditory function (Lomber *et al.*, 2007). Some authors have pointed to inter-hemispheric competition of subcortical structures as being a critical mechanism in this effect (Hilgetag *et al.*, 1999). More recent evidence from a study of cats points to the role of secondary alterations after visual cortex lesions, these alterations being mediated by NMDA-mediated excitoxicity which may in turn be prevented by

Figure 3.8 James Sprague (1916–2002), after whom the 'Sprague Effect' was named (University of Pennsylvania. Reproduced with permission).

pre-treatment administration of an NMDA receptor antagonist (Jiang *et al.*, 2009). Thus, Jiang *et al.* concluded that visual neglect which results from cortical lesions is due to NMDA-mediated excitoxic events in subcortical structures that alter communication between such structures, and lead to inhibitory effects on the functioning of specific structures such as the superior colliculus.

Weddell (2004) reported the first clinical case study to document a human analogue of the Sprague Effect. A patient with a midbrain tumour developed left-sided neglect as the result of subsequent right frontal damage. When the midbrain tumour progressed to involve the left superior colliculus, bilateral visual orientation returned. Sustained right-sided visual neglect developed after further progression of the tumour, when there was probable additional damage to the right superior colliculus. A follow-up report of this case (Weddell, 2008) highlighted relative sparing of memory functioning.

In a further clinical study, Vuilleumier *et al.* (1996) found that left-sided neglect that followed a right parietal infarct disappeared after subsequent left frontal infarction (Figures 3.9, 3.10 and 3.11). As will be described in Chapter 13, this observation has led to a number of studies using left frontal TMS to alleviate left-sided neglect.

(b) Double-hit recovery in language

Relatively few studies have been reported on paradoxical facilitation effects associated with language functioning. Two relevant studies have both reported a dramatic improvement in stuttering after brain injury or brain disease. Thus, Helm-Estabrooks *et al.* (1986) reported the case of an ambidextrous man who ceased to stutter after suffering a head injury. Some years later, Muroi *et al.* (1999) found that a patient with long-standing stuttering dramatically improved his speech after incurring bilateral thalamic infarction (Figure 3.12).

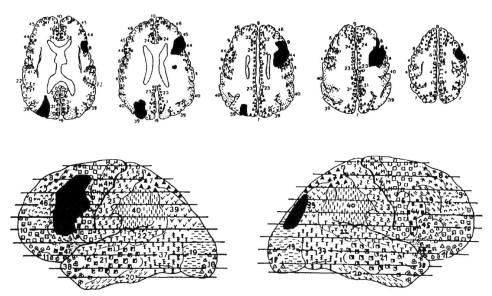

Figure 3.9 Plotting of the lesions seen on CT scans on anatomical templates that show the first parietal infarct involving mainly the dorsal portion of Brodmann's area 39, just below its junction with area 7, and the second frontal infarct that involved the caudal end of the middle frontal gyrus (Brodmann's area 8), together with areas 9, 44 and 45. (Vuilleumier *et al.*, 1996. Reproduced with permission.)

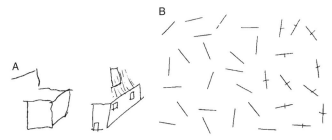

Figure 3.10 Left spatial neglect shown in (A) drawings of a cube and a house, and in (B) a line crossing task, four days after the first right-sided parietal stroke. (Vuilleumier *et al.*, 1996. Reproduced with permission.)

In view of the similarities between the site of the thalamic lesion shown in Figure 3.12 and those thalamic sites associated with improvements in movement disorder after planned ablation, it is possible that amelioration of some form of motor coordination deficit, rather than a primary language disorder, lies behind the improvement found by Muroi *et al.*

Although it is considered by some to be a controversial phenomenon (Miller, 2007), a few patients with a focal brain lesion may find themselves speaking in a foreign accent, one that is quite different to their native accent. Cohen *et al.* (2009) have described the case of an American patient who developed a distortion in her speech pattern with what sounded to her country folk like a German accent, following a left temporo-parietal stroke. Three-and-a-half years later, she suffered a further stroke in the cerebellum. Following this second stroke, her 'foreign accent syndrome' disappeared, and she recovered her normal American-English accent (Figure 3.13).

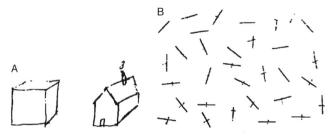

Figure 3.11 Resolution of neglect shown in (A) drawings of a cube and a house, and in (B) a line crossing task, six days after the second left-sided frontal stroke. (Vuilleumier *et al.*, 1996. Reproduced with permission.)

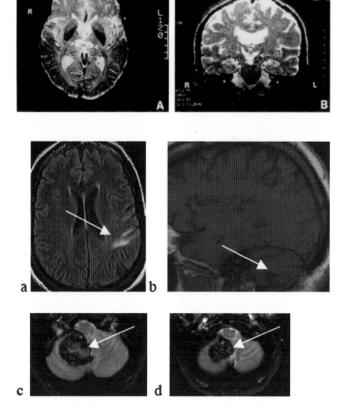

Figure 3.12 Axial (A) and Coronal (B) MRI scans showing bilateral thalamic infarction (arrowed). (Muroi *et al.*, 1999. Reproduced with permission.)

Figure 3.13 Axial (a) and sagittal (b) MRI scans showing left temporo-parietal and cerebellar lesions respectively, the latter also being evident on the dedicated views of the cerebellum (c, d). (Cohen *et al.*, 2009. Reproduced with permission.)

Hinder–help effect

In general, those variables that are detrimental or beneficial to cognitive functioning in healthy individuals are also detrimental and beneficial to cognitive functioning in brain damaged individuals. However, exceptions to this rule have been noted, which I have termed 'hinder–help' effects, and a number of these studies will be reviewed in this section. The following review is not meant to be exhaustive, but should alert the reader to this general phenomenon.

Several 'hinder–help' effects have been reported in the condition known as 'optic ataxia', where bilateral posterior parietal lesions are associated with marked impairments in spatial selective attention and visuomotor control. Such patients, who are impaired when told to immediately grasp or point to an object in their proximal environment, have been found to show a surprising improvement in performance when a delay is introduced between the command and the execution of the command (Milner *et al.*, 1999, 2001, 2003; Rossetti *et al.*, 2005; Rice *et al.*, 2008). To account for this finding, authors have generally resorted to implicating two distinct streams of communication from the back to the front of the brain in each hemisphere – the upper dorsal stream, which emanates from superior parietal regions to frontal regions, and the lower ventral stream, that has a trajectory from lower occipital regions to regions in the anterior temporal lobe. The paradoxical phenomenon noted in visuomotor control has been interpreted as reflecting an impaired dorsal stream in the superior parietal region (immediate pointing/grasping) in conjunction with a relatively spared ventral stream (delayed pointing/grasping) in temporal lobe neocortex, although Himmelbach *et al.* (2009) have provided functional imaging evidence inconsistent with this idea.

A form of the hinder–help effect was reported by Warrington and Davidoff (2000) in a patient with visual object recognition difficulties, related to the presence of probable Alzheimer's disease. This patient was strikingly better at matching mirror representations of objects that she was unable to identify, compared to ones that she was able to correctly recognize. It would seem that in this case performance solely on the basis of spatial attributes may have been a better strategy, with object-related representations having an interfering effect on such spatial processing where they are intact. In the case of face processing, a well-established hinder–help effect has been found in patients with prosopagnosia, a condition where there is a major impairment in the identification of familiar faces. Thus, Farah *et al.* (1995), de Gelder and Rouw (2000), and Rouw and de Gelder (2002) reported that, while normal participants were better at matching upright compared to upside-down faces, the reverse effect was found in prosopagnosic patients, who were better at matching upside-down faces (cf. Busigny and Rossion, 2010). De Gelder and Rouw (2000) and Rouw and de Gelder (2002) also found that the inverse superiority effect applied to non-faces stimuli.

In a standard memory experiment, retention is usually tested by asking for recall of material presented sometime earlier. The effects of retention test trials on subsequent memory and learning have yielded sets of contrasting findings in respective literatures dealing with healthy individuals in the normal population, and some neurological patients who have suffered a brain injury or brain illness that resulted in marked memory impairment or marked executive dysfunction. Thus, Karpicke and Roediger (2008) have reviewed evidence, dating back to the beginning of the twentieth century, which shows that in most learning settings normal individuals show better long-term retention of material if the initial learning session included a greater number of retention test trials, rather than simply repeated occurrence of presentation trials. In contrast, over the past 20 years, there has been a growing literature (see Clare and Jones, 2008 and Wilson, 2009 for reviews) which has shown that for certain neurological patients, such as those with an amnesic syndrome or who have marked executive dysfunction, the reverse may be the case – that is, test trials may inevitably result in many errors being made, and such patients will tend to perseverate with those errors on later retention trials, apparently unable to distinguish them from earlier correct responses. For those patients, repeated

57

presentation trials (encouraging 'errorless' compared to 'errorful' learning) may therefore represent the best strategy to be used in a learning setting.

Increased cognitive load, as in the form of dual-task performance, will usually result in more impaired level of functioning. However, in a recent study of a group of confabulating patients (Ciaramelli *et al.*, 2009) noted that introducing a divided attention task during recognition memory performance produced fewer false recognition responses to semantically related distractor items (e.g. saying that the word 'sleep' was presented when the list of words may have included words such as 'bed, night, pillow', etc., but not 'sleep'), with the opposite effect being found in healthy participants and non-confabulating patients.

In the realm of language functioning, naming of pictures is normally helped by prior exposure to a related written word ('prime'), but the opposite effect has been found in patients with primary progressive aphasia, who named a picture more slowly after a related prime word compared with an unrelated prime word (Vandenberghe *et al.*, 2005).

In a case where paradoxically inverse effects were found in neurological patients, Boyd and Winstein (2004) found that providing explicit information during an implicit motor sequencing test hindered the performance of patients with basal ganglia lesions, but helped the performance of healthy control participants. Similarly, Behrmann *et al.* (2005) reported that training a prosopagnosic patient to categorize biological-like forms (Greebles) resulted in enhanced performance on that task, and generalized to untrained Greebles and recognizing common objects, but that there was a concomitant deterioration in performance on a faces identification task.

An intriguing series of studies have pointed to an unusual form of the 'hinder–help' effect – epsilon 4, a version of the apolipoprotein E gene (APOE), is a risk factor for developing Alzheimer's disease late in life, but in earlier years it is associated with enhanced performance on memory and problem-solving tasks (Callaway, 2010; Han and Bondi, 2008; Han *et al.*, 2007; Marchant *et al.*, 2010; Zetterberg *et al.*, 2009). The mechanisms for such a paradoxical advantage remain to elucidated, although it is of note that functional imaging studies have shown greater task-based activation of temporal lobe and related brain structures in such gene carriers (Filippini *et al.*, 2009).

Lesion-load paradox

One of the basic principles of the lesion-deficit model is that larger lesions will result in greater deficits and disability. ('Lesion load' will usually refer to the size/volume of a lesion, but may also encompass some indices of tissue integrity, or the presence of multifocal lesions.) Clinical findings that appear anomalous to this principle include instances where large, benign brain tumours, such as meningiomas, may be associated with minimal outward signs of dysfunction (e.g. Kuratsu *et al.*, 2000; Jovanovic *et al.*, 2006). This has been attributed to the slow-growing nature of such lesions, and related compensation/ reorganization that takes place in the brain. In conditions such as multiple sclerosis, some researchers (e.g. Strasser-Fuchs *et al.*, 2008) have commented on the paradoxical presence of large lesion load in clinically benign forms of the condition. Similarly, chronic large cystic lesions have been noted to be associated with minimal cognitive or everyday difficulties (e.g. Trabacca and DiCuonzo, 2009). More dramatically, there have been cases of long-standing hydrocephalus (enlarged ventricles of the brain), with often only a thin layer of neocortex appearing to be present (Figure 3.14), but where the individual functions normally in society or even functions at an above-average level (Lewin, 1980; Feuillet

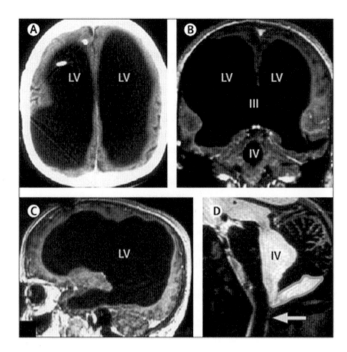

Figure 3.14 Chronic enlargement of ventricles in a healthy individual. (Feuillet *et al.*, 2007. Reproduced with permission.)

et al., 2007). Again, some form of neural compensation/reorganization has generally been invoked to account for this unusual finding.

A related set of paradoxical effects, sometimes seen in animal lesion studies (Irle, 1987, 1990) and very occasionally evident in human studies (Irle *et al.*, 1992, 1994; Cavaco *et al.*, 2004), arises when there is a reverse of the usual relationship between lesion size and functional deficit, with larger lesions leading to less marked functional impairment. In the case of sectioning of the corpus callosum, the fibre tract connecting the two hemispheres, while the general rule is that total sectioning compared to partial sectioning will result in better clinical outcome (Sunaga *et al.*, 2009), and more marked cognitive deficits (Fabri *et al.*, 2005), instances of greater inter-hemispheric transfer deficits after partial compared to total sectioning of the corpus callosum have been reported (Aglioti *et al.*, 1998).

Keidel *et al.* (2010) have outlined a computational model of neuroplasticity that takes into account phenomena such as the lesion-load paradox, a model that attempts to balance modularity and equipotentiality views of brain organization.

Paradoxical positive outcome

Traumatic brain injury (TBI) usually results in impaired functioning in the realms of cognition, emotion and behaviour, with resultant handicaps in everyday adjustment. The traumatic event itself will generally be associated with negative connotations, and, in some patients post-traumatic stress disorder (PTSD) will be a major residual disability. PTSD will tend to consist of intrusive thoughts related to the trauma that may include nightmares or distress on exposure to trauma-related cues; anxiety and avoidance behaviour; and general cognitive and somatic symptoms associated with a degree of hyperarousal. In TBI, especially blunt head injury associated with concussion, there is usually amnesia for circumstances surrounding the event. Drawing on earlier clinical observations (Adler, 1943; O'Brien, 1993), several studies have therefore reported a paradox, whereby some cases of TBI may have a lower incidence of PTSD. Thus, Gil *et al.* (2005) reported that the less patients recalled of the event associated with their head injury, the less likely they were to develop symptoms associated with PTSD. A later study by Bryant *et al.* (2009) noted that longer periods of post-traumatic amnesia seemed to be protective against the occurrence of severe intrusive memories. Other studies, however, have not found such a protective effect (e.g. Greenspan *et al.*, 2006). Harvey *et al.* (2003) have noted that some of the divergence in findings between studies may in part be related to ambiguity in the criteria for diagnosing PTSD, and that TBI patients may perhaps have PTSD symptoms, but that the symptoms differ in content from those of other PTSD patients.

While insight and accurate awareness of deficits following conditions such as TBI are generally important for good outcomes, a few anomalies to this relationship have been noted. Thus, Herbert and Powell (1989) reported that clients with TBI who over-rated their abilities did better following a period of rehabilitation than clients who were more realistic or under-confident, although somewhat conflicting findings were reported in a later study (Malia *et al.*, 1993). More recently, Cooper-Evans *et al.* (2008) noted that survivors of TBI who were more impaired cognitively and/or less aware of their deficits reported higher-self esteem than other TBI survivors.

More generally, in recent years there has been an increased focus on the notion that positive changes may be seen in some patients who survive a brain injury or brain illness – 'post-traumatic growth'. This term is usually meant to refer to beneficial psychological changes that occur following the occurrence of some stressful event. While the concept also applies to disciplines other than neurology (Joseph and Linley, 2008), relevant observations in neurological conditions are particularly paradoxical in view of the generally negative outcomes that are highlighted after an insult to the brain. Both McGrath and Linley (2006) and Powell *et al.* (2007) noted that in a group of patients with TBI, long-term follow-up indicated that post-traumatic growth appeared to increase over time after the head injury. Hawley and Joseph (2008) found that on long-term follow-up (an average of 11 years) after TBI, around half of their participants showed evidence of post-traumatic growth on a structured questionnaire, responding positively to items such as 'I don't take life for granted any more' and 'I value my relationships much more now'.

Psychiatric disorders

In general, psychiatric disorders are associated with distress and with difficulties in coping with everyday demands. In addition, there are negative effects on cognition from distracting, anxious preoccupations; from difficulties initiating activities in depression; from irrational feelings of persecution in schizophrenia, etc. In this section, I consider positive consequences of these disorders which, together with the established negative features, may help to shed light on the disorders in question.

(a)   Anxiety and related conditions

Ehlers and Breuer (2006) have reviewed studies in which participants were asked to monitor their own heart rates. Some anxious individuals, including those with a full-blown panic disorder, were more accurate in this perception than healthy controls, suggesting enhanced somatic awareness in this population. Whilst that may be deleterious in some settings, there may be advantages in the early detection of abnormal body states. In an elegant demonstration of how fear can focus the mind, Li *et al.* (2008) presented healthy participants with a series of smells. Some were paired with an electric shock. Discrimination of odours was enhanced by this aversive conditioning. They further noted that this improvement in discrimination was accompanied by spatial reorganization of sensory coding in olfactory (piriform) cortex. In a case of 'help–hinder' effects (see page 56), Dalgleish *et al.* (2009) reported that whereas instructions to suppress negative emotions generally result in a beneficial decrease in such feelings, participants with initially high levels of negative affect showed the opposite trend, with an increase in negative emotions compared to a no-instruction condition.

One can imagine how attention to detail and adherence to strict rules that are part of obsessive–compulsive disorder could be advantageous to particular professions, e.g. where safety-critical procedures must be followed rigidly. Such processing, it seems, can also result in above-average recall of information. Reed (1977) examined patients suffering from obsessional personality disorder compared to psychiatric control subjects who suffered from some other psychiatric disorder. They noted that while long-term recall of factual material was the same as that of controls, in patients suffering from obsessional personality disorder there was better immediate memory span and enhanced superior recall of ambiguous anecdotal material. Over-activation of the striatum (caudate and putamen) has been noted in brain imaging studies of those with obsessive–compulsive disorder (Mataix-Cols *et al.*, 2004), and it is interesting to note that Roth *et al.* (2004) reported such individuals as showing enhanced procedural memory compared to controls, as evident on the initial trials of a pursuit learning task.

(b) Depression and bipolar disorder

Keedwell (2008) has argued for the evolutionary benefits of depression, with a chapter in his book covering 'beneficial by-products of depression', including enhanced ability to cope with suffering, greater empathy and compassion, and more humility. In a similar vein, Andrews and Thomson (2009, 2010) have proposed specific cognitive mechanisms that may accompany enhanced psychological functioning in depression. In particular, they argue that improved problem-solving can result from the intense ruminative focus sometimes associated with depression, in which distractions by social contact, sexual behaviour, and even eating are minimized (cf. Dreisbach and Goschke, 2004). In a review of studies that have highlighted positive aspects of bipolar disorder, Galvez *et al.* (2011) have found evidence for enhancement in a number of traits, including empathy, creativity, realism and resilience (see Chapter 16 for links between bipolar disorder and creativity).

Turning to experimental studies, there are reports that depressed individuals may be more accurate than non-depressed individuals in judging the impact of their actions. For example, Alloy and Abramson (1979), gave participants a task where on each trial the participant could choose to make an action or not, and in which subsequently an event might or might not occur – a light might switch on. They found that when an event occurred very frequently, typical volunteers over-estimated the causal link between this event and their actions. By contrast, relatively depressive individuals were less likely to fall for the illusion. This phenomenon has been termed 'depressive realism'. It should be noted that more recent studies have suggested greater complexity to the concept of 'depressive realism' than simply 'negative-but-accurate' expectations, with factors such as severity of depression (Carson *et al.*, 2010), and context factors/degree of contextual processing (Benassi and Mahler, 1985; Allan *et al.*, 2007; Msetfi *et al.*, 2005) influencing the effects that are found. A recent experimental study has pointed to possible neural mechanisms that may underlie enhanced cognitive functioning in depression. Golomb *et al.* (2009) reported enhanced motion perception of large high-contrast stimuli in patients with major depressive disorder compared to control participants, and speculated that this may have been due to low levels of the inhibitory neurotransmitter GABA in depressed patients (see Commentary by Wallisch and Kumbhani, 2009). Chase *et al.* (2010) have also found evidence of enhanced perceptual functioning, on this occasion in an odd-one-out reaction time task where performance could be rewarded, with visual cues indicating the probability of a reward occurring.

Patients with depression tend to focus on negative features of past events and of their current environment, and it is therefore not a great surprise that Ridout *et al.* (2003) found better recognition memory performance for sad facial expressions in depressed subjects compared to control participants.

(c)　Schizophrenia

Although schizophrenia is a devastating condition, and is associated with a higher-than-average suicide risk, there has been an increasing recognition that it may be associated with some positive features (see Chapter 16). Amongst those who have spearheaded such a movement have been sufferers of the disease who have written eloquently about it, including Peter Chadwick, a former Professor of Psychology (Chadwick, 2009). He remarked that vulnerability to schizophrenia 'is associated also with the workings of the creative process, with language, high sensitivity and imaginativeness generally and in many instances with enhanced spiritual sensitivity and empathy' (2009, p. ix).

Patients with schizophrenia have been reported to be less susceptible to various visual illusions. Dima *et al.* (2009) examined one such illusion, where patients suffering from schizophrenia showed a reduced tendency to see a face in a hollow mask. Dima *et al.* argued from functional imaging findings that such patients have a greater reliance on stimulus-driven processing, and are less able to employ conceptually driven top-down strategies during perception. Williams *et al.* (2010) found that patients with schizophrenia were less susceptible to the 'size–weight illusion' – in this illusion, when healthy individuals are shown two similar objects of identical mass, but of different sizes, the smaller object is perceived as significantly heavier. The authors interpreted this finding in terms of a 'forward model of motor control', where prediction of sensory feedback from a motor command is matched to actual feedback when an object is lifted. Mismatch of the two sets of feedback helps to produce the visual illusion, and predictive deficits in schizophrenic patients mean that such mismatching is less likely to occur.

In their perception of the world, healthy people unconsciously take into account their own actions. This is the reason that we are not able to tickle ourselves – we know what's coming! Blakemore *et al.* (2000) noted that psychiatric patients with auditory hallucinations and/or passivity experiences did not show this phenomenon, reporting self-generated and other-generated tickles as equivalent. In a follow-up study by Shergill *et al.* (2005), which overcame the limitations of relying on self-report, participants received a push on their finger. The push varied in its force, and the participants' task was to reproduce a given force. This was done either using a joystick to control a motor that pushed a bar onto the same finger, or by pressing on the bar/finger with the other hand. Although accurate when using the joystick, when pushing directly with their hands healthy controls applied excess force. This is consistent with self-generated force being perceived as 'weaker'. In contrast, patients with schizophrenia were accurate in both conditions, and showed evidence of enhanced performance relative to controls (cf. Synofzik *et al.*, 2010).

Menon *et al.* (2005) found that patients with schizophrenia who also had active delusions were less likely than controls to suffer from the 'famous names illusion'. This refers to a phenomenon whereby when people are given a list that contains famous and non-famous names, they judge the famous names to be more numerous. This is due to a mechanism known as the 'availability heuristic', where a presumed increase in trace strength makes items easier to recall, and thus seem more frequent. For patients with schizophrenia who also have severe thought disorder, more specific alterations in the semantic associative networks have been implicated in several studies (Pomarol-Clotet *et al.*, 2008; Lecardeur *et al.*, 2008). For example, a study by Kiefer *et al.* (2009) found increases in masked semantic priming in such patients compared to control participants. They suggested that such increases in unconscious activation of related concepts, a form of 'hyperpriming', may interfere with more explicit, goal-directed behaviour in such patients. Enhanced discrimination of movement in large high-contrast stimuli in schizophrenic patients compared to controls was reported by Tadin *et al.* (2006), who hypothesized that this was due to a weakening in patients of suppressive centre-surround mechanisms in motion perception. Similarly, decreased centre-surround antagonism was implicated in a study by Dakin *et al.* (2005), who focused on an illusion where the contrast of a small textured disk appears reduced when presented within a high-contrast surround, compared to when shown in isolation. Patients with schizophrenia were much less susceptible to this illusion than healthy controls (cf. Crawford *et al.*, 2010).

In an intriguing study that somewhat departs from the content of the studies cited above, Owen *et al.* (2007) found that people with schizophrenia performed better than controls on syllogistic reasoning tasks, e.g. deciding the truth/falsity of statements such as 'If the sun rises, then the sun is in the East; the sun is in the East; therefore, the sun rises'. Owen *et al.* argued that their patients were less biased by general knowledge in making logical decisions.

(d)   Post-traumatic growth

The concept of 'post-traumatic' growth has generally been used to refer to positive psychological perspectives on post-traumatic stress (Joseph and Linley, 2008). Some authors have attempted to apply the concept more generally to psychiatric disorders and to adverse life events (Haidt, 2006; Peterson *et al.*, 2008), and to conditions such as cardiac disease (Leung *et al.*, 2010). In the case of mental stress, Taku *et al.* (2008) attempted a factor analysis of the components of post-traumatic growth, and identified five factors: Relating to Others, New Possibilities, Personal Strength, Spiritual Change and Appreciation of Life. It is of course important to see such instances of 'post-traumatic growth' in the context of the usually disabling and distressing nature of psychiatric disorder and negative life events, and to take account of general reservations such as those outlined by Coyne and Tennen (2010) in the case of cancer patients, but these instances of positive outcomes in psychiatric disorder may offer clues as to what may or not be fruitful avenues in therapeutic intervention.

Conclusions

(a)   Implications for theory

The findings reviewed in this chapter point to the brain operating as a dynamic system, with inhibitory–excitatory interactions contributing to function, and multiple routes having the potential to contribute to cognitive activity ('multicausality'). This is evident not only from the Sprague Effect, but also from improvement in speech fluency after thalamic lesions. Some of the evidence relating to false recognition and priming point to a hierarchical representation of information, which enables the co-existence within representation formats of features such as both gist and specificity. The findings relating to reduced interference in learning paradigms point to competitive harmony between neural systems, which helps to maintain a balance between influences that may achieve similar goals, but do so by differing mechanisms (Poldrack and Packard, 2003; Martel et al., 2007). This principle has some overlap with the multicausality principle outlined above.

(b)   Implications for therapy

The Sprague Effect raises the possibility that, as in Parkinson's disease, some forms of subcortical stimulation or lesion ablation may be worth exploring as a therapeutic option for treating unilateral neglect. The better-than-normal performance of some aphasic patients on the detection of deception points to the value of compensatory strategies using other modalities, and the extent to which practice in the use of strategies may result in more general cognitive enhancement. If aphasic patients perform well on certain meaningful tasks, these may in themselves be worth noting as 'therapeutic pastime' activities, ones which patients find easy, meaningful and enjoyable. In the case of speech expression, the few clinical case reports of improvement in speech fluency after thalamic lesions suggest that deep brain stimulation and/or selective ablation may be worth considering in cases of severe, intractable dysfluency. 'Constraint-induced therapy', where neurological patients with a disability are actively discouraged from using their remaining intact system, and are actively encouraged to use their remaining, partially disabled, system – its success in a number of rehabilitation settings (Wittenberg and Schaechter, 2009) highlights the unhelpful inhibition that may sometimes emanate from an intact brain system.

(c)   Future challenges and questions

Many of the papers reviewed in this chapter have been one-off studies, and there is therefore a need to replicate a number of the findings, and in particular to establish any boundary conditions for the particular effects to occur. Most of the paradoxical effects arise from studies of patients with focal or static brain lesions. Can we find evidence for similar observations in patients with primary degenerative dementia? A major remaining challenge is to develop a biologically plausible conceptual framework that will account for paradoxical functional facilitation effects. A further challenge is to harmonize paradoxical functional facilitation effects in human lesion studies with those in animal lesion studies. Whilst evidence is inherently scarce (given the nature of the studies that would be required), the preceding discussion would predict that in some progressive neurological conditions, there may be disappearance and paradoxical re-emergence of function A, because function B, which inhibited function A, is itself compromised. These observations may have both prognostic and theoretical implications.

References

Adler, A. (1943). Neuropsychiatric complications in victims of Boston's Cocoanut Grove Disaster. *Journal of the American Medial Association*, **123**: 1098–101.

Adolphs, R., Denberg, N. L., & Tranel, D. (2001b). The amygdala's role in long-term declarative memory for gist and detail. *Behavioural Neuroscience*, **115**: 983–92.

Adolphs, R., Jansari, A., & Tranel, D. (2001a). Hemispheric perception of emotional valence from facial expressions. *Neuropsychology*, **15**: 516–24.

Adolphs, R., Tranel, D., & Buchanan, T. W. (2005). Amygdala damage impairs emotional memory for gist but not details of complex stimuli. *Nature Neuroscience*, **8**: 512–18.

Aglioti, S., & Fabbro, F. (1993). Paradoxical selective recovery in a bilingual aphasic following subcortical lesions. *NeuroReport*, **30**: 1359–62.

Aglioti, S., Beltramello, A., Girardi, F., & Fabbro, F. (1996). Neurolinguistic and follow-up study of an unusual pattern of recovery from bilingual subcortical aphasia. *Brain*, **119**: 1551–64.

Aglioti, S., Beltramello, A., Tassinari, G., & Berlucchi, G. (1998). Paradoxically greater interhemispheric transfer deficits in partial than complete callosal agenesis. *Neuropsychologia*, **36**: 1015–24.

Allan, L. G., Siegel, S., & Hannah, S. (2007). The sad truth about depressive realism. *Quarterly Journal of Experimental Psychology*, **60**: 482–95.

Alloy, L. B., & Abramson, L. Y. (1979). Judgment of contingency in depressed and nondepressed students: sadder but wiser? *Journal of Experimental Psychology: General*, **108**: 441–85.

Andrews, P., & Thomson, J. (2010). Depression's evolutionary roots. *Scientific American Mind*, **20**: 57–61.

Andrews, P. W., & Thomson, J. A. (2009). The bright side of being blue: depression as an adaptation for analyzing complex problems. *Psychological Review*, **116**: 620–54.

Appenzeller, O., & Bicknell, J. (1969). Effects of nervous system lesions on phantom experience in amputees. *Neurology*, **19**: 141–6.

Baxendale, S. (2004). Memories aren't made of this: amnesia at the movies. *British Medical Journal*, **329**: 1480–3.

Behrmann, M., Marotta, J., Gauthier, I., Tarr, M. J., & McKeeff, T. J. (2005). Behavioural change and its neural correlates in visual agnosia after expertise training. *Journal of Cognitive Neuroscience*, **17**: 554–68.

Benassi, V., & Mahler, H. (1985). Contingency judgments by depressed college students: sadder but not always wiser. *Journal of Personality and Social Psychology*, **49**: 1323–9.

Beste, C., Saft, C., Gunturkun, O., & Falkenstein, M. (2008). Increased cognitive functioning in symptomatic Huntington's Disease as revealed by behavioral and event-related potential indices of auditory sensory memory and attention. *The Journal of Neuroscience*, **28**: 11695–702.

Beversdorf, D. Q., Smith, B. W., Crucian, G. P., et. al. (2000). Increased discrimination of 'false memories' in autism spectrum disorder. *Proceedings of the National Academy of Sciences*, **97**: 8734–7.

Blakemore, S. J., Smith, J., Steel, R., Johnstone, C. E., & Frith, C. D. (2000). The perception of self-produced sensory stimuli in patients with auditory hallucinations and passivity experiences: evidence for a breakdown in self-monitoring. *Psychological Medicine*, **30**: 1131–9.

Bornstein, B. (1949). Sur le phénomène du member fantomea *L'encéphale*, **38**: 32–46.

Bowles, B., Crupi, C., Mirsattari, S. M, et al. (2007). Impaired familiarity with preserved recollection after anterior temporal-lobe resection that spares the hippocampus. *Proceedings of the National Academy of Sciences*, **104**: 16,382–7.

Boyd, L., & Winstein, C. (2004) Providing explicit information disrupts implicit motor learning after basal ganglia stroke. *Learning and Memory*, **11**: 388–96.

Bryant, R. A., Creamer, M., O'Donnell, M., Silove, D., Clark, C. R., & McFarlane, A. C. (2009). Post-traumatic amnesia and the nature of post-traumatic stress disorder after mild traumatic brain injury. *Journal of the*

International Neuropsychological Society, **15**: 862–7.

Buchanan, T., Tranel, W. D., & Adolphs, R. (2005). Emotional autobiographical memories in amnesic patients with medial temporal lobe damage. *The Journal of Neuroscience*, **25**: 3151–60.

Buchanan, T., Tranel, W. D., & Adolphs, R. (2006). Memories for emotional autobiographical events following unilateral damage to medial temporal lobe. *Brain*, **129**: 115–27.

Budson, A. E., Daffner, K. R., Desikan, R., & Schacter, D. L. (2000). When false recognition is unopposed by true recognition: gist-based memory distortion in Alzheimer's disease. *Neuropsychology*, **14**: 277–87.

Busigny, T., & Rossion, B. (2010). Acquired prosopagnosia abolishes the face inversion effect. *Cortex*, **46**: 965–81.

Callaway, E. (2010). Alzheimer's gene makes you smart. *New Scientist*, **2747**: 12–13.

Canavero, S., Bonicalzi, V., Lacerenza, M., *et al.* (2001). Disappearance of central pain following iatrogenic stroke. *Acta Neurologica Belgica*, **101**: 221–3.

Carson, R. C., Hollon, S. D., & Shelton, R. C. (2010). Depressive realism and clinical depression. *Behaviour Research and Therapy*, **48**: 257–65.

Cavaco, S., Anderson, S., Allen, J., Castro-Caldas, A., & Damasio, H. (2004). The scope of preserved procedural memory in amnesia. *Brain*, **127**: 1853–67.

Cermak, L., Mather, M. & Hill, R. (1997). Unconscious influences on amnesics' word-stem completion. *Neuropsychologia*, **35**: 605–10.

Cermak, L. S., Bleich, R. P. & Blackford, S. P. (1988). Deficits in the implicit retention of new associations by alcoholic Korsakoff patients. *Brain and Cognition*, **7**: 312–23.

Cermak, L. S., Verfaellie, M., Sweeney, M. & Jacoby, L. L. (1992). Fluency versus conscious recollection in the word completion performance of amnesic patients. *Brain and Cognition*, **20**: 367–77.

Chadwick, P. (2009). *Schizophrenia: The Positive Perspective. Second Edition*. London: Routledge.

Chase, H., Michael, A., Bullmore, E., Sahakian, B., & Robbins, R. (2010). Paradoxical enhancement of choice reaction time performance in patients with depression. *Journal of Psychopharmacology*, **24**: 471–9.

Chertkow, H., Bub, D., Bergman, H., Bruemmer, A., Merling, A., & Rothfleisch, J. (1994). Increased semantic priming in patients with dementia of the Alzheimer's type. *Journal of Clinical and Experimental Neuropsychology*, **16**: 608–22.

Ciaramelli, E., Ghetti, S., & Borsotti, M. (2009). Divided attention during retrieval suppresses false recognition in confabulation. *Cortex*, **45**: 141–53.

Clare, L., & Jones, R. (2008). Errorless learning in the rehabilitation of memory impairment: a critical review. *Neuropsychology Review*, **18**: 1–23.

Cohen, D. A., Kurowski, K., Steven, M. S., Blumstein, S. E. & Pascual-Leone, A. (2009). Paradoxical facilitation: the resolution of foreign accent syndrome after cerebellar stroke. *Neurology*, **73**: 566–7.

Cools, R., Miyakawa, A., Sheridan, M. & D'Esposito, M. (2010). Enhanced frontal function in Parkinson's Disease. *Brain*, **133**: 225–33.

Cooper-Evans, S., Alderman, N., Knight, C., & Oddy, M. (2008). Self-esteem as a predictor of psychological distress after severe acquired brain injury: an exploratory study. *Neuropsychological Rehabilitation*, **18**: 607–26.

Corballis, M. C., Hamm, J. P., Barnett, K. J., & Corballis, P. M. (2002). Paradoxical inter-hemispheric summation in the split brain. *Journal of Cognitive Neuroscience*, **14**: 1151–7.

Coyne, J. C., & Tennen, H. (2010). Positive psychology in cancer care: bad science, exaggerated claims, and unproven medicine. *Annals of Behavioural Medicine*, **39**: 16–26.

Cramer, S. (2008). Repairing the human brain after stroke I. Mechanisms of spontaneous recovery. *Annals of Neurology*, **63**: 272–87.

Crawford, T., Hamm, J., Kean, M., *et al.* (2010). The perception of real and illusory motion in schizophrenia. *Neuropsychologia*, **48**: 3121–7.

Cumming, T. B., Graham, K. S., & Patterson, K. (2006). Repetition priming and hyperpriming in semantic dementia. *Brain and Language*, **98**: 221–34.

Dakin, S., Carlin, P., & Hemsley, D. (2005). Weak suppression of visual context in chronic schizophrenia. *Current Biology*, **15**: R822–4.

Dalgleish, T., Yiend, J., Schweizer, S. & Dunn, B. D. (2009). Ironic effects of emotion suppression when recounting distressing memories. *Emotion*, **9**: 744–9.

Daniele, O., Fierro, B., Brighina, F., Magaudda, A., & Natalè, E. (2003). Disappearance of haemorrhagic stroke-induced thalamic (central) pain following a further (contralateral ischaemic) stroke. *Functional Neurology*, **18**: 95–6.

Deese, J. (1959). On the prediction of occurrence of particular verbal intrusions in immediate recall. *Journal of Experimental Psychology*, **58**: 17–22.

De Gelder, B., & Rouw, R. (2000). Paradoxical configuration effects for faces and objects in prosopagnosia. *Neuropsychologia*, **38**: 1271–9.

De Martino, B., Camerer, C., & Adolphs, R. (2010). Amygdala damage eliminates monetary loss aversion. *Proceedings of the National Academy of Sciences*, **107**: 3788–92.

Dima, D., Roiser, J. P., Dietrich, D. E., *et al.* (2009). Understanding why patients with schizophrenia do not perceive the hollow-mask illusion using dynamic causal modelling. *Neuroimage*, **46**: 1180–6.

Dreisbach, G., & Goschke, T. (2004). How positive affect modulates cognitive control: reduced perseveration at the cost of increased distractibility. *Journal of Experimental Psychology: Learning, Memory and Cognition*, **30**: 343–53.

Ehlers, A., & Breuer, P. (2006). How good are patients with panic disorders at perceiving their heartbeats? *Biological Psychology*, **42**: 165–82.

Etcoff, N. L., Ekman, P., Magee, J. J., & Frank, M. G. (2000). Lie detection and language comprehension. *Nature*, **405**: 139.

Evans, J., & Dennis, I. (1982). Brain lesions and reasoning: a note on Golding. *Cortex*, **18**: 317–8.

Fabri, M., Del Pesce, M., Paggi, A., *et al.* (2005). Contribution of posterior corpus callosum to the interhemispheric transfer of tactile information. *Brain Research. Cognitive Brain Research*, **24**: 73–80.

Farah, M. J., Wilson, K. D., Drain, H. M., & Tanaka, J. R. (1995). The inverted face inversion effect in prosopagnosia: evidence for mandatory, face-specific perceptual mechanisms. *Vision Research*, **35**: 2089–93.

Feuillet, L., Dufour, H., & Pelletier, J. (2007). Brain of a white-collar worker. *Lancet*, **370**: 262.

Filippini, N., MacIntosh, B. J., Hough, M. G., *et al.* (2009). Distinct patterns of brain activity in young carriers of the *APOE*-ε4 allele. *Proceedings of the National Academy of Sciences of the USA*, **106**: 7209–14.

Galvez, J. F., Thommi, S., & Ghaemi, S. N. (2011). Positive aspects of mental illness: a review in bipolar disorder. *Journal of Affective Disorders*, **128**: 185–90.

Gardner, H., Boiler, F., Moreines, J., & Butters, N. (1973). Retrieving information from Korsakoff patients: effects of categorical cues and reference to the task. *Cortex* **9**: 165–75.

Giffard, B., Desgranges, B. N., Nore-Mary, F., *et al.* (2001). The nature of semantic memory deficits in Alzheimer's disease: new insights from hyperpriming effects. *Brain*, **124**: 1522–32.

Gil, S., Caspi, Y., Ben-Ari, I. Z., Koren, D., & Klein, E. (2005). Does memory of a traumatic event increase the risk for posttraumatic stress disorder in patients with traumatic brain injury? A prospective study. *American Journal of Psychiatry*, **162**: 963–9.

Glickstein, M. (2009). Paradoxical inter-hemispheric transfer after section of the cerebral commissures. *Experimental Brain Research*, **192**: 425–9.

Glickstein, M., & Sperry, R. (1960). Intermanual somesthetic transfer in split-brain rhesus monkeys. *Journal of Comparative and Physiological Psychology*, **53**: 322–7.

Golding, E. (1981). The effect of unilateral brain lesion on reasoning. *Cortex*, **17**: 31–40.

Golomb, J. D., McDavitt, J. R., Ruf, B. M., *et al.* (2009). Enhanced visual motion perception in major depressive disorder. *Journal of Neuroscience*, **29**: 9072–7.

Greenspan, A. I., Stringer, A. Y., Phillips, V. L., Hammond, F. M., & Goldstein, F. C. (2006). Symptoms of post-traumatic stress: intrusion and avoidance 6 and 12 months after TBI. *Brain Injury*, **20**: 733–42.

Haidt, J. (2006). The uses of adversity. *In The Happiness Hypothesis*. New York, NY: Basic Books.

Han, S., & Bondi, M. W. (2008). Revision of the apolipoprotein E compensatory mechanism recruitment hypothesis. *Alzheimer's & Dementia*, **4**: 251–4.

Han, S. D., Drake, A. I., Cessante, L. M., *et al.* (2007). Apolipoprotein E and traumatic brain injury in a military population: evidence of a neuropsychological compensatory mechanism? *Journal of Neurology, Neurosurgery, and Psychiatry*, **78**: 1103–08.

Harvey, A. G., Brewin, C. R., Jones, C., & Kopelman, M. D. (2003). Coexistence of posttraumatic stress disorder and traumatic brain injury: towards a resolution of the paradox. *Journal of the International Neuropsychological Society*, **9**: 663–76.

Hawley, C. A., & Joseph, S. (2008). Predictors of positive growth after traumatic brain injury. *Brain Injury*, **22**: 427–35.

Head, H., & Holmes, G. (1911). Sensory disturbances from cerebral lesions. *Brain*, **34**: 102–254.

Heindel, W. C., Salmon, D. P., & Butters, N. (1990). Pictorial priming and cued recall in Alzheimer's and Huntington's disease. *Brain and Cognition*, **13**: 282–95.

Helm-Estabrooks, N., Yeo, R., Geschwind, N., Freedman, M., & Weinstein, C. (1986). Stuttering: disappearance and reappearance with acquired brain lesions. *Neurology*, **36**: 1109–12.

Helmchen, C., Lindig, M., Petersen, D., & Tronnier, V. (2002). Disappearance of central thalamic pain syndrome after contralateral parietal lobe lesion: implications for therapeutic brain stimulation. *Pain*, **98**: 325–30.

Herbert, C. M., & Powell, G. E. (1989). Insight and progress in rehabilitation. *Clinical Rehabilitation*, **3**: 125–30.

Hilgetag, C., Kotter, R., & Young, M. (1999). Inter-hemispheric competition of sub-cortical structures is a crucial mechanism in paradoxical lesion effects and spatial neglect. In: Reggia, J., Ruppin, E. & Glanzman, D. (Eds). *Progress in Brain Research, Vol 121*. Amsterdam: Elsevier, pp. 121–41.

Himmelbach, M., Nau, M., Zündorf, I., Erb, M., Perenin, M. T., & Karnath, H. O. (2009). Brain activation during immediate and delayed reaching in optic ataxia. *Neuropsychologia*, **47**: 1508–17.

Hudon, C., Belleville, S., Souchay, C., Gély-Nargeot, M. C., Chertkow, H., & Gauthier, S. (2006). Memory for gist and detail information in Alzheimer's disease and mild cognitive impairment. *Neuropsychology*, **20**: 566–77.

Hughes, J. (2010). A review of the Savant Syndrome and its possible relationship to epilepsy. *Epilepsy and Behavior*, **17**: 147–52.

Iacoboni, M. (2005). Divided attention in the normal and the split brain: chronometry and imaging. In: Itti, L., Rees, G., & Tsotsos, J. (Eds). *Neurobiology of Attention*. New York, NY: Academic Press, pp. 363–7.

Irle, E. (1987). Lesion size and recovery of function: some new perspectives. *Brain Research*, **434**: 307–20.

Irle, E. (1990). An analysis of the correlation of lesion size, localization and behavioural effects in 283 published studies of cortical and subcortical lesions in old-world monkeys. *Brain Research, Brain Research Reviews*, **15**: 181–213.

Irle, E., Peper, M., Wowra, B., & Kunze, S. (1994). Mood changes after surgery for tumors of the cerebral cortex. *Archives of Neurology*, **51**: 164–74.

Irle, E., Wowra, B., Kunert, H., Hampl, J., & Kunze, S. (1992). Memory disturbances following anterior communicating artery rupture. *Annals of Neurology*, **31**: 473–80.

Jacoby, L. L., & Witherspoon, D. (1982). Remembering without awareness. *Canadian Journal of Psychology*, **36**: 300–24.

Jiang, H., Stein, B., & McHaffie, J. (2009). Cortical lesion-induced visual hemineglect is prevented by NMDA antagonist pretreatment. *The Journal of Neuroscience*, **29**: 6917–25.

Joseph, S., & Linley, P. (Eds). (2008). *Trauma, Recovery and Growth. Positive Psychological Perspectives on Posttraumatic Stress*. Hoboken, NJ: Wiley.

Jovanovic, M. B., Berisavac, I., Perovic, J. V., Grubor, A., & Milenkovic, S. (2006). Huge extracranial asymptomatic frontal invasive meningioma: a case report. *European Archive of Otorhinolaryngology*, **263**: 223–7.

Kapur, N. (1980). Recognition of word associates in semantic paralexia. *British Journal of Psychology*, **71**: 401–05.

Kapur, N. (1996). Paradoxical functional facilitation in brain–behaviour research: a critical review. *Brain*, **119**: 1775–90.

Kapur, N., Heath, P., Meudell, P., & Kennedy, P. (1986). Amnesia can facilitate memory performance: evidence from a patient with dissociated retrograde amnesia. *Neuropsychologia*, **24**: 215–22.

Karpicke, J., & Roediger, III H. (2008). The critical importance of retrieval for learning. *Science*, **319**: 966–8.

Keedwell, P. (2008). *How Sadness Survived: The Evolutionary Basis of Depression*. Oxford: Radcliffe Publishing Ltd.

Keidel, J., Welbourne, S., & Lambon Ralph, M. (2010). Solving the paradox of the equipotential and modular brain: a neurocomputational model of stroke vs slow-growing glioma. *Neuropsychologia*, Feb 24 [Epub ahead of print].

Kiefer, M., Martens, U., Weisbrod, M., Hermle, L., & Spitzer, M. (2009). Increased unconscious semantic activation in schizophrenia patients with formal thought disorder. *Schizophrenia Research*, **114**: 79–83.

Kim, J. (1999). Aggravation of post-stroke sensory symptoms after a second stroke on the opposite side. *European Neurology*, **42**: 200–04.

Klimkowicz-Mrowiec, A., Slowikm, A., Krzywoszanski, L., Herzog-Krzywoszanska, R., & Szczudlik, A. (2008). Severity of explicit memory impairment due to Alzheimer's disease improves effectiveness of implicit learning. *Journal of Neurology*, **255**: 502–09.

Kuratsu, J., Kochi, M., & Ushio, Y. (2000). Incidence and clinical features of asymptomatic meningiomas. *Journal of Neurosurgery*, **82**: 766–70.

Lecardeur, L., Dollfus, S., & Stip, E. (2008). Semantic hyperpriming in schizophrenia. *British Journal of Psychiatry*, **193**: 82.

Leung, Y. W., Gravely-Witte, S., Macpherson, A., Irvine, J., Stewart, D. E., & Grace, S. L. (2010). Post-traumatic growth among cardiac outpatients: degree comparison with other chronic illness samples and correlates. *Journal of Health Psychology*, **15**: 1049–63.

Lewin, R. (1980). Is your brain really necessary? *Science*, **210**: 1232–4.

Li, W., Howard, J. D., Parrish, T. B., & Gottfried, J. A. (2008). Aversive learning enhances perceptual and cortical discrimination of indiscriminable odor cues. *Science*, **319**: 1842–5.

Lomber, S., Malhotra, S., & Sprague, J. (2007). Restoration of acoustic orienting into a cortically deaf hemifield by reversible deactivation of the contralesional superior colliculus: the acoustic 'Sprague Effect'. *Journal of Neurophysiology*, **97**: 979–93.

Lorenzen, B., & Murray, L. (2008). Bilingual aphasia: a theoretical and clinical review. *American Journal of Speech–Language Pathology*, **17**: 299–317.

Luck, S. J., Hillyard, S. A., Mangun, G. R., & Gazzaniga, M. S. (1989). Independent hemispheric attentional systems mediate visual search in split-brain patients. *Nature*, **342**: 543–5.

Malia, K., Torode, S., & Powell, G. (1993). Insight and progress in rehabilitation after brain injury. *Clinical Rehabilitation*, 7: 23–9.

Marchant, N. L., King, S. L., Tabet, N., & Rusted, J. M. (2010). Positive effects of cholinergic stimulation favor young *APOE*ϵ-4 carriers.

Neuropsychopharmacology, epub ahead of print.

Marsh, E. J., Balota, D. A., & Roediger, H. L. III (2005). Learning facts from fiction: effects of healthy aging and early-stage dementia of the Alzheimer type. *Neuropsychology*, **19**: 115–29.

Martel, G., Blanchard, J., Mons, N., Gastambide, F., Micheau, J., & Guillou, J. L. (2007). Dynamic interplays between memory systems depend on practice: the hippocampus is not always the first to provide solution. *Neuroscience*, **50**: 743–53.

Mataix-Cols, D., Wooderson, S., Lawrence, N., Brammer, M. J., Speckens, A., & Phillips, M. L. (2004). Distinct neural correlates of washing, checking, and hoarding symptom dimensions in obsessive–compulsive disorder. *Archives of General Psychiatry*, **61**: 564–76.

McGrath, J., & Linley, A. (2006). Post-traumatic growth in acquired brain injury. *Brain Injury*, **20**: 767–73.

McNeil, J., & Warrington, E. (1991). Prosopagnosia: a reclassification. *Quarterly Journal of Experimental Psychology A*, **43**: 267–87.

Menon, M., Woodward, T. S., Pomarol-Clotet, E., McKenna, P. J., & McCarthy, R. (2005). Heightened stimulus salience renders deluded schizophrenics less susceptible to the 'famous names illusion'. *Schizophrenia Research*, **80**: 369–71.

Miller, N. (2007). The merry vibes of Wintzer: the tale of foreign accent syndrome. In: Della Sala, S. (Ed), *Tall Tales about the Mind and Brain*. Oxford: Oxford University Press, pp. 204–17.

Milner, A. D., Dijkerman, H. C., McIntosh, R. D., Rossetti, Y., & Pisella, L. (2003). Delayed reaching and grasping in patients with optic ataxia. *Progress in Brain Research*, **142**: 225–42.

Milner, A. D., Dijkerman, H. C., Pisella, L., *et al.* (2001). Grasping the past. Delay can improve visuomotor performance. *Current Biology*, **11**: 1896–901.

Milner, A. D., Paulignan, Y., Dijkerman, H. C., Michel, F., & Jeannerod, M. (1999). A paradoxical improvement of misreaching in optic ataxia: new evidence for two separate neural systems for visual localization. *Proceedings of the Royal Society B*, **266**: 2225–9.

Mitchell, J. P., Schacter, D. L., Schacter, D. L., & Budson, A. E. (2006). Mis-attribution errors in Alzheimer's disease: the illusory truth effect. *Neuropsychology*, **20**: 185–92.

Moscovitch, M., Wincour, G., & Behrmann, M. (1997). What is special about face recognition? Nineteen experiments on a person with visual object agnosia and dyslexia but normal face recognition. *Journal of Cognitive Neuroscience*, **9**: 555–604.

Msetfi, R. M., Murphy, R. A., Simpson, J., & Kornbrot, D. E. (2005). Depressive realism and outcome density bias in contingency judgement: the effect of the context and inter-trial interval. *Journal of Experimental Psychology: General*, **134**: 10–22.

Muroi, A., Hirayama, K., Tanno, Y., Shimizu, S., Watanabe, T., & Yamamoto, T. (1999). Cessation of stuttering after bilateral thalamic infarction. *Neurology*, **53**: 890.

Musen, G., Shimamura, A., & Squire, L. R. (1990). Intact text-specific reading skill in amnesia. *Journal of Experimental Psychology: Learning, Memory and Cognition*, **16**: 1068–76.

Myers, C. E., McGlinchey-Berroth, R., Warren, S., Monti, L., Brawn, C. M., & Gluck, M. A. (2000). Latent learning in medial temporal amnesia: evidence for disrupted representational but preserved attentional processes. *Neuropsychology*, **14**: 3–15.

Myers, C. E., Shohamy, D., Gluck, M. A., Grossman, S., Onlaor, S., & Kapur, N. (2003). Dissociating medial temporal and basal ganglia memory systems with a latent learning task. *Neuropsychologia*, **41**: 1919–28.

Nathaniel-James, D., & Frith, C. (2002). The role of the dorsolateral prefrontal cortex: evidence from the effects of contextual restraint in a sentence completion task. *Neuroimage*, **16**: 1094–102.

O'Brien, M. (1993). Loss of memory is protective [Letter]. *British Medical Journal*, **307**: 1283.

Ogourtsova, T., Korner-Bitensky, N., & Ptito, A. (2010). Contribution of the superior colliculi to post-stroke unilateral spatial neglect and recovery. *Neuropsychologia*, **48**: 2407–16.

Ovsiew, F. (1997). Paradoxical functional facilitation in brain–behaviour research: a critical review [Letter]. *Brain*, **120**: 1261–4.

Owen, G. S., Cutting, J., & David, A. S. (2007). Are people with schizophrenia more logical than healthy volunteers? *British Journal of Psychiatry*, **191**: 453–4.

Packard, M. (2009). Anxiety, cognition and memory: a multiple memory systems perspective. *Brain Research*, **1293**: 121–8.

Peterson, C., Park, N., Pole, N., D'Andrea, W., & Seligman, M. E. (2008). Strengths of character and post-traumatic growth. *Journal of Trauma and Stress*, **21**: 214–7.

Poldrack, R. A., & Packard, M. G. (2003). Competition amongst multiple memory systems: converging evidence from animal and human brain studies. *Neuropsychologia*, **41**: 245–51.

Pollman, S., & Zaidel, E. (1999). Redundancy gains for visual search after complete commissurotomy. *Neuropsychology*, **13**: 246–58.

Pomarol-Clotet, E., Oh, T. M., Laws, K. R., & McKenna, P. J. (2008). Semantic priming in schizophrenia: systematic review and meta-analysis. *British Journal of Psychiatry*, **192**: 92–7.

Powell, T., Ekin-Wood, A., & Collin, C. (2007). Post-traumatic growth after head injury: a long-term follow-up. *Brain Injury*, **21**: 31–8.

Pujol, J., Vendrell, P., Deus, J., et al. (2001). The effect of medial frontal and posterior parietal demyelinating lesions on Stroop interference. *NeuroImage*, **13**: 68–75.

Randolph, C. (1991). Implicit, explicit, and semantic memory functions in Alzheimer's disease and Huntington's disease. *Journal of Clinical and Experimental Neuropsychology*, **13**: 479–94.

Reed, G. F. (1977). Obsessional personality disorder in remembering. *British Journal of Psychiatry*, **130**: 177–83.

Regard, M., Cook, N., Wieser, H., & Landis, T. (1994). The dynamics of cerebral dominance during unilateral seizures. *Brain*, **117**: 91–104.

Reverberi, C., Toraldo, A., D'Agostini, S., & Skrap, M. (2005). Better without (lateral) frontal cortex? Insight problems solved by frontal patients. *Brain*, **128**: 2882–90.

Rice, N. J., Edwards, M. G., Schindler, I., et al. (2008). Delay abolishes the obstacle avoidance deficit in unilateral optic ataxia. *Neuropsychologia*, **46**: 1549–57.

Riddoch, M. J., Johnston, R., Bracewell, R., Boutsen, L., & Humphreys, G. (2008). Are faces special? A case of pure prosopagnosia. *Cognitive Neuropsychology*, **25**: 3–26.

Ridout, N., Astell, A. J., Reid, I. C., Glen, T., & O'Carroll, R. E. (2003). Memory bias for emotional facial expressions in major depression. *Cognition and Emotion*, **17**: 101–22.

Rosenquist, A., & Sherman, S. (2007). *James Mather Sprague, 1916–2002. Biographical Memoirs, Volume 89*. Washington, DC: National Academy of Sciences.

Rossetti, Y., Revol, P., McIntosh, R., et al. (2005). Visually guided reaching: bilateral posterior parietal lesions cause a switch from fast visuomotor to slow cognitive control. *Neuropsychologia*, **43**: 162–77.

Roth, R. M., Baribeau, J., Milovan, D., O'Connor, K., & Todorov, C. (2004). Procedural and declarative memory in obsessive–compulsive disorder. *Journal of the International Neuropsychological Society*, **10**: 647–54.

Rouw, R., & de Gelder, B. (2002). Impaired face recognition does not preclude intact whole face perception. *Visual Cognition*, **9**: 689–718.

Sacks, O. (1985). *The Man Who Mistook His Wife for a Hat*. London: Duckworth.

Sato, W., Kubota, Y., Okada, T., Murai, T., Yoshikawa, S., & Sengoku, A. (2002). Seeing happy emotion in fearful and angry faces: qualitative analysis of facial expression recognition in a bilateral amygdala-damaged patient. *Cortex*, **38**: 727–42.

Schacter, D. L. (1996). Illusory memories: a cognitive neuroscience analysis. *Proceedings of the National Academy of Science USA*, **93**: 13,527–33.

Shergill, S., Samso, G., Bays, P., Frith, C., & Wolpert, D. (2005). Evidence for sensory prediction deficits in schizophrenia. *American Journal of Psychiatry*, **162**: 2384–6.

Shiv, B., Loewenstein, G., Bechara, A., Damasio, H., & Damasio, A. R. (2005). Investment behaviour and the negative side of emotion. *Psychological Science*, **16**: 435–9.

Soria, E., & Fine, E. (1991). Disappearance of thalamic pain after parietal subcortical stroke. *Pain*, **44**: 285–8.

Sprague, J. M. (1966). Interaction of cortex and superior colliculus in mediation of visually guided behaviour in the cat. *Science*, **153**: 1544–7.

Sprague, J. M. (1996). Neural mechanisms of visual orienting responses. *Progress in Brain Research*, **112**: 1–15.

Squire, L. R., & McKee, R. (1993). Declarative and nondeclarative memory in opposition: when prior events influence amnesic patients more than normal subjects. *Memory and Cognition*, **21**: 424–30.

Strasser-Fuchs, S., Enzinger, C., Ropele, S., Wallner, M., & Fazekas, F. (2008). Clinically benign multiple sclerosis despite large T2 lesion load: can we explain this paradox? *Multiple Sclerosis*, **14**: 205–11.

Sunaga, S., Shimizu, H., & Sunago, H. (2009). Long-term follow-up of seizure outcomes after corpus callosotomy. *Seizure*, **18**: 124–8.

Synofzik, M., Their, P., Leube, D., Schlotterbeck, P., & Lindner, A. (2010). Misattributions of agency in schizophrenia are based on imprecise predictions about the sensory consequences of one's actions. *Brain*, **133**: 262–71.

Tadin, D., Kim, J., Doop, M. L., *et al.* (2006). Weakened center-surround interactions in visual motion processing in schizophrenia. *The Journal of Neuroscience*, **26**: 11,403–12.

Taku, K., Cann, A., Calhoun, L. G., & Tedeschi. (2008). The factor structure of the posttraumatic growth inventory: a comparison of five models using confirmatory factor analysis. *Journal of Trauma and Stress*, **21**: 158–64.

Trabacca, A., & DiCuonzo, F. (2009). Living with one hemisphere – a large porencephalic cyst. *The New England Journal of Medicine*, **361**: 16.

Treffert, D. (2010). *Islands of Genius*. London: Jessica Kingsley Publishers.

Trevethan, C., Sahraie, A., & Weiskrantz, L. (2007). Can blindsight be superior to 'sighted sight'? *Cognition*, **103**: 491–501.

Vandenberghe, R., Vandenbulcke, E., Weintraub, S., *et al.* (2005). Paradoxical features of word finding difficulty in primary progressive aphasia. *Annals of Neurology*, **57**: 204–09.

Verfaellie, M., Schacter, D. L., & Cook, S. P. (2002). The effect of retrieval instructions on false recognition: exploring the nature of the gist memory impairment in amnesia. *Neuropsychologia*, **40**: 2360–8.

Vuilleumier, P., Hester, D., Assal, G., & Regli, F. (1996). Unilateral spatial neglect recovery after sequential strokes. *Neurology*, **19**: 184–9.

Wallisch, P., & Kumbhani, R. (2009). Can major depression improve the perception of visual motion? *The Journal of Neuroscience*, **29**: 14,381–2.

Warrington, E. K., & Davidoff, J. (2000). Failure at object identification improves mirror image matching. *Neuropsychologia*, **38**: 1229–34.

Warrington, E. K., & Weiskrantz, L. (1978). Further analysis of the prior learning effect in amnesic patients. *Neuropsychologia*, **16**: 169–77.

Weddell, R. (2004). Subcortical modulation of spatial attention including evidence that the Sprague effect extends to man. *Brain and Cognition*, **55**: 497–506.

Weddell, R. (2008). The effects of midbrain glioma on memory and other functions: a longitudinal single case study. *Neuropsychologia*, **46**: 1135–50.

Williams, L. E., Ramachandran, V. S., Hubbard, E. M., Braff, D. L., & Light, G. A. (2010). Superior size–weight illusion performance in patients with schizophrenia: evidence for deficits in forward models. *Schizophrenia Research*, **121**: 101–06.

Wilson, B. A. (2009). *Memory Rehabilitation.* New York, NY: The Guilford Press.

Wilson, B. A., Watson, P. C., Baddeley, A. D., Emslie, H., & Evans, J. J. (2000). Improvement or simply practice? The effects of twenty repeated assessments on people with and without brain injury. *Journal of the International Neuropsychological Society*, **6**: 469–79.

Wingard, J., & Packard, M. (2008). The amygdala and emotional modulation of competition between cognitive and habit memory. *Behavioral Brain Research*, **19**: 126–31.

Wittenberg, G., & Schaechter, J. (2009). The neural basis of constraint-induced movement therapy. *Current Opinion in Neurology*, **22**: 582–8.

Yarnitsky, D., Barron, S., & Bental, E. (1988). Disappearance of phantom pain after focal brain infarction. *Pain*, **32**: 285–7.

Zetterberg, H., Alexander, D. M., Spandidos, D. A., & Blennow, K. (2009). Additional evidence for antagonistic pleiotrophic effects of *APOE. Alzheimer's & Dementia*, **5**: 75.

Paradoxes in neurorehabilitation

Tom Manly, Ian H. Robertson and Narinder Kapur

Summary

We consider how a number of interventions that would normally interfere with function have paradoxically improved symptoms in patients with neurological conditions. These include distorting reality, constraining patients' ability to perform everyday tasks, impeding vision, temporarily disabling healthy brain tissue, and distracting patients from the task at hand. We argue that the effects of these diverse interventions can be understood within a general framework of brain function that emphasizes competition for limited capacity resources. We discuss how this competition can be biased to produce rehabilitation benefits.

Introduction

Neurorehabilitation refers to any intervention that aims to reduce impairment caused by brain injury, disease or developmental abnormality. It also refers to techniques that help compensate for such impairments or that facilitate adjustment (Wilson, 1996). Much that is effective in rehabilitation is far from paradoxical. People relearn and improve through practice, encouragement and the setting of incremental, achievable goals (e.g. Wilson *et al.*, 2009). Where full restoration of a function is not possible, as is often the case, compensatory aids such as diaries and communication devices can facilitate independence (Kime, 2006; Kapur and Wilson, 2009). Patients and families can gain comfort, perspective and realistic hope from discussion with professionals and other patients.

In line with the focus of this book, here we concentrate on particular interventions that under normal circumstances may be considered deleterious or contrary to perceived wisdom, but which have been shown to reduce or offset impairment in people with brain injuries. These include inducing visual illusions, hindering the use of intact body systems, exposure to noise and other distractions, obstruction of vision and even the pouring of cold water into one ear.

Rehabilitation is ultimately concerned with helping people to live independently, and to make their own choices. Here, we take a less stringent definition, including interventions that have been shown to modulate symptom severity, whether or not the long-term impact on general outcome has been fully explored. This fits in with a second focus of the book, in exploring how paradoxical effects can illuminate underlying processes of brain function, change and recovery. At the end of the chapter, we discuss how a number of

Figure 4.1 From John Tenniel's illustrations for Lewis Carroll's *Through the Looking Glass.*

these apparently disparate findings can be integrated within a general framework in which objects and mental control programs for different tasks ('task-sets') are viewed as competing for neural representation.

Through the looking glass: the value of illusions in neurorehabilitation

The brain constructs and constantly updates models of the world that allow fast and accurate action. If those models are wrong in important ways, the consequences can be very serious. Accordingly, perceptual illusions such as visual and auditory hallucinations and distorted spatial representations normally have a highly disruptive effect on behaviour. Here, however, we consider some ways in which deliberately inducing illusions has improved function.

One illusion to which we are all prone is the idea that, when our foot hurts, the pain is in our foot .rather than in our brain. This illusion is no more dramatically revealed than when, following limb amputation, people experience crippling pain in the now absent limb. This 'phantom pain' is disturbing, not least because normal strategies such as rubbing or flexing the hurt area are not available. One ingenious approach to helping such patients has been to create the illusion that the absent limb is still present. This is achieved using a mirror to reflect the remaining limb in the location of the missing limb (see Figure 4.2). Remarkably, despite the patients knowing that they are not seeing their absent limb, over a large number of trials the illusion of cramp-relieving movement can reduce the pain, sometimes permanently (Sumitani *et al.*, 2008). The technique has also been used to help patients with reduced movement, sensation or increased pain in a limb following brain damage. Again, with sufficient practice, the illusion that one's

Figure 4.2 Mirror Therapy. The powerful illusion that the man is looking through a window at his (amputated) right hand, rather than seeing a mirror reflection of his left hand. This has been used to treat 'phantom pain' in patients with amputated limbs and to facilitate physical and sensory recovery following brain injury.

affected limb is moving appears to enhance its neural representations and promote recovery (Ramachandran and Altschuler, 2009; Moseley *et al.*, 2008; McCabe *et al.*, 2008; Cacchio *et al.*, 2009; Serino *et al.*, 2007).

Unilateral (i.e. one-sided) spatial neglect is a debilitating consequence of brain injury in which patients have difficulty in noticing and acting on information from one side of space (Brain, 1941). Patients may ignore people approaching from one side, eat food from only one side of the plate or fail to wash or dress one side of the body. Spatial neglect can occur despite intact vision (Walker *et al.*, 1991), and can operate across sensory modalities (Robertson and Halligan, 1999). As such, it has fascinated researchers because of the insights it offers into attention and conscious awareness. Persistent neglect is a serious

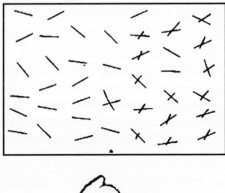

disorder that compromises many activities of daily living (including mobility, self-care and reading), and appears to slow recovery more generally (Paolucci *et al.*, 2003). It is therefore an important target for rehabilitation. Most patients with persistent neglect have damage to the right hemisphere of the brain and ignore information on the left (Stone *et al.*, 1993), and this is the group that we will generally be talking about where we mention spatial neglect in this chapter.

Figure 4.3 Presentation of unilateral spatial neglect in (1) cancellation task where the instruction is to cross out all lines on the page; (2) drawing a stick man from memory.

Most patients with unilateral spatial neglect (see Box) can look and become aware of information on the left for a short time if they are reminded to do so (Riddoch and Humphreys, 1983). Accordingly, many early rehabilitation studies focused on increasing leftward visual scanning. Although there have been exceptions (Antonucci et al., 1995), a general view has been that this tends to produce limited and poorly generalized gains (Robertson, 1999). Other interventions that might assist patients to regain awareness of neglected space have therefore been explored.

Among the most recent and high profile of these interventions involves deliberate distortion of patients' spatial awareness. Glass prisms worn as goggles provide a form of illusion by bending the light. If you put on prism goggles that caused a 10-degree rightward shift, the first time you reached out for an object you would have the unsettling experience of watching your hand miss the target by about 10 degrees. Quite quickly, however, you would learn to correct for the distortion and would regain accuracy. Take the prism goggles off and many people find that they now miss the target, this time overshooting to the *left*. They know that the prisms have gone, but their brains are correcting as if they were still present. Fortunately, this is only temporarily debilitating and normality is restored with a few more reaches. Researchers asked, what would occur if patients showing left visual neglect adapted to rightward deviating prisms; could they benefit from this leftward, post-adaptation rebound effect? Remarkably, Rossetti et al. (1998) reported that, after just 5 minutes of making reaches while wearing prism goggles, patients showed significantly greater awareness of the left. Rather than the effect fading, as it does in non-brain injured people, it was if anything stronger 2 hours after the prism exposure. Subsequent work has shown that detectable positive effects of approximately 100 minutes of rightward prism adaptation were detectable 6 weeks later (Frassinetti et al., 2002). Whilst, in common with a number of techniques that we will discuss, not all studies using prism adaptation in neglect have returned positive results (Turton et al., 2009; Nys et al., 2008), it seems clear that the effect works for some patients. What is particularly surprising is that the benefits are not simply attributable to patients reaching further to the left (as would be expected), but appear to reflect a genuine recalibration of their spatial awareness across even non-reaching tasks, such as reading.

Our sense of location and orientation is influenced by information from vision, touch, audition, balance and proprioception (feedback on the relative location of limbs). It is not surprising that our brains are intolerant of discrepancies between these sources – you cannot be facing one way and the other at the same time. If such disparities occur, the brain seems to find a single, 'best fit' solution. This means that induced distortions in one source of information can bias another sense. Caloric vestibular stimulation (CVS) is a good example. Here, one ear is chilled with cold water to produce a temperature difference between the left and right sides of the vestibular (balance) system. This induces an illusion of head rotation that in turn triggers compensatory eye movements in the opposite direction – the vestibulo-ocular reflex. A number of studies have demonstrated how this illusion can, at least temporarily, increase the number of leftward eye movements made by patients with left spatial neglect, with resulting gains for awareness (Adair et al., 2003; Cappa et al., 1987; Rubens, 1985). As with the effects of prisms, the improvements in visual awareness may be accompanied by more generalized changes, including improved motor function, sensation and sense of ownership for neglected limbs (Rode et al., 1992; Bottini et al., 2005). These changes are not simply a result of the novelty of a cold, wet ear (although as we discuss later, this may help!), the effect crucially depends upon which ear is chilled. In a surprising demonstration of how general the biasing effects of CVS can be, Bächtold *et al.* (2001) found differentially improved nonverbal and verbal memory following left and right CVS. This suggests that even non-spatial functions associated with one or other cerebral hemisphere can be modulated with this technique.

Another distortion to our sense or orientation can be induced by mechanical muscle vibration 'fooling' the proprioceptive system about the relative positions of our limbs. Even with our eyes open, unilateral vibration of the back muscles can cause us to deviate from an intended straight path when walking (Schmida *et al.*, 2005). Similarly, vibrating of posterior neck muscle on one side (at a rate of about 80 pulses per second) can induce an illusion of head rotation. Following the work of Karnath (1994), Schindler *et al.* (2002) exposed patients with unilateral neglect to approximately 10 hours of such neck stimulation (in daily sessions of 40 minutes), producing demonstrable gains to their awareness of the left. The gains persisted long after the end of the intervention and, as we see with other treatments for spatial neglect, generalized across sensory modalities.

Refusing a helping hand – constraint-induced therapy in rehabilitation

It is natural to try to compensate for disability using any means, including making the most of one's residual abilities. Where one limb has been paralysed by stroke, for example, it seems sensible to use the intact limb to complete tasks where possible. Given that rehabilitation is ultimately about working with patients to help them achieve functional goals as easily and independently as possible, artificially hindering people by deterring the use of intact functions appears paradoxical and perverse. That, however, is the essence of various forms of 'constraint-induced therapy'. The idea in its original manifestation in motor recovery was simple: if we do not use a limb, prolonged non-use will compound the initial damage and the full potential for recovery may not be realized. Instead, patients should be encouraged not to use their good limbs, and instead attend to and practise using their impaired limbs as much as possible. The easiest way to remember to do this is to constrain the good limb in some manner (see Blanton *et al.*, 2008 for a review of Constraint Induced Therapy for movement disorders).

These ideas have become influential in other areas of function. For example, Pulvermüller and Berthier (2008) provide a useful historical perspective to 'constraint-induced aphasia therapy' (CIAT) for people with language disorders following brain injury. An example of this approach is shown in Figure 4.4. Here, each patient has a set of cards showing various items and is playing a game where they have to ask for a matching card from the other players. Because each person cannot see the others' cards or gestures, the game specifically encourages expressive speech. Researchers who use the technique argue for a relatively intensive schedule ('massed practice'; e.g. 2-hour therapy sessions taking place over 10 consecutive days) to consolidate the gains and prevent alternative forms of communication developing. Reviewing the area, Cherney *et al.* (2008) report generally positive outcomes, but argue that further, well-controlled studies are warranted. Clearly, attempting to communicate with impaired speech can be frustrating and embarrassing for patients and care is needed to provide the appropriate supportive setting.

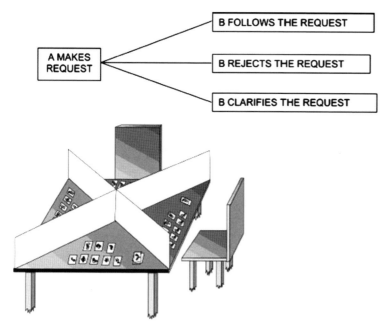

Figure 4.4 A paradigm for 'language-action therapy', as discussed by Pulvermüller and Berthier (2008).

Another obvious candidate for constraint-induced therapy is unilateral neglect: if patients spend all of their time looking at the right side of space, what happens if they are prevented from doing so? Beis *et al.* (1989) asked patients to wear glasses with patches over the right half of each lens for approximately 12 hours a day. The patches are not as noticeable and debilitating as you might expect, unless of course if you look to the right (try it with your fingers!). After three months and following the removal of the patches, the patients showed increased spontaneous eye movements to the left and improvements in some everyday activities in comparison to a control group who had worn patches that blocked vision from the right eye (i.e. which reduces information from the right side of space to a much lesser degree). Again, it is important to state that, as with much in rehabilitation, this technique does not always produce positive effects (e.g. Tsang *et al.*, 2009; Fong *et al.*, 2007).

A final and somewhat extreme form of constraint-induced therapy is not the temporary disablement of a limb, speech or vision, but of part of the brain itself. The two hemispheres of the brain are, in some respects, in competition with each other. In the case of our spatial awareness, the left side of the brain appears primarily concerned with 'pushing' attention over to the right. Fortunately, the right side of the brain is generally pushing back with equal vigour, leaving us with balanced perception. Where one hemisphere is compromised by injury, the competition can become very one-sided and perception will become markedly skewed. This idea of finely balanced competition has been used to explain why unilateral neglect is so common and why it occurs following damage to such an apparently wide variety of brain structures (Mesulam, 2002; Kinsbourne, 1977). If the functioning left hemisphere is impeding potential function of the right, might there be benefits if the left hemisphere's ability to compete is weakened? There are obvious and dramatic ways in which this could be achieved. Thankfully, repetitive transcranial magnetic stimulation (rTMS) offers a more benign and temporary means to suppress regional brain activity. As is discussed fully in Chapter 13, TMS uses rapidly changing magnetic fields in a coil held near the scalp to induce weak electrical currents in underlying brain tissue. After a period of rTMS, stimulated cortical regions may show reduced excitability for a period. As would be predicted by the hemispheric competition model, rTMS over the *left* parietal cortex has been shown to reduce left spatial neglect shown by patients with right hemisphere damage, apparently with lasting effects (Koch *et al.*, 2008; Fierro *et al.*, 2006; Brighina *et al.*, 2002).

Interruptions! Interruptions! Interruptions!

There is nothing so annoying as to have two people talking when you're busy interrupting.

Mark Twain

So far we have considered interventions that induce distortions in perception or constrain aspects of function. Now we turn to distraction. It is pretty clear that, when we are trying to do any kind of demanding task, distraction is a nuisance. Why then would clinicians wish to deliberately distract patients, particularly those whose attention is already impaired?

In our first two examples that follow below, which again focus on patients with unilateral neglect, distraction may be seen as an incidental rather than the key aim of the strategy. Dividing attention between two tasks, stimuli or information streams is, compared with single tasks, almost always associated with a performance cost (Duncan, 2006). Finding *better* performance under dual- than single-task conditions is therefore highly paradoxical, particularly in a patient group who often show profound problems in maintaining attention (Robertson *et al.*, 1997a; Samuelsson *et al.*, 1998; Husain and Rorden, 2003). Despite this, following the observations of Halligan *et al.* (1991) that a patient showed less left spatial neglect when using his left rather than right hand to perform a task, Robertson and colleagues performed a series of studies in which patients were asked, in effect, to focus simultaneously on two activities. Typically, the task was to name objects or read words scattered over the table top whilst, at the same time, remembering to move their left, right or both hands, hidden from sight beneath the table. Taken together, the results suggested that *despite* the dual task nature of the activity, and despite the hands forming no sort of visual cue, movements of the left hand in space to the left side of the body significantly enhanced patients' ability on the spatial naming tasks. This did not occur if patients moved both hands at the same time, if they moved their left hand but to the right of the body midline, or if they moved the right hand to the left of midline. There was something, in short, about the interaction between the laterality of the limb and the space in which the action occurred that supported visual awareness for the left. Whilst the effect does not occur in all patients, and indeed many patients with neglect are simply unable to move their left limbs, the technique has been used as a tractable therapy with demonstrable and lasting functional gains (Robertson and North, 1992, 1993, 1994; Robertson *et al.*, 1992, 1994, 1998a).

One thing that is almost always distracting is the occurrence of a loud, unexpected noise. If sufficiently startling, this will cause us to immediately disengage from ongoing activity, prioritize information gathering, and potentiate possible action (e.g. running away!).

Robertson *et al.* (1998b) investigated what would occur if, just before making a spatial judgement, patients with left neglect were exposed to a moderately loud and somewhat unexpected tone. The rather surprising result was that, on these trials, the patients showed significantly reduced or even reversed neglect compared with the standard trials in the task. The results were not, of course, so surprising to the authors. The intervention was based on the observation that persistent neglect often co-occurs with a drowsy, unresponsive state and tested the prediction that elevating alertness (biological readiness to respond) with the loud tone could reduce neglect. George *et al.* (2008) demonstrated that stimulating thoughts could have a similar effect. Sadly perhaps, the thoughts were at the milder end of the stimulating spectrum, based on the observation that perceived time-pressure is associated with moderate increases in arousal (Slobounov *et al.*, 2000). They asked patients with left neglect to find and cross out visual targets scattered over a sheet of paper. Paradoxically, when the patients thought they were acting under time pressure, rather than missing more targets in their haste (the standard 'speed–accuracy trade-off'), they missed significantly *fewer* than under open-ended testing conditions. Consistent findings from the use of stimulant medication (Malhotra *et al.*, 2006) and through monitoring spontaneous changes in alertness levels (Dodds *et al.*, under review) have been reported.[1] One recent study even showed that listening to the music of Kenny Rogers during a spatial task reduced left neglect. In this case, however, the benefits were attributed to enhanced positive affect rather than heightened alertness in response to an aversive stimulus (Soto *et al.*, 2009).

Aside from spatial awareness, paradoxical improvement in performance on certain tasks from potentially distracting 'stressors' has been observed. Robert Yerkes and John Dodson famously reported in 1908 that, whilst a series of mild electric shocks interfered with performance on a difficult task, it *facilitated* performance on an easier version (Yerkes and Dodson, 1908). Broadbent (1971) similarly describes performance gains on dull, repetitive activities by simultaneous exposure to unpleasant noise or temperatures. Consistent 'inverted U-shaped functions', in which performance in a particular task increases in proportion to neural activity up to a certain point but is then impaired by further increases, have been reported in relation to the locus coeruleus (implicated in arousal) and dopamine and noradrenaline levels (Arnsten *et al.*, 1996; Usher *et al.*, 1999; see also Chapter 23). The full implications for neurorehabilitation of such findings have yet to be fully explored. As we will discuss further, attention is a crucial mediating variable in recovery and rehabilitation. Identifying optimal levels of stimulation that best allow sustained engagement in adaptive activities is likely to be beneficial. In this respect, it is a sobering thought that, in a recent observational study of *specialist* stroke units in the UK, patients were reported to spend less than an hour a day in any sort of structured therapy and more than 60% of their day in isolation (De Wit *et al.*, 2005).

We now turn to rehabilitation in which interruption of current activity is not incidental but *essential* to the effect. A key human ability is to plan an action that is not a response to one's immediate environmental contingencies but which will serve to achieve a goal in some

---

[1] Interestingly, recent evidence suggests a similar, although much more subtle, interaction between alertness and spatial awareness in the healthy population and in children with the diagnosis of Attention Deficit Hyperactivity Disorder (see Manly *et al.*, 1997, 2005; Dobler *et al.*, 2001, 2005; Fimm *et al.*, 2006; Dodds *et al.*, 2008; Sheppard *et al.*, 1999; George *et al.*, 2005; Nigg *et al.*, 1997; and Voeller and Heilman, 1988).

probable future context. Various categories of such 'prospective memories' have been proposed including *event-based* (when I see Jane I need to ask her for a book), *time-based* (I need to phone the bank at 2:00), or *pulse* (I need to write this report at some stage) (Ellis, 1988; Einstein and McDaniel, 1996). Prospective memory is probably best thought of not as a single process but as the functional result of a series of interacting stages; having the intention, storing it, retrieving it at the appropriate point, acting on it, and remembering that you have already acted on it so as to avoid repetition. Given the complex interplay between planning, memory, and attention and the consequently rather distributed neural processes involved, it is not surprising that prospective memory complaints are common across many patient groups (Fish *et al.*, 2010). The multi-stage model is useful in appropriately targeting rehabilitation. If a person has great difficulty remembering their own intentions or others' instructions, alternative means of storing specific content can be explored. These could include the use of diaries, calendars, white-boards, personal organizers and specialist systems such as the *Neuropage* service – in which predictable events such as when to take medication are entered by an operator and automatically sent to a pager worn by the patient at the correct time (Wilson *et al.*, 2001). Such techniques can greatly increase independence and reduce carer strain (Teasdale *et al.*, 2009).

A rather different experience is one where we *know* what it is that we intended to do (in the sense that, if asked, we would remember it) and yet, when the relevant triggering event or time arrives, it does not spring to mind. Damage to the prefrontal cortex has long been associated with an exaggerated form of this type of prospective memory lapse (Luria, 1966; Shallice and Burgess, 1991; Duncan, 1986). Shallice and Burgess (1991), for example, describe a series of patients with frontal lesions, all of whom performed very well on standardized IQ measures, who nevertheless showed profound levels of disorganization in everyday life. One patient, who left the clinic to get a drink, was later found playing golf on an adjacent course apparently with no real idea why – as if his behaviour was determined almost entirely by immediate contextual cues rather than his stated intentions. Shallice and Burgess developed a novel test to examine this behaviour. In the 6-Element test, participants were asked to attempt 6 simple tasks. Crucially, they were told that they would not have time to complete all of the items in every test. To meet the main requirement (i.e. to do something from all 6), participants had therefore to spontaneously switch between the tasks during the 15 minutes available to them. Despite being tested on their comprehension of the rules before and after the test, and their above average IQ scores, the patients with frontal lesions showed a strong tendency to get caught up in one or other of the tasks to the detriment of the overall goal. Similar results in a much larger group of brain injured participants has been reported (Wilson *et al.*, 1996).

As discussed, in a limited capacity system, attentional engagement in one task is almost invariably at the cost of another. When the patients were engaged in a component task of the 6-Element test (e.g. doing simple mental arithmetic tasks), the main goal of switching between the tasks was not kept sufficiently active to interrupt this engagement. Manly *et al.* (2002a) examined what happened if participants were deliberately interrupted. Working with patients who showed disorganization in daily life consequent upon TBI (in which the frontal lobes often take disproportionate damage), they used a variant of the 6-Element test, The Hotel Test. Here, participants were asked to sample a series of simple tasks involved in running a hotel, such as sorting conference labels into alphabetical order and looking up telephone numbers. As with the 6-Element test, they were explicitly told that they could not fully complete even one of the tasks during the 15 minutes available, meaning that they should occasionally switch between activities such that they spent an approximately equal time on each. Under standard conditions, the patients were again significantly worse than IQ-matched controls. In a condition in which they were asked to 'think about what they were doing' if they heard a tone, and during which 6 tones were presented at random intervals, however, their performance became *indistinguishable* from that of healthy volunteers (Manly *et al.*, 2002a). In itself, the effect suggests that poor performance under standard conditions was not generally related to frank forgetting of the goal or a lack of motivation – the interrupting tone is unlikely to have helped in these respects. Rather, by temporarily disengaging attention from the current task and cueing a moment of reflection, the main goal was more likely to be expressed.

Fish *et al.* (2007) extended this approach to a prospective memory task (making phone calls at certain times) that needed to be executed by patients during normal daily life over a period of two weeks. In training, a particular cue phrase ('STOP': Stop Think Organize Plan) was associated with reviewing one's intentions. Over the study phase, 'STOP' text (SMS) messages were sent to the patient participants' mobile phones on half of the days selected at random. The messages were sent at random times during the working day but, crucially, not within half-an-hour of the time a call was due. Despite this, success in the telephone task was substantially greater on days with cues than days without. Even given the delay between a cue and the execution of the intention, this periodic interruption/review facilitated performance.

Further work is required looking at the persistence and generality of this effect. A merit of the approach, however, lies in its potential flexibility. It does not require intentions to be pre-specified. It aims to assist patients to actively manage their *own* goals, however recently these were formed.

Rehabilitation, attention and integrated competition

In our discussion of paradoxes in rehabilitation so far, we have generally steered away from precise mechanisms, in that these may be rather specific to a given technique or system (e.g. prism adaptation, vestibulo-ocular reflex, etc.). Here, we attempt to couch the findings within a general framework that can, in principle, be used to generate new interventions.

In this respect it is important first to say something about attention. William James wrote in 1890:

> Everyone knows what attention is. It is the taking possession by the mind, in clear and vivid form, of one out of what seem several simultaneous possible objects or trains of thought. Focalisation, concentration of consciousness are of its essence. It implies withdrawal from some things in order to deal effectively with others. (James, 1890)

Despite 60 years of experimental research into attention, the essence of this definition remains uncontroversial. Attention is about selection. It is about the one thing, from a multitude of candidates (sights, sounds, thoughts), that at any one time dominates conscious awareness. It is about limited capacity; that we cannot attend to one thing without withdrawing attention from another.

Subjectively, attention is arguably akin to focusing a camera (or its auditory or other sensory equivalents) on a given stimulus, sensation or thought. It feels as if there is an 'us' seated in the theatre of our mind, choosing what to focus upon. Neuroscience has, however, made increasingly untenable the view that attention is conscious selection only at the *end* of a series of neural processes.

Let us consider one well worked through example of how attention operates in vision (and, in this, we lean heavily on two seminal papers by Duncan, 2006 and Desimone and Duncan, 1995). Early visual processes in the occipital cortex can respond to a large amount of information simultaneously. If a neuron is, say, sensitive to a particular angle, colour or movement and such a feature occurs within its receptive field, the neuron will tend to fire regardless of what else is going on in the scene. To a first approximation, the output of these visual areas then moves forward through the brain in two major streams. There is a ventral stream, via the inferior temporal lobe, that is primarily concerned with identifying objects (Ungerleider and Mishkin, 1982), and a dorsal stream, via the parietal lobes, primarily coding spatial locations to facilitate action (Ungerleider and Mishkin, 1982; Goodale and Milner, 1992). Something important happens as various visual features coalesce into representations of objects in the infero-temporal cortex. The level of neural response associated with a particular object will vary in relation to how many other objects are in the scene (Chelazzi et al., 1993). In effect, objects now 'compete' with each other for representation. If, by chance, representations associated with a particular object happened to be relatively high, those associated with other objects would accordingly reduce and the favoured object would begin to dominate awareness. In addition to chance, however, there are inherent characteristics of stimuli (sudden appearance, intensity, movement, biological significance, etc.) that bias competition in their favour. They may also gain competitive weight from long-term learning – for example, the way that an arbitrary stimulus such as one's own name tends to capture attention. If these were the only factors, our attention system would be at the mercy of whatever was most salient around us. Whilst this sometimes seems to be the case, in addition we clearly have mechanisms that can bias this competition in an intentional, top-down manner related to our goals. The crucial observation by Desimone and Duncan (1995) was that such top-down bias cannot purely operate at the end of the visual streams, because selection according to salience, etc., *would have already occurred*. Rather, these top-down signals join the general competitive affray across multiple levels of processing, at early and later stages.

So far we have considered a single visual pathway. There are, of course, many streams relating to visual location, auditory, tactile, olfactory, and proprioceptive information as well as processes relating to memories, thoughts and other internal content. Life would be rather complex if information about lots of different sorts of events were to dominate competition at each of these levels – for example, simultaneously being most aware of different objects in each modality. In addition to bottom-up characteristics of a stimulus, and top-down task-based control, a crucial additional factor biasing competition at a given level of processing has therefore been argued to be the degree to which that object/event currently dominates in other levels (Desimone and Duncan, 1995). A number of everyday experiences – including the way sights and smells associated with food take on particular salience in the hungry, or the 'Proustian rush' of involuntary memories triggered by an object – can be couched in such an 'integrated competition' framework. In the experimental literature, priming (in which one stimulus speeds recognition of related content in other domains) is perhaps the clearest example. Other examples include the tendency, if you turn towards a particular location, for sounds and tactile sensations from that location also to be enhanced (Driver and Spence, 1994).

With this framework in mind, turning to our series of paradoxical interventions, it is useful to ask: *in any given case, what can we do that is likely to bias competition at one or more levels in favour of reduced impairment and enhanced recovery?*

Let us first take the example of an impairment in hand motor function following stroke. Where patients make little use of one hand, it is likely that attention tends to become biased in favour of the still-functioning limb now being used to complete most tasks. A technique such as Mirror Therapy (in which the reflection of the functioning limb appears in the location of the impaired limb), creates conditions under which the competitive weight of representations of the impaired limb throughout the brain are likely to be enhanced. By representations, we do not mean simply that patients will pay more attention to that limb (although that may be the subjective experience), but that via integrated competition, the competitive weight of *all content* relating to that limb is likely to be enhanced. Sensations in the hand that, following the stroke, may have fallen below a threshold for conscious detection may now, for example, be just sufficient to cross that barrier. Motor commands may be more likely, and more likely to lead to action. It is easy to see how forced use of an impaired hand (by constraint of the unimpaired hand) could have similar consequences.

Turning to prism adaptation and other rehabilitation effects in unilateral neglect, it is important to first emphasize the rather volatile, unreliable characteristics of this condition. Patients do not have a stable dividing line, to the left of which everything is neglected and to the right of which everything is detected. Rather there is a left–right gradient affecting the *probability* that a given object will be seen (Kinsbourne, 1993). In repeating the same spatial task, patients can on one go miss the majority of targets on the left and on another perform almost at normal levels (Dodds *et al.*, under review). Where information is close to conscious representation, even small gains in competitive weight may be sufficient to tip the balance and produce awareness. This volatility may account for why spatial neglect reappears so frequently in our examination of paradoxes in rehabilitation.

Considering prism adaptation in this light, it is known that an instruction to attend to a particular spatial location increases firing in neural populations sensitive to that region even before a stimulus appears (Luck *et al.*, 1997) and that a general leftward cue can increase neglect patients' awareness of subsequently presented left stimuli (Riddoch and Humphreys, 1983). Adapting to rightward deviating prisms causes a rebound reach bias to the left which, through integrated competition, may increase the competitive weight of other left-located content. Similar arguments could be advanced in the case of the beneficial effects on neglect from induced illusions (from neck muscle vibration and caloric vestibular stimulation); constraining awareness from the right with eye-patches; induced temporary under-function of left hemisphere with transcranial magnetic stimulation; and encouraging left-sided hand movements.

The reduction in spatial neglect that follows increases in alertness is more difficult to explain. One possibility in patients is that, in addition to a general rightward bias, their often rather drowsy state is associated with a narrowing of attention (Halligan and Marshall, 1994) and a difficulty in disengaging from right-sided details (Posner *et al.*, 1984). Enhanced alertness may increase available capacity and thereby increase the likelihood that left-located stimuli will have some competitive weight. A second possibility is that alertness changes are not symmetrical across the brain. The right hemisphere is thought to have a particular role in developing and maintaining an alert state and is possibly the primary or initial beneficiary of such increases (Pardo *et al.*, 1991; Wilkins *et al.*, 1987; Sturm *et al.*, 1999). Because left-located objects are represented in the right side of the brain, this shift in the balance may be sufficient to enhance their representation. A third possibility is that a degree of alertness or arousal is necessary for the maintenance of an appropriate top-down signal. Drowsy people are prone to distraction and action lapses (Manly *et al.*, 2002b;

85

Horne, 1993). It is possible that, when relatively awake, patients are better able to will themselves to attend to the left, this intention allowing left-located stimuli to better compete at early levels of processing. The benefits of increases in alertness for spatial neglect may, of course, be an additive or nonlinear combination of these factors.

A final component to the integrated competition framework concerns competition, not between events vying for representation, but between 'programmes' vying for control of the cognitive system. For well over a century, disturbance arising from damage to the prefrontal cortex has led many researchers to conclude that this region performs a special role in self-organization and behavioural control (Harlow, 1848; Luria, 1966; Shallice, 1988). Patients with frontal damage may, for example, get components in tasks out of sequence, repeat some segment of behaviour over and over again without obvious cause ('perseveration') or completely fail to follow important aspects of their own stated strategy (Luria, 1965; Duncan, 1986). In line with this suggested role in organizing goal-directed responses, recent research has demonstrated a remarkable degree of flexibility in prefrontal neurons. Unlike other brain regions, which may show rather fixed preferences for certain stimuli (such as a colour, frequency or a face), prefrontal neurons appear to respond to *whatever is relevant to the task at hand* (Everling *et al.*, 2002; Miller and Cohen, 2001). Take the example of an experimenter giving rather arbitrary instructions to a participant such as: 'Watch the screen – respond with one button push to a presented green square, two button pushes to a blue square but do not respond to a red square'. The idea would be that the frontal cortex uses these instructions to build a model of the task. It will quickly become differentially responsive to the red, blue and green squares and not, for example, to irrelevant details of the monitor. Through integrated competition, this activity will tend to produce coherent responses in other systems relating to colour, button pushing and so forth. After a few trials, the frontal system (at least, an efficient one) will be producing smooth, accurate behaviour to these new arbitrary constraints (Duncan, 2006).

In this example, the experimenter has set up a single-goal situation. In real life, there are many tasks that you could complete at any one time. The novel you are reading is, in a sense, in competition with the washing up that you could be doing, which is in competition with that chair that needs repairing. This competition is pretty much a winner-takes-all affair because we are only capable of doing well one thing at a time. Just as we saw that various factors could influence competition between objects at a given level of processing (salience, relevance to current task and the weighting of the object at other levels of processing), various factors are likely to influence competition between goals/task sets. One probable factor is anticipated reward; all else being equal, we will do the task that we most enjoy, is easiest, or from which we stand most to benefit. Other factors might include the strength of relevant triggers in the environment (if I see a toaster and bread, I am more likely to make toast) and the level of activation of a particular task set (such that we may be more likely to continue with the same task than to switch). Just as with other forms of attentional competition, it is the interplay between different levels (reward, environment and recent activity) that will determine the behavioural outcome at a particular time. In addition, to produce adaptive, goal-directed behaviour, we will sometimes want to act on a plan in a way that is not immediately rewarding or strongly triggered by the current context. An interesting question is how such a stored intention – a prospective memory – is ever able to compete against current activity. The most likely opportunities may be when the current task has been completed, when it is inherently unrewarding, or when an impasse, or other barrier to continuation, has been reached. Another may be when attention is disengaged from current activity by an interruption, particularly when that interruption is designed to bias attention towards neglected goals. This was the thinking behind the last of our paradoxical rehabilitation examples in which the performance of patients, who had a tendency to neglect important goals, was improved by interruptions, associated in training with a process of goal review (Manly *et al.*, 2002a; Fish *et al.*, 2007).

Conclusions

In this chapter we have considered a number of interventions which, in healthy people, may be considered deleterious but which have reduced symptom severity in patients with neurological conditions. These have included inducing illusory distortions via mirrors, prisms, vestibular stimulation and muscle vibration, impeding neural function with magnetic stimulation, and constraining action and communication. In the latter section we examined how ostensibly distracting left-hand movements and loud tones nevertheless produced benefits even in patients with very fragile attention function and how deliberate periodic interruption of ongoing activity may facilitate completion of important but currently ignored goals.

We have couched these rather diverse effects within a general framework of integrated competition, the idea that objects and tasks compete for representation and that this competition can be adaptively biased in a variety of ways at a number of levels (Desimone and Duncan, 1995; Duncan, 2006). One value of this account is that it can be used to generate ideas for remediation of function in other domains: If a patient is deficient at function X, what inputs in any modality or strategies are likely to favourably bias the system in terms of enhancing X? Such interventions do not, of course, need to be paradoxical. For example, we have seen how focusing attention on an impaired limb (using mirrors or constraint-induced therapies) can produce advantages. Competition may also be favourably biased by attending to others' actions (see Pomeroy *et al.*, 2005), by reading about or imagining actions or by using virtual reality to exaggerate existing function (see Sveistrup, 2004). One strength of paradoxical findings is not that they form better interventions but that, in going against expected outcome, they help us to focus on what may be important underlying principles. Rather than thinking of 'attention' as a sort of final stage in cognition, for example, the insights of integrated competition help us to explain why patients' capacity to sustain attention – to maintain top-down biasing during recovery – may be an important factor determining outcome across a range of impairments, including in motor function and spatial neglect (Robertson *et al.*, 1997a, 1997b). In turn, this should lead us to try and develop interventions that best support these crucial functions.

Future challenges and questions

- Relatively few of the studies described in this chapter have investigated the long-term effects of interventions. In many cases, the effects have been evaluated using tests rather than everyday activities and investigators have been aware of the treatments received by patient participants. There are pragmatic reasons for this. Investigating long-term effects is expensive and often hampered by the accumulation of other medical problems in patient groups. Carefully controlled tests allow researchers to examine effects in detail not easily achieved in ecological tasks. Blind assessment is complicated and expensive to achieve. However, a Cochrane review of interventions for neglect argued that conclusions on efficacy were premature due to too few randomized control trials and too little information on reduction in disability (Bowen and Lincoln, 2007). If clinicians are to adopt potentially useful techniques in daily practice, authoritative, well-funded trials are required.

- Unilateral neglect is a very interesting and salient aspect of patients' presentations. As discussed, in its chronic forms it is associated with slowed recovery and poor outcome. Clearly the hope is that reducing the definitive spatial biases of the condition would therefore *improve* outcome. However, we have also seen that neglect tends to persist in patients with more general attentional limitations which in themselves may impede recovery; it is not difficult to imagine how a drowsy, unresponsive state could undermine rehabilitation, motor relearning, and so on. It may be that rehabilitation of these basic problems will be an important additional aspect in producing generalized and lasting gains.

- Although constraining normal function should always be used with caution, further investigations of this 'use it or lose it' approach to shaping recovery in neurological disorder are warranted. However, there may be limits. In the case of memory, for example, asking patients to repeatedly learn lists of words without writing them down or using other external aids could be considered a form of 'constraint-induced therapy'. Very little evidence of generalized benefits from such approaches has been reported (Wilson, 1996).

- In its potential to determine every aspect of a patients' experience, virtual reality (VR) may well become an increasingly important tool in rehabilitation. Elegant experiments have already shown how quickly people can come to feel that an electronic representation of a body is their own, even one of an obviously different gender! Accordingly, small movements made by patients' impaired limbs could be greatly amplified in a VR world and missing limbs temporarily reinstated. Spatial distortions equivalent to prism exposure could be easily contrived and VR could allow long exposure to engaging exercises that, with a real therapist, might be prohibitively expensive. A crucial issue, of course, is the degree to which gains generalize to the real world. In this respect, funding for developing clinical VR applications is always likely to be relatively modest in comparison with that of the general consumer market, and some current clinical implementations could be argued to be at best, *virtual* VR. Hopefully, however, commercial packages will become available that allow researchers to tailor convincing and attractive virtual worlds without these substantial development costs.

Acknowledgements

We gratefully acknowledge the financial support of the UK Medical Research Council (MRC U.1055.01.003.00001.01) to the first author.

References

Adair, J. C., Na, D. L., Schwartz, R. L., & Heilman, K. M. (2003). Caloric stimulation in neglect: evaluation of response as a function of neglect type. *Journal of the International Neuropsychological Society*, **9**: 983–8.

Antonucci, G., Guariglia, C., Judica, A., *et al.* (1995). Effectiveness of neglect rehabilitation in a randomized group study. *Journal of Clinical and Experimental Neuropsychology*, **17**: 383–9.

Arnsten, A. F. T., Steere, J. C., & Hunt, R. D. (1996). The contribution of α-2 noradrenergic mechanisms to prefrontal cortical cognitive function: potential significance to Attention Deficit Hyperactivity Disorder. *Archives of General Psychiatry*, **53**: 448–55.

Bächtold, D., Baumann, T., Sándor, P. S., Kritos, M., Regard, M., & Brugger, P. (2001). Spatial- and verbal-memory improvement by cold-water caloric stimulation in healthy subjects. *Experimental Brain Research*, **136**: 128–32.

Beis, J. M., Andre, J. M., Baumgarten, A., & Challier, B. (1989). Eye patching in unilateral spatial neglect: efficacy of two methods. *Archives of Physical Medicine and Rehabilitation*, **80**: 71–6.

Blanton, S., Wilsey, H., & Wolf, S. L. (2008). Constraint-induced movement therapy in stroke rehabilitaiton: perspectives on future clinical applications. *Neurorehabilitation*, **23**: 15–28.

Bottini, G., Paulesu, E., Gandola, M., *et al.* (2005). Left caloric vestibular stimulation ameliorates right hemianesthesia. *Neurology*, **65**, 1278–83.

Bowen, A., & Lincoln, N. B. (2007). Rehabilitation for spatial neglect improves test performance but not disability. *Stroke*, **38**: 2869–70.

Brain, R. (1941). Visual disorientation with special reference to lesions of the right hemisphere. *Brain*, **64**: 244–72.

Brighina, F., Bisiach, E., La Bua, V., Piazza, A., & Fierro, B. (2002). Low-frequency repetitive transcranial magnetic stimulation of left parietal cortex ameliorates contralesional visuospatial hemineglect. *Neurology*, **58**: A320.

Broadbent, D. B. (1971). *Decision and Stress*. London: Academic Press.

Cacchio, A., De Blasis, E., De Blasis, V., Santilli, V., & Spacca, G. (2009). Mirror therapy in complex regional pain syndrome type 1 of upper limb in stroke patients. *Neurorehabilitation and Neural Repair*, **23**: 792–9.

Cappa, S. F., Sterzi, R., Vallar, G., & Bisiach, E. (1987). Remission of hemineglect and anosognosia during vestibular stimulation. *Neuropsychologia*, **25**: 775–82.

Chelazzi, L., Miller, E. K., Duncan, J., & Desimone, R. (1993). A neural basis for visual search in inferior temporal cortex. *Nature*, **363**: 345–7.

Cherney, L. R., Patterson, J. P., Raymer, A., Frymark, T., & Schooling, T. (2008). Evidence-based systematic review: effects of intensity of treatment and constraint-induced language therapy for individuals with stroke-induced aphasia. *Journal of Speech, Language, and Hearing Research*, **51**: 1282–99.

De Wit, L., Putman, K., Dejaeger, E., *et al.* (2005). Use of time by stroke patients: a comparison of four European rehabilitation centers. *Stroke*, **36**: 1977–83.

Desimone, R., & Duncan, J. (1995). Neural mechanisms of selective visual attention. *Annual Review of Neuroscience*, **18**: 193–222.

Dobler, V., Manly, T., Robertson, I. H., *et al.* (2001). Modulation of hemispatial attention in a case of developmental unilateral neglect. *Proceedings of the British Neuropsychological Society Neurocase*, **7**: 186.

Dobler, V. B., Anker, S., Gilmore, J., Robertson, I. H., Atkinson, J., & Manly, T. (2005). Asymmetric deterioration of spatial awareness with diminishing levels of alertness in normal children and children with ADHD. *Journal of Child Psychology and Psychiatry*, **46**: 1230–48.

Dodds, C. M., Dove, A., & Manly, T. (under review). Spontaneous fluctuations in alertness modulate the severity of unilateral spatial neglect: two demonstrations.

Dodds, C. M., Van Belle, J., Peers, P. V., *et al.* (2008). The effects of time-on-task and concurrent cognitive load on normal visuospatial bias. *Neuropsychology*, **22**: 545–52.

Driver, J., & Spence, C. J. (1994). Spatial synergies between auditory and visual attention. In: Milta, C. & Moscovitch, M. (Eds.). *Attention and Performance*. Cambridge, MA: MIT Press.

Duncan, J. (1986). Disorganisation of behaviour after frontal lobe damage. *Cognitive Neuropsychology*, **3**: 271–90.

Duncan, J. (2006). EPS mid-career award 2004: brain mechanisms of attention. *Quarterly Journal of Experimental Psychology*, **59**: 2–27.

Einstein, G. O., & Mcdaniel, M. A. (1996). Retrieval processes in prospective memory: Theoretical approaches and some new empirical findings. In: Brandimonte, M. A., Einstein, G. O. & Mcdaniel, M. A. (Eds.). *Prospective Memory: Theory and Application.* Mahwah, NJ: Lawrence Erlbaum Associates.

Ellis, J. (1988). Memory for future intentions: Investigating pulses and steps. In: Gruneberg, M. M., Morris, P. E. & Sykes, R. N. (Eds.). *Practical Aspects of Memory: Current Research and Issues.* Chichester: Wiley.

Everling, S., Tinsley, C. J., Gaffan, D., & Duncan, J. (2002). Filtering of neural signals by focused attention in the monkey prefrontal cortex. *Nature Neuroscience*, 5: 671–6.

Fierro, B., Brighina, F., & Bisiach, E. (2006). Improving neglect by TMS. *Behavioural Neurology*, 17: 169–76.

Fimm, B., Willmes, K., & Spijkers, W. (2006). The effect of low arousal on visuo-spatial attention. *Neuropsychologia*, 44: 1261–8.

Fish, J., Evans, J. J., Nimmo, M., *et al.* (2007). Rehabilitation of executive dysfunction following brain injury: 'content-free cueing' improves everyday prospective memory performance. *Neuropsychologia*, 45: 1318–30.

Fish, J., Wilson, B. A., & Manly, T. (2010). The assessment and rehabilitation of prospective memory problems in people with neurological disorders: a review. *Neuropsycholgical Rehabilitation*, 4: 1–19.

Fong, K. N., Chan, M. K., Ng, P. P., *et al.* (2007). The effect of voluntary trunk rotation and half-field eye-patching for patients with unilateral neglect in stroke: a randomized control trial. *Clinical Rehabilitation*, 21: 729–41.

Frassinetti, F., Angeli, V., Meneghello, F., Avanzi, S., & Ladavas, E. (2002). Long-lasting amelioration of visuospatial neglect by prism adaptation. *Brain*, 125: 608–23.

George, M., Dobler, V. B., Nicholls, E., & Manly, T. (2005). Spatial awareness, alertness and ADHD: the re-emergence of unilateral neglect with time-on-task. *Brain and Cognition*, 57: 264–75.

George, M. S., Mercer, J. S., Walker, R., & Manly, T. (2008). A demonstration of endogenous modulation of unilateral spatial neglect: the impact of apparent time–pressure on spatial bias. *Journal of the International Neuropsychological Society*, 14: 33–41.

Goodale, M. A., & Milner, A. D. (1992). Separate visual pathways for perception and action. *Trends in Neurosciences*, 15: 20–5.

Halligan, P. W., Manning, L., & Marshall, J. C. (1991). Hemispheric activation vs spatio-motor cueing in visual neglect: a case study. *Neuropsychologia*, 29: 165–76.

Halligan, P. W., & Marshall, J. C. (1994). Focal and global attention modulate the expression of visuo-spatial neglect: a case study. *Neuropsychologia*, 32: 13–21.

Harlow, J. M. (1848). Passage of an iron rod through the head. *Boston Medical and Surgical Journal*, 39: 389–93.

Horne, J. A. (1993). Human sleep, sleep deprivation and behaviour: implications for the prefrontal cortex and psychiatric disorder. *British Journal of Psychiatry*, 162: 413–9.

Husain, M., & Rorden, C. (2003). Non-spatially lateralized mechanisms in hemispatial neglect. *Nature Reviews Neuroscience*, 4: 26–36.

James, W. (1890). *The Principles of Psychology, Vol. 2.* New York, NY: Dover (1950; reprint of original edition published by Henry Holt & Co.).

Kapur, N., & Wilson, B. A. (2009). Compensating for memory deficits with memory aids. In: Wilson, B. (Ed.). *Memory Rehabilitation* (pp. 52–73). London: Guilford Press.

Karnath, H. O. (1994). Subjective body orientation in neglect and the interactive contribution of neck muscle proprioception and vestibular stimulation. *Brain*, 117: 1001–12.

Kime, S. K. (2006). *Compensating for Memory Deficits using a Systematic Approach.* Bethesda, MD: AOTA Press.

Kinsbourne, M. (1977). Hemi-neglect and hemisphere rivalry. In: Weinstein, E. A. & Friedland, R. P. (Eds.). *Advances in Neurology, vol. 18.* New York, NY: Raven.

Kinsbourne, M. (1993). Orientation bias model of unilateral neglect: evidence from attentional gradients within hemispace. In: Robertson, I. & Marshall, J. (Eds.). *Unilateral*

Neglect: Clinical and Experimental Studies. Hillsdale. NJ: Lawrence Erlbaum Associates.

Koch, G., Oliveri, M., Cheeran, B., *et al.* (2008). Hyperexcitability of parietal-motor functional connections in the intact left-hemisphere of patients with neglect. *Brain*, **131**: 3147–55.

Luck, S. J., Chelazzi, L., Hillyard, S. A., & Desimone, R. (1997). Mechanisms of spatial selective attention in areas V1, V2, and V4 of macaque visual cortex. *Journal of Neurophysiology*, 77: 24–42.

Luria, A. R. (1965). Two kinds of motor perseveration in massive injury of the frontal lobes. *Brain*, **88**: 1–10.

Luria, A. R. (1966). *Higher Cortical Functions in Man.* London: Tavistock.

Malhotra, P. A., Parton, A. D., Greenwood, R., & Husain, M. (2006). Noradrenergic modulation of space exploration in visual neglect. *Annals of Neurology*, **59**: 186–90.

Manly, T., Dobler, V. B., Dodds, C. M., & George, M. A. (2005). Rightward shift in spatial awareness with declining alertness. *Neuropsychologia*, **43**: 1721–8.

Manly, T., Hawkins, J., Evans, J. J., Woldt, K., & Roberson, I. H. (2002a). Rehabilitation of executive function: facilitation of effective goal management on complex tasks using periodic auditory alerts. *Neuropsychologia*, **40**: 271–81.

Manly, T., Lewis, G. H., Robertson, I. H., Watson, P. C., & Datta, A. K. (2002b). Coffee in the cornflakes: time-of-day as a modulator of executive response control. *Neuropsychologia*, **40**: 1–6.

Manly, T., Robertson, I. H., & Verity, C. (1997). Developmental unilateral visual neglect: a single case study. *Neurocase*, **3**: 19–29.

McCabe, C. S., Haigh, R. C., & Blake, D. R. (2008). Mirror visual feedback for the treatment of complex regional pain syndrome (type 1). *Current Pain and Headache Reports*, **12**: 103–07.

Mesulam, M. (2002). Functional anatomy of attention and neglect: from neurons to networks. In: Karnath, H.-O., Milner, D. & Vallar, G. (Eds.). *The Cognitive and Neural Basis of Spatial Neglect.* Oxford: Oxford University Press.

Miller, E. K., & Cohen, J. D. (2001). An integrative theory of prefrontal cortex function. *Annual Review of Neuroscience*, **24**: 167–202.

Moseley, G. L., Gallace, A., & Spence, C. (2008). Is mirror therapy all it is cracked up to be? Current evidence and directions. *Pain*, **138**: 7–10.

Nigg, J. T., Swanson, J. M., & Hinshaw, S. P. (1997). Covert spatial attention in boys with attention deficit hyperactivity disorder: lateral effects, methylphenidate response and results for parents. *Neuropsychologia*, **35**: 165–76.

Nys, G. M., De Haan, E. H., Kunneman, A., De Kort, P. L., & Dijkerman, H. C. (2008). Acute neglect rehabilitation using repetitive prism adaptation: a randomised placebo-controlled trial. *Restorative Neurology and Neuroscience*, **26**: 1–12.

Paolucci, S., Antonucci, G., Grasso, M. G., *et al.* (2003). Functional outcome of ischemic and hemorrhagic stroke patients after inpatient rehabilitation a matched comparison. *Stroke*, **34**: 2861–5.

Pardo, J. V., Fox, P. T., & Raichle, M. E. (1991). Localization of a human system for sustained attention by positron emission tomography. *Nature*, **349**: 61–4.

Pomeroy, V. M., Clark, C. A., Miller, J. S. G., Baron, J., Markus, H. S., & Tallis, R. C. (2005). The potential for utilizing the 'mirror neuron system' to enhance recovery of the severely affected upper limb early after stroke: a review and hypothesis. *Neurorehabilitation and Neural Repair*, **19**: 4–13.

Posner, M. I., Walker, J. A., Fredrich, F. J., & Rafal, R. B. (1984). The effects of parietal lobe injury on covert orienting of visual attention. *Journal of Neuroscience*, **4**: 1863–74.

Pulvermüller, F., & Berthier, M. L. (2008). Aphasia therapy on a neuroscience basis. *Aphasiology*, **22**: 563–99.

Ramachandran, V. S., & Altschuler, E. L. (2009). The use of visual feedback, in particular mirror visual feedback, in restoring brain function. *Brain*, **132**: 1693–710.

Riddoch, M. J., & Humphreys, G. W. (1983). The effect of cueing on unilateral neglect. *Neuropsychologia*, **21**: 589–99.

Robertson, I. H. (1999). Cognitive rehabilitation: attention and neglect. *Trends in Cognitive Science*, **3**: 385–93.

Robertson, I. H., & Halligan, P. W. (1999). *Spatial Neglect: A Clinical Handbook for Diagnosis and Treatment*. Hove: Psychology Press.

Robertson, I. H., & North, N. (1992). Spatio-motor cueing in unilateral neglect: the role of hemispace, hand and motor activation. *Neuropsychologia*, **30**: 553–63.

Robertson, I. H., & North, N. (1993). Active and passive activation of left limbs: influence on visual and sensory neglect. *Neuropsychologia*, **31**: 293–300.

Robertson, I. H., & North, N. (1994). One hand is better than two: motor extinction of left hand advantage in unilateral neglect. *Neuropsychologia*, **32**: 1–11.

Robertson, I. H., Hogg, K., & Mcmillan, T. M. (1998a). Rehabilitation of unilateral neglect: improving function by contralesional limb activation. *Neuropsychological Rehabilitation*, **8**: 19–29.

Robertson, I. H., Manly, T., Beschin, N., *et al.* (1997a). Auditory sustained attention is a marker of unilateral spatial neglect. *Neuropsychologia*, **35**: 1527–32.

Robertson, I. H., Mattingley, J., Rorden, C., & Rorden, J. (1998b). Phasic alerting of neglect patients overcomes their spatial deficit in visual awareness. *Nature*, **395**: 169–72.

Robertson, I. H., North, N., & Geggie, C. (1992). Spatio-motor cueing in unilateral neglect: three single case studies of its therapeutic effectiveness. *Journal of Neurology, Neurosurgery and Psychiatry*, **55**: 799–805.

Robertson, I. H., Ridgeway, V., Greenfield, E., & Parr, A. (1997b). Motor recovery after stroke depends on intact sustained attention: a two-year follow-up study. *Neuropsychology*, **11**: 290–5.

Robertson, I. H., Tegnér, R., Goodrich, S. J., & Wilson, C. (1994). Walking trajectory and hand movements in unilateral left neglect: a

vestibular hypothesis. *Neuropsychologia*, **32**: 1495–502.

Rode, G., Charles, N., Perenin, M.-T., Vighetto, A., Trillet, M., & Aimard, G. (1992). Partial remission of hemiplegia and somatoparaphrenia through vestibular stimulation in a case of unilateral neglect. *Cortex*, **28**: 203–08.

Rossetti, Y., Rode, G., Pisella, L., *et al.* (1998). Prism adaptation to a rightward optical deviation rehabilitates left hemispatial neglect. *Nature*, **395**: 166–9.

Rubens, A. B. (1985). Caloric stimulation and unilateral visual neglect. *Neurology*, **35**: 1019–24.

Samuelsson, H., Hjelmquist, E., Jensen, C., Ekholm, S., & Blomstrand, C. (1998). Nonlateralized attentional deficits: an important component behind persisting visuospatial neglect? *Journal of Clinical and Experimental Neuropsychology*, **20**: 73–88.

Schindler, I., Kerkhoff, G., Karnath, H.-O., Keller, I., & Goldenberg, G. (2002). Neck muscle vibration induces lasting recovery in spatial neglect. *Journal of Neurology Neurosurgery and Psychiatry*, **73**: 412–9.

Schmida, M., De Nunzioa, A. M., & Schieppatia, M. (2005). Trunk muscle proprioceptive input assists steering of locomotion. *Neuroscience Letters*, **384**: 127–32.

Serino, A., Farnè, A., Rinaldesi, M. L., Haggard, P., & Làdavas, E. (2007). Can vision of the body ameliorate impaired somatosensory function? *Neuropsychologia*, **45**: 1101–07.

Shallice, T. (1988). *From Neuropsychology to Mental Structure*. Cambridge: Cambridge University Press.

Shallice, T., & Burgess, P. (1991). Deficit in strategy application following frontal lobe damage in man. *Brain*, **114**: 727–41.

Sheppard, D. M., Bradshaw, J. L., Mattingley, J. B., & Lee, P. (1999). Effects of stimulant medication on the lateralisation of line bisection judgements of children with attention deficit hyperactivity disorder. *Journal of Neurology, Neurosurgery and Psychiatry*, **66**: 57–63.

Slobounov, S. M., Fukada, K., Simon, R., Rearick, M., & Ray, W. (2000).

Neurophysiological and behavioural indices of time pressure effects on visuomotor task performance. *Cognitive Brain Research*, **9**: 287–98.

Soto, D., Funes, M., Guzmán-García, A. T. W., & Humphreys, G. W. (2009). Pleasant music overcomes the loss of visual awareness in patients with visual neglect. *Proceedings of the National Academy of Sciences*, **106**: 6011–16.

Stone, S. P., Halligan, P. W., & Greenwood, R. J. (1993). The incidence of neglect phenomena and related disorders in patients with an acute right or left-hemisphere stroke. *Age and Ageing*, **22**: 46–52.

Sturm, W., Simone, A. D., Krause, B. J., *et al.* (1999). Functional anatomy of intrinsic alertness: evidence for a fronto-parietal–thalamic–brainstem network in the right hemisphere. *Neuropsychologia*, **37**: 797–805.

Sumitani, M., Miyauchi, S., Mcabe, C. S., *et al.* (2008). Mirror visual feedback alleviates deafferentation pain, depending on qualitative aspects of the pain: a preliminary report. *Rheumatology*, **47**: 1038–43.

Sveistrup, H. (2004). Motor rehabilitation using virtual reality. *Journal of Neuroengineering and Rehabilitation*, **1**: 10.

Teasdale, T. W., Emslie, H., Quirk, K., Evans, J. J., Fish, J., & Wilson, B. A. (2009). Alleviation of carer strain during the use of the NeuroPage device by people with acquired brain injury. *Journal of Neurology Neurosurgery and Psychiatry*, **80**: 781–3.

Tsang, M. H., Sze, K. H., & Fong, K. N. (2009). Occupational therapy treatment with right half-field eye-patching for patients with subacute stroke and unilateral neglect: a randomised controlled trial. *Disability and Rehabilitation*, **31**: 630–7.

Turton, A. J., O'leary, K., Gabb, J., Woodward, R., & Gilchrist, I. D. (2009). A single blinded randomised controlled pilot trial of prism adaptation for improving self-care in stroke

patients with neglect. *Neuropsychological Rehabilitation*, **21**: 1–17.

Ungerleider, L., & Mishkin, M. (1982). Two cortical visual systems. In: Ingle, D., Mansfield, R. & Goodale, M. (Eds.). *The Analysis of Visual Behaviour*. Cambridge, MA: MIT Press.

Usher, M., Cohen, J. D., Servan-Schreiber, S., Rajkowski, J., & Aston-Jones, G. (1999). The role of locus cueruleus in the regulation of cognitive performance. *Science*, **283**: 549–53.

Voeller, K. K. S., & Heilman, K. M. (1988). Attention deficit disorder in children: a neglect syndrome? *Neurology*, **38**: 806–08.

Walker, R., Findlay, J. M., Young, A. W., & Welch, J. (1991). Disentangling neglect and hemianopia. *Neuropsychologia*, **29**: 1019–27.

Wilkins, A. J., Shallice, T., & Mccarthy, R. (1987). Frontal lesions and sustained attention. *Neuropsychologia*, **25**: 359–65.

Wilson, B. A. (1996). Cognitive rehabilitation: how it is and how it might be. *Journal of the International Neuropsychological Society*, **3**: 487–96.

Wilson, B. A., Alderman, N., Burgess, P. W., Emsley, H., & Evans, J. (1996). *Behavioural Assessment of the Dysexecutive Syndrome*. Bury St Edmunds: Thames Valley Test Company.

Wilson, B. A., Emslie, H. C., Quirk, K., & Evans, J. J. (2001). Reducing everyday memory and planning problems by means of a paging system: a randomised control crossover study. *Journal of Neurology, Neurosurgery & Psychiatry*, **70**: 477–82.

Wilson, B. A., Evans, J. J., Gracey, F., & Bateman, A. (2009). *Neuropsychological Rehabilitation: Theory Therapy and Outcomes*. Oxford: Oxford University Press.

Yerkes, R. M., & Dodson, J. D. (1908). The relation of strength of stimulus to rapidity of habit-formation. *Journal of Comparative and Neurological Psychology*, **18**: 459–82.

Chapter 5

The paradoxical self

Vilayanur Ramachandran and William Hirstein

Summary

We consider a number of syndromes incorporating paradoxical phenomena that lie at the boundary between neurology and psychiatry. Amongst the phenomena we examine are Cotard's Syndrome (belief that one is dead/dying), Capgras Syndrome (belief that a personally familiar person has been replaced by an imposter), and Apotemnophilia (desire to have a limb amputated). We use these phenomena to speculate on the manner in which the brain constructs a sense of self. We propose that, despite the extraordinary variety of paradoxical symptoms encountered in neuropsychiatry, certain key assumptions can help explain most of these self-related phenomena. (1) Discrepancies and conflict between the information dominating different brain systems. (2) Disturbance of Me/Other distinctions caused by dysfunctional interactions between the mirror neuron system, frontal lobe structures and sensory input. (3) Misattribution of symptoms to spurious causes, so as to minimize internal discrepancies. (4) The existence of three functionally distinct visual systems, as opposed to the two conventionally accepted ones, with selective damage or uncoupling between them. (5) Recruiting one neural map for another unrelated function, or one neural structure serving as a template for transcribing on to another neural structure. We suggest that, paradoxically, the mechanisms that give rise to psychiatric delusions and illusions may themselves sometimes have adaptive value in evolutionary terms.

Introduction

An approach we have pursued in our laboratory involves exploring precisely those phenomena that have long been regarded as paradoxical or anomalous, that do not fit the overall framework of science as currently practised, or that appear to violate established conventional assumptions. Neurology and psychiatry are full of such examples. What can be more paradoxical than a person with Cotard's Syndrome denying his own existence, when the very denial implies existence? Conditions such as Cotard's Syndrome, and many others, have shown that the self is not the monolithic entity it often believes itself to be. Our unitary sense of self may well be an illusion that incorporates distinct components, each of which may be studied separately. If it is an illusion, it is not enough to merely state that fact; we need to explain how it arises. An interesting question is, for example, whether it is an adaptation acquired through natural selection (cf. McKay and Dennett, 2009).

Our emphasis in this chapter will be on 'borderline' syndromes that straddle the boundary between neurology and psychiatry, with a focus on delusions directly or indirectly

The Paradoxical Brain, ed. Narinder Kapur. Published by Cambridge University Press. © Cambridge University Press 2011.

involving the concept of self (Hirstein and Ramachandran, 2009). Consider the following disorders that illustrate different aspects of self.

1. Cotard's Syndrome – a patient claiming he is dead or that he does not exist (Pearn and Gardner-Thorpe, 2002).
2. Capgras Delusion – a patient claims that his mother looks like his mother but is in fact an imposter (Sinkman, 2008).
3. Apotemnophilia – an otherwise apparently normal person develops an intense desire to have his arm or leg amputated (Money et al., 1977).
4. A person with temporal lobe epilepsy (TLE) claims to see or feel God (Devinsky and Lai, 2008).
5. Somatoparphrenia – a patient with right superior parietal lobule (SPL) damage and insula damage claims his left arm doesn't belong to him (Berlucchi and Aglioti, 1997; Bisiach and Geminiani, 1991).
6. Tactile hyperempathy in amputees – a patient who has had his arm amputated watches another's arm being touched. Astonishingly, he feels the touch on his own phantom arm, an extreme form of 'tactile empathy' (Ramachandran and Brang 2009; Case and Ramachandran, 2010) – the barrier between him and others has been dissolved.
7. Out-of-body experiences – following a right hemisphere stroke, a patient reports floating out into space and being able to see her own body. Paradoxically, she says that she feels the sensation of pain 'in that other body down below' but not in herself (Blanke et al., 2004).

Can we resolve these paradoxes of consciousness and self using our knowledge of neuroanatomy? Here we offer proposals, some still speculative, to help to resolve these paradoxes.

Three visual pathways

Our scheme, introducing three parallel visual pathways (Figure 5.1), emerged initially from our attempt to deal with the Capgras Syndrome. In this disorder, an apparently lucid patient claims, for example, that his mother is an imposter – a woman who *looks* identical to his mother but is not (Capgras and Reboul-Lachaux, 1923; Young et al., 1994; Devinsky, 2009).

To understand this disorder we will start with the notion that there are three function-ally distinct, quasi-autonomous intra-cortical visual pathways in man (see Jeannerod and Jacob, 2005 for a discussion of the two-pathway model). We will mainly focus on the feed-forward features of these pathways, recognizing that they may also have important feed-backward components – e.g. the amygdala feeds back to the temporal cortex (Amaral and Price, 1984), allowing, for example, for the response of the fusiform gyrus to be modified by emotional faces (Hung et al., 2010).

Pathway 1 ('dorsal stream') is well known – it goes from the superior colliculus to the parietal lobe via the pulvinar and is involved in navigation and spatial vision (e.g. avoiding obstacles, reaching for objects, stepping over branches, dodging missiles). It is not involved in identifying objects, this is achieved by pathways 2 and 3.

Focusing on the most salient of objects, the human face is initially processed in the fusiform gyrus. Here, faces are discriminated, dropped into 'bins' (as being different faces) and tagged; in much the same way that an entomologist might classify and label

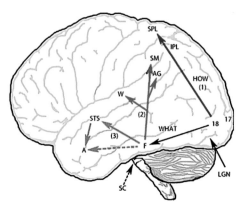

Figure 5.1 Diagram of postulated pathways (1), (2) and (3), and related neural structures. In this schematic representation, locations are approximate and readers should be aware that structures such as the amygdala, lateral geniculate nucleus and superior colliculus are deep within the brain and not on its surface. The superior colliculus has direct connections with the parietal lobe. The HOW pathway (1) is also likely to represent WHERE information in relation to any particular stimulus. 17 and 18 refer to Brodmann areas. A, amygdala; AG, angular gyrus; F, fusiform gyrus; IPL, inferior parietal lobule; LGN, lateral geniculate nucleus; SC, superior colliculus; SM, supramarginal gyrus; SPL, superior parietal lobule; STS, superior temporal sulcus; W, Wernicke's area.

hundreds of different butterflies without knowing anything about them. The fusiform face area projects to dozens of higher areas but, crudely speaking, the output segregates into two pathways (which we call 2 and 3). One of these, *Pathway 2* (the semantic pathway), evokes a halo of memories associated with the face, and has an inferior, ventral route that terminates in the anterior temporal lobe. *Pathway 3* (the emotional pathway) is involved in the early detection of biologically salient (e.g. terrifying, sexually evocative) objects. Pathway 3 gives you that jolt of familiarity when you recognize important people, such as your mother or spouse. It projects mainly via the superior temporal sulcus (STS) and amygdala to evoke both subjective manifestations (fear, joy, familiarity) and physiological manifestations (sweating, heart racing) of the emotional response, mediated through the hypothalamic output. This superior temporal sulcus is rich in mirror neurons (Aziz-Zadeh *et al.*, 2006; Noordzij *et al.*, 2009), cells that are active during the planning of an action and when that action is observed in others (Di Pellegrino *et al.*, 1992; see further below). Here they respond to changing facial expressions and biological motion. Pathway 3 is functionally distinct from Pathway 2, although perhaps with some overlap. The degree to which Pathway 3 is anatomically segregated from Pathway 2 remains to be seen.

Pathway 3 is also connected (via STS) to the insular cortex, which has cells that both *respond* to changing facial expressions of disgust and also fire when the individual *produces* the corresponding expression. These could be regarded as 'emotional expression' mirror neurons that require cross-modal abstraction of information from the motor system about one's own face-muscle twitches and visually perceived facial features of others. We suggest that the insula's proximity to left hemisphere language areas makes it ideally suited for transforming literal expressions of disgust (e.g. facial expression of disgust to faeces) to metaphorical ones ('he is disgusting' or 'that was a tasteless remark'). Our bold prediction is that such verbal expressions would be incomprehensible to someone with insular damage.

The insula also receives information about the relative locations of our limbs, our orientation with respect to gravity, and from our internal viscera – in other words, somatic data that help keep the 'self' anchored in the body. If these data are discrepant with those from other systems, parts of our body may simply not feel 'right'. Perhaps for this reason, somatoparaphrenia (the delusional denial that a body part is one's own) has sometimes been observed following insular damage (Vallar and Ronchi, 2009).

Interactions between Pathways 2 and 3

If the amygdala's role in Pathway 3 is to imbue familiarity and emotional salience to faces and other objects, what is its role in Pathway 2? We can speculate that, together with the hippocampus, it may draw on accumulating semantic and contextual associations to direct attention to particular faces and objects marked as salient (familiar, attractive, distorted). The amygdala is a highly differentiated structure and it's also possible that Pathways 2 and 3 initially activate different portions of it before salient inputs get 'transferred' from Pathway 2 to Pathway 3.

This scheme requires the additional, somewhat radical, postulate that a neural algorithm that is initially set up in one brain region can, with repeated stimulation, serve as a template to entrain another brain region which initially has only crude responses. Thus, non-automatic and initially slow responses to complex stimuli in Pathway 2 become transcribed onto Pathway 3, which would then start responding automatically and rapidly to the trained stimuli – thereby making it emotionally salient and familiar.

Summary of pathways

In summary, the amygdala receives both direct projections from fusiform (Pathway 2) and indirect ones via STS (Pathway 3) (Amaral and Price, 1984; Freese and Amaral, 2006; Smith *et al.*, 2009). Pathway 2 is responsible for evoking emotions, including familiarity. From a phylogenetic standpoint, it evolved as an early warning system with circuits 'hardwired' to quickly detect eyes, faces, etc. (in the generic sense), snakes, bananas, water (Rolls, 1999) and sexually attractive characteristics – in short, biologically salient stimuli. This system is characterized by rapid processing of a small but important class of specific inputs (visual and auditory) leading to rapid – almost reflexive – action. Response to breasts, for example, is hardwired in this pathway, manifesting as the mammo-ocular reflex in humans (S. M. Anstis, personal communication). More complex objects – e.g. mother or father – are initially processed by circuits in Pathway 2 (acquired by associative learning). The result is sophisticated recognition but slower response. However, with repeated stimulation, according to our speculation, responses to such complex stimuli get 'transferred' to Pathway 3; so 'wife' becomes as salient as water, breasts or snakes, in addition to being imbued with familiarity. Whether originating from hardwired circuits in Pathway 3 or acquired initially in Pathway 2 and 'transferred' to Pathway 1, the emotions cascade from the basolateral amygdala via the amygdalofugal pathways and stria terminalis to generate hypothalamic outflow – influencing a range of responses such as fighting, fleeing, feeding, reproduction, hormonal regulation, subjective emotions, etc.

Obviously these anatomical flow diagrams are a gross oversimplification. However, a simplified picture is not a bad place to start, especially given that it has already proved to be of heuristic value in explaining aspects of psychopathology such as misidentification syndromes (see below).

Capgras Syndrome and abhorrence of discrepancy

We suggested that the Capgras Syndrome, where a familiar person has been replaced by an imposter, arises because the fusiform area becomes disconnected from the STS and amygdala, but remains connected to relevant semantic processes (as represented in structures such as Wernicke's area and the left angular gyrus): a face is recognized and a penumbra of associated memories activated, but it does not evoke emotion – there is no jolt of familiarity. Our patient, David, on recognizing his mother, is therefore forced to rationalize away his curious sensations by concluding that she is an imposter. We tested this idea by measuring changes in skin sweating (skin conductance response, SCR) when David looked at photographs. For healthy volunteers, photos of their mothers typically evoke reliable SCR in a way that pictures of strangers do not. In David, there was no difference, supporting the disconnection hypothesis (Hirstein and Ramachandran, 1997; cf. Ellis *et al.*, 1997). It is worth noting similarities with a theory proposed by Young *et al.* (1993). A difference is that, in their scheme, the disconnection was between Pathways 1 and 2 (in our terms), rather than between Pathways 2 and 3.

One might ask: why doesn't a patient with Capgras Syndrome merely say, 'I know it *is* my mother, but she doesn't feel familiar for some reason', instead of saying she is an imposter or even (in some cases) developing paranoid ideation about the imposter's intent? To account for this, we introduce one of our key postulates – abhorrence of discrepancies between outputs of brain modules and/or a lack of consistency between expected and actual input (cf. Coltheart *et al.*, 2009). In Capgras Syndrome, the patient is confronted with a peculiar dilemma. He 'recognizes' his mother from a semantic standpoint, but fails to do so from an emotional standpoint. This creates a paradox, a peculiar discrepancy in his brain that he is unable to interpret or convey and which produces distress or even paranoia. Additionally, there may also be some damage to frontal (especially right frontal) structures, which makes individuals more prone to delusions (Ramachandran and Blakeslee, 1998; Hirstein and Ramachandran, 1997).

David also had difficulty abstracting across successive encounters of a new person seen in different contexts. Without the flash of recognition he ought to have experienced in the second, third or *n*th exposure, we hypothesize that he was unable to bind these experiences together to form an enduring identity for the other person. Even more remarkably, this may also have applied to his experience of himself across successive episodes. He would, for example, refer to 'The other David who is on vacation' as if, unable to bind these experiences together, his conclusion was that he existed in a form of temporal multiplicity.

Prosopagnosia and Capgras

A specific difficulty in recognizing faces despite intact basic visual processes is called prosopagnosia. It seems at first peculiar that a person with such 'face blindness' can nevertheless show a relatively normal emotional response to familiar faces, as indexed, for example, by changes in skin conductance (Bauer, 1984). However, we have all had an inkling of it when we run into someone completely out of context, someone we 'know' well (e.g. an ex-student, dentist, etc.). He looks completely familiar yet his identity eludes you – you do not know who he is and cannot quite place him. As we shall see later, the fact that such a dissociation can occur at all in healthy people suggests some separation between recognition and familiarity, although it could be that familiarity is a necessary precursor for recognition. Capgras Syndrome, in which people recognize others but do not experience familiarity, provides the crucial 'double dissociation' suggesting complete independence of process (Young *et al.*, 1994). In our scheme, this double dissociation is explained by the partial segregation between the semantic and emotional Pathways (2 and 3): damage to Pathway 2 leads to no semantic recognition but normal emotional responses (prosopagnosia), whereas damage to Pathway 3 leads to preserved recognition but anomalous emotional responses (Capgras).

A strange feature of the Capgras Syndrome is that it can be modality-specific. A patient may claim that his mother is an imposter when he sees her, but has no delusion when he talks to her on the phone (Ramachandran and Hirstein, 1998). We suggested that this might be caused by selective damage to Pathway 3 with simultaneous preservation of input from the auditory cortex to the amygdala.

Apotemnophilia

Apotemnophilia refers to a condition in which an apparently neurologically normal person has had – from early childhood – an intense desire to have a limb amputated, often going to the extreme of actually having it removed (Money et al., 1977; Bayne and Levy, 2005; First, 2005). What causes this?

Based on several lines of evidence we proposed that the disorder has a neurological rather than a purely 'psychological' basis. We will mention two sets of evidence. First, the patient can use a pen to precisely draw the line along which he desires amputation. Second, as in somatoparaphrenia (limb ownership denial), the left limb is more commonly involved than the right. We therefore suggested and provided the first experimental evidence that the right superior parietal lobe (SPL) is implicated in the condition (Brang et al., 2008). An identical theory, based on the same line of reasoning, was later proposed by Blanke et al. (2009).

The SPL in the right hemisphere has a complete representation of the body (body image or 'body schema'). It is probably topographically organized and receives its input from several primary sensory areas. Although malleable, through experience, the map in SPL is probably hard-wired (for example, those who have never had a limb due to congenital malformation may nevertheless experience a 'phantom' of that limb; Ramachandran and Blakeslee, 1998). We recently postulated (Ramachandran and McGeoch, 2007) and found evidence that, in apotemnophiliacs, the arm (or leg) portion is congenitally absent from the SPL body map (Brang et al., 2008). Since the sensory input from the leg is intact but there is no corresponding recipient zone in SPL, the result is once again a discrepancy that leads to stressful aversion. Indeed, we have found that touching the affected limb produces a much higher SCR than touching the normal limb (McGeoch et al., 2007) and substantially *lower* activation in SPL, as measured by MEG (magnetoencephalography; Ramachandran et al., 2008). On the other hand, if the sensory input itself is lost (as in brachial plexus avulsion), then there is no activation of either S1 or SPL so there is no discrepancy and no desire for amputation. The same holds for a limb that has had deafferentation from stroke. Finally, in somatoparaphrenia, both S1/S2 and SPL are damaged in the right hemisphere. Since there is no discrepancy between S1 and SPL, no desire for amputation emerges.

One might predict, therefore, that if the limb is anaesthetized in an apotemnophiliac (and the arm made to appear to be visually missing using an optical trick) there might be a temporary alleviation of the desire for amputation. Merely occluding the limb may not suffice – one may need to make it *look* amputated. (For absence of evidence for the limb is not the same thing as evidence of absence.)

We recently invoked a similar theory to account for the intense desire that male to female transsexual men develop for amputation of the penis (Ramachandran and McGeoch, 2007). We suggested that these men have no representation of the penis in SPL, so they develop a form of specific 'apotemnophilia' caused again by the discrepancy between body image and afferent input. Conversely, we have seen (Ramachandran and McGeoch, 2007) that a majority of female to male transsexuals who have been asked, report having had a phantom penis ever since childhood and request genital reassignment surgery to correct the mismatch between external anatomy and the map in SPL.

Apotemnophila and sexual preferences

One curious aspect of apotemnophilia that is unexplained by our model is the associated sexual inclinations in some individuals, namely a desire for intimacy with another amputee. These sexual overtones are probably what misled people to propose a Freudian view of the disorder.

We postulate that one's sexual 'aesthetic preference' for certain body morphology, even across the obvious sexual differences between men and women, is dictated in part by the shape of one's own body image, hardwired into the right superior parietal, and possibly insular cortex (Ramachandran *et al.*, 2009). Expanding on this, we suggest that there is a genetically specified mechanism that allows a template of one's body image to act on limbic connections thereby determining aesthetic visual preference for one's own body image 'type'. Consequently, if a person with apotemnophilia has an arm missing in his internal (genetically hardwired) body image, then that would affect his limbic circuits and explain his sexual affinity for amputees. The pathways that enable limbic structures to determine visual aesthetic preference remain obscure, but there are known back-projections from basolateral amygdala to almost every stage of extrastriate visual processing. (These pathways may also be involved in art appreciation; patients with Capgras Syndrome sometimes lose interest in art and natural beauty.)

This notion of the circuitry in one brain region serving as a template for being transcribed onto another region may have more general applicability in helping us understand brain development and function.

Mirror neurons in psychopathology

We will now consider two aspects of self that are considered almost axiomatic. First, its essentially private nature. You can empathize with someone, but never to the point of experiencing his sensations or dissolving into him (except in pathological states like *folie à deux* and romantic love). Second, it is aware of its own existence. A self that negates itself is an oxymoron. Yet both these axioms can collapse in disease, without affecting other aspects of self. For example, an amputee can literally feel his phantom being touched when he merely watches a normal person being touched (Ramachandran and Brang, 2009). A person with Cotard's Syndrome will deny that he exists, claiming that his body is merely an empty shell. Explaining these disorders in neural terms can help illuminate how the *normal* self is constructed, especially its peculiar recursive quality.

To account for some of these syndromes we need to again invoke mirror neurons (Di Pellegrino *et al.*, 1992; see reviews by Rizzolatti and Craighero, 2004 and Iacoboni, 2009). Neurons in the prefrontal cortex send signals down the spinal cord that orchestrate skilled and semi-skilled movements such as putting food in your mouth, pulling a lever, pushing a button, etc. These are 'ordinary' motor command neurons, but some of them, known as mirror neurons, also fire when you merely *watch* another person perform a similar act. It's as if the neuron (more strictly the network of which the neuron is part) was using the visual input to do a sort of 'virtual reality simulation' of the other person's actions, allowing you to empathize with her and view the world from her point of view. We have previously speculated that these neurons cannot only help simulate other people's behaviour, but can also be turned 'inward' – as it were – to create second-order representations or 'meta-representations' of your *own* earlier first-order brain processes. This could be the neural basis of introspection, and of the reciprocity of self-awareness and other awareness. This complements Humphrey's ingenious hypothesis (Humphrey, 1978) that the selection pressure for the emergence of introspection in humans came from the need to model and predict other people's behaviour. There is obviously a chicken-or-egg question here as to which evolved first, but that is tangential to our main argument. The main point is that the two co-evolved, mutually enriching each other to create the mature representation of self that characterizes modern humans. Our ordinary language illustrates this, as when we say, 'I feel a bit self-conscious', when we really mean that I am conscious of others being conscious of me. Or when I speak of being self-critical or experiencing self-pity. It is arguable whether an ape can experience pity (as when responding to a beggar), but it is almost certainly incapable of self-pity, let alone *knowing* that it is engaging in self-pity.

We also suggest that, although these neurons initially emerged in our ancestors to adopt another's allocentric *visual* point of view, they evolved further in humans to enable the adoption of another's *metaphorical* point of view ('I see the idea from his point of view', etc.). Our idea that metaphorical thinking is parasitic on, and has evolved from, early brain processes is similar to Lakoff and Johnson's (1980) ingenious speculations. We are merely trying to flesh it out by referring it to actual brain structures. Just as we might model another's metaphorical point of view via structures developed for the prediction of motor acts, we suggest that many gestures produced by the motor system may be 'metaphorical' echoes of concepts. For example, when trying to convey a conceptually precise point we oppose thumb and index finger in a 'precision grip' unique to humans. Or we clench our fist literally to metaphorically convey that we have 'come to grips' with the situation.

As we have seen, there are also 'touch mirror neurons' that fire not only when your skin is touched, but when you watch someone else being touched (Keysers *et al.*, 2004). This raises an interesting question – how does the neuron know what the stimulus is? Why doesn't the activity of these neurons lead you to literally experience the touch delivered to another person? There are two answers. First, the tactile receptors in your skin tell the other touch neurons in the cortex (the non-mirror neurons) that they are *not* being touched and this null signal selectively vetoes some of the outputs of mirror neurons. This would explain why our amputee experienced touch sensations when he watched our student being touched, a phenomenon that we have dubbed 'tactile hyperempathy' – the amputation had removed the vetoing (Ramachandran and Brang, 2009). Astonishingly, the same kind of referral is seen immediately following a brachial plexus block (Case and Ramachandran, 2010).

A second reason why your mirror neurons do not lead you to mime everyone you watch or to literally experience their tactile sensations might be that your frontal lobes send feedback signals to partially inhibit the mirror neurons' output (cf. Brass *et al.*, 2009). It cannot completely inhibit them, otherwise there would be no point having mirror neurons in the first place. As expected, if the frontal lobes are damaged, you *do* start imitating people ('echopraxia'). Recent evidence suggests that there may also be mirror neurons for pain, disgust, facial expression – perhaps for all outwardly visible expression of emotions. Some of these are in the anterior cingulate, others in the insula.

We suggest that many otherwise inexplicable neuropsychiatric symptoms may arise from flaws in the three-way interactions between the mirror neuron system, frontal structures and external sensory input, systems that are normally in dynamic equilibrium. These circuits allow you to have deep empathy while at the same time maintaining your distinctiveness – your brain holds on to two parallel representations. Where this goes wrong, 'you–me' confusion and impoverished ego-differentiation would occur. Our group has seen strong preliminary hints that autistic children have a paucity of mirror neurons (Altschuler *et al.*, 1997; Oberman *et al.*, 2005; Oberman and Ramachandran, 2007) which would not only explain their poor imitation, empathy and 'pretend play' (which requires role-playing), but also why they sometimes confuse the pronouns 'I' and 'You', and have difficulty with introspection.

At this juncture, we should point out that some scholars have recently raised questions about the significance of mirror neurons for cognitive functions like theory of mind, and indeed about their very existence in humans (Hickok, 2008; Lotto *et al.*, 2009; Lingnau *et al.*, 2009). Some of this, we would argue, may be a manifestation of 'neuron envy' – a deep-seated fear of reductionism. This is irrational because mirror neurons are not meant to replace the theory of mind any more than DNA replaces heredity. On the contrary, the mirror neuron system (MNS) provides a mechanism by which theory of mind can be instantiated in the brain and might have emerged in evolution. A second criticism is that there is too much hype surrounding it, but the existence of media hype in itself does not invalidate a theory. A third criticism is that although the MNS exists in monkeys, it has not been unequivocally shown to exist in humans; the brain imaging techniques are inherently unreliable. However, absence of evidence is not evidence of absence – to a biologist it would be strange to suggest that a system of neurons demonstrated in monkeys would have suddenly disappeared in humans; in fact, the default position is the opposite (we never went through a phase when people claimed that Hubel and Wiesels' discovery of orientation selective cells is applicable only to monkeys). A fourth criticism is that the neurons with MNS-like properties are simply the result of Hebbian associative conditioning, that there's nothing special about them. There are two answers to this. First, even if the statement were true, it would not detract from their importance for understanding brain function. The whole brain could be set up through associative conditioning, but no one would argue from this that studying the actual circuitry in the brain is useless for our understanding of how the brain works. The second answer is that if it is all a matter of associative learning then why are only a *subset* of V5 neurons (or S2 neurons) – about 20% – capable of this? Why not the other 80%? You cannot argue that only 20% are wired up genetically to acquire MNS-like properties – that just takes you back to square one. If we are right about MNS deficiency in autism spectrum disorder (ASD) then one might be able to devise new therapies to tap into any residual MNS function and enhance or rejuvenate their function. For example, one could create multiple mirror images of a 'trainer' dancing to a rhythm and have the child synchronize with the multiple images. This might revive MNS function and its benefits might spill over into other more cognitive domains.

Cotard's Syndrome

Let us return to Cotard's Syndrome – the ultimate paradox of the self-negating its own existence (sometimes claiming 'I am dead'). We postulate that this arises from a combination of two lesions, resulting in something akin to derealization. First, a lesion that is analogous to that which causes the Capgras familiarity impairment, but which is far more pervasive. Instead of emotions being disconnected just from visual centres, they are disconnected from all sensations and even memories of sensations. So, rather than just familiar people, the entire world becomes an imposter, it feels unreal. Second, there may be dysfunctional interaction between the mirror neurons and frontal inhibitory structures leading to a dissolution of the sense of self as being distinct from others (or indeed from the world). Lose the world and lose yourself – and it's as close to death as you can get.

Geschwind Syndrome and hyper-religiosity

Now, imagine if these same circuits that were outlined above became *hyper*active. This can happen during seizures originating in the temporal lobes (TLE or temporal lobe epilepsy). The result would be an intense heightening of the patient's sensory appreciation of the world (Ramachandran *et al.*, 1997) and intense empathy for all beings, to the extent of perceiving no barriers between himself and the cosmos. In that this may be interpreted as a religious experience, it is perhaps not surprising that hyper-religiosity can occur in a disorder particularly associated with TLE, Geschwind Syndrome (Benson, 1991). Other features of the syndrome can include hypergraphia (excessive written output), altered sexuality (often reduced sexual drive), and a degree of viscosity/'stickiness' in interpersonal interactions (inappropriate over-attachment). Whilst retrospective diagnosis from selective contemporary accounts is always dangerous, arguments have been made that some of history's religious leaders have had TLE. We hasten to add that the fact that fervent belief can arise in the context of TLE neither refutes nor supports the existence of God(s).

Let us turn now to out-of-body experiences (Easton *et al.*, 2009). Even a normal person, perhaps such as yourself, can at times adopt a 'detached' allocentric stance, but this does not become a full-blown delusion because other neural systems keep you anchored. However, damage to the right fronto-parietal regions or ketamine anaesthesia (which may influence the same circuits) removes the inhibition and you can feel that 'you' have left your body, even to the extent of not feeling your own pain (Muetzelfeldt *et al.*, 2008). You see your pain 'objectively' as if someone else was experiencing it. Out-of-body experiences can also be produced by using a system of parallel multiple-reflecting mirrors (Altschuler and Ramachandran, 2007) or video cameras (Ehrsson, 2007). This raises the possibility of using such systems to allow patients with chronic pain – such as fibromyalgia – to dissociate themselves from their pain (Ramachandran and Rogers-Ramachandran, 2008), mimicking ketamine anaesthesia.

Unity and discrepancy

The purported unity or internal consistency of self is also a myth, or highly tenuous at best. Most patients with left arm paralysis caused by right hemisphere stroke complain about it as, indeed, they should. However, a subset of patients who have additional damage to the 'body image' representation in the right SPL (superior parietal lobule; and possibly also the insula) claim that their paralysed left arm does not belong to them (Critchley, 1953). The patient may assert that it belongs to his father or spouse (as if he had a selective 'Capgras' for his arm). Such syndromes challenge even basic assumptions such as 'I am anchored in this body' or 'This is my arm'. They suggest that 'belongingness' is a primal brain function hardwired through natural selection because of its obvious selective advantage to our hominid ancestors. It makes one wonder if a Californian with this disorder would deny ownership of (or damage to) the left fender of his car and ascribe it to his mother's car.

There appears to be almost no limit to this. An intelligent and lucid patient we saw recently claimed that her own left arm was not paralysed and that the lifeless left arm on her lap belonged to her father who was 'hiding under the table'. Yet when we asked her to touch her nose with her left hand she used her intact right hand to grab and raise the paralysed left hand – using the latter as a 'tool' to touch her nose! Clearly somebody in there knew that her left arm was paralysed and that the arm on her lap was her own, but 'she' – the person we were talking to – did not.

Finally, we have speculated that some aspects of pain in phantom limbs may arise from discrepancies between visual input and corollary discharge to the (now) missing limb. Restoring visual/motor congruence using visual feedback ('mirror visual feedback', MVF) reduces pain in many patients possibly by restoring the congruence (Ramachandran *et al.*, 1995; Ramachandran and Hirstein, 1998; Ramachandran nd Altschuler, 2009). Even more intriguingly, we (Altschuler *et al.*, 1999) found that MVF could produce substantial recovery of function in the paralysed arm, following stroke.

Discrepancy between sensory and motor signals may also be involved in producing the excruciating, intractable pain that arises in reflex sympathetic dystrophy (RSD) or complex regional pain syndrome (CRPS). In 1996, we proposed (Ramachandran, 1996) using mirrors for treating this condition and recent double-blind placebo-controlled clinical trials have shown striking reduction of pain (Cacchio *et al.*, 2009).

Hemispheric specialization

Confabulation refers to a memory (or report of a memory) for events that did not happen, but which feel to the reporter to be true. There is evidence from a number of sources that language centres in the left hemisphere tend to 'patch up' discrepancies in sensory input (or indeed between inputs and pre-existing stable beliefs) by engaging in confabulation (Gazzaniga and LeDoux, 1978). In fact, we have suggested (Ramachandran, 1998; Ramachandran and Blakeslee, 1998; Pettigrew and Miller 1998) that many of the so-called Freudian defences (of which confabulation is one example; others include 'projection' rationalization, 'reaction formation', etc.) are mainly attempts by the more 'action'-oriented left hemisphere to confer stability and coherence on behaviour – you do not want to orient to every small discrepancy. On the other hand, if this is overdone, it can lead to delusions even of manic proportions (it is hardly ever adaptive to deny poverty and over-use a credit card). We therefore postulated, albeit a gross over-simplification, a 'devil's advocate' in the right hemisphere that constantly questions the status quo instead of clinging to it (Ramachandran, 1998). Thus, damage to the right frontoparietal region destroys the devil's advocate leading to florid delusions such as denial of paralysis and even denial of arm ownership (when the STS and right insula are also damaged) tinged with aversion because of the discrepancy, as noted above.

In the final section of this chapter, we consider how the patterns that we have seen in neurological illness, including paradoxical denial of the self, may illuminate general human responses to extreme conditions, anxiety problems such as panic attacks, and depression.

Panic attacks, depersonalization and derealization

In emergency situations, such as during an assault, people can experience significant alterations in state, including a sense of depersonalization, in which they feel apart or separated from the outside world. These responses can sometimes be set off by no obvious external threat, and the result is a panic attack. For example, if the neural circuitry responsible for a reflexive response to an emergency is triggered accidentally – caused by a mini TLE-type 'seizure' – it sets in motion an autonomic storm: your heart rate and blood pressure go up and you start sweating. You continue to be vigilant as well, and the anterior cingulate mediates this. But this time there is no tangible external danger to ascribe it to. Once again, an inexplicable discrepancy is set up leading to acute distress. So you ascribe the physiological changes to an impending heart attack or some other inexplicable danger – a foreboding of death that is vague yet deeply disturbing.

If this theory is correct, it immediately suggests a therapy for panic attacks. Since the main problem is a discrepancy arising from the absence of a target, one could substitute a false target. During the premonition of the attack, the patient could view a short horrifying video clip on, say, his iPhone. On the assumption that a tangible threat (anxiety that can be attributed to a specific external trigger) is less disturbing than an intangible one, the film clip may abort the attack. The fact that you know 'It's only a film clip' may not matter much – no more than knowing you are merely watching horror movie prevents you from vicariously 'enjoying' the horror. Now consider what would happen if the same circuitry starts malfunctioning on an extended timescale rather than just a few seconds. There is an increase in vigilance combined with no external cause and (possibly) lack of emotions as well (Sierra and Berrios, 2001). Additionally, there may be dysfunctional MNS causing poor ego differentiation and recursive representation of self (shades of Cotard's Syndrome here). Once again the organism – the brain – is confronted with a peculiar set of discrepancies that it would never ordinarily encounter; hence the patient concludes that the world does not exist or is not real (derealization), or that he does not exist or is not real (depersonalization). In desperate attempts to regain their sense of being anchored in reality, or indeed in their bodies, such patients may deliberately self-harm.

Self/other confusion

One of our propositions is that many neuropsychiatric disturbances arise from dysfunction of self/other differentiation, which in turn is based on deranged interactions between MNS and frontal inhibitory circuits. The result is a range of behaviour spanning the gradient from normalcy to pathology; from (1) *lack of empathy* – seen in some autism spectrum disorders; (2) *sympathy* – I sympathize with your plight, but maintain the clinical detachment of a surgeon; (3) *empathy* – I actually adopt your world view, to gain the deeper appreciation towards a close friend; (4) *hyperempathy* – a profound sense of feeling the other's emotional responses; (5) *pathological empathy* – experiencing the other's qualia as your own (e.g. a patient feeling his phantom being touched when watching someone else being touched); (6) *cosmic union* – a sense of relatedness with all beings and with the cosmos (God delusions).

Future challenges and questions

Some of the ideas and formulations outlined in this chapter are speculative, but we hope nevertheless that it will help generate testable predictions and new therapies and provide a starting point for a more comprehensive explanation of self-related paradoxes in neuropsychiatry.

One issue that needs to be addressed in future research is the role of individual differences in the manifestation of these syndromes. If there is an explanation in terms of particular networks and pathways, why do we not see these syndromes more often? Could it be the case that the syndromes will only become apparent in individuals with a particular set of past experiences and repositories of knowledge, and/or individuals who happen to have particular goals that they need to achieve, and that the syndromes emerge due to pressures from these two factors?

In the last decade there has been a tremendous resurgence of interest among neuroscientists in the nature of consciousness and self. The goal is to explain specific details of certain complex mental capacities in terms of equally specific activity of specialized neural structures. Just as the functional logic of heredity (pigs give birth to pigs, not donkeys) was mapped precisely on to the structural logic of the DNA molecule (the complementarity of the two strands), we need to map the mental phenomena on to specialized neural structures and their interactions.

As we have seen, one way to achieve this might be to explore inherently paradoxical syndromes that lie at the interface between neurology and psychiatry, using them to illuminate both normal and abnormal mental functions. We have used this strategy to provide a conceptual framework for thinking about neuropsychiatric disturbances. Many of the ideas have been proposed by others, but the particular synthesis we present may have some novel features.

Acknowledgements

The ideas we have expressed in this article are an attempt to provide a novel synthesis, but rely a great deal on the work of many researchers – most notably Francis Crick, Pat Churchland, Antonio Damasio, Nick Humphrey, Joe LeDoux, Orrin Devinsky, Haydn Ellis, Andrew Young, Mauricio Berrios, M. Sierra, Jack Pettigrew and many others.

References

Altschuler, E. L., & Ramachandran, V. S. (2007). A simple method to stand outside oneself. *Perception*, **36**: 632–4.

Altschuler, E. L., Vankov, A., Wang, V., Ramachandran, V. S. & Pineda, J. A. (1997). *Person see, person do: human cortical electrophysiological correlates of monkey see monkey do cells* (poster session presented at the 27th annual meeting of the society for neuroscience, New Orleans, LA).

Altschuler, E. L., Wisdom, S. B., Stone, L., *et al.* (1999). Rehabilitation of hemiparesis after stroke with a mirror. *Lancet*, **353**: 2035–6.

Amaral, D. G., & Price, J. L. (1984). Amygdalo-cortical projections in the monkey (*Macaca fascicularis*). *The Journal of Comparative Neurology*, **230**: 465–96.

Aziz-Zadeh, L., Koski, L., Zaidel, E., Mazziotta, J., & Iacoboni, M. (2006). Lateralization of the human mirror neuron system. *Journal of Neuroscience*, **26**: 2964–70.

Bauer, R. (1984). Autonomic recognition of names and faces in prosopagnosia: a neuropsychological application of the Guilty Knowledge Test. *Neuropsychologia*, **22**: 457–69.

Bayne, T., & Levy, N. (2005). Amputees by choice: body integrity disorder and the ethics of amputation. *Journal of Applied Philosophy*, **22**: 75–86.

Benson, D. (1991). The Geschwind Syndrome. *Advances in Neurology*, **55**: 411–21.

Berlucchi, G., & Aglioti, S. (1997). The body in the brain: neural bases of corporeal awareness. *Trends in Neuroscience*, **20**: 560–4.

Bisiach, E., & Geminiani, G. (1991). Anosognosia related to hemiplegia and hemianopia. In: Priganto, G. P. and Schacter, D. L. (Eds.). *Awareness of Deficit After Brain Injury: Clinical and Theoretical Issues*. Oxford: Oxford University Press.

Blanke, O., Landis, T., Spinelli, L., & Seeck, M. (2004). Out-of-body experience and autoscopy of neurological origin. *Brain*, **127**: 243–58.

Blanke, O., Morgenthaler, F. D., Brugger, P., & Overney, L. S. (2009). Preliminary evidence for a fronto-parietal dysfunction in able-bodied participants with a desire for a limb amputation. *Journal of Neuropsychology*, **3**: 181–200.

Brang, D., McGeoch, P., & Ramachandran, V. S. (2008). Apotemnophilia: a neurological disorder. *Neuroreport*, **19**: 1305–06.

Brass, M., Ruby, P., & Spengler, S. (2009). Inhibition of imitative behaviour and social cognition. *Philosophical Transactions of the Royal Society of London. Series B, Biological Sciences*, **364**: 2359–67.

Cacchio, A., De Blasis, E., Necozione, S., di Orio, F., & Santilli, V. (2009). Mirror therapy for chronic complex regional pain syndrome type 1 and stroke. *New England Journal of Medicine*, **361**: 634–6.

Capgras, J., & Reboul-Lachaux, J. (1923). L'illusion des 'sosies' dans un délire systématisé chronique. *Bulletin de la Société Clinique de Medicine Mentael*, **11**: 6–16. Reprinted in H. D. Ellis, J. Whitley and J. P. Luauté (Eds.). (1994) Delusional misidentification: the three original papers on the Capgras, Fregoli and intermetamorphosis delusions. *History of Psychiatry*, **5**: 117–46.

Case, L., & Ramachandran, V. S (2010). Immediate interpersonal and intermanual referral of tactile sensation following anesthetic block of the brachial plexus. *Archives of Neurology*, **57**: 1521–3.

Coltheart, M., Menzies, P., & Sutton, J. (2009). Abductive inference and delusional belief. *Cognitive Neuropsychiatry*, **15**: 1–27.

Critchley, M. (1953). *The Parietal Lobes*. London: Edward Arnold.

Devinsky, O. (2009). Delusional misidentifications and duplications: right brain lesions, left brain delusions. *Neurology*, **72**: 80–7.

Devinsky, O., & Lai, G. (2008). Spirituality and religion in epilepsy. *Epilepsy and Behavior*, **12**: 636–43.

Di Pellegrino, G., Fadiga, L., Fogassi, L., Gallese, V., & Rizzolatti, G. (1992). Understanding motor events: a neurophysiological study. *Experimental Brain Research*, **91**: 176–80.

Easton, S., Blanke, O., & Mohr, C. (2009). A putative implication for fronto-parietal connectivity in out-of-body experiences. *Cortex*, **45**: 216–27.

Ehrsson, H. H. (2007). The experimental induction of out-of-body experience. *Science*, **317**: 1048.

Ellis, H., Young, A., Quayle, A., & De Pauw, K. (1997). Reduced autonomic responses to faces in Capgras Delusion. *Proceedings of the Royal Society, Biological Sciences*, **264**: 1085–92.

First, M. B. (2005). Desire for an amputation of a limb: paraphilia, psychosis, or a new type of identity disorder. *Psychological Medicine*, **35**: 919–28.

Freese, J. L., & Amaral, D. G. (2006). Synaptic organization of projections from the amygdala to visual cortical areas TE and V1 in the Macaque monkey. *The Journal of Comparative Neurology*, **496**: 655–67.

Gazzaniga, M., & LeDoux, J. (1978). *The Integrated Mind*. New York, NY: Springer.

Hickok, G. (2008). Eight problems for the mirror neuron theory of action understanding in monkeys and humans. *Journal of Cognitive Neuroscience*, **21**: 1229–43.

Hirstein, W., & Ramachandran, V. (2009). He is not my father, and that is not my arm: accounting for misidentification of people and limbs. In: Hirstein, W. (Ed.). *Confabulation. Views from Neuroscience, Psychiatry, Psychology and Philosophy*. Oxford: Oxford University Press, pp. 109–38.

Hirstein, W., & Ramachandran, V. S. (1997). Capgras syndrome: a novel probe for understanding the neural representation and familiarity of persons. *Proceedings of the Royal Society of London*, **264**: 437–44.

Humphrey, N. (1978). Nature's psychologists. In Ramachandran, V. S. and Josephson, B. (Eds.). *Consciousness and the Physical World*. Oxford: Pergamon Press.

Hung, Y., Smith, M. L., Bayle, D. J., *et al.* (2010). Unattended emotional faces elicit early lateralized amygdala–frontal and fusiform activations. *Neuroimage*, **50**: 727–33.

Iacoboni, M. (2009). Imitation, empathy, and mirror neurons. *Annual Review of Psychology*, **60**: 653–70.

Jeannerod, M., & Jacob, P. (2005). Visual cognition: a new look at the two-visual systems model. *Neuropsychologia*, 43: 301–12.

Keysers, C., Wicker, B., Gazzola, V., Anton, J. L., Fogassi, L., & Gallese, V. (2004). A touching sight: SII/PV activation during the observation and experience of touch. *Neuron*, 42: 335–46.

Lakoff, G., & Johnson, M. (1980). *Metaphors We Live By*. Chicago, IL: University of Chicago Press.

Lingnau, A., Gesierich, B., & Caramazza, A. (2009). Asymmetric fMRI adaptation reveals no evidence for mirror neurons in humans. *Proceedings of the National Academy of Sciences*, 106: 9925–30.

Lotto, A., Hickok, G. S., & Holt, L. L. (2009). Reflections of mirror neurons and speech perception. *Trends in Cognitive Sciences*, 13: 110–4.

McGeoch, P. D., Brang, D., & Ramachandran, V. S. (2007). Apraxia, metaphor and mirror neurons. *Medical Hypotheses*, 69:1165–8.

McKay, R., & Dennett, D. (2009). The evolution of misbelief. *Behavioral and Brain Sciences*, 32: 493–510.

Money, J., Jobaris, R., & Furth, G. (1977). Apotemnophilia: two cases of self-demand amputation as a paraphilia. *Journal of Sex Research*, 13: 115–25.

Muetzelfeldt, L., Kamboj, S. K., Rees, H., *et al.* (2008). Journey through the K-hole: phenomenological aspects of ketamine use. *Drug and Alcohol Dependence*, 95: 219–29.

Noordzij, M. L., Newman-Norlund, S. E., de Ruiter, J. P., *et al.* (2009). Brain mechanisms underlying human communication. *Frontiers in Human Neuroscience*, 3: 14.

Oberman, L. M., & Ramachandran, V. S. (2007). The stimulating social mind: the role of the mirror neuron system and simulation in the social and communicative deficits of autism spectrum disorders. *Psychological Bulletin*, 133: 310–27.

Oberman, L. M., Hubbard, E. M., McCleery, J. P., Altschuler, E. L., & Ramachandran, V. S. (2005). EEG evidence for mirror neuron dysfunction in autism spectrum disorders. *Cognitive Brain Research*, 24: 190–8.

Pearn, J., & Gardner-Thorpe, C. (2002). Jules Cotard (1840–1899): his life and the unique syndrome that bears his name. *Neurology*, 58: 1400–03.

Pettigrew, J. D., & Miller, S. M. (1998). A 'sticky' interhemispheric switch in bipolar disorder? *Proceeding of the Royal Society of London, Series B, Biological Sciences*, 265: 2141–8.

Ramachandran, V. S. (1996). What neurological syndromes can tell us about human nature: some lessons from phantom limbs, Capgras syndrome, and anosognosia. *Cold Spring Harbor Symposia on Quantitative Biology*, 61: 115–34.

Ramachandran, V. S. (1998). Consciousness and body image. *Philosophical transactions of the Royal Society of London. Series B, Biological Sciences*, 353: 1851–9.

Ramachandran, V. S., & Altschuler, E. L. (2009). The use of visual feedback, in particular mirror visual feedback, in restoring brain function. *Brain*, 132: 1693–710.

Ramachandran, V. S., & Blakeslee, S. (1998). *Phantoms in the Brain: Probing the Mysteries of the Human Mind*. New York, NY: William Morrow.

Ramachandran, V. S., & Brang, D. (2009). Sensations evoked in patients with amputation from watching an individual whose corresponding intact limb is being touched. *Archives of Neurology*, 66: 1281–4.

Ramachandran, V. S., & Hirstein, W. (1998). The perception of phantom limbs. The D. O. Hebb lecture. *Brain*, 121: 1603–30.

Ramachandran, V. S., & McGeoch, P. D. (2007). Occurrence of phantom limb genitalia after gender reassignment surgery. *Medical Hypotheses*, 69: 1001–03.

Ramachandran, V. S., & Rogers-Ramachandran, D. (2008). Sensations referred to a patient's phantom arm from another subject's intact arm: perceptual correlates of mirror neurons. *Medical Hypotheses*, 70: 1233–4.

Ramachandran, V. S., Brang, D., McGeoch, P. D., & Rosar, W. (2009). Sexual and food preference in apotemnophilia and anorexia: interactions between 'beliefs' and 'needs' regulated by two-way connections between body image and limbic structures. *Perception*, **38**: 775–7.

Ramachandran, V. S., McGeoch, P. D., & Brang, D. (2008). *Apotemnophilia: a neurological disorder with somatotopic alterations in SCR and MEG activation*. Society for Neuroscience Meeting, Washington, D.C.

Ramachandran, V. S., Rogers-Ramachandran, D., & Cobb, S. (1995). Touching the phantom limb. *Nature*, **377**: 489–90.

Ramachandran, V. S., Vilayanur, S., Hirstein, W. S., Armel, K. C., Tecoma, E., & Iragul, V. (1997). The neural basis of religious experience (paper presented at the 27th Annual Meeting of the Society for Neuroscience, New Orleans, LA).

Rizzolatti, G., & Craighero, L. (2004). The mirror neuron system. *Annual Reviews of Neuroscience*, **27**: 169–92.

Rolls, E. T. (1999). Spatial view cells and the representation of place in the primate hippocampus. *Hippocampus*, **9**: 467–80.

Sierra, M., & Berrios, G. E. (2001). The phenomenological stability of depersonalisation: comparing the old with the new. *Journal of Nervous and Mental Disorders*, **189**: 629–36.

Sinkman, A. (2008). The syndrome of Capgras. *Psychiatry*, **71**: 371–8.

Smith, C. D., Lori, N. F., Akbudak, E., *et al.* (2009). MRI diffusion tensor tracking of a new amygdalo-fusiform and hippocampo-fusiform pathway system in humans. *Journal of Magnetic Resonance Imaging*, **29**: 1248–61.

Vallar, G., & Ronchi, R. (2009). Somatoparaphrenia: a body delusion. A review of the neuropsychological literature. *Experimental Brain Research*, **192**: 533–1.

Young, A. W., Leafhead, K. M., & Szulecka, T. K. (1994). The Capgras and Cotard delusions. *Psychopathology*, **27**: 226–31.

Young, A. W., Reid, I., Wright, S., & Hellawell, D. J. (1993). Face-processing impairments and the Capgras delusion. *British Journal of Psychiatry*, **162**: 695–8.

Chapter 6

Paradoxical psychological functioning in early child development

David J. Lewkowicz and Asif A. Ghazanfar

Summary

Development is a progressive process that results in the growth and proliferation of motor, perceptual and cognitive skills. A growing body of evidence shows, however, that seemingly paradoxical regressive processes also contribute to perceptual development and to the emergence of specialization. This evidence shows that unisensory perceptual sensitivity in early infancy is so broadly tuned that young infants respond to, and discriminate, native sensory inputs (e.g. speech sounds in their own language and faces from their own species and race) as well as non-native sensory inputs (e.g. speech sounds from other languages and faces from other species and other races). In contrast, older infants only respond to native inputs. For example, younger but not older infants discriminate monkey, human, and other-race faces, native and foreign speech contrasts, and musical rhythms from different cultures. Here, we review new findings indicating that perceptual narrowing is not just a unisensory developmental process, but a general, pan-sensory one. These new data reveal that young infants can perceive non-native (monkey) faces and vocalizations as well as non-native speech gestures and vocalizations as coherent multisensory events, and that this broad multisensory perceptual tuning is present at birth. These data also reveal that this broad tuning narrows by the end of the first year of life, leaving older infants only with the ability to perceive the multisensory coherence of native sensory inputs. Together, these findings suggest that perceptual narrowing is a pan-sensory process, force us to reconsider the traditional progressive theories of multisensory development, and open up several new evolutionary questions.

Introduction

Most developmental theories reflect the conventional view that life begins with a set of narrow behavioural capacities and that these then broaden in scope and complexity as children grow (Werner, 1973; Gottlieb, 1996; Piaget, 1952; Gibson, 1969). A prototypic example of this developmental broadening view is Piaget's (1952) theory of cognitive development. According to Piaget, life begins with a set of rudimentary sensorimotor abilities that then gradually become transformed into sophisticated symbolic representational and logico-deductive skills. The broadening view has great intuitive appeal and is supported by a wealth of empirical evidence. For example, newborn infants have poor visual acuity and poor spatial resolution skills, do not perceive the affect that faces convey, do not understand that objects are bounded and have an independent existence, can hear speech

The Paradoxical Brain, ed. Narinder Kapur. Published by Cambridge University Press. © Cambridge University Press 2011.

but cannot segment it into its meaningful components, cannot link specific speech sounds to the objects that they represent, cannot understand the meanings inherent in the temporal structure of events, do not perceive depth nor have a fear of heights, and cannot self-locomote. As infants grow and as they experience the world around them, however, they gradually acquire all of these skills.

Despite the obvious validity of the developmental broadening view, a growing body of evidence has begun to show that broadening does not fully represent the developmental process. This evidence shows that a developmental narrowing process operates side-by-side with the broadening process. At first blush, the process of narrowing seems to be a paradoxical phenomenon because it leads to the unexpected decline in various sensory, perceptual, and cognitive capacities at a time in development when they should all be improving and proliferating. In this chapter, we show that contrary to its seemingly paradoxical nature, the process of perceptual narrowing is actually a crucial part of the developmental process, and we argue that it probably evolved as an adaptation that permits developing organisms to tune their sensory/perceptual abilities to best match their eco-logical setting – an adaptation that may be particularly important for humans given the very immature neurodevelopmental state of human newborns relative to other primate species. At the end of this process, organisms become experts at processing inputs that are the most socioecologically relevant.

We will discuss two sets of findings related to perceptual narrowing. The first set comes from studies of unisensory perceptual narrowing in human infants showing that infant perception of non-native speech, faces and music narrows during the first year of life. The second comes from our recent studies of intersensory perception in human and animal infants showing that perceptual narrowing is not solely a unisensory process, but that it also affects the interactions among the different sensory modalities. In other words, our studies indicate that perceptual narrowing is a *pan-sensory* developmental phenomenon.

The developmental problem and the broadening view

Given the essentially multisensory character of our perceptual world, a developing infant's primary task is to discover the multisensory coherence of the objects and events that constitute his/her normal ecological setting. This task is complicated by the fact that the infant's nervous system is immature and constantly changing and the fact that the infant is perceptually inexperienced. Despite these limitations, research over the last three decades has shown that infants are able to overcome them gradually during the first year of life and that they end up being able to detect multisensory coherence (Lewkowicz, 2000, 2002; Bahrick and Lickliter, 2000; Walker-Andrews, 1997; Lewkowicz and Lickliter, 1994). There are at least two reasons for this. First, much of the multisensory perceptual array consists of invariant amodal attributes. That is, much of the multisensory information in our everyday world is characterized by overlapping and highly correlated streams of information. For example, when we speak with another person we can simultaneously see that person's articulations and hear them as the person speaks. The visual and auditory information specifying the person's speech is usually not only temporally synchronized but its duration, tempo, and rhythmical pattern is the same in each modality. It is this kind of intersensory equivalence that is the source of the multisensory invariance in our perceptual array. Its detection is what makes it easier for infants to discover the multisensory coherence of their world (Gibson, 1969). Second, the developmental limitations that are present early in life actually facilitate the emergence of multisensory perceptual skills. They do so by reducing the number of potential concurrent multisensory interactions and, as a result, promote the orderly integration of sensory modalities in a nervous system that might otherwise get easily overwhelmed (Turkewitz and Kenny, 1982).

Most studies yielding evidence of multisensory perception in infancy have been driven either explicitly or implicitly by one of two theoretical views. The first, the developmental integration view, holds that basic multisensory perceptual abilities are not present at birth and that they emerge gradually during the first years of life as a result of the child's active exploration of the world (Birch and Lefford, 1967; Piaget, 1952). The second, the developmental differentiation view, holds that multisensory perceptual abilities are present at birth and that they become increasingly differentiated and refined over time (Gibson, 1984). Importantly, in both theoretical views, multisensory development is thought of as a progressive process that results in the improvement of early-emerging multisensory perceptual abilities and the proliferation of new ones with development and increasing experience.

On the surface, most of the empirical evidence to date appears to be consistent with the developmental differentiation view. It indicates that basic multisensory perceptual abilities are present in infancy and that as infants grow these abilities change and improve in significant ways. For example, even though very young infants can match faces and voices and, thus, perceive them as unitary events (Kuhl and Meltzoff, 1982; Patterson and Werker, 2003; Walton and Bower, 1993), it is not until many months later, and after the acquisition of considerable experience with conspecific (i.e. the same species) faces and voices, that infants become capable of perceiving higher-order multisensory attributes such as affect and gender (Patterson and Werker, 2002; Kahana-Kalman and Walker-Andrews, 2001). These kinds of findings suggest a pattern consisting of the initial emergence of low-level multisensory abilities that permit infants to detect simple, synchrony-based relations (Lewkowicz, 2010; Lewkowicz et al., 2010), followed by a subsequent age- and experience-dependent emergence of new higher-level multisensory abilities – a scenario consistent with developmental broadening.

Historical ideas regarding developmental regression and perceptual narrowing

There is no doubt that functional as well as structural broadening is part-and-parcel of the developmental process. It is also true, however, that regressive processes play an important role in development. This was first noted in the behavioural sphere by Holt (1931), who pointed out the importance of the process of behavioural narrowing in his studies of the development of organized motor activity patterns in fetuses. Holt observed that the sensorimotor activity of the chick is initially very diffuse and that as the chick develops this activity gradually becomes canalized into organized motor patterns. According to Holt, the process of canalization was driven by behavioural conditioning.

Holt's inference that canalization of motor activity was driven by conditioning was incomplete because of his failure to recognize the critical contribution of various organismic and extra-organismic factors; however, his concept of canalization was still conceptually valuable and, indeed, presaged its more modern version. This can be seen in dynamic systems theories of development (Lewis, 2000; Thelen and Smith, 1994), where developmental regression and the concept of canalization are considered to play key roles in the development of motor behaviour. In essence, these theories assume that the degrees of freedom that define the critical parameters that control various motor skills are reduced during motor learning and development. For example, when infants are first learning to walk, the many parts of their motor system are free to assemble into many functional patterns and are free to do so in many different ways. As infants begin to move and interact with the physical substrate on which they locomote, the various subparts of the motor system begin to cooperate with one another and begin to assemble into stable and efficient patterns of action. As a result, the functionally useful patterns are selected during development from many possible ones through a reduction in the degrees of freedom underlying the various subsystems that participate in the control of locomotion.

Kuo (1976) also found the concept of canalization to be useful in describing the development of behaviour. For Kuo, however, Holt's concept was too limited and, as a result, he proposed that the narrowing of behavioural potential was not merely the result of the individual's history of reinforcement, but that it included the individual's entire developmental history, context and experience. Subsequently, Gottlieb (1991) adopted this broader concept of canalization in his studies of the development of species recognition in mallard ducks. Gottlieb hypothesized that recognition of species-specific duck calls is actually the result of the influence of non-obvious experiential factors *in ovo*. In this case, he hypothesized that it is due to the embryo listening to its own prenatal vocalizations. Indeed, Gottlieb found that embryos who were prevented from producing, and thus hearing, their own vocalizations – by being devocalized – failed to exhibit socially affiliative responses toward their conspecifics. Thus, Gottlieb showed that when embryos vocalize and listen to their own vocalizations, they not only learn some of the critical features of their species-specific call but, critically, also learn *not to respond* to the social signals of other species because of the lack of exposure to heterospecific signals. In other words, experience with their own embryonic vocalizations narrows the embryos' initially broadly tuned auditory sensitivity. This highly compelling example of the importance of canalization in perceptual development, and of the fact that it is driven by experience, is consistent with the many other examples of the same phenomenon.

Unisensory perceptual narrowing in human infants

It has now become clear that a number of human perceptual functions undergo canalization (i.e. narrowing) as a function of early experience. As a result, they narrow their tuning early in life and this leads to the eventual development of species-specific patterns of perceptual expertise. This body of evidence consists of findings from studies of speech, face and music perception and shows that perceptual tuning is so broad at first that it allows young infants to respond to native as well as non-native perceptual attributes. As development proceeds, and as infants are selectively exposed to native perceptual attributes, this tuning narrows in scope, leaving older infants with a perceptual insensitivity to non-native attributes. We first describe this unisensory evidence and then move on to the most recent evidence for perceptual narrowing in the multisensory perceptual domain.

Speech perception

In a landmark study, Werker and Tees (1984) showed that narrowing occurs in infant perception of non-native speech contrasts. They found that 6–8-month-old English-learning infants discriminated non-native consonants – the Hindi retroflex /Da/ versus the dental /da/ as well as the Thompson glottalized velar /k'i/ versus the uvular /q'i/ – but that 10–12-month-old infants did not. Based on these findings, Werker and Tees concluded that the decline in the salience of non-native phonetic contrasts is due to language-specific experience that provides infants with continuing experience with native consonant contrasts and none with the non-native ones. Subsequent cross-linguistic consonant and vowel discrimination studies have provided additional evidence of this type of narrowing (Best et al., 1995; Kuhl et al., 1992; Cheour et al., 1998), as well as direct evidence that narrowing of speech perception is due to experience-dependent processes. This latter evidence comes from a study in which English-learning infants were exposed to natural Mandarin Chinese during 12 play sessions between 9 and 10 months of age (Kuhl et al., 2003). Following such exposure, these infants were better able to discriminate a Mandarin Chinese phonetic contrast that does not occur in English when compared to control infants.

Face perception

As in the speech processing domain, human infants are better at recognizing and discriminating non-native faces than are adults. Pascalis, de Haan and Nelson (2002) showed that 6-month-old infants can discriminate both human and monkey faces, but that 9-month-old infants can only discriminate human faces. As in the case of speech perception, the decline in non-native face discrimination is also the result of selective perceptual experience. In this case, it is the result of selective experience with human faces. This is evident from studies in which it has been found that responsiveness to non-native faces can be maintained in older infants by providing them with additional experience with such faces. That is, infants exposed to monkey faces at home during the 3-month period between 6 and 9 months of age, when sensitivity to non-native faces declines, exhibit successful discrimination of monkey faces at 9 months of age (Pascalis et al., 2005; Scott and Monesson, 2009). A similar pattern of perceptual narrowing is thought to underlie the 'other race effect' (ORE). This effect is characterized by adults' poorer discrimination of faces of people from other races relative to the faces of people from their own race (Chiroro and Valentine, 1995) and it is independent of culture (Pascalis and Kelly, 2009). The ORE emerges gradually in infancy between 3 and 9 months of age (Kelly et al., 2007) and, like the perception of non-native speech contrasts and the faces of other species, is experience-dependent (Sangrigoli and De Schonen, 2004). This is evident in a study that investigated the interaction between gender discrimination and the ORE. Results revealed that 3-month-old Caucasian infants show a preference for female over male faces when the faces are Caucasian, but not when the faces are Asian (Quinn et al., 2008). This is in contrast to newborn Caucasian infants who do not demonstrate a preference for female over male faces when looking at Caucasian faces.

Music perception

Simple musical meters, defined by simple duration ratios of inter-onset intervals of sounds (e.g. 2:1), predominate in North American music whereas complex musical meters, defined by complex duration ratios (e.g. 3:2), predominate in many other musical cultures (e.g. in the Balkans). North American adults can detect differences in melodies based on alterations of simple meters, but not when the differences are based on alterations of complex meters characteristic of Balkan music (Hannon and Trehub, 2005a). Adults of Bulgarian or Macedonian origin detect melodic differences in both simple and complex metrical structure. The same is true for 6-month-old North American infants but not for 12-month-old infants (Hannon and Trehub, 2005b). As is the case for the positive effects of exposure to non-native speech and faces in infants who no longer exhibit discrimination, 12-month-old North American infants can discriminate the complex meters inherent in Balkan music after a 2-week exposure to such meters (Hannon and Trehub, 2005b).

Multisensory perceptual narrowing in human infants

The objects and events that make up our everyday experience provide us with a constant flow of sensory signals in multiple modalities. Although such inputs can potentially create confusion, our ability to integrate the information available in different modalities enables us to have coherent and meaningful perceptual experiences. For example, talking faces are typically specified by various modality-specific attributes (e.g. colour, pitch) that are usually synchronous and spatially co-located as well as by a host of invariant amodal attributes (e.g. duration, tempo, rhythm). The former include facial configuration cues, skin colour, facial hair and the pitch and timbre of the voice. The latter, which provide information about the relations between visible and audible articulator actions, include such amodal attributes as intensity, duration, tempo, and rhythm (Chandrasekaran *et al.*, 2009; Munhall and Vatikiotis-Bateson, 2004). Our ability to integrate the diverse multisensory perceptual attributes representing talking faces is critical to our ability to extract coherent meanings from such ubiquitous sources of communicative signals. Indeed, multisensory integration is central to adaptive cognitive functioning, because it not only allows us to perceive a world of coherent perceptual entities, but also because it enables us to take advantage of the increased salience that the normally available redundant sources of information provide (Bahrick *et al.*, 2004; Lewkowicz and Kraebel, 2004).

That multisensory perception is so central to cognition naturally raises questions about its developmental and evolutionary origins and, ultimately, about the relationship between these two processes (Kingsbury and Finlay, 2001; Krubitzer, 2007; Oyama, 2000). Recent studies challenge extant theories of multisensory perceptual development and the conventional view that development is a progressive process. These results show that unisensory and multisensory perceptual tuning to faces and vocalizations and to the relationship between them is initially broad in infancy. This enables infants to respond to native as well as non-native perceptual attributes. In addition, these results show that as infants grow and as they acquire massive perceptual experience with native perceptual attributes and virtually no experience with non-native ones, their unisensory and multisensory tuning gradually narrows leaving them with the ability to respond primarily to native multisensory perceptual attributes.

Given that multisensory perception is essentially the default mode of functioning (Rosenblum, 2005; Ghazanfar, 2010), this raises the possibility that perceptual narrowing is not a unisensory but, rather, a pan-sensory process. If that is the case, then this would suggest that the progressive developmental theoretical framework and the broadening view of perceptual development provide an incomplete description of the processes underlying the emergence of multisensory perception. An early hint that this might be the case came from a study that pre-dates the various findings of narrowing in the unisensory domain. In it, Lewkowicz and Turkewitz (1980) investigated audio-visual (A-V) intensity matching in 3-week-old infants and adults. Infants were first habituated to a constant-intensity patch of white light. Then, they were tested on separate trials for response generalization to a series of white noise stimuli varying in intensity (one of these stimuli was known to match the light based on a prior study in which adults were explicitly asked to match the same visual and auditory stimuli presented to the infants). Results indicated that infants made spontaneous A-V matches in that they exhibited the smallest response recovery to the auditory stimulus that the adults found to match the visual stimulus and increasingly greater response recovery to the auditory stimuli that were both higher and lower in intensity. In contrast, when adults were tested for response generalization with the same procedure as used with infants, they failed to exhibit evidence of matching. Moreover, when adults were explicitly instructed to match in a separate study, they indicated that that they found the task 'bizarre'. Originally, it was not clear how to interpret the infant–adult response difference, but in hindsight, and in the context of the more recent findings on perceptual narrowing in early development, it has become clear that this difference probably reflects the process of *multisensory* perceptual narrowing. That is, this difference probably reflects the narrowing of an initially broadly tuned response system that at first integrates multisensory information regardless of its specific nature but that eventually narrows in its tuning as a result of perceptual differentiation, learning and the development of perceptual expertise.

Response to non-native faces and vocalizations

Recently, we conducted several studies designed to investigate the possibility that perceptual narrowing is a pan-sensory phenomenon and obtained empirical support for this hypothesis. The first one of these to provide direct evidence of narrowing was a study by Lewkowicz and Ghazanfar (2006). In this study, we presented side-by-side movies of the faces of a rhesus monkey producing a coo call on one side and a grunt call on the other side. We showed these movies to 4-, 6-, 8- and 10-month-old infants and measured their preferences for each of the visual calls when they were presented in silence and then in the presence of one of the corresponding audible vocalizations. Consistent with the hypothesis of multisensory narrowing, we found that the 4- and 6-month-old infants readily matched the visual and audible calls – they looked longer at the visible call in the presence of the corresponding vocalization than in its absence – whereas the 8- and 10-month-old infants did not (Figure 6.1).

Because the onsets of the facial gestures and the corresponding audible calls were in temporal synchrony in this experiment, it was likely that synchrony mediated successful matching in the younger infants. We tested this hypothesis in a follow-up study in which we disrupted the synchrony between the matching facial and vocal expressions by having the vocalization occur 666 ms prior to the time when the lips could be seen moving. As predicted, we found that the younger infants no longer performed multisensory matches (Lewkowicz et al., 2008). In addition to testing whether synchrony was involved in matching at the younger ages, in this latter study we asked whether the failure of the older infants to match was due to unisensory deficits and whether the decline in multisensory matching persists into later development. The answer to the first question was that 8–10-month-old infants easily discriminated the different call gestures and the different audible calls, respectively. The answer to the second question was that the decline in multisensory matching of non-native faces and vocalizations persists to 18 months of age, because both 12- and 18-month-old infants failed to make matches (Figure 6.1).

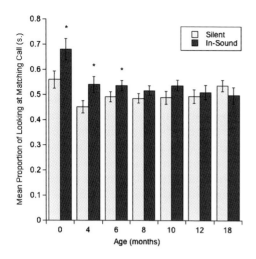

Figure 6.1 Composite figure of the findings on cross-species multisensory matching in human infants from birth up to 18 months of age. Shown is the mean proportion of looking time directed at the matching silent visible call out of the total amount of looking time directed at both silent calls, versus the mean proportion of looking at the matching call in the presence of the audible call (in-sound condition). The results from newborns are from Lewkowicz et al. (2010), from 4–10-month-olds from Lewkowicz and Ghazanfar (2006), and from 12–18-month-olds from Lewkowicz et al. (2008). The figure shows that infants exhibited matching of the visible and audible calls from birth up to 6 months of age and that older infants did not. Error bars indicate standard error of the mean and asterisks indicate that looking at the matching face in the in-sound condition was significantly greater than in the silent condition.

This developmental pattern of initial multisensory matching at younger ages and the absence of such matching at older ages is in direct contrast with all previous findings on face–voice matching in human infants. That is, all studies to date that investigated whether human infants are able to match human faces with human vocalizations found that infants as young as two months of age and as old as 18 months of age can make such matches and, critically, that this ability does *not* decline at the older ages (Patterson and Werker, 1999, 2002, 2003; Kuhl and Meltzoff, 1982; Kahana-Kalman and Walker-Andrews, 2001; Walker-Andrews, 1986; Walker-Andrews *et al.*, 1991; Poulin-Dubois *et al.*, 1994, 1998). As a result, when our findings on infant response to non-human faces and vocalizations are considered together with the findings on infant response to human faces and vocalizations, it is clear that infants' ability to perceive non-native face–voice relations is initially present and then declines, whereas infants' ability to perceive various types of native face–voice relations not only does not decline but actually improves. For example, whereas young infants do not perceive the amodal affective invariance of the faces and vocalizations of human strangers, older infants do (Walker-Andrews, 1986).

The fact that infants undergo a period of multisensory perceptual narrowing raised at least three questions for us. First, does the broad multisensory perceptual tuning found at 4 months of age, and the consequent ability to perceive the multisensory coherence of the social signals of another species, represent the initial developmental condition in humans (i.e. is it present at birth)? Second, does this broad multisensory perceptual tuning extend to other domains (e.g. speech)? Third, does multisensory perceptual narrowing occur in other primate species?

Is broad multisensory tuning present at birth?

To investigate the first question, Lewkowicz, Leo and Simion (2010) used the same testing methods and materials that Lewkowicz and Ghazanfar (2006) used. They found that newborns also matched monkey facial gestures and vocalizations (Figure 6.1), indicating that the broad multisensory tuning that Lewkowicz and Ghazanfar (2006) initially found in older infants characterizes perceptual functioning from birth onwards. Given these results,

Lewkowicz *et al.* (2010) then conducted a second experiment in which they investigated the mechanism underlying the successful multisensory matching found in the first experiment. Specifically, they tested the possibility that when newborns were matching the monkey faces and vocalizations, they were doing so on the basis of the synchronous onsets and offsets of stimulus energy in the two modalities. Thus, they repeated the original experiment, except that this time they presented a complex tone signal instead of the natural audible call. Results indicated that despite the absence of the temporal formant structure of the call, and despite the absence of the dynamic relation between the audible stimulus and the visible gesture, the newborns still made intersensory matches. These findings – that synchronous multisensory energy onsets and offsets mediated responsiveness in the newborns – are consistent with previous work (Lewkowicz and Ghazanfar, 2006; Lewkowicz *et al.*, 2008) and suggest that the broad multisensory perceptual tuning found at birth and up to 6 months of age is based on sensitivity to low-level A-V temporal synchrony cues and an insensitivity to higher-level intersensory cues. Furthermore, when these findings are considered together with the finding that starting at 8 months of age infants no longer match non-native faces and vocalization, regardless of whether they are synchronized or not (Lewkowicz and Ghazanfar, 2006; Lewkowicz *et al.*, 2008), they suggest that the decline in infant ability to perceive non-native face–voice relations is not due to a decline in the ability to perceive A-V synchrony. Rather, they suggest that the decline is due to perceptual differentiation and the emergence of the ability to perceive higher-level intersensory relational cues (e.g. affect, gender, identity). In other words, the decline in responsiveness to non-native faces and vocalizations is due to an attentional shift to increasingly more complex types of perceptual cues and their relations and to a specialization for human faces and vocalizations (Lewkowicz and Ghazanfar, 2009).

Response to native and non-native auditory and visual speech

The second question posed earlier was whether the broad multisensory perceptual tuning observed in infant response to non-native faces and vocalizations extends to other domains. To answer this question, Pons *et al.* (2009) conducted a study in which they investigated 6- and 11-month-old infants' ability to match native and non-native auditory and visual speech. They tested this ability at these two ages based on the Lewkowicz and Ghazanfar (2006) findings of multisensory narrowing between 6 and 8 months and the Werker and Tees (1984) findings of narrowing in the speech domain by 11 months. Thus, Pons *et al.* predicted that narrowing of responsiveness to non-native audiovisual speech would occur by 11 months of age. To investigate this possibility, Pons *et al.* tested 6- and 11-month-old Spanish- and English-learning infants' ability to match the visual and auditory phonemes /ba/ and /va/. Because the phonetic distinction between a /b/ and a /v/ does not exist in the Spanish language, it was expected that the Spanish-learning infants would exhibit narrowing but that English-learning infants would not. At the start of the experiment, infants were presented with side-by-side silent facial gestures of a /ba/ and a /va/ produced by the same person and their visual preferences were recorded. Next, infants heard one or the other syllable in the absence of the faces. This was then followed by the silent presentation of the two facial gestures of the /ba/ and /va/ again to determine whether having just heard the syllable would cause the infants to now look longer at the visual gesture that corresponded to the previously heard syllable. As predicted, the 6-month-old but not the 11-month-old Spanish-learning infants matched the visible and audible syllables, whereas both English-learning age-groups matched (Figure 6.2).

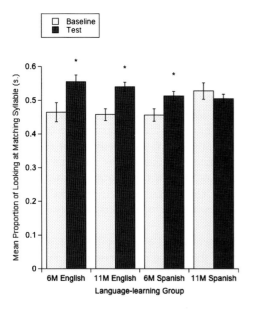

Figure 6.2 Mean proportion of looking time directed at the matching syllable out of the total amount of time of looking time directed at both syllables during the baseline trials, versus the mean proportion of total amount of looking time directed at the matching syllable following familiarization with the audible syllable for each language group. Error bars indicate standard error of the mean and asterisks indicate that looking at the matching syllable following familiarization was significantly greater than in the baseline trials.

Finally, to determine whether the decline in matching observed in the Spanish-learning infants persists into adulthood for native Spanish speakers, and whether such a decline does not occur for native English speakers, adult subjects in each language group were tested in a forced-choice multisensory discrimination task. The subjects were asked to indicate which of the two facial gestures representing the /ba/ and /va/ syllables corresponded to an immediately preceding presentation of one or the other audible syllable. As expected, the Spanish-speaking subjects made random choices whereas the English-learning adults made correct intersensory matches on over 90% of the trials. In sum, the findings from this study indicate that responsiveness to non-native audiovisual speech narrows in infancy just like responsiveness to non-native faces and vocalizations does.

Does multisensory perception narrow in non-human primates?

The evidence for multisensory perceptual narrowing raises interesting questions about the evolution of this developmental process. Naturally, the only way to get at this issue is through comparative studies with non-human primates (hereafter, *primates*). Given that both humans and other extant primates use both facial and vocal expressions as communication signals, it is perhaps not surprising that many primates recognize the correspondence between the visual and auditory components of vocal signals. Macaque monkeys (*Macaca mulatta, Macaca fuscata*), capuchins (*Cebus apella*) and chimpanzees (*Pan troglodytes*) all perceive the A-V coherence of multisensory vocalizations (Ghazanfar and Logothetis, 2003; Izumi and Kojima, 2004; Parr, 2004; Adachi *et al.*, 2006; Jordan *et al.*, 2005; Ghazanfar *et al.*, 2007).

Although the apparent cross-species homology in the multisensory perception of communication signals is interesting, it begs the question of whether the developmental processes leading to the emergence of these abilities are similar or different across species. The most likely answer is that, because the timing of neural development in primates and humans differs (this phenomenon is known as *heterochrony*), the developmental emergence of multisensory perception probably also differs across species. For example, relative to humans, the rate of neural development in Old World monkeys is faster. As a result, monkeys are neurologically precocial, possessing ~65% of their adult brain size at birth whereas human infants only possess ~25% of their adult brain size at birth (Malkova *et al.*, 2006, Sacher and Staffeldt, 1974). In addition, the myelination of fibre tracts is more mature in monkeys than in humans at the same postnatal age (Malkova *et al.*, 2006; Gibson, 1991). Thus, while all the primate species investigated to date show evidence of multisensory perception of social signals, whether or not their underlying developmental mechanisms are similar is not known. In particular, until recently, it has not been known whether the development of multisensory perception in primates is influenced by postnatal experience to the extent that it is in humans and, thus, whether primates go through a process of perceptual narrowing as well. Certainly the neural precocity of non-human primates relative to humans suggests that they may not be so 'open' to the effects of early sensory experience.

If a relatively immature state of neural development leaves a developing human infant more open to the effects of early sensory experience, then it stands to reason that the more advanced state of neural development in monkeys might result in one of two possible outcomes. One is that monkeys may be born with a perceptual system that is already tuned to a much narrower range of sensory input and, thus, may only be able to integrate the faces and vocalization of their own species. This, in turn, would mean that they are relatively closed to the effects of early sensory experience. Conversely, like humans, monkeys may be born with a perceptual system that is tuned to a broad range of sensory input, but because of their advanced state of neural development may not be as susceptible to the effects of early experience and, as a result, may either be permanently tuned to a broader range of sensory input or may require a greater amount of experience before perceptual narrowing exerts its full effects. In either scenario, monkeys would not be expected to exhibit perceptual narrowing effects in the same way and its timing would be different than in humans.

Zangenehpour *et al.* (2009) investigated these possibilities in developing infant vervet monkeys (an Old World monkey species; formerly *Cercopithecus aethiops*, now classified as *Chlorocebus pygerethrus*) by testing their ability to match the faces and vocalizations of another species with which they had no prior experience. The design, procedure and materials of this study were identical to those used in the human infant study described above (Lewkowicz and Ghazanfar, 2006). Thus, infant vervets ranging in age from 23 to 65 weeks (~6–18 months) were tested in a paired-preference task in which they viewed pairs of the same rhesus monkey face producing a coo call on one side and a grunt call on the other side and heard one of the calls at the same time. Even though the vervets had no prior exposure to rhesus monkey faces and vocalizations, they recognized the correspondence between the rhesus monkey faces and vocalizations. Interestingly, however, they did so by looking at the non-matching face for a greater proportion of overall looking time (Figure 6.3A). This is a bit strange, but not uncommon. Typically in this type of experiment (with either adult monkeys or infant humans), an understanding of the correspondence between a face and voice is revealed by the subjects looking longer at the face that matches the voice. However, understanding that correspondence can also be revealed by looking longer at what is odd in the experimental scenario – the non-matching face. Thus, most pertinent to the question of narrowing, the vervets *recognized the correspondence between non-native faces and voices well beyond the age of perceptual narrowing in human infants.*

(A)

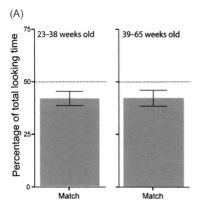

(B)

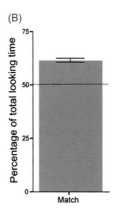

Figure 6.3 Cross-species multisensory matching in young vervet monkeys. (A) The percentage of total time the vervets looked at the matching video in the presence of the naturalistic vocalization at two different ages. (B) The percentage of total time the vervets looked at the matching video in the presence of the tone, collapsed over the two ages (because there was no age difference). Error bars indicate standard error of the mean.

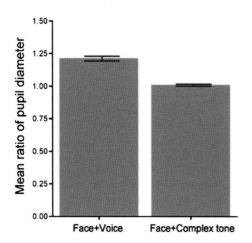

Figure 6.4 The mean ratio of pupil dilation when vervets were looking at a visible call and the matching natural audible call versus dilation when they were looking at the visible call and listening to the tone.

The seemingly 'opposite' pattern of the vervets' responsiveness (i.e. looking more at the non-matching face) turned out to be due to the increased affective salience of the matching face–vocalization combination. That is, it appeared that a combination of a particular facial call (e.g. a coo) and the matching audible coo, or a facial grunt and the matching audible grunt, elicited greater fear than did a combination of the mismatching visible and audible calls. This conclusion was supported by an experiment where the voice was replaced with a complex tone and, thus, the affective value of the audible call was eliminated. In this case, the pattern of looking reversed (Figure 6.3B). Moreover, an analysis of pupillary responses revealed that the vervets' pupils were more dilated (an affective response) when they looked at the matching natural face/vocalization combination than when they looked at the face/tone combination (Figure 6.4). Because the infant vervets in this study exhibited cross-species multisensory matching far later in development than do human infants, the findings suggest either that multisensory perceptual narrowing does not occur in Old World monkeys or that it occurs later in development.

Why do infant vervets continue to match heterospecific faces and voices at a postnatal and neurological age that, relative to human infants, is beyond the time when intersensory perceptual narrowing should have occurred? As suggested earlier, there are two possible explanations. One possibility is that monkeys are less plastic in the same sense that magnitude of sensory cortical plasticity in older animals is not as great as it is in younger animals (Kaas, 1991). According to this latter scenario, vervets may still be sensitive to social experience, but it may take them longer to incorporate the effects of such experience. That is, they may need considerably more postnatal experience to exhibit perceptual narrowing. The other possibility is that they are actually 'stuck' with a broader range of sensitivity because of the more precocial nature of their nervous system. As a result, they can integrate the multisensory social signals of their own species as well as those of other related species.

Perceptual narrowing in monkeys beyond the multisensory domain

The possibility that monkeys are sensitive to social experience, but are slower to incorporate it, is consistent with the development of vocal behaviour in vervets. Their ability to produce vocalizations, use them in appropriate contexts, and respond appropriately to the vocalizations of conspecifics, emerges gradually during the first four years of life (Seyfarth and Cheney, 1986). For example, adult vervets produce 'eagle' alarm calls when they see a Marshall eagle in the sky, causing conspecifics to run for cover (Marshall eagles are one of the few birds of prey that hunt and kill vervets). In contrast, infant vervets produce 'eagle' alarm calls to a very broad class of visual stimuli found in the air above (both harmful and harmless bird species, falling leaves, etc.). When they do so, other vervets tend to ignore these inappropriate calls and, as a result, these vocalizations are not reinforced. Perhaps precisely because they are not reinforced for such inappropriate calls, over time infant vervets learn to limit their alarm calls to the very small set of genuinely dangerous raptor species. In other words, they undergo a form of perceptual narrowing for aerial predators (Seyfarth et al., 1980).

In addition to perceptual narrowing in the vocal domain, vervets also seem to undergo 'narrowing' in their motor response to the alarm calls produced by others. This is generally consistent with the proposals of Holt (1931) and Thelen and Smith (1994). There are two examples of motor narrowing. The first comes from playback experiments showing that very young infants respond to alarm calls by running to their mothers, while slightly older infants often run in such a manner as to *increase* their likelihood of being preyed upon (Seyfarth and Cheney, 1986). It is only when vervets reach 6 months of age that they begin to respond appropriately. In other words, functionally useful patterns of motor output seem to be selected during development from many possible ones. The second example comes from studies showing that there is an apparent decline in infant vervet monkeys' ability to produce 'wrr' vocalizations initially, followed by its return later in life (Hauser, 1989). That is, very young infants produce 'wrrs' that sound adult-like whereas older infants no longer do. Later, they seem to go through a process of learning how to produce an adult-like 'wrr' all over again. Although this developmental pattern is interesting, caution needs to be exercised in its ultimate interpretation because it is very difficult to determine (particularly in field studies) whether a vocalization is truly absent from the repertoire or whether the appropriate context to elicit the vocalizations simply did not arise during the periods when the infant monkeys were observed. If, however, this developmental pattern is confirmed in other studies, it will provide additional evidence of narrowing in the sensorimotor domain. Finally, some neonatal (1- to 3-day-old) rhesus monkeys imitate lip-smacking and tongue-protrusion gestures, but lose this ability after a few days (Ferrari *et al.*, 2006). This is in stark contrast to chimpanzees and humans: both species exhibit neonatal imitation but retain this capacity (i.e. there is no narrowing) (Bard, 2007; Meltzoff and Moore, 1977), again suggesting the importance of neural developmental differences across primate species and individuals (Ferrari *et al.*, 2009).

Earlier we suggested that the absence of narrowing in vervet monkeys may be due either to monkeys being relatively closed to the effects of early experience or to their being broadly tuned to non-native inputs far beyond infancy. There is no doubt that experience plays a role in monkey development as evidenced in studies of Japanese macaques (another Old World monkey species) showing that unisensory and multisensory representations are influenced by the amount of exposure they have to conspecifics and heterospecifics (Adachi *et al.*, 2009; Sugita, 2008). Thus, the effects of experience are there but may play a different role. In addition, our studies of vervets' multisensory responsiveness suggest that they are broadly tuned later into development. Thus, there is evidence for both factors playing a role. Nonetheless, there is a third possibility. That is, the absence of narrowing may be due to a combination of being relatively closed to experience and, at the same time, of being broadly tuned. Monkey studies to date do not provide sufficient information to determine the extent to which the 'slowness' of monkey perceptual and sensorimotor narrowing is due to their precocial (and presumably, less plastic) neural state, their broad tuning, and/or the amount of experience that they may require in the wild to eventually narrow their perceptual tuning and responsiveness. This information is necessary if we are to better understand the relationship between variations in neural plasticity and the amount of exposure that organisms have in their environments. For example, in the case of vervet alarm calls, it is possible that the reason that it takes vervets a long time to learn whether to produce alarm calls in response to aerial predators is because predators occur relatively rarely under natural conditions.

Putative neural mechanisms underlying perceptual narrowing

The kinds of narrowing effects found in the development of speech, face and music perception, as well as in the development of the perception of vocalizing faces, raise obvious questions regarding the putative neural mechanisms that might underlie perceptual narrowing effects. The first and natural inclination is to link 'selectionist' or regressive theories of neural development (Cowan *et al.*, 1984; Low and Cheng, 2006) with the regressive nature of perceptual narrowing. These theories postulate that neural development occurs in two stages, the first of which is the construction of neuronal networks that are initially diffuse and somewhat global in nature. This first stage is constructed through genetic and epigenetic factors and sets up what will ultimately be considered 'exuberant' connections. The second stage involves the selective elimination of some of the connections in this initial network, leading to a more modularized network that is better adapted to mediate mature perceptual and motor skills needed in the current species-typical environment. In this stage, the reshaping (or 'pruning') of the network occurs through the competitive stabilization of some synapses versus others. The competition is decided through experience. This neurodevelopmental scheme fits perfectly with the phenomena related to perceptual narrowing: the initially diffuse network mediates the broad tuning of early infant perception and experience subsequently sculpts the network to generate more finely tuned perceptual capacities.

Although conceptually elegant, there are many problems with the selectionist scheme. First, the basic premise of the theory is that there are extra synapses in the initial developmental state and that this results in extra-exuberant axonal and dendritic arbors. Although this may be true in some cases – the transient connections between the visual cortex and the spinal cord in the developing rodent brain – it is not true for many others (e.g. the axonal arborizations of thalamocortical neurons in layer 4 of the rodent somato-sensory cortex (Agmon et al., 1993) and ferret visual cortex (Crowley and Katz, 1999)). Thus, it is not a general property of brain development and, therefore, its link to cognitive development is weak (Quartz and Sejnowski, 1997). The most damning evidence against the selectionist theories is quite simple: as the brain matures, it grows in size (Purves et al., 1996). This growth is attributable, in part, to neurons increasing their morphological complexity through the elaboration of axonal and dendritic processes. For example, there is an explosive rise in the number of synapses in the perinatal rhesus monkey brain, followed by a long period of time during which a steady number of synapses is present (Bourgeois and Rakic, 1993). In other words, *there is a net gain in synapses over the course of development*. As a result, the narrowing that is observed at the functional level is most likely due to the formation of new neural connections rather than to the loss of neurons and/or their connections through a Darwinian-like process of selective pruning. This is evident, in part, by the increase in white matter over postnatal development (Malkova et al., 2006; Gibson, 1991). What does this all mean for the neural basis of perceptual narrowing? The neural developmental data suggest that perceptual narrowing is more likely the result of a *selective elaboration* of synapses, whose relevance is determined by postnatal experience, rather than the selective pruning of irrelevant synapses.

Conclusions

Experience can have two complementary effects on the development of perceptual functions. On the one hand, it can induce and facilitate the emergence of a particular perceptual function and, through continued exposure to specific sensory input, maintain that function. On the other hand, experience can have the seemingly opposite and seemingly paradoxical effect of leading to a decline in certain early-appearing functions. In reality, however, this process serves to calibrate and fine-tune initially broadly tuned perceptual abilities so that what remains best matches the ecological and species-specific demands of the infant's environment. At the perceptual level, the seemingly paradoxical regressive processes are reflected in a decline in responsiveness to non-native sensory attributes, whereas at the neural level these processes are likely reflected in increasing synaptic connections rather than the selective pruning of an excess of neurons and exuberant connections. Overall, regardless of whether we consider narrowing at the behavioural or neural levels, the effects of early experience can differ for different functions, leading to their emergence at different times in development (heterochrony). For example, narrowing of responsiveness to non-native vowels occurs several months before the narrowing of responsiveness to consonants. Similar developmental heterochronies have been found in the development of multisensory perceptual abilities (Lewkowicz, 2002). This suggests that the specific timing of developmental narrowing of multisensory perceptual abilities also may depend on the nature of the information to be processed, the modality within which it is processed, the specific modalities involved, the timing of sensory system development, the rate of neural development and the ecological context of the organism (i.e. the species involved).

Future challenges and questions

There are two possible ways to achieve perceptual expertise in development. One way is for an organism to begin life with a set of primitive and diffusely organized sensory/perceptual sensitivities that are initially tuned to the perceptual attributes that are native to the organism's typical ecology. As the organism acquires experience with its native world, these sensitivities gradually improve and this ultimately leads to the emergence of perceptual expertise. Underlying this improvement is a progressive developmental process that gradually produces more efficient perceptual detection, discrimination and learning abilities. The other way is for an organism to begin life with a set of primitive and diffusely organized sensory/perceptual sensitivities that are so broadly tuned that initially the organism can respond to native as well as non-native stimulation. As the organism acquires experience with its typical sensory environment, these sensitivities gradually improve but, as we have shown here, their improvement is the result of a complex and, as yet, poorly understood interaction between progressive and regressive developmental processes. Although the regressive processes seem to be paradoxical, they can be particularly useful for organisms with relatively extended ontogenies because the longer the ontogeny the greater the organism's developmental plasticity and ability to profit from early experience. The addition to early development of what appears to be a paradoxical regressive process may reflect an evolutionary adaptation that ended up endowing the young of some species with an added degree of plasticity. Future studies need to investigate the extent to which this is the case and how widespread the role of perceptual narrowing is in the animal kingdom. These studies might be guided by the following specific questions.

1. Is multisensory perceptual narrowing a general developmental phenomenon and, if so, does it occur in other species besides humans?
2. Is the operation of multisensory perceptual narrowing dependent on the ecological milieu of a particular species? In other words, does it only occur in species that are in close proximity to other similar looking species?
3. Does multisensory perceptual narrowing depend on the rate of neural development and/ or the species' ecological context or does one factor dominate the other?
4. Is the process of multisensory perceptual narrowing restricted to auditory-visual pairings or is it general across any combination of modalities?

References

Adachi, I., Kuwahata, H., Fujita, K., Tomonaga, M., & Matsuzawa, T. (2006). Japanese macaques form a cross-modal representation of their own species in their first year of life. *Primates*, **47**: 350–4.

Adachi, I., Kuwahata, H., Fujita, K., Tomonaga, M., & Matsuzawa, T. (2009). Plasticity of the ability to form cross-modal representations in infant Japanese macaques. *Developmental Science*, **12**: 446–52.

Agmon, A., Yang, L. T., O'Dowd, D. K., & Jones, E. G. (1993). Organized growth of thalamocortical axons from the deep tier of terminations into layer IV of developing mouse barrel cortex. *Journal of Neuroscience*, **13**: 5365–82.

Bahrick, L. E., & Lickliter, R. (2000). Intersensory redundancy guides attentional selectivity and perceptual learning in infancy. *Developmental Psychology*, **36**: 190–201.

Bahrick, L. E., Lickliter, R., & Flom, R. (2004). Intersensory redundancy guides the development of selective attention, perception, and cognition in infancy. *Current Directions in Psychological Science*, **13**: 99–102.

Bard, K. (2007). Neonatal imitation in chimpanzees (*Pan troglodytes*) tested with two paradigms. *Animal Cognition*, **10**: 233–42.

Best, C. T., McRoberts, G. W., Lafleur, R., & Silver-Isenstadt, J. (1995). Divergent developmental patterns for infants' perception of two non-native consonant contrasts. *Infant Behavior & Development*, **18**: 339–50.

Birch, H. G., & Lefford, A. (1967). Visual differentiation, intersensory integration, and voluntary motor control. *Monographs of the Society for Research in Child Development*, **32**: 1–87.

Bourgeois, J. P., & Rakic, P. (1993). Changes of synaptic density in the primary visual cortex of the macaque monkey from fetal to adult stage. *Journal of Neuroscience*, **13**: 2801–20.

Chandrasekaran, C., Trubanova, A., Stillittano, S., Caplier, A., & Ghazanfar, A. A. (2009). The natural statistics of audiovisual speech. *PLoS Computational Biology*, 5: el000436.

Cheour, M., Ceponiene, R., Lehtokoski, A., *et al.* (1998). Development of language-specific phoneme representations in the infant brain. *Nature Neuroscience*, **1**: 351–3.

Chiroro, P., & Valentine, T. 1995. An investigation of the contact hypothesis of the own-race bias in face recognition. *The Quarterly Journal of Experimental Psychology A: Human Experimental Psychology*, **48A**: 879–94.

Cowan, W. M., Fawcett, J. W., O'Leary, D. D., & Stanfield, B. B. (1984). Regressive events in neurogenesis. *Science*, **225**: 1258–65.

Crowley, J. C., & Katz, L. C. (1999). Development of ocular dominance columns in the absence of retinal input. *Nature Neuroscience*, **2**: 1125–30.

Ferrari, P., Paukner, A., Ruggiero, A., Darcey, L., Unbehagen, S., & Suomi, S. (2009). Interindividual differences in neonatal imitation and the development of action chains in rhesus macaques. *Child Development*, **80**: 1057–68.

Ferrari, P., Visalberghi, E., Paukner, A., Fogassi, L., Ruggiero, A., & Suomi, S. (2006). Neonatal imitation in rhesus macaques. *PLoS Biology*, **4**: 1501.

Ghazanfar, A., Turesson, H., Maier, J., Van Dinther, R., Patterson, R., & Logothetis, N. (2007). Vocal-tract resonances as indexical cues in rhesus monkeys. *Current Biology*, **17**: 425–30.

Ghazanfar, A. A. (2010). The default mode of primate vocal communication and its neural correlates. In: Naumer, M. J. & Kaiser, J. (Eds.). *Multisensory Object Perception in the Primate Brain*. New York, NY: Springer.

Ghazanfar, A. A., & Logothetis, N. K. (2003). Facial expressions linked to monkey calls. *Nature*, **423**: 937–8.

Gibson, E. J. (1969). *Principles of Perceptual Learning and Development*. New York, NY: Appleton.

Gibson, E. J. (1984). Perceptual development from the ecological approach. In: Lamb, M. E., Brown, A. L. & Rogoff, B. (Eds.). *Advances in Developmental Psychology*. Hillsdale, NJ: Lawrence Erlbaum Associates.

Gibson, K. R. (1991). Myelination and behavioral development: a comparative perspective on questions of neoteny, altriciality and intelligence. In: Gibson, K. R. & Petersen, A. C. (Eds.). *Brain Maturation and Cognitive Development: Comparative and Cross-cultural Perspectives*. New York, NY: Aldine de Gruyter.

Gottlieb, G. (1991). Experiential canalization of behavioral development: results. *Developmental Psychology*, **27**: 35–9.

Gottlieb, G. (1996). Developmental psychobiological theory. In: Cairns, R. B. & Elder, G. H., Jr. (Eds.). *Developmental Science. Cambridge Studies in Social and Emotional Development*. New York, NY: Cambridge University Press.

Hannon, E. E., & Trehub, S. E. (2005a). Metrical categories in infancy and adulthood. *Psychological Science*, **16**: 48–55.

Hannon, E. E., & Trehub, S. E. (2005b). Tuning in to musical rhythms: infants learn more readily than adults. *Proceedings of the National Academy of Science USA*, **102**: 12639–43.

Hauser, M. D. (1989). Ontogenetic changes in the comprehension and production of vervet monkey (*Cercopithecus aethiops*) vocalizations. *Journal of Comparative Psychology*, **103**: 149–58.

Holt, E. B. (1931). *Animal Drive and the Learning Process*. New York, NY: Holt.

Izumi, A., & Kojima, S. (2004). Matching vocalizations to vocalizing faces in a chimpanzee (*Pan troglodytes*). *Animal Cognition*, 7: 179–84.

Jordan, K., Brannon, E., Logothetis, N., & Ghazanfar, A. (2005). Monkeys match the number of voices they hear to the number of faces they see. *Current Biology*, 15: 1034–8.

Kaas, J. H. (1991). Plasticity of sensory and motor maps in adult animals. *Annual Review of Neuroscience*, 5: 137–67.

Kahana-Kalman, R., & Walker-Andrews, A. S. (2001). The role of person familiarity in young infants' perception of emotional expressions. *Child Development*, 72: 352–69.

Kelly, D. J., Quinn, P. C., Slater, A., Lee, K., Ge, L., & Pascalis, O. (2007). The other-race effect develops during infancy: evidence of perceptual narrowing. *Psychological Science*, 18: 1084–9.

Kingsbury, M. A., & Finlay, B. L. (2001). The cortex in multidimensional space: where do cortical areas come from? Commentary. *Developmental Science*, 4: 125–42.

Krubitzer, L. (2007). The magnificent compromise: cortical field evolution in mammals. *Neuron*, 56: 201–08.

Kuhl, P. K., & Meltzoff, A. N. (1982). The bimodal perception of speech in infancy. *Science*, 218: 1138–41.

Kuhl, P. K., Tsao, F. M., & Liu, H. M. (2003). Foreign-language experience in infancy: effects of short-term exposure and social interaction on phonetic learning. *Proceedings of the National Academy of Science USA*, 100: 9096–101.

Kuhl, P. K., Williams, K. A., Lacerda, F., Stevens, K. N., & Lindblom, B. (1992). Linguistic experience alters phonetic perception in infants by 6 months of age. *Science*, 255: 606–08.

Kuo, Z. Y. (1976). *The Dynamics of Behavior Development: An Epigenetic View*. New York, NY: Plenum.

Lewis, M. D. (2000). The promise of dynamic systems approaches for an integrated account of human development. *Child Development*, 71, 36–43.

Lewkowicz, D. J. (2000). The development of intersensory temporal perception: an epigenetic systems/limitations view. *Psychological Bulletin*, 126: 281–308.

Lewkowicz, D. J. (2002). Heterogeneity and heterochrony in the development of intersensory perception. *Cognitive Brain Research*, 14: 41–63.

Lewkowicz, D. J. (2010). Infant perception of audio-visual speech synchrony. *Developmental Psychology*, 46: 66–77.

Lewkowicz, D. J., & Ghazanfar, A. A. (2006). The decline of cross-species intersensory perception in human infants. *Proceedings of the National Academy of Science USA*, 103: 6771–4.

Lewkowicz, D. J., & Ghazanfar, A. A. (2009). The emergence of multisensory systems through perceptual narrowing. *Trends in Cognitive Sciences*, 13: 470–8.

Lewkowicz, D. J., & Kraebel, K. (2004). The value of multimodal redundancy in the development of intersensory perception. In: Calvert, G., Spence, C. & Stein, B. (Eds.). *Handbook of Multisensory Processing*. Cambridge, MA: MIT Press.

Lewkowicz, D. J., & Lickliter, R. (Eds.) (1994). *The Development of Intersensory Perception: Comparative Perspectives*. Hillsdale, NJ: Lawrence Erlbaum Associates, Inc.

Lewkowicz, D. J., Leo, I., & Simion, F. (2010). Intersensory perception at birth: newborns match non-human primate faces & voices. *Infancy*, 15: 46–60.

Lewkowicz, D. J., & Turkewitz, G. (1980). Cross-modal equivalence in early infancy: auditory-visual intensity matching. *Developmental Psychology*, 16: 597–607.

Lewkowicz, D. J., Sowinski, R., & Place, S. (2008). The decline of cross-species intersensory perception in human infants: underlying mechanisms and its developmental persistence. *Brain Research*, 1242: 291–302.

Low, L. K., & Cheng, H. J. (2006). Axon pruning: an essential step underlying the developmental plasticity of neuronal connections. *Philosophical Transactions of the Royal Society of London, Series B, Biological Sciences,* **361**: 1531–44.

Malkova, L., Heuer, E., & Saunders, R. C. (2006). Longitudinal magnetic resonance imaging study of rhesus monkey brain development. *European Journal of Neuroscience,* **24**: 3204–12.

Meltzoff, A. N., & Moore, M. K. (1977). Imitation of facial and manual gestures by human neonates. *Science,* **198**: 75–8.

Munhall, K. G., & Vatikiotis-Bateson, E. (2004). Spatial and temporal constraints on audiovisual speech perception. In: Calvert, G. A., Spence, C. & Stein, B. E. (Eds.). *The Handbook of Multisensory Processes.* Cambridge, MA: MIT Press.

Oyama, S. (2000). *The Ontogeny of Information.* Durham, NC: Duke University Press.

Parr, L. A. (2004). Perceptual biases for multimodal cues in chimpanzee (*Pan troglodytes*) affect recognition. *Animal Cognition,* 7: 171–8.

Pascalis, O., & Kelly, D. J. (2009). The origins of face processing in humans: phylogeny and ontogeny. *Perspectives on Psychological Science,* **4**: 200–09.

Pascalis, O., Haan, M. D., & Nelson, C. A. (2002). Is face processing species-specific during the first year of life? *Science,* **296**: 1321–3.

Pascalis, O., Scott, L. S., Kelly, D. J., *et al.* (2005). Plasticity of face processing in infancy. *Proceedings of the National Academy of Sciences USA,* **102**: 5297–300. Epub 2005 Mar 24.

Patterson, M. L., & Werker, J. F. (1999). Matching phonetic information in lips and voice is robust in 4.5-month-old infants. *Infant Behavior & Development,* **22**: 237–47.

Patterson, M. L., & Werker, J. F. (2002). Infants' ability to match dynamic phonetic and gender information in the face and voice. *Journal of Experimental Child Psychology,* **81**: 93–115.

Patterson, M. L., & Werker, J. F. (2003). Two-month-old infants match phonetic information in lips and voice. *Developmental Science,* **6**: 191–6.

Piaget, J. (1952). *The Origins of Intelligence in Children.* New York, NY: International Universities Press.

Pons, F., Lewkowicz, D. J., Soto-Faraco, S., & Sebastián-Gallés, N. (2009). Narrowing of intersensory speech perception in infancy. *Proceedings of the National Academy of Science USA,* **106**: 10,598–602.

Poulin-Dubois, D., Serbin, L. A., & Derbyshire, A. (1998). Toddlers' intermodal and verbal knowledge about gender. *Merrill-Palmer Quarterly,* **44**: 338–54.

Poulin-Dubois, D., Serbin, L. A., Kenyon, B., & Derbyshire, A. (1994). Infants' intermodal knowledge about gender. *Developmental Psychology,* **30**: 436–42.

Purves, D., White, L. E., & Riddle, D. R. (1996). Is neural development Darwinian? *Trends in Neuroscience,* **19**: 460–4.

Quartz, S. R., & Sejnowski, T. J. (1997). The neural basis of cognitive development: a constructivist manifesto. *Behavioral and Brain Sciences,* **20**: 537–56.

Quinn, P. C., Uttley, L., Lee, K., *et al.* (2008). Infant preference for female faces occurs for same- but not other-race faces. *Journal of Neuropsychology (Special Issue on Face Processing),* **2**: 15–26.

Rosenblum, L. D. (2005). The primacy of multimodal speech perception. In: Pisoni, D. and Remez, R. (Eds.), *Handbook of Speech Perception.* Malden, MA: Blackwell.

Sacher, G. A., & Staffeldt, E. F. (1974). Relation of gestation time to brain weight for placental mammals: implications for the theory of vertebrate growth. *American Naturalist,* **108**: 593–615.

Sangrigoli, S., & De Schonen, S. (2004). Recognition of own-race and other-race faces by three-month-old infants. *Journal of Child Psychology and Psychiatry,* **45**: 1219–27.

Scott, L. S., & Monesson, A. (2009). The origin of biases in face perception. *Psychological Science,* **20**: 676–80.

Seyfarth, R. M., & Cheney, D. L. (1986). Vocal development in vervet monkeys. *Animal Behaviour,* **34**: 1640–58.

Seyfarth, R. M., Cheney, D. L., & Marler, P. (1980). Vervet monkey alarm calls – semantic communication in a free-ranging primate. *Animal Behaviour*, **28**: 1070–94.

Sugita, Y. (2008). Face perception in monkeys reared with no exposure to faces. *Proceedings of the National Academy of Science USA*, **105**: 394–8.

Thelen, E., & Smith, L. B. (1994). *A Dynamic Systems Approach to the Development of Cognition and Action*. Cambridge, MA: MIT Press.

Turkewitz, G., & Kenny, P. A. (1982). Limitations on input as a basis for neural organization and perceptual development: a preliminary theoretical statement. *Developmental Psychobiology*, **15**: 357–68.

Walker-Andrews, A. S. (1986). Intermodal perception of expressive behaviors: relation of eye and voice? *Developmental Psychology*, **22**: 373–7.

Walker-Andrews, A. S. (1997). Infants' perception of expressive behaviors:

differentiation of multimodal information. *Psychological Bulletin*, **121**: 437–56.

Walker-Andrews, A. S., Bahrick, L. E., Raglioni, S. S., & Diaz, I. (1991). Infants' bimodal perception of gender. *Ecological Psychology*, **3**: 55–75.

Walton, G. E., & Bower, T. G. (1993). Amodal representations of speech in infants. *Infant Behavior & Development*, **16**: 233–43.

Werker, J. F., & Tees, R. C. (1984). Cross-language speech perception: evidence for perceptual reorganization during the first year of life. *Infant Behavior & Development*, 7: 49–63.

Werner, H. (1973). *Comparative Psychology of Mental Development*. New York, NY: International Universities Press.

Zangenehpour, S., Ghazanfar, A. A., Lewkowicz, D. J., & Zatorre, R. J. (2009). Heterochrony and cross-species intersensory matching by infant vervet monkeys. *PLoS ONE*, **4**, e4302.

Chapter

7

Cognitive ageing: a positive perspective

Shira Zimerman, Lynn Hasher and David Goldstein

Summary

Ageing is characterized by decreased brain volume, changes in general neuronal efficacy and connectivity and by a number of medical conditions, any or all of which contribute to widely reported age-related declines in cognition and memory. However, a number of findings in the recent literature suggest that the age-related declines do not characterize all of cognition, and that there may even be domains in which older adults outperform younger adults. We offer an overview of this evidence along with a review of ways in which standard laboratory procedures may be biased against older adults, leading to an underestimation of their true abilities, as well as to an overestimation of the magnitude of age differences. These two sections raise questions regarding how brain functions compensate in the face of widely reported neurobiological differences with age, and suggest that the full abilities of older adults have yet to be recognized.

Introduction

On 15 January 2009, Captain Chesley Sullenberger landed an engineless plane in the Hudson River, saving the lives of all 154 people aboard. Similar dramatic rescues of crippled aircraft have occurred over the years and most have had one thing in common: a highly experienced pilot was flying the plane. Professional pilots agreed that it was the training and experience of these pilots that enabled them to respond successfully to the extreme challenges their planes faced. Each of these pilots (Captains C. Sullenberger, G. Hersche, D. M. Cronin) was nearing his 60th birthday, an age at which airline pilots prior to 2007 were required to retire in the United States, and an age which the cognitive gerontology literature considers 'old'. These pilots may have been exceptional individuals (see also reports of the cognitive functioning of a 112–115-year-old woman; den Dunnen *et al.*, 2008), but it is nevertheless worth noting at this point that the vast majority of research on ageing and cognition (e.g. Park *et al.*, 2002; Salthouse, 2004; Craik & Salthouse, 2008) and on the underlying neuroanatomy (e.g. Raz *et al.*, 2005) and neurofunctioning (Grady, 2008) reports age-related declines from young adulthood to an age range that includes these pilots.

How are we to reconcile the dramatic skills of these pilots with a behavioural and neuropsychological literature reporting declines? To address this question, we review surprising data showing that, relative to young adults, older adults show spared (and occasionally even superior) cognitive functioning. We also review evidence suggesting that standard laboratory

---

The Paradoxical Brain, ed. Narinder Kapur. Published by Cambridge University Press. © Cambridge University Press 2011.

procedures may be biased against older adults, leading to what may well be an overestimation of age differences in cognition and memory. Taken together, these two sections suggest the possibility that the full cognitive abilities of older adults have yet to be recognized.

In the behavioural and neurocognitive literatures, one goal is to compare the performance of healthy, well-educated older adults to that of healthy well-educated younger adults.[1] When age differences are reported (and they most often are), their magnitude is presumed to be even greater in groups of older adults who are less healthy and less well educated (i.e. who have lower levels of cognitive reserve; see Stern, 2002, 2009). For example, younger adults are widely reported to be faster than older adults, to have better episodic and autobiographical memory, better problem-solving skills and superior language comprehension (see Craik and Salthouse, 2008). In addition, the neuroanatomical literature reports that older adults have diminished frontal lobes, hippocampal shrinkage, thinning of grey matter and reductions in white matter integrity (Persson et al., 2006; Raz et al., 2004, 2005), all areas involved in memory and cognition. In addition to structural changes, there are also age-related changes in the brain's vasculature system (e.g. Hillary and Biswal, 2007).

The literature using functional imaging techniques reports that when performing a cognitive task, older adults may have less activity in some brain regions, along with over-recruitment of others, relative to young adults (for review see e.g. Grady, 2008). Broader areas of neural activation among older adults are often thought to reflect a compensatory mechanism in response to decreases in neural networks' effectiveness (e.g. Cabeza, 2002). These findings, coupled with negative Western stereotypes about ageing and cognition (Hess, 2006), make it quite unsurprising that it is often even difficult to get papers published that report no age differences (Rose Zacks 2007, personal communication). Nonetheless, there are such findings, and the contrast between these behavioural results on the one hand and the neurocognitive findings on the other forms the basis of the paradox addressed in this chapter[2] (see also Goldberg, 2005).

The first section of this chapter highlights findings of preserved and even superior performance by older as compared to younger adults. For example, older adults outperform younger adults on general knowledge and vocabulary tests (e.g. Park et al., 2002), demonstrate superior motion discrimination abilities (which may well be a result of poor centre-surround discrimination; Betts et al. 2005; Tadin and Blake, 2005) and, in at least some cases, make better decisions compared to young adults (e.g. Kim and Hasher, 2005). In addition, older adults generally report being in a better mood than young adults (e.g. Thomas and Hasher, 2006) and rate their job satisfaction more highly than younger adults (Clark et al., 1996) which, given life facts, suggests superior emotional regulation (see Charles and Carstensen, 2010). Findings from longitudinal studies also suggest that

---

[1] There are inherent problems in making comparisons between different age cohorts due to factors such as differential cultural exposure, and the artefactual findings that may sometimes ensue (see e.g. Nilsson et al., 2009). However, efforts are made to rule out confounding variables and currently the cross sectional research paradigm is more prevalent than longitudinal studies in cognitive ageing research [for examples of the latter, see e.g. Dixon and deFrias, 2004 (The Victoria Longitudinal Study); Finkel and Pedersen, 2004 (The Swedish Adoption/Twin Study of Ageing); Lovden et al., 2004 (The Berlin Aging Study); Nilsson et al., 2004 (The Betula cohort study); Yu et al., 2009 (The Seattle Longitudinal Study)].

[2] One longitudinal study reports brain changes over an 8-year period without associated behavioural changes, in itself a paradox (Beason-Held et al., 2008a, 2008b).

subjective well-being remains relatively stable into old age, despite mental and physical declines (e.g. Kunzmann *et al.*, 2000).

The second section of this chapter highlights findings suggesting that typical laboratory experiments tend to underestimate older adults' true abilities, resulting in overestimates of the magnitude of age differences between young and older adults. For example, despite their generally positive affect, older adults tend to feel more anxious regarding their cognitive abilities than the university students to whom they are being compared. Stress reactions to testing situations are known to negatively affect cognition (Lupien *et al.*, 2007). In addition, older adults are on a different circadian cycle than young adults (see May *et al.*, 1993, 2005a; Rowe *et al.*, 2009) and experiments that use ad-lib testing schedules may well advantage young adults and disadvantage older adults. Furthermore, the standard laboratory practice of using materials that have no particular interest for older adults may also lead to an overestimation of their cognitive and memory difficulties (see e.g. Castel, 2005; Rahhal *et al.*, 2002).

It is important to note that we do not make the claim that there are no age differences in cognitive functioning. As mentioned above, ageing is by and large a negative process, partly due to deleterious brain changes, and partly due to the medical conditions such as vascular disease, cancer and diabetes that often accompany ageing. These conditions may have direct, adverse effects on brain function or may give rise to conditions such as depression and high levels of stress, which also affect cognitive efficiency. Different cognitive problems such as psychomotor slowing, reduced episodic and autobiographical memory, and impaired executive functions are, as a rule, more common in the elderly (see Craik and Salthouse, 2008 for a review). Nonetheless, we do suggest that age differences may be exaggerated and that the skills that older adults actually do have may not be a central focus of research, resulting in a skewed picture of cognitive ageing.

Positive aspects of cognitive ageing

(a) Memory functioning

One of the most common complaints among older adults is that their memory is 'not what it used to be' and numerous studies report age-related memory problems across a range of tasks, including episodic memory (memory for events), working memory (holding information in mind while mentally manipulating it or other information), and source memory (e.g. remembering how or when one learned a known fact; see Craik, 2002; Balota *et al.*, 2000 for reviews). However, ageing does not impair all memory functions uniformly. For example, one of the earliest findings regarding memory and ageing suggests that age-related memory impairments are greater in recall tasks than in recognition tasks (e.g. Schonfield and Robertson 1966; Craik and McDowd, 1987). Craik (1983) suggested that recall and recognition differ in the amount of effortful 'self-initiated' processing involved, with recall tasks requiring more effortful processing than recognition since, in the latter, mental operations are driven largely by the external stimuli associated with the task itself. In recall, by comparison, very few retrieval cues are provided and the participant must necessarily initiate demanding mental operations. Supportive findings were reported by Nyberg *et al.* (2003), who studied the memory performance of 925 community-dwelling individuals ranging in age from 35 to 80. Both recall and recognition memory tests were administered (e.g. face recognition, item and source recall) and age-related memory deficits were more pronounced for recall than for recognition (although differences in recognition may appear when task difficulty increases, e.g. Prull *et al.*, 2006). These findings suggest that the age-related recall deficit is not due to a failure to encode critical information, or to differential decay rates over time, but instead they point directly to age-related retrieval problems.[3]

Another common distinction in memory performance refers to episodic memory (or memory for specific events) in contrast to semantic memory (or memory for general knowledge, facts and schemas). While age differences are commonly found in the episodic domain (at least when recall is the measure), the semantic memory domain remains intact or even improves as we age. In the Nyberg *et al.* (2003) study, semantic memory tests (e.g. vocabulary and general knowledge) were administered along with episodic memory tasks (e.g. face/name recognition, item/source recall). Overall, the results support the view that episodic memory is more age-sensitive than is semantic memory, with older adults showing generally preserved performance on semantic memory tasks reflecting their accumulated knowledge about different facts and events, and the wider experience one gains across a lifetime (see also Goldberg, 2005).

Another way to think of different memory domains is to focus on what may be two separate routes for retrieval: a deliberate or intentional one, as in explicit memory tasks, and an unintentional one, as when one's behaviour is triggered by a cue without one's knowledge or awareness (or, implicit memory). When implicit memory measures are used, the ageing picture is quite different, with older adults usually showing intact performance (see Balesteros *et al.*, 2009; Jennings and Jacoby, 1993; Light *et al.*, 2000). In addition, recent research suggests older adults are more likely than young adults to rely on implicit memory or contextually driven, automatic retrieval (e.g. Spieler *et al.*, 2006). For example, Rowe *et al.* (2006) showed that older adults implicitly acquire information in one situation and tacitly use it in another, resulting in superior performance in the second situation by older, as compared to younger, adults. In this study, young and older adults were first shown overlapping pictures and letter strings (words and nonwords) and were told to press a button whenever the same picture was shown twice in a row. They were also instructed to ignore the distracting verbal items. After a brief filled interval, memory for the distracting words was tested implicitly with a word fragment completion test (e.g. a_i_g for ageing) which included a number of fragments that could be solved with distracting words from the previous task. As shown in Figure 7.1, priming scores (the difference between the proportion of target word fragments correctly solved and the baseline completion rates for those fragments) were substantial for older adults, but not for young adults. Moreover, reliable age differences were found only in the afternoon, while performance of young and older participants did not differ in the morning. (We elaborate on the time of day differences seen in this figure in a later section.)

These findings corroborate the notion that older adults are more likely to encode both relevant and irrelevant information possibly due to impaired inhibitory mechanisms which are critical for selection, while younger adults are better able to ignore/suppress distractors both at encoding and retrieval (e.g. Healey *et al.*, 2008, 2010). Other work using this and related procedures also suggests that older adults differentially rely on previous experience, without being aware of doing so, to a greater extent than younger adults (e.g. Kim

---

[3] Elsewhere, we have attributed the source of age-related retrieval deficits to two factors that can be seen as part of inhibitory deficits: encoding too much information in the first instance, including irrelevant information, and the much reduced ability of older adults to suppress competitors at retrieval (see Campbell *et al.*, 2010; Ikier and Hasher, 2006; Ikier *et al.*, 2008).

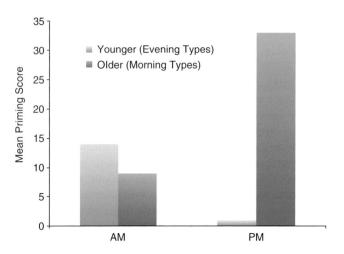

Figure 7.1 Mean priming scores as a function of age and testing time. The morning (a.m.) is peak time for older adults and off-peak time for young adults, and the evening (p.m.) is the reverse. Adapted from Rowe *et al.*, 2006.

et al., 2007). According to views suggesting that implicit memory and learning processes are part of the cognitive substrate of social intuition (e.g. Lieberman, 2000), we would expect that intact implicit processes will result in improved performance on complex tasks such as decision-making and emotional regulation, and indeed – as will be seen in the following section – there are cases in which older adults show improved performance in those domains compared to younger adults.

(b) Mood and emotions

Mood and emotions are not widely considered as components of cognitive functioning and neither is the ability to regulate emotion. As it happens, recent work suggests that these factors likely play a role in contributing to age differences in cognition (e.g. Charles and Carstensen, 2010). In fact, social, familial and personal factors may be just as relevant as biological ones in determining cognitive performance.

There are certainly reasons to expect that well-being should decline as people grow old. Physical health declines and the span of the future shortens. Opportunities for satisfying occupational activities are limited, income may diminish, loved ones die, social circles shrink. Yet research suggests that many older adults are in a more positive mood than younger adults (Mather and Carstensen, 2005). In addition, older adults sometimes show positivity biases in memory that manifest themselves in a variety of ways, including selectively remembering a higher proportion of happy rather than sad or disturbing materials (Charles *et al.*, 2003; see also Thomas and Hasher, 2006); older adults recall negative emotions less intensely, and remember past choices more positively (Mather and Johnson, 2000). These biases may be the result of elevated mood, or may contribute to the maintenance of elevated mood status, or both. It is important to note at this point that the increased positivity with ageing has been demonstrated mainly among healthy, well-educated, middle-class individuals in western countries (see Stone *et al.*, 2010 for data from a very large sample of US citizens). To what degree this finding (and others) will generalize (see Henrich *et al.*, 2010) to others with poorer health and less education and other resources, not to mention to those from non-Western cultures, remains to be seen.

An important aspect of well-being is emotional regulation, a domain in which older adults outperform young adults (Charles and Carstensen, 2010). Compared with younger adults, older adults report that they focus more on self-control of their emotions and rate their emotion regulation skills as better than young adults do. For example, when dealing with an upsetting interpersonal situation, older adults report being less likely to engage in negative, destructive behavioural responses such as shouting or name calling and better able to 'pick their battles', choosing to first wait and see if things improve (Birditt and Fingerman, 2005). Of course, it might also be the case that older adults avoid conflicts that they may lose due to limited physical and mental resources (but see Grossmann et al., 2010).

In addition, the goal of regulating emotion may well underlie the differential attention that older adults pay to positive as compared to negative events and information (see also Goeleven et al., 2010; Mather and Carstensen, 2005). A study supporting this possibility (Isaacowitz et al., 2006) used eye-tracking measures to assess attentional preference toward faces; young adults preferred fearful faces, whereas older adults preferred happy faces. This is consistent with the suggestion that the age-related attentional preference serves a motivational purpose: to keep negatively valenced information out of the 'spotlight' of attention and to maintain a focus on positive information (but see Murphy and Isaacowitz, 2008).

It is clear that older adults recognize the importance of positive information in their lives. For example, Sullivan et al. (2010) demonstrated that older adults included a greater proportion of positive words when retelling a story to a 75-year-old listener than when retelling the story to a 25-year-old listener. Young adults did not appreciate this lifespan change, as their retellings included the same proportion of positive words whether the listener was 25 or 75. This pattern of storytelling suggests that older adults are more sensitive to their audience's interest than are younger adults, a finding also reported by Adams et al. (2002), here with respect to telling stories to young adult versus child listeners.

Neuroimaging data demonstrate that both younger and older adults recruit the amygdala and the orbito-frontal cortex during the successful encoding of emotional information (Kensinger and Schacter, 2008). In other words, the same neuroanatomical structures are used over the adult's life span, suggesting that the emotional memory network is preserved across age groups. Another study (Williams et al., 2006) revealed that age-related improvement in emotional stability is predicted by a shift in activity toward greater medial prefrontal control over negative emotional input and less control over positive input. In addition, there are data to suggest that neural activity to negative images declines linearly with age, while activity toward positive images is invariant across the adult lifespan (Kisely et al., 2007).

These findings raise the question of whether there is an age-related loss of cognitive control in general (as many views in cognitive neuroscience assume; e.g. Friedman et al., 2009), or rather, whether age differences lie in the use of those mechanisms, with younger adults invoking them for cognitive targets and older adults invoking them for emotional targets, as the views of Carstensen et al. (2003) might suggest. If so, this argument suggests that there is no age-related decline in control mechanisms themselves, merely differences in the targets to which those mechanisms are applied. These differences could well be thought of as adaptive to changing life circumstances or to the ecological niches in which individuals of different ages live (Baltes, 1997).

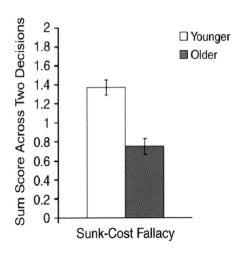

Figure 7.2 Mean sunk-cost fallacy scores by age group. Scores were computed by comparing each subject's decisions for the investment and no-investment analogues within each pair: if a subject indicated more time for the investment than for the no-investment analogue, a score of 1 was assigned to indicate the fallacy occurred; otherwise, the score was 0. Scores from the two pairs of vignettes were summed (range: 0–2). Adapted from Strough *et al.* (2008).

(c)   Decision-making and problem-solving

Whereas advancing age is associated with cognitive decline, such declines do not readily translate into impaired everyday problem-solving. In fact, the recent literature includes a number of findings suggesting that some decision-making abilities are preserved or even improved with advanced age. For example, older adults seem to be less susceptible to classic decision biases than younger adults. Consider the 'sunk-cost fallacy', or the tendency to continue with an action once an investment has been made, a fallacy widely shown by young adults and likely adopted in order to avoid losses. Strough *et al.* (2008) argued that young adults (on whom this large literature is based) show both loss aversion and the sunk-cost fallacy because of their general negative bias. Older adults, by contrast, do not share this negativity bias – and so should not show the sunk-cost fallacy. To test this, younger and older adults were presented with two pairs of vignettes. In each pair, one involves an investment and one does not. For example, the investment vignette stated 'you paid $10.95 to see a movie on pay TV. After 5 minutes, you are bored and the movie seems pretty bad'. In the no-investment analogue, the sentence about the payment was removed. After reading each vignette, participants decided on their future time investment (e.g. stop watching entirely, watch for 20 more min, watch until the end). As shown in Figure 7.2, younger adults were willing to make a larger future investment in response to the vignette involving an investment compared to the vignette involving no investment. However, older adults chose to make a similar future investment regardless of whether the vignette includes an investment or not. In other words, older adults were less likely than younger adults to commit the sunk-cost fallacy, potentially tied to their greater knowledge of their own values. This suggests as well that older adults' loss function may be quite different from the one reported by Kahneman and Tversky (1979), who argued that, generally, losses tend to have a bigger impact on behaviour than gains, again based largely on findings from young adult samples.

Another demonstration of more rational choices made by older adults compared to college students refers to making more 'regular' decisions. A regular decision occurs when you do not change your choice between two options (white bread vs. whole wheat, or chocolate vs. vanilla ice cream), when a third option (a bagel in the one example, and strawberry ice cream in the other) is added. There is a rich literature showing that across a range of choices, young adults are 'irregular', in that they switch from, say, white bread in the pair-wise choice to whole wheat in the three-option choice. Regularity is widely assumed to be a necessary condition for rational choice (Sen, 1971). Tentori *et al.* (2001) found virtually no sign of irregular choice by seniors in any of three experiments in which people have to pick a supermarket discount card. They suggest that everyday experience in the marketplace teaches a person to beware of contextual effects in judging the value of merchandise. Older adults benefit from greater experience and thus manifest more regular choice. Indeed, in this study, seniors demonstrated more judgemental wisdom than students. In a following study, Kim and Hasher (2005) demonstrated that older adults showed consistent choice both in the familiar context of grocery shopping and in the unfamiliar context of earning extra credit in a university course, while younger adults showed consistent choice only in the familiar context of earning extra credit. In other words, while younger adults chose consistently only in familiar contexts, older adults demonstrated consistent choices in familiar as well as unfamiliar contexts.

In addition to evidence of some spared decision-making skills, there is also evidence that older adults have spared and even superior problem solving skills. For example, a study by Blanchard-Fields *et al.* (2007) reported that older adults were more effective than younger adults when solving hypothetical interpersonal problems (see also the wisdom work of Baltes and colleagues, e.g. Baltes and Smith, 2008). As well, there is now evidence that across all education, social class and IQ levels (in a United States sample), greater age is associated with greater wisdom in both interpersonal and societal conflict domains (Grossmann *et al.*, 2010).

Another surprising source of superior problem solving by older adults is tied to their greater distractability. Kim *et al.* (2007) explored whether or not distraction that disrupts performance in one situation results in enhancement on a subsequent problem-solving task. They found that older adults solved more verbal problems using previous distraction than younger adults, consistent with the idea that older adults transfer past knowledge to new situations, possibly automatically. These findings are consistent with the view that younger adults are better able to ignore distracting information compared to older adults. Alternatively, if young adults do encode the distraction, retrieval cues do not appear to spontaneously trigger the past, unless perhaps the relevance of that information is pointed out to them. In the studies above, older adults appear to make decisions and solve problems better than young adults. This might be based on greater knowledge about their priorities (see Kim *et al.*, 2008) than is the case for many younger adults. Alternatively, given older adults' reliance on automatic processes, they may have an increased propensity to rely on heuristic or intuitive information processing, coupled with younger adults' greater reliance on analytic, systematic information processing (e.g. Kim *et al.*, 2005). It is well known that there are many decision situations in which intuitive or heuristic processing yields effective solutions (e.g. Gigerenzer and Selten, 2001).

There is also recent evidence (Mikels *et al.*, 2010) that older adults are more effective decision-makers when they approach a problem focusing on emotional responses instead of details. This study asked both older and younger adults to make decisions about health care options. Younger adults made better decisions when focusing on details rather than on emotions while older adults did better while focusing on emotions rather than on details – a finding that suggests that control processes might be spared with age, but focused on different aspects of information than is the case for young adults (see also May *et al.*, 2005b; Rahhal *et al.*, 2002).

(d)   Creativity

For decades, art critics agreed that the quality and importance of Pablo Picasso's work declined as he aged. However, a 2009 exhibition in New York of his late paintings and prints suggested the need for a revision: Picasso's last period was described as a demonstration of his constant invention of the new, with the conclusion that 'in the main Picasso only got better' (Smith, 2009). Examples of late creativity come from the fine arts (e.g. Cezanne, Titian), music (e.g. Handel, Bach, Verdi) and film (e.g. John Ford, Clint Eastwood, Alfred Hitchcock). However, there is not a large literature on creativity and the elderly (see e.g. Runco, 2007). The little empirical work that has been done on creativity in the elderly has relied primarily on longitudinal studies using psychometric tests of divergent thinking. These studies invariably suggest that creativity reaches its peak in mid-adulthood and declines thereafter (e.g. McCrae *et al.*, 1987). The historiometric approach, which relies heavily on case studies of eminent individuals, has yielded a comparable conclusion, namely, that – depending on the discipline – creativity peaks anywhere from the third to the sixth decade of life (Simonton, 1990).

Nevertheless, large individual differences in creativity over the life span have been reported in the psychological literature as well as in other social sciences and the human-ities. Simonton (2004), for example, has argued that highly creative individuals are charac-terized by high rates of productivity. This productivity has a 'constant probability of success' over time, meaning that creative contributions are as likely to occur at older ages as at younger ones. Some investigators have proposed the existence of an 'old age style' characterized by a 'summing up' or integration of ideas from earlier work (Lehman, 1953; Sternberg and Lubart, 2001; see also Said, 2006). Galenson (2005) has argued that there are two types of creative artists, conceptualists and experimentalists. The latter show late peaking creativity, consistent with the idea that for some, creativity is not only maintained in old age, but is enhanced (see Simonton, 2007 for a critique of this view). In sum, it seems clear that among *some* creative writers, artists and composers a unique type of creative output occurs in old age and further, that a decline in creativity with age is not inevitable (Galenson, 2005; Lindauer, 2003).

Summary

In this section we reviewed findings suggesting preserved and even superior performance of older adults across a range of cognitive abilities including decision making, emotional regulation and some aspects of memory retrieval. This review stands in sharp contrast to the typically reported findings in the cognitive ageing literature (see Figure 7.3), in which younger adults are virtually always at an advantage relative to older adults (but contrast these findings with those reported in a longitudinal study of memory by Rönnlund *et al.*, 2005). In the second section of this chapter we will address the gap between these two sets of findings.

Measuring older adults' cognition: methodological biases

As many have suggested (e.g. Lupien *et al.*, 2007; Zacks and Hasher, 2006), typical laboratory tasks may systematically underestimate the true abilities of older adults. For example, testing in a university-based laboratory setting may be differentially disruptive to older adults, whose performance in a more familiar setting may well be better than in the

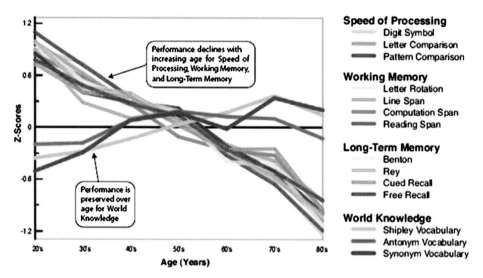

Figure 7.3 Cross-sectional ageing data showing behavioural performance on measures of speed of processing, working memory, long-term memory and world knowledge. All measures of cognitive function show decline with age, except for world knowledge. Adapted from Park and Reuter-Lorenz (2009).

laboratory. Consider the example of prospective memory, or memory for future intentions (e.g. when we need to remember to turn off the stove in an hour, or to make an appointment with our physician to get the latest test results). A meta-analysis of age differences in prospective memory studies (Henry *et al.*, 2004) revealed that although in laboratory settings younger participants often outperform older participants, in naturalistic conditions older participants appear able to not only compensate for any age-related decline in basic processing mechanisms but also to substantially outperform their younger counterparts (see also Bailey *et al.*, 2010). This may reflect older adults' experience with time management, belief in their memory's fallibility, fewer distractions and possibly greater opportunity to plan how they will remember to execute the tasks (see also Kvavilashvili and Fisher, 2007).[4] Spared functioning of prospective memory is especially surprising in the light of the reported age-related declines in executive functions, including planning (Sorel and Pennequin, 2008).

There are several other factors that can account for the discrepancy between older adult's poor performances in the laboratory and their improved performance in their daily lives and we address these next.

(a)   Stress and cognition

Extensive research documents that the experience of stress can impair performance on a range of cognitive tasks (for review see Lupien *et al.*, 2007), and numerous studies demonstrate that under stress both younger and older adults tend to show reduced cognitive performance. To take an example, Neupert *et al.* (2006) investigated the

---

[4] We are unaware of published research in which older adults have been systematically tested in familiar environments, such as their homes or in senior centres that are attended for social purposes, but such a project is ongoing in Montreal (S. Lupien, personal communication).

relationship between stressors and memory failures in a naturalistic setting via a daily diary study of 333 older adults. On days when people experienced stressors, particularly interpersonal stressors, they were more likely to report memory failures. In addition, evidence of the negative impact of stress on cognitive functioning in middle-aged and older adults can be seen in research with an unusual sample of older adults, those giving care to seriously ill family members (Mackenzie et al., 2007, 2009).

Lupien et al. (2007) proposed three important psychological determinants of a stressful situation – novelty, unpredictability and lack of control over the situation – and argued that participating in a cognitive study may include all three factors for older, but not for younger, adults. Young participants in most studies are university students tested in their own departments, often after learning about cognitive experiments and taking part in a number of them. They are familiar with the psychological and social setting of university life and so may likely have a sense of control in the situation. For older adults, however, the situation is different. The need to navigate their way to the university, enter an unfamiliar building, and meet with new people who are going to test their 'cognitive functions', constitutes the perfect cocktail of novelty, unpredictability and uncontrollability that defines a stressful circumstance. In addition, there is evidence that older adults are significantly more reactive to the testing environment than are their younger counterparts (Kudielka et al., 2004), making older adults even more prone to feel stressed when participating in experiments.[5]

Stress can be triggered by subtle cues in the experimental setting. One example for a cue that may well evoke stress among older but not younger adults is the examiner, who is most often a university student. As a result, younger participants will be tested by a person who is similar in age and background to the students they are testing, but of course quite different from those of older adults. We are unaware of studies that have manipulated the age of the examiner directly, but there is evidence that older adults vary their responses considerably to audiences of different ages (e.g. Adams et al., 2002) just as young children do (e.g. Zigler et al., 1973). These findings suggest the possibility that reducing stress responses created by unfamiliar testing circumstances may well reduce age-related differences in cognitive performance (Lupien et al., 2007).

In addition, evidence from the stereotype threat literature is also relevant here. This phenomenon occurs when an individual is a member of a negatively stereotyped group (as older adults are vis-a-vis memory performance) and when the stereotype is triggered subtly in the context of an experiment. Negative stereotypes of ageing that are held by both young and older adults include perceptions of slowing, decreased competence and increasing forgetfulness (e.g. Kwong See and Heller, 2004). Older adults have more negative beliefs about memory than do younger adults: they believe they will do less well on memory tasks (Berry et al., 1989), they feel their memory will worsen with increasing age and they report less control over memory function as they age (Lachman et al., 1995). Furthermore, recent evidence demonstrates that older adults overestimate the degree to which their memories have actually declined over time (Hultsch et al., 2009). It is not surprising, then, that triggering a stereotype of ageing can at least modestly lower the performance of

---

[5] In this light, it is interesting to speculate that older participants in longitudinal studies may be less stressed than those in cross-sectional studies, in part because participants in those studies will likely have greater knowledge of laboratory settings and tasks than will participants in cross sectional studies.

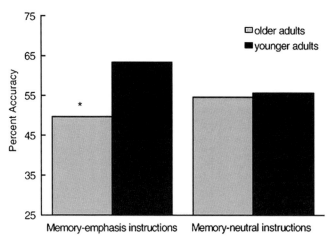

Figure 7.4 Memory accuracy as function of age and instructions type. Asterisk denotes a significant difference ($p < .001$) in accuracy between older and younger adults. Adapted from Rahhal *et al.* (2001).

older adults, in the same way as triggering a negative stereotype of other targeted groups has been shown elsewhere (e.g. Spencer *et al.*, 1999).

How might a stereotype be triggered in a typical cognitive psychology laboratory? There are many possibilities, since the literature suggests that triggers are subtle. These might include using testers who are the age of the grandchildren of older participants, and instructions that include extensive use of the word 'memory'. With respect to the latter suggestion, in one study (Rahhal *et al.*, 2001) younger and older adults viewed trivia sentences such as 'about 4 hours are required to boil an ostrich egg'. During the learning phase participants read each statement, and then, for some sentences, received feedback that the fact was true or false. Their knowledge was tested in a final phase. Prior to the task, one group received 'memory emphasis' instructions while a second group was given 'memory neutral' instructions, which warned of a test but avoided use of the word 'memory' in the instructions. As shown in Figure 7.4, younger adults outperformed older adults when the task used traditional memory instructions, replicating a large body of research that shows age related differences in performance on explicit memory tasks. However, when the instructions de-emphasized memory, older and younger adults did not differ in their performance on the identical explicit memory test. The lack of age differences on this memory task is in sharp contrast with the large cognitive ageing literature on memory.

These data suggest how small details in a study (e.g. the use of a stereotyped word and possibly of a young tester) can influence older adults' performance. It is possible that merely having the experiment conducted in a university setting (i.e. having the older participants surrounded mainly by young college students) might implicitly prime older adults with the concept of their age, which in turn can trigger a stereotype threat response, lowering performance.

Arbitrary materials and tasks

Laboratory memory tasks often include arbitrary materials that lack meaning (e.g. a random list of words). While such tasks may be close to the academic lives of the university students to whom older adults are typically compared, there is evidence that the poor

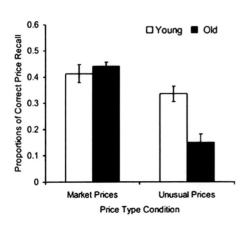

Figure 7.5 The proportions of correct price recall for the market value and unusual priced items by younger and older adults. Error bars represent standard error of the mean. Adapted from Castel (2005).

performance of older adults on cognitive tasks can sometimes be the result of lack of interest in the task. Indeed, when the information to be learned makes sense, has meaning and/or is related to one's goals, age differences are diminished. For example, Castel (2005) tested older and younger adults' memory for grocery price information. Participants studied prices for grocery items that were either priced at market value (e.g. butter $2.99) or not (soup $14.39). When asked to recall the prices, younger adults displayed better recall performance for unrealistic prices than older adults, but, as can be seen in Figure 7.5, differences disappeared for realistic prices. In addition, both groups were equally accurate at remembering the general price range of the items. These findings stand in stark contrast to the memory literature using arbitrary materials.

A second line of work has yielded similar findings (May et al., 2005b; Rahhal et al., 2002). These investigators gave participants materials that can be presented as emotionally meaningful (whether food is safe to eat or not) versus neutral (the same food, located on the left or right side of a table). When tested for the arbitrary knowledge (location), young adults showed an advantage. When tested for the meaningful knowledge (food safety), age differences disappeared. This work can be thought of as testing source memory and, as such, is consistent with the Castel findings, in that source for meaningful materials can be remembered quite well by older adults.

A similar example offers supportive findings using two variants of a working memory task. As mentioned before, ageing is typically associated with a deficit in working memory, which is virtually always demonstrated using tests of memory for neutral (i.e. nonemotional) verbal and visual information. In a study by Mikels et al. (2005), age differences in working memory were measured using emotional material, thought to be goal-relevant for both age groups. The modified task was modeled after standard delayed-response tasks used to test working memory. It required that participants experience a negative or positive feeling elicited by a visual image, maintain that feeling during a delay when the image was no longer present, and compare it with a feeling from a second image. By contrast with a large literature on working memory (e.g. see Lustig et al., 2001), there were no age differences in working memory scores for the emotionally relevant materials.

People develop expertise with time and experience, and there are some studies demonstrating age-related sparing on tasks on which individuals have substantial experience, often attained over many decades. In a recent study, Nunes and Kramer (2009) examined whether decades of experience in air traffic control would enable older controllers to perform at high levels of proficiency. Both young and old controllers and non-controllers performed standard traffic control tasks. The authors observed experience-based sparing on simulated air traffic control tasks, with the sparing being most evident on the more complex air traffic control tasks. These results suggest that given substantial experience, older adults may be quite capable of performing at high levels of proficiency even on fast-paced, demanding real-world tasks. There are of course, many studies that do not show such sparing, although they often show ways in which older experts can compensate to some degree for their losses (Morrow et al., 1994).

One reading of the literature suggests, therefore, that when testing is adjusted to the interests, knowledge, goals or values of older adults, some age-related differences in memory are at least minimized, if not abolished.

(c)   Time-of-day effects

There is considerable evidence, from samples taken around the world, that older and younger adults are on different circadian (approximately 24-hour) arousal cycles. Older adults tend to be morning-type people (i.e. they wake early and their peak mental and physical performance is in the morning) while young adults are likely to reach their peak later in the day (e.g. May et al., 1993; Yoon et al., 2000). Failing to take this difference into account when testing participants can have substantial effects on performance on a range of cognitive tasks, including for example those measuring fluid intelligence (Goldstein et al., 2007). In addition, there is a substantial literature showing large differences across the day on a variety of memory tasks, with morning-type older adults' performance declining from morning to afternoon and evening-type young adults' performance improving across the day. Among these findings are ones showing that susceptibility to interference (a key process that disrupts retrieval, see note 1) varies across the day (Hasher et al., 2002). Furthermore, attentional control, executive control and motor control also vary across the day, in a manner that is different for younger and older adults (Goldstein et al., 2007). Conducting studies beginning in the late morning or early afternoon (which is frequently the case; May et al., 1993) biases the data in favour of young adults (who are then tested at or near their peak time of day) and against older adults (who are tested at an off-peak time). This work suggests that failing to attend to age differences in circadian arousal patterns and time of testing (and these are rarely reported in either the behavioural and/or neuroscience literatures) may lead to an overestimation of age differences on all but highly skilled and automatic tasks. As an example, return to Figure 7.1, reporting data from a study in which distracting words occurred in the first phase and were tested for implicitly (using fragments) after a delay. Note the very large age differences seen in the afternoon testing session and the far smaller differences seen in the morning session.

This reading of the literature suggests the possibility that the full abilities of older adults may not yet be known – and will not be until circadian arousal patterns and times of testing are in synchrony for both younger and older adults in studies.

Conclusions

The process of ageing is traditionally associated with a decline in cognitive abilities, as any text book will tell us, and as most of us believe. These beliefs are buttressed by findings in cognitive neuroscience pointing to changes in brain structure and function that are correlated with behavioural measures, and that may even be viewed as causal. Here we reviewed findings demonstrating areas in which older adults' performance is intact or even superior to their younger counterparts. Older adults do not show a decline in encoding information into memory (some have argued they encode too much, not too little; see note 1), nor do they show a decline in implicit memory or automatic retrieval. They have greater general knowledge and vocabulary skills, their general mood is more positive and they are better able to regulate their emotions than are young adults. In addition, under some circumstances, older adults are more likely to reach normatively correct decisions, they show greater wisdom in some reasoning tasks and some, at least, can be as creative as younger adults.

We also reviewed evidence which reported that age differences may be overestimated under a variety of laboratory conditions. For example, older adults are more concerned about their memory performance than younger adults, and so tend to be more anxious when their cognitive ability is being assessed. This feeling of stress can negatively affect older adults' performance, while having little impact on younger adults, who do not share these concerns and who are familiar with testing situations. The majority of older adults are on a different circadian cycle than are the young to whom they are compared, and it appears that more older adults are tested at disadvantageous times than are young adults, another factor that increases the magnitude of age differences.

Nonetheless, it is important to note that age-related cognitive declines are widely reported, and findings such as age-related sensory acuity, psychomotor slowing and increased distractibility do not seem to be context-dependent. Having said that, the data that we reviewed suggest that the relation between ageing and cognitive decline is not as straightforward as might be thought from a perusal of text books, review and journal articles in both the behavioural and neuroscience literatures (however, see Park and Reuter-Lorenz, 2009). We discussed a number of findings that do not fit the common stereotype about ageing, and that seem to stand in contrast to known declines in brain volume and functioning with age. However, we do not see these positive aspects of ageing as puzzling or inexplicable. Rather, they likely represent adaptive changes in goals and capacities that enable older adults to compensate for decline in other areas, and to use the experience and knowledge they have gathered over the years (Baltes and Smith, 2008; Grossmann et al., 2010).

Future challenges and questions

Cognitive ageing is characterized by changes that manifest as a distinct pattern of impaired, preserved and even improved performance. In this chapter, we have mentioned factors that can hinder performance in some situations but improve it in others. To take an example, increased susceptibility to distraction can disrupt older adults' cognitive performance in some cases but improve it in others (see evidence presented in the memory and problem-solving section; also see Healey et al., 2008). In other words, whether a specific feature that characterizes ageing helps or hinders performance might depend entirely on the situation. In addition, it is important to note that there are high levels of individual variability in cognitive aspects of ageing (Rabbitt, 2000). The performance of young and old groups can overlap, such that a 70-year-old may outperform a 20-year-old. Gaining a better understanding of the factors contributing to these individual differences can help us identity the factors related to 'successful ageing'.

We end with the caution that it is not fully known to what degree the factors reviewed here (circadian rhythms, stereotype threat, the relevance of materials to age-related goals) influence age differences in cognitive performance. It is critical that we begin to understand these because only then can we assess the paradox between the ageing brain and true levels of cognitive competence of older adults. As well, it is likely that the development of effective behavioural interventions for individuals experiencing cognitive declines will also require this knowledge.

Authors' note

The research reviewed in this chapter was supported by a Rotman Research Institute fellowship to SZ and by grants from the US National Institute on Aging and the Canadian Institutes of Health Research to LH.

References

Adams, C., Smith, M. C., Pasupathi, M., & Vitolo, L. (2002). Social context effects on story recall in older and younger women: does the listener make a difference? *Journals of Gerontology: Psychological Sciences*, **57**: 28–40.

Bailey, P. E., Henry, J. D., Rendell, P. G., Phillips, L. H., & Kliegel, M. (2010). Dismantling the 'age–prospective memory paradox': the classic laboratory paradigm simulated in a naturalistic setting. *The Quarterly Journal of Experimental Psychology*, **63**: 646–52.

Balesteros, S., Montserrat, G., Mayas, J., Garcia-Rodriguez, B., & Reales, J. M. (2009). Cross-modal repetition priming in young and old adults. *European Journal of Cognitive Psychology*, **21**: 366–87.

Balota, D. A., Dolan, P. O., & Duchek, J. M. (2000). Memory changes in healthy older adults. In: Endel, T. & Craik, F. I. M. (Eds.). *The Oxford Handbook of Memory*. New York, NY: Oxford University Press, 395–409.

Baltes, P. A. (1997). On the incomplete architecture of human ontogeny: selection, optimization, and compensation as foundations of developmental theory. *American Psychologist*, **52**: 366–80.

Baltes, P. A., & Smith, J. (2008). The fascination of wisdom: its nature, ontogeny, and function. *Perspectives on Psychological Science*, **3**: 56–64.

Beason-Held, L. L., Kraut, M. A., & Resnick, S. M. (2008a). I. Longitudinal changes in aging brain function. *Neurobiology of Aging*, **29**: 483–96.

Beason-Held, L. L., Kraut, M. A., & Resnick, S. M. (2008b). II. Temporal patterns of longitudinal change in aging brain function. *Neurobiology of Aging*, **29**: 497–513.

Berry, J. M., West, R. L., & Dennehey, D. M. (1989). Reliability and validity of the Memory Self-Efficacy Questionnaire. *Developmental Psychology*, **25**: 701–13.

Betts, L. R., Taylor, C. P., Sekuler, A. B., & Bennett, P. J. (2005). Aging reduces center-surround antagonism in visual motion processing. *Neuron*, **45**: 361–6.

Birditt, K. S., & Fingerman, K. L. (2005). Do we get better at picking our battles? Age group differences in descriptions of behavioral reactions to interpersonal tensions. *Journals of Gerontology, Series B: Psychological Sciences and Social Sciences*, **60**: 121–8.

Blanchard-Fields, F., Mienaltowski, A., & Baldi, S. R. (2007). Age differences in everyday problem-solving effectiveness: older adults select more effective strategies for interpersonal problems. *Journals of Gerontology: Series B, Psychological Sciences and Social Sciences*, **62**: 61–4.

Cabeza, R. (2002). Hemispheric asymmetry reduction in older adults: the HAROLD model. *Psychology & Aging*, **17**: 85–100.

Campbell, K. L., Hasher, L., & Thomas, R. C. (2010). Hyper-binding: a unique age effect. *Psychological Science*, **21**: 399–401.

Carstensen, L. L., Fung, H. H., & Charles, S. T. (2003). Socioemotional selectivity theory and the regulation of emotion in the second half of life. *Motivation and Emotion*, **27**: 103–23.

Castel, A. D. (2005). Memory for grocery prices in younger and older adults: the role of schematic support. *Psychology and Aging*, **20**: 718–21.

Charles, S. T., & Carstensen, L. L. (2010). Social and emotional aging. *Annual Review of Psychology*, **61**: 383–409.

Charles, S. T., Mather, M., & Carstensen, L. L. (2003). Aging and emotional memory: the forgettable nature of negative images for older adults. *Journal of Experimental Psychology: General*, **132**: 310–24.

Clark, A., Oswald, A., & Warr, P. (1996). Is job satisfaction U-shaped in age? *Journal of Occupational and Organizational Psychology*, **69**: 57–81.

Craik, F. I. M. (1983). On the transfer of information from temporary to permanent memory. *Philosophical Transactions of the Royal Society of London*, **B302**: 341–59.

Craik, F. I. M. (2002). Human memory and aging. In Bäckman, L. & von Hofsten, C. (Eds.). *Psychology at the Turn of the Millennium*. Hove: Psychology Press, 261–80.

Craik, F. I. M., & McDowd, J. M. (1987). Age differences in recall and recognition. *Journal of Experimental Psychology: Learning, Memory, & Cognition*, **13**: 474–9.

Craik, F. I. M., & Salthouse, T. A. (Eds.) (2008). *Handbook of Aging and Cognition. 3rd Edition*. New York, NY: Psychology Press.

Dixon, R. A., & deFrias, C. M. (2004). The Victoria longitudinal study: from characterizing cognitive aging to illustrating changes in memory compensation. *Aging, Neuropsychology, and Cognition*, **11**: 346–76.

den Dunnen, W. F. A., Brouwer, W. H., Bijlard, E., *et al.* (2008). No disease in the brain of a 115-year-old woman. *Neurobiology of Aging*, **29**: 1127–32.

Finkel, D., & Pedersen, N. L. (2004). Processing speed and longitudinal trajectories of change for cognitive abilities: the Swedish adoption/twin study of aging. *Aging, Neuropsychology, and Cognition*, **11**: 325–45.

Friedman, D., Nessler, D., Cycowicz, Y. M., & Horton, C. (2009). Development of and change in cognitive control: a comparison of children, young adults, and older adults. *Cognitive, Affective and Behavioral Neuroscience*, **9**: 91–102.

Galenson, D. (2005). *Old Masters and Young Geniuses: The Two Life Cycles of Artistic Creativity*. Princeton, NJ: Princeton University Press.

Gigerenzer, G., & Selten, R. (2001). *Bounded Rationality: The Adaptive Toolbox*. Cambridge, MA: The MIT Press.

Goeleven, E., De Raedt, R., & Dierckx, E. (2010). The positivity effect in older adults: the role of affective interference and inhibition. *Aging & Mental Health*, **14**: 129–37.

Goldberg, E. (2005). *The Wisdom Paradox: How Your Mind Can Grow Stronger as Your Brain Grows Older*. New York, NY: Penguin Group.

Goldstein, D., Hahn, C., Hasher, L., Wiprzycka, U. J., & Zelazo, P. D. (2007). Time of day, intellectual performance, and behavioral problems in Morning versus Evening type adolescents: is there a synchrony effect? *Personality and Individual Differences*, **42**: 431–40.

Grady, C. L. (2008). Cognitive neuroscience of aging. In: Kingstone, A., & Miller, M. B. (Eds.). *The Year in Cognitive Neuroscience 2008. Annals of the New York Academy of Sciences*. Malden, MA: Blackwell Publishing, 127–44.

Grossmann, I., Na, J., Varnum, M. E. W., Park, D. C., Kitayama, S., & Nisbett, R. W. (2010). Reasoning about social conflicts improves into old age. *Proceedings of the National Academy of Science*, **107**: 7246–50.

Hasher, L., Chung, C., May, C. P., & Foong, N. (2002). Age, time of testing, and proactive interference. *Canadian Journal of Experimental Psychology*, **56**: 200–07.

Healey, M. K., Campbell, K. L., & Hasher, L. (2008). Cognitive aging and increased distractibility: costs and potential benefits. In Sossin, W. S., Lacaille, J. C., Castellucci, V. F. & Belleville, S. (Eds.). *Progress in Brain Research*, Vol **169**. Amsterdam: Elsevier, 353–63.

Healey, M. K., Campbell, K. L., Hasher, L., & Ossher, L. (2010). Direct evidence for the role of inhibition in resolving interference. *Psychological Science*, **21**: 1464–70.

Henrich, J., Heine, S. J., & Norenzayan, A. (2010). The weirdest people in the world. *Behavioural and Brain Sciences*, **33**: 61–83.

Henry, J. D., MacLeod, M. S., Phillips, L. H., & Crawford, J. R. (2004). Meta-analytic review of prospective memory and aging. *Psychology and Aging*, **19**: 27–39.

Hess, T. M. (2006). Attitudes toward aging and their effects on behaviour. In: Buren, J. E. & Schaie, K. W. (Eds.). *Handbook of the Psychology of Aging. 6th edition.* San Diego, CA: Academic Press, 379–406.

Hillary, F. G., & Biswal, B. (2007). The influence of neuropathology on the fMRI signal: a measurement of brain or vein? *The Clinical Neuropsychologist*, **21**: 38–72.

Hultsch, D. F., Bielak, A. A. M., Crow, C. B., & Dixon, R. A. (2009). The way we were: perceptions of past memory change in older adults. In: Bosworth, H. B. & Hertzog, C. (Eds.). *Cognition in Aging: Methodologies and Applications.* Washington, DC: American Psychological Association, 197–216.

Ikier, S., & Hasher, L. (2006). Age differences in implicit interference. *Journals of Gerontology: Psychological Sciences*, **61B**: 278–84.

Ikier, S., Yang, L., & Hasher, L. (2008). Implicit proactive interference, age, and automatic versus controlled retrieval strategies. *Psychological Science*, **19**: 456–61.

Isaacowitz, D. M., Wadlinger, H. A., Goren, D., & Wilson, H. R. (2006). Selective preference in visual fixation away from negative images in old age? An eye tracking study. *Psychology and Aging*, **21**: 40–8.

Jennings, J. M., & Jacoby, L. L. (1993). Automatic versus intentional uses of memory: aging, attention, and control. *Psychology & Aging*, **8**: 283–93.

Kahneman, D., & Tversky, A. (1979). Prospect theory: an analysis of decision under risk. *Econometrica*, **47**: 263–91.

Kensinger, E. A., & Schacter, D. L. (2008). Neural processes supporting young and older adults' emotional memories. *Journal of Cognitive Neuroscience*, **20**: 1161–73.

Kim, S., & Hasher, L. (2005). The attraction effect in decision making: superior performance by older adults. *Quarterly Journal of Experimental Psychology*, **58A**: 120–33.

Kim, S., Goldstein, D., Hasher, L., & Zacks, R. (2005). Framing effects in younger and older adults. *Journals of Gerontology: Series B: Psychological Sciences and Social Sciences*, **60**: 215–8.

Kim, S., Hasher, L., & Zacks, R. T. (2007). Aging and a benefit of distractability. *Psychonomic Bulletin & Review*, **14**: 301–05.

Kim, S., Healey, M. K., Goldstein, D., Hasher, L., & Wiprzycka, U. J. (2008). Age differences in choice satisfaction: a positivity effect in decision making. *Psychology & Aging*, **23**: 33–8.

Kisely, M. A., Wood, S., & Burrows, C. L. (2007). Looking at the sunny side of life. Age-related change in an event-related potential measure of the negativity bias. *Psychological Science*, **18**: 838–43.

Kudielka, B. M., Buske-Kirschbaum, A., Hellhammer, D. H., & Kirschbaum, C. (2004). HPA axis responses to laboratory psychosocial stress in healthy children, younger adults and elderly adults: impact of age and gender. *Psychoneuroendocrinology*, **29**: 83–98.

Kunzmann, U., Little, T. D., & Smith, J. (2000). Is age-related stability of subjective well-being a paradox? Cross-sectional and longitudinal evidence from the Berlin Aging Study. *Psychology & Aging*, **15**: 511–26.

Kvavilashvili, L., & Fisher, L. (2007). Is time-based prospective remembering mediated by self-initiated rehearsals? Role of incidental cues, ongoing activity, age, and motivation. *Journal of Experimental Psychology: General*, **136**: 112–32.

Kwong See, S. T., & Heller, R. B. (2004). Judging older targets' discourse: how do age stereotypes influence evaluations. *Experimental Aging Research*, **30**: 63–73.

Lachman, M. E., Bandura, M., Weaver, S. L., & Elliott, E. (1995). Assessing memory control beliefs: the memory controllability inventory. *Aging & Cognition*, **2**: 67–84.

Lehman, H. C. (1953). *Age and Achievement.* Princeton, NJ: Princeton University Press.

Lieberman, M. D. (2000). Intuition: a social cognitive neuroscience approach. *Psychological Bulletin*, **126**: 109–37.

Light, L. L., Prull, M. W., La Voie, D. J., & Healy, M. R. (2000). Dual process theories of memory in old age. In: Perfect, T. J. & and Maylor, E. A. (Eds.). *Models of Cognitive Aging*. Oxford: Oxford University Press, 238–300.

Lindauer, M. S. (2003). *Aging, Creativity, and Art*. New York, NY: Plenum.

Lovden, M., Ghisletta, P., & Lindenberger, U. (2004). Cognition in the Berlin Aging Study (BASE): the first 10 years. *Aging, Neuropsychology and Cognition*, **11**: 104–33.

Lupien, S. J., Maheu, F. S., Tu, M., Fiocco, A., & Schramek, T. E. (2007). The effects of stress and stress hormones on human cognition: implications for the field of brain and cognition. *Brain and Cognition*, **65**: 209–37.

Lustig, C., May, C. P., & Hasher, L. (2001). Working memory span and the role of proactive interference. *Journal of Experimental Psychology: General*, **130**: 199–207.

MacKenzie, C. S., Smith, M. C., Hasher, L., Leach, L., & Behl, P. (2007). Cognitive functioning under stress: evidence from informal caregivers of palliative patients. *Journal of Palliative Medicine*, **10**: 749–58.

Mackenzie, C. S., Wiprzycka, U. J., Hasher, L., & Goldstein, D. (2009). Associations between psychological distress, learning and memory in spouse caregivers of older adults. *The Journals of Gerontology, Series B. Psychological Sciences and Social Sciences*, **64**: 742–6.

Mather, M., & Carstensen, L. L. (2005). Aging and motivated cognition: the positivity effect in attention and memory. *Trends in Cognitive Sciences*, **9**: 496–502.

Mather, M., & Johnson, M. K. (2000). Choice-supportive source monitoring: do our decisions seem better to us as we age? *Psychology & Aging*, **15**: 596–606.

May, C. P., Hasher, L., & Foong, N. (2005a). Implicit memory, age, and time of day: paradoxical priming effects. *Psychological Science*, **16**: 96–100.

May, C. P., Hasher, L., & Stoltzfus, E. R. (1993). Optimal time of day and the magnitude of age differences in memory. *Psychological Science*, **4**: 326–30.

May, C. P., Rahhal, T., Berry, E. M., & Leighton, E. A. (2005b). Aging, source memory, and emotion. *Psychology and Aging*, **20**: 571–8.

McCrae, R. R., Arenberg, D., & Costa, P. T., Jr. (1987). Declines in divergent thinking with age: cross-sectional, longitudinal, and cross-sequential analyses. *Psychology and Aging*, **2**: 130–7.

Mikels, J. A., Larkin, G. R., Reuter-Lorenz, P. A., & Carstensen, L. L. (2005). Divergent trajectories in the aging mind: changes in working memory for affective versus visual information with age. *Psychology and Aging*, **20**: 542–53.

Mikels, J. A., Lockenhoff, C. E., Maglio, S. J., et al. (2010). Following your heart or your head: focusing on emotions versus information differentially influences the decisions of younger and older adults. *Journal of Experimental Psychology: Applied*, **16**: 87–95.

Morrow, D., Leirer, V., Altieri, P., & Fitzsimmons, C. (1994). When expertise reduces age differences in performance. *Psychology and Aging*, **9**: 134–48.

Murphy, N. A., & Isaacowitz, D. M. (2008). Preferences for emotional information in older and younger adults: a meta-analysis of memory and attention tasks. *Psychology and Aging*, **23**: 263–86.

Neupert, S. D., Almeida, D. M., Mroczek, D. K., & Spiro, A., III (2006). Daily stressors and memory failures in a naturalistic setting: findings from the VA normative aging study. *Psychology and Aging*, **21**: 424–9.

Nilsson, L-G., Adolfsson, R., Bäckman, L., de Frias, C., Molander, B., & Nyberg, L. (2004). Betula: a prospective cohort study on memory, health and aging. *Aging, Neuropsychology and Cognition*, **11**: 134–48.

Nilsson, L-G., Sternäng, O, Rönnland, M., & Nyberg, L. (2009). Challenging the notion of an early-onset of cognitive decline. *Neurobiology of Aging*, **30**: 521–4.

Nunes, A., & Kramer, A. F. (2009). Experience-based mitigation of age-related performance declines: evidence from air traffic control. *Journal of Experimental Psychology: Applied*, **15**: 12–24.

Nyberg, L., Maitland, S. B., Rönnlund, M., *et al.* (2003). Selective adult age differences in an age-invariant multifactor model of declarative memory. *Psychology and Aging*, **18**: 149–60.

Park, D. C., & Reuter-Lorenz, P. (2009). The adaptive brain: aging and neurocognitive scaffolding. *Annual Review of Psychology*, **60**: 173–96.

Park, D. C., Lautenschlager, G., Hedden, T., Davidson, N. S., Smith, A. D., & Smith, P. K. (2002). Models of visuospatial and verbal memory across the adult life span. *Psychology & Aging*, **17**: 299–320.

Persson, J., Nyberg, L., Lind, J., *et al.* (2006). Structure–function correlates of cognitive decline in aging. *Cerebral Cortex*, **16**: 907–15.

Prull, M. W., Dawes, L. L. C., Martin, A.M., III, Rosenberg, H. F., & Light, L. L. (2006). Recollection and familiarity in recognition memory: adult age differences and neuropsychological test correlates. *Psychology and Aging*, **21**: 107–18.

Rabbitt, P. M. A. (2000). Measurement indices, functional characteristics, and psychometric constructs in cognitive aging. In: Perfect, T. J. & Maylor, E. A. (Eds.). *Models of Cognitive Aging*. New York, NY: Oxford University Press, 160–87.

Rahhal, T. A., Hasher, L., & Colcombe, S. (2001). Instructional manipulations and age differences in memory: now you see them, now you don't. *Psychology and Aging*, **16**: 697–706.

Rahhal, T. A., May, C. P., & Hasher, L. (2002). Truth and character: sources that older adults can remember. *Psychological Science*, **13**: 101–05.

Raz, N., Gunning-Dixon, F., Head, D., Rodrigue, K. M., Williamson, A., & Acker, J. D. (2004). Aging, sexual dimorphism, and hemispheric asymmetry of the cerebral cortex: replicability of regional differences in volume. *Neurobiology of Aging*, **25**: 377–96.

Raz, N., Lindenberger, U., Rodrigue, K. M., Kennedy, K. M., Head, D., & Williamson, A. (2005). Regional brain changes in aging healthy adults: general trends, individual differences and modifiers. *Cerebral Cortex*, **15**: 1679–89.

Rönnlund, M., Nyberg, L., Bäckman, L., & Nilsson, L.-G. (2005). Stability, growth and decline in adult life-span development of declarative memory: cross-sectional and longitudinal data from a population-based sample. *Psychology and Aging*, **20**: 3–18.

Rowe, G., Turcotte, J., & Hasher, L. (2009). Age and synchrony effects in visuospatial cognition. *Quarterly Journal of Experimental Psychology*, **62**: 1873–80.

Rowe, G., Valderrama, S., Hasher, L., & Lenartowicz, A. (2006). Attentional disregulation: a benefit for implicit memory. *Psychology and Aging*, **21**: 826–30.

Runco, M. A. (2007). *Creativity*. New York, NY: Academic Press.

Said, E. W. (2006). *On Late Style: Music and Literature Against the Grain*. New York, NY: Pantheon Books.

Salthouse, T. A. (2004). What and when of cognitive aging. *Current Directions in Psychological Science*, **13**: 140–4.

Schonfield, D., & Robertson, B. (1966). Memory storage and aging. *Canadian Journal of Psychology*, **20**: 228–36.

Sen, A. (1971). Choice functions and revealed preference. *Review of Economic Studies*, **38**: 307–17.

Simonton, D. K. (1990). Creativity and wisdom in aging. In: Birren, J. E. & Schaie, K. W. (Eds.). *Handbook of the Psychology of Aging (3rd ed)*. San Diego, CA: Academic Press, 320–9.

Simonton, D. K. (2004). *Creativity in Science: Chance, Logic, Genius, and Zeitgeist*. Cambridge: Cambridge University Press.

Simonton, D. K. (2007). Creative life cycles in literature: poets versus novelists or conceptualists versus experimentalists? *Psychology of Aesthetics, Creativity, and the Arts*, **1**: 133–9.

Smith, R (2009, April 16). Going all out, right to the end. *New York Times*. Retrieved July 9, 2009, from http://www.nytimes.com.

Sorel, O., & Pennequin, V. (2008). Aging of the planning process: the role of executive functioning. *Brain and Cognition*, **66**: 196–201.

Spencer, S. J., Steele, C. M., & Quinn, D. M. (1999). Stereotype threat and women's math performance. *Journal of Experimental Social Psychology*, **35**: 4–28.

Spieler, D. G., Mayr, U., & LaGrone, S. (2006). Outsourcing cognitive control to the environment: adult age differences in the use of task cues. *Psychonomic Bulletin and Review*, **13**: 787–93.

Stern, Y. (2002). What is cognitive reserve? Theory and research application of the reserve concept. *Journal of the International Neuropsychological Society*, **8**: 448–60.

Stern, Y. (2009). Cognitive reserve. *Neuropsychologia*, **47**: 2015–28.

Sternberg, R. J., & Lubart, T. I. (2001). Wisdom and creativity. In: Birren, J. E., & Schaie, K. W. (Eds.). *Handbook of the Psychology of Aging (5th edn)*. San Diego, CA: Academic Press, 500–22.

Stone, A. A., Schwartz, J. E., Broderick, J. E., & Deaton, A. (2010). A snapshot of the age distribution of psychological well-being in the United States. *Proceedings of the National Academy of Sciences*, **107**: 9985–90.

Strough, J., Mehta, C. M., McFall, J. P., & Schuller, K. L. (2008). Are older adults less subject to the sunk-cost fallacy than younger adults? *Psychological Science*, **19**: 650–2.

Sullivan, S. J., Mikels, J. A., & Carstensen, L. L. (2010). You never lose the ages you've been: affective perspective taking in older adults. *Psychology and Aging*, **25**: 229–34.

Tadin, D., & Blake, R. (2005). Motion perception getting better with age? *Neuron*, **45**: 325–7.

Tentori, K., Osherson, D., Hasher, L., & May, C. (2001). Wisdom and aging: irrational preferences in college students but not older adults. *Cognition*, **81**: 87–96.

Thomas, R. C., & Hasher, L. (2006). The influence of emotional valence on age differences in early processing and memory. *Psychology and Aging*, **21**: 821–5.

Williams, L. M., Brown, K. J., Palmer, D., *et al.* (2006). The mellow years? Neural basis of improving emotional stability over age. *Journal of Neuroscience*, **26**: 6422–30.

Yoon, C., May, C. P., & Hasher, L. (2000). Aging, circadian arousal patterns and cognition. In: Park, D. & Schwarz, N. (Eds.). *Cognitive Aging: A Primer*. Philadelphia, PA: Psychology Press, 151–72.

Yu, F., Ryan, L. H., Schaie, K. W., Willis, S. L., & Kolanowski, A. (2009). Factors associated with cognition in adults: the Seattle Longitudinal Study. *Research in Nursing & Health*, **32**: 540–50.

Zacks, R. T., & Hasher, L. (2006). Aging and long term memory: deficits are not inevitable. In: Bialystok, E. & Craik, F. I. M. (Eds.). *Lifespan Cognition: Mechanisms of Change*. New York, NY: Oxford University Press, 162–77.

Zigler, E., Abelson, W. D., & Seitz, V. (1973). Motivational factors in the performance of economically disadvantaged children on the Peabody Picture Vocabulary Test. *Child Development*, **44**: 294–303.

Chapter 8

Paradoxes of learning and memory

Henry L. Roediger, III and Andrew C. Butler

Summary

We explore 12 paradoxes of learning, memory and knowing in our chapter. These are mysteries in which subjective experience – what we think we know or remember – does not correspond to objective facts. In some cases, we hold false memories: we are utterly confident in our memories that events happened one way, but they did not. Another example is hindsight bias: we may believe that we knew (after the fact) how an event would turn out, but controlled experiments show people cannot predict the event. Another category of illusion occurs with learning. Often students judge one method of learning to be superior to a second method, but their actual performance shows the reverse to be true. The paradox of interference creates other puzzles: when people try to remember similar events, they will often confuse one for another. We discuss 12 paradoxes and their implications for cognitive functioning. Some of these errors may implicate cognitive strategies that we use because they often lead to correct answers in many situations, but can produce errors in other instances.

Introduction

Psychologists love mysteries and paradoxes. They always have, they always will. There is nothing surprising here; all people like paradoxes and puzzles. Look at Figure 8.1 and ask yourself which surface of the two boxes is longer, the one on the left or the one on the right? Every person naïve to the situation will answer the one on the left. However, the two surfaces are exactly congruent. They are the same. Try tracing over one and laying it over the other if you don't believe us. Even if you are aware that it is an illusion (created by Shepard, 1981), you still fall for it every time. Knowing the two surfaces are the same does not correct our perception of the boxes. Psychologists studying perception have discovered hundreds of remarkable illusions like this one and people generally find them fascinating.

Cognitive and social psychologists also love illusions. Our journals are filled with puzzles of the following sort: clever experimenters manipulate a variable that has a large effect on some judgement or behaviour, then they ask subjects to predict their own behaviour in the situation and show that, lo and behold, the subjects either give random predictions or make completely wrong ones. For example, variable A increases a behaviour whereas the subject thinks the variable decreased it or had no effect. A variant on this theme is to show how human behaviour violates the rules of some normative theory about behaviour. The field of behavioural economics has grown up around observations that

---

The Paradoxical Brain, ed. Narinder Kapur. Published by Cambridge University Press. © Cambridge University Press 2011.

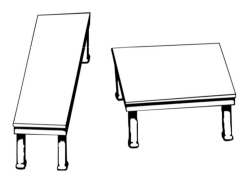

Figure 8.1 A spatial illusion created by Roger Shepard (1981). The surface of the left box appears much wider than the one on the right, but the two are actually congruent.

people fail to follow the rational models of 'economic man' in making decisions about money. The predictions work neither on the microeconomic scale of individual human behaviour (e.g. Kahneman, 2003) nor the macroeconomic scale of national and international finance (e.g. witness the world's economies thrown into complete disarray in 2007–2008, which virtually no economist predicted).

When subjects in our experiments are asked to explain their behaviour, they often make up a coherent story, even if it is one that is wildly inaccurate and does not account for the facts. Nisbett and Wilson (1977) reviewed many studies from social and cognitive psychology and argued that people 'tell more than they can know'. If we clearly do not know the real causes of the behaviour (the independent variable that the experimenter manipulated), we make up a good enough story, nonetheless. In a later book, Wilson (2002) argued that these tendencies at self-delusion are so pervasive that we are 'strangers to ourselves' (the title of his book). Books by Dunning (2005) and Gilovich (1991) make similar points.

Psychologists are much less successful at explaining the mysteries they raise. We report interesting puzzles, we explore them experimentally, we root around in them for a while, and then we move on to the next puzzle (as has been pointed out by critics; e.g. Newell, 1973). This may be an unfortunate tradition, but it is one we generally follow in writing this chapter. We write about 12 interesting paradoxes that have been uncovered using behavioural paradigms (our chapter is a 'no-brainer'). Yes, we know that the title of the book involves the brain, but we will have nothing whatsoever to say about the neural bases of the illusions and puzzles that we review. We can be confident that the brain holds the secrets to all these phenomena, but neural explanations for them are not at hand (but for a few potential leads, see the section on *Future Challenges and Questions* at the end of the chapter).

We organize our chapter into four main parts. The first section is concerned with paradoxes of remembering and knowing. Why do people suffer false memories, remembering some event differently from the way it happened, or remembering an event that never happened at all? Often these erroneous memories are held with high confidence. Or why does our knowledge sometimes blind us to the way others see the world? An expert has trouble seeing the world through the eyes of the novice, even though the expert was once a novice (see Chapter 9). The second section of the chapter is concerned with paradoxes of task difficulty and students' judgements of their own learning and memory as a function of difficulty. The surprising finding is that people often misjudge the conditions of learning that lead to good retention later. Even students, who are expert learners, have such erroneous beliefs.

A third section is concerned with paradoxes of interference. The basic feature of these puzzles is that when people try to remember an event that happened some time ago, they can become confused by events that happened more recently, during the intervening time since the original event. The more recent events can interfere with memory for the original event that the person is trying to retrieve. A final section of the chapter deals with puzzles caused by the fluency with which cognitive processes are carried out. Our being able to perceive or remember something easily colours the weight we give that information in making judgements of the world. We often overweight information that is easy to perceive or retrieve.

We cover these illusions and paradoxes as though they are separate, but they probably have some common causes. We pause along the way to make connections where appropriate. Our chapter is perforce rather superficial – we identify a paradox, puzzle or illusion, and then we move on to the next. Many articles, chapters and even books have been written about these phenomena. Following the citations in each section via Google or some other search engine would bring about a wealth of information. Pohl's (2004) edited volume is a good place to find more information about many of these phenomena.

Paradoxes of remembering and knowing

We all believe in our memories, the record of our lives. Memories contain our identity; to believe that cherished memories might be false could mean that our self-image is wrong, too. Yet even strongly held memories can turn out to be wrong. Jean Piaget, a pioneer in the study of cognitive development, had an early memory of this sort. A critical moment in his life occurred when his nanny was walking him in a carriage on a street in Paris. A kidnapper tried to steal him, but his nanny fought back and saved him. Piaget later wrote: 'I was held in by the strap fastened round me while my nurse bravely tried to stand between me and the thief. She received various scratches, and I can still vaguely see those on her face'. However, when he was 15, Piaget's parents received a letter from the nurse, who had recently been converted and was confessing past sins. She had made up the whole story, faking the scratches, and she returned a valuable watch she had been given for her bravery in the situation. Piaget remarked 'I therefore must have heard, as a child, the account of this story . . . and projected it into the past in the form of a visual memory'. He further opined that 'Many real memories are doubtless of the same order' (quotes are from Piaget, 1962, pp. 187–8).

Of course, we do not normally have our cherished memories so rudely shaken from us. Still, psychologists have shown in many studies over the past 40 years that our memories are surprisingly malleable. We can often remember things quite differently from the way they happened or, as in Piaget's case, have vivid, detailed memories of events that never happened at all. We next consider a laboratory paradigm that captures the effect in an easily studied manner.

Associative memory illusions: the DRM effect

You have probably had the experience of listening to a story or a lecture and then something the speaker said led you to think further on the topic before your attention snapped back to the speaker. Later, if you are trying to recount the story to a friend, you might begin to relate a detail and then stop and wonder: did the speaker say that or was that something I thought while listening to her? Or, worse yet, maybe you never even wonder,

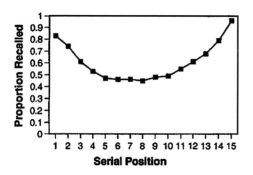

Figure 8.2 Mean proportion recall of words as a function of list position (data are averaged over 24 lists). Data are from Roediger and McDermott (1995, Experiment 2).

but you confidently assert that she said something that you only thought. The events of life go whirling by, and the memorial residue is some combination of what really happened with how we recoded the information given our own background, interests and proclivities (Bartlett, 1932). The problem of discerning which of our thoughts came from real events and which were ones we inferred or imagined is called 'reality monitoring' (Johnson and Raye, 1981).

Roediger and McDermott (1995) developed a paradigm, first introduced by Deese (1959) for other purposes, to get at these issues. Subjects heard lists of words such as *hard, light, pillow, plush, loud, cotton, fur, touch, fluffy, feather, furry, downy, kitten, skin, tender.* They were instructed to listen carefully and, immediately after hearing the list, to write down all the words they could recall in any order they wanted (free recall). They were told to be very careful and to recall only items that they had just heard. The subjects' recall is shown in Figure 8.2 plotted against the input position of the words in the list (the data are averaged over 24 lists and many subjects). The figure reveals a standard U-shaped serial position function: subjects recalled the most words from the beginning of the series (the primacy effect) and from the end (the recency effect) – a standard finding. However, something unusual occurred in this experiment. When recalling each list, subjects tended to recall a particular word. The recalled word for this sample list was *soft*; in fact, the list was generated from the 15 words most closely associated from the word *soft* in norms of word association. That is, if students are given the word *soft* and asked to think of the first word that comes to mind, the 15 words in the list are the 15 most popular associates. Interestingly, subjects recalled the associated word that was never presented 55% of the time – about the same level or even slightly higher than recall of words that actually were presented in the middle of the list (like *cotton, fur,* etc. in this list). This illusory recall of a word not presented in a list (but strongly associated to the ones that were presented) is called the DRM (for Deese–Roediger–McDermott) effect.

Unlike Piaget's false memory, this one (albeit much more prosaic) appears immediately after study, with no appreciable delay between study of the list and its test. But is memory for the non-event rich and detailed? Do people really remember it? Roediger and McDermott (1995, Experiment 2) asked this question by giving a recognition test after the recall test. Subjects looked at words that were studied (*hard, cotton*) and words that were not studied in any list (*eagle, typhoon*) and, critically, the word implied by the list but not actually studied (*soft*). They asked the subjects to judge each word on the test as old (studied) or new (non-studied). If a word was judged old, subjects were asked to make a second judgement: did they really remember the moment the word occurred in the list

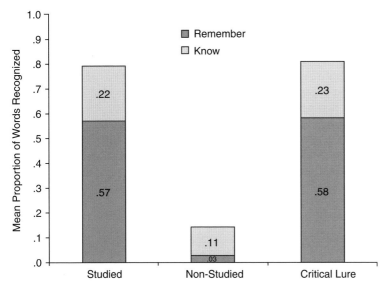

Figure 8.3 Mean proportion recognition for studied, non-studied and critical lure words broken down as a function of remember/know judgements. Data are from Roediger and McDermott (1995, Experiment 2).

(e.g. the sound of a person's voice, the words before or after it), or did they just know it was on the list (but they could not remember the moment of presentation)? Tulving (1985) and others (Gardiner, 1988; Rajaram, 1993) developed this remember/know procedure to analyse a person's subjective experience during retrieval.

The results from the recognition test are shown in Figure 8.3. Studied words were recognized (called old) about 79% of the time; further, for those words called old, about 75% of the time subjects reported remembering the moment of the item's occurrence by providing a *remember* judgement. For the non-studied and unrelated words (the standard kind of lures on most recognition tests), the results were quite different. Subjects rarely called these items old (10% or so), and when they did make this mistake, they nearly always judged the item to be known and not remembered. After all, the item was not studied, so how could someone (just a few minutes later) have a strong experience of false remembering? The answer to this question lies in the bar on the far right in Figure 8.3: when the test item was strongly associated to one of the studied lists (like *soft* in our example list), a vivid false memory occurred. Subjects called such items old 81% of the time and, even more remarkably, they said they remembered the occurrence of the word in the list about 75% of those times. In fact, the results for the associated lure items like *soft* show about the same performance as items from the lists that were actually studied!

Of course, this laboratory sort of false memory does not rival the Piaget anecdote in its sweep and scale. Nonetheless, it provides a carefully controlled procedure by which genesis of false memories can be studied. One prominent theory to account for the effect (at a psychological level) is the activation-monitoring framework (Roediger *et al.*, 2001a; Balota *et al.*, 1999). Briefly, the idea is that the list of associates sparks thoughts (conscious or unconscious) of associated words (so people hear *hard, fur, cotton* and the word *soft* becomes highly activated). Once an item has been activated, then the subject has a reality-monitoring problem when retrieving words during the test, asking: 'Was this word presented or is it activated for some other reason?' Subjects often fail this reality monitoring test and report or recognize the associated word like *soft* as though it had actually been presented.

155

A large amount of research has grown up about this DRM paradigm, and Gallo (2006) has written an entire book towards understanding it and related phenomena. The DRM effect is large, persistent and robust across many conditions and subject groups. It provides a compelling and perplexing experience for all who try it. Piaget's false memory presumably developed over the years and we can understand how someone may not recall his childhood accurately so many years later, but the DRM illusion (which also involves remembering concrete details of an event that never happened) develops over seconds. The power of the demonstration, and our surprise in seeing that our recall is wrong, present a paradox to our understanding of how memory works. Of course, we are not arguing that the mechanisms of the Piaget false memory and those of the DRM illusion are the same; they surely are not. However, both phenomena indicate how people can remember events that never occurred.

The curse of knowledge

The brilliant statistician, a leader in his field, is assigned to teach introductory statistics. This should be a breeze, he thinks. However, he is confounded by his class; they know nothing, they cannot understand anything he says. The students are similarly confounded. The teacher talks in equations, does not give concrete examples, and seems to assume that they have already had several statistics courses. They have not. The professor in this instance is hampered by the curse of knowledge – he knows so much about the field that he can no longer put himself in the place of a student in college who has never had a statistics course.

Similarly, computers and all sorts of other technologies (think of your TV, DVD player and cable box) are designed by electrical engineers, computer scientists and others of their ilk. The early personal computers were maddeningly difficult to use, and sales suffered. The reason was that engineers designed them so other engineers could use them – not normal people with no engineering background. Apple and some other far-sighted computer companies started hiring human factors psychologists to help engineers to redesign the computer to take people – the human factor – into account. The psychologists had to get the engineers to overcome the curse of their knowledge and make the equipment so that nearly any slob could use it.

Elizabeth Newton (1990) conducted an experiment that reveals the curse of knowledge. She made up a list of tunes that nearly every American grows up knowing – Happy Birthday to You; Shave and a Haircut, Two Bits; The Star Spangled Banner, etc. Two students sat on opposite sides of a screen in a room unable to see each other, though they could hear each other, with the screen on a desk between them. One student, the sender, tapped out a given tune with their knuckles on the table. The sender had to judge whether or not his/her performance was successful in revealing the song to the other person, while the receiver's job was to guess the identity of the song from a list of 20.

The senders, as a group, seemed relatively modest. They thought that the receivers would be able to identify the tune they played about 50% of the time. However, the receivers were able to identify the tune correctly only 3% of the time, just at chance levels! The senders were actually wildly optimistic. One plausible reason is the curse of knowledge: when the sender was tapping her knuckles on the table, she was mentally hearing the music and words of 'Happy Birthday' or some other song. This vivid imagery made her sure she was tapping out a great song, but of course what the receiver was hearing was some knocks on the table (not the music, not the words). The sender could not appreciate how difficult a

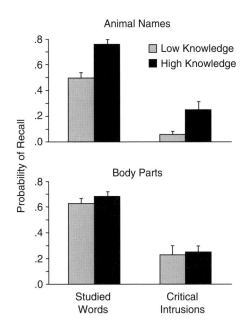

Figure 8.4 Recall of animal names (top panel) and body parts (bottom panel) as a function of football knowledge (high versus low). Data are from Castel *et al.* (2007).

job the receiver faced because she was cursed with knowledge of the song. Similarly, the statistics professor giving his lecture can imagine that he is making brilliant connections among topics, dazzling the students with his knowledge and erudition. However, the students do not know enough to be dazzled; they are hearing a lot of jargon that bounces off them rather than being absorbed. They do not have the knowledge structures (the schema, to use jargon from cognitive psychology) that would permit the lecture to be understood.

The curse of knowledge can also show up in DRM-type memory studies. Castel *et al.* (2007) tested students who were either avid and knowledgeable football fans or who were not. They gave them two lists of material to remember. One list was animal names, but the names all belonged to professional US football teams (*dolphins, broncos, falcons, colts, jaguars, bengals, seahawks, rams, lions, ravens* and *bears*), but some other team names were omitted (*eagles, panthers* and *cardinals*). The other list was composed of body parts, and again 11 items were presented (*arm, knee, mouth, stomach*, etc.) and three common items were omitted from the list (*leg, head, nose*). Thus, the lists are like DRM lists in that they both cluster about a theme (animals, body parts) with some items presented and some omitted. Students studied both lists and, after a 10-minute delay, tried to recall each one when cued with the category name (animals or body parts).

The results are shown in Figure 8.4, with recall of animal names shown at the top and body parts shown below. The bars represent the students who were either high or low in football knowledge. Those with great football knowledge recalled the animal names (belonging to team mascots) better than those students who did not know as much about football. This pattern shows the positive effect of expertise, of a case where knowledge is not a curse but a blessing. However, notice that there is a downside, too. Those with high football knowledge were also more likely to falsely recall animal mascot names that were not on the list (see the bars labeled critical intrusions). Thus, increased knowledge cursed these students with higher levels of false memories.

However, maybe those students with high football knowledge were just different somehow from the other students. That possibility seems unlikely as judged by the other data in Figure 8.4. When recalling body parts, both groups looked quite similar in terms of both accurate and false recall, so there was probably no general difference in ability across groups. The difference between the groups was in terms of expertise for football – this knowledge was both a blessing, in helping recall of animal names actually presented, and a curse in promoting false recall (see Chapter 9 for discussion on the curse of expert knowledge).

The knew-it-all-along effect (hindsight bias)

This common illusion is a cousin of the curse of knowledge, or perhaps a species of it. People have great confidence (after the fact) that they knew something (or could have predicted something) when in fact they could not have. This bias shows the value of the proverb that 'hindsight is 20/20'. Foresight is typically myopic. As we write this chapter, many books are appearing claiming that the factors that caused the economy to crash in 2007–2008 were huge (mortgage risks, all kinds of risky investments built on unsound mortgages and so on; e.g. Foster and Magdoff, 2009). However, all these factors were clear before the crash and yet practically no one predicted it. In hindsight, the crash and its causes seem obvious, but no one in power displayed the foresight to identify and prevent them.

A laboratory paradigm to identify and study hindsight bias was identified in two important papers by Baruch Fischhoff in 1975 (Fischhoff, 1975; Fischhoff and Beyth, 1975). Students were told they were to assess the likelihood of the outcome of events. An event was described, they were provided with four possible outcomes and they had to assign probabilities for each possible outcome. In one study, students read brief passages (about 150 words) describing a historical or clinical event that was true but would be unknown to most of them. For example, one incident was about a battle in 1814 in India between the British and Gurkas of Nepal. After the description was given, students were given the four outcomes (the British won; the Gurkas won; a military stalemate ensued; or a military stalemate occurred followed by a peace treaty). Two groups of students were given the same description, but with one difference. One group was told how the event actually came out in the last sentence of the paragraph, while the other was not. The students' task was to assign probabilities to the four possible outcomes so that they would sum to 100. After that, they justified their responses by saying which parts of the passage were most relevant in making their judgements.

The basic finding, which has been replicated many times, is that students who knew the outcome deemed it much more probable than students who were not told the outcome. When students know an outcome, they selectively choose the evidence to justify why they thought they would have predicted it. However, students in the other group who did not know the outcome and actually did have to predict it generally did not arrive at the same conclusion. Their probabilities were more evenly split among the alternatives. In other studies, Fischhoff (1975) demonstrated that people are generally unaware of this hindsight bias. They fully believe that they could have predicted the events given the other information in the paragraph, even though the control groups show that this is not so. In a later replication and extension of this work, Wood (1978) provided another descriptive label – the 'knew-it-all-along effect'. Keep this in mind as you hear media figures or friends pontificate on why the stock market did what it did during the day, why the President acted as he did, and so on. In the case of the stock market, you can ask: if you saw this trend coming so clearly, why didn't you get rich?

Paradoxes of difficulty

People want learning to be quick and easy. If you need to be convinced that this statement is true, then do a quick Google search for 'learning' paired with 'fast' (or any synonym of your choosing). Among the millions of website hits that result, you will find products, programs and other tools that all claim to speed up the learning process. Why spend a year living abroad in Peru when you can learn to speak fluent Spanish in mere weeks through a language-learning program like Rosetta Stone? Why read *A Midsummer Night's Dream* when you can learn all about Shakespeare's romantic comedy by consulting a study guide like Cliff's Notes? Obviously, these hypothetical questions ignore the richness of learning that accompanies the experience of living in a foreign country or reading a literary classic. Yet, they raise an important point: if the goal is to attain some criterion level of learning (e.g. fluency in speaking Spanish, knowledge of the plot of *A Midsummer Night's Dream*, etc.), why not do so in the quickest and easiest way possible?

The problem with this line of reasoning is that the level of performance during learning is a poor indicator of whether the knowledge or skill will be retained over longer periods of time. That is, reaching some criterion level of performance during learning does not guarantee that the knowledge or skill will be well remembered in the future. As Bjork and Bjork (1992) have argued, performance during learning reflects momentary accessibility of knowledge or skill (i.e. *retrieval strength*), rather than how well it has been stored in memory (i.e. *storage strength*). When retrieval strength is high, but storage strength is low, performance will be excellent in the short term, but it will suffer in the long term. An example would be remembering what you had for breakfast this morning (assuming you don't have the same breakfast every morning) – you will have no trouble retrieving that information today, but you would probably fail to retrieve it if you tried again a month from now. Thus, the key to ensuring that knowledge or skill is retained over the long term is building up high levels of storage strength.

Based on this analysis, R.A. Bjork and colleagues (Bjork, 1994a, 1994b; Christina and Bjork, 1991; Schmidt and Bjork, 1992) proposed the paradoxical concept of 'desirable difficulties' in learning. They argued that introducing difficulties during learning can actually increase long-term retention because the greatest gains in storage strength occur when retrieval strength is low. In other words, successfully retrieving information under difficult circumstances will lead to greater increments of storage strength relative to retrieving that information under easy circumstances. For example, imagine you are introduced to someone new at a cocktail party – if you retrieve that person's name immediately (i.e. when retrieval strength is high), the gains in storage strength will be much smaller than if you retrieve the name after 5 minutes of conversation (i.e. when retrieval strength is low). The idea of 'desirable difficulties' in learning is paradoxical in that it contradicts the commonly held belief that factors which enhance performance or speed improvement during learning also produce superior long-term retention. We now turn to three examples of such 'desirable difficulties' in learning, each of which could be considered paradoxical as well.

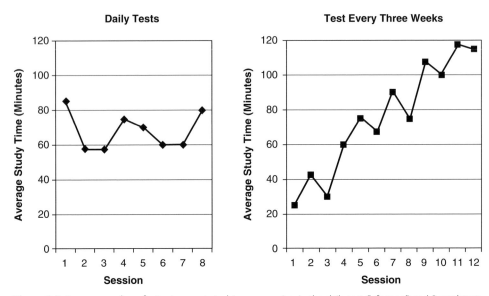

Figure 8.5 Average number of minutes spent studying per session in the daily test (left panel) and 3-week test (right panel) conditions. Data are from Mawhinney *et al.* (1971).

Spacing

Mark Twain once said, 'never put off till tomorrow what you can do the day after tomorrow'. People are masters at the art of procrastination, especially when it comes studying for a test. As anyone reading this book can readily attest, procrastination inevitably leads to cramming. In general, students spend relatively little time studying until immediately before the test, a pattern of behaviour that has been referred to as the 'procrastination scallop' (Michael, 1991). Figure 8.5 shows the results of an experiment conducted by Mawhinney *et al.* (1971) in which students were either tested every day or every three weeks. In the daily testing condition (left panel), the average number of minutes that students spent studying each day remained high and relatively constant; however, when tests were given every three weeks (right panel), the students' study behaviour exhibited the usual scalloping pattern leading up to the test that occurred after the twelfth study session.

Of course, cramming is a perfectly good way to maximize performance on an immediate test, but much of the information is quickly forgotten after the test. If long-term retention is the goal (which is certainly true of formal education generally, but perhaps not for students individually), then it is much better to space out or distribute study over time. The mnemonic benefit of spaced practice over massed practice (i.e. cramming) is one of the most robust and well-replicated findings in research on human memory and learning (Glenberg, 1976; Melton, 1970; for a review, see Cepeda *et al.*, 2006; Dempster, 1989). Indeed, the spacing effect, as it is often called, is also one of the oldest findings – it was described by Ebbinghaus ([1885]1967) in the first experimental investigation of human memory.

Spaced practice constitutes a 'desirable difficulty' in that it takes longer to reach the criterion level of performance during learning relative to massed practice, but it leads to better long-term retention. Prior research has found spacing effects for inter-study intervals ranging from several seconds (see Underwood, 1961) to years (e.g. Bahrick *et al.*, 1993). However, a recent meta-analysis performed by Cepeda and colleagues (2006) showed that the optimal spacing interval seems to depend on how long the information needs to be retained: final test performance is maximized when the inter-study interval is roughly 20% of the retention interval. Although subsequent research suggests that the retention-maximizing ratio may vary slightly depending on the retention interval (see Cepeda *et al.*, 2008), a general rule of thumb is that greater spacing will be beneficial for longer retention intervals.

Variability

When people are learning to perform a task or attempting to acquire some knowledge, often they will repeatedly practice the same action or study the same material. Children who are learning to write in cursive often practise writing one letter many times before moving on to the next letter. Professional basketball players spend a great deal of time practising how to shoot a free throw. During an exam period, students often concentrate on studying for one exam before moving on to study for another exam. Consistent practice in massed fashion often enables learners to reach some criterion of performance very quickly. However, as we discuss above, fast learning does not always lead to good long-term retention.

Although consistently practising the same action or studying the same material may have benefits in certain circumstances, many studies show that introducing variability during practice can produce superior performance on later tests. For example, Kerr and Booth (1978) conducted an experiment in which two groups of 8-year-old children practised throwing beanbags at targets during a learning phase. In the variable group, the children threw beanbags at targets that were 2 feet and 4 feet away. In the constant group, they threw beanbags at targets that were 3 feet away. After completing the learning phase, the children received a final test on a target placed 3 feet away. It would be easy to assume that the constant group would perform better on this final test than the variable group because the constant group had practiced this distance, but the variable group had not. However, contrary to one's intuition, it was the variable group that produced the superior final test performance. Indeed, many other studies of motor skill learning have shown a benefit of variable practice relative to a consistent practice schedule (for review see Shapiro and Schmidt, 1982).

Interestingly, the benefits of introducing variability during learning that occur in motor learning seem to hold for the learning of verbal information as well. Goode *et al.* (2008) compared variable and consistent practice in an experiment that involved solving anagrams. In the 'same' condition, students had to repeatedly solve a set of anagrams, each of which was always presented in the same way (e.g. LDOOF; to which the answer is FLOOD). In the 'varied' condition, they also repeatedly solved a set of anagrams, but they received a different variation of the anagram (e.g. FOLOD, OOFLD, and DOLOF) each time they had to solve it. Once the practice phase was completed, students were tested with the variation of the anagram that was practised three times in the same condition, but never practised in the varied condition. As Figure 8.6 shows, students who received varied practice produced a greater proportion of correct solutions to the anagrams on the final test relative to those who had practised with the same variation of anagram.

Introducing variability during learning can be considered a 'desirable difficulty' in that variability often slows learning and requires greater effort on the part of the learner; however, as the findings described above demonstrate, variable practice often produces

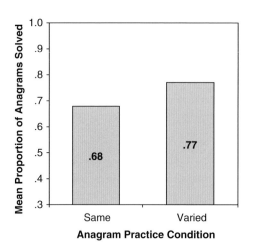

Figure 8.6 Mean proportion of correct solutions to the anagrams on the final test in the same and varied practice conditions. Data are from Goode *et al.* (2008).

better subsequent performance than consistent practice. A related idea is the concept of interleaving tasks during learning. If one must learn to perform three tasks (A, B and C) during a fixed period of time (e.g. a 3-hour training session), then one must decide how to distribute practice on these three tasks. One possibility is to practise Task A for an hour, then practise Task B for an hour, and so on for Task C. However, one could also practise each task for 10 minutes at a time, continuing to switch between tasks over the 3 hours. Research has shown that the latter schedule of practice, often called interleaving, leads to better subsequent performance (e.g. Shea and Morgan, 1979; for review see Magill and Hall, 1990). The benefits of interleaving are likely derived in part from the effects of spacing practice (as discussed above), but presumably these benefits also result from introducing variability during practice.

Testing

What activities produce learning? The first answer that comes to mind for most people is probably studying. Indeed, when students are asked about their study habits, they often report that their top strategy for learning is to repeatedly read information (e.g. Karpicke *et al.*, 2009; see too Kornell and Bjork, 2007). In contrast, testing is an answer that would be at the end of most people's list, if they include it at all. One reason that testing is likely to be omitted from a list of activities that produce learning is that people generally conceptualize testing as an assessment tool. That is, testing is assumed to be a neutral event in which knowledge is assessed without changing memory, much as stepping on a scale does not alter a person's weight. However, research on memory and learning has shown that the act of retrieving information from memory actually changes memory (e.g. Bjork, 1975), often leading to better retention over time (e.g. Carrier and Pashler, 1992).

The finding that practice in retrieving information from memory (i.e. testing) produces superior long-term retention is commonly referred to as *the testing effect* (for review see Roediger and Karpicke, 2006a). Critically, the mnemonic benefits of retrieval practice emerge even when neither feedback nor further study opportunities are provided and when compared to a control condition that re-studies the information for an equivalent amount of time (e.g. Glover, 1989; Roediger and Karpicke, 2006b). An experiment by Karpicke and Roediger (2008) provides a simple, yet powerful illustration of this robust phenomenon. In

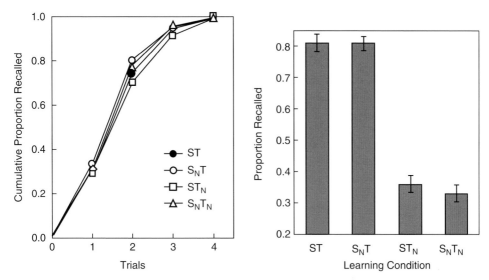

Figure 8.7 Proportion of correct responses on the initial learning tests (left panel) and the delayed final test (right panel). Data are from Karpicke and Roediger (2008).

a first phase, all students studied a list of 40 Swahili–English word pairs (e.g. mashua–boat) and then they were tested on each pair from the list (e.g. mashua– ?). When a student successfully recalled the English word on a test trial, then that pair moved into a second phase that consisted of four additional trials in one of four experimental conditions. In the 'standard' (ST) condition, students repeatedly studied and took tests on all the word pairs. In the 'repeated testing' condition, they took tests on the word pairs, but they did not study them any more (S_NT). In the 'repeated study' condition, they studied the pairs, but did not take any more tests (ST_N). Finally, in the 'drop' condition, students neither studied nor took a test again ($S_N T_N$).

The left panel of Figure 8.7 shows the cumulative learning curves (giving credit for recall the first time an item was recalled and ignoring repeated recall of the same item in some conditions) for all four experimental conditions. The rate of learning did not differ among the conditions, and every student had successfully recalled the correct English word for each pair in the list by the end of the learning session. Thus, if performance during initial learning is the criterion by which the efficacy of any learning strategy is judged, then all four experimental conditions would be assumed to be equally effective. However, this assessment changes drastically when long-term retention of the word pairs is considered. As the right panel of Figure 8.7 shows, the pattern of performance on a final test given one week later was very different. Students in the repeated study and drop conditions recalled 36 and 33%, respectively – a substantial decline when compared with performance at the end of learning. In contrast, students in the standard and repeated testing conditions recalled approximately 80% of the word pairs, which means there was relatively little forgetting in these conditions. What was the critical difference between these conditions? Retrieval practice. In the standard and repeated testing conditions, students continued to be tested, but they did not take any further tests in the repeated study and drop conditions.

Returning to the central theme of this section, testing clearly represents a 'desirable difficulty' in learning. The act of retrieving information from memory requires greater effort than passively studying that information, but this difficulty during learning leads to superior performance over the long term. The mnemonic benefits of retrieval practice are particularly interesting in light of the fact that most people do not think of testing as a way to promote learning. Rather, they report studying as their top learning strategy. Looking at the results of the Karpicke and Roediger (2008) experiment, it is important to note that the standard condition produced equivalent retention to the repeated testing condition, even though the standard condition contained many more study trials. This result suggests that continuing to study an item once it has been recalled does little to improve retention. It also fits nicely with the findings of other studies which have shown that after an initial reading of the material, re-reading it produces relatively limited memorial benefits (see Callender and McDaniel, 2009).

Paradoxes of interference

Interference from other events is perhaps the most potent cause of forgetting any particular event. Suppose you are a frequent traveller and you are asked to remember in great detail the airplane trip you took five flights ago. The four flights since that trip would provide retroactive interference as you tried to retrieve the critical trip, and all the trips you took before that critical trip (but especially the ones immediately before it) would provide proactive interference. The difficulty is to hone in on the particular event and ignore ones like it that occurred before it (creating proactive interference) and after it (creating retroactive interference). Interference occurs in many forms, but we will concentrate on three interesting interference phenomena in this section of the chapter.

The misinformation effect

Loftus and Palmer (1974) were interested in interference in a situation that has great implications. When a person is a witness to a crime, they may have to testify in a court of law months (or even years) later about what they saw or heard. Can information that occurs after an event be incorporated into memory of the event? Can the interfering information change or override what one actually saw? Loftus and Palmer (1974), and many other researchers since then, have shown that the answer to this question is yes.

The typical misinformation experiment involves three stages. First, a person witnesses a simulated crime (e.g. a repairman fixing a desk in an office steals money from a wallet). During a second phase, the person reads a report ostensibly produced by some other witness to the event, but there are errors in the report. For example, if the thief had been using a screwdriver to repair the desk, the report might refer to him using pliers. The third part of the experiment involves a test in which questions are asked about the original event (sometimes with subjects being warned that the reports they read might have errors). The subject might be asked 'What tool did the man use to fix the desk?' The finding is that the misinformation presented in the post-event report can alter the subjects' response. Relative to a control condition in which no misinformation is presented, subjects will recall items suggested in the report as actually having been present in the scene (Loftus et al., 1978). Further, people will often say they actually remember the item in the scene (Roediger et al., 1996), using Tulving's (1985) remember/know procedure.

The fact that information which is presented after an event can alter the memory of that event has enormous implications for the legal profession and the veracity of eyewitness testimony. After all, once a person has witnessed a crime, he/she will think about and

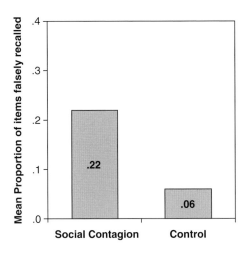

Figure 8.8 Proportion of items falsely recalled for the social contagion and control conditions. Data are from Roediger *et al.* (2001b).

recount the event in response to questions from police, friends and lawyers long before testifying in court. Each remembrance of the event may (depending on the context, the questions asked, etc.) alter it in subtle ways.

The misinformation provided in the experiments just discussed was from a written source. Roediger *et al.* (2001b) developed a paradigm to see whether similar effects would occur when students took turns recalling items from a scene. The two people came to the lab together and watched the same scenes. However, one person was an experimental confederate. The pair watched 6 scenes together and then took turns recalling 12 items from the scenes, 6 apiece. The confederate accurately recalled 6 items from 3 scenes, but for the other 3 scenes he recalled 4 correctly and got 2 wrong (producing items that might have been in the scene but were not). Finally, at the end of the experiment, the students were separated and tested separately (of course, only the real subject got the test). The subject was told to try to recall as accurately as possible the items that were in the original 6 scenes as the scenes were cued one by one. The interest was in whether the subjects would 'remember' items as being in the scene that the confederate suggested (and which were not in the scene). The answer is Yes, and the results are shown in Figure 8.8. The authors called this effect 'the social contagion of memory', because the confederate's erroneous memories 'infected' those of the subject. This effect is another example of how retroactive interference can create illusory memories.

In both the standard misinformation effect experiment and the social contagion variation on the theme, people are unaware of how their memories have been affected by information occurring after the events. As noted above, they often display high confidence in their illusory memories and claim to remember them in Tulving's (1985) special sense of the term. Warnings that the report includes errors or that the confederate made mistakes weaken but do not eliminate the effect (e.g. Meade and Roediger, 2002). Thus, as in the DRM effect, we are left in the paradoxical state where people cannot distinguish real events they actually experienced or saw from ones that were merely suggested, which leads to yet another paradox of memory. Of course, the misremembered events in the cases above were ones that were suggested to have been in the scene. Surely people would not misremember things they actually did (not just things they saw). Or would they?

Imagination inflation

Forming images is an age-old way to improve memory for verbal items (e.g. Bower and Reitman, 1972). Many mnemonic devices depend on imagery (e.g. Roediger, 1980). However, imagining events can also create errors. In experiments by Johnson and colleagues (1979), subjects either saw pictures of a butterfly various numbers of times or saw the word butterfly various numbers of times. Later they were asked to judge the frequency that a particular word or picture was observed. Subjects were generally fairly accurate at this task. However, in a condition in which subjects saw words but were asked to form mental images of the words' referents (see the word butterfly but form a mental image of a butterfly), the authors showed that the estimates of having seen the pictures of butterflies were increased. That is, subjects confused some of their own images for actually occurring pictures.

Goff and Roediger (1998) asked whether a similar effect would occur with behaviours people performed. Based on earlier work on action memory involving 'subject-performed tasks', they developed a set of 60 tasks that people could do while sitting at a desk either with small objects ('pick up the paper clip') or with hand movements ('touch your left ear with your right hand'). On a first day in the experiment, students heard instructions to perform tasks like these between one and six times; they performed some tasks but only listened to the instructions for others. They came back on a second day for a second session in which they now imagined performing tasks. Some of the tasks were ones they performed the first day, whereas others were new. Again, they were asked to imagine performing the tasks from one to six times. Then the students had a long break. They came back to the lab two weeks later. They were told that they would be given a test for the events they actually performed on the first day. They were told to ignore any events they heard on the second day and to concentrate on remembering only what happened on the first day.

The results showed that, despite the instructions, the act of imagining events on Day 2 inflated the judgements of the number of times they were performed on Day 1. This was true for events that actually had been performed on Day 1, but more importantly, it was true for events that were not performed on Day 1. That is, repeatedly imagining doing something made people believe they had actually done it. This effect has been called 'imagination inflation' and is studied in the laboratory, as here, or in more natural settings with events from childhood. In this latter case, imagining events from childhood (e.g. running through the house, slipping, and cutting one's hand on broken glass in a window) increased the probability that people thought the events had actually happened to them. Thomas *et al.* (2003) showed that instructing people to vividly imagine events (colours, sounds, etc.) increased imagination inflation. Imagination inflation shows that when we imagine ourselves performing actions we may later believe we actually did the action. Once again, our imaginations can play tricks on our memories.

The self-limiting nature of retrieval

Think back to a recent time that you were together with a large group of people – maybe 10 to 15 individuals – all of whom you know. It could be a dinner party, a work meeting, or any other type of gathering. Now try to list the names of all the people at this event. The first couple of names will be easy; however, you will probably find that it becomes progressively harder as you continue to retrieve names from memory. You may even fail

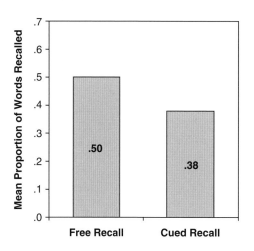

to remember the last two or three people – a frustration that we have all experienced before. This phenomenon presents a paradox because the retrieval of some information is generally thought to facilitate the retrieval of associated information. For example, the use of mnemonic devices, such as the peg-word method, is predicated on the idea that associations between memories enhance retrieval (Roediger, 1980). Why, then, does remembering sometimes grow harder as we successfully remember more related information?

One potential answer to this question is that, under certain circumstances, recall is a self-limiting process because the act of retrieving a memory can interfere with the retrieval of related memories, a phenomenon that is often referred to as 'output interference' (see Roediger, 1974, 1978; Tulving and Arbuckle, 1963) and has more recently been called retrieval-induced forgetting (Anderson *et al.*, 1994). The part-list (or part-set) cueing paradigm is one method that has been used in the laboratory to investigate output interference. In a typical experiment, subjects study a list of words and then they attempt to recall all the words in the list or they are 'cued' with a subset of the words in the list and must recall the other words in the list. For example, Slamecka (1968, Experiment 2) showed subjects a list of 30 words and then had them either recall all 30 words (free recall) or presented them with 15 of the words and had them recall the other 15 words (cued recall). Figure 8.9 shows the mean proportion recall in each group for the 15 words that were not presented in the cued recall condition. As you can see, subjects in the free recall group recalled a significantly greater proportion of the words relative to the cued recall group. That is, the presence of some of the words from the list seems to interfere with recall of the remaining words.

Why is recall a self-limiting process? Rundus (1973) offered an explanation in which knowledge is conceptualized as a hierarchical structure with groups of associated items connected to a common node (e.g. a category label). When recalling items associated with a given node, those items are retrieved through a process of sampling with replacement. The act of retrieving an item strengthens that item, which increases the probability that that item will be recalled again in the future. Thus, as more items from the set are recalled, these 'old' items begin to be repeatedly recalled, preventing the recovery of non-recalled items from the same set. Several other theories of these effects also exist (see Bäuml, 2008).

Paradoxes caused by fluency of cognitive processing

Try to remember a long trip that you took as a child. Perhaps you went to explore another country, or to visit relatives that live far away, or maybe you travelled to attend some unique event. Now, ask yourself, 'What makes me sure that I really experienced this event and that it is not a product of my imagination?' One way of answering this question is to evaluate the contents of the memory. Real memories tend to contain more idiosyncratic details, a greater amount of sensory, spatial or temporal information, and vivid imagery relative to imagined events (see Johnson *et al.*, 1993). In addition to the objective contents of the memory, people often rely upon the subjective experience of remembering in order to make such a determination. The act of remembering a past experience is often accompanied by a feeling of familiarity, which is interpreted as a signal that the memory truly represents a past experience. In the absence of this subjective experience, we may know that a particular experience occurred, but the feeling of ownership is lost.

One idea is that the subjective experience of remembering is derived directly from the memory trace. However, a problem with this idea is that the act of retrieving a memory does not always give rise to a feeling of remembering. For example, people with amnesia utilize representations of past experiences to facilitate performance on implicit memory tasks, but do not 'remember' those past experiences (see Roediger, 1990). In addition, people can experience a feeling of remembering in the absence of a memory trace – such as when an amnesic patient confabulates by making up a false response to a question but strongly believes it to be true. Thus, the existence of a memory trace is neither necessary nor sufficient for a person to experience a feeling of remembering.

An alternative idea, proposed by Jacoby and colleagues (1989), is that the subjective experience of remembering results from an attribution or inference about the fluency of cognitive processing. For example, when we re-read an old book, we process the prose more fluently and we (correctly) attribute that ease of processing to having read the book before. Similarly, when you tried to remember a long trip during childhood a few moments ago, the full memory likely came to mind relatively quickly after you had identified it and you (correctly) inferred that this fluency was due to you having previously experienced this event. Of course, these two examples illustrate instances in which fluent cognitive processing results from the existence of a memory trace and that fluency is correctly attributed to the memory trace. However, many other factors can also influence the fluency of cognitive processing – the use of overly complex words in prose can decrease perceptual fluency (e.g. Oppenheimer, 2006), priming people with the answer before displaying a question can increase the retrieval fluency (Kelley and Lindsay, 1993).

In addition, the attributions that people make about the origin of such fluent processing are often driven by the goals of the ongoing task. Increased fluency may be attributed (either correctly or incorrectly) to a prior experience if the current goal is to remember, but it may be attributed (again either correctly or incorrectly) to another factor if remembering is not the current goal. For example, if you are evaluating a piece of writing that is printed in a hard-to-read font, you might (incorrectly) attribute the decrease in perceptual fluency to the quality of writing and give it a poor evaluation (see Oppenheimer, 2006, Experiment 4). Thus, the accuracy of people's attributions about their subjective experience of remembering depends on both the source of the fluency of cognitive processing (prior experience versus other factors) and the current goal of the ongoing task (remembering versus another goal). Generally speaking, fluency is a good indicator of previous experience (i.e. the retrieval of a memory trace often produces a feeling of familiarity), and we often interpret this fluency correctly. However, under certain circumstances, our reliance on fluency can paradoxically result in misattributions. We now turn to describing three examples of paradoxes caused by the fluency of cognitive processing.

Cryptomnesia

Helen Keller was an American author and political activist, whose accomplishments are amazing because she was born deaf and blind. In 1892, an 11-year-old Keller published a story called *The Frost King*. Readers immediately noticed a striking similarity to a story called *The Frost Fairies* that appeared in a book written by Margaret Canby and published in 1874. Keller was accused of plagiarism – a charge that she vehemently denied. She claimed to have no recollection of being told *The Frost Fairies* story, but it later emerged that a family friend had communicated the story to her via her teacher, Anne Sullivan, tracing letters on her hand several years earlier. Made to stand trial before a tribunal of the Perkins Institute for the Blind, Keller was acquitted of intentional plagiarism in a close vote. The members of the tribunal who voted 'not guilty' were convinced that it was a case of cryptomnesia or unconscious plagiarism.

Cryptomnesia occurs when people retrieve other people's ideas and mistakenly believe that they generated them, either at that moment or at an earlier time. Helen Keller may have inadvertently plagiarized *The Frost Fairies* because it came to mind without any feeling of familiarity, and the absence of a subjective experience of remembering led her to believe that it was her own idea. Alternatively, if she did experience fluency in retrieving the story, she may have misattributed that fluency to the quality of the story because the goal of the ongoing task was creating a story (i.e. not remembering the previous experience of being told a story).

In the laboratory, cryptomnesia has been investigated using a paradigm in which two or more students collaborate on a generation task and then later try to remember who generated each idea and/or generate new ideas. For example, students might be asked to generate exemplars from categories (e.g. Brown and Murphy, 1989) or identify words in a word-search puzzle (e.g. Marsh and Bower, 1993). After the initial generation phase, they might have to recall the items that they generated earlier, generate new items, and/or take a recognition test that includes items that were generated by themselves and their partner as well as new items. In such experiments, cryptomnesia can occur in two ways: students can recall another person's item as their own, or they can generate a (seemingly) new item that was actually generated in the initial task.

Studies using this paradigm have shown that both types of unconscious plagiarism are quite common (e.g. Brown and Murphy, 1989; Marsh and Bower, 1993). The incidence of cryptomnesia increases when the final test phase is delayed rather than given immediately (e.g. Brown and Halliday, 1991). The goals of the ongoing task can also influence the amount of cryptomnesia observed. For example, a greater incidence of cryptomnesia is generally observed in tasks that involve generating new items relative to a recognition test in which students must categorize items as their own, someone else's or new (e.g. Marsh *et al.*, 1997). In addition, the incidence of cryptomnesia increases when people experience high incidental effort while working to generate items, but low effort when the solutions appear (Preston and Wegner, 2007). Presumably, this effect occurs because people misattribute the feeling of greater effort and subsequent release from effort to their own successful generation of the item. Interestingly, recent research suggests that separate processes might give rise to the two types of plagiarism described above because certain manipulations (e.g. feedback on the quality of the ideas generated; Perfect and Stark, 2008) and individual difference variables (e.g. age; McCabe *et al.*, 2007) affect each type of plagiarism differently.

Availability

Fluency can also affect people's judgements when relevant information comes to mind with ease. Consider the following question: Are you more likely to die from a car accident or a medical error? If you answered 'car accident', like many other people would, then you are wrong – assuming that you live in the United States of America, but it is probably the wrong answer in other countries too. While the number of fatalities from car accidents in USA has averaged between 40,000 and 45,000 each year over the past decade, medical error accounts for up to 225,000 deaths per year by one estimate (Starfield, 2000).

People make errors like this one because they often base their judgements on how easily relevant instances come to mind, a strategy that Tversky and Kahneman (1973, 1974) have called the 'availability heuristic'. When searching for relevant information on which to produce an answer to the question above, you likely had an easier time retrieving instances in which people died from a car crash than from medical error because the former is more prominently featured in the news, TV shows, books, etc. Reliance on the availability heuristic does not always result in an erroneous judgement because, generally speaking, availability is correlated with ecological frequency; however, it consistently leads to system-atic biases under some circumstances.

In studies that investigate the circumstances under which people rely on the availability heuristic, the critical manipulation often involves a factor that affects the fluency or ease with which information comes to mind. For example, Carroll (1978) explored whether having people imagine the outcome of a future event would increase the availability of that outcome and thus bias subsequent judgements. In one experiment, he had people imagine either Jimmy Carter or Gerald Ford winning the upcoming US presidential election. When people were later asked to predict who was more likely to win the election, they tended to pick the candidate that they had imagined earlier. In another experiment, he had people imagine a good season or a bad season for the US college football team that had won the national championship during the prior year. When asked about whether that team would get a bowl bid (i.e. an invitation to participate in prestigious post-season game) at the end of the upcoming season, people were more likely to predict a bowl bid if they had imagined a good season.

Although factors that increase the availability of relevant information can influence judgements, the way in which such information is used depends upon the fluency or ease with which it is retrieved. Schwarz *et al.* (1991, Experiment 1) manipulated the number of examples that people had to generate about one of two types of behaviour – acting assertively or unassertively. Subjects recalled either 6 or 12 examples of situations in which they behaved assertively or unassertively. In the two groups that recalled 12 examples of assertive or unassertive behaviours, retrieval was difficult because it was hard to generate such a large number of examples. In contrast, retrieval was relatively easy for the two groups that recalled six examples of assertive and unassertive behaviours. Later, subjects were asked to answer some general questions as part of an unrelated task, including a question on which they had to evaluate their assertiveness on a 10-point scale (where 1 equalled

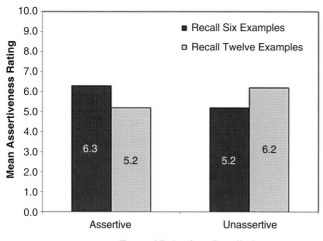

Figure 8.10 Mean assertiveness rating as a function of number of examples and type of behaviour recalled. High values represent higher assertiveness ratings. Data are from Schwarz et al. (1991, Experiment 1).

unassertive and 10 equalled assertive). As Figure 8.10 shows, subjects who experienced the difficulty of retrieving 12 examples of assertiveness rated themselves as less assertive relative to those who had to recall 6 examples (and vice versa for the subjects who were recalling examples of unassertiveness). As this example illustrates, judgements can be influenced by the availability of relevant information, but that influence depends on the fluency with which that information is retrieved.

Implicit theories of stability and change

The fluency with which memories are retrieved also plays an important role in how we construct our personal histories. As this chapter has undoubtedly convinced you by now, human memory is a constructive process, and the way in which we remember the narrative of our lives is no exception. Much like the availability heuristic, our knowledge about our current self can bias our judgements about our past self. As Michael Ross (1989) has argued, people possess implicit theories about stability and change, and they use these implicit theories to construct their personal histories. If people believe that they have been consistent over time with respect to a certain attribute (e.g. extraversion) or attitude (e.g. stance on abortion), then they will consider current status and then judge their past self to be similar. Alternatively, if people believe that they have changed, then they will judge their past self to be different. Much of the time people's implicit theories of stability or change are correct, and they can more or less accurately recall their past self. However, when their implicit theories are wrong it can lead to biases in recall and judgement.

A study by McFarland and Ross (1987) provides a prime example of how people's implicit theories of stability can lead them to overestimate the similarity between their present and past selves. In an initial session, they had undergraduate students with steady dating partners rate themselves and their partner on the expected stability of 25 traits (e.g. honesty, intelligence, reliability) over the next two months. In a follow-up session two months later, the students re-rated themselves and their partners on the same traits and tried to recall their earlier ratings. Students whose ratings were more positive relative to their earlier rating tended to recall their earlier rating as more positive than it was, and vice versa for students whose ratings became more negative. Presumably, the bias that the students exhibited in remembering their past impressions resulted from their implicit theory of stability and the ease with which they could retrieve their current impressions of themselves and their partner.

Ross and Wilson have gone on to explore the related idea of how people's implicit theory of stability or change affects the 'subjective temporal distance' of events (for a brief review see Ross and Wilson, 2003). Subjective temporal distance is a measure of how far away people feel from past selves. In general, people view their present self more favourably than their past self, and they judge their own self-improvement over time to be greater than that of their peers (e.g. Wilson and Ross, 2001). When people evaluate past selves, they often exhibit a bias in their judgement of the distance of past events in which they judge successes to be closer in time and failures to be further in past (e.g. Ross and Wilson, 2002). Interestingly, subjective temporal distance can be manipulated by making events seem more recent or distant, and people tend to be more critical of their former self when an event seems more distant (Ross and Wilson, 2003).

Future challenges and questions

This chapter has covered paradoxes of behaviour that result from remembering and knowing, task difficulty, interference and the fluency of cognitive processing. We have described 12 paradoxes that all follow the same general form: people behave in a certain way, but their judgements about their behaviour are somehow wrong-headed. They tell an erroneous story about why they behaved as they did, or they predict the opposite of what will happen (e.g. students think repeated reading will produce better recall later than practice in retrieving, yet the recall results later show exactly the opposite). The purpose of our chapter is to call these puzzles to the attention of researchers.

A target for future research, which would make good on the promise implicit in the title of the book, is to discover the neural basis for these puzzles and paradoxes. We did not attempt to describe the neural bases of the illusions and puzzles that we reviewed, but this omission is only partly our fault. If we had tried to link some of these behavioural findings to brain research, our efforts would have been futile because there is a paucity of research in the neuroscience literature about these topics. Although cognitive neuroscientists are starting to look for answers to some of these questions (e.g. Kuhl *et al.*, 2007; Mobbs *et al.*, 2009; Trepel *et al.*, 2005), a more concerted effort is surely needed.

References

Anderson, M. C., Bjork, R. A., & Bjork, E. L. (1994). Remembering can cause forgetting: retrieval dynamics in long-term memory. *Journal of Experimental Psychology: Learning, Memory and Cognition*, **20**: 1063–87.

Bahrick, H. P., Bahrick, L. E., Bahrick, A. S., & Bahrick, P. E. (1993). Maintenance of foreign language vocabulary and the spacing effect. *Psychological Science*, **4**: 316–21.

Balota, D. A., Cortese, M. J., Duchek, J. M., *et al.* (1999). Veridical and false memories in healthy older adults and in dementia of the Alzheimers type. *Cognitive Neuropsychology*, **16**: 361–84.

Bartlett, F. C. (1932). *Remembering: A Study in Experimental and Social Psychology.* Cambridge: Cambridge University Press.

Bäuml, K. H. (2008). Inhibitory processes. In: Roediger, H. L. (Ed.). *Cognitive Psychology of Memory.* Oxford: Elsevier, 195–220.

Bjork, R. A. (1975). Retrieval as a memory modifier. In: Solso, S. (Ed.). *Information Processing and Cognition: The Loyola Symposium*. Hillsdale, NJ: Lawrence Erlbaum Associates, 123–44.

Bjork, R. A. (1994a). Memory and metamemory considerations in the training of human beings. In: Metcalfe, J. & Shimamura, A. (Eds.). *Metacognition: Knowing About Knowing*. Cambridge, MA: MIT Press, 185–205.

Bjork, R. A. (1994b). Institutional impediments to effective training. In: Druckman, D. and Bjork, R. A. (Eds.). *Learning, Remembering, Believing: Enhancing Human Performance*. Washington, DC: National Academy Press, 295–306.

Bjork, R. A., & Bjork, E. L. (1992). A new theory of disuse and an old theory of stimulus fluctuation. In: Healy, A., Kosslyn, S. & Shiffrin, R. (Eds.). *From Learning Processes to Cognitive Processes: Essays in Honor of William K. Estes, Volume. 2*. Hillsdale, NJ: Erlbaum, 35–67.

Bower, G. H., & Reitman, J. S. (1972). Mnemonic elaboration in multilist learning. *Journal of Verbal Learning & Verbal Behaviour*, **11**: 478–85.

Brown, A. S., & Halliday, H. E. (1991). Crytomnesia and source memory difficulties. *American Journal of Psychology*, **104**: 475–90.

Brown, A. S., & Murphy, D. R. (1989). Cryptomnesia: delineating inadvertent plagiarism. *Journal of Experimental Psychology: Learning, Memory, and Cognition*, **15**: 432–42.

Callender, A. A., & McDaniel, M. A. (2009). The limited benefits of rereading educational texts. *Contemporary Educational Psychology*, **34**: 30–41.

Carrier, M., & Pashler, H. (1992). The influence of retrieval on retention. *Memory & Cognition*, **20**: 632–42.

Carroll, J. S. (1978). The effect of imagining an event on expectations for the event: an interpretation in terms of the availability heuristic. *Journal of Experimental Social Psychology*, **14**: 88–96.

Castel, A. D., McCabe, D. P., & Roediger, H. L., & Heitman, J. (2007). The dark side of

expertise: domain specific memory errors. *Psychological Science*, **18**: 3–5.

Cepeda, N. J., Vul, E., Rohrer, D., Wixted, J. T., & Pashler, H., (2008). Spacing effect in learning: a temporal ridgeline of optimal retention. *Psychological Science*, **19**: 1095–102.

Cepeda, N. J., Pashler, H., Vul, E., Wixted, J. T., & Rohrer, D. (2006). Distributed practice in verbal recall tasks: a review and quantitative synthesis. *Psychological Bulletin*, **132**: 354–80.

Christina, R. W., & Bjork, R. A. (1991). Optimizing long-term retention and transfer. In: Druckman, D. & Bjork, R. A. (Eds.). *In The Mind's Eye: Enhancing Human Performance*. Washington, DC: National Academy Press, 23–56.

Deese, J. (1959). On the prediction of occurrence of particular verbal intrusions in immediate recall. *Journal of Experimental Psychology*, **58**: 17–22.

Dempster, F. N. (1989). Spacing effects and their implications for theory and practice. *Educational Psychology Review*, **1**: 309–30.

Dunning, D. (2005). *Self-insight: Roadblocks and Detours on the Path to Knowing Thyself*. New York, NY: Psychology Press.

Ebbinghaus, H. (1967). *Memory: A Contribution to Experimental Psychology* (H. A. Ruger & C. E. Bussenius, Trans.). New York, NY: Dover. (Original work published 1885.)

Fischhoff, B. (1975). Hindsight is not equal to foresight: the effect of outcome knowledge on judgement under uncertainty. *Journal of Experimental Psychology: Human Perception and Performance*, **1**: 288–99.

Fischhoff, B., & Beyth, R. (1975). 'I knew it would happen': remembered probabilities of once-future things. *Organizational Behaviour & Human Performance*, **13**: 1–16.

Foster, J. B., & Magdoff, F. (2009). *The Great Financial Crisis: Causes and Consequences*. New York, NY: Monthly Review Press.

Gallo, D. A. (2006). *Associative Illusions of Memory*. New York, NY: Psychology Press.

Gardiner, J. M. (1988). Functional aspects of recollective experience. *Memory & Cognition*, **16**: 309–13.

Gilovich, T. (1991). *How We Know What Isn't So: The Fallibility of Human Reason in Everyday Life*. New York, NY: The Free Press.

Glenberg, A. M. (1976). Monotonic and nonmonotonic lag effects in paired-associate and recognition memory paradigms. *Journal of Verbal Learning and Verbal Behavior*, **15**: 1–16.

Glover, J. A. (1989). The 'testing' phenomenon: not gone but nearly forgotten. *Journal of Educational Psychology*, **81**: 392–9.

Goff, L. M., & Roediger, H. L. (1998). Imagination inflation for action events: repeated imaginings lead to illusory recollections. *Memory & Cognition*, **26**: 20–33.

Goode, M. K., Geraci, L., & Roediger, H. L., III (2008). Superiority of variable to repeated practice in transfer on anagram solution. *Psychonomic Bulletin & Review*, **15**: 662–6.

Jacoby, L. L., Kelley, C. M., & Dywan, J. (1989). Memory attributions. In: Roediger, H. L. & Craik, F. I. M. (Eds.). *Varieties of Memory and Consciousness: Essays in Honour of Endel Tulving*. Hillsdale, NJ: Erlbaum, 391–422.

Johnson, M. K., & Raye, C. L. (1981). Reality monitoring. *Psychological Review*, **88**: 67–85.

Johnson, M. K., Hashtroudi, S., & Lindsay, D. S. (1993). Source monitoring. *Psychological Bulletin*, **114**: 3–28.

Johnson, M. K., Raye, C. L., Wang, A. Y., & Taylor, T. H. (1979). Fact and fantasy: the roles of accuracy and variability in confusing imaginations with perceptual experiences. *Journal of Experimental Psychology: Human Learning and Memory*, **5**: 229–40.

Kahneman, D. (2003). Maps of bounded rationality: psychology for behavioral economics. *American Economic Review*, **93**: 1449–75.

Karpicke, J. D., & Roediger, H. L. (2008). The critical importance of retrieval for learning. *Science*, **15**: 966–8.

Karpicke, J. D., Butler, A. C., & Roediger, H. L. (2009). Metacognitive strategies in student learning: do students practice retrieval when they study on their own? *Memory*, **17**: 471–9.

Kelley, C. M., & Lindsay, D. S. (1993). Remembering mistaken as knowing: ease of generation as a basis for confidence in answers to general knowledge questions. *Journal of Memory and Language*, **32**: 1–24.

Kerr, R., & Booth, B. (1978). Specific and varied practice of a motor skill. *Perceptual and Motor Skills*, **46**: 395–401.

Kornell, N., & Bjork, R. A. (2007). The promise and perils of self-regulated study. *Psychonomic Bulletin & Review*, **14**: 219–24.

Kuhl, B. A., Dudukovic, N. M., Kahn, I., & Wagner, A. D. (2007). Decreased demands on cognitive control reveal the neural processing benefits of forgetting. *Nature Neuroscience*, **10**: 908–14.

Loftus, E., Miller, D., & Burns, H. (1978). Semantic integration of verbal information into a visual memory. *Journal of Experimental Psychology: Human Learning and Memory*, **4**: 19–31.

Loftus, E. F., & Palmer, J. C. (1974). Reconstruction of automation destruction: an example of the interaction between language and memory. *Journal of Verbal Learning and Verbal Behavior*, **13**: 585–9.

Magill, R. A., & Hall, K. G. (1990). A review of the contextual inference effect in motor skill acquisition. *Human Movement Science*, **9**: 241–89.

Marsh, R. L., & Bower, G. H. (1993). Eliciting cryptomnesia: unconscious plagiarism in a puzzle task. *Journal of Experimental Psychology: Learning, Memory, and Cognition*, **19**: 673–88.

Marsh, R. L., Landau, J. D., & Hicks, J. L. (1997). Contributions of inadequate source monitoring to unconscious plagiarism during idea generation. *Journal of Experimental Psychology: Learning, Memory, and Cognition*, **23**: 886–97.

Mawhinney, V. T., Bostow, D. E., Laws, D. R., Blumenfeld, G. J., & Hopkins, B. L. (1971). A comparison of students studying-behavior produced by daily, weekly, and three-week testing schedules. *Journal of Applied Behavior Analysis*, **4**: 257–64.

McCabe, D. P., Smith, A. D., & Parks, C. M. (2007). Inadvertent plagiarism in young and older adults: the role of working memory capacity in reducing memory errors. *Memory & Cognition*, **35**: 231–41.

McFarland, C., & Ross, M. (1987). The relation between current impressions and memories of self and dating partners. *Personality and Social Psychology Bulletin*, **12**: 228–38.

Meade, M. L., & Roediger, H. L. (2002). Explorations in the social contagion of memory. *Memory & Cognition*, **30**: 995–1009.

Melton, A. W. (1970). The situation with respect to the spacing of repetitions and memory. *Journal of Verbal Learning and Verbal Behavior*, **9**: 596–606.

Michael, J. (1991). A behavioral perspective on college teaching. *The Behavior Analyst*, **14**: 229–39.

Mobbs, D., Hassabis, D., Seymour, B., *et al.* (2009). Choking on the money: reward-based performance decrements are associated with midbrain activity. *Psychological Science*, **20**: 955–62.

Newell, A. (1973). You can't play 20 questions with nature and win: projective comments on the papers of this symposium. In: Chase, W. G. (Ed.). *Visual Information Processing*. New York, NY: Academic Press, 283–308.

Newton, L. (1990). Overconfidence in the communication of intent: heard and unheard melodies. Unpublished doctoral dissertation, Department of Psychology, Stanford University.

Nisbett, R. E., & Wilson, T. D. (1977). Telling more than we can know: verbal reports on mental processes. *Psychological Review*, **84**: 231–59.

Oppenheimer, D. M. (2006). Consequences of erudite vernacular utilized irrespective of necessity: problems with using long words needlessly. *Applied Cognitive Psychology*, **20**: 139–56.

Perfect, T. J., & Stark, L. (2008). Why do I always have the best ideas? The role of idea quality in unconscious plagiarism. *Memory*, **16**: 386–94.

Piaget, J. (1962). *Play, Dreams and Imitation in Childhood*. New York, NY: Norton.

Pohl, R. F. (2004). *Cognitive Illusions: A Handbook on Fallacies and Biases in Thinking, Judgement and Memory*. Hove: Psychology Press.

Preston, J., & Wegner, D. M. (2007). The eureka error: inadvertent plagiarism by misattributions of effort. *Journal of Personality and Social Psychology*, **92**: 575–84.

Rajaram, S. (1993). Remembering and knowing: two means of access to the personal past. *Memory & Cognition*, **21**: 89–102.

Roediger, H. L. (1974). Inhibiting effects of recall. *Memory & Cognition*, **2**: 261–9.

Roediger, H. L. (1978). Recall as a self-limiting process. *Memory & Cognition*, **6**: 54–63.

Roediger, H. L. (1980). Memory metaphors in cognitive psychology. *Memory & Cognition*, **8**: 231–46.

Roediger, H. L. (1990). Implicit memory: retention without remembering. *American Psychologist*, **45**: 1043–56.

Roediger, H. L., & Karpicke, J. D. (2006a). The power of testing memory: basic research and implications for educational practice. *Perspectives on Psychological Science*, **1**: 181–210.

Roediger, H. L., & Karpicke, J. D. (2006b). Test-enhanced learning: taking memory tests improves long-term retention. *Psychological Science*, **17**: 249–55.

Roediger, H. L., & McDermott, K. B. (1995). Creating false memories: remembering words that were not presented in lists. *Journal of Experimental Psychology: Learning, Memory and Cognition*, **21**: 803–14.

Roediger, H. L., Balota, D. A., & Watson, J. M. (2001a). Spreading activation and the arousal of false memories. In: Roediger, H. L., Nairne, J. S., Neath, I. & Surprenant, A. M. (Eds.). *The Nature of Remembering: Essays in Honor of Robert G. Crowder*. Washington, D.C.: American Psychological Association Press, 95–115.

Roediger, H. L., Jacoby, D., & McDermott, K. B. (1996). Misinformation effects in recall: creating false memories through repeated retrieval. *Journal of Memory and Language*, **35**: 300–18.

Roediger, H. L., Meade, M. L., & Bergman, E. (2001b). Social contagion of memory. *Psychonomic Bulletin & Review*, **8**: 365–71.

Ross, M. (1989). Relation of implicit theories to the construction of personal histories. *Psychological Review*, **96**: 341–57.

Ross, M., & Wilson, A. E. (2002). It feels like yesterday: self-esteem, valence of personal past experiences, and judgments of subjective distance. *Journal of Personality and Social Psychology*, **82**: 792–803.

Ross, M., & Wilson, A. E. (2003). Autobiographical memory and conceptions of self: getting better all the time. *Current Directions in Psychological Science*, **12**: 66–9.

Rundus, D. (1973). Negative effects of using list items as recall cues. *Journal of Verbal Learning & Verbal Behavior*, **12**: 43–50.

Schmidt, R. A., & Bjork, R. A. (1992). New conceptualizations of practice: common principles in three paradigms suggest new concepts for training. *Psychological Science*, **3**: 207–17.

Schwarz, N., Bless, H., Strack, F., Klumpp, G., Rittenauer-Schatka, H., & Simons, A. (1991). Ease of retrieval as information: another look at the availability heuristic. *Journal of Personality and Social Psychology*, **61**: 195–202.

Shapiro, D. C., & Schmidt, R. A. (1982). The schema theory: recent evidence and developmental implications. In: Kelso, J. A. S. & Clark, J. E. (Eds.). *The Development of Movement Control and Co-ordination*. New York, NY: Wiley, 113–50.

Shea, J. B., & Morgan, R. L. (1979). Contextual interference effects on the acquisition, retention, and transfer of a motor skill. *Journal of Experimental Psychology: Human Learning and Memory*, **5**: 179–87.

Shepard, R. N. (1981). Psychological complementarity. In: Kubovy, M. & Pomerantz, J. R. (Eds.). *Perceptual Organization*. Hillsdale, NJ: Lawrence Erlbaum Associates, 279–342.

Slamecka, N. J. (1968). An examination of trace storage in free recall. *Journal of Experimental Psychology*, **76**: 504–13.

Starfield, B. (2000). Is US health really the best in the world? *Journal of the American Medical Association*, **284**: 483–5.

Thomas, A. K., Bulevich, J. B., & Loftus, E. F. (2003). Exploring the role of repetition and sensory elaboration in the imagination inflation effect. *Memory & Cognition*, **31**: 630–40.

Trepel, C., Fox, C. R., & Poldrack, R. A. (2005). Prospect theory on the brain: toward a cognitive neuroscience of decision under risk. *Cognitive Brain Research*, **23**: 34–50.

Tulving, E. (1985). Memory and consciousness. *Canadian Psychologist*, **26**: 1–12.

Tulving, E., & Arbuckle, T. Y. (1963). Sources of intratrial interference in paired-associate learning. *Journal of Verbal Learning & Verbal Behavior*, **1**: 321–34.

Tversky, A., & Kahneman, D. (1973). Availability: a heuristic for judging frequency and probability. *Cognitive Psychology*, **5**: 207–32.

Tversky, A., & Kahneman, D. (1974). Judgments under uncertainty: heuristics and biases. *Science*, **185**: 1124–31.

Underwood, B. J. (1961). Ten years of massed practice on distributed practice. *Psychological Review*, **68**: 229–47.

Wilson, A. E., & Ross, M. (2001). From chump to champ: people's appraisals of their earlier and current selves. *Journal of Personality and Social Psychology*, **80**: 572–84.

Wilson, T. D. (2002). *Strangers to Ourselves: Discovering the Adaptive Unconscious*. Cambridge, MA: Harvard University Press.

Wood, G. (1978). The knew-it-all-along effect. *Journal of Experimental Psychology: Human Perception and Performance*, **4**: 345–53.

Chapter 9

The paradox of human expertise: why experts get it wrong

Itiel E. Dror

Summary

Expertise is correctly, but one-sidedly, associated with special abilities and enhanced performance. The other side of expertise, however, is surreptitiously hidden. Along with expertise, performance may also be degraded, culminating in a lack of flexibility and error. Expertise is demystified by explaining the brain functions and cognitive architecture involved in being an expert. These information processing mechanisms, the very making of expertise, entail computational trade-offs that sometimes result in paradoxical functional degradation. For example, being an expert entails using schemas, selective attention, chunking information, automaticity and more reliance on top-down information, all of which allows experts to perform quickly and efficiently; however, these very mechanisms restrict flexibility and control, may cause the experts to miss and ignore important information, introduce tunnel vision and bias and can cause other effects that degrade performance. Such phenomena are apparent in a wide range of expert domains, from medical professionals and forensic examiners, to military fighter pilots and financial traders.

Expertise is highly sought after – only those with special abilities, after years of training and experience, can achieve those exceptional brain powers that make them experts. Indeed, being an expert is most often prestigious, well-paid, respected and in high demand. However, examining expertise in depth raises some interesting and complex questions. In this chapter, I will take apart and reject the myth that experts merely have superior performance per se. I will not only show that experts are not exclusively superior or infallible, but that they are in fact sometimes prone to specific types of degradations and errors.

Examining expertise from a cognitive neuroscientific perspective offers an opportunity to understand that expertise is not about being faster and more efficient, but rather that experts go about things differently. This leads to high performance in most cases, but not always. Paradoxically, the very underpinning of expertise can entail degradation in performance as well, such as tunnel vision and biases. These are inherent computational and cognitive trade-offs resulting from the brain functions of experts. These trade-offs mean that as you enhance performance in some aspects, you may decrease it in others. For example, as experts modify their mental representations, they form very efficient brain

The Paradoxical Brain, ed. Narinder Kapur. Published by Cambridge University Press. © Cambridge University Press 2011.

mechanisms, but these very mechanisms are inherently automatic and rigid, causing vulnerabilities that may result in degradation and error (Sternberg, 2002; Stanovich, 2009).

To understand these mechanisms and their trade-offs, I start off with a discussion about the world of experts and expertise. Then, I explore the brains and cognitive mechanisms of experts, examining specific mental representations and architectures. Their paradoxical nature will be highlighted by computational trade-offs, and their functional degradation will be illustrated through expertise in real-world domains.

Recognizing and labelling an individual as an expert is to a large extent a social construct, often based on education, certification and social acceptance. These are not considered here, because the focus is on the actual expertise *de facto*. In other words, what are the brain and cognitive makings of an expert, rather than the external social issues involved (there may well be experts who are not socially recognized as experts, and – conversely – there may be recognized 'experts' who in fact do not possess sufficient – or any – expertise). Hence, I examine expertise from its *actual* brain and cognitive underpinning, rather than addressing social notions of expertise. I am interested in the ontology of what *actually* constitutes expertise, rather than the epistemological questions of how we recognize and know who an expert is.

Even within the brain and cognitive literature, sometimes the notion of expertise has been diluted and even dissolved by attributing it to everyone. For example, many researchers regard people as 'experts' in face recognition (e.g. Schwaninger *et al.*, 2003; Carey, 1992; Tanaka, 2001). Indeed, people have an excellent ability to recognize faces. However, since everyone possesses this ability[1] (effortlessly and without needing specialized training), it does not, in essence, constitute expertise in the way I conceptualize and address it.

Expertise is discussed and conceptualized in terms of expert performance, expertise in the sense of special abilities that only some people possess, in contrast to others who are not experts – the novices – who cannot perform to the levels of experts (e.g. Dror *et al.*, 1993; Wood, 1999). These abilities may entail different types of knowledge and performance characteristics associated with different expertise. For example, declarative vs. procedural knowledge (Squire, 1994; see 'knowing that' vs. 'knowing how,' Ryle, 1946, 1949). Declarative knowledge, *knowing that*, is more factually based and may be more related to academic and intellectual experts who understand certain things (but may not be able to 'do' anything with it), whereas procedural knowledge, *knowing how*, is more related to performing an act, where an expert knows how to do certain things (but may not understand much or anything about it). For instance, an expert physicist knows the laws of physics, but may not know how to ride a bicycle, drive a car or fly an airplane. In contrast, expert drivers and pilots will know how to drive and race a car, or fly an aircraft, but may have no knowledge of the physics underlying their expert performance. Indeed, trying to access declarative knowledge can even interfere with expert performance that relies on procedural knowledge, e.g. expert golfers (Flegal and Anderson, 2008).

The distinction between expertise being based on *knowing that* or on *knowing how* is directly related to the real-world domains of expertise. For example, in the medical domain some specialists may have expertise in diagnosis, knowing how to read, for instance, X-rays; being able to *know that* a 'tumour is present', whereas other experts,

---

[1] Except patients with developmental or acquired prosopagnosia, who have specific impairments in recognizing faces.

such as surgeons, may specialize and have expertise in executing medical procedures, i.e. *know how* to remove the tumour. Some expert domains are clearly characterized more by one type of knowledge, e.g. music, sports and other performing experts are based on knowing how. Although experts may have both types of knowledge, often they need to rely on one type of knowledge rather than the other (e.g. in policing, see Dror, 2007). The type of expert knowledge that is most appropriate depends on the situational demands and on the cognitive mechanisms involved in operationalizing this knowledge; e.g. time constraints (e.g. Beilock *et al.*, 2004; Dror, 2007).

Experts often have special 'talent'; in other words, special and specific cognitive abilities needed to perform tasks associated with their expert domain. Astronauts have mental imagery abilities that are important for controlling a robotic arm during Space Shuttle and International Space Station missions (Menchaca-Brandan *et al.*, 2007). Cognitive ability to inhibit an ongoing action in response to a signal from the environment is important for expert baseball batting (Gray, 2009). Many specific cognitive abilities are important in the medical domain, and specifically in surgery (e.g. Tansley *et al.*, 2007). These examples of baseball batting and surgical competence relate to expertise that are characterized by knowing how, as they require, and extensively rely on, the ability to perform an action – executing a motor command.

If cognitive abilities are important for such expertise, then domains that are much more cognitively oriented, such as requiring visualization and pattern matching, are critically dependent on cognitive abilities. Take, for example, the reliance on spatial visualization in technical graphics and engineering design (Yue, 2007); the examination and comparison of impression and pattern evidence in forensic domains (Dror and Cole, 2010); the visualization of three-dimensional structures of molecules from two-dimensional representations in chemistry (Pribyl and Bodner, 1987); or the visualization of body parts and their spatial relations by clinical anatomists (Fernandez *et al.*, 2011) and verbal and visuospatial abilities of expert Scrabble players (Halpern and Wai, 2007).

Experts have abilities and capabilities that enable them to perform at much higher levels than non-experts, the novices.[2] To achieve such performance levels, experts need to have well-organized knowledge, use sophisticated and specific mental representations and cognitive processing, apply automatic sequences quickly and efficiently, be able to deal with large amounts of information, make sense of signals and patterns even when they are obscured by noise, deal with low quality and quantity of data, or with ambiguous information and many other challenging task demands and situations that otherwise paralyse the performance of novices (e.g. Patel *et al.*, 1999; Wood, 1999; Dror *et al.*, 1993). Such expert abilities and cognitive performance have been associated with specialized brains; for example, in musicians (Gaser and Schlaug, 2003), radiologists (Harley *et al.*, 2009), mathematicians (Aydin *et al.*, 2007), forensic examiners (Busey and Vanderkolk, 2005), taxi drivers (Maguire *et al.*, 2000) and even jugglers (Draganski *et al.*, 2004).

Experts have abilities and knowledge that has been acquired by repeated exposure to the tasks they need to perform. With time, they tune into and pick out the important and relevant information, learning how to detect and use it well while ignoring and filtering

---

[2] I conceptualize expertise as a continuum with different levels of performance abilities rather than a dichotomy. Indeed, in some domains there is clear quantification of expert levels, such as chess (e.g. Elo, 2008). In other domains which are not so well-defined, it is more difficult to clearly quantify levels of expertise, but there is nevertheless a range of levels.

out everything else (e.g. Kundel and Nodine, 1983; Wood, 1999). Experts are driven by knowledge contained in specific mental representations and schemas which they have acquired by learning and experience (see Russell, 1910, for the distinction between knowledge by *description* vs. knowledge by *acquaintance*). Armed with these expert tools, they select and focus on the specific signals that are relevant, and perform quickly and efficiently even in environments that contain little data or noise (e.g. Gold *et al.*, 1999; Lu and Dosher, 2004).

Training of experts can be improved and enhanced by helping them learn the important and critical signals. For example, expertise in aircraft identification requires knowledge of the distinguishing and distinctive features of each aircraft, and how to utilize them to identify aircraft in a whole spectrum of orientations. Initially identification is difficult, if not impossible. However, through repeated exposure to aircraft, experts learn the critical signals that characterize each aircraft, and use these for identification. Dror *et al.* (2008) enhanced the efficiency and effectiveness of acquiring this expertise by artificially *exaggerating the distinctive and unique features* of each aircraft during training. The enhanced training not only reduced the time needed to acquire this expertise, but it also produced more effective mental representations that improved performance later during testing (see Dror *et al.*, 2008, for more details). With such knowledge, experts can deal with complex and difficult tasks with relative ease, seemingly performing instantaneously and effortlessly.

Experts' ability to perform with relative ease is surprising given the brain's limited capacity and resources to process information. However, this is exactly the point: experts deal with *cognitive load* by mental representations and cognitive processes that are computationally efficient. This enables them to perform at high levels in the face of constraints imposed by the brain. Certainly, one of the impediments on the performance of novices is the brain's limited capacity to process information. Experts overcome these constraints in a number of ways that allow them to perform well; however, these solutions also entail a cost – the associated degradation.

Experts often report that they 'see things differently'. Indeed, a cornerstone of expertise is that they modify how they represent information and the brain's neuronal mechanisms that process it. There are a few typical changes in *knowledge organization* with expertise, which affect mental representations and processing. The common denominator of such changes is that they re-package the information in ways that make it more efficient to perform certain tasks. An everyday example of how people do such cognitive 're-packaging' is when we 'chunk' information together. Chunking means that cognitive load is reduced by lumping things together in mental representations that fit the task demands. For instance, consider how people memorize and use phone numbers. They start off with singular digits, but as they gain experience and use a number, they often 'chunk' some of the digits together, re-packing the phone number (or area code) to a smaller number of units of information. Using different mental representations to reduce cognitive load and increase efficiency is a general cognitive and brain mechanism that is used when the available resources are stretched; for example, older people may adopt more computationally efficient mental representations (Dror *et al.*, 2005).

With expertise, mental representations are formed to fit the specific task demands while controlling for cognitive load. For example, Czerwinski *et al.* (1992) suggest 'perceptual unitization', whereby conjunctions of features are chunked together so they are perceived as a single entity. Unitization creates new entities and neural processing that causes components that were once perceived separately to become fused together (Schyns and Rodet,

1997). Such new brain organization plays an important role in expertise (Goldstone, 2000; Shiffrin and Lightfoot, 1997). However, the price of making such expertise-based unitizations is that the components are less available, if not inaccessible altogether (Fusi *et al.*, 2005; Kepecs *et al.*, 2002).

The re-occurrence of typical configuration arrangements in expert domains results in lumping them and jointly putting them together within a mental representation. Expert chess players are a good illustration of this mechanism, exemplifying its advantages as well as its functional degradation. Expert chess players do not represent board positions by constituting individual pieces on the board; rather, they often chunk them together into meaningful patterns. Indeed, expert chess players are much better than novices in encoding and remembering board positions. However, the more efficient representations are constructed to fit certain situations and address specific task demands and experiences. That means that these mechanisms of representing information are effective and efficient, but only under certain conditions. The enhanced functional performance is limited; the chess experts are indeed better than novices in encoding and remembering board positions, but this is limited only to realistic board positions. Experts are no better, and are even worse than novices, in board positions in which the constituting individual pieces are placed at random (Chase and Simon, 1973; Gobet and Simon, 1996). The reason for this is that the experts' mental representations are based on their experience with real games and real board positions. Hence, their expert knowledge is helpful in those situations, but it does not help, and it even hinders performance, when the knowledge is not applicable (as in random board positions). The use of mental representations that capture configural arrangements rather than single pieces is typical of experts across domains, from forensic fingerprint experts to experts in the recognition of cars, dogs and birds (e.g. Busey and Vanderkolk, 2005; Gauthier *et al.*, 2000; Tanaka and Curran, 2001; Rhodes and McLean, 1990).

The brain changes that occur with expertise reflect the optimization of the brain to carry out the cognitive information processing needed for specific expert performance. As such, the brain adapts, taking advantage of neuronal plasticity. However, as the brain develops to accomplish specific expertise, there are a number of resulting limitations and even degradations that can occur. For example, professional London taxi drivers develop specific brains that underpin their expertise, with greater grey matter volume in the posterior hippocampi (Maguire *et al.*, 2000, 2006). However, such changes in the brain are not mere improvement and enhancement across the board. Along with greater grey matter volume in the posterior hippocampi, Maguire *et al.* found less grey matter volume in the anterior hippocampi. The accompanying behavioural performance levels showed that the London taxi drivers' superior knowledge of London landmarks and their spatial relationships came at a cost of degraded performance in anterograde visuo-spatial memory (see Maguire *et al.*, 2000, 2006). A further study showed that, although London taxi drivers were significantly more knowledgeable about London landmarks and their spatial relationships, they were significantly worse at forming and retaining new associations involving visual information (Woollett and Maguire, 2009).

The same type of trade-offs are apparent in other expert domains. For example, while detecting abnormalities in chest X-rays, expert radiologists show brain activity in the right fusiform face area (FFA) that is correlated with visual expertise. However, it seems that this comes at a price, as activity in left lateral occipital cortex correlated negatively with expertise, and was reduced in experts compared to novices. Hence, achieving expert visual performance may involve developing new neural representations while simultaneously suppressing other existing structures (for details, see Harley *et al.*, 2009). Part of the explanation of some of these brain trade-offs has to do with narrow neural tuning that may accompany specialization and expertise (e.g. Jiang *et al.*, 2007).

Other brain changes reflect higher cognitive mental representations that characterize expertise. For example, Busey and Vanderkolk (2005) studied expert fingerprint examiners and observed brain activity that shows configural processing in fingerprint experts (but not novices). At a higher level of information processing, cognition depends both on bottom-up and top-down information. Bottom-up refers to the incoming data, where as top-down relies on pre-existing knowledge. Top-down has many forms and manifestations, which include the context in which the data is presented, past experience and knowledge, expectations, etc. Experts rely more on top-down information, which allows efficient and effective processing of the bottom-up data, but it can distort and bias how the data are processed. For example, detectives and forensic experts may contaminate and bias investigations because of such top-down processes (see Dror, 2008, 2009; Dror and Cole, 2010).

Experts often consolidate and integrate complex sequences of steps into a unified routine and schemata. By chunking steps together into a single entity or action, the experts not only achieve quick performance in terms of execution time, but they are able to do more because these processes are more computationally efficient. Such mental representations and information processing many times give rise to *automatization* (Schneider and Shiffrin, 1977; Shiffrin and Schneider, 1977). Experts rely on such processes especially in domains that require complex decisions and actions under time pressure and risk. Automaticity is so efficient that many times it does not require conscious initiation or control, and it may even occur without awareness (Norman and Shallice, 1986).

Once the experts acquire the automated skills, they can perform them effortlessly. However, the change in processes also degrades performance in a number of ways. Given the nature of automaticity, experts cannot fully account and explain, or even recall, their actions. This makes training difficult, as the expert knowledge is not accessible. It is further problematic in expert domains, such as policing and medicine, where accountability is expected and important. The lack of accessibility to knowledge in expert automaticity is so engrained and inherent to the process that trying to access it can reduce performance efficiency (e.g. Beilock *et al.*, 2002; Flegal and Anderson, 2008).

Automaticity that often accompanies the development of expertise can also degrade performance because it introduces different types of slips (Norman, 1981). An expert can make a slip because an uncontrolled automated process has taken place rather than what was actually needed, which may result in expert errors (Reason, 1979, 1990). The lack of conscious awareness and monitoring, as well as lack of control, bring about *rigidity and minimize mindfulness* (Langer, 1989). Expert performance many times requires flexibility and creativity, but with automaticity it is reduced (if not eliminated altogether), resulting in degradation of expert performance (e.g. Frensch and Sternberg, 1989).

Many times experts are required to act very quickly, without time to fully and logically consider all options. These situations entail, at best, minimal flexibility and creativity (whether it is needed or not), as they require very rapid responses (such as in the military, police and medical settings). Actions in such situations rely on 'experiential' knowledge and decision-making brain mechanisms, whereas other situations enable individuals to process and consider information in a more 'analytic' fashion, utilizing different brain structures and decision-making mechanisms (Dror, 2007; Johnson, 1988; Reyna, 2004; Sloman, 1996).

Experts have better 'intuitive' experientially based decision mechanisms, but these may be problematic (Kahneman and Klein, 2009). These mainly develop on the job, through hands-on experience.

As we have seen, many of the underpinnings of expertise involve ways of dealing with cognitive load. They enable the experts to 'do more for less', that is, achieve higher levels of performance with less cognitive effort, giving them enhanced cognition. *Selective attention* is another way of achieving expert-level performance. In fact, one of the most important characteristics of expertise is the ability to pay attention and focus on the important information while filtering out and ignoring the rest (e.g. Wood, 1999). As one becomes a greater expert, one becomes more selective, filtering out more and more information, at an ever-increased rate. While a novice is still trying to absorb the information and make sense of it, the expert has already focused on the critical information (e.g. de Valk and Eijkman, 1984), processed it and solved the problem. Training of experts can focus on enhancing the cognitive system's ability to detect and pick up the important information. Earlier in the chapter we described how enhancing unique aircraft features during training increases acquiring expertise in aircraft recognition (Dror *et al.*, 2008).

The process of attention and selection of information is critical. Experts must select the 'right' information, and they use their experience and expectations to guide this process. For example, expert radiologists selectively process X-ray films according to clinically relevant abnormalities (Myles-Worsley *et al.*, 1988; de Valk and Eijkman, 1984). This results in efficient and effective processing. However, the superior selective processing of the expert radiologists is restricted to abnormalities, and was associated with degradation in their ability to detect variations in normal features that did not contain abnormalities. Moreover, selection processes are also highly vulnerable to biases and to other functional degradations.

What happens, for example, when experts filter out and ignore important information because they regard it as irrelevant? Imagine a police detective gathering information in a criminal investigation, guided by expectations that a certain suspect is guilty. If the expectation or 'hunch' is correct, then information is effectively filtered out; however, if they are incorrect, then important information is ignored (Dror, 2008; Rossmo, 2008). Such confirmation bias is more likely to cause an expert to notice and focus on information that validates and confirms their expectation, extraneous information, context, a belief or a hope. These affect the way the expert allocates attention and examines information. The result is possible degradation in performance, since confirming data are weighted highly and emphasized, while conflicting data are weighted low (sometimes even filtered out and ignored altogether).

Dror and Charlton (2006) and Dror *et al.* (2006) examined potential expert error in the domain of forensic fingerprinting. In a couple of studies, expert fingerprint examiners were presented with prints and were required to determine whether the prints matched. Unknown to the experts, they were in fact presented with fingerprints they had judged in the past, and the experimental set-up was designed to examine if performance would degrade because of extraneous contextual cues. For example, fingerprints that were matched as a definite identification by an examiner a few years ago were re-presented to the same expert examiner as normal routine criminal case work. However, when the prints were re-presented, they were presented within an extraneous context that suggested that they were not a match (e.g. someone else confessed to the crime). Many of the expert examiners contradicted their own past conclusions, exhibiting degradation in performance, and resulting in erroneous conclusions as a result of the contextual influences (see Dror and

Charlton, 2006; Dror *et al.*, 2006; Dror and Rosenthal, 2008 for details). Such findings are not limited to forensic examiners, e.g. see Potchen (2006) for inter-observer variability among radiologists, and Patel and Cohen (2008) for general medical errors in critical care.

One of the main themes of this paper is to demystify expertise. Taking experts off the high pedestal and examining expertise from a scientific viewpoint, showing that expertise is not 'all good', and demonstrating the existence of paradoxical functional degradation with expertise (e.g. Hecht and Proffitt, 1995). I have focused on cognitive and brain elements of expertise, such as unitization, configural processing, automaticity and attention. However, there are other psychological effects that can degrade the performance of experts. For example, over-confidence, and sometimes even arrogance, can be an Achilles heel of experts. As they become greater and greater experts, their confidence increases. This can result in refusal to listen to others, take advice, pay attention to detail, etc. This is especially problematic in expert domains that involve risk-taking and uncertainty. For example, a doctor who is over-confident may not follow procedures in detail and take shortcuts; a fighter pilot with over self-confidence may take inappropriate risks; and an over-confident financial banker may make unbalanced and too high-risk investment decisions. Wishful thinking, escalation of commitment, tunnel vision, belief perseverance, cognitive dissonance, group think, and other phenomena can also cause functional degradation with experts (e.g. errors by expert referees of scientific journal articles, see Peters and Ceci, 1982; Rothwell and Martyn, 2000).

To summarize, I have tried to illustrate the paradoxical nature of expertise, showing that with extraordinary abilities come vulnerabilities and pitfalls (e.g. Dror *et al.*, 1993; Busey and Dror, 2009). These paradoxical elements represent inherent computational trade-offs in brain and cognitive mechanisms that govern expertise, many of which are unavoidable. The view that experts optimize performance overall is rejected, but rather experts specialize and adapt their cognitive processing, optimizing to certain and specific scenarios, but these changes do not always result in enhanced performance overall. Paradoxically, in some cases they cause performance degradation (e.g. Hecht and Proffitt, 1995). The paradoxical functional degradation of expertise is important to study and understand as it gives a realistic picture of expertise, and also has implications on how to maximize expert performance.

For enhancing expert performance, and minimizing the vulnerabilities that come with it, one can use technology to support and overcome potential weaknesses. By 'off-loading' elements of expertise onto computers, one can extend the expert's ability and distribute cognition more appropriately (Dror and Harnad, 2008). However, throwing technology at experts is by no means a solution – in fact, not only may it not help experts, it may even degrade their performance. How best to use technology to help experts, how to optimize the distribution of cognition and expert–technology collaboration, is a complex issue that has to be carefully considered (Dror and Mnookin, 2010).

Expert performance depends mainly on two elements – the expert and their training. Both elements pose interesting challenges for further research. In relation to the experts themselves, critical factors include how to select the right people for domains in which they can excel, how best to fit the person's ability to the job requirements, and how to take advantage of their cognitive profile and relate it to those cognitive abilities that are needed.

Once you select the right person, then further research can guide the way to how best to train them. The two issues, of selection and training, are related. Abilities that are relatively hard-wired in the brain should be the focus of initial selection and screening, whereas those abilities that can be acquired through neuronal plasticity and, thus, are more trainable should be the focus of training (see Dror *et al.*, 1993; Jiang *et al.*, 2007; Munte *et al.*, 2002; Draganski *et al.*, 2004).

The nature of expertise, its cognitive underpinning and its architecture have been discussed and considered, and pose complex challenges which more research can further enlighten. However, any future steps in improving expert performance must be scientifically guided, with an understanding of the vulnerabilities of experts (the enhanced performance along with the potential pitfalls), and not through the naive view that experts are merely superior.

Acknowledgements

For more information related to this article, see www.cci-hq.com. This research was supported by grants from the National Institute of Justice, National Institute of Standards and Technology, Federal Bureau of Investigation, and Department of Defence (Contracts N41756–10-C-3307, N41756–10-C-3382, 2009-DNBX-K225, and 2009-DN-BX-K224). Any opinions, findings and conclusions or recommendations expressed in this chapter are those of the author and do not necessarily reflect the views of any of the funding agencies.

References

Aydin, K., Ucar, A., Oguz, K. K., *et al.* (2007). Increased gray matter density in the parietal cortex of mathematicians: a voxel-based morphometry study. *American Journal of Neuroradiology*, 28: 1859–64.

Beilock, S. L., Bertenthal, B. I., McCoy, A. M., & Carr, T. H. (2004). Haste does not always make waste: expertise, direction of attention, and speed versus accuracy in performing sensorimotor skills. *Psychonomic Bulletin and Review*, 11: 373–9.

Beilock, S. L., Carr, T. H., MacMahon, C, & Starkes, J. L. (2002). When paying attention becomes counterproductive: impact of divided versus skill-focused attention on novice and experienced performance of sensorimotor skills. *Journal of Experimental Psychology: Applied*, 8: 6–16.

Busey, T., & Dror, I. E. (2009). Special abilities and vulnerabilities in forensic expertise. In McRoberts, A. (Ed.). *Friction Ridge Sourcebook*. Washington, DC: NIJ Press.

Busey, T. A., & Vanderkolk, J. R. (2005). Behavioral and electrophysiological evidence for configural processing in fingerprint experts. *Vision Research*, 45: 431–48.

Carey, S. (1992). Becoming a face expert. *Philosophical Transactions of the Royal Society of London*, 335: 95–103.

Chase, W. G., & Simon, H. A. (1973). Perception in chess. *Cognitive Psychology*, 4: 55–81.

Czerwinski, M., Lightfoot, N., & Shiffrin, R. M. (1992). Automatization and training in visual search. *American Journal of Psychology*, 105: 271–315.

Draganski, B., Gaser, C., Busch, V., Schuierer, G., Bogdahn, U., & May, A. (2004). Neuroplasticity: changes in grey matter induced by training. *Nature*, 427: 311–2.

Dror, I. E. (2007). Perception of risk and the decision to use force. *Policing*, 1: 265–72.

Dror, I. E. (2008). Biased brains. *Police Review*, 116: 20–3.

Dror, I. E. (2009). How can Francis Bacon help forensic science? The four idols of human biases. *Jurimetrics: The Journal of Law, Science, and Technology*, 50: 93–110.

Dror, I. E., & Charlton, D. (2006). Why experts make errors. *Journal of Forensic Identification*, 56: 600–16.

Dror, I. E., & Cole, S. (2010). The vision in 'blind' justice: expert perception, judgment and visual cognition in forensic pattern recognition. *Psychonomic Bulletin & Review*, 17: 161–7.

Dror, I. E., & Harnad, S. (2008). Offloading cognition onto cognitive technology. In Dror, I., & Harnad, S. (Eds.). *Cognition Distributed: How Cognitive Technology Extends Our Minds*. Amsterdam: John Benjamins Publishing.

Dror, I. E., & Mnookin, J. (2010). The use of technology in human expert domains: challenges and risks arising from the use of automated fingerprint identification systems in forensics. *Law, Probability and Risk*, 9: 47–67.

Dror, I. E., & Rosenthal, R. (2008). Meta-analytically quantifying the reliability and biasability of fingerprint experts' decision making. *Journal of Forensic Sciences*, 53: 900–03.

Dror, I. E., Charlton, D., & Péron, A. E. (2006). Contextual information renders experts vulnerable to make erroneous identifications. *Forensic Science International*, 156: 74–8.

Dror, I. E., Kosslyn, S. M., & Waag, W. (1993). Visual–spatial abilities of pilots. *Journal of Applied Psychology*, 78: 763–73.

Dror, I. E., Schmitz-Williams, I. C., & Smith, W. (2005). Older adults use mental representations that reduce cognitive load: mental rotation utilises holistic representations and processing. *Experimental Aging Research*, 31: 409–20.

Dror, I. E., Stevenage, S. V., & Ashworth, A. (2008). Helping the cognitive system learn: exaggerating distinctiveness and uniqueness. *Applied Cognitive Psychology*, 22: 573–84.

Elo, A. E. (2008). *The Rating of Chessplayers, Past and Present*. San Rafael, CA: Ishi Press.

Fernandez, R., Dror, I. E., & Smith, C. (2011). Spatial abilities of expert clinical anatomists: comparison of abilities between novices, intermediates and experts in anatomy. *Anatomical Sciences Education*, 4: 1–8.

Flegal, K. E., & Anderson, M. C. (2008). Overthinking skilled motor performance: or why those who teach can't do. *Psychonomic Bulletin & Review*, 15: 927–32.

Frensch, P. A., & Sternberg, R. J. (1989). Expertise and intelligent thinking: when is it worse to know better? In Sternberg, R. J. (Ed.). *Advances in the Psychology of Human Intelligence*. Hillsdale, NJ: Erlbaum, 157–88.

Fusi, S., Drew, P., & Abbott, L (2005). Cascade models of synaptically stored memories. *Neuron*, 45: 599–611.

Gaser, C., & Schlaug, G. (2003). Gray matter differences between musicians and nonmusicians. *Annals of the New York Academy of Sciences*, 999: 514–7.

Gauthier, I., Skudlarski, P., Gore, J. C., & Anderson, A. W. (2000). Expertise for cars and birds recruits brain areas involved in face recognition. *Nature Neuroscience*, 3: 191–7.

Gobet, F., & Simon, H. A. (1996). Recall of rapidly presented random chess positions is a function of skill. *Psychonomic Bulletin & Review*, 3: 159–63.

Gold, J., Bennett, P. J., & Sekuler, A. B. (1999). Signal but not noise changes with perceptual learning. *Nature*, 402: 176–8.

Goldstone, R. L. (2000). Unitization during category learning. *Journal of Experimental Psychology: General*, 123: 178–200.

Gray, R. (2009). A model of motor inhibition for a complex skill: baseball batting. *Journal of Experimental Psychology: Applied*, 15: 91–105.

Halpern, D. F., & Wai, J. (2007). The world of competitive scrabble: novice and expert differences in visuospatial and verbal abilities. *Journal of Experimental Psychology: Applied*, 13: 79–94.

Harley, E. M., Pope, W. B., Villablanca, P., *et al.* (2009). Engagement of fusiform cortex and disengagement of lateral occipital cortex in the acquisition of radiological expertise. *Cerebral Cortex*, 19: 2746–54.

Hecht, H., & Proffitt, D. R. (1995). The price of expertise: effects of experience on the water-level task. *Psychological Science*, 6: 90–5.

Jiang, X., Bradley, E., Rini, R. A., Zeffiro, T., Vanmeter, J., & Riesenhuber, M. (2007). Categorization training results in shape- and category-selective human neural plasticity. *Neuron*, 53: 891–903.

Johnson, E. J. (1988). Expertise and decision under uncertainty: performance and process. In: Chi, M. T. H., Glaser, R., & Farr, M. J.

(Eds). *The Nature of Expertise*. Hillsdale, NJ: Erlbaum, 209–28.

Kahneman, D., & Klein, G. (2009). Conditions for intuitive expertise. *American Psychologist*, **64**: 515–26.

Kepecs, A., Wang, X., & Lisman, J. (2002). Bursting neurons signal input slope. *Journal of Neuroscience*, **22**: 9053–62.

Kundel, H. L., & Nodine, C. F. (1983). A visual concept shapes image perception. *Radiology*, **146**: 363–8.

Langer, E. J. (1989). *Mindfulness*. New York, NY: Addison-Wesley.

Lu, Z. L., & Dosher, B. A. (2004). Perceptual learning retunes the perceptual template in foveal orientation identification. *Journal of Vision*, **4**: 44–56.

Maguire, E. A., Gadian, D. G., Johnsrude, I. S., *et al.* (2000). Navigation-related structural change in the hippocampi of taxi drivers. *Proceedings of the National Academy of Sciences USA*, **97**: 4398–403.

Maguire, E. A., Woollett, K., & Spiers, H. J. (2006). London taxi drivers and bus drivers: a structural MRI and neuropsychological analysis. *Hippocampus*, **16**: 1091–101.

Menchaca-Brandan, A., Liu, A. M., Oman, C. M., & Natapoff, A. (2007). Influence of perspective-taking and mental rotation abilities in space teleoperation. *Proceedings of the ACM/IEEE International Conference on Human-robot interaction*, 8–11 March. New York, NY: ACM Press, pp. 271–8.

Munte, T. F., Altenmuller, E., & Jancke, L. (2002). The musician's brain as a model of neuroplasticity. *Nature Reviews Neuroscience*, **3**: 473–8.

Myles-Worsley, M., Johnston, W. A., & Simons, M. A. (1988). The influence of expertise on X-ray image processing. *Journal of Experimental Psychology: Learning, Memory, and Cognition*, **14**: 553–7.

Norman, D. A. (1981). Categorization of action slips. *Psychological Review*, **88**: 1–15.

Norman, D. A., & Shallice, T. (1986). Attention to action: willed and automatic control of behaviour. In: Davison, R., Schwartz, G., & Shapiro, D. (Eds.). *Consciousness and Self-regulation: Advances in Research and Theory*. New York, NY: Plenum.

Patel, V. L., & Cohen, T. (2008). New perspectives on error in critical care. *Current Opinion in Critical Care*, **14**: 456–9.

Patel, V. L., Arocha, J. F., & Kaufman, D. R. (1999). Expertise and tacit knowledge in medicine. In: Sternberg, R. J., & Horvath, J. A. (Eds). *Tacit Knowledge in Professional Practice: Researcher and Practitioner Perspectives*. Mahwah, NJ: Basic Books, 75–99.

Peters, D. P., & Ceci, S. J. (1982). Peer-review practices of psychological journals: the fate of published articles, submitted again. *Behavioural Brain Science*, **5**: 187–96.

Potchen, E. (2006). Measuring observer performance in chest radiology: some experiences. *Journal of the American College of Radiology*, **3**: 423–32.

Pribyl, J. R., & Bodner, G. M. (1987). Spatial ability and its role in organic chemistry: a study of four organic courses. *Journal of Research in Science Teaching*, **24**: 229–40.

Reason, J. (1979). Actions not as planned: the price of automatization. In: Underwood, G., & Stephens, R. (Eds). *Aspects of Consciousness, Volume* **1**. London: Academic Press.

Reason, J. (1990). *Human Error*. New York, NY: Cambridge University Press.

Reyna, V. F. (2004). How people make decisions that involve risk: a dual-processes approach. *Current Directions in Psychological Science*, **13**: 60–6.

Rhodes, G., & McLean, I. G. (1990). Distinctiveness and expertise effects with homogeneous stimuli: towards a model of configural coding. *Perception*, **19**: 773–94.

Rossmo, D. K. (2008). *Criminal Investigative Failures*. New York, NY: Taylor & Francis.

Rothwell, P., & Martyn, C. (2000). Reproducibility of peer review in clinical neuroscience. Is agreement between reviewers any greater than would be expected by chance alone? *Brain*, **123**: 1964–9.

Russell, B. (1910). Knowledge by acquaintance and knowledge by description. *Proceedings of the Aristotelian Society*, **11**: 108–28.

Ryle, G. (1946). Knowing how and knowing that. *Proceedings of the Aristotelian Society*, **46**: 1–16.

Ryle, G. (1949). *The Concept of Mind*. London: Hutchinson.

Schneider, W., & Shiffrin, R. M. (1977). Controlled and automatic human information processing. *Psychological Review*, **84**: 1–66.

Schwaninger, A., Carbon, C. C., & Leder, H. (2003). Expert face processing: specialization and constraints. In: Schwarzer, G., & Leder, H. (Eds). *Development of Face Processing*. Göttingen: Hogrefe, 81–97.

Schyns, P. G., & Rodet, L. (1997). Categorization creates functional features. *Journal of Experimental Psychology: Learning, Memory and Cognition*, **23**: 681–96.

Shiffrin, R. M., & Lightfoot, N. (1997). Perceptual learning of alphanumeric-like characters. In: Goldstone, R. L., Schyns, P. G. & Medin, D. L. (Eds.). *The Psychology of Learning and Motivation, Volume* **36**. San Diego, CA: Academic Press, 45–82.

Shiffrin, R. M., & Schneider, W. (1977). Controlled and automatic human information processing: II. Perceptual learning, automatic attending, and a general theory. *Psychological Review*, **84**: 127–90.

Sloman, S. A. (1996). The empirical case for two systems of reasoning. *Psychological Bulletin*, **119**: 3–21.

Squire, L. R. (1994). Declarative and nondeclarative memory. In: Schacter, D. L.

& Tulving, E. (Eds.). *Memory Systems 1994*. Cambridge, MA: MIT Press, 204–31.

Stanovich, K. (2009). *What Intelligence Tests Miss*. New Haven, CT: Yale University Press.

Sternberg, R. J. (Ed) (2002). *Why Smart People Can Be So Stupid*. New Haven, CT: Yale University Press.

Tanaka, J. W. (2001). The entry point of face recognition: evidence for face expertise. *Journal of Experimental Psychology: General*, **130**: 534–43.

Tanaka, J. W., & Curran, T. (2001). A neural basis for expert object recognition. *Psychological Science*, **12**: 43–7.

Tansley, P., Kakar, S., Withey, S., & Butler, P. (2007). Visuospatial and technical ability in the selection and assessment of higher surgical trainees in the London deanery. *Annual Royal College of Surgery England*, **89**: 591–5.

de Valk, J. P. J., & Eijkman, E. G. J. (1984). Analysis of eye fixations during the diagnostic interpretation of chest radiographs. *Medical and Biological Engineering and Computing*, **22**: 353–60.

Wood, B. P. (1999). Visual expertise. *Radiology*, **211**: 1–3.

Woollett, K., & Maguire, E. A. (2009). Navigational expertise may compromise anterograde associative memory. *Neuropsychologia*, **47**: 1088–95.

Yue, J. (2007). Spatial visualization by isometric view. *Engineering Design Graphics Journal*, **71**: 5–19.

Chapter 10

Paradoxes in Parkinson's disease and other movement disorders

Ashwani Jha and Peter Brown

Summary

The phenomenon of paradoxical facilitation has its greatest clinical impact in the field of movement disorders. Tens of thousands of people suffering from Parkinson's disease have spectacularly improved thanks to precisely placed surgical lesions or electrical stimulation deep in the centre of the brain. This chapter reports how this paradoxical benefit has driven science and medicine to unravel some of the secrets of one of the most complex circuits in the brain – the basal ganglia. We describe how careful anatomical studies of the basal ganglia have exposed their underlying circuitry, allowing scientists to ascribe function and capture dysfunction in disease. Against this background, we set a number of clinical paradoxes that challenge this model. These force us to take a leap in our conceptualization of the brain, considering it as a plastic network, perturbed by one or more disruptive signals in disease.

Meyers' observation – the paradox

As a young neurosurgeon in the Brooklyn Hospital, New York, Russell Meyers was inspired by an anecdote from his supervisor E. Jefferson Browder. Whilst performing a frontal lobectomy (presumably to remove a tumour), Browder had to extend the lesion far back into an unaffected area deep in the centre of the brain known as the basal ganglia. Coincidentally this patient also had early signs similar to Parkinson's disease, a degenerative condition causing slow, stiff movement and shaking. When the patient awoke after surgery, Browder noted something very unexpected. The patient's Parkinsonian symptoms had disappeared, completely (Meyers, 1940; Clower, 2002).

At first this seemed counter-intuitive. How could removing a *healthy* part of the brain improve its function? Was it in fact an abnormal area? Meyers persisted with this paradox and pioneered surgical removal of sections of the basal ganglia as a treatment for Parkinson's disease. Indeed, descendents of this technique are still popular today in countries in which financial constraints are key. Elsewhere, deep brain stimulation (DBS) is preferred to lesioning. DBS is a rapidly advancing field of neurosurgery which relies on continuous electrical stimulation at a very high frequency to effectively disable or over-ride activity in discrete parts of the brain (Rezai *et al.*, 2008). The effects can be dramatic. Parkinson's disease patients with slow stiff legs have been able to walk freely for the first time in years. Patients with uncontrolled hand shaking have once again been able to write, hold a cup, have breakfast without help – all things crucial for independence.

The Paradoxical Brain, ed. Narinder Kapur. Published by Cambridge University Press. © Cambridge University Press 2011.

As the field of DBS neurosurgery surged forward, neuroscientists tried to get to grips with the unanswered central question of paradoxical improvement. How could interventions deep within normal brain tissue improve function?

To truly appreciate this and many more paradoxes, we need to put them in context; we need to set them against our continuously changing understanding of how we move. This is a story of how surgeons, physicians, anatomists, patients and scientists have worked together to understand the function of what Kinnear Wilson, a famous British neurologist, referred to as the dark basement of the mind – the basal ganglia (Wilson, 1925). One of the most complex networks of cells in the brain, this area hides information on not only how we organize our movements but also how we learn, how we make decisions and how we combine subconscious urges with conscious planning to create our actions. In order to begin to understand this system, we will start where neuroscience has traditionally started, the lesion-deficit model.

The lesion-deficit model

This models the effect of damage to a part of the brain. Whichever brain function is lost can then be assigned to the damaged area. The model describes some of the basic structure of the motor system quite well. Neighbouring muscles are controlled by nerves that originate at neighbouring levels in the spinal cord. In this way, nerves supplying the legs originate in the lower back and nerves supplying the arms originate at the level of the neck. These spinal motor nerve cells are directly controlled by a sheet of cells folded around the surface of the brain called the cerebral cortex. The lesion-deficit model assumes that the cortex can be divided into distinct areas, and certainly most of the cells that directly connect to spinal motor cells are located in the middle, in an area called the primary motor cortex. Additionally, cells in this region are ordered in a similar way to the parts of the body and the lesion-deficit model comfortably predicts the consequences. Damage to the hand area in the left primary motor cortex causes right hand weakness (the left brain controls the right side of the body), as does damage to the spinal motor nerve cells in the neck. In addition, damage to any part of the *pathway* from the primary motor cortex to the spine causes similar predictable problems, since these two areas have become disconnected. This pathway of the motor system is called the pyramidal tract (because it passes through parts of the brainstem which look like pyramids) and is interconnected to the other parts of the motor system. For example, the supplementary motor area, just in front of the primary motor cortex, has a crucial role in linking cognition to action (Nachev *et al.*, 2007). The cerebellum, located at the back of the brain, behind the brainstem, is known to be involved in coordination. Lesions outside the pyramidal system show less-consistent clinical effects and are less faithful to the lesion-deficit model. However, this is a good model with which to start unravelling the functions of the basal ganglia.

Obviously, scientists cannot permanently damage the brains of healthy humans. Clinicians, however, have the opportunity to observe the effects of damage to the human basal ganglia by disease processes. So, if the basal ganglia help to organize movement, does damage to this region result in less movement? Well, yes, but – paradoxically – also no.

We have known for a long time that the consequences of basal ganglia damage can be classified into two groups: slowness, or too little movement, called akinesia, and involuntary or too much movement, called hyperkinesia. The latter is made up of different subdivisions including chorea and dyskinesias (semi-purposeful and jerky movements), dystonia (sustained spasms) and tremor (rhythmic shaking). The pathologies which can involve the basal ganglia are varied and include slowly progressive degenerative conditions such as Parkinson's disease (predominant akinesia and tremor) and Huntington's disease (predominant chorea), and also more rapid onset conditions such as strokes, infections and immune mediated phenomena (Piccolo *et al.*, 2003).

In 1994, Kailash Bhatia and David Marsden reviewed a large series of patients with lesions localized in the caudate, putamen and globus pallidus of the basal ganglia (Bhatia and Marsden, 1994). They found that the majority of lesions in the motor input zone, the putamen, caused dystonia (16 out of 19), whereas far fewer led to the slowed movements of akinesia (2 out of 19). Unfortunately, this contradicts the predominantly akinetic findings in Parkinson's disease which has mainly putamenal dysfunction secondary to dopamine depletion, consequent on degeneration in another brain area, the substantia nigra pars compacta. The results of damage to the globus pallidus (GP) were more variable. Seven out of 12 patients with GP lesions suffered from akinesia, whilst 4 out of the 12 lesions caused dystonia. One reason for these conflicting results is that the comparisons made are between different things. It is likely that selective dysfunction to the cohort of putamenal cells receiving dopaminergic input in Parkinson's disease causes a different impairment to damage to the whole of the putamen, including cells with and without dopaminergic input. Thus, the variable type of underlying disease pathology makes comparisons difficult. Even if we look at one disease by itself, such as Huntington's disease, it is well known that as the disease progresses, symptoms can progress from initially excessive movements to slowness and stiffness. Another point is that the actual lesions in the seminal study by Bhatia and Marsden were of different sizes. Finally the GP lesions did not differentiate between the globus pallidus interna (GPi) and the globus pallidus externa (GPe), which have similar names but very different proposed functions. In summary, the above analysis of lesion deficits is interesting but too inconsistent to answer our questions.

So what can we take from the fact that basal ganglia damage can leave movement seemingly untouched, or cause either too much or too little movement? Although we cannot be specific about their function, we can say that they are in some way involved in motor action control, rather than the direct motor (muscle) activation coordinated by the pyramidal system. Damage to the 'brakes' of this control system could conceivably result in uncontrolled excess movements, whilst damage to the 'accelerator' could cause movements to slow down. However, to complicate matters, damage to the basal ganglia has also been associated with a reduction in spatial working memory, a decreased ability to manipulate objects stored in the working memory (Owen, 2004) and changes in mood, decision-making and value learning (Voon *et al.*, 2007; Frank *et al.*, 2007).

So how do we sort this out? Do different parts of the basal ganglia do different things and therefore damage to different parts cause different impairments? Do the basal ganglia really incorporate something akin to an 'accelerator' or 'brake'? Fortunately, a surge of scientific research in the 1980s–1990s revolutionized our anatomical knowledge in this area and allowed scientists to begin to answer these questions.

Setting the scene – the components of the basal ganglia

If we unravel the basal ganglia, we see that they are made up of parallel circuits designed to harness information from different parts of the cortex, process it and then send it back out to the cortex via what has been pejoratively called the brain's junction box, the thalamus

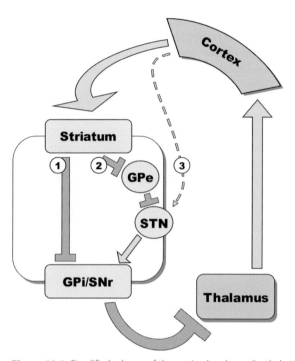

Figure 10.1 Simplified schema of the cortico-basal ganglia–thalamic loop. The cerebral cortex sends information directly to the input zone (striatum) of the basal ganglia. Thereafter, information proceeds through two pathways. The first 'direct' pathway (1) goes straight to the output of the basal ganglia, the GPi/SNr complex. The second 'indirect' pathway (2) passes through the GPe and STN to reach the GPI/SNr output. Different groups of cells either stimulate (green arrows) or inhibit (red flat-ended line) their projection targets. This means that, in the default state, the GPi/SNr 'holds the reigns' of the thalamus, which is primed to stimulate the cortex. Activation of the 'direct' pathway (1) loosens the reigns and therefore the cortex is activated. Activation of the 'indirect' pathway (2) tightens the reigns, and no cortical activation takes place. New connections are constantly being discovered, such as the 'hyperdirect' pathway (3) which connects the cortex to the STN. The function of this pathway still remains unclear. The neurotransmitter dopamine influences many parts of this circuit, most notably the striatum. Here it facilitates activity in the direct pathway, and suppresses activity in the indirect pathway. Parkinson's disease involves a deficiency of striatal dopamine, therefore causing overactivity of the indirect pathway. This may explain the slowness of movement associated with the condition. *Abbreviations:* GPe, globus pallidus externa; GPi, globus pallidus interna; SNr, substantia nigra pars reticulata; STN, subthalamic nucleus.

(see Figure 10.1 – diagram of basal ganglia loop). A highly influential group of papers in the 1980s (Albin *et al.*, 1989; Alexander *et al.*, 1986; DeLong, 1990) suggested that there were several such circuits in the basal ganglia, separately processing information about motor control, eye movements, cognitive functions (such as working memory) and emotion. The implication is that the basal ganglia are involved in all sorts of functions, not just motor function, and that damage here can result in all sorts of dysfunction, not just movement disorders.

The same, primarily anatomical, studies also revealed the remarkable similarity in layout of these different functional circuits. This provided a tempting but unproved supposition. Could the basal ganglia process cognitive and motor information in the same basic way (Marsden and Obeso, 1994)? The consequence of such speculation is that if we can find out how the basal ganglia influence something that is relatively simple to quantify, motor control, we would have a head start in determining how it modulates higher cognitive processes such as working memory. So let us take a closer look at the motor control circuit.

Cortical information from motor and sensory areas of the cortex is channelled into the major input zone of the basal ganglia, the striatum. In fact, incoming motor information is concentrated in a particular part of the striatum known as the putamen (the other main area of the striatum is called the caudate and receives inputs from cortical areas concerned with cognition and emotion). Then the pathway splits into two, the direct and indirect pathways which bypass and relay through the GPe and subthalamic nucleus, respectively (Figure 10.1). The pathways project to the output stations of the basal ganglia, the GPi and the substantia nigra pars reticulata. Here, the pathway is sent via the thalamus back to the cerebral cortex, especially the supplementary motor cortex, an area crucial for linking cognition to action, and down to the brainstem where many ancillary motor systems reside. The above pattern of anatomical connectivity was quickly equated with function by introducing an extra variable, the overall rate of neuronal discharge at each connection. This schema became known as the rate model of basal ganglia function and, as we will see, it beautifully captured dysfunction of the basal ganglia caused by disease, but did rather less well in explaining the effects of functional neurosurgery.

Paradoxical functional improvement by 'double hits'

So far we have reviewed the circuitry of the basal ganglia and used this to model the effects of damage to discrete locations within it. Whether causing increased or decreased movements, these effects tend to impair motor function. However, can damage to the basal ganglia ever be helpful? Do lesions sometimes paradoxically facilitate motor function? This can certainly occur if movement is already imperfect, in other words when a second lesion seems to right an earlier one. For example, Nakashima *et al.* described a 67-year-old telegrapher who developed occupational cramp in his right hand after typing. Eventually, he also developed painful and disabling dystonic cramps triggered by writing (Nakashima *et al.*, 1993). In time, he was forced to give up writing altogether, but was still able to use his hands well for other purposes, such as holding chopsticks. This is not out of the ordinary, as dystonias can be task-specific. Many years later, a stroke affecting his left striatum caused weakness and numbness in the right side of his body. After a week, these symptoms had almost gone, although he was still too weak to use chopsticks with ease. However, paradoxically, his dystonic cramp had disappeared. Ten months later, he was able to use chopsticks normally and his dystonic cramp never returned. The second lesion from the stroke, a double-hit, had improved his motor function (Figure 10.2).

Double-hits can also improve tremor due to a variety of causes. Kim *et al.* reported a 70-year-old patient who developed a right hand tremor triggered by writing (Kim *et al.*, 2006a). Again, after a stroke affecting the left striatum, and temporarily causing right hand weakness, his tremor vanished. This time the tremor took a few weeks to disappear, suggesting that, in this case, the brain needed time to remodel. Constantino and Lewis (2003) reported a different example: a 75-year-old dentist who had suffered from a form of familial tremor in both hands known as essential tremor. After two strokes affecting the right fronto-parieto-temporal region, he developed left arm and leg weakness. Although the weakness persisted, presumably because of the involvement of the primary motor cortex, his left-sided tremor resolved. Other groups have reported improvement of essential tremor following strokes involving the thalamus (Barbaud *et al.*, 2001), frontal cortex (Kim *et al.*, 2006b) and the central structure in the brainstem, the pons (Nagaratnam and Kalasabail, 1997). Further reports have suggested that thalamic strokes can resolve the tremor caused by Parkinson's disease (Probst-Cousin *et al.*, 2003; Choi *et al.*, 2008) (Figure 10.2). The effects of these double-hits are broadly consistent

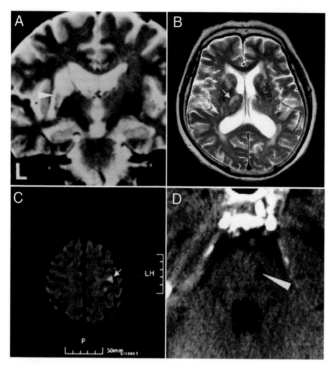

Figure 10.2 The double-hit phenomenon. (A) A coronal T2 MR scan showing a left putamenal stroke (yellow arrowhead), which relieved occupational and writer's cramp in the right hand of this 67-year-old telegrapher (Nakashima *et al.*, 1993). (B) An axial T2 MR scan demonstrating a right anterior thalamic stroke (yellow arrow), which improved the Parkinsonian tremor in the left hand of this 46-year-old lady (Choi *et al.*, 2008). (C) An axial diffusion-weighted MR scan showing a left frontal cortical stroke (yellow arrow). This lesion improved essential tremor in the right hand of this 63-year-old lady (Kim *et al.*, 2006b). (D) An axial CT scan showing a left pontine stroke (yellow arrowhead) which improved essential tremor in this 90-year-old man's right hand (Nagaratnam and Kalasabail, 1997). *Abbreviations*: MR, magnetic resonance; CT, computed tomography. Reprinted with permission from John Wiley and Sons (images A and C) and Elsevier (images B and D).

with the rate model. Damage to parts of the cortex, striatum and thalamus would all tend to suppress extra involuntary movements such as tremor and dystonia. However, the rate model does not model all types of paradoxical facilitation.

Double-hits also provide a framework to understand some of the less explained phenomena of Parkinson's disease. As above, the first lesion in Parkinson's disease is pathological, this time striatal dopaminergic denervation, but what if the second 'hit' is not a lesion at all, but a change in environment or arousal? Could such transient changes of state temporarily disengage the standard basal ganglia circuit and improve motor function? The first clinical paradox that can be understood in this way is paradoxical kinesis, which was initially described by Souques, a leading French neurologist, in 1921. Paradoxical kinesis consists of the dramatic but temporary reversal of Parkinsonism in the face of highly alerting situations, such as the sudden appearance of an on-coming automobile or the cry of 'fire'. Patients otherwise barely able to move because of their disease are momentarily able to flee the threat. A common theme is the presence of a startling stimulus and it is known that such stimuli can lead to the bypassing of normal motor pathways so that movement is elicited unusually rapidly, even in healthy subjects (Valls-Sole *et al.*, 1999). The paradoxical improvement in

Parkinson's disease could be due to the functional hit of the startling stimulus bypassing the standard pathways afflicted by the disease so that movement is produced that is surprising in its swiftness. Although dramatic, this phenomenon remains rare, mysterious and difficult to harness. A remarkable questionnaire based study revealed that only 1 out of 50 Israeli patients with Parkinson's disease experienced paradoxical kinesis whilst their homes were under missile attack for 1 month (Schlesinger *et al.*, 2007). Conversely an ex-footballer with Parkinson's disease was able to exploit an environmental stimulus, in this case kicking a ball, to improve his walking, although it is debated whether this phenomenon was truly paradoxical kinesia (Asmus *et al.*, 2008; Robottom *et al.*, 2009).

The second clinical paradox is one that was only thoroughly documented as recently as 2007 (De Cock *et al.*, 2007). This consists of the remarkably improved movements that occur during rapid eye movement (REM) sleep in patients with Parkinson's disease. This is the stage of sleep in which we dream, but usually brainstem centres disengage motor responses so that we do not physically act out our dreams. However, there is a common sleep disturbance called REM sleep behavioural disorder (RBD) in which this fails to occur. Dreams are enacted, as in the infamous case of partners strangling their spouses. When RBD co-exists with Parkinson's disease, movements during REM sleep not only occur but are fast and vigorous. Speech that is usually low and monotonous becomes loud and clear. An otherwise akinetic patient is able to fight with an invisible foil with great agility whilst shouting a war cry as he dreams of saving his endangered lady-love (De Cock *et al.*, 2007). REM sleep somehow disengages the basal ganglia contribution to movement so that movements become temporally vigorous (De Cock *et al.*, 2007). What is tantalizing about these clinical observations is that they suggest that impaired movement is potentially reversible, if we could only define and promote the pathways responsible for paradoxical movement.

Back to the neurosurgical paradoxes

With early neurosurgical observations, and anecdotal 'double-hit' cases, all suggesting that localized damage to areas of brain could improve symptoms, surgeons began to empirically explore different targets for the treatment of Parkinson's disease. Meyers (1940) eventually favoured targeting the region of the ansa lenticularis, just below the thalamus, which links the globus pallidus to the thalamus. Earlier surgical approaches to Parkinson's disease targeted the motor cortex or its descending connections to the spinal cord and usually caused weakness, spasticity or reduction in motor skills. Meyers showed that a lesion in the basal ganglia could ameliorate the tremor and rigidity associated with Parkinson's disease without causing such complications. However, Meyers' procedures were risky, inconsistent and – by modern standards – imprecise.

A major leap came in 1947 with the development of human stereotactic neurosurgery by Ernest Spiegel in the USA (Spiegel *et al.*, 1947). Here, a precise frame could be mounted onto the patient's head allowing millimetre accurate localization in the brain. This dramatically improved the accuracy of targeting smaller structures deep within the brain such as the basal ganglia. Neurosurgeons such as Rolf Hassler and Irving S. Cooper capitalized and tried many different locations in the 1950s–1960s, some with dramatic therapeutic effects (Rezai *et al.*, 2008). One of the most popular regions to be targeted was the motor thalamus. Deliberate damage to this region (thalamotomy) proved highly effective for tremors due to Parkinson's disease, essential tremor and multiple sclerosis. However, it was noted that this treatment had minimal impact on the other motor symptoms of Parkinson's disease – akinesia and stiffness (Marsden and Obeso, 1994; Rezai *et al.*, 2008).

Surgeons moved onto the preceding part of the basal ganglia circuit and lesioned the globus pallidus interna. This was again highly successful at treating tremor, but additionally improved akinesia and the abnormal excessive movements resulting from long-term dopamine therapy called dyskinesias (Marsden and Obeso, 1994; Rezai *et al.*, 2008).

So, how does the rate model of basal ganglia circuitry and functioning, established in the late 1980s, fare in explaining these neurosurgical observations? The underlying abnormality in conditions with too much movement, such as tremor and chorea, was presumed to be an underactive GPi, a faulty break. This would in turn allow the thalamus to activate the cortex in an unrestrained fashion causing too much movement. So we would expect that a surgical lesion in the thalamus would improve tremor – precisely what happens. However, the follow-on question that emerges is – why doesn't a thalamic lesion, which occupies the whole motor thalamus, *cause* prominent akinesia and rigidity? In fact, destruction of the thalamus on both sides of the brain causes the latter signs in less than 20% of patients (Marsden and Obeso, 1994).

A closer look at GPi surgery reveals even more paradoxes. Too little movement, exemplified by akinesia in Parkinson's, is thought to be due to a continuously overactive output from the basal ganglia, which in turn reduces thalamic activation of the cortex. The GPi brake is jammed on and patients are unable to move. So we would expect that damage to the GPi would free up the thalamus to once again allow movement – precisely what happens. Except that the same GPi lesion also improves excessive uncontrolled movements such as dystonia, tremor and levodopa-induced dyskinesias in Parkinson's disease. From our predictions, it should make them worse.

The rate model of basal ganglia circuitry and functioning did, however, serve to inspire scientists and neurosurgeons to trial what has turned out to be the most popular current surgical target for the treatment of Parkinson's disease, the subthalamic nucleus. This nucleus is a key component of the indirect pathway and continuously excites the GPi (Figure 10.1). It was posited that removal of this excitement would stem the excessive inhibition of the thalamus by the GPi and it soon became apparent that interventions aimed at this nucleus were very effective in treating Parkinson's disease. At almost the same time, Alim Louis Benabid, in Grenoble, France initiated another revolution in the neurosurgery of the basal ganglia, deep brain stimulation (DBS). For many years, neurosurgeons had used electrical stimulation of the brain to temporarily reverse Parkinsonian symptoms intraoperatively and help to functionally identify deep brain structures for subsequent lesioning. In the late 1980's, Benabid and colleagues developed a long-term implantable brain stimulator which could locally override brain function but at the same time avoid irreversible lesioning and any associated potential side-effects (Benabid *et al.*, 1987). Now, if the patient was worse after the procedure, the stimulator could simply be turned off. A roughly equivalent functional improvement, reduced side-effects and reversibility meant that this technique gained popularity and its use rapidly spread to the treatment of essential tremor, dystonia, and Tourette's syndrome.

A new model

Despite the success of the rate model of the basal ganglia in predicting the benefits of targeting the subthalamic nucleus in Parkinson's disease, there remained no clear explanation of how lesioning or DBS worked at other sites and, indeed, for different conditions. These paradoxes were highlighted in David Marsden's and José Obeso's classic paper in 1994. There seemed no easy solution. It was time to move on from the lesion-deficit way of thinking. In fact, the conceptual limitations of this type of analysis were first described by the famous nineteenth-century British neurologist, Hughlings Jackson. If a lesion causes *impaired* function, the model works well and, indeed, most cortical lesions do cause impaired function. However, if the lesion causes a *positive* function (i.e. manifestation of a new piece of behaviour) we should be more cautious. In fact, these positive functions more precisely reflect the 'liberated activity of the remaining nervous system' (Bhatia and Marsden, 1994, p. 859). Tremor and dyskinesias are obvious positive symptoms, but it is unclear whether akinesia and rigidity are similar or negative phenomena. Indeed, it is probably unrealistic to consider parts of the basal ganglia in isolation. We must think of them working together in a network (McIntyre and Hahn, 2010). Different brain regions communicate via the electrical activity of neurons and so damaging one part of the system would cause abnormal electrical activity throughout the remaining network. Therefore, symptoms would reflect the abnormal remaining activity, and crucially not merely the opposite of normal function of the damaged area. Marsden and Obeso briefly considered this among several possible solutions (Marsden and Obeso, 1994). Could there be some sort of disruptive electrical network activity, a noisy signal in Parkinson's disease? Could different symptoms reflect different types of disruptive signal within the same anatomical network? The advantage of this hypothesis was that it meant that the same lesion, for example in the GPi, could plausibly reduce different types of disruptive noisy signal and improve contrasting movement disorders such as dyskinesias and akinesia.

This concept gained momentum after Bergman and Delong's landmark paper in 1994, establishing the abnormal pattern of activity in STN and pallidum in the primate model of Parkinsonism (Bergman *et al.*, 1994). To confirm this in humans, however, scientists would have to directly record the electrical activity of elements of the basal ganglia. This is easier said than done and so many groups used indirect measures of neuronal activity, such as functional imaging of cerebral blood flow, to study changes related to Parkinson's disease and its treatments (McIntyre and Hahn, 2010). Although these techniques captured the spatial distribution of the groups of neurons involved, inferences regarding the electrical activity of the underlying neurons remained limited. Fortunately, direct recording of the activity of basal gangia neurons became easier thanks to the arrival of DBS. In addition to intraoperative recordings, scientists could record for a few days after DBS operations before the stimulation electrodes were internalized and connected to a stimulator and battery under the skin. Either one cell at a time could be recorded, or the combined output of a large population of cells could be recorded. The latter, known as the local field potential, proved particularly informative as it would naturally pick out any dominant or disruptive signals which were saturating the motor network and causing symptoms (Hammond *et al.*, 2007). Oscillations in local field potentials largely reflect the degree to which neurons synchronize their activity, and when this synchronization becomes exaggerated it is disruptive. One way of classifying the synchronized electrical activity of a group of cells is to determine its frequency, measured in Hertz (Hz). A large body of work has now built up in this area (Brown and Eusebio, 2008) and we will take the opportunity to review some of it.

The disruptive signal in Parkinson's disease

In akinetic patients with Parkinson's disease, a dominant noisy signal has been recorded in the basal ganglia–cortical circuit. This signal is usually found between 10 and 30 Hz, which is often termed the beta range. There is persuasive evidence that the suppression of this signal correlates with the improvement of Parkinsonism. Beta activity in the basal ganglia and cortex is suppressed by treatment with anti-Parkinsonian (dopaminergic) medications and DBS of the subthalamic nucleus, and the degree of beta suppression correlates well with the reduction in akinesia and rigidity (Kuhn *et al.*, 2006; Silberstein *et al.*, 2005).

However, the correlation of the disruptive beta signal with akinesia and rigidity does not mean it is necessarily causative. It could merely be an innocent bystander. One way to approach this would be to temporarily stimulate the subthalamic nucleus in the beta range with DBS, rather than use the very high frequencies of stimulation employed for therapy. If the beta signal is disruptive, stimulation at this frequency should slow movement. This has been confirmed, although the effect is quite small (Chen *et al.*, 2007).

If beta activity does slow movement, the next question is how. Low amounts of beta activity are normal and have been suggested to favour a stable state where postural muscles would remain continuously activated, allowing us to hold a certain position (Androulidakis *et al.*, 2007a; Gilbertson *et al.*, 2005). This 'hold steady' signal is usually switched off prior to any movement, but in Parkinson's disease the disruptive beta signal is much stronger and more distributed. It proves to be more difficult to switch off, causing slowness of movement (Androulidakis *et al.*, 2007b; Doyle *et al.*, 2005). The upshot of all this is that there is now fairly good evidence that beta activity contributes to akinesia and rigidity in Parkinson's disease. But what about other symptoms?

The disruptive signal in dystonia and levodopa-induced dyskinesias

Is there a different disruptive signal causing too much movement in conditions such as dystonia and related Parkinsonian levodopa-induced dyskinesias? Several studies have suggested that there is excessive activity at less than 10 Hz, in the theta range, in the local field potential recorded in the pallidum of patients with dystonia (Liu *et al.*, 2002; Silberstein *et al.*, 2003). Activity in this range in the basal ganglia has been implicated in the integration of sensory and motor signals (Bland and Oddie, 2001; DeCoteau *et al.*, 2007; Gengler *et al.*, 2005) in keeping with the proposed abnormal mechanism behind dystonia.

One quirk of dystonia is that patients often have a 'sensory trick'. The act of touching a specific part of the body (usually near the dystonic muscle) somehow temporarily suppresses dystonic movements. As predicted, the theta signal transiently abates during a sensory trick (Tang *et al.*, 2007). It also seems that the specific frequency characteristics of this signal are linked to activity in the dystonic muscle itself (Chen *et al.*, 2006b), and that activity appears in the pallidum before the dystonic muscle, suggesting a driving role for the theta activity (Foncke *et al.*, 2007).

A similar correlation between levodopa-induced dyskinesias and theta activity in the local field potential has also been noted, suggesting that this abnormality may be common to conditions associated with excessive movements (Silberstein *et al.*, 2003; Alonso-Frech *et al.*, 2006). After receiving dopaminergic medication, beta activity in the basal ganglia is suppressed in patients with Parkinson's disease, but as patients' dyskinesias supervene, activity in the theta range increases, as does that at frequencies of 60–95 Hz, a range called high gamma (Alonso-Frech *et al.*, 2006). However, so far there is little evidence that stimulation of components of the basal ganglia at these frequencies causes dystonia or dyskinesias.

As always, in reality the picture is probably more complex. It may be that the relative amounts of different disruptive signals, rather than absolute amount of one signal, correlates with clinical symptoms. Indeed, early work in rats and humans suggest a reciprocal relationship between the 'hold steady' beta signal and presumably prokinetic theta and gamma activities (Fogelson *et al.*, 2006; Costa *et al.*, 2006). Where tremor fits into all this remains unclear, with some authors suggesting that it is predominantly a feature of dysfunction in cerebellar loops (Rivlin-Etzion *et al.*, 2006).

Paradoxes do not just go away – they are replaced by others

So we have succeeded in explaining one paradox – how lesioning the same area, for example the GPi, can reduce different types of disruptive signal and therefore help seemingly opposite types of abnormal movement. But we are still left with another paradox. Why does a thalamic lesion, and indeed over-riding activity with high frequency stimulation in the basal ganglia, not affect any preserved motor functioning? How are people able to move at all if any physiological basal ganglia output has been blocked or over-ridden? Are the normal functions of the basal ganglia not that important?

Recent work has updated the previous notion that DBS causes no deficit in motor functioning in patients with Parkinson's disease. Simple motor functions like finger tapping (Chen *et al.*, 2006a) and more complex visuomotor tasks (Brown *et al.*, 2006) are variably affected in patients undergoing therapeutic high-frequency electrical stimulation of the subthalamic nucleus. Patients who initially performed badly, as expected, improved after the stimulation is switched on. However, patients that initially performed well, had subtly worse functioning during stimulation. It seems that there may be a small worsening of movement induced by subthalamic nucleus DBS, but that in most patients this is dramatically out-weighed by the removal of the beta noisy signal (Chen *et al.*, 2006a). This also explains why DBS can sometimes cause significant speech (Pinto *et al.*, 2005; Rodriguez-Oroz *et al.*, 2005), cognitive (Rodriguez-Oroz *et al.*, 2005; Smeding *et al.*, 2006; Saint-Cyr *et al.*, 2000) and postural impairments (Guehl *et al.*, 2006; Maurer *et al.*, 2003; Rodriguez-Oroz *et al.*, 2005). Still, these deficits may well underestimate the importance of the basal ganglia under normal conditions, since Parkinsonism is a slowly progressive disease, affording the brain time to reorganize and compensate. Thus, although the observation that DBS of the subthalamic nucleus may actually impair certain functions in some patients is relevant, it may go only a small way in explaining what the basal ganglia normally do.

So what do the basal ganglia do?

Although many hypotheses have sprung up from different groups, we still do not know precisely what the basal ganglia do in healthy brains. One popular hypothesis of basal ganglia function considers it the brain's action selector (Redgrave *et al.*, 1999). For example, multiple different movement choices are presented to the striatum by the cortical inputs. Dopaminergic inputs to the striatum help weight the various choices according to their behavioural value. The striatum selects the choice with the strongest weighting and sends it down the 'accelerator' direct pathway. All other choices are sent down the 'brake' indirect pathway and are inhibited. The resting activity of the basal ganglia inhibits the thalamus and therefore removes tonic facilitation from the cortex. This continuous brake is lifted momentarily when a new movement is selected by the striatum, releasing the thalamus and allowing it to activate the cortex. In this way, the basal ganglia are thought to select the best of the options presented to them by the cortex.

How can we reconcile this view of the basal ganglia with the idea that disease disrupts the system with noisy signals? Perhaps the synchronized activities that characterize disease states are themselves pathological exaggerations of normal rhythms. As mentioned before, there is some evidence to support this and to suggest that the beta and gamma/theta activities can be seen as the embodiment of the brake and accelerator functions, respectively. This idea is attractive as it puts the emphasis on the balance of spectral activities in determining movement and any disturbance of movement rather than on the power of any single activity. However, although the brake and accelerator functions of the basal ganglia are seen as the products of the competing indirect and direct pathways, thus far there is little to tie different spectral activities to these pathways.

Summary

After almost a century of research, major achievements have been made in understanding the organization of the motor system, and the pathological basis of movement disorders such as Parkinson's disease. There is increasing evidence to suggest that the basal ganglia–cortical circuit forms a plastic network, the function of which is disturbed by multiple patterns of disruptive signals in disease. It is these disruptive signals, which reflect abnormally synchronized neuronal activity, that lie at the heart of a number of otherwise insoluble paradoxes. Whilst some phenomena such as paradoxical kinesis remain remarkably poorly understood, other clinical phenomena such as improvement after double-hits have been harnessed as a therapy. Surgeons now routinely damage or electrically stimulate parts of the motor system to successfully treat Parkinson's disease and dystonia.

Future challenges and questions

Two priorities exist for future research. The first is to establish the quantitative importance of these disruptive signals in the genesis of disorders such as Parkinson's disease. Questions remain regarding the relatively small impairments caused by direct stimulation at pathological frequencies and whether synchrony is an early or even obligatory feature of Parkinsonism. Regardless, beta synchrony provides an excellent biomarker of the clinical state of the patient which is responsive to both drug therapy and DBS. The same may turn out to be true of synchronization in the theta and gamma bands, which may afford biomarkers of hyperkinetic movement disorders like dystonia. This brings us to the second priority, which is to harness this advance in our understanding of basal ganglia conditions like Parkinson's disease and develop a new generation of feedback controlled stimulation devices which sense the level of the relevant biomarker and adapt stimulation voltage and form accordingly, ensuring more effective therapy.

References

Albin, R. L., Young, A. B., & Penney, J. B. (1989). The functional anatomy of basal ganglia disorders. *Trends in Neuroscience*, **12**: 366–75.

Alexander, G. E., Delong, M. R., & Strick, P. L. (1986). Parallel organization of functionally segregated circuits linking basal ganglia and cortex. *Annual Review of Neuroscience*, **9**: 357–81.

Alonso-Frech, F., Zamarbide, I., Alegre, M., et al. (2006). Slow oscillatory activity and levodopa-induced dyskinesias in Parkinson's disease. *Brain*, **129**: 1748–57.

Androulidakis, A., Doyle, L., Yarrow, K., Litvak, V., Gilbertson, T., & P., B. (2007a). Anticipatory changes in beta synchrony in the human corticospinal system and associated improvements in task performance. *European Journal of Neuroscience*, **25**: 3758–65.

Androulidakis, A. G., Kuhn, A. A., Chen, C. C., et al. (2007b). Dopaminergic therapy promotes lateralized motor activity in the subthalamic area in Parkinson's disease. *Brain*, **130**: 457–68.

Asmus, F., Huber, H., Gasser, T., & Schols, L. (2008). Kick and rush: paradoxical kinesia in Parkinson disease. *Neurology*, **71**: 695.

Barbaud, A., Hadjout, K., Blard, J. M., & Pages, M. (2001). Improvement in essential tremor after pure sensory stroke due to thalamic infarction. *European Neurology*, **46**: 57–9.

Benabid, A. L., Pollak, P., Louveau, A., Henry, S., & De Rougemont, J. (1987). Combined (thalamotomy and stimulation) stereotactic surgery of the VIM thalamic nucleus for bilateral Parkinson disease. *Applied Neurophysiology*, **50**: 344–6.

Bergman, H., Wichmann, T., Karmon, B., & Delong, M. R. (1994). The primate subthalamic nucleus. II. Neuronal activity in the MPTP model of parkinsonism. *Journal of Neurophysiology*, **72**: 507–20.

Bhatia, K. P., & Marsden, C. D. (1994). The behavioural and motor consequences of focal lesions of the basal ganglia in man. *Brain*, **117**: 859–76.

Bland, B. H., & Oddie, S. D. (2001). Theta band oscillation and synchrony in the hippocampal formation and associated structures: the case for its role in sensorimotor integration. *Behaviour and Brain Research*, **127**: 119–36.

Brown, P., & Eusebio, A. (2008). Paradoxes of functional neurosurgery: clues from basal ganglia recordings. *Movement Disorders*, **23**: 12–20.

Brown, P., Chen, C. C., Wang, S., et al. (2006). Involvement of human basal ganglia in offline feedback control of voluntary movement. *Current Biology*, **16**: 2129–34.

Chen, C. C., Brucke, C., Kempf, F., et al. (2006a). Deep brain stimulation of the subthalamic nucleus: a two-edged sword. *Current Biology*, **16**: R952–3.

Chen, C. C., Kuhn, A. A., Hoffmann, K. T., et al. (2006b). Oscillatory pallidal local field potential activity correlates with involuntary EMG in dystonia. *Neurology*, **66**: 418–20.

Chen, C. C., Litvak, V., Gilbertson, T. G., et al. (2007). Excessive synchronisation of basal ganglia neurons at 20 Hz slows movement in Parkinson's disease. *Experimental Neurology*, **205**: 214–21.

Choi, S. M., Lee, S. H., Park, M. S., Kim, B. C., Kim, M. K., & Cho, K. H. (2008). Disappearance of resting tremor after thalamic stroke involving the territory of the tuberothalamic artery. *Parkinsonism Related Disorders*, **14**: 373–5.

Clower, W. (2002). Lesions as therapy: surgical intervention in Parkinson's Disease prior to L-Dopa. *Journal of the History of the Neurosciences*, **11**: 375–91.

Constantino, A. E., & Louis, E. D. (2003). Unilateral disappearance of essential tremor after cerebral hemispheric infarct. *Journal of Neurology*, **250**: 354–5.

Costa, R. M., Lin, S. C., Sotnikova, T. D., et al. (2006). Rapid alterations in corticostriatal ensemble coordination during acute dopamine-dependent motor dysfunction. *Neuron*, **52**: 359–69.

De Cock, V. C., Vidailhet, M., Leu, S., et al. (2007). Restoration of normal motor control in Parkinson's disease during REM sleep. *Brain*, **130**: 450–6.

Decoteau, W. E., Thorn, C., Gibson, D. J., et al. (2007). Learning-related coordination of striatal and hippocampal theta rhythms during acquisition of a procedural maze task. *Proceedings of the National Academy of Sciences of the United States of America*, **104**: 5644–9.

Delong, M. R. (1990). Primate models of movement disorders of basal ganglia origin. *Trends in Neuroscience*, **13**: 281–5.

Doyle, L. M., Kuhn, A. A., Hariz, M., Kupsch, A., Schneider, G. H., & Brown, P. (2005). Levodopa-induced modulation of subthalamic beta oscillations during self-paced movements in patients with

Parkinson's disease. *European Journal of Neuroscience*, **21**: 1403–12.

Fogelson, N., Williams, D., Tijssen, M., Van Bruggen, G., Speelman, H., & Brown, P. (2006). Different functional loops between cerebral cortex and the subthalmic area in Parkinson's disease. *Cerebral Cortex*, **16**: 64–75.

Foncke, E. M., Bour, L. J., Speelman, J. D., Koelman, J. H., & Tijssen, M. A. (2007). Local field potentials and oscillatory activity of the internal globus pallidus in myoclonus-dystonia. *Movement Disorders*, **22**: 369–76.

Frank, M. J., Samanta, J., Moustafa, A. A., & Sherman, S. J. (2007). Hold your horses: impulsivity, deep brain stimulation, and medication in Parkinsonism. *Science*, **318**: 1309–12.

Gengler, S., Mallot, H. A., & Holscher, C. (2005). Inactivation of the rat dorsal striatum impairs performance in spatial tasks and alters hippocampal theta in the freely moving rat. *Behaviour and Brain Research*, **164**: 73–82.

Gilbertson, T., Lalo, E., Doyle, L., Di Lazzaro, V., Cioni, B., & Brown, P. (2005). Existing motor state is favored at the expense of new movement during 13–35 Hz oscillatory synchrony in the human corticospinal system. *Journal of Neuroscience*, **25**: 7771–9.

Guehl, D., Dehail, P., De Seze, M. P., *et al.* (2006). Evolution of postural stability after subthalamic nucleus stimulation in Parkinson's disease: a combined clinical and posturometric study. *Experimental Brain Research*, **170**: 206–15.

Hammond, C., Bergman, H., & Brown, P. (2007). Pathological synchronization in Parkinson's disease: networks, models and treatments. *Trends in Neuroscience*, **30**: 357–64.

Kim, D. H., Kim, J., Kim, J. M., & Lee, A. Y. (2006a). Disappearance of writing tremor after striatal infarction. *Neurology*, **67**: 362–3.

Kim, J. S., Park, J. W., Kim, W. J., Kim, H. T., Kim, Y. I., & Lee, K. S. (2006b). Disappearance of essential tremor after frontal cortical infarct. *Movement Disorders*, **21**: 1284–5.

Kuhn, A. A., Kupsch, A., Schneider, G. H., & Brown, P. (2006). Reduction in subthalamic

8–35 Hz oscillatory activity correlates with clinical improvement in Parkinson's disease. *European Journal of Neuroscience*, **23**: 1956–60.

Liu, X., Griffin, I. C., Parkin, S. G., *et al.* (2002). Involvement of the medial pallidum in focal myoclonic dystonia: a clinical and neurophysiological case study. *Movement Disorders*, **17**: 346–53.

Marsden, C. D., & Obeso, J. A. (1994). The functions of the basal ganglia and the paradox of stereotaxic surgery in Parkinson's disease. *Brain*, **117**: 877–97.

Maurer, C., Mergner, T., Xie, J., Faist, M., Pollak, P., & Lucking, C. H. (2003). Effect of chronic bilateral subthalamic nucleus (STN) stimulation on postural control in Parkinson's disease. *Brain*, **126**: 1146–63.

McIntyre, C. C., & Hahn, P. J. (2010). Network perspectives on the mechanisms of deep brain stimulation. *Neurobiology of Disease*, **38**: 329–37.

Meyers, R. (1940). Surgical proceedure for the postencephalitic tremor, with notes on the physiology of premotor fibres. *Archives of Neurology and Psychiatry*, **44**: 455–7.

Nachev, P., Wydell, H., O'Neill, K., Husain, M., & Kennard, C. (2007). The role of the pre-supplementary motor area in the control of action. *National Review of Neuroscience*, **11**: 856–69.

Nagaratnam, N., & Kalasabail, G. (1997). Contralateral abolition of essential tremor following a pontine stroke. *Journal of Neurological Science*, **149**: 195–6.

Nakashima, K., Takahashi, K., & Ota, M. (1993). Cessation of writer's cramp after stroke. *Movement Disorders*, **8**: 249–51.

Owen, A. M. (2004). Cognitive dysfunction in Parkinson's disease: the role of frontostriatal circuitry. *Neuroscientist*, **10**: 525–37.

Piccolo, I., Defanti, C. A., Soliveri, P., Volonte, M. A., Cislaghi, G., & Girotti, F. (2003). Cause and course in a series of patients with sporadic chorea. *Journal of Neurology*, **250**: 429–35.

Pinto, S., Gentil, M., Krack, P., *et al.* (2005). Changes induced by levodopa and subthalamic nucleus stimulation on parkinsonian speech. *Movement Disorders*, **20**: 1507–15.

Probst-Cousin, S., Druschky, A., & Neundorfer, B. (2003). Disappearance of resting tremor after 'stereotaxic' thalamic stroke. *Neurology*, **61**: 1013–4.

Redgrave, P., Prescott, T. J., & Gurney, K. (1999). The basal ganglia: a vertebrate solution to the selection problem? *Neuroscience*, **89**: 1009–23.

Rezai, A. R., Machado, A. G., Deogaonkar, M., Azmi, H., Kubu, C., & Boulis, N. M. (2008). Surgery for movement disorders. *Neurosurgery*, **62**(Suppl 2): 809–38.

Rivlin-Etzion, M., Marmor, O., Heimer, G., Raz, A., Nini, A., & Bergman, H. (2006). Basal ganglia oscillations and pathophysiology of movement disorders. *Current Opinions in Neurobiology*, **16**: 629–37.

Robottom, B. J., Weiner, W. J., Asmus, F., Huber, H., Gasser, T., & Schols, L. (2009). Kick and rush: paradoxical kinesia in Parkinson disease. *Neurology*, **73**: 328; author reply 328–9.

Rodriguez-Oroz, M. C., Obeso, J. A., Lang, A. E., *et al.* (2005). Bilateral deep brain stimulation in Parkinson's disease: a multicentre study with 4 years follow-up. *Brain*, **128**: 2240–9.

Saint-Cyr, J. A., Trepanier, L. L., Kumar, R., Lozano, A. M., & Lang, A. E. (2000). Neuropsychological consequences of chronic bilateral stimulation of the subthalamic nucleus in Parkinson's disease. *Brain*, **123**: 2091–108.

Schlesinger, I., Erikh, I., & Yarnitsky, D. (2007). Paradoxical kinesia at war. *Movement Disorders*, **22**: 2394–7.

Silberstein, P., Kuhn, A. A., Kupsch, A., *et al.* (2003). Patterning of globus pallidus local field potentials differs between Parkinson's disease and dystonia. *Brain*, **126**: 2597–608.

Silberstein, P., Pogosyan, A., Kuhn, A. A., *et al.* (2005). Cortico-cortical coupling in Parkinson's disease and its modulation by therapy. *Brain*, **128**: 1277–91.

Smeding, H. M., Speelman, J. D., Koning-Haanstra, M., *et al.* (2006). Neuropsychological effects of bilateral STN stimulation in Parkinson disease: a controlled study. *Neurology*, **66**: 1830–6.

Souques, M. (1921). Rapport sur les syndrome parkinsoniens. Séance du 3–4 Juin 1921. *Review of Neurology*, **1**: 534.

Spiegel, E. A., Wycis, H. T., Marks, M., & Lee, A. J. (1947). Stereotaxic apparatus for operations on the human brain. *Science*, **106**: 349–50.

Tang, J. K., Mahant, N., Cunic, D., *et al.* (2007). Changes in cortical and pallidal oscillatory activity during the execution of a sensory trick in patients with cervical dystonia. *Experimental Neurology*, **204**: 845–8.

Valls-Sole, J., Rothwell, J. C., Goulart, F., Cossu, G., & Munoz, E. (1999). Patterned ballistic movements triggered by a startle in healthy humans. *Journal of Physiology*, **516**: 931–8.

Voon, V., Potenza, M. N., & Thomsen, T. (2007). Medication-related impulse control and repetitive behaviors in Parkinson's disease. *Current Opinions in Neurology*, **20**: 484–92.

Wilson, S. (1925). Disorders of motility and of muscle tone, with special reference to the corpus striatum. *Lancet*, **2**: 1–10, 53–62, 169–78, 215–19, 268–76.

Paradoxical phenomena in epilepsy

Steven C. Schachter

Summary

The impact of epilepsy on patients is determined by the frequency and severity of seizures, seizure-related symptoms, medication side-effects, the underlying cause and associated psychosocial issues. Paradoxical phenomena have been described in each of these domains, including unexpected worsening or improvement in seizure frequency, causes of epilepsy that can also precipitate a remission, extraordinary seizure-related experiences and psychiatric consequences. This chapter provides a brief overview of these and related topics. A fuller understanding of these paradoxical phenomena should yield unique insights into the development and pathophysiology of epilepsy, as well as illuminate the borderlands between mind and brain, and between neurology and psychiatry.

Introduction

Epilepsy is a common neurological disorder that affects persons of all ages and socio-economic backgrounds. An estimated 2 to 4 million people in the United States have epilepsy (Hauser and Hesdorffer, 1990), with approximately 200,000 newly diagnosed cases each year. Worldwide, approximately 50 million persons have epilepsy, the large majority of whom do not receive therapy, largely because of limited access to medical care and due to the costs of treatment.

The many causes of epilepsy include congenital brain malformations, metabolic diseases, brain trauma, brain tumours and abscesses, stroke, vascular malformations and cerebral degeneration. The most common causes vary as a function of age, degree of treatment resistance and whether the anatomic origin of seizure onset is focal, regional or diffuse. The most common pathology seen in the resected brain tissue of patients who undergo temporal lobectomies for focal-onset treatment-resistant epilepsy is hippocampal sclerosis.

Nearly half of all patients with epilepsy do not have an identifiable underlying cause; among this group, the term 'paradoxical temporal lobe epilepsy' has been used to describe those patients with normal neuroimaging studies who undergo medial temporal lobectomy for intractable hippocampal-onset seizures and are not found to have any histopathological abnormalities of the removed tissue (Cohen-Gadol *et al.*, 2005).

Persons with epilepsy, by definition, have a tendency for recurrent epileptic seizures. Seizures are sudden changes in behaviour, which may or may not be apparent to others, that result when interconnected (and perhaps over-connected; Hsu *et al.*, 2008)

The Paradoxical Brain, ed. Narinder Kapur. Published by Cambridge University Press. © Cambridge University Press 2011.

neuronal networks in the brain suddenly become hypersynchronized in their func-tioning. The ictal behavioural manifestations, which vary between patients, are deter-mined by the specific neuronal networks that are affected pathologically. Consciousness may or may not be altered, in which case the patient may be aware of motor, sensory, autonomic or subjective experiences. Contrary to everyday experience in which consciousness and wakefulness are directly correlated, consciousness may be impaired by a seizure and yet the affected individual remains awake, perhaps engaged in complicated behaviours, suggesting that there are neuroanatomical and functional distinctions between consciousness, complex behaviours and wakefulness (Yu and Blumenfeld, 2009).

Epilepsy is associated with an increased risk of injuries and mortality. Causes of death include accidents, drowning and homicide in the home (Bowman *et al.*, 2010), sudden and unexplained death in epilepsy (SUDEP), status epilepticus (repeated seizures over a defined period of time without recovery of consciousness between seizures), the underlying brain disease (such as brain tumours) and suicide, which is up to 10 times higher than in the general population and as much as 25 times higher in patients with seizures of temporal lobe origin (Harden and Goldstein, 2002).

The goals of conventional epilepsy therapy are to treat the underlying cause, if known, and to completely suppress further seizures from occurring without causing troublesome side-effects. As such, treatment is typically begun after seizures become manifest. Anti-epileptic drugs (AEDs) are the mainstay of therapy. Seizures in up to 70% of patients completely respond to AED treatment. The other 30% of patients are candidates for combination AED therapy and adjunctive nonpharmacological treatments such as vagus nerve stimulation, brain surgery, special diets, stress reduction techniques, investigational drugs and brain stimulation devices (Villanueva *et al.*, 2007; Cascino, 2008). No known therapy prevents the development of epilepsy, although cannabinoid antagonists may hold promise, which is paradoxical because these agents are acutely proconvulsant in animal models (Armstrong *et al.*, 2009).

A large proportion of patients with epilepsy experience an unsatisfactory quality of life because of seizures, medication side-effects and such psychosocial factors as cognitive dysfunction, stigma and psychiatric disorders, including depression and anxiety, which occur in up to 60% of patients with treatment-resistant seizures (Beyenburg *et al.*, 2005; LaFrance *et al.*, 2008).

Therefore, the full impact of epilepsy is determined by symptoms, treatment-related side-effects, the underlying cause, and associated psychosocial issues, including stigma. This makes it a difficult, but somewhat unique and rewarding, chronic medical condition to treat. In the light of all these factors, a number of paradoxical phenomena have been observed in patients with epilepsy. The term *paradoxical* is used here to refer to subjective observations by patients with epilepsy or objective results obtained from their medical evaluations that are counter-intuitive, go against common wisdom, or defy ready explan-ation. Such paradoxical phenomena should encourage a reappraisal of relevant underlying assumptions or principles, following which the same observations and results may eventu-ally become intuitively obvious rather than surprising.

This chapter first reviews factors that paradoxically worsen or improve the occurrence of seizures and then discusses mood disorders in patients with epilepsy, unexpected effects of seizure control on psychiatric function, unusual manifestations of seizures and living with epilepsy.

Paradoxical worsening of seizures

Antiepileptic drugs

Paradoxically, the same drugs used to treat seizures (AEDs) may produce an increase in frequency or severity of existing seizure types, emergence of new seizure types, or the development of status epilepticus (Bauer, 1996; Gayatri and Livingston, 2006). The epilepsy syndromes of infancy and childhood are especially susceptible to AED-induced seizure exacerbation (Sazgar and Bourgeois, 2005). Physicians unfamiliar with this phenomenon are usually inclined to increase AED dosages if seizures continue or worsen, which only further exacerbates the situation.

In some cases, AEDs are not only ineffective against certain seizure types but can increase the occurrence of these seizures if inappropriately prescribed. For example, carbamazepine and vigabatrin are ineffective against absence seizures and can increase their frequency in patients with absence epilepsy (Guerrini et al., 1998). In other instances, AEDs at high doses may increase the frequency of seizure types against which they are effective at lower doses. This manifestation of drug intoxication may be due to depression of the inhibitory actions of interneurons (Perucca et al., 1998). This phenomenon is particularly well-described for phenytoin, especially when present in supratherapeutic serum concentrations (Schachter, 1998), but can be seen with other AEDs, including carbamazepine and valproate (Perucca et al., 1998; Thundiyil et al., 2007).

Non-antiepileptic drugs (non-AEDs)

A variety of non-AEDs have been linked to seizure worsening in patients with epilepsy (Schachter, 1998). This is somewhat paradoxical, because they target disorders other than epilepsy and are often assumed to have a sedating effect that would at first glance be considered to be anticonvulsant in nature. Because of the high frequency of psychiatric co-morbidities in patients with epilepsy, clinicians are particularly concerned that antipsychotic and antidepressant drugs (ADs) may worsen seizures (Haddad and Dursun, 2008). Many clinicians erroneously believe that all ADs should therefore be avoided (Mula et al., 2008). This may arise largely from the overgeneralization of data showing that seizures can be caused by AD overdoses (Citak et al., 2006). Indeed, therapeutic doses of ADs, such as the selective serotonin reuptake inhibitors, may actually have *anticonvulsant* properties (Jobe, 2004). Notwithstanding this paradoxical concept, certain ADs, including bupropion, maprotiline, clomipramine and amoxapine, are probably best avoided in patients with epilepsy because of their apparent propensity for causing seizures in a dose-responsive fashion (Sarko, 2000; Eyer et al., 2009).

The potential for oestrogen, whether as hormone replacement therapy or endogenously produced, to cause seizures may seem counter-intuitive because it is a naturally occurring hormone and not generally associated with seizures or epilepsy. Yet, as stated by Chakraborti et al. (2007), oestrogen 'is not solely an endocrine factor but plays important but hitherto largely unrecognized physiological and pathophysiological roles that are not directly involved in reproductive processes'. In fact, the gonadal hormones oestrogen and progesterone have significant effects on cortical excitability, the former by modulation of gene expression, regulation of neurotransmitter release or direct interactions with neurotransmitter receptors (Veliskova, 2007), and the latter through actions of a metabolite on gamma-aminobutyric acid (GABA) receptors (Frye, 2008).

Whereas oestrogen may be either pro-convulsant or anticonvulsant depending on a variety of factors, including treatment duration, latency prior to seizure testing, mode of administration, dose, hormonal status, seizure type/model and the specific effects mentioned in the previous paragraph (Veliskova, 2007), progesterone is generally viewed as anticonvulsant and may have antiepileptic effects in women with catamenial epilepsy, which refers to a pattern of seizure occurrence in menstruating women with epilepsy in whom seizures happen disproportionately during menses (Herzog *et al*, 2004; Scharfman and MacLusky, 2006).

Endogenously produced oestrogen may worsen seizures in women with catamenial epilepsy (Scharfman and MacLusky, 2006). Women with reproductive endocrine disorders characterized by inadequate secretion of progesterone during the luteal phase of the menstrual cycle are particularly vulnerable (Harden, 2005). Similarly, exogenous oestrogen taken by post-menopausal women with epilepsy can exacerbate seizures (Harden, 2008). While a catamenial relationship to seizure occurrence has been described for well over 100 years and has been supported by substantial laboratory and clinical evidence, many physicians remain skeptical.

Paradoxical relationships between epilepsy and psychiatric co-morbidities

Depression

Depression occurs in 10–20% of patients with epilepsy whose seizures are controlled and up to 60% of patients with treatment-resistant seizures (Figure 11.1; Mendez *et al.*, 1986; O'Donoghue *et al.*, 1999). Depression may occur between seizures, usually in association with variable levels of irritability and emotionality, during a seizure (ictal depression), or the initial 72 h following a seizure (Kanner *et al.*, 2004).

Depression may arise from specific brain pathology, as well as a response to the social and vocational disabilities associated with having epilepsy (Gilliam and Kanner, 2002). Interestingly, depression is a risk factor for the development of epilepsy (Kanner and Barry, 2003), perhaps owing to common pathogenic mechanisms (Jobe, 2003). While this may seem surprising, it was predicted by Hippocrates around 400 BC, when he wrote, 'Melancholics ordinarily become epileptics, and epileptics, melancholics: what determines the preference is the direction the malady takes; if it bears upon the body, epilepsy, if upon the intelligence, melancholy' (Lewis, 1934).

Depression may also be caused by AEDs. Mula and Sander (2007) identified the following variables as relevant to the development of depressive symptoms in association with AED therapy: enhanced GABA neurotransmission (e.g. with barbiturates, vigabatrin, tiagabine and topiramate), folate deficiency, AED polytherapy, the presence of hippocampal sclerosis, dramatic improvement in seizures (forced normalization, see below) and a past history of affective disorders.

In as much as electroconvulsive therapy has antidepressant effects in non-epileptic patients, the consequences of spontaneous convulsions in depressed patients with epilepsy are of interest, although not often documented in the literature or noted clinically. Seethalakshmi and Krishnamoorthy (2007) reported a 41-year-old widow with a 15-year history of epilepsy who had periods of sadness and crying spells that resolved when she had generalized tonic–clonic seizures.

Figure 11.1 Abstract face (computer-generated), by Jude Rouslin (Schachter, 2003, p. 68). Reproduced with permission.

Psychosis

Psychosis has been described as a 'broad and elusive mental expanse reflecting a fundamental disintegration of self and its connection to nonself' (Nadkarni *et al.*, 2007). A relationship between epilepsy and psychosis might be unexpected, given their distinctly different clinical presentations, and yet the incidence of psychosis varies from about 0.6 to 7% of patients with epilepsy in the community to 19–27% of epilepsy patients requiring hospitalization (Torta and Keller, 1999).

Psychosis may be seen during the first 72 h of the post-ictal period (Kanner *et al.*, 2004), between seizures (chronic, interictal psychosis), in the setting of improvement in seizures and/or resolution of epileptiform abnormalities on the EEG (referred to as 'forced normalization' – see below – or alternative psychosis) and *de novo* after epilepsy surgery (Kanner, 2000). Psychosis may also be an ictal phenomenon. The most intriguing presentations are post-ictal psychosis and forced normalization, which themselves are paradoxically related to one another, since one follows a series of seizures while the other develops in the setting of sustained seizure control.

Post-ictal psychosis typically occurs within several days following a cluster of seizures or status epilepticus, often after a prolonged period with good seizure control. Post-ictal psychosis after a single seizure is rare. Symptoms begin after 24–48 h of normal baseline behaviour, often referred to as the 'lucid interval', although a recent study suggests that cognition may be altered during this period (Schulze-Bonhage and Tebartz van Elst, 2010). The psychosis may last up to several weeks, with nearly all episodes ending within one month. Symptoms include visual or auditory hallucinations, paranoia, delusions, confusion, affective changes, violence and amnesia. Kanner and Ostrovskaya (2008) showed in a retrospective study that post-ictal psychotic episodes are associated with bilateral independent ictal foci; they did not report the results of EEG monitoring during the post-ictal psychoses.

Forced normalization

Originally described by Landolt (1953), some patients develop severe mood changes or psychosis in the setting of sustained seizure control (Trimble and Schmitz, 1998). Landolt correlated this syndrome with normalization of the patient's EEG, hence the term 'forced normalization', whereas others have not required a normal EEG to make the diagnosis, therefore referring to this phenomenon as 'alternative psychosis'. This syndrome has been seen with virtually all forms of seizure treatments, including drugs, vagus nerve stimulation and resective brain surgery. A particularly fascinating case was described by Ohara *et al.* (2006) in which intermittent seizures in a 56-year-old woman with longstanding epilepsy were completely eliminated by a left temporoparietal stroke, only to be followed 4 months later by the paradoxical development of psychosis.

Krishnamoorthy and colleagues (2002) observed that 'a number of clinicians continue to deny the very existence of the forced normalization phenomenon'. One of the contributing factors is that the understanding of the pathophysiology of forced normalization is incomplete. Hypotheses have been proposed based on the limbic kindling model and neurochemical/neurotransmitter changes, particularly of dopamine, glutamate, GABA, catecholamines, opiates, adenosine and nitric oxide (Krishnamoorthy *et al.*, 2002; Sachdev, 2007); active inhibitory processes leading to insomnia, hypervigilance and dysphoria (Krishnamoorthy *et al.*, 2002); and the phenomenon of long-term potentiation (Smith and Darlington, 1996). The lack of animal models and biomarkers hamper further progress in this area. However, a report of two cases supports the relationship of epileptiform discharges rather than overt seizures with this phenomenon (Clemens, 2005).

Psychiatric disorders following temporal lobectomy

A variety of mood and behavioural disorders as well as psychosis can paradoxically begin following temporal lobectomy for treatment-resistant epilepsy, when common wisdom would suggest that patients would do well, having been 'freed' of their epilepsy and the associated medical and psychosocial consequences. Depression may occur in up to 30% of patients after temporal lobectomies, typically within the first 6 months, varying from mild to severe with suicidality (LaFrance *et al.*, 2008). A previous history of depression is a risk factor, as may be poor post-surgical control of seizures.

One study of a series of 11 patients with *de novo* psychosis following temporal lobectomy out of 320 operated patients identified preoperative bilateral EEG abnormalities, pathologies other than mesial temporal sclerosis in the excised lobe and a smaller amygdala on the unoperated side as risk factors for the development of psychosis (Shaw *et al.*, 2004). Thus, evidence of more widespread abnormalities of function or structure suggested a higher possibility of poor outcome.

It is not only in neurological or psychiatric terms that seizure freedom following epilepsy surgery may portend an unfavourable outcome. Wilson *et al.* (2007) have described 'the burden of normality' as a paradoxical consequence of brain surgery for the treatment of epilepsy. In this conceptual framework, the patient for whom epilepsy is fully incorporated into their self-identity is seen as unable to adapt to the new psychological, behavioural, affective and sociological realities of living without epilepsy, following otherwise successful surgery. Symptoms include anxiety, depression, psychotic ideation, alterations in behaviour and social functioning, grief and bitterness, and changed relationships with family and friends. Wilson *et al.* suggest that the broad psychosocial changes associated with becoming seizure-free following brain surgery provide an essential framework for post-operative rehabilitation to help patients successfully transition from chronic disability to sudden wellness (Wilson *et al.*, 2004).

A similar phenomenon may be seen in non-operated patients with epilepsy and severe learning disabilities with a prolonged course of frequent and nearly continuous clinical and electrographic seizures who then become seizure-free. Such patients, typically children and adolescents, may exhibit deteriorating behaviour while seizure-free to the extent they become difficult to manage. This is clinically different from forced normalization and has been referred to as the 'release phenomenon' (Besag, 2004), which is explained by Mula and Monaco (2009) as the patient not knowing 'how to express his or her new-found ability in an acceptable way'.

A profound change in sexual behaviour following temporal lobectomy for control of seizures would not be an obvious consequence compared to changes in cognitive functioning. Blumer (1970) described three patients who underwent temporal lobectomies for control of treatment-resistant seizures. After 3–6 weeks, they developed persistent sexual arousal, homosexual behaviour, changes in their eating habits and loss of anger. Cogen *et al.* (1979) explain this as a form of Klüver Bucy syndrome in which one temporal lobe has been removed leaving behind another with underlying pathology.

Paradoxical improvement in seizures

Brain electrical stimulation

If seizures result from the propagation of electrical impulses along hyper-synchronized neuronal networks, then it may seem paradoxical that electrical brain stimulation could have an antiepileptic effect (Cascino, 2008). Yet, a number of groups have used direct or noninvasively applied electrical stimulation to treat seizures in the laboratory or the clinic (Santiago-Rodriguez *et al.*, 2008; Nitsche and Paulus, 2009; Saillet *et al.*, 2009). Targets for direct electrical stimulation include the cerebellum, hippocampus, centromedian thalamic nucleus, subthalamic nucleus (Pollo and Villemure, 2007; Ellis and Stevens, 2008) and the seizure focus (Theodore and Fisher, 2007). One recent approach is based on deep brain stimulation for the treatment of Parkinson's disease, with the target changed from the subthalamic nucleus to the anterior nucleus of the thalamus bilaterally (Graves and Fisher, 2005). Electroconvulsive therapy, an extreme form of brain electrical stimulation, was reported to successfully, if not paradoxically, terminate status epilepticus (Lisanby *et al.*, 2001).

The counter-intuitive nature of applying electrical stimulation to the brain for treating seizures is supported by the observations that stimulation of the subthalamic nucleus in rodents is pro-convulsant at specific frequencies (Lado *et al.*, 2003) and may increase the duration of focal seizures (Usui *et al.*, 2005). Further, the thalamus, especially the reticular nucleus, appears to play a major role in the pathogenesis of human absence epilepsy (Hughes, 2009).

Brain injuries

An iatrogenic brain injury that may improve seizures is a callosotomy, which is a sectioning of otherwise healthy fibres of the corpus callosum to reduce the frequency of drug-resistant tonic and atonic seizures (Heick, 1996; Rosenfeld and Roberts, 2009). A rat model suggests that a callosotomy blocks repetitive transcallosal neuronal discharges that, when present, serve to enhance cortical reactivity (Ono *et al.*, 2002). Other theories concern the role of homeostatic mechanisms in certain forms of epilepsy, which have evolved to elaborate computer simulations that may eventually yield accurate seizure prediction and closed-loop feedback devices to prevent seizures in susceptible patients (Chakravarthy *et al.*, 2009). This illustrates how the study of a paradoxical phenomenon can illuminate mechanisms underlying epilepsy with therapeutic implications that might otherwise have not been investigated.

Epilepsy can develop from traumatic brain injury. How can subsequent brain trauma other than resective brain surgery do anything but potentially worsen seizures, for example, from trauma-induced apoptosis, gliosis and maladaptive neuroplastic changes? While exacerbation of pre-existing epilepsy from head injury has been documented (Tai and Gross, 2004), there are, surprisingly, case reports suggesting that some acquired brain injuries can improve seizures (Trinka *et al.*, 2000). For example, in a retrospective study of 63 patients with chronic epilepsy, Marosi *et al.* (1994) found that nearly 1 in 3 patients with epilepsy became seizure-free after brain injuries, including trauma, stroke and haemorrhages, which was statistically significant compared to a control group. Spitz *et al.* (2000) described a 31-year-old woman who averaged five seizures per month despite aggressive pharmacological attempts to control her seizures. Consequent to a seizure, she fell down a flight of stairs, sustaining a head injury that resulted in a right temporal lobe contusion and a mild left hemiparesis that lasted for seven months. Following the head injury, she became seizure-free for one year, after which seizures reoccurred, leading the authors to speculate that the injury-induced inhibition of her epileptogenic zone had resolved. Similarly, Cukiert *et al.* (1992) reported a 33-year-old woman with epilepsy whose seizures significantly improved after a traumatic callosotomy.

Two additional reports are especially ironic, in that brain injuries occurred during tests to determine the suitability of patients with epilepsy for potentially curative brain resection that paradoxically resolved their epilepsy without the need for surgery. One case involved an infarction of the epileptic focus during an intracarotid sodium amobarbital procedure (Ammerman *et al.*, 2005), and the other report documents seizure remission in a series of six patients following the temporary insertion of intracerebral or subdural electrodes for seizure localization (Katariwala *et al.*, 2001).

In addition to seizures, co-morbid disorders may also improve following acquired or iatrogenic brain lesions. Levine *et al.* (2003) reported two patients with epilepsy and eating disorders; the latter resolved after a right temporal lobectomy in one patient and a right infero-frontal and temporal traumatic injury in the other.

Finally, several reports document significant improvement or resolution of seizures in association with bacterial or viral illnesses in patients with epilepsy (Sasaki *et al.*, 2000; Yamamoto *et al.*, 2004, 2007). These outcomes are counter-intuitive since a common trigger for seizures in patients with epilepsy is systemic or intracranial infection.

Spontaneous remission

Common wisdom suggests that adult patients with chronic epilepsy rarely undergo spontaneous remission. Yet studies of untreated patients with chronic epilepsy imply that a substantial proportion, perhaps up to 30%, paradoxically undergo a spontaneous remission (Placencia *et al.*, 1994; Nicoletti *et al.*, 2009). This suggests that not all patients whose seizures appear to respond to AEDs may actually be benefitting directly from the treatment.

Figure 11.2 Brainstorm #23 (oil and acrylic), by Craig Getzlaff (Schachter, 2003, p. 28). Reproduced with permission.

Dietary therapies

It is not intuitively obvious that diet can reduce seizures in persons with epilepsy, or that starvation and fasting, as observed in the New Testament (St. Mark; 9:29; King James version), can be antiepileptic. Nonetheless, the high-fat, adequate protein and low-carbohydrate diet known as the ketogenic diet, often initiated with a period of fasting, can be quite effective at reducing seizures in patients with treatment-resistant seizures, as can related diets such as the medium-chain triglyceride and Atkins diets (Papandreou *et al.*, 2006). The underlying mechanism of action is not fully known, but when elucidated may hold clues for the development of new treatments (Kossoff, 2004; Mainardi and Albano, 2008).

Paradoxical, positive consequences of seizures

There are numerous examples of positive seizure experiences that defy ready explanation, including visual hallucinations (Figure 11.2) and abnormal self-location (Figure 11.3; Lopez *et al.*, 2010; also see below). Among the more interesting positive ictal experiences are ecstatic seizures and orgasmic seizures.

Ecstatic seizures

Picard and Craig (2009) describe ecstasy as a 'state of heightened consciousness in which an individual has a transcendent capacity for exceptional mental clarity and an intensely positive emotional experience'. These authors state that affected individuals may have a strongly altered subjective perception of time, space and the self, and that 'the experience can permanently change an individual's world view'.

Given that seizures often have an impairing effect on consciousness, and that achieving an ecstatic state as defined by Picard and Craig would seem to require a brain functioning to its maximum capability, it is therefore paradoxical that seizures in some patients are associated with ecstasy, as made famous by Fyodor Dostoevsky in *The Idiot* (Hughes, 2005b). Picard and Craig (2009) describe a series of five patients with ectastic seizures.

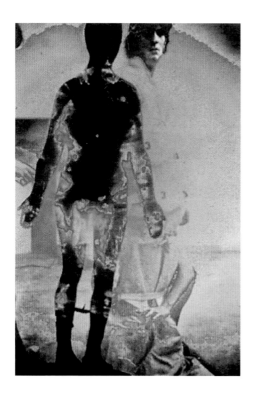

Figure 11.3 Transcending (computer graphic), by Jennifer Hall (Schachter, 2003, p. 30). Reproduced with permission.

Based on the neurophysiological and neuroradiological evidence in these patients, they argue that their ecstatic states result from hyperactivation of the anterior insula. This localization is consistent with the putative role of the anterior insular cortex, both in time perception (Craig, 2009) and in the subjective feeling states that underlie self-awareness and self-consciousness (Critchley *et al.*, 2004; Craig, 2009).

In their series of 11 patients with ecstatic seizures, Hansen and Brodtkorb (2003) found a tendency for seizure self-induction and treatment non-compliance, which may not seem paradoxical, except that ecstatic seizures in some patients may potentially become generalized tonic–clonic seizures, putting patients at risk. Interestingly, the patients of Hansen and Brodtkorb 'felt that the symptoms of their ictal events did not have a counterpart in human experience and could not be fully described in words'. Five of their patients experienced religious phenomena with their seizures, leading the authors to speculate that religious experiences in historical figures said to have epilepsy such as St. Paul, Joan of Arc and St. Birgitta may have been ictal in nature, though this is controversial (Hughes, 2005a).

Case reports of ecstatic seizures highlight the unusual nature of these episodes and challenge us to describe the neuronal circuitry underlying these experiences. Clues may be found in the circumstances under which they occur and the associated symptoms. Ecstatic seizures have been associated with specific triggers, such as watching television (Binnie and Wilkins, 1997), and may occur in conjunction with other difficult-to-explain phenomena such as abnormal self-location (also called out-of-body episodes), described in one case report as 'ecstatic astral journeys' (Vuilleumier *et al.*, 1997). Cirignotta *et al.* (1980) reported a 30-year-old man with episodes of 'psychomotor arrest, slight lapse of consciousness, and above all, an ineffable sensation of "joy"'. The joy he felt was 'so intense that he cannot find its match in reality . . . His mind, his whole being is pervaded by a sense of total bliss'. Naito and Matsui (1988) reported a 62-year-old woman with no prior psychiatric history, but who was described as pious and possessing 'a strong faith in the god of a new religion in Japan'. Five years after suffering a head injury, she had the first of several ecstatic episodes, for which she was occasionally, but not always, amnesic. For example, she would suddenly cry out 'I saw my God! I saw my God!', or 'A halo appeared around God. Thank my God! Oh! Thank my God!' Another type of episode occurred once while she watched the rising sun, which she described as follows: 'Triple haloes appeared around the sun. Suddenly the sunlight became intense. I experienced a revelation of God and all creation glittering under the sun. The sun became bigger and engulfed me. My mind, my whole being was pervaded by a feeling of delight'.

In the context of ecstatic seizures, gelastic seizures are of interest because of two counter-intuitive features. First, they are often seen in association with hypothalamic hamartomas rather than with pathologies affecting the cortex, and second, they are characterized by episodes of laughing without the simultaneous experience of ecstasy, mirth or joy (Harvey and Freeman, 2007).

Orgasmic seizures

Orgasmic seizures were described in 1983 by Remillard *et al.* (1983) and since then have been the subject of scattered case reports and case series (Fadul *et al.*, 2005; Aull-Watschinger *et al.*, 2008), including a 41-year-old patient in whom all orgasmic seizures were brought on by brushing her teeth (Chuang *et al.*, 2004). Janszky *et al.* (2004) reported seven patients with temporal lobe epilepsy (six with right-sided seizure onset and one left) who experienced an orgasmic sensation at the start of their seizures, including one patient who (understandably) declined treatment. Based on the similar description of these auras to non-ictal orgasms by their patients, the authors speculated that orgasmic seizures result from ictal activation of the same brain regions that are responsible for physiological orgasms during coitus or masturbation. A candidate region is the right amygdala, which was the site of seizure onset of another patient with orgasmic auras and whose symptoms were reproduced with electrical stimulation of the same area (Bancaud *et al.*, 1970), and which has been shown to be activated during non-ictal orgasm (Heath, 1972). A related but rare phenomenon has been described in patients whose seizures are triggered by sexual intercourse and orgasms (Ozkara *et al.*, 2006).

Paradoxical accomplishments in persons with epilepsy

A diagnosis of epilepsy is generally equated with a challenging life, particularly if seizures are not fully controlled. Hence it may be surprising that a number of famous people have had intractable seizures, including such notable military and political leaders as Peter the Great (Hughes, 2007), Julius Caesar (Hughes, 2004) and Napoleon Bonaparte (Hughes, 2003). While the list of artists and geniuses said to have epilepsy is quite long, with little credible support other than speculation (Hughes, 2005a), macro- and microscopic examination of the brains of creative persons with a firm diagnosis of epilepsy may provide a scientific basis for the relationship of creativity to epilepsy, and suggest mechanisms by which epilepsy may enhance creativity (see, for example, Murai *et al.*, 1998), or, paradoxically, the converse.

Conclusions

Paradoxical phenomena have been described in a number of areas related to epilepsy, including unexpected worsening or improvement in seizures, causes of epilepsy that under certain circumstances can be a cure, inter-relationships with psychiatric disorders and extraordinary seizure-related experiences.

Whether paradoxical worsening or improvement in seizures from brain injuries or antiepileptic drugs may be specific to, or more common in, certain forms of epilepsy – for example, focal or lesion-based epilepsies compared to channelopathy-based epilepsies – is not clear, but deserves further study. One intriguing hypothesis is that idiopathic generalized epilepsy may be less susceptible to paradoxical effects, and that epilepsy due to ion channelopathies might not be improved by selective trauma but have more 'paradoxical' effects from non-AED membrane-affecting drugs (Jonathan Cole, personal communication).

Future challenges and questions

Identifying those aspects of epilepsy that seem paradoxical serves to illustrate the gaps in our current understanding of the underlying mechanisms of epilepsy and indeed the neural basis of human behaviour, and should stimulate researchers to close those gaps. Yet for every paradoxical observation published in the medical literature there are probably dozens that have been mentioned by patients to physicians only to be ignored by the physician or dismissed by journal editors because there was no rational explanation.

These observations should be vigorously pursued because they may turn out to be the keys to unlocking current mysteries and advancing the fields of epilepsy and behavioural neurology. Such advances will surely be made in parallel with technological improvements in functional imaging, neurophysiological monitoring and the development of surrogate markers. However, the rate-limiting step, and therefore the primary challenge before us, is cultural. For paradoxical phenomena to move the field of epilepsy forward, we must first suspend disbelief, recognize unexpected outcomes and truly listen to our patients. Then we must be willing as a scientific community to explore these phenomena as potential Black Swan Events, a phrase used by Taub (2007) to describe infrequent, unexpected and seemingly random events that nonetheless have the potential to be high-impact with significant consequences.

References

Ammerman, J. M., Caputy, A. J., & Potolicchio, S. J. (2005). Endovascular ablation of a temporal lobe epileptogenic focus – a complication of Wada testing. *Acta Neurologica Scandinavica*, 112: 189–91.

Armstrong, C., Morgan, R. J., & Soltesz, I. (2009). Pursuing paradoxical proconvulsant prophylaxis for epileptogenesis. *Epilepsia*, 50: 1657–69.

Aull-Watschinger, S., Pataraia, E., & Baumgartner, C. (2008). Sexual auras: predominance of epileptic activity within the mesial temporal lobe. *Epilepsy & Behavior*, 12: 124–7.

Bancaud, J., Favel, P., Bonis, A., Bordas-Ferrer, M., Miravet, J., & Talairach, J. (1970). Manifestations sexuelles paroxytiques et épilepsie temporal. *Revue Neurologique*, 123: 217–30.

Bauer, J. (1996). Seizure-inducing effects of antiepileptic drugs: a review. *Acta Neurologica Scandinavica*, 94: 367–77.

Besag, F. M. (2004). Behavioural effects of the newer antiepileptic drugs: an update. *Expert Opinion on Drug Safety*, 3: 1–8.

Beyenburg, S., Mitchell, A. J., Schmidt, D., Elger, C. E., & Reuber, M. (2005). Anxiety in patients with epilepsy: systematic review and suggestions for clinical management. *Epilepsy & Behavior*, 7: 161–71.

Binnie, C. D. & Wilkins, A. J. (1997). Ecstatic seizures induced by television. *Journal of Neurology, Neurosurgery, and Psychiatry*, 63: 273.

Blumer, D. (1970). Hypersexual episodes in temporal lobe epilepsy. *American Journal of Psychiatry*, 126: 1099–106.

Bowman, S. M., Aitken, M. E., & Sharp, G. B. (2010). Disparities in injury death location for people with epilepsy/seizures. *Epilepsy & Behavior*, 17: 369–72.

Cascino, G. D. (2008). When drugs and surgery don't work. *Epilepsia*, 49(Suppl. 9): 79–84.

Chakraborti, A., Gulati, K., & Ray, A. (2007). Estrogen actions on brain and behavior: recent insights and future challenges. *Reviews in the Neurosciences*, 18: 395–416.

Chakravarthy, N., Tsakalis, K., Sabesan, S., & Iasemidis, L. (2009). Homeostasis of brain dynamics in epilepsy: a feedback control systems perspective of seizures. *Annals of Biomedical Engineering*, 37: 565–85.

Chuang, Y.-C., Lin, T.-K., Lui, C.-C., Chen, S.-D., & Chang, C.-S. (2004). Tooth-brushing epilepsy with ictal orgasms. *Seizure*, 13: 179–82.

Cirignotta, F., Todesco, C. V., & Lugaresi, E. (1980). Temporal lobe epilepsy with ecstatic seizures (so-called Dostoevsky epilepsy). *Epilepsia*, 21: 705–10.

Citak, A., Soysal, D. D., Ucsel, R., Karabocuoglu, M., & Uzel, N. (2006). Seizures associated with poisoning in children: tricyclic antidepressant intoxication. *Pediatrics International*, 48: 582–5.

Clemens, B. (2005). Forced normalisation precipitated by lamotrigine. *Seizure*, 14: 485–9.

Cogen, P. H., Antunes, J. L., & Correll, J. W. (1979). Reproductive function in temporal lobe epilepsy: the effect of temporal lobectomy. *Surgical Neurology*, 12: 243–6.

Cohen-Gadol, A. A., Bradley, C. C., Williamson, A., et al. (2005). Normal magnetic resonance imaging and medial temporal lobe epilepsy: the clinical syndrome of paradoxical temporal lobe epilepsy. *Journal of Neurosurgery*, 102: 902–09.

Craig, A. D. (2009). How do you feel – now? *Nature Reviews Neuroscience*, 10: 59–70.

Critchley, H. D., Wiens, S., Rotshtein, P., Ohman, A., & Dolan, R. J. (2004). Neural systems supporting interoceptive awareness. *Nature Neuroscience*, 7: 189–95.

Cukiert, A., Haddad, M. S., Mussi, A., & Marino Júnior, R. (1992). Traumatic callosotomy. *Arquivos de Neuro-Psiquiatria*, 50: 365–8.

Dostoyevsky, F. (1959). *The Idiot*. New York, NY: Dell Publishing Company, p. 259.

Ellis, T. L. & Stevens, A. (2008). Deep brain stimulation for medically refractory epilepsy. *Neurosurgical Focus*, 25: 1–11.

Eyer, F., Stenzel, J., Schuster, T., et al. (2009). Risk assessment of severe tricyclic antidepressant overdose. *Human & Experimental Toxicology*, 28: 511–19.

Fadul, C. E., Stommel, E. W., Dragnev, K. H., Eskey, C. J., & Dalmau, J. O. (2005). Focal paraneoplastic limbic encephalitis presenting as orgasmic epilepsy. *Journal of Neuro-Oncology*, 72: 195–8.

Frye, C. A. (2008). Hormonal influences on seizures: basic neurobiology. *International Review of Neurobiology*, 83: 27–77.

Gayatri, N. A., & Livingston, J. H. (2006). Aggravation of epilepsy by anti-epileptic drugs. *Developmental Medicine & Child Neurology*, 48: 394–8.

Gilliam, F., & Kanner, A. M. (2002). Treatment of depressive disorders in epilepsy patients. *Epilepsy & Behavior*, 3: 2–9.

Graves, N. M., & Fisher, R. S. (2005). Neurostimulation for epilepsy, including a pilot study of anterior nucleus stimulation. *Clinical Neurosurgery*, 52: 127–34.

Guerrini, R., Belmonte, A., & Genton, P. (1998). Antiepileptic drug-induced worsening of seizures in children. *Epilepsia*, 39(Suppl. 3): S2–10.

Haddad, P. M., & Dursun, S. M. (2008). Neurological complications of psychiatric drugs: clinical features and management. *Human Psychopharmacology*, 23: 15–26.

Hansen, B. A., & Brodtkorb, E. (2003). Partial epilepsy with 'ecstatic' seizures. *Epilepsy & Behavior*, **4**: 667–73.

Harden, C. L. (2005). Sexuality in women with epilepsy. *Epilepsy & Behavior*, 7: S2–6.

Harden, C. L. (2008). Hormone replacement therapy: will it affect seizure control and AED levels? *Seizure*, **17**: 176–80.

Harden, C. L., & Goldstein, M. A. (2002). Mood disorders in patients with epilepsy: epidemiology and management. *CNS Drugs*, **16**: 291–302.

Harvey, A. S., & Freeman, J. L. (2007). Epilepsy in hypothalamic hamartoma: clinical and EEG features. *Seminars in Pediatric Neurology*, **14**: 60–4.

Hauser, W. A., & Hesdorffer, D. C. (1990). *Epilepsy: Frequency, Causes, and Consequences*. New York, NY: Demos.

Heath, R. G. (1972). Pleasure and brain activity in man. *The Journal of Nervous and Mental Disease*, **154**: 3–18.

Heick, A. (1996). The thalamic commissure in generalized epilepsy. *British Journal of Neurosurgery*, **10**: 309–10.

Herzog, A. G., Harden, C. L., Liporace, J., et al. (2004). Frequency of catamenial seizure exacerbation in women with localization-related epilepsy. *Annals of Neurology*, **56**: 431–4.

Hsu, D., Chen, W., Hsu, M., & Beggs, J. M. (2008). An open hypothesis: is epilepsy learned, and can it be unlearned? *Epilepsy & Behavior*, **13**: 511–22.

Hughes, J. R. (2003). Emperor Napoleon Bonaparte: did he have seizures? Psychogenic or epileptic or both? *Epilepsy & Behavior*, **4**: 793–6.

Hughes, J. R. (2004). Dictator Perpetuus: Julius Caesar – did he have seizures? If so, what was the etiology? *Epilepsy & Behavior*, **5**: 756–64.

Hughes, J. R. (2005a). Did all those famous people really have epilepsy? *Epilepsy & Behavior*, **6**: 115–39.

Hughes, J. R. (2005b). The idiosyncratic aspects of the epilepsy of Fyodor Dosteovsky. *Epilepsy & Behavior*, 7: 531–8.

Hughes, J. R. (2007). The seizures of Peter Alexeevich = Peter the Great, father of modern Russia. *Epilepsy & Behavior*, **10**: 179–82.

Hughes, J. R. (2009). Absence seizures: a review of recent reports with new concepts. *Epilepsy & Behavior*, **15**: 404–12.

Janszky, J., Ebner, A., Szupera, Z., et al. (2004). Orgasmic aura – a report of seven cases. *Seizure*, **13**: 441–4.

Jobe, P. C. (2003). Common pathogenic mechanisms between depression and epilepsy: an experimental perspective. *Epilepsy & Behavior*, **4**: S14–24.

Jobe, P. C. (2004). Affective disorder and epilepsy comorbidity: implications for development of treatments, preventions and diagnostic approaches. *Clinical EEG and Neuroscience*, **35**: 53–68.

Kanner, A. M. (2000). Psychosis of epilepsy: a neurologist's perspective. *Epilepsy & Behavior*, **1**: 219–27.

Kanner, A. M., & Barry, J. J. (2003). The impact of mood disorders in neurological diseases: should neurologists be concerned? *Epilepsy & Behavior*, **4**: 3–13.

Kanner, A. M., & Ostrovskaya, A. (2008). Long-term significance of postictal psychotic episodes. I. Are they predictive of bilateral ictal foci? *Epilepsy & Behavior*, **12**: 150–3.

Kanner, A. M., Soto, A., & Gross-Kanner, H. (2004). Prevalence and clinical characteristics of postictal psychiatric symptoms in partial epilepsy. *Neurology*, **62**: 708–13.

Katariwala, N. M., Bakay, R. A., Pennell, P. B., Olson, L. D., Henry, T. R., & Epstein, C. M. (2001). Remission of intractable partial epilepsy following implantation of intracranial electrodes. *Neurology*, **57**: 1505–07.

Kossoff, E. H. (2004). More fat and fewer seizures: dietary therapies for epilepsy. *Lancet Neurology*, **3**: 415–20.

Krishnamoorthy, E. S., Trimble, M. R., Sander, J. W. A. S., & Kanner, A. M. (2002). Forced normalization at the interface between epilepsy and psychiatry. *Epilepsy & Behavior*, **3**: 303–08.

Lado, F. A., Velisek, L., & Moshe, S. L. (2003). The effect of electrical stimulation of the subthalamic nucleus on seizures is frequency dependent. *Epilepsia*, **44**: 157–64.

LaFrance, C. W., Kanner, A. M., & Hermann, B. (2008). Psychiatric comorbidities in epilepsy. *International Review of Neurobiology*, **83**: 347–83.

Landolt, H. (1953). Some clinical electroencephalographical correlations in epileptic psychosis (twilight states). *Electroencephalography and Clinical Neurophysiology*, **5**: 121.

Levine, R., Lipson, S., & Devinsky, O. (2003). Resolution of eating disorders after right temporal lesions. *Epilepsy & Behavior*, **4**: 781–3.

Lewis, A. (1934). Melancholia: a historical review. *Journal of Mental Science*, **80**: 1–42.

Lisanby, S. H., Bazil, C. W., Resor, S. R., Nobler, M. S., Finck, D. A., & Sackeim, H. A. (2001). ECT in the treatment of status epilepticus. *The Journal of ECT*, **17**: 210–15.

Lopez, C., Heydrich, L., Seeck, M., & Blanke, O. (2010). Abnormal self-location and vestibular vertigo in a patient with right frontal lobe epilepsy. *Epilepsy & Behavior*, **17**: 289–92.

Mainardi, P., & Albano, C. (2008). Is the antiepileptic effect of the ketogenic diet due to ketones? *Medical Hypotheses*, **70**: 536–9.

Marosi, M., Luef, G., Schett, P., Graf, M., Sailer, U., & Bauer, G. (1994). The effects of brain lesions on the course of chronic epilepsies. *Epilepsy Research*, **19**: 63–9.

Mendez, M. F., Cummings, J. L., & Benson, D. F. (1986). Depression in epilepsy. Significance and phenomenology. *Archives of Neurology*, **43**: 766–70.

Mula, M., & Sander, J. W. (2007). Negative effects of antiepileptic drugs on mood in patients with epilepsy. *Drug Safety*, **30**: 555–67.

Mula, M., & Monaco, F. (2009). Antiepileptic drugs and psychopathology of epilepsy: an update. *Epileptic Disorders*, **11**: 1–9.

Mula, M., Schmitz, B., & Sander, J. W. (2008). The pharmacological treatment of depression in adults with epilepsy. *Expert Opinion on Pharmacotherapy*, **9**: 3159–68.

Murai, T., Hanakawa, T., Sengoku, A., *et al.* (1998). Temporal lobe epilepsy in a genius of natural history: MRI volumetric study of postmortem brain. *Neurology*, **50**: 1373–6.

Nadkarni, S., Arnedo, V., & Devinsky, O. (2007). Psychosis in epilepsy patients. *Epilepsia*, **48**: 17–19.

Naito, H., & Matsui, N. (1988). Temporal lobe epilepsy with ictal ecstatic state and interictal behavior of hypergraphia. *The Journal of Nervous and Mental Disease*, **176**: 123–4.

Nicoletti, A., Sofia, V., Vitale, G., *et al.* (2009). Natural history and mortality of chronic epilepsy in an untreated population of rural Bolivia: a follow-up after 10 years. *Epilepsia*, **50**: 2199–206.

Nitsche, M. A., & Paulus, W. (2009). Noninvasive brain stimulation protocols in the treatment of epilepsy: current state and perspectives. *Neurotherapeutics*, **6**: 244–50.

O'Donoghue, M. F., Goodridge, D. M., Redhead, K., Sander, J. W., & Duncan, J. S. (1999). Assessing the psychosocial consequences of epilepsy: a community-based study. *The British Journal of General Practice*, **49**: 211–14.

Ohara, T., Monji, A., Onitsuka, T., *et al.* (2006). Interictal psychosis after stroke with forced normalization. *The Journal of Neuropsychiatry and Clinical Neurosciences*, **18**: 557–8.

Ono, T., Fujimura, K., Yoshida, S., & Ono, K. (2002). Suppressive effect of callosotomy on epileptic seizures is due to the blockade of enhancement of cortical reactivity by transcallosal volleys. *Epilepsy Research*, **51**: 117–21.

Ozkara, C., Ozdemir, S., Yilmaz, A., Uzan, M., Yeni, N., & Ozmen, M. (2006). Orgasm-induced seizures: a study of six patients. *Epilepsia*, **47**: 2193–7.

Papandreou, D., Pavlou, E., Kalimeri, E., & Mavromichalis, I. (2006). The ketogenic diet in children with epilepsy. *British Journal of Nutrition*, **95**: 5–13.

Perucca, E., Gram, L., Avanzini, G., & Dulac, O. (1998). Antiepileptic drugs as a cause of worsening seizures. *Epilepsia*, **39**: 5–17.

Picard, F., & Craig, A. D. (2009). Ecstatic epileptic seizures: a potential window on the neural basis for human self-awareness. *Epilepsy & Behavior*, **16**: 539–46.

Placencia, M., Sander, J. W. A. S., Roman, M., et al. (1994). The characteristics of epilepsy in a largely untreated population in rural Ecuador. *Journal of Neurology, Neurosurgery, and Psychiatry*, **57**: 320–5.

Pollo, C., & Villemure, J. G. (2007). Rationale, mechanisms of efficacy, anatomical targets and future prospects of electrical deep brain stimulation for epilepsy. *Acta Neurochirurgica, Supplement*, **97**: 311–20.

Remillard, G. M., Andermann, F., Testa, G. F., et al. (1983). Sexual ictal manifestations predominate in women with temporal lobe epilepsy: a finding suggesting sexual dimorphism in the human brain. *Neurology*, **33**: 323–30.

Rosenfeld, W. E., & Roberts, D. W. (2009). Tonic and atonic seizures: what's next-VNS or callosotomy? *Epilepsia*, **50**(Suppl 8), 25–30.

Sachdev, P. S. (2007). Alternating and postictal psychoses: review and a unifying hypothesis. *Schizophrenia Bulletin*, **33**: 1029–37.

Saillet, S., Langlois, M., Feddersen, B., et al. (2009). Manipulating the epileptic brain using stimulation: a review of experimental and clinical studies. *Epileptic Disorders*, **11**: 100–12.

Santiago-Rodríguez, E., Cárdenas-Morales, L., Harmony, T., Fernández-Bouzas, A., Porras-Kattz, E., & Hernández, A. (2008). Repetitive transcranial stimulation decreases the number of seizures in patients with focal neocortical epilepsy. *Seizure*, **17**: 677–83.

Sarko, J. (2000). Antidepressants, old and new. A review of their adverse effects and toxicity in overdose. *Emergency Medicine Clinics of North America*, **18**: 637–54.

Sasaki, M. Matsuda, H., Omura, I., Sugai, K., & Hashimoto, T. (2000). Transient seizure disappearance due to bilateral striatal necrosis in a patient with intractable epilepsy. *Brain Development*, **22**: 50–5.

Sazgar, M., & Bourgeois, B. F. D. (2005). Aggravation of epilepsy by antiepileptic drugs. *Pediatric Neurology*, **33**: 227–34.

Schachter, S. C. (1998). Iatrogenic seizures. *Neurologic Clinics of North America*, **16**: 157–70.

Schachter, S. C. (2003). *Visions: Artists Living with Epilepsy*. San Diego, CA: Academic Press.

Scharfman, H. E., & MacLusky, N. J. (2006). The influence of gonadal hormones on neuronal excitability, seizures, and epilepsy in the female. *Epilepsia*, **47**: 1423–40.

Schulze-Bonhage, A., & Tebartz van Elst, L. (2010). Postictal psychosis: evidence for extrafocal functional precursors. *Epilepsy & Behavior*, **18**: 308–12.

Seethalakshmi, R., & Krishnamoorthy, E. S. (2007). The complex relationship between seizures and behavior: an illustrative case report. *Epilepsy & Behavior*: **10**: 203–05.

Shaw, P., Mellers, J., Henderson, M., Polkey, C., David, A. S., & Toone, B. K. (2004). Schizophrenia-like psychosis arising *de novo* following a temporal lobectomy: timing and risk factors. *Journal of Neurology, Neurosurgery, and Psychiatry*, **75**: 1003–08.

Smith, P. F., & Darlington, C. L. (1996). The development of psychosis in epilepsy: a reexamination of the kindling hypothesis. *Behavioral Brain Research*, **75**: 59–66.

Spitz, M. C., Towbin, J. A., & Shantz, D. (2000). Closed head injury resulting in paradoxical improvement of a seizure disorder. *Seizure*, **9**: 142–4.

Tai, P. C., & Gross, D. W. (2004). Exacerbation of pre-existing epilepsy by mild head injury: a five patient series. *Canadian Journal of Neurological Science*, **31**: 394–7.

Taub, N. N. (2007). *The Black Swan: The Impact of the Highly Improbable*. New York, NY: Random House.

Theodore, W. H., & Fisher, R. (2007). Brain stimulation for epilepsy. *Acta Neurochirurgica, Supplement*, **97**: 261–72.

Thundiyil, J. G., Kearney, T. E., & Olson, K. R. (2007). Evolving epidemiology of drug-induced seizures reported to a poison control system. *Journal of Medical Toxicology*, **3**: 15–9.

Torta, R., & Keller, R. (1999). Behavioral, psychotic, and anxiety disorders in epilepsy:

etiology, clinical features, and therapeutic implications. *Epilepsia*, **40**(Suppl 10): S2–20.

Trimble, M. R., & Schmitz, B. (1998). *Forced Normalization and Alternative Psychoses of Epilepsy*. Petersfield: Wrightson Biomedical Publishing Ltd.

Trinka, E., Luef, G., & Bauer, G. (2000). Closed head injury resulting in paradoxical improvement of a seizure disorder. *Seizure*, **9**: 531–2.

Usui, N., Maesawa, S., Kajita, Y., Endo, O., Takebayashi, S., & Yoshida, J. (2005). Suppression of secondary generalization of limbic seizures by stimulation of subthalamic nucleus in rats. *Journal of Neurosurgery*, **102**: 1122–9.

Veliskova, J. (2007). Estrogens and epilepsy: why are we so excited? *The Neuroscientist*, **13**: 77–88.

Villanueva, V., Carreno, M., Herranz Fernandex, J. L., & Gil-Nagel, A. (2007). Surgery and electrical stimulation in epilepsy: selection of candidates and results. *Neurologist*, **13**(6 Suppl 1): S29–37.

Vuilleumier, P., Despland, P. A., Assal, G., & Regli, F. (1997). Astral and out-of-body voyages. Heautoscopy, ecstasy and experimental hallucinations of epileptic origin. *Revue Neurologique*, **153**: 115–19.

Wilson, S. J., Bladin, P. F., & Saling, M. M. (2004). Paradoxical results in the cure of chronic illness: the 'burden of normality' as exemplified following seizure surgery. *Epilepsy & Behavior*, **5**: 13–21.

Wilson, S. J., Bladin, P. F., & Saling, M. M. (2007). The burden of normality: a framework for rehabilitation after epilepsy surgery. *Epilepsia*, **48**: 13–16.

Yamamoto, H., Kamiyama, N., Murakami, H., Miyamoto, Y., & Fukuda, M. (2007). Spontaneous resolution of intractable epileptic seizures following HHV-7 infection. *Brain Development*, **29**: 185–8.

Yamamoto, H., Yamano, T., Niijima, S., Kohyama, J., & Yamanouchi, H. (2004). Spontaneous improvement of intractable epileptic seizures following acute viral infections. *Brain Development*, **26**: 377–9.

Yu, L. & Blumenfeld, H. (2009). Theories of impaired consciousness in epilepsy. *Annals of the New York Academy of Sciences*, **1157**: 48–60.

Chapter 12

Paradoxical creativity and adjustment in neurological conditions

Indre V. Viskontas and Bruce L. Miller

Summary

In recent years, the paradoxical occurrence of creativity and related behaviours in patients with neurological conditions has begun to gain attention. Relevant examples include the emergence of previously unrecognized visual and musical creativity in the context of the neurodegenerative illnesses such as Alzheimer's disease and frontotemporal dementia, and also in some cases of stroke. The description of these phenomena has helped to influence models of the neural underpinnings of creativity. Specifically, it is possible that down-regulation of frontal or anterior temporal function may enable spontaneous creative insights that originate in other regions of the brain. However, other explanations may also be tenable, and further research needs to be carried out to gauge why certain individuals and not others with neurological conditions become creative, and how this enhanced creativity may be understood in terms of specific cognitive processes and neural systems.

Introduction

Neurological conditions are inevitably accompanied by deficits, disabilities and handicaps – problems that are emphasized by the patients' loved ones, clinicians and researchers alike. In rare instances, however, neurological changes have led to observations of enhanced function, including the domain of creativity. For example, Lythgoe and colleagues described a patient who, following a subarachnoid haemorrhage, showed an all-encompassing com-pulsion to sculpt, draw and paint, having shown no premorbid interest in art (Lythgoe *et al.*, 2005). Defining and measuring creativity has proven to be a monumental task, and taken together with the considerable individual differences in response to brain damage, evidence unambiguously demonstrating increased creativity is scarce. Here, we focus on studies that are at least suggestive of such links and the mechanisms whereby creativity may be increased. We do, however, discuss limitations in these studies and possible alternative explanations of findings. Since psychiatric conditions, epilepsy and autism are covered in other chapters in this book, we will limit our discussion to degenerative diseases, trauma and stroke.

In recent years, some authors have chosen to highlight certain positive aspects of neurological conditions; this emphasis on the positive serves to humanize these diseases, as well as to provide insights into the neural underpinnings of positive behaviours such as creating art, and perhaps most importantly, it may help to ease patient suffering. Relevant examples include the emergence of previously unrecognized artistic and musical creativity

---

in the context of the neurodegenerative illnesses such as Alzheimer's disease (Beatty *et al.*, 1994; Cummings *et al.*, 1987) and frontotemporal dementia (Miller *et al.*, 1998, 2000). Understanding which skills are retained or even emerge in the setting of a neurological condition may not only aid in differential diagnosis, but can also help clinicians design appropriate treatment options and diminish the frustration that patients and their care-givers experience on a daily basis by finding activities that bring satisfaction and pleasure to patients. Furthermore, as many neurological conditions are closely related to ageing, highlighting the positive changes that can accompany these conditions may also aid in decreasing the prevalence of prejudicial attitudes towards the elderly.

Given that neurodegenerative diseases, by definition, show progressive and focal loss of function over time, patients with these conditions represent an opportunity to study the reorganization of regional functional specialization. By following these patients longitudin-ally, clinicians and researchers can observe how focal degeneration can change behaviour and, recently, with the application of functional imaging techniques, how neural activity related to specific behavioural changes might reflect functional reorganization. Neural plasticity remains a central topic in neuroscience and much remains to be investigated. Better understanding of plastic processes in the brain should ultimately lead to major improvements in the quality of life of many neurological patients in particular, and the ageing public in general.

One might speculate that a possible force behind creative behaviour is the pleasure inherent in achieving what Mihaly Csikszentmihalyi has called 'flow' (Csikszentmihalyi, 1991). Csikszentmihalyi has proposed that the state of flow emerges when two or more of nine separable factors co-exist: (1) the delineation of clear goals, wherein expectations and rules are discernible, goals which are attainable and goals which align appropriately with one's skill set and abilities; (2) a high degree of concentration on a limited number of items; (3) a loss of the feeling of self-consciousness, via the merging of action and awareness; (4) a distorted sense of subjective time; (5) direct and immediate feedback, that makes successes and failures apparent, so that behaviour can be adjusted as needed; (6) a balance between ability level and challenge, such that the activity is neither too easy nor too difficult; (7) a sense of personal control over the situation or activity; (8) the activity is intrinsically rewarding, so that action feels effortless; and finally, (9) the activity is all-encompassing. Finding activities and creating situations in which patients are able to achieve flow could yield immeasurable enhancements of the quality of life. One might further speculate that some neurological patients engage in creative behaviours such as writing, painting or gardening, because they are able to experience 'flow' within these contexts.

Brain regions involved in creativity

The neural basis of creativity has proven difficult to outline in part because researchers do not agree on a single definition. Most scientists in this field do, however, concede that at least two components are necessary for creative output: (1) the work must be novel in its domain, be it music, visual art, literature or other, and (2) the work must have some usefulness, be it to inspire, move, explain or so forth in its particular social setting (Csikszentmihalyi, 1999; Perkins, 1988). For example, the creation of a wheel would be creative for a caveman but not in today's society, and a child's finger painting might be novel but does not necessarily contain the added utility necessary for a truly creative work. A wealth of research on insightful problem solving, creative thinking, expertise acquisition and exceptional individuals has demystified creativity, to a large extent, by demonstrating that talent is largely an enhancement, mainly by practice, of ordinary mental and/or physical processes (Boden, 1998; Gardner, 1993; Gladwell, 2008; Simonton, 2000). This paradigm shift has led researchers away from the relatively simplistic view that the neural basis of creativity can be explained by hemispheric asymmetry alone and that it cannot be taught (Bogen and Bogen, 1969; Martindale, 1999), and towards the view that different creative behaviours are subserved by the same discrete neural circuits that drive those behaviours in non-creative contexts (Dietrich, 2004). Finally, the emphasis on the importance of the non-dominant hemisphere in creativity (Bogen and Bogen, 1988) has been gradually diminished in concert with an increase in interest in the interaction between the frontal and temporal lobes, and the important role that the limbic and dopaminergic systems play in generating the drive to create (Flaherty, 2005; Martindale, 1999).

Although creativity itself is made up of several stages, each requiring a different skill set, arguably the most critical component involves the mechanism of 'insights'. Here, we define 'insights' as the building blocks of creativity: that is, the new ideas, concepts, associations or other manifestations of expression that characterize the products of the creative process. Creative insights can be dissociated into two domains, depending on the knowledge set tapped: the insight can be largely *cognitive* or *emotional* in content (Dietrich, 2004). Similarly, the process by which the creative insight is delivered can also be divided into two types: *spontaneous* or *deliberate* (Dietrich, 2004). This framework for categorizing creativity is useful in the study of neural circuits involved in these different types of insights. Thus, these two dimensions yield four distinct classes by crossing the type of content with the type of processing mode: creative insights might be cognitive and deliberate, emotional and deliberate, cognitive and spontaneous, or emotional and spontaneous.

Dietrich (2004) demonstrates how each of these classes may be served by distinct neural circuitry, with deliberate processing involving the prefrontal cortex, spontaneous insight likely resulting from activity in regions outside the prefrontal cortex, cognitive content being largely organized by dorsolateral prefrontal cortex and emotional content emerging from ventromedial prefrontal cortex and its interactions with the limbic system, including the cingulate cortex. Following from these assumptions, an anatomically-specific model of creative insights can be proposed (see Figure 12.1).

According to Dietrich (2004), deliberate cognitive insights are likely generated within the prefrontal cortex, via its search processes of stored information in the temporal, occipital and parietal cortices. Deliberate emotional insights also require the prefrontal cortex, but instead of searching neocortical association areas for relevant information, attentional resources are directed towards retrieving affective memories that are stored in regions conducting emotional processing such as the amygdala, cingulate cortex and ventromedial prefrontal regions. Spontaneous cognitive insights would originate in posterior association areas, during associative unconscious thinking. These thoughts probably involve the basal ganglia, given its role in automatic behaviours, and enter consciousness, or working memory, during the periodic down-regulation of the frontal attentional system. Finally, spontaneous emotional insights emerge when neural activity in structures that process emotional information is also spontaneously represented in working memory. Often, during biologically significant events and/or intense emotional experiences, information processed in emotion regions takes priority and overrides voluntary attention. Understanding how each of these types of insights is subserved by specific neural circuits aids in the interpretation of the paradoxical facilitation of creativity with

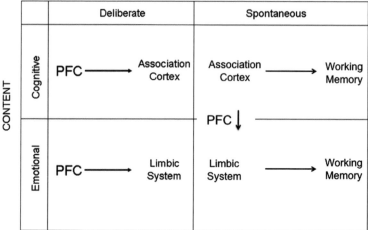

Figure 12.1 Simple model of brain regions involved in creative insights.

brain injury or psychiatric conditions. Furthermore, this classification scheme might also help clinicians find domains in which patients might experience flow.

The role of the frontal lobes in creativity then, seems to depend on the extent to which the process is spontaneous. No creative behaviours, however, seem to be fully independent of frontal lobe function, and there are several characteristics of the frontal lobes that make them critical for creativity. The pioneering work of Dean Keith Simonton introduced the idea that creative works that meet both the uniqueness and appropriateness criteria are almost always a function of a highly developed skill used in a novel fashion (Simonton, 1994). Before a novel creative masterpiece is produced, artists spend years developing the necessary skills in painting, music, writing, and science (Gladwell, 2008).

Cortical plasticity facilitates fine-tuning of motor and sensory skills and allows the formation of novel associations that make up the building blocks of creativity, and has been observed in both the frontal and medial temporal lobes. For example, extensive practice of a musical instrument results in reorganization of motor and sensory regions involved in the activity, with a larger proportion of cortical real estate devoted to the sensory and motor processing of the relevant body part (Elbert and Rockstroh, 2004). The flexible and dynamic nature of brain regions such as the hippocampus and prefrontal cortex, where plasticity is most pronounced, enables creativity. In addition, ventromedial frontal regions which are critical for social function may be responsible for internalizing the values and societal standards of a person's culture – a skill that is necessary for the second criterion of creativity: namely, assessing the usefulness or appropriateness of the creative product, and knowing when and how to break the rules of society in order to create.

Another feature of frontal lobe neuroanatomy that supports creativity is its connectivity. The frontal cortex receives information from regions throughout the brain, including motor, sensory and emotion areas, and via reciprocal connections controls attention, language, memory and other cognitive functions. The prefrontal cortex in particular receives highly processed information, allowing this region to achieve still higher cognitive functions such as self-construct (Keenan et al., 2000), self-reflective consciousness (Courtney et al.,

1998a, 1998b), complex social function (Damasio *et al.*, 1994), cognitive flexibility, planning, willed action, source memory and theory of mind. With changes in frontal lobe functioning and representations, one expects to see effects on creativity, although the exact nature of these effects is difficult to predict given the complexity of frontal lobe function.

Paradoxical facilitation of creativity with neurodegenerative disease

Paradoxically, new or preserved musical or visual artistic abilities have been described in the setting of frontotemporal dementia, which causes progressive atrophy of frontal and anterior temporal lobes (Miller *et al.*, 1998, 2000). Given the putative role of the frontal lobes in creativity, it is not surprising that the emergence of these abilities is often linked to degeneration of the anterior temporal lobe, particularly in the left hemisphere. These patients show progressive loss of conceptual knowledge, and their creative output tends to be devoid of verbal or symbolic content (see Figure 12.2) (Miller *et al.*, 2000).

Specifically, patients paint realistic landscapes, animals or detailed geometric designs that do not seem to contain meaning beyond the visual characteristics. Musicians continue to perform music, but even with popular songs do not necessarily pay attention to the

Figure 12.2 Typical examples of art produced in the context of temporal lobe degeneration. Note that images are largely devoid of conceptual or symbolic representations.

verbal realm. This observation was particularly striking in the case of one individual, LF, who did not notice when the words of a famous folk song (My Bonny Lies over the Ocean) were altered to the point of being incomprehensible, during a sing-a-long (Sacks, 2007). In our experience, much of the work created by these patients contains some recollections from the past, although, as mentioned above and demonstrated in the examples in Figure 12.2, they tend to avoid verbal or symbolic representations.

Despite their progressive neurodegeneration, these patients share many features with great creative minds in history. They show increasing interest and/or obsessions with their subjects, they neglect social and occupational responsibilities in favour of their art production, and they continue to produce work even in the absence of any encouragement or support from others (Miller et al., 1998). It is likely that within their artistic context, they are able to achieve the rewarding state of flow. Notably, as suggested earlier, the patients that show emergence of new or preservation of old artistic skills generally do not show extensive frontal lobe degeneration, which is characteristic of the disorder (Miller et al., 2000). This observation is in line with the wealth of research on creativity in neurologically intact individuals, which suggests that certain components of frontal lobe function are critical for the many organizational and motivational components of creativity (Chavez-Eakle et al., 2007).

While exploring the connection between anterior temporal lobe degeneration and visual art, Rankin and colleagues (2007) used both standardized tests to probe creative cognition and novel tests of visual art creation in a study of art in patients with dementia. Patients with both the frontal and temporal variants of frontotemporal dementia produced artwork that was rated as more bizarre and distorted than patients with Alzheimer's disease and healthy age-matched controls. Notably, however, in the *verbal* tests of creative cognition, patients with semantic dementia (anterior temporal lobe damage) showed decreased fluency, originality and elaboration in concert with a tendency toward ending the test prematurely. On standardized visuospatial creativity testing, which involved creating drawings based on incomplete meaningless doodles, these patients were more likely than participants from any of the other groups to produce drawings devoid of meaning, and to choose conventional or obvious markings, such as closing an open-ended figure. In contrast, the paintings that they created, and indeed much of the artwork from this patient group, was striking in the aesthetic dimension, characterized by the unorthodox use of vivid and unconventional colours, intricate and repetitive geometrical designs, underscoring the unique perception as well as the obsessive nature of their work. One caveat when interpreting this work that is worth considering is the notion that as the patients' ability to make representational drawings might be hailed as more creative by the artistic community, the brain networks underlying the drive to make these choices may not necessarily be the same as that upon which healthy artists rely. These findings also suggest that the enhancements in creativity that may accompany a particular degenerative pattern may remain domain-specific. Just as mastery of skills in one domain such as music can improve creative output in that domain but not necessarily transfer to other artistic realms, so too might the paradoxical facilitation of creativity with neurological disease remain tied to a single type of output.

The dominance of the visual domain and the perseverative or obsessive behaviours characteristic of semantic dementia can also be seen in the large proportion (~25%) of these patients for whom the completion of jigsaw puzzles becomes an important, or even the primary, activity of daily living (Green and Patterson, 2009), likely because they are able to achieve 'flow' by working on these puzzles. In a controlled study of jigsaw puzzle activity, Green and Patterson (2009) found that semantic dementia patients have preserved jigsaw skills, sometimes even above and beyond the performance of age-matched controls. In fact, these patients were superior to controls in completing 'reality-disrupted' puzzles, in which expectations based on knowledge of the real world can interfere with puzzle completion, and on 'grain' jigsaw puzzles, characterized by the fact that conceptual knowledge would not benefit performance. Most encouraging, from a clinical standpoint, semantic dementia patients, who often exhibit flat affect and demeanour, were observed to display signs of pleasure and pride during the completion of jigsaw puzzles, even if the activity was not a primary one for that particular person, suggesting that this task might be a good candidate for enabling flow in many patients with semantic dementia.

In a comprehensive case study, Seeley et al. (2008) described a visual artist, Anne Adams, who suffered from progressive non-fluent aphasia (PNFA). Although she had painted as a hobby throughout her life, with disease progression painting became progressively more important, until it became her primary daily activity. Note that she might have chosen any number of hobbies that were less complex, or related to her profession (she was a biologist), and yet she, and other similar patients, chose visual art. Likewise, another semantic dementia patient who was a lawyer by profession and a musician by vocation also chose to produce visual art when he became ill, rather than resorting to music or other hobbies (Miller et al., 1998). Anne's most stunning works of art were produced at a time when the disease was already progressing. In PNFA, the main site of atrophy is the left fronto-opercular cortex, leaving patients with effortful, non-fluent and apractic speech (Gorno-Tempini et al., 2004), and difficulties with grammar and articulation. In an interesting twist of fate, Anne chose to create an elaborate painting inspired by Maurice Ravel's (1875–1937) famous 'Bolero' (Seeley et al., 2008). Ravel himself suffered from a progressive aphasia, and composed his most famous piece, the Bolero, set to the rhythms of the Moorish-Spanish dance, in the early stages of his disease, at age 53. The piece is a study of compulsions and perseverations (Amaducci et al., 2002), with the repetition of a simple melodic theme, accompanied by an extraordinarily repetitive and simple bass line. Interestingly, Ravel considered the Bolero as a rather trivial work, describing it once as 'a piece for orchestra without music'. 'I'm going to try and repeat [the theme] a number of times without any development, gradually increasing the orchestra as best I can' (Orenstein, 1991). After writing Bolero, Ravel's illness gradually progressed until he died, eight years later, of complications related to an attempted treatment. Unaware of Ravel's illness, Anne Adams was inspired to paint the Bolero, representing the piece in a precise and compulsive fashion, with the height of each row signifying the increasing texture and volume of the orchestra (see Figure 12.3).

Notably, structural and functional imaging findings in the case of Anne Adams demonstrated enhanced grey matter and activation in heteromodal associative (IPS/SPL) and polymodal (STS) neocortex in the right hemisphere (Seeley et al., 2008). These areas are involved in visuomotor search and attentional control (Corbetta and Shulman, 2002; Seeley et al., 2007) and sensory transcoding, which is necessary for sight-reading music (Schon et al., 2002; Sergent et al., 1992). In addition, voxel-based morphometry (VBM) has demonstrated enhancements in these same regions in professional musicians (Gaser and Schlaug, 2003). We have recently completed a study of dementia patients in which we found enhanced visual search in patients with semantic dementia, which in turn correlated with greater grey matter in the right superior parietal lobe in both patients and controls when

Figure 12.3 'Unraveling Bolero', 1994. Anne Adam's portrayal of Maurice Ravel's *Bolero*.

measured with VBM (Viskontas *et al.*, 2011). That is to say, that the more grey matter found in this region, the better the performance in conjunction search. We suspect that enhancement of function in the right posterior brain may account for the increase in focused visuospatially based activities in our patients, such as the tendency to engage in jigsaw puzzles, design beautiful gardens, or even create visual art. For example, this alteration in visual search may be one mechanism by which patients with semantic dementia described above create paintings with vivid and repetitive geometric patterns.

The role of inhibition in creativity

The finding that damage to the left anterior temporal lobes might facilitate the emergence of creativity in semantic dementia patients led Miller and colleagues (2000) to suggest that the mechanism by which this behavioural change operates might involve releasing the right hemisphere from inhibition. In line with this idea, besides having the necessary skills in a given field, creative individuals often lack inhibition in both behaviour and cognition (Martindale, 1999; Martindale and Hines, 1975). Anecdotally, creative people describe themselves as lacking self-control and the creative process in those who achieve their goals via spontaneous insights is described as effortless and without deliberation (Csikszentmihalyi, 1996). Moreover, the psychiatric and neurological disorders that have been associated with creativity, such as frontotemporal dementia and bipolar disorder, usually include impulsive behaviours in their symptomatology (Martindale, 1971). Might decreased activation of the frontal lobes, in the dominant hemisphere in particular, be the source of the disinhibition that has been associated with creativity, particularly in patients with neurodegenerative disease? In a doctoral dissertation, Hudspeth (1985) demonstrated that more creative people show higher amplitude frontal lobe theta wave activity, which possibly indicates lower frontal lobe activation. These results are consistent with findings reported by Carlsson *et al.* (2000) who found that decreases in regional blood flow (rCBF) in both the left and right superior frontal lobes correlated with superior performance on the Alternate Uses Task. In addition, Lythgoe and colleagues (2005) described a patient who, following a subarachnoid haemorrhage, showed an all-encompassing compulsion to create visual art, along with mild frontal symptoms such as disinhibition and an impairment in task switching. Taken together, these findings highlight the complexity of the creative process and demonstrate that, whereas the frontal lobes are involved in creative cognition and the organization of deliberate creative behaviours as described in the model presented earlier in this chapter, many of the spontaneous aspects of creative output seem to be supported by regions outside of the frontal cortex. One might even go a step further and suggest that in some cases the frontal lobes need to be 'turned off' in order to facilitate the emergence of these spontaneous behaviours.

The paradoxical facilitation of creativity seen in patients with semantic dementia and progressive non-fluent aphasia has inspired studies of the effect of deactivating dominant hemisphere function on creativity using repetitive transcranial magnetic stimulation (rTMS), a non-invasive method of transiently deactivating parts of the cortex in awake humans (Miller *et al.*, 1998). Snyder *et al.* (2003) used rTMS to investigate the hypothesis that left temporal lobe function may inhibit artistic processes in the right hemisphere, specifically by 'blocking' access to creative thoughts. Decline in language function might overcome these blocks, allowing spontaneous insights to enter working memory more readily.

Accordingly, Snyder *et al.* (2003) demonstrated that rTMS of the left fronto-temporal lobe enhanced the creative components of certain skills, such as drawing (although not necessarily drawing ability per se, but rather the ability to capture perspective, kinetics and certain highlighted details), and the ability to detect commonly overlooked duplicate words while proof-reading. It is interesting to note that these proof-reading skills rely on similar perceptual and attentional processes as visual search in general, which seems to be preserved or enhanced in some SD patients (Viskontas *et al.*, in preparation). Notably, these effects were seen only in a subset of their participants (4/11 in drawing, 2/11 in proof-reading). Although these initial reports are still in the preliminary stages, the results are nonetheless intriguing. The results are consistent with the general notion that deliberate language-based focus can inhibit spontaneous creative thinking and that the absence of these constraints may enable the dynamic processes which lead to the novel recombination of ideas in areas such as visual art (Bristol and Viskontas, 2006).

Additional evidence that inhibitory processes are reduced in creative individuals comes from studies showing that highly creative people are overly reactive to external stimuli. For example, Martindale (1977) found that a series of mild electric shocks were rated as more intense by creative subjects. Subsequently, Martindale *et al.* (1996) showed that galvanic skin responses of creative subjects were greater than non-creative subjects to series of moderately intense auditory tones. In addition, the creative subjects took twice as long to habituate to the tones, and for some subjects this effect appeared to have been due more to the higher baseline response than to a difference in the rate of habituation. Higher baseline responses to external stimuli might represent a greater sensitivity to the environment. If such models are correct, then patients with semantic dementia and non-fluent aphasia might be experiencing greater sensitivity to visual stimuli as their language skills deteriorate, and conscious thoughts take up fewer cognitive resources in working memory.

Dopamine and the paradoxical facilitation of creativity

Given the central role that the neurotransmitter dopamine (DA) plays in motivation, it is not surprising that disruptions in DA have affected creative behaviour. As alluded to above, low latent inhibition[1] gives artists a heightened awareness of sensations (Carson *et al.*, 2003). DA has been shown to decrease latent inhibition (Swerdlow *et al.*, 2003), and increase baseline arousal, which has also been shown to be a trait of highly creative individuals (Martindale, 1999). Reward-seeking behaviour is mediated via DA activity (Pessiglione *et al.*, 2006), and DA is likely involved in the appreciation of beauty, as aesthetic evaluations in many domains, including visual art, faces and music, have been shown to activate regions modulated by DA such as the striatum and orbitofrontal cortex (Aharon *et al.*, 2001; Altarescu *et al.*, 2001; Breiter *et al.*, 2001; Kawabata and Zeki, 2004). Mink (1996) has suggested that DA facilitates goal-directed activity and inhibits competing behaviours. Further underscoring the role of DA in creativity is the finding that an allele of the D4 receptor may be a novelty-seeking gene (Keltikangas-Jarvinen *et al.*, 2003; Savitz and Ramesar, 2004). In addition, hypomania induced by DA agonists in patients with Parkinson's disease (PD) has been associated with the emergence of poetic talent and an increase in artistic productivity related to compulsive behaviour (Chatterjee *et al.*, 2006; Schrag and Trimble, 2001; Walker *et al.*, 2004). Kulisevsky *et al.* (2009) recently reported a case of a painter with PD, who showed a great increase in artistic productivity and commercial art success specifically following DA therapy. His art, now showing greater emotional content, suggest that perhaps the facilitation of creativity related to DA function acts via the limbic system, characterized by what Dietrich (2004) might describe as spontaneous emotional insights.

Summary

Neurological and psychiatric conditions that disrupt the interactions between the frontal lobes and the temporal, parietal and occipital lobes, or between the dominant and non-dominant hemispheres have been shown to affect creativity in a myriad of ways. Diminished language function in neurodegenerative diseases that target the left frontal or left anterior temporal lobes sometimes leads to the emergence of previously unrecognized visual and musical creativity, possibly by facilitating function in posterior brain regions. Down-regulation of frontal function may enable spontaneous creative insights, but as patients with frontal lobe dysfunction demonstrate, the frontal lobes are necessary for many components of creativity, including organization, monitoring and other executive functions. The importance of studying the paradoxical facilitation of behaviours that can help patients achieve 'flow' is underscored by the observation that patients who engage in creative activities display many signs of improved quality of life.

---

[1] Latent inhibition is a process by which exposure to an irrelevant stimulus reduces the likelihood that subsequent associative learning will occur and be manifest to that stimulus. It is argued that individuals with low latent inhibition may be unable to ignore/shut out the constant stream of environmental stimuli that occurs naturally. Latent inhibition has been implicated in a wide range of phenomena, including mental disorder and creativity (Lubow and Weiner, 2010).

Future challenges and questions

Our understanding of the neural underpinnings of creativity remains in its infancy. As theories of creativity become more comprehensive and complete, we will be in a better position to assess the paradoxical facilitation of related processes in patients with neurological damage and dysfunction. Many of the studies described in this chapter were performed on relatively small patient groups and therefore need to be replicated with larger samples and better controls. In addition, while certain artistic skills are only seen in a fairly small percentage of patients, precursors of these skills need to be identified and assessed in larger samples, to understand whether the patients are predisposed towards their artistic endeavours. Our study of conjunction search in semantic dementia patients is a first step in this direction (Viskontas et al., 2011). Future studies should also consider individual differences, and what might account for the proliferation of talent in one patient and not in another. Further work is also needed to investigate the role of dopamine and other neurotransmitter systems in creativity, particularly in patients whose pharmacotherapy includes manipulation of these systems. Finally, rTMS studies in healthy subjects which induce creative processes can help test the theories generated by patient studies.

References

Aharon, I., Etcoff, N., Ariely, D., Chabris, C. F., O'Connor, E., & Breiter, H. C. (2001). Beautiful faces have variable reward value: fMRI and behavioral evidence. *Neuron*, 32: 537–51.

Altarescu, G., Hill, S., Wiggs, E., et al. (2001). The efficacy of enzyme replacement therapy in patients with chronic neuronopathic Gaucher's disease. *Journal of Pediatrics*, 138: 539–47.

Amaducci, L., Grassi, E., & Boller, F. (2002). Maurice Ravel and right-hemisphere musical creativity: influence of disease on his last musical works? European *Journal of Neurology*, 9: 75–82.

Beatty, W. W., Winn, P., Adams, R. L., et al. (1994). Preserved cognitive skills in dementia of the Alzheimer type. *Archives of Neurology*, 51: 1040–6.

Boden, M. A. (1998). Creativity and artificial intelligence. *Artificial Intelligence*, 103: 347–56.

Bogen, J. E., & Bogen, G. M. (1969). The other side of the brain III: the corpus callosum and creativity. *Bulletin of the Los Angeles Neurological Society*, 34: 191–203.

Bogen, J. E., & Bogen, G. M. (1988). Creativity and the corpus callosum. *Psychiatric Clinics of North America*, 11: 293–301.

Breiter, H. C., Aharon, I., Kahneman, D., Dale, A., & Shizgal, P. (2001). Functional imaging of neural responses to expectancy and experience of monetary gains and losses. *Neuron*, 30: 619–39.

Bristol, A. S., & Viskontas, I. V. (2006). Dynamic processes within associative memory stores: piecing together the neural basis of creativity. In: Kaufman, J. C. & Baer, J. (Eds.). *Creativity, Knowledge and Reason*. Cambridge: Cambridge University Press, 60–80.

Carlsson, I., Wendt, P. E., & Risberg, J. (2000). On the neurobiology of creativity. Differences in frontal activity between high and low creative subjects. *Neuropsychologia*, 38: 873–85.

Carson, S. H., Peterson, J. B., & Higgins, D. M. (2003). Decreased latent inhibition is associated with increased creative achievement in high-functioning individuals. *Journal of Personality and Social Psychology*, 85: 499–506.

Chatterjee, A., Hamilton, R. H., & Amorapanth, P. X. (2006). Art produced by a patient with Parkinson's disease. *Behavioural Neurology*, 17: 105–08.

Chavez-Eakle, R. A., Graff-Guerrero, A., Garcia-Reyna, J. C., Vaugier, V., & Cruz-Fuentes, C. (2007). Cerebral blood flow associated with creative performance: a comparative study. *Neuroimage*, 38: 519–28.

Corbetta, M., & Shulman, G. L. (2002). Control of goal-directed and stimulus-driven attention in the brain. *Nature Reviews. Neuroscience*, **3**: 201–15.

Courtney, S. M., Petit, L., Haxby, J. V., & Ungerleider, L. G. (1998a). The role of prefrontal cortex in working memory: examining the contents of consciousness. *Philosophical Transactions of the Royal Society of London Series B, Biological Sciences*, **353**: 1819–28.

Courtney, S. M., Petit, L., Maisog, J. M., Ungerleider, L. G., & Haxby, J. V. (1998b). An area specialized for spatial working memory in human frontal cortex. *Science*, **279**: 1347–51.

Csikszentmihalyi, M. (1991). *Flow: the Psychology of Optimal Experience*. New York, NY: Harper and Row.

Csikszentmihalyi, M. (1996). *Creativity*. New York, NY: Harper Collins.

Csikszentmihalyi, M. (1999). Implications of a systems perspective for the study of creativity. In: Sternberg, R. J. & Smith, E. E. (Eds.). *Handbook of Creativity*. New York, NY: Cambridge University Press, 313–35.

Cummings, J. L., Miller, B., Hill, M. A., & Neshkes, R. (1987). Neuropsychiatric aspects of multi-infarct dementia and dementia of the Alzheimer type. *Archives of Neurology*, **44**: 389–93.

Damasio, H., Grabowski, T., Frank, R., Galaburda, A. M., & Damasio, A. R. (1994). The return of Phineas Gage: clues about the brain from the skull of a famous patient. *Science*, **264**: 1102–05.

Dietrich, A. (2004). The cognitive neuroscience of creativity. *Psychonomic Bulletin & Review*, **11**: 1011–26.

Elbert, T., & Rockstroh, B. (2004). Reorganization of human cerebral cortex: the range of changes following use and injury. *Neuroscientist*, **10**: 129–41.

Flaherty, A. W. (2005). Frontotemporal and dopaminergic control of idea generation and creative drive. *Journal of Comparative Neurology*, **493**: 147–53.

Gardner, H. (1993). *Creating Minds: an Anatomy of Creativity Seen Through the Lives of Freud, Einstein, Picasso, Stravinsky, Eliot, Graham and Gandhi*. New York, NY: Basic Books.

Gaser, C., & Schlaug, G. (2003). Brain structures differ between musicians and non-musicians. *Journal of Neuroscience*, **23**: 9240–5.

Gladwell, M. (2008). *Outliers*. New York, NY: Little, Brown and Company.

Gorno-Tempini, M. L., Dronkers, N. F., Rankin, K. P., *et al*. (2004). Cognition and anatomy in three variants of primary progressive aphasia. *Annals of Neurology*, **55**: 335–46.

Green, H. A., & Patterson, K. (2009). Jigsaws – a preserved ability in semantic dementia. *Neuropsychologia*, **47**: 569–76.

Hudspeth, S. (1985). The neurological correlates of creative thought. Unpublished PhD dissertation, University of Southern California, Los Angeles, CA.

Kawabata, H., & Zeki, S. (2004). Neural correlates of beauty. *Journal of Neurophysiology*, **91**: 1699–705.

Keenan, J. P., Wheeler, M. A., Gallup, G. G., Jr., & Pascual-Leone, A. (2000). Self-recognition and the right prefrontal cortex. *Trends in Cognitive Science*, **4**: 338–44.

Keltikangas-Jarvinen, L., Elovainio, M., Kivimaki, M., Lichtermann, D., Ekelund, J., & Peltonen, L. (2003). Association between the type 4 dopamine receptor gene polymorphism and novelty seeking. *Psychosomatic Medicine*, **65**: 471–6.

Kulisevsky, J., Pagonabarraga, J., & Martinez-Corral, M. (2009). Changes in artistic style and behaviour in Parkinson's disease: dopamine and creativity. *Journal of Neurology*, **256**: 816–19.

Lubow, R., & Weiner, I. (2010). *Latent Inhibition. Cognition, Neuroscience and Applications to Schizophrenia*. Cambridge: Cambridge University Press.

Lythgoe, M. F., Pollak, T. A., Kalmus, M., de Haan, M., & Chong, W. K. (2005). Obsessive, prolific artistic output following subarachnoid hemorrhage. *Neurology*, **64**: 397–8.

Martindale, C. (1971). Degeneration, disinhibition, and genius. *Journal of the History of the Behavioural Sciences*, **7**: 177–82.

Martindale, C. (1977). Creativity, consciousness, and cortical arousal. *Journal of Altered States of Consciousness*, **3**: 69–87.

Martindale, C. (1999). Biological bases of creativity. In: Sternberg, R. J. (Ed.). *Handbook of Creativity*. Cambridge: Cambridge University Press, 137–52.

Martindale, C., & Hines, D. (1975). Creativity and cortical activation during creative, intellectual and EEG feedback tasks. *Biological Psychology*, 3: 91–100.

Martindale, C., Anderson, K., Moore, K., & West, A. N. (1996). Creativity, oversensitivity, and rate of habituation. *Personality and Individual Differences*, 20: 423–7.

Miller, B. L., Boone, K., Cummings, J. L., Read, S. L., & Mishkin, F. (2000). Functional correlates of musical and visual ability in frontotemporal dementia. *British Journal of Psychiatry*, 176: 458–63.

Miller, B. L., Cummings, J., Mishkin, F., et al. (1998). Emergence of artistic talent in frontotemporal dementia. *Neurology*, 51: 978–82.

Mink, J. W. (1996). The basal ganglia: focused selection and inhibition of competing motor programs. *Progress in Neurobiology*, 50: 381–425.

Orenstein, A. (1991). *The Ballets of Maurice Ravel: creation and interpretation.* Burlington, VT: Ashgate.

Perkins, D. N. (1988). Creativity and the quest for mechanism. In: Sternberg, R. J. & Smith, E. E. (Eds.). *Psychology of Human Thought*. New York, NY: Cambridge University Press, 309–36.

Pessiglione, M., Seymour, B., Flandin, G., Dolan, R. J., & Frith, C. D. (2006). Dopamine-dependent prediction errors underpin reward-seeking behaviour in humans. *Nature*, 442: 1042–5.

Rankin, K. P., Liu, A. A., Howard, S., et al. (2007). A case-controlled study of altered visual art production in Alzheimer's and FTLD. *Cognitive and Behavioural Neurology*, 20: 48–61.

Sacks, O. W. (2007). *Musicophilia: Tales of Music and the Brain* (1st ed.). New York, NY: Alfred A. Knopf.

Savitz, J. B., & Ramesar, R. S. (2004). Genetic variants implicated in personality: a review of the more promising candidates. *American*

Journal of Medical Genetics Part B, Neuropsychiatric Genetics, 131B: 20–32.

Schon, D., Anton, J. L., Roth, M., & Besson, M. (2002). An fMRI study of music sight-reading. *Neuroreport*, 13: 2285–9.

Schrag, A., & Trimble, M. (2001). Poetic talent unmasked by treatment of Parkinson's disease. *Movement Disorders*, 16: 1175–6.

Seeley, W. W., Allman, J. M., Carlin, D. A., et al. (2007). Divergent social functioning in behavioral variant frontotemporal dementia and Alzheimer disease: reciprocal networks and neuronal evolution. *Alzheimer Disease & Associated Disorders*, 21: S50–7.

Seeley, W. W., Matthews, B. R., Crawford, R. K., et al. (2008). Unravelling Bolero: progressive aphasia, transmodal creativity and the right posterior neocortex. *Brain*, 131: 39–49.

Sergent, J. Z., Terriah, S., & MacDonald, B. (1992). Distributed neural network underlying musical sight-reading and keyboard performance. *Science*, 257: 106–09.

Simonton, D. K. (1994). *Greatness: Who Makes History and Why*. New York, NY: Guildford Press.

Simonton, D. K. (2000). Creativity. Cognitive, personal, developmental, and social aspects. *American Psychologist*, 55: 151–8.

Snyder, A. W., Mulcahy, E., Taylor, J. L., Mitchell, D. J., Sachdev, P., & Gandevia, S. C. (2003). Savant-like skills exposed in normal people by suppressing the left fronto-temporal lobe. *Journal of Integrative Neuroscience*, 2: 149–58.

Swerdlow, N. R., Stephany, N., Wasserman, L. C., Talledo, J., Sharp, R., & Auerbach, P. P. (2003). Dopamine agonists disrupt visual latent inhibition in normal males using a within-subject paradigm. *Psychopharmacology (Berlin)*, 169: 314–20.

Viskontas, I. V., Boxer, A. L., Fesenko, J., et al. (2011). Visual search patterns in semantic dementia show paradoxical facilitation of binding processes. *Neuropsychologia*, 40: 468–78.

Walker, Z., Costa, D. C., Walker, R. W., et al. (2004). Striatal dopamine transporter in dementia with Lewy bodies and Parkinson disease: a comparison. *Neurology*, 62: 1568–72.

Chapter 13

Paradoxical functional facilitation with noninvasive brain stimulation

Umer Najib and Alvaro Pascual-Leone

Summary

Noninvasive brain stimulation with transcranial magnetic stimulation (TMS) or transcranial direct current stimulation (tDCS) is valuable in research and has potential therapeutic applications in cognitive neuroscience, neurophysiology, psychiatry, neurology and neurorehabilitation. TMS and tDCS allow diagnostic and interventional neurophysiology applications, targeted neuropharmacology delivery and systematic exploration of local cortical plasticity and brain network dynamics. Repetitive TMS or tDCS can modulate cortical excitability of the directly targeted brain region beyond the duration of the brain stimulation train by the induction of phenomena similar to long-term potentiation (LTP) or long-term depression (LTD), which may increase or decrease cortical excitability respectively. The effects of TMS or tDCS do not remain limited to the targeted brain region, and thus disruption of brain activity by TMS or tDCS can result in behavioural facilitation via distant cortical or subcortical structures. In addition, state-dependent effects of noninvasive brain stimulation condition the impact of TMS and tDCS and may result in paradoxical behavioural effects of the stimulation. Greater understanding of the neurobiological mechanisms involved in such intances may allow us to systematically use TMS or tDCS to leverage paradoxical functional facilitation for therapeutic applications.

Introduction

In the past decades, neuroimaging techniques such as computerized tomography (CT), magnetic resonance imaging (MRI), positron emission tomography (PET), magnetoencephalography (MEG) and electro-encephalography (EEG) have shaped the ways in which we model behaviour. Anatomical neuroimaging techniques produce ever more detailed descriptions of the extent of lesions produced by brain injury. Functional neuroimaging methods reveal associations between various behaviours and patterns of activity in cortical and subcortical structures. Functional MRI and PET can inform us about the *spatial network* of a brain activity associated with a function, while event-related potentials using EEG or MEG can provide information about the *timing* of a brain activation during a task. Careful design of neuroimaging experiments may allow us to conclude with reasonable certainty that the correlation of brain activity with behaviour is likely to be due to a causal connection (i.e. that the brain activity produces the behaviour). Nevertheless, imaging alone can never provide absolute proof of that assertion.

The Paradoxical Brain, ed. Narinder Kapur. Published by Cambridge University Press. © Cambridge University Press 2011.

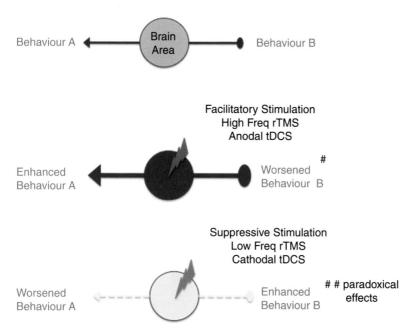

Figure 13.1 Schematic representation of the behavioural effects of TMS on a given brain area. Application of TMS can enhance (red) or reduce (green) activation of a certain brain region. Enhancing activation would be expected to enhance behaviour while suppressing activation would be expected to worsen behaviour. However, if the targeted area exerts inhibitory control onto the behaviour (right side of the figure), paradoxical (opposite) effects are possible. Notice that a given area may in fact promote one and suppress another behaviour.

Transcranial magnetic stimulation (TMS) allows us to actively *interfere* with brain function, and thus investigate the relationship between focal cortical activity and behaviour. It also allows us to trace the timing at which a cortical region contributes to a given task, and map the functional connectivity between brain regions. In addition, repetitive TMS and other methods of noninvasive brain stimulation, such as transcranial direct current stimulation (tDCS), provide means of modulating cortical excitability and hence possibly modifying behaviour, guiding plasticity and treating neuropsychiatric disorders.

Using TMS or tDCS, it is possible to suppress brain activity in discrete brain regions, assess the impact on behaviour in the form of worsening task performance, and thus reveal causal relations between brain activity and behaviour with great temporal resolution (Figure 13.1). In addition, it is possible to increase activity in certain brain areas and ultimately improve behaviour and performance in specific tasks mediated by the stimulated brain region (Figure 13.1). However, in some instances, TMS or tDCS applied with parameters aimed at suppressing brain activity can result in a paradoxical behavioural improvement. In addition, TMS or tDCS at parameters that increase activity in the targeted brain region may on occasions paradoxically disrupt behaviour. It has become increasingly apparent that complex brain functions, such as coordinated movement, memory and language, depend critically on dynamic interactions between brain areas, leading to the concept of *functional connectivity networks* – distributed brain regions transiently interacting to perform a particular neural function. Abnormalities in the interactions of network components play a critical role in common and devastating neurological and psychiatric disorders ranging from epilepsy to depression, and damage to specific functional connectivity networks can lead to distinct neurological syndromes.

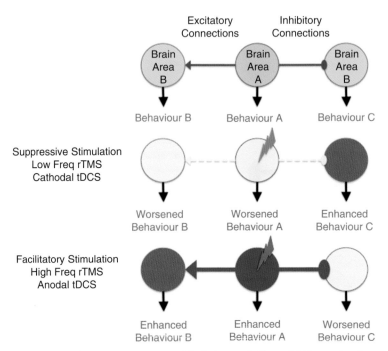

Figure 13.2 Schematic representation of the behavioural effects of TMS on a given functional network. Behaviours mediated by brain areas not directly targeted by TMS or tDCS, may get paradoxically enhanced or worsened depending on the type of connections between the targeted brain area and the brain region that mediates the behaviour.

Furthermore, both the deficits and functional recovery after damage from strokes or traumatic brain injury may be a function of the architecture and adaptability of these networks. Consistent with such notions of distributed brain networks, it has become increasingly clear that modulation of activity in a discrete brain region by TMS or tDCS is associated with distributed neural network effects that depend on the anatomical and functional connectivity between the directly targeted brain regions and the rest of the brain. Thus, TMS or tDCS to a given brain region modulates local brain activity, but also changes activity in distant cortical and subcortical structures via trans-synaptic effects. The sign of the connections (excitatory or inhibitory) between the targeted brain region and the distant brain areas, and the type of local modulation of excitability induced by the stimulation in the directly targeted brain region, determine the impact that stimulation will have on distributed nodes of a network (Figure 13.2). For example, enhancement of activity in a discrete brain region that sends inhibitory projections to a second, distant region, will suppress activity in that distant region.

Conversely, enhancement of activity in the same brain region will increase activity in a distant region that receives excitatory connections from the stimulated brain area. Behaviours mediated by brain areas that are not directly targeted by TMS or tDCS, but whose activity is modified by such trans-synaptic effects, may thus be paradoxically disrupted or facilitated by virtue of the type of connections between the targeted brain area and the brain region that mediates the behaviour (Figure 13.2). It is thus possible to use TMS or tDCS to systematically explore the phenomenon of paradoxical facilitation in healthy subjects and in patients with a variety of neuropsychiatric conditions, and even consider leveraging the controlled induction of paradoxical functional facilitation for neurological or psychiatric therapeutics. This requires knowledge of the connectivity between brain regions, as well as careful assessment of the physiological as well as behavioural impact of TMS or tDCS. The combination of brain stimulation with EEG, PET, fMRI or other brain mapping techniques is promising, because one can apply a noninvasive input of known spatial and temporal characteristics to study interactions between different brain regions as captured by such brain mapping techniques.

A few historical insights about paradoxical uses of noninvasive brain stimulation

As far back as 43 AD, Scribonious Largus, a court physician to the Roman emperor Claudius, recorded in his book 'Compositiones Medicamentorum' the use of electrical currents to treat headaches and gout by applying electric torpedo fish to the affected regions or by placing painful extremities into a pool of water containing torpedo fish. The resulting electrical shocks presumably stunned the peripheral skin receptors and affected spinal or brain structures, inducing numbness in the extremity and an associated transient period of pain relief. In this application, electrical torpedo fish were a very early means of transcutaneous electrical nerve stimulation (TENS) for therapeutic purposes. Arguably this is one of the first paradoxical 'therapeutic applications': the disruption of normal activity of peripheral neural structures leading to an improvement of symptoms, rather than to a loss of function.

In the late eighteenth century, the French physician Charles Le Roy, among others, experimented with the use of electricity to influence nervous system physiology and improve function. In one application, Le Roy wound conducting wires around the head of a blind man and led one wire to his leg. The wires were connected to an array of Leyden jars and 12 shocks were administered in the hope that sight would be restored (Figure 13.3A). Along with the pain of the stimulation the patient did perceive vivid flashes of light (phosphenes) and underwent the treatment several times in the following days with the aim of restoring his sight. He remained blind, but the explicit intent of Le Roy, restoration of sight by disruption of nervous system function, represents another early example of paradoxical facilitation attempts with noninvasive brain stimulation.

Duchenne de Boulogne (1806–1875) became the first to systematically use electricity in the study of disease, both for diagnostic as well as therapeutic goals (faradization; Figure 13.3B). In 'L'Electrisation Localisee' (1855), Duchenne de Boulogne describes the method founded on the observation that a current from two electrodes applied to the wet skin can stimulate muscles without damaging the skin (Duchenne, 1855). Among other applications of faradization, he describes the case of a woman admitted to the Charité 'whither she had been brought the night before stifled by carbonic oxide'. Duchenne de Boulogne 'very soon brought back the pulse and breathing, and caused the coma to disappear' by applying 'faradization of the skin of the praecordia', an early form of cardioversion. In addition, Duchenne experimented extensively with the distortion of facial expression and the stimulation of neural structures via application of current in order to enhance motor control, improve function and modify mood. Along the same lines, in 1871 Beard and Rockwell published in the USA, their 'Practical Treatise of the Medical and Surgical Uses of Electricity', arguing for the utility of faradizations for a wide

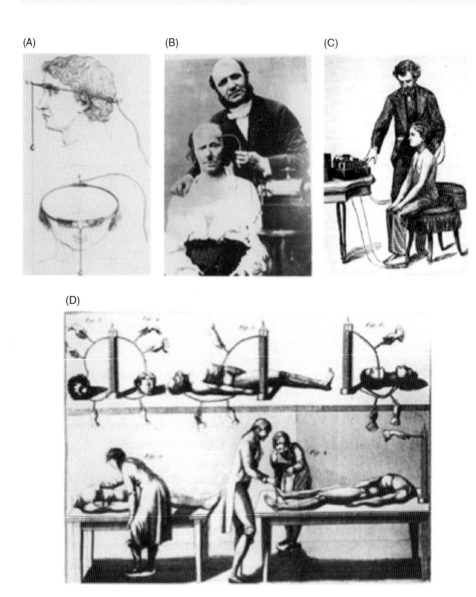

Figure 13.3 (A), Charles Le Roy's stimulation of a blind person. (B), Duchenne de Boulogne applying faradization. (C), Beard and Rockwell's application of faradization. (D), Aldini's experiments attempting to revive the dead.

range of indications (Beard and Rockwell, 1871; Figure 13.3C). Even before, in 1804, Giovanni Aldini (1762–1834) reported in his 'Essai Theorique et Experimental sur le Galvanisms' experiments with electric 'therapy' to treat psychoses and melancholia, and even to revive the dead (Aldini, 1804). Here lie the origins of electroshock and cardioversion, but Aldini became a sort of travelling showman, demonstrating the effect of application of current to cadavers (Figure 13.3D). Perhaps, the popularization of such 'circus acts' may have contributed to the fact that in scientific circles, noninvasive brain stimulation was mostly ignored for over 100 years. However, all these and other attempts

(A) (B) (C)

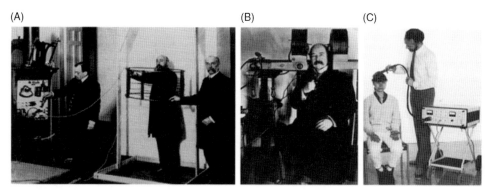

Figure 13.4 (A), D'Arsonval (right) demonstrating the application of electromagnetic stimulation. (B), Sylvanus P. Thompson demonstrating electromagnetic stimulation on himself. (C), Anthony Barker demonstrating the application of TMS.

reflect the early realization that disruption of normal neural activity may paradoxically lead to behavioural and functional gains in certain instances. In the 1960s, researchers began experimenting with the use of weak DC (direct current) applied directly to the exposed cortex of animals, and in recent years it has become apparent that transcranial DC can influence cortical activity in humans in a similar way to that seen in those early experiments (Wagner *et al.*, 2007).

Electromagnetic stimulation in its most primitive form was first investigated at the end of the nineteenth century by physicists studying fundamental aspects of electromagnetics and in particular the implications of Faraday's Law. In 1896, Jaques-Arsène d'Arsonval (Figure 13.4A) reported, 'an intensity of 110 volts, 30 amperes with a frequency of 42 cycles per second, gives rise to, when one places the head into the coil, phosphenes and vertigo' (d'Arsonval, 1896). Independently in 1910, Sylvanus P. Thompson (Figure 13.4B) reported similar findings of perceived magnetophosphenes, the visual excitations of the retina induced by the time varying magnetic fields (it is now understood that magneto-phosphenes can also be induced from the stimulation of the occipital brain cortex) (Thompson, 1910). In 1965, Brickford and Fremming non-invasively stimulated peripheral nerves within intact frogs, rabbits and humans through a pulsed magnetic field (2–3 Tesla pulse over 300 µs) (Brickford and Fremming, 1965). In the 1970s and 1980s, Anthony Barker and his group at the University of Sheffield overcame many of the earlier technical problems and developed a device capable of generating peak fields of 2 Tesla with an approximate rise time of 100 µs for the study of velocity-selective stimulation of neural structures (Barker, 1976). Eventually, in 1985 they introduced transcranial magnetic stimulation (TMS, Figure 13.4C), a noninvasive technique that uses the principles of electromagnetic induction to focus currents in the brain and modulate the function of the cortex (Barker *et al.*, 1985). Today, numerous TMS devices are commercially available and techniques abound in the clinic and laboratory settings. All these and other scientists realized that stimulation of the nervous system might give rise to positive phenomena, e.g. the perception of a flash of light (phosphene), but also to negative phenomena, e.g. blocking of visual perception by occipital stimulation or delaying motor movement by motor cortex stimulation. Based on such observations, attempts of enhancing function and improving behaviour have been linked with the history of noninvasive brain stimulation from its earliest beginning.

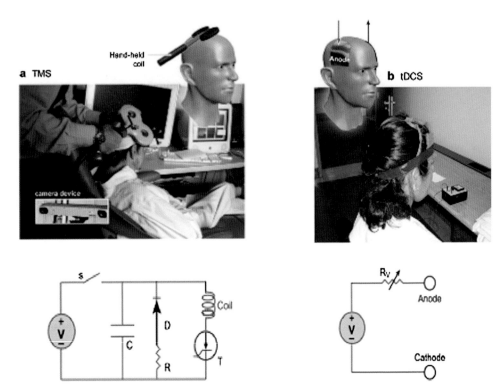

Figure 13.5 (a) TMS application along with a simplified circuit diagram of a single pulse magnetic stimulator. (b) tDCS application along with a circuit diagram of a tDCS stimulator unit. V, voltage source; S, switch; C, capacitator; D, diode; R, resistor; T, thyristor; Rv, variable resistor. Modified from Wagner *et al.* (2007).

What are TMS and tDCS?

The two most commonly used techniques for noninvasive brain stimulation are transcranial magnetic stimulation (TMS) and transcranial direct current stimulation (tDCS). Both take advantage of electromagnetic principles to non-invasively influence neural activity. TMS is a neurostimulation and neuromodulation application, while tDCS is a purely neuromodulatory intervention (Figure 13.5). TMS uses the principle of electromagnetic induction to focus induced currents in the brain. These currents can be of sufficient magnitude to depolarize neurons. When these currents are applied repetitively – repetitive transcranial magnetic stimulation, rTMS – they can modulate cortical excitability, decreasing or increasing it, depending on the parameters of stimulation, beyond the duration of the train of stimulation. During tDCS, low amplitude direct currents are applied via scalp electrodes and penetrate the skull to enter the brain. Although the applied currents do not usually elicit action potentials, they modify the transmembrane neuronal potential and thus influence the level of excitability and modulate the firing rate of individual neurons in response to additional inputs. As with TMS, when tDCS is applied for a sufficient duration, cortical function can be altered beyond the stimulation period.

Magnetic stimulators consist of two main components: a capacitive high-voltage, high-current charge–discharge system and a magnetic stimulating coil that produces pulsed fields of 1–4 Tesla in strength with durations of approximately a millisecond for single pulse stimulators and a quarter of a millisecond for rapid stimulators. The charge–discharge system is composed of a charging unit, a bank of storage capacitors, switching circuitry and control electronics. In 'repetitive stimulators' the essential circuitry remains the same, except modifications are made to the switching system to allow pulse rates of many times per second. The second key hardware component of magnetic stimulators is the current-carrying coil, which serves as the electromagnet source during stimulation. Design of the coil is critically important because it is the only component that comes in direct contact with the subject undergoing stimulation and the coil's shape directly influences the induced current distribution and, thus, the site of stimulation. While many researchers have explored unique coil designs for increased focality of specified stimulation, the most common coils used nowadays are single circular loop or figure of eight shaped (i.e. two circular coils in parallel, also referred to as double or butterfly coils; see Figure 13.5).

DC stimulation is applied via a constant current source attached via patch electrodes (surface areas from 25–35 mm^2) to the scalp surface. Currents usually range in magnitude from a constant 0.5 to 2 mA, and are applied from seconds to minutes. The electrodes can be simple saline soaked cotton pads or specifically designed sponge patches covered with conductive gel. There is no complex circuitry comprising the stimulators and in its simplest form a DC source is placed in series with the scalp electrodes and a potentiometer to adjust for constant current.

In order to track and predict the location of neural stimulation using TMS or tDCS, one can use image guided frameless stereotaxic systems similar to those used for intracranial navigation during minimally invasive neurosurgery. The frameless stereotaxic systems rely on the subject's head MRI data and coil geometry or electrode montage to digitally track the position of the current source relative to the subject's head and register the predicted stimulation location in MRI space.

Induction of a virtual lesion

TMS provides a means of interfering with the activity in a specific cortical area and probing the functional changes that may result. The effects can be transient or extend beyond the duration of a train of stimuli, depending on the parameters of stimulation. Applied as trains of repetitive stimuli at appropriate frequency and intensity, TMS can be used to transiently disrupt the function of a given cortical target thus creating a temporary, 'virtual brain lesion' (Pascual-Leone et al., 1999). The use of rTMS to disrupt brain function stems from studies of the motor cortex, where it has been shown that, applied to the primary motor area, a train of TMS pulses at a frequency of 1 Hz induces a transient reduction of cortical excitability in most subjects that outlasts the stimulation itself (Chen et al., 1997; Maeda et al., 2000). The notion that cortical excitability can be reduced in the motor cortex following low-frequency rTMS suggested that it could also modulate behavioural output when applied to non-motor areas. This idea was first applied to the visual cortex, where it was shown that a 1 Hz, 10 min rTMS train to the occipital pole could impair performance in a visual perception and imagery task (Kosslyn et al., 1999). This rationale has since then been applied to a variety of cortical areas, including parietal (Hilgetag et al., 2001; Lewald et al., 2002; Sack et al., 2002; Brighina et al., 2003), somatosensory (Satow et al., 2003), visual (Thut et al., 2003) and prefrontal (Mottaghy et al., 2002; Robertson et al., 2001; Shapiro et al., 2001) cortices, as well as to the cerebellum (Théoret et al., 2001).

However, it is important to realize that disruption of behaviour, or reduction of the amplitude of motor evoked potentials following rTMS, does not actually prove that the stimulation was suppressing cortical activity or that the suppression is responsible for the worsening in task performance (see Figures 13.1 and 13.2). In order to assess such issues, it is necessary to evaluate behaviour and at the same time capture the changes in brain activity induced by the rTMS. Only then is it really possible to ascertain whether the impairment of behaviour, motor, perceptual or cognitive ability is due to a directly induced disruption of brain activity, or possibly due to the modification of activity in some other distant brain region.

Mottaghy *et al.* (2000) studied the effects of repetitive TMS of the prefrontal cortex as subjects performed a 2-back working memory task. In this task, subjects had to say whether a current stimulus within a train of stimuli was the same as, or different to, one that had occurred two trials previously. TMS to the right or left dorsolateral prefrontal cortex, but not to the midline frontal cortex, significantly worsened performance in the task, hence establishing a causal role of these regions for the behaviour under study. Disruption of task performance was measured as a change in reaction time and left and right dorsolateral prefrontal cortex lengthened reaction time by a similar amount. Therefore, it would appear that both of these areas contribute similarly to the 2-back task studied. Mottaghy *et al.* conducted the study while measuring changes in regional cerebral blood flow as revealed by positron emission tomography or PET (Figure 13.6). This allows one to investigate the effects of TMS at the level of compensatory, rather than (virtual) lesion analysis. The changes in task performance following TMS to the right and the left dorsolateral prefrontal cortex were associated with similar reduction in the regional cerebral blood flow in the targeted brain regions, but different effects on distant brain areas. Residual task performance during the TMS-induced disruption of the right and left dorsolateral prefrontal cortex is related to the capacity of the brain to react to the temporary lesion and differential effects of left and right prefrontal TMS must account for the differences in brain activity in that setting. Task performance during TMS to the left dorsolateral prefrontal cortex was associated, as compared with baseline performance during sham stimulation, with decreased regional cerebral blood flow in the targeted left dorsolateral prefrontal cortex. On the other hand, task performance during TMS to the right dorsolateral prefrontal cortex was associated with decreased regional cerebral blood flow in the targeted right dorsolateral prefrontal cortex, and also in the left dorsolateral prefrontal cortex and bilateral parietal cortices (Figure 13.6). A correlation analysis of the change in cerebral blood flow and the behavioural disruption, as indexed by the change in reaction time, shows that whether TMS is applied to the right or the left dorsolateral prefrontal cortex, the change in left-sided activity is the most critical predictor of the behavioural effects.

Indeed, as mentioned before, TMS to a given brain region does not only lead to changes in activity in the directly targeted cortex, but also to rapid modulation of established network interactions, in animal as well as human studies. Valero-Cabre *et al.* (2005, 2007, 2008) combined rTMS with 2-deoxyglucose uptake labelling in cats. These studies provided direct evidence of the network effects of cortical TMS upon an extended network of cortical, subcortical and midbrain nodes linked by specific anatomical pathways (Figure 13.7). High-frequency stimulation generated a mean 14% decrease in cortical activity (^{14}C-2DG uptake activity), affecting a radial area of $\sim$12 mm^2, and a $\sim$1.25% attenuation effect per each mm of cortical depth across a sulcus separating two banks of cortex. Further findings

(A)

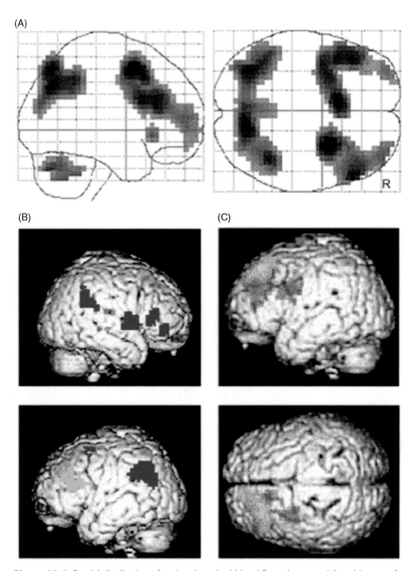

(B)   (C)

Figure 13.6 Spatial distribution of regional cerebral blood flow changes while subjects perform a 2-back working memory task with or without concurrent TMS to the right or left dorsolateral prefrontal cortex. In A, the spatial distributions of significantly activated voxels are shown as integrated projections along sagittal and axial axes while subjects performed the working memory task during sham TMS (R, right). The voxels show levels of significance above a threshold of $p = 0.001$ and a cluster size of $k = 20$ (SPM glass brain projections). In B, the deactivations induced by rTMS of the left (green) and the right (blue) dorsolateral prefrontal cortex are shown as an overlay on a 3D surface rendered anatomical MR ($p < 0.01$; $k = 20$). Note that deactivations induced by left-sided rTMS (green) are limited to the frontal region directly targeted by TMS. However, deactivation during rTMS to the right hemisphere presents at the prefrontal site of stimulation, bilateral parietal cortices, and left dorsolateral prefrontal region. Despite these differences in cerebral blood flow results, the behavioural effects of right and left prefrontal rTMS, as indexed by the changes in response time, were not statistically different. C shows the overlay of the negative correlations between regional cerebral blood flow and performance (as indexed by the response time) in the 2-back working memory task. Red represents the trials without rTMS, green those during rTMS to the left dorsolateral prefrontal cortex, and blue the trials with right-prefrontal rTMS. Note that regardless of site of rTMS (right or left), the disruption of left-sided prefrontal activity is only correlated with task performance. Modified from Mottaghy et al. (2000).

243

(A)

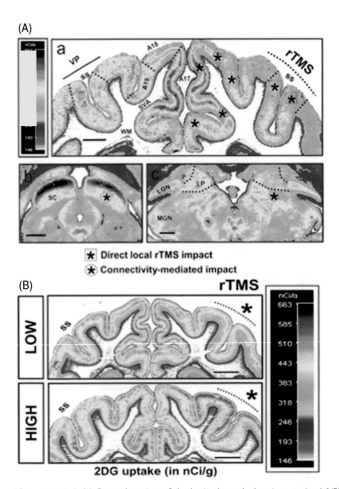

(B)

Figure 13.7 A, (a) Coronal section of the brain through the visuo-parietal (VP) cortex showing direct and connectivity-mediated impact of rTMS on ^{14}C-2DG uptake. (b) and (c) Impact of rTMS on subcortical sites (b, superior colliculus; c, pulvinar nucleus and lateral posterior complex). Impact of rTMS is identified by predominant green compared to predominant yellow shading of the homologous region of the contralateral hemisphere. Absence of impact is identified by matching yellows in homologous structures on the two hemispheres. B, ^{14}C-2DG uptake densities following stimulation of the VP cortex in the following conditions, LOW: 1 Hz off-line, HIGH: 20 Hz off-line. Notice the relative decrease of ^{14}C-2DG uptake in the stimulated VP (with respect to the contralateral VP area) in the LOW condition and increase of ^{14}C-2DG uptake in the HIGH condition. Modified from Valero-Cabre et al. (2005, 2007).

demonstrated that local and trans-synaptic effects of TMS depend upon stimulation frequency and time of the assessment in a rather complex way. During the delivery of the TMS pulses ('on line impact'), cortical activity is strongly depressed locally, inducing prominent trans-synaptic effects. This is likely the result of significant pools of the targeted cortical neurons being repetitively depolarized, thus interfering with their normal encoding firing rhythms. Opposite modulation in cortical metabolism dependent upon stimulation frequency patterns was found to outlast the delivery of TMS trains ('off-line' impact or 'after effects'). High- or low-frequency patterns of stimulation resulted in significant increases and decreases of local glucose consumption, respectively, thus providing support to uses of rTMS in neuromodulation of brain systems (Figure 13.7B). This frequency-dependent

Before   After

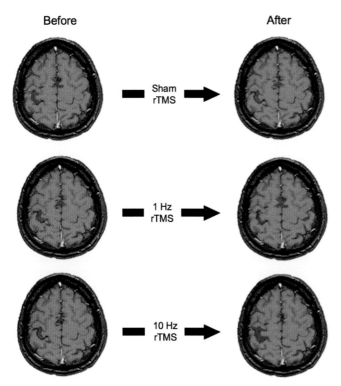

Sham
rTMS

1 Hz
rTMS

10 Hz
rTMS

Figure 13.8 Brain activation in functional magnetic resonance imaging while subjects performed the same rhythmic hand movement (under careful kinematic control) before and after repetitive transcranial magnetic stimulation (rTMS) of the contralateral motor cortex. Following sham rTMS (top row) there is no change in the significant activation of the motor cortex (M1) contralateral to the moving hand and of the supplementary motor cortex (SMA). After M1 activity is suppressed using 1 Hz rTMS (1600 stimuli, 90% of motor threshold intensity; middle row), there is an increased activation of the rostral SMA and of M1 ipsilateral to the moving hand. Increasing excitability in the contralateral M1 using high-frequency rTMS (20 Hz, 90% of motor threshold intensity, 1600 stimuli; bottom row) results in a decrease in activation of rostral SMA. Importantly, despite the modulation of brain activity, behaviour remains unchanged. The shift in activity at the targeted brain region and across network might be considered an example of rapid plasticity to sustain behavioural integrity.

effect seems to suggest LTP-, LTD-like modulation of the targeted systems and might also reflect the contribution of compensatory mechanisms emerging from unaffected brain networks.

Parallel examples of local and network effects of repetitive TMS being dependent on connectivity across neural networks and stimulation parameters have also been obtained in humans. For example, subjects were asked to open and close their fist deliberately at a self-paced rhythm of approximately one movement every second while lying in an fMRI scanner. As compared with rest, during movement there was a significant activation of the motor cortex (M1) contralateral to the moving hand and of the rostral supplementary motor cortex (SMA). If motor cortex activity is modified by rTMS, the pattern of brain activation changes as behavioural integrity is maintained (Figure 13.8). Application of slow rTMS to the contralateral M1, which is presumed to suppress neuronal firing (Walsh and Pascual-Leone 2003), results in increased activation of the rostral SMA and of M1 ipsilateral to the moving hand. Conversely, increasing excitability in the contralateral M1, by application of fast rTMS, leads to a decrease in activation of rostral SMA. In a very elegant study, Lee *et al.* (2003) – combining TMS and PET – have provided supporting evidence to these notions and critically extended them by revealing the shifts in cortico-cortical and cortico-subcortical connectivity underlying the changes in cortical activation patterns.

Facilitating behaviour by suppressing local activity so as to release activity in a distant area

Following a brain lesion, plasticity may not lead to recovery, but rather provide the substrate for deficits to become chronically established. In such instances, focal disruption of brain activity may lead to behavioural improvement. For example, it has been hypothesized that the phenomenon of 'extinction to double simultaneous stimulation' and 'neglect' is related to an imbalance between the hemispheres resulting from the release of reciprocal inhibitory influences (Kinsbourne, 1977). Lesion of one hemisphere results in trans-hemispheric release of inhibition onto the healthy hemisphere that becomes 'hyperactive', creating 'hyper-attention' to the ipsilesional side. In humans, support for this hypothesis first came from the report of a patient who suffered from severe spatial neglect (the failure to explore contralesional space) following a right parietal lesion (Vuilleumier *et al.*, 1996). After a second lesion to the left frontal cortex, the neglect symptoms completely and abruptly disappeared, supporting the concept of a dynamic balance between the two hemispheres for the allocation of attentional resources.

The idea that transient disruption of the healthy hemisphere can temporarily alleviate extinction symptoms was further supported by a study which showed that in a group of 14 right brain-damaged patients, application of single-pulse TMS to the left prefrontal cortex significantly reduced contralateral extinction when the TMS pulse was applied 40 ms after bilateral electrical stimulation of the fingers (Oliveri *et al.* 1999). These results were later replicated by the same group in a visuospatial task, using high-frequency repetitive TMS (Oliveri *et al.*, 2001). The performance of five right brain-damaged patients on a line bisection task was significantly improved following parietal rTMS of the unaffected hemisphere. Again, in right brain-damaged patients suffering from visuospatial neglect, Brighina *et al.* (2003) showed that a two-week regimen of low-frequency repetitive TMS to the healthy hemisphere could reduce visuospatial neglect beyond the period of stimulation. One hertz rTMS was applied to the left parietal cortex in three patients with a right parieto-temporal lesion every other day for 14 days. Visuospatial performance (clock drawing and line bisection tasks) was significantly improved immediately after treatment and for at least 15 days. Koch *et al.* tested the same hemispheric rivalry in hemispatial neglect patients after unilateral brain damage, particularly to perisylvian structures in the right-hemisphere (Koch *et al.*, 2008). The twin-coil TMS approach was used to measure excitability within the intact left hemisphere of the neglect patients. This involved applying a conditioning TMS pulse over left posterior parietal cortex (PPC), in order to test its effect on the amplitude of motor evoked potentials produced by a subsequent test pulse over left motor cortex (M1). It was found that excitability of left PPC–M1 circuits was higher in neglect patients than the other groups (RH stroke patients without neglect and healthy controls), and related to the degree of neglect on clinical cancellation tests. A follow-up study found that 1 Hz repetitive TMS over left PPC normalized this over-excitability, and also ameliorated visual neglect on an experimental measure with chimeric objects.

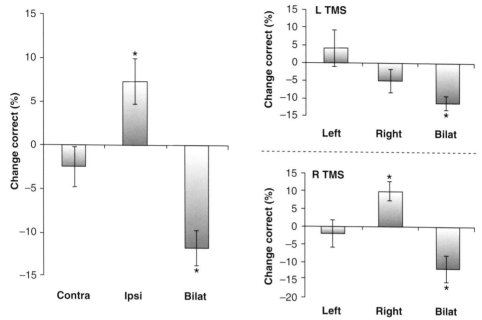

Figure 13.9 Modified from Hilgetag *et al.* (2001) with permission. Changes in correct stimulus detection after parietal rTMS. The diagrams are based on changes in the number of correctly detected stimuli (relative to the total number of presented stimuli) averaged for both stimulus sizes and all subjects. (a) The pooled data show a significant increase in performance ipsilateral to the parietal rTMS location (increase in relative percentage points: 7.3% SEM: 2.6%), and a trend to decreased contralateral performance (reduction by 2.5%, SEM: 2.3%). In addition, detection of bilateral stimuli decreased significantly (−11.7%, SEM: 2.0%). These trends are also apparent after separating data for (b) left parietal TMS and (c) right parietal rTMS. Significant trends (as determined by z-tests), are marked by asterisks.

The reciprocal inter-hemispheric inhibition, and its proposed link to attentional performance, can lead to the hypothesis that suppression of one parietal cortex would lead to contralateral neglect. However, at the same time, the disinhibition of structures involved in inter-hemispheric competition might lead to a functional release in the opposite hemisphere, which could result in a measurable ipsilateral behavioural enhancement (Hilgetag *et al.* 2001). To verify this hypothesis, normal subjects were asked to detect small rectangular stimuli briefly presented on a computer monitor either unilaterally in the left or right periphery, or bilaterally in both. Spatial detection performance was tested before and immediately after a 10-min, 1 Hz rTMS train to: (a) right parietal cortex, (b) left parietal cortex, (c) right primary motor cortex, and (d) sham stimulation. It was observed that a clear extinction phenomenon for stimuli presented contralaterally to the stimulated hemisphere (right or left parietal cortex) existed. This deficit was accompanied by increased detection for unilateral stimuli presented on the side of the stimulated hemisphere compared to baseline (Figure 13.9). None of the control stimulation sites had any effect on the detection performance. Detailed investigation revealed that although trends were mirror-symmetric for rTMS of left and right parietal cortex, the enhancement produced by right-hemispheric rTMS was significantly greater than that after left hemisphere stimulation and only right hemispheric stimulation produced a significant ipsilateral detection enhancement.

These series of experiments in patients with focal lesions and in normal subjects provide empirical support and proof-of-principle evidence for the potential of TMS to induce and reveal paradoxical functional facilitation. In normal subjects, decreasing excitability in one parietal cortex with rTMS disinhibits the contralateral cortex, leading to improvements in performance. In patients, the balance of interactions across the parietal regions is already shifted, and in this setting, the effect of TMS, while again paradoxical, may effectively restore function. Rushmore *et al.* (2006) have discussed such notions of interhemispheric cortico-subcortical network dynamics in relation to spatial attention on the basis of careful anatomical description of established connectivities, essentially expanding on Sprague's classic insights (see Chapter 3).

Data from inter-hemispheric interactions in the realm of attention illustrate the notion that disruption of a given brain region may ultimately lead to paradoxical behavioural improvement on the basis of releasing inhibition of a distant area (e.g. in the unstimulated hemisphere). In fact, such interactions can be specifically tested and characterized in humans using paired-pulse stimulation (Kobayashi and Pascual-Leone, 2003). Similar paradoxical effects of suppressing activity in a given brain area resulting in behavioural enhancement, presumably medicated by a distant brain region being released on inhibition, can be demonstrated systematically with TMS across cognitive domains.

Consider the motor system after stroke. There is an increase in the excitability of the unaffected hemisphere, presumably owing to reduced transcallosal inhibition from the damaged hemisphere and increased use of the intact hemisphere. For example, in patients with acute cortical stroke, TMS measures reveal that intracortical inhibition is decreased and intracortical. facilitation increased in the unaffected hemisphere (Liepert *et al.*, 2000). Furthermore, the inter-hemispheric inhibitory drive from the unaffected to the affected motor cortex in the process of voluntary movement generation is abnormal (Murase *et al.*, 2004). The paradoxical effects of an rTMS-induced 'virtual lesion' can be applied in such a case for suppression of the ipsilateral motor cortex through slow rTMS (Pascual-Leone *et al.*, 1998; Maeda *et al.*, 2000), which may enhance motor performance in stable patients following a stroke. In patients 1–2 months after a stroke, Mansur *et al.* (2005) applied 0.5 Hz rTMS for 10 min to the unaffected hemisphere to suppress cortical activity and thus release the damaged hemisphere from potentially excessive transcallosal inhibition. The results of this study support the notion that the over-activity of the unaffected hemisphere (ipsilateral hemisphere) may hinder hand function recovery, and neuromodulation can be an interventional tool to accelerate this recovery. The findings are consistent with results in normal subjects, where ipsilateral motor cortex activation, in functional MRI during unilateral hand movements, is related primarily to interhemispheric interactions (Kobayashi *et al.*, 2003). Here, disruption of the activity of one hemisphere reduces transcallosal inhibition to the contralateral hemisphere and can indeed improve ipsilateral motor function (Figure 13.10). More recently, Kobayashi *et al.* (2009) applied low-frequency (1 Hz) rTMS over the primary motor cortex to suppress cortical excitability and revealed that while motor learning with the hand contralateral to the stimulation M1 was disrupted, motor learning with the hand ipsilateral to the stimulation was facilitated. This provides direct support for the notion of inter-hemispheric competition and provides novel insights that may be applicable to neurorehabilitation. The paradoxical effects of TMS on motor learning with the hand ipsilateral to the stimulated motor cortex were presumably mediated by interhemispheric inhibitory connections. Suppression of one motor cortex leads to the release of interhemispheric inhibition onto the unstimulated motor cortex, and thus

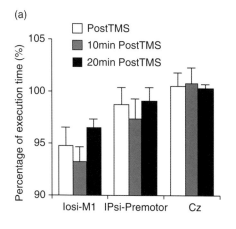

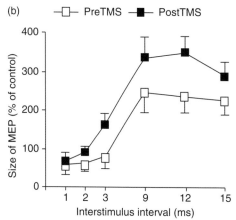

Figure 13.10 Modified from Kobayashi *et al.* (2003) with permission. (a) Ratio of execution times following rTMS at three different sites (ipsilateral M1, ipsilateral premotor cortex and Cz). Reaction times were significantly shorter after ipsilateral rTMS over primary motor cortex. (b) Changes in MEP sizes of the left first dorsal interosseus muscle with various interstimulus intervals.

a secondary enhancement in excitability (Figure 13.11). Conceptually similar is the finding of Seyal *et al.* (1995), who observed increases in tactile sensitivity as a result of stimulation of the somatosensory cortex ipsilateral to the fingers being tested.

Research in patients with aphasia (Knecht *et al.*, 2002; Martin *et al.*, 2004; Naeser *et al.*, 2005a, 2005b) serves to illustrate the same principles. Functional neuroimaging studies of patients with residual non-fluent aphasia have observed unusually high activation levels in right perisylvian language homologues (Belin *et al.*, 1996; Rosen *et al.*, 2000), which are not correlated with improved language performance (Naeser *et al.*, 2004; Perani *et al.*, 2003; Rosen *et al.*, 2000). Slow, 1 Hz rTMS applied to suppress activity of right hemispheric language homologue areas can induce significant naming and overall language enhancement in patients with left hemispheric, chronic strokes. In different rTMS sessions, 1 Hz rTMS was applied to transiently suppress activity in one of several distinct cortical areas; right pars triangularis; right pars opercularis; right motor cortex–mouth (M1, orbicularis oris); right posterior, superior temporal gyrus (R BA 22) or anterior supramarginal gyrus (BA 40). In all patients studied, application of rTMS to right pars triangularis, right BA 45, significantly increased the number of pictures named correctly and significantly reduced response time. Conversely, rTMS to the right pars opercularis significantly reduced the number of pictures named correctly

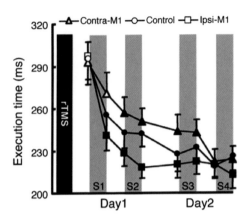

Figure 13.11 Changes in execution time. Each plot represents mean execution time in one practice block. Data from the initial block on day 1 (baseline), the first block on day 2 and the last one in each practice session are plotted. Execution time improved with practice sessions. In the group with repetitive transcranial magnetic stimulation (rTMS) to the ipsilateral M1, the execution time at the end of day 1 (after S2) was significantly shorter than in the other two groups ($P < 0.05$). The group with rTMS of the contralateral M1 improved their execution times slower than the other two groups, but not significantly. Filled symbols indicate significantly shorter values than baseline ($P < 0.05$). Error bars represent standard error. (B) Changes of execution time during the 10 blocks of the first session (S1). Modified from Kobayashi et al. (2009).

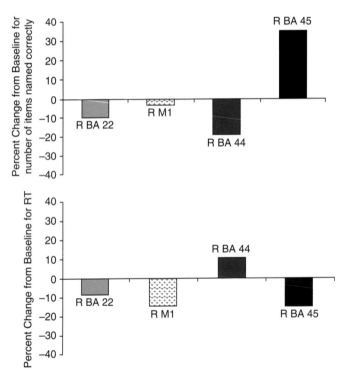

Figure 13.12 Modified from Naeser et al. (2005). Mean percent change from Baseline Naming score (and RT) for Snodgrass and Vanderwart lists pre-rTMS, and post-rTMS naming scores (and RT) after each of four right ROIs was stimulated at 1-Hz rTMS for 10 min. Note the increase in number of pictures named correctly and decrease in RT for right BA 45; however, it is the reverse for right BA 44.

and slowed down the response time (Figure 13.12). The behavioural benefit following rTMS suggests that disruption of a specific node in the involved neural network, the right pars triangularis, may have led to a shift in weighted activity across the involved neural network and possibly promoted alterations in brain-behavioural mapping. This effect might have been due to inter-hemispheric effects, but it is possible that the suppression of the pars triangularis may have led to the release of inhibition of the pars opercularis. Inhibitory connections between pars triangularis and opercularis have indeed been described (Rosen *et al.*, 2000; Nagai *et al.*, 2010; Xiang *et al.*, 2010).

Finally, let's consider verbal memory. Functional neuroimaging data indicate that episodic encoding during phonological task performance is correlated with activation in bilateral posterior ventrolateral prefrontal cortex (pVLPFC) (Clark and Wagner, 2003; Otten *et al.*, 2002), although uncertainty remains regarding whether these prefrontal regions make necessary contributions to episodic memory formation. Using functional MRI data to guide application of single-pulse transcranial magnetic stimulation (spTMS), Kahn *et al.* (2005) examined the necessity of left and right pVLPFC for episodic encoding (as expressed through subsequent memory performance). To assess the timing of critical computations, pVLPFC function was transiently disrupted at different post-stimulus onset times while subjects made syllable decisions about visually presented familiar and unfamiliar words, and subsequent memory for these stimuli was measured. Left pVLPFC disruption during encoding of familiar words impaired subsequent memory. However, right pVLPFC disruption facilitated subsequent memory for familiar words, expressed as an increase in confidence recognition, with this facilitation being maximal at 380 ms. Furthermore, phonological decision accuracy was also facilitated by right pVLPFC disruption, but was unaffected by left pVLPFC disruption. These findings suggest that left pVLPFC mechanisms are necessary for effective episodic encoding. In contrast, disruption of correlated mechanisms in right pVLPFC facilitates encoding, perhaps by inducing a functional shift in the mechanisms engaged during learning. Furthermore, research in reciprocal interactions between declarative and procedural memories has shown that disruption of the dorsolateral prefrontal cortex facilitates the consolidation of procedural skills (Galea *et al.*, 2010; Brown and Robertson, 2007). Galea *et al.* used TMS to test the hypothesis that functions in the dorsolateral prefrontal cortex (DLPFC) that support declarative memory formation indirectly reduce the formation of procedural representations. Inhibitory theta-burst TMS was applied to the left DLPFC, to the right DLPFC or to an occipital cortical control site immediately after training on the serial reaction time task (SRTT). All groups were retested after eight daytime hours without sleep. TMS of either left or right DLPFC led to skill improvements on the SRTT, but there was no improvement in skill for the control group. These findings support the hypothesis of paradoxical facilitatory response in procedural consolidation by disruption of declarative consolidation processes.

In all these and several other reported instances, it is important to remember that behavioural enhancement following rTMS does not necessarily demonstrate a paradoxical effect (see Figures 13.1 and 13.2). The above examples illustrate the fact that, even if activity in the directly targeted brain region is disrupted by a certain TMS pattern of stimulation, known functional brain connectivities and measurable neurophysiologic modulations at a distance from the stimulated brain area can provide a sensible explanation for the behavioural consequences (Figure 13.2). Computational modelling may be useful in imposing some direction and also constraints on the search for, and interpretation of, facilitatory effects of TMS (Hilgetag *et al.*, 1999; Young *et al.*, 2000). One simulation, for example, showed that the connectivity of a cortical area was a strong predictor of the effects of lesions on the rest of the network, as well as for how that area responded to a lesion elsewhere in the network. This may seem like a truism, but the kind of connectivity analysis offered by these models is not really taken into account in classical lesion analysis, even though modelling work has begun to make these predictions explicit and testable. The combination of TMS with careful measurement of its direct neurophysiologic impact (e.g. with fMRI and EEG), along with anatomical-connectivity restrained neurocomputing modelling, may help establish TMS-induced paradoxical functional facilitations as a reliable therapeutic intervention in certain conditions.

Facilitating behaviour by leveraging state-dependent effects of TMS

We have discussed facilitation in visual attention, motor, somatosensory, language and memory systems on the basis of the distributed network effects of TMS. Inter-hemispheric interactions with release of inhibition may account for many of these cases. However, the local effects of TMS themselves might result in paradoxical behavioural effects, by virtue of state dependency modulation of the neurophysiologic impact of the stimulation. The behavioural effects of TMS are ultimately a complex interaction between the stimulation applied and the state of brain activity at the time. Thus, under certain conditions, the effects of TMS might be unexpected and paradoxical.

For example, Fierro *et al.* (2005) used rTMS to explore the effects of light deprivation on visual cortex excitability. Healthy subjects reporting reliable induction of phosphenes by occipital TMS underwent 60 min of complete light deprivation. Phosphene threshold was measured serially as an indicator of visual cortical excitability. Repetitive TMS at 1 or 10 Hz was applied in separate sessions during the last 15 min of light deprivation. Low-frequency rTMS at 1 Hz induces a suppression of cortical excitability under normal circumstances. Therefore, following 1 Hz rTMS, phosphene thresholds would be expected to increase, as visual cortical activity would be predicted to be suppressed. On the other hand, high-frequency rTMS at 10 Hz generally induces an enhancement of excitability and thus phosphene thresholds would be expected to be decreased. Paradoxically, following light deprivation, 10 Hz rTMS significantly increased phosphene thresholds while 1 Hz rTMS decreased them. The findings are reminiscent of those of Brighina *et al.* (2002), who showed that 1 Hz rTMS over the occipital cortex led to a paradoxical increase in visual cortex excitability in subjects affected by migraine with aura. In contrast, in normal subjects a decrease in visual cortex excitability (inferred from phosphene thresholds) was observed. This study shows that changes in cortical excitability induced by neurological conditions such as migraine, or by manipulations such as light deprivation, can have a major impact on the neurophysiologic and behavioural impact of TMS.

Beyond that, disruption of a certain neuronal population may suppress the behavioural relevance of certain information and, in that setting, TMS may paradoxically improve performance in certain tasks. For example, Walsh *et al.* (1998) applied TMS to visual area V5/MT and showed that this impaired performance in visual search tasks that involved scanning complex motion displays. The findings are consistent with the concept of a TMS-induced 'virtual lesion' and extensive data showing that suppression of V5/MT results in akinetopsia, the selective inability or disruption to process visual motion stimuli. However, Walsh *et al.* elegantly showed that on displays in which motion was absent or irrelevant to task performance, subjects were faster following TMS-induced disruption of V5/MT than in control trials at the discrimination of colour or form (Figure 13.13). This suggests that separate visual modalities may compete for resources and that the disruption of the motion system may liberate other visual areas from its influence. In this experiment, the subjects received blocks of trials of a single type and therefore knew whether the forthcoming

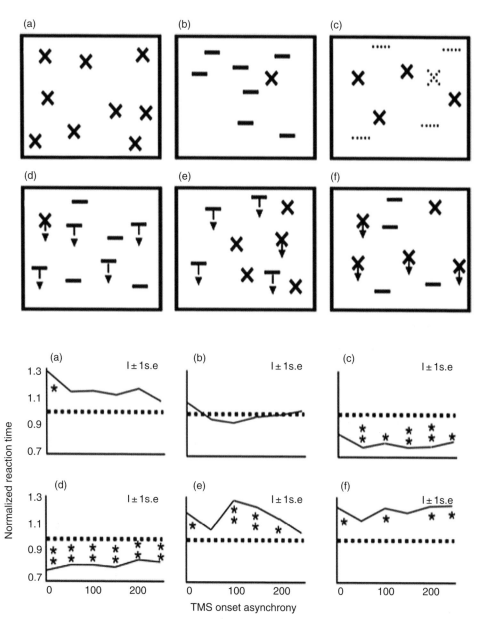

Figure 13.13 Applying TMS to a region of cortex can enhance or inhibit performance on different tasks. (a) Shows six visual search tasks in which subjects were required to detect the presence or absence of a target. (b) Below shows the effects of applying TMS to area V5. In two tasks (tasks a and b) there is little or no effect of TMS. When TMS is applied to V5 during a search requiring attention to motion (tasks e and f) performance is significantly slower with TMS. Tasks on which attention to attributes other than motion is required are facilitated by TMS over V5. Dotted line at 1 represents reaction times without TMS. Solid lines show reaction times with TMS relative to without. From Walsh et al. (1998) with permission.

stimulus array would contain movement or colour or form as the important parameter. When the types of trials are interleaved such that the subject does not have advance information, the enhancing effects of TMS were not obtained. Therefore, it seems that a combination of priming (due to the advanced knowledge of the stimuli) and suppression of activity in motion brain area V5/MT by TMS were required to enhance performance on colour and form tasks.

Consideration of priming mechanisms raises the concept of state-dependent effects of TMS (Silvanto and Pascual-Leone, 2008). It seems quite clear that the effects of TMS, or any other form of brain stimulation, represent a complex interaction between the stimulation applied, and the state of activity in the brain at the time of stimulation. Such effects were demonstrated, for example, by Silvanto et al. (2007) by manipulating the initial cortical activation state of functionally distinct neural populations by the use of adaptation prior to the application of TMS. Adaptation is the phenomenon in which changes in neural tuning and excitability induced by prolonged exposure to sensory stimulation bias the perception of subsequently presented stimuli. The interaction between the neural activation state and the effects of TMS was assessed by TMS-induced visual percepts (phosphenes) as well as using a psychophysical task. After adaptation to a colour stimulus, phosphenes induced from the early visual cortex took on the colour qualities of the adapting stimulus. In the psychophysical task in which TMS was applied at an intensity below the phosphene threshold, TMS similarly facilitated the perception of the adapted attributes. As neurons encoding the adapted attribute were made less excitable by adaptation, the finding that phosphenes took on the colour of the adapting stimulus implies that TMS behaviourally facilitates the less excitable neural populations relative to the more active neural populations.

Similar findings have been obtained in motion perception after adaptation to simple translational motion, with TMS facilitating the detection of the adapted direction and impairing the detection of the opposite direction (Cattaneo and Silvanto, 2008a, 2008b). Romei et al. (2007) reported similar state-dependent effects of TMS in the context of multisensory interaction. They noted that single-pulse TMS over the occipital pole produced opposing behavioural effects during a simple reaction time task to visual and auditory stimuli, with TMS slowing down reaction times to visual stimuli but facilitating reaction times to auditory stimuli.

Priming can also be used to manipulate the state of activity of the brain prior to TMS. In priming, repetition of an object's feature or spatial position facilitates subsequent detection or identification of that object. At a neural level, various theories have been put forward to account for the effects of priming – for example, that priming occurs because neurons activated by the prime are still active when the test stimulus is presented. This elevated activity level facilitates target detection if those pre-activated neurons are involved in encoding the target stimulus. Priming has also been proposed to reflect changes in neural tuning. In this view, neurons that code features irrelevant to identification of a stimulus become less responsive to that stimulus, leading to a sparser representation of stimuli. Because tuning curves become narrower, neurons become more sensitive to change, enabling more efficient or faster processing of repeated stimuli. Regardless of the underlying neural mechanism, experimental findings support the conclusion that TMS preferentially facilitates the attributes encoded by the less active neural populations. Specifically, Cattaneo et al. (2008) compared the state-dependent effects of TMS when the initial activation states had been modulated either with adaptation or priming. In the adaptation experiment, TMS facilitated the detection of the adapted attributes. In the priming paradigm, TMS facilitated the detection of non-primed targets. As the activity level of neurons encoding the non-primed targets was lower at the time of TMS application than the activity level of neurons encoding primed targets, this finding provides further evidence for the view that TMS preferentially facilitates the less-active neural populations. This is an important finding, as it demonstrates that the principle of TMS facilitating less active neural populations is not simply restricted to adaptation, but can also be observed in other paradigms.

State-dependent effects of online TMS have also been observed when the stimulated region has been uniformly suppressed by 1 Hz repetitive TMS prior to application of online TMS. In a recent study by Silvanto *et al.* (2008), TMS was applied over the motion-selective region V5/MT during a simple motion detection task and subjects' motion detection ability was impaired. Similarly, suppression of V5/MT activity using offline 1 Hz rTMS disrupted performance in a subsequent motion detection task. However, paradoxically, online V5/MT TMS facilitated motion detection if V5/MT had been suppressed by offline 1 Hz rTMS prior to the motion detection task. These results demonstrate that online TMS can have an unexpected facilitatory effect on behaviour when the targeted neural population is in a suppressed state. This finding provides further evidence for the view that the effects of TMS are modulated by the initial activation state of the targeted neural population. It appears, that at the behavioural level, the effects of TMS are akin to microstimulation of the less active neural populations. The concept of TMS as a tool for disrupting cognitive function by inducing reversible 'lesions' does not do justice to these subtle effects.

Paradoxical functional facilitation following tDCS

Transcranial application of weak direct currents induces an intracerebral current flow sufficiently large to alter neuronal activity and behaviour. DCS differs qualitatively from TMS by not inducing neuronal action potentials; static fields in this range do not yield the rapid depolarization required to produce action potentials in neural membranes. Hence, tDCS might be considered a purely neuromodulatory intervention. The exposed tissue is polarized and tDCS modifies spontaneous neuronal excitability and activity by a tonic depolarization or hyper-polarization of resting membrane potential (Creutzfeldt *et al.*, 1962; Purpura and McMurtry, 1965). The efficacy of tDCS in inducing acute modifications of membrane polarity depends on current density, which determines the induced electrical field strength, and is the quotient of current strength and electrode size. Another important parameter of tDCS is the stimulation duration. tDCS electrodes' positions and polarity play an important role to achieve the intended electrical stimulation effects. Anode is defined as the positively charged electrode, whereas the cathode is the negatively charged one. Current flows from cathode to anode.

In the motor cortex, anodal or cathodal tDCS performed for seconds results in a motor cortical excitability increase or decrease, which does not outlast the stimulation itself (Nitsche and Paulus, 2000; Priori *et al.*, 1998). With two electrodes over the scalp, excitability is enhanced following tDCS with the anode positioned over the primary motor cortex and the cathode over the contralateral orbit, thus causing an anterior–posterior directed current flow. By contrast, the reversed electrode position, with the cathode over the primary motor cortex and thus a posterior–anterior current flow, reduces excitability.

When applied for several minutes, tDCS produces lasting effects in the human motor cortex. These effects are stable for up to about an hour if tDCS is applied for 9–13 min

(Nitsche and Paulus, 2001, Nitsche *et al.*, 2003; Ardolino *et al.*, 2005). Anodal stimulation enhances, whereas cathodal tDCS diminishes excitability, as measured by motor-evoked potential (MEP) amplitude.

Various studies have investigated paradoxical functional facilitation resulting from tDCS disruption of the brain activity. Fregni *et al.* (2005) asked whether reduction of the excitability in the unaffected hemisphere by cathodal tDCS could result in motor performance improvement in stroke patients. The results were compared with excitability-enhancing anodal tDCS of the affected hemisphere and sham tDCS. Both cathodal stimulation of the unaffected hemisphere and anodal stimulation of the affected hemisphere (but not sham tDCS) improved motor performance significantly, suggesting that the appropriate modulation of bi-hemispheric brain structures can promote motor function recovery.

In another study, Monti *et al.* (2008) evaluated the effects of tDCS over the left frontotemporal areas in eight chronic non-fluent post-stroke aphasic patients. The study assessed picture naming (accuracy and response time) in the aphasic patients, before and immediately after anodal or cathodal tDCS, and sham stimulation. Whereas anodal tDCS and sham tDCS failed to induce any changes, cathodal tDCS significantly improved the accuracy of the picture naming task by a mean of 33.6% (SEM 13.8%).

Thus, paralleling studies and approaches using TMS discussed above, it appears possible to induce similar paradoxical functional facilitation phenomena with tDCS. Noninvasive brain stimulation has therefore proved to be a powerful tool in cognitive neuroscience to probe paradoxical functional facilitations that may occur following lesions to a particular node of a complex and distributed neural network. TMS studies on visual attention, motor, somatosensory, language and memory systems have highlighted the mechanisms that may underlie functional facilitation by providing experimental support for the hypothesis that some brain functions operate in a state of dynamic hemispheric competition. Manipulation of this hemispheric balance with repetitive TMS thus enables investigation of the neural mechanisms underlying plasticity following brain lesions and can provide valuable knowledge on the inner workings of the normal brain. In that sense, noninvasive brain stimulation provides a unique tool to disrupt specific brain regions and guide brain plasticity, promoting shifts in brain-behaviour mapping and the establishment of new strategies that might be more adaptive for a given individual.

Future challenges and questions

Noninvasive brain stimulation can thus offer unique approaches to the study and characterization of brain network dynamics and of paradoxical functional facilitation in healthy participants, as well as in patients with neuropsychiatric disorders. Furthermore, probing plasticity with noninvasive brain stimulation can offer a unique insight into the physiological consequences of functional human polymorphisms. However, beyond cognitive neuroscience questions, noninvasive brain stimulation can allow leverage of paradoxical functional facilitation for neurotherapeutics. This offers the exciting future potential of using this approach to reduce symptoms and disabilities. However, such approaches require detailed control of the effects of TMS, tDCS or other noninvasive brain stimulation methods at an individual level, and tailoring of the stimulation parameters to online measured effects. At this point we lack such approaches, but the technology is being developed. For example, personally tailored therapeutic applications of paradoxical functional facilitation may be enabled by close-loop systems that use individual brain anatomy and connectivity information – e.g. derived from morphometric and functional brain magnetic resonance and diffusion tensor imaging. They may also be enabled by brain stimulation and by on-line recording of brain activity – e.g. using electroencephalogram or near-infrared spectroscopy. Such targeted approaches can further benefit from the use of noninvasive brain stimulation to leverage the effect of pharmacotherapy, especially in neurorehabilitation.

References

Aldini, G. (1804). *Essai théorique et expérimental sur le galvanisme*. Paris: Fournier Fils.

Ardolino, G., Bossi, B., Barbieri, S., & Priori, A. (2005). Non-synaptic mechanisms underlie the after-effects of cathodal transcutaneous direct current stimulation of the human brain. *Journal of Physiology*, **568**: 653–63.

Barker, A. T. (1976). *Determination of the Distribution of Conduction Velocity in Human Nerve Trunks*. Sheffield: University of Sheffield.

Barker, A. T., Jalinous, R., & Freeston, I. L. (1985). Non-invasive stimulation of human motor cortex. *Lancet*, **1**: 1106–07.

Beard, G. M., & Rockwell, A. D. (1871). *A Practical Treatise on the Medical and Surgical Use of Electricity, Including Localized and General Electrization*. New York, NY: William Wood.

Belin, P., Van Eeckhout, P., Zilbovicious, M., *et al.* (1996). Recovery from nonfluent aphasia after melodic intonation therapy: a PET study. *Neurology*, **47**: 1504–11.

Brickford, R. G., & Fremming, B. D. (1965). Neural stimulation by pulsed magnetic fields in animals and man. In: Iwai, Y. (Ed.). *Digital 6th International Conference on Medical and Biological Engineering*. Tokyo: Japan Society of Medical Electronics and Biological Engineering, p. 112.

Brighina, F., Bisiach, E., Oliveri, M., *et al.* (2003). 1 Hz repetitive transcranial magnetic stimulation of the unaffected hemisphere ameliorates contralesional visuospatial neglect in humans. *Neuroscience Letters*, **16**: 131–3.

Brighina, F., Piazza, A., Daniele, O., & Fierro, B. (2002). Modulation of visual cortical excitability in migraine with aura: effects of 1 Hz repetitive transcranial magnetic stimulation. *Experimental Brain Research*, **145**: 177–81.

Brown, R. M., & Robertson, E. M. (2007). Off-line processing: reciprocal interactions between declarative and procedural memories. *Journal of Neuroscience*, **27**: 10,468–75.

Cattaneo, Z., & Silvanto, J. (2008a). Investigating visual motion perception using the transcranial magnetic stimulation-adaptation paradigm. *Neuroreport*, **19**: 1423–7.

Cattaneo, Z., & Silvanto, J. (2008b). Time course of the state-dependent effect of transcranial magnetic stimulation in the TMS-adaptation paradigm. *Neuroscience Letters*, **443**: 82–5.

Cattaneo, Z., Rota, F., Vecchi, T., & Silvanto, J. (2008). Using state-dependency of transcranial magnetic stimulation (TMS) to investigate letter selectivity in the left posterior parietal cortex: a comparison of TMS-priming and TMS-adaptation paradigms. *European Journal of Neuroscience*, **28**: 1924–9.

Chen, R., Classen, J., Gerloff, C., *et al.* (1997). Depression of motor cortex excitability by low-frequency transcranial magnetic stimulation. *Neurology*, **48**: 1398–403.

Clark, D., & Wagner, A. D. (2003). Assembling and encoding word representations: fMRI subsequent memory effects implicate a role for phonological control. *Neuropsychologia*, **41**: 304–17.

Creutzfeldt, O. D., Fromm, G. H., & Kapp, H. (1962). Influence of transcortical D-C currents on cortical neuronal activity. *Experimental Neurology*, **5**: 436–52.

d'Arsonval, A. (1896). Dispositifs pour la mesure des courants alternatifs de toutes frequences. *CR Soc Bid (Paris)*, **21**: 450–1.

Duchenne, G. B. A. (1855). *De l'Électrisation Localisée et de son Application à la*

Physiologie, à la Pathologie et à la Thérapeutique. Paris: J.B. Baillière.

Fierro, B., Brighina, F., Vitello, G., *et al.* (2005). Modulatory effects of low- and high-frequency repetitive transcranial magnetic stimulation on visual cortex of healthy subjects undergoing light deprivation. *Journal of Physiology,* **565**: 659–65.

Fregni, F., Boggio, P. S., Mansur, C. G., *et al.* (2005). Transcranial direct current stimulation of the unaffected hemisphere in stroke patients. *Neuroreport,* **16**: 1551–5.

Galea, J. M., Albert, N. B., Ditye, T., & Miall, R. C. (2010). Disruption of the dorsolateral prefrontal cortex facilitates the consolidation of procedural skills. *Journal of Cognitive Neuroscience,* **22**: 1158–64.

Hilgetag, C. C., Kötter, R., & Young, M. P. (1999). Inter-hemispheric competition of sub-cortical structures is a crucial mechanism in paradoxical lesion effects and spatial neglect. *Progress in Brain Research,* **121**: 121–41.

Hilgetag, C. C., Theoret, H., & Pascual-Leone, A. (2001). Enhanced visual spatial attention ipsilateral to rTMS-induced 'virtual lesions' of human parietal cortex. *Nature Neuroscience,* **4**: 953–7.

Kahn, I., Pascual-Leone, A., Theoret, H., Fregni, F., Clark, D., & Wagner, A. D. (2005). Transient disruption of ventrolateral prefrontal cortex during verbal encoding affects subsequent memory performance. *Journal of Neurophysiology,* **94**: 688–98.

Kinsbourne, M. (1977). Hemi-neglect and hemisphere rivalry. In: Weinstein, E. A. & Friedland, R. P. (Eds.). *Hemi-inattention and Hemisphere Specialization. Advances in Neurology, Volume* **18**. New York, NY: Raven Press, 41–9.

Knecht, S., Floel, A., Drager, B., *et al.* (2002). Degree of language lateralization determines susceptibility to unilateral brain lesions. *Nature Neuroscience,* **5**: 695–9.

Kobayashi, M., & Pascual-Leone, A. (2003). Transcranial magnetic stimulation in neurology. *Lancet Neurology,* **2**: 145–56.

Kobayashi, M., Hutchinson, S., Schlaug, G., & Pascual-Leone, A. (2003). Ipsilateral motor cortex activation on functional magnetic resonance imaging during unilateral hand movements is related to interhemispheric interactions. *Neuroimage,* **20**: 2259–70.

Kobayashi, M., Théoret, H., & Pascual-Leone, A. (2009). Suppression of ipsilateral motor cortex facilitates motor skill learning. *European Journal of Neuroscience,* **29**: 833–6.

Koch, G., Oliveri, M., Cheeran, B., *et al.* (2008). Hyperexcitability of parietal-motor functional connections in the intact left-hemisphere of patients with neglect. *Brain,* **131**: 3147–55.

Kosslyn, S. M., Pascual-Leone, A., Felician, O., *et al.* (1999). The role of area 17 in visual imagery: convergent evidence from PET and rTMS. *Science,* **284**: 167–70.

Lee, L., Siebner, H. R., Rowe, J. B., *et al.* (2003). Acute remapping within the motor system induced by low-frequency repetitive transcranial magnetic stimulation. *Journal of Neuroscience,* **23**: 5308–18.

Liepert, J., Storch, P., Fritsch, A., & Weiller, C. (2000). Motor cortex disinhibition in acute stroke. *Clinical Neurophysiology,* **111**: 671–6.

Lewald, J., Foltys, H., & Töpper, R. (2002). Role of the posterior parietal cortex in spatial hearing. *Journal of Neuroscience,* **22**: RC207.

Maeda, F., Keenan, J. P., Tormos, J. M., Topka, H., & Pascual-Leone, A. (2000). Modulation of corticospinal excitability by repetitive transcranial magnetic stimulation. *Clinical Neurophysiology,* **111**: 800–05.

Mansur, C. G., Fregni, F., Boggio, P. S., *et al.* (2005). A sham-stimulation controlled trial of rTMS of the unaffected hemisphere on hand motor function after stroke. *Neurology,* **64**: 1802–04.

Martin, P. I., Naeser, M. A., Theoret, H., *et al.* (2004). Transcranial magnetic stimulation as a complementary treatment for aphasia. *Seminars in Speech and Language,* **25**: 181–91.

Monti, A., Cogiamanian, F., Marceglia, S., *et al.* (2008). Improved naming after transcranial direct current stimulation in aphasia. *Journal of Neurology, Neurosurgery and Psychiatry,* **79**: 451–3.

Mottaghy, F. M., Gangitano, M., Sparing, R., Krause, B. J., & Pascual-Leone, A. (2002).

Segregation of areas related to visual working memory in the prefrontal cortex revealed by rTMS. *Cerebral Cortex*, **12**: 369–75.

Mottaghy, F. M., Krause, B. J., Kemna, L. J., *et al.* (2000). Modulation of the neuronal circuitry subserving working memory in healthy human subjects by repetitive transcranial magnetic stimulation. *Neuroscience Letters*, **280**: 167–70.

Murase, N., Duque, J., Mazzocchio, R., & Cohen, L. G. (2004). Influence of interhemispheric interactions on motor function in chronic stroke. *Annals of Neurology*, **55**: 400–09.

Naeser, M. A., Martin, P. I., Baker, E. H., *et al.* (2004). Overt propositional speech in chronic nonfluent aphasia studied with the dynamic susceptibility contrast fMRI method, *Neuroimage*, **22**: 29–41.

Naeser, M. A., Martin, P. I., Nicholas, M., *et al.* (2005a). Improved naming after TMS treatments in a chronic, global Aphasia patient – case report. *Neurocase*, **11**: 182–93.

Naeser, M. A., Martin, P. I., Nicholas, M., *et al.* (2005b). Improved picture naming in chronic Aphasia after TMS to part of right Broca's area, an open-protocol study. *Brain and Language*, **93**: 95–105.

Nagai, C., Inui, T., & Iwata, M. (2010). Role of Broca's subregions in syntactic processing: a comparative study of Japanese patients with lesions in the pars triangularis and opercularis. *European Neurology*, **63**: 79–86.

Nitsche, M. A., & Paulus, W. (2000). Excitability changes induced in the human motor cortex by weak transcranial direct current stimulation. *Journal of Physiology*, **527**: 633–9.

Nitsche, M. A., & Paulus, W. (2001). Sustained excitability elevations induced by transcranial DC motor cortex stimulation in humans. *Neurology*, **57**: 1899–901.

Nitsche, M. A., Nitsche, M. S., Klein, C. C., *et al.* (2003). Level of action of cathodal DC polarisation induced inhibition of the human motor cortex. *Clinical Neurophysiology*, **114**: 600–04.

Oliveri, M., Bisiach, E., Brighina, F., *et al.* (2001). rTMS of the unaffected hemisphere transiently reduces contralesional visuospatial hemineglect. *Neurology*, **57**: 1338–40.

Oliveri, M., Rossini, P. M., Traversa, R., *et al.* (1999). Left frontal transcranial magnetic stimulation reduces contralesional extinction in patients with unilateral right brain damage. *Brain*, **122**: 1731–9.

Otten, L. J., Henson, R. N., & Rugg, M. D. (2002). State-related and item-related neural correlates of successful memory encoding. *Nature Neuroscience*, **5**: 1339–44.

Pascual-Leone, A., Bartres-Faz, D., & Keenan, J. P. (1999). Transcranial magnetic stimulation: studying the brain–behaviour relationship by induction of 'virtual lesions'. *Philosophical Transactions of the Royal Society London, Part B – Biological Sciences*, **354**: 1229–38.

Pascual-Leone, A., Tormos, J. M., Keenan, J., Tarazona, F., Canete, C., & Catala, M. D. (1998). Study and modulation of human cortical excitability with transcranial magnetic stimulation. *Journal of Clinical Neurophysiology*, **15**: 333–43.

Perani, D., Cappa, S. F., Tettamanti, M., *et al.* (2003). An fMRI study of word retrieval in aphasia. *Brain and Language*, **85**: 357–68.

Priori, A., Berardelli, A., Rona, S., Accornero, N., & Manfredi, M. (1998). Polarization of the human motor cortex through the scalp. *Neuroreport*, **9**: 2257–60.

Purpura, D. P., & McMurtry, J. G. (1965). Intracellular activities and evoked potential changes during polarization of motor cortex. *Journal of Neurophysiology*, **28**: 166–85.

Robertson, E. M., Tormos, J. M., Maeda, F., & Pascual-Leone, A. (2001). The role of the dorsolateral prefrontal cortex during sequence learning is specific for spatial information. *Cerebral Cortex*, **11**: 628–35.

Romei, V., Murray, M. M., Merabet, L. B., & Thut, G. (2007). Occipital transcranial magnetic stimulation has opposing effects on visual and auditory stimulus detection: implications for multisensory interactions. *Journal of Neuroscience*, **27**: 11,465–72.

Rosen, H. J., Petersen, S. E., Linenweber, M. R., *et al.* (2000). Neural correlates of recovery from aphasia after damage to left inferior frontal cortex. *Neurology*, **55**: 1883–94.

Rushmore, R. J., Valero-Cabre, A., Lomber, S. G., Hilgetag, C. C., & Payne, B. R. (2006). Functional circuitry underlying visual neglect. *Brain*, **129**: 1803–21.

Sack, A. T., Sperling, J. M., Prvulovic, D., *et al.* (2002). Tracking the mind's image in the brain II: transcranial magnetic stimulation reveals parietal asymmetry in visuospatial imagery. *Neuron*, **35**: 195–204.

Satow, T., Mima, T., Yamamoto, J., *et al.* (2003). Short-lasting impairment of tactile perception by 0.9 Hz-rTMS of the sensorimotor cortex. *Neurology*, **60**: 1045–7.

Seyal, M., Ro, T., & Rafal, R. (1995). Increased sensitivity to ipsilateral cutaneous stimuli following transcranial magnetic stimulation of the parietal lobe. *Annals of Neurology*, **38**: 264–7.

Shapiro, K. A., Pascual-Leone, A., Mottaghy, F. M., Gangitano, M., & Caramazza, A. (2001). Grammatical distinctions in the left frontal cortex. *Journal of Cognitive Neuroscience*, **13**: 713–20.

Silvanto, J., & Pascual-Leone, A. (2008). State-dependency of transcranial magnetic stimulation. *Brain Topography*, **21**: 1–10.

Silvanto, J., Cattaneo, Z., Battelli, L., & Pascual-Leone, A. (2008). Baseline cortical excitability determines whether TMS disrupts or facilitates behavior. *Journal of Neurophysiology*, **99**: 2725–30.

Silvanto, J., Muggleton, N. G., Cowey, A., & Walsh, V. (2007). Neural adaptation reveals state-dependent effects of transcranial magnetic stimulation. *European Journal of Neuroscience*, **25**: 1874–81.

Théoret, H., Haque, J., & Pascual-Leone, A. (2001). Increased variability of paced finger tapping accuracy following repetitive magnetic stimulation of the cerebellum in humans. *Neuroscience Letters*, **306**: 29–32.

Thompson, S. P. (1910). A physiological effect of an alternating magnetic field. *Proceedings of the Royal Society, London*, **B82**: 396–9.

Thut, G., Théoret, H., Pfennig, A., *et al.* (2003). Differential effects of low- frequency rTMS at the occipital pole on visual-induced alpha desynchronization and visual-evoked potentials. *Neuroimage*, **18**: 334–47.

Valero-Cabré, A., Pascual-Leone, A., & Rushmore, R. J. (2008). Cumulative sessions of repetitive transcranial magnetic stimulation (rTMS) build up facilitation to subsequent TMS-mediated behavioural disruptions. *European Journal of Neuroscience*, **27**: 765–74.

Valero-Cabré, A., Payne, B. R., & Pascual-Leone, A. (2007). Opposite impact on ^{14}C-2-deoxyglucose brain metabolism following patterns of high and low frequency repetitive transcranial magnetic stimulation in the posterior parietal cortex. *Experimental Brain Research*, **176**: 603–15.

Valero-Cabré, A., Payne, B. R., Rushmore, J., Lomber, S. G., & Pascual-Leone, A. (2005). Impact of repetitive transcranial magnetic stimulation of the parietal cortex on metabolic brain activity: a 14C-2DG tracing study in the cat. *Experimental Brain Research*, **163**: 1–12.

Vuilleumier, P., Hester, D., Assal, G., & Regli, F. (1996). Unilateral spatial neglect recovery after sequential strokes. *Neurology*, **46**: 184–9.

Wagner, T., Valero-Cabre, A., & Pascual-Leone, A. (2007). Noninvasive human brain stimulation. *Annual Review of Biomedical Engineering*, **9**: 527–65.

Walsh, V., & Pascual-Leone, A. (2003). *Neurochronometrics of Mind: TMS in Cognitive Science*. Cambridge, MA: MIT Press.

Walsh, V., Ellison, A., Battelli, L., & Cowey, A. (1998). Task-specific impairments and enhancements induced by magnetic stimulation of human visual area V5. *Proceedings of the Royal Society, Biological Sciences*, **265**: 537–43.

Xiang, H. D., Fonteijn, H. M., Norris, D. G., & Hagoort, P. (2010). Topographical functional connectivity pattern in the perisylvian language networks. *Cerebral Cortex*, **20**: 549–60.

Young, M. P., Hilgetag, C. C., & Scannell, J. W. (2000). On imputing function to structure from the behavioural effects of brain lesions. *Philosophical Transactions of the Royal Society, Biological Sciences*, **355**: 147–61.

Chapter 14

Unexpected benefits of allergies and cigarette smoking: two examples of paradox in neuroepidemiology

Judith Schwartzbaum, Linda Karavodin, Narinder Kapur and James L. Fisher

Summary

This chapter explores puzzling paradoxes that apply to two major neurological diseases. The first involves allergies which range in severity from allergic rhinitis, which may cause only mild discomfort, to allergic asthma which can be life-threatening. It has been repeatedly demonstrated that people with malignant brain tumours have fewer allergies than people who do not. The reasons for this association are unknown, but it is possible that allergies reflect an active immune system that is also able to destroy nascent tumours. Alternatively, it is well known that malignant brain tumours suppress anti-tumour immunity, so it is possible that they suppress allergies as well. The second paradox involves cigarette smoking, well known to cause lung cancer, heart disease, chronic respiratory disease and other harmful effects that have been extensively documented. Yet cigarette smokers have a lower risk of Parkinson's disease than do people who have never smoked cigarettes. Epidemiologic evidence indicates that this paradox is not an artefact, but that cigarette smokers actually enjoy lower risks of Parkinson's disease as a result of smoking. These reduced risks probably result from nicotine's observed protective effects on the nervous system.

Introduction

Conventional wisdom maintains that an illness or assault on one organ should not have a beneficial effect on another. Yet in neurology, as in other branches of medicine, there are cases where harm to one biological system appears to benefit another. This chapter focuses on the protective effects of allergy on glioma, and of smoking on Parkinson's disease. However, several other neurologic paradoxes are worthy of brief mention.

One such anomaly involves the metabolic disease, diabetes. Patients with diabetes (DM) are at increased risk of developing Alzheimer's disease (AD) (Mielke *et al.*, 2007; Regan *et al.*, 2006; Helzner *et al.*, 2009). However, cognitive decline is slower in AD patients with DM than in their non-diabetic AD counterparts (Sanz *et al.*, 2009). Age or sex differences between AD patients with and without DM may explain these disparities. Nevertheless, these differences may also be attributed to the fact that DM patients often

---

receive cardiovascular medications, possibly contributing to a slower cognitive decline in patients with both DM and AD.

Anti-inflammatory medications given for rheumatoid arthritis (RA) may also reduce the risk of, or delay the onset of, AD (McGeer et al., 1996). Although there is no evidence that RA itself is protective against AD, AD lesions are typified by a chronic neuro-inflammatory state that may promote neuronal destruction. Anti-inflammatory agents may therefore delay AD progression (Norhashemi, 1999).

Genetic variation does appear to play a part in another neurologic inconsistency. Although individuals with Down's syndrome have an increased risk of childhood leukaemia, their incidence of most solid tumours is reduced among all age-groups (Hasle et al., 2000; Satge et al., 1998; Patja et al., 2006). Mortality from non-leukaemia cancers is 10% lower than expected (Yang et al., 2002). This finding suggests that genes on chromosome 21 responsible for Down's syndrome may also protect against malignancy. Down's syndrome patients have reduced incidence of other diseases related to formation of new blood vessels (angiogenesis), such as diabetic retinopathy (Fulcher et al., 1998) and atherosclerosis (Murdoch et al., 1977), indicating that cancer protection in the Down's syndrome population may be related to suppression of angiogenesis (Baek et al., 2009), with consequent failure of nascent tumours to develop an adequate blood supply.

Patients with schizophrenia also have a reduced risk of malignancy, including stomach, rectal, prostate, breast and brain cancer (Barak et al., 2005). The controlled diet and smoking limitations of extended hospitalization were once thought to contribute to this phenomenon (Fox and Howell, 1974). More recent theories propose that polymorphism of the p53 tumour suppressor gene, essential to the regulation of programmed cell death (apoptosis), and found in patients with schizophrenia, may be associated with a reduced vulnerability to lung cancer (Park et al., 2004). This hypothesis is supported by a large Chinese cohort study (Yang et al., 2004).

Another link between neurologic disease and cancer is suggested by the observation that multiple sclerosis (MS) patients have a 10% lower risk of cancer than do people without MS, which cannot be explained by a simple inherited characteristic (Bahmanyar et al., 2009). MS is associated with reduced risks of digestive, respiratory, prostate and ovarian cancers, and non-Hodgkin lymphoma (Soderberg et al., 2006), but increased risks of urinary tract and nasopharyngeal cancers (Nielsen et al., 2006). Behavioural changes or treatment might contribute to a decline in cancer risk among MS patients, or it could be that some immunologic characteristic of MS actually improves antitumour surveillance. A recent report proposes that the sequence of certain common infections may result in an immune shift away from protection and towards enhancement of MS risk (Krone et al., 2009).

Infectious burden has also been identified as a risk factor for stroke (Mitchell et al., 2009). However, another physical assault, ischaemia, appears to provide a more favourable clinical outcome for stroke victims (Moncayo et al., 2000). Transient ischaemic attack (TIA) refers to the restriction of blood supply in the blood vessels, and affords protection against cardiac disease (Hausenloy et al., 2007). Stroke patients with a prior history of TIA have less tissue damage after their strokes than do their non-TIA controls (Wegener et al., 2004), contributing to their decreased morbidity. It is possible that the natural repair mechanisms which occur after TIA upregulate protective mechanisms to block injury induced by subsequent stress (O'Duffy et al., 2007).

Allergies and glioma

Why would a condition that most immunologists describe as a disorder of the immune system be implicated in a protective response to one of the most deadly neurological cancers? This is the paradox linking the hypersensitive immune response known as allergy, and the malignant brain tumour, glioma.

Gliomas are malignant tumours of brain tissue which normally provide support, nutrition and facilitate signal transmission. Glial cells are known as the 'glue' of the nervous system. Tumours of these cells account for nearly 80% of adult malignant tumours that start in the brain, and contribute to more years of life lost than any other malignant tumour (Burnet *et al.*, 2005). Glioblastoma is the most common subtype and has an average survival time of only 14 months from the time of diagnosis. Glioma incidence rates have increased over time and are associated with the tumour's histologic subtype as well as the patient's age, sex and geographic location (Hoffman *et al.*, 2005). However, an unexpected association has been observed. Comparative analyses of patients with and without glioma show a strong inverse association with allergic conditions; that is, within a population, as the average proportion with a history of allergy increases, the average risk of glioma decreases (Linos *et al.*, 2007). This result has been consistently observed in more than 12 large epidemiologic studies conducted since 1990 (e.g. Linos *et al.*, 2007). Although these findings suggest that allergies reduce glioma risk, they are also consistent with known brain tumour-induced immunosuppression. That is, the tumour itself may suppress allergic reactions via immunosuppressive immune system proteins found in the tumour microenvironment (Schwartzbaum *et al.*, 2010a; Schwartzbaum *et al.*, 2010b) and peripheral blood.

Allergic reactions are characterized by an exaggerated immune response to normally harmless environmental substances, resulting in an extreme inflammatory immune response in the lung and directly affected tissues. These reactions include hay fever, asthma, eczema, hives or localized inflammation. Mild allergies are highly prevalent among residents of industrialized countries, but can occasionally become serious, with environmental, dietary or medication allergens resulting in life-threatening reactions. The factors that mediate the symptoms of allergy are all part of a normal immune response to an immunological challenge, but in allergy the brakes on the system are less effective – the immune response is in overdrive.

The mechanisms responsible for this potentially protective allergic response are not well defined, but recent observations have focused on two regulatory proteins (cytokines), interleukin (IL)-4 and IL-13. These are two potent anti-inflammatory agents, paradoxically active in allergic and autoimmune disease (Dinarello, 2003), that may also contribute to increased tumour immunosurveillance among patients with allergies and autoimmune disease (Dunn *et al.*, 2002). Although IL-4 is not expressed in the normal adult brain, it is strongly expressed during brain injury (Liu *et al.*, 2000a), when invading T cells may be a source of this cytokine (Barna *et al.*, 1995). There is a defective blood–brain barrier in advanced glioma (gliobastoma) that allows passage of larger molecules, such as cytokines or antibodies, into brain tissue.

Evidence for the suppressive effects of these cytokines on glioma comes from several sources. IL-4 and IL-13 added to cultures of glioma cell lines in vitro were found to inhibit cell growth (Barna *et al.*, 1995; Liu *et al.*, 2000b). Cell surface receptors for IL-4 (IL-4R) were evaluated on three normal astrocytic, two low-grade astrocytoma and four glioblastoma cell lines, and were found on all but one glioblastoma cell line (Barna *et al.*, 1995), indicating that a majority of these cell lines can bind this cytokine.

Next, investigations were taken to the level of the gene itself. Schwartzbaum *et al.* (2005) examined the distribution of asthma and allergy-related genetic polymorphisms in patients with glioblastoma as compared to controls, and found that the genetic variants that increase asthma risk were associated with a decreased risk of developing glioblastoma. IL-4Ralpha and IL-13, genetic variants known as single nucleotide polymorphisms (SNPs) were among several SNPs evaluated in this study; these were related to increased risk of allergic conditions. This was a necessary piece of the puzzle, since self-reporting of allergic conditions may be affected by the patient's memory of allergy incidents, or even by tumour immunosuppression itself. Although these germline genetic variants do not indicate the presence of allergic conditions per se, they point to increased risk of allergic conditions among people without brain tumours and so provide a way to measure these associations free of patient recall bias. Our working hypothesis was that individuals with IL-4Ralpha or IL-13 polymorphisms, who are at increased risk for allergic conditions, would also demonstrate decreased risk for glioblastoma. A large study of IL-4 and IL-13 genetic variants was undertaken (Schwartzbaum *et al.*, 2007), but it did not provide strong support for our hypothesis. Nonetheless, we found an IL-4Ralpha haplotype associated with glioblastoma and inversely related to the self-reporting of hay fever or asthma among controls.

It is still possible, however, that allergy-related cytokines regulate the growth of glioma by suppressing the process of inflammation, an early component of tumour establishment (Gomez and Kruse, 2006). Investigators have found that the signalling of IL-13 via the IL-13Ralpha 2 receptor leads to the production of tumour growth factor (TGF-beta1), a major immunosuppressive and anti-inflammatory cytokine (Terabe *et al.*, 2006). Similarly, a recurring allergic reaction can, in some cases, lead to anergy, an immunologically unresponsive state. Bee keepers who have been stung multiple times develop T cells that are no longer able to respond to bee venom antigens due to increased production of the regulatory cytokine, IL-10 (Akdis *et al.*, 2001).

Another well-known mediator of allergic response, the antibody IgE, has been implicated in this protective role. Wiemels *et al.* (2004) found that total serum IgE levels were lower in glioma patients than in controls, although a later study suggests that this may be a function of treatment rather than a reflection of differences in the prevalence of allergies (Wiemels *et al.*, 2009). Wrensch *et al.* (2006) reported an increase of 9 months survival time for glioblastoma patients with elevated IgE, compared to those with lower or normal IgE levels. This finding is especially important because it suggests that immunological factors can be used to predict glioblastoma prognosis. Glioblastoma patients with higher IgE levels may have better antitumour defences, less-aggressive tumours with weaker antiimmunological effects, or IgE itself may have antitumour activity through direct activity on glioma or other nearby cells (Wrensch *et al.*, 2006).

As we noted previously, the inverse association between glioma risk and allergic response may be due to immune suppression caused directly by the tumour. The tumour itself has mechanisms that inhibit the immune system's ability to eradicate it. Human glioma cell lines secrete immunosuppressive cytokines that selectively recruit regulatory T cells directly into the tumour microenvironment (Jordan *et al.*, 2008). IL-10 and TGF-beta, two major immunosuppressive cytokines detected both in the glioma tumour microenvironment and in the blood of glioma patients, induce immune tolerance and thereby limit allergic responses (Umetsu and DeKruyff, 2006).

Although there is no direct evidence for suppression of allergic disease by glioma there are suggestive results indicating that non-Hodgkin's lymphoma (NHL), a tumour also inversely related to self-reported history of allergic disease, is itself responsible for reduction of serum IgE levels. Specifically, in an analysis of the Finnish Maternity Cohort Study data, where serum IgE levels were measured prior to NHL diagnosis, Melbye et al. (2007) found that the closer the time of NHL diagnosis the lower serum IgE levels. Ten years prior to diagnosis there was no association between IgE levels and NHL, but the time of IgE levels diminished as the time of diagnosis approached.

There is limited evidence for a similar process in glioma. Self-reported incidence of hay fever and eczema, two common allergic syndromes, was examined in a recent large study of glioma patients and controls (Wigertz, 2008). The authors found that hay fever present at the time of glioma diagnosis was associated with reduced glioma risk. However, glioma cases were more likely to have a past history of hay fever than were controls, perhaps suggesting that the preclinical tumour had suppressed allergic symptoms, thus causing more cases than controls to report a past history of allergy. Additional data, consistent with this finding, indicates that allergy-related cytokines and IgE binding genes show reduced expression as glioblastoma progresses (Schwartzbaum et al., 2010a).

Infectious diseases are equally strong stimulators of the immune system. In line with the initial paradox, there is some evidence that the immune response to certain infectious organisms may also reduce glioma risk. As detailed in two case-control series, prior clinical disease associated with chicken pox (varicella zoster virus) infection and IgG antibodies to chicken pox is inversely associated with adult glioma risk (Scheurer et al., 2008; Wrensch et al., 1997, 2001, 2005).

As we have discussed throughout this chapter, there is consistent and compelling evidence of a negative association between glioma and allergies and immune-related conditions. The concept that a highly stimulated immune response against an allergen might contribute to a survival advantage against an unrelated tumour may seem at first counter-intuitive. However, this paradox may be resolved by taking into consideration the variety of non-specific molecules generated during an elevated immune response to any allergen or infection. It may be that these ancillary mediators are capable of providing some limited defences of a non-specific nature that, under certain circumstances, can halt or slow tumour growth. If true, then understanding the relationships between immune mediators, regulatory T cells, tumour-generated modulators, the allergic response and infection, could provide both a means of predicting and preventing glioma tumour progression.

In contrast, if the inverse association between glioma and immune-related conditions is due to the immunosuppressive effects of the preclinical tumour, this information may be used to identify the tumour before the usual time of diagnosis, and understand the mechanisms by which the tumour bypasses antitumour immunity.

Parkinson's disease and cigarette smoking

During the last 60 years, medical problems associated with cigarette smoking have been documented extensively. Tobacco smoking results in increased risks of cancer at several sites including the lung, head and neck, bladder and of emphysema, and heart attacks (Surgeon General's Report, 2004).

Controversy has occasionally surrounded the attribution of causality to smoking in human disease (Eysenck, 1991, 1995), and anomalies have sometimes been noted in the form of reduced mortality and complications in smokers with heart disease (Kievit *et al.*, 2009; Fonarow *et al.*, 2008; Katayama *et al.*, 2008). Yet, smoking appears to offer protection against one neurological condition, Parkinson's disease (PD). In the text that follows, we describe and evaluate evidence for the paradoxical protective effect of cigarette smoking on PD.

PD is a progressive degenerative disease of the brain and central nervous system that is classified as a motor system disorder. The primary symptoms of PD are muscle rigidity in the limbs and trunk; tremor in the hands, arms, legs and face; a slowness of movement; and impaired balance and coordination. These symptoms are the result of the loss of dopamine-producing brain cells. Although many genetic mutations associated with PD have been discovered, most cases are classified as 'idiopathic PD', i.e. having no known cause. Secondary cases of PD may result from drug toxicity, head trauma, cerebrovascular disease or other medical disorders.

Epidemiologic evidence of an inverse association between tobacco smoking and PD risk (as the proportion of cigarette smokers in a population increases their risk of PD decreases) is strong and consistent. Most studies divide smoking habits of the participants into several classifications. There are those who have never smoked, as well as current smokers and former smokers (both groups when combined are called 'ever-smokers'). Findings from combined results from several epidemiologic investigations (referred to as meta-analysis), suggest that risk of PD among individuals who have never smoked is approximately double that of those who ever smoked in their lifetime (Fratiglioni and Wang, 2000). The largest known meta-analysis of smoking and PD risk (including 48 studies) revealed that, compared with never-smokers, PD risk was 41, 20 and 61% lower in ever, former and current smokers, respectively. A systematic review of 4 cohort studies – smoking data obtained before PD diagnosis (Allam *et al.*, 2004a) – and a review of these same 4 studies and 21 additional case-control studies (smoking data obtained after PD diagnosis) (Allam *et al.*, 2004b) produced similar estimates comparing PD risk in current and former smokers. These findings suggest that the greater the dose or 'pack-years' of smoking, the more pronounced the reduction of risk of PD (Checkoway *et al.*, 2002; Galanaud *et al.*, 2005; Hernan *et al.*, 2001, 2002; Kandinov *et al.*, 2009; Ritz *et al.*, 2007; Scott *et al.*, 2005; Weisskopf *et al.*, 2007). Further support for these findings comes from investigators comparing smoking behaviour and PD incidence in men versus women. They found that the relative frequency of PD among women declined when the proportion of women smoking increased, and that these results were unlikely to have occurred if there was really no association between smoking and PD (Morozova *et al.*, 2008).

A patient's smoking history may not be the only factor contributing to the inverse association between smoking and PD. Tobacco smoking may confer more protection against PD among men than among women (Hernan *et al.*, 2001), but results of studies conflict and further research is needed (Scott *et al.*, 2005; Thacker *et al.*, 2007). Race or ethnic group may also alter the effect of smoking on PD, but this area also requires further research (Ritz *et al.*, 2007).

There are several possible reasons for the observed association between tobacco smoking and PD. These are: (1) some aspect of subclinical PD causes patients to quit smoking (for example, palsy), thus the association actually represents the effects of PD on smoking; (2) cigarette smokers are less likely to survive to be diagnosed with PD than are non-smokers; (3) an as-yet-unidentified factor related to both smoking and PD risk (such as age) is actually responsible for the inverse association; and (4) a component of tobacco has a neuroprotective biologic effect thereby reducing PD risk.

We can probably rule out the idea that some aspect of PD causes patients to quit smoking, since the results of studies where smoking information is obtained before PD diagnosis are consistent with the results of studies where smoking data is obtained after PD diagnosis. However, we do not know when the symptoms of PD actually begin relative to the usual time of clinical diagnosis (Marder and Logroscino, 2002). If PD has a long prediagnostic period, its possible effects on cigarette consumption might be observed many years before diagnosis and be falsely attributed to a protective effect of cigarettes. Nonetheless, evidence that pre-diagnostic PD is not causing people to quit smoking is based on the fact that, if PD itself were responsible for a decline in cigarette consumption, we would observe an apparent increased risk of PD among former smokers and an apparent decreased risk among current smokers at the time of PD diagnosis. We do not observe this pattern. Rather a meta-analysis of 25 observational studies found relative consistency of the effects of cigarette consumption at the time of diagnosis and prior to that time (Allam *et al.*, 2004b).

A second reason that the association between smoking and PD may be non-causal is that smokers may die from heart and other diseases, thus leaving non-smokers to be diagnosed with PD. The average age at diagnosis of PD is 60 years, which is relatively young for competing risks from major causes of mortality, but possible nonetheless. A similar scenario occurred in the study of smoking and its apparent effect of decreasing Alzheimer's disease risk. Although results from case-control studies suggested such protection, results from cohort studies – which are superior in the capacity to determine if an effect [smoking] actually resulted in an outcome [Alzheimer's disease], rather than vice versa – did not confirm this protection. Conflicting results of case-control and cohort studies resulted from an increased risk of (especially early) mortality among smokers (Debanne *et al.*, 2007). Further analyses of cohort data need to be conducted that account for mortality among cigarette smokers.

A third possible explanation for the smoking-PD association depends on the presence of a potentially confounding factor, i.e. a factor that distorts a true association because it is related to both smoking and PD risk. The smoking–PD association could simply be the result of a common factor causing both PD and an aversion to smoking. If there is such a common factor, then results from studies of smoking and PD risk should be statistically adjusted to remove the effect of this factor; not adjusting for this confounding factor could distort the findings in such a way that smoking would appear to protect against PD, when, in fact, the result is merely the consequence of associations between the confounding factor and smoking, and the confounding factor and PD risk. Certainly, the identification of a genetic factor associated with decreased risk of smoking and increased risk of PD would provide compelling evidence of confounding. Coffee, tea and alcohol have each been considered potential confounders of the smoking–PD risk association, and each may affect PD risk independent of smoking (Benedetti *et al.*, 2000; Checkoway *et al.*, 2002; Deleu, 2001; Dong *et al.*, 2003; Evans *et al.*, 2006; Hancock *et al.*, 2007; Hernan *et al.*, 2001; James, 2003; Kandinov *et al.*, 2007, 2009; Powers *et al.*, 2008; Tan *et al.*, 2003a). Based on results that are statistically adjusted for these factors, there has been no consistent evidence that the smoking–PD risk association is the result of confounding by coffee, tea or alcohol.

The final possible explanation for the inverse association between smoking and the risk of PD is that an actual biological mechanism accounts for this relation. A number of theories have been presented, although none have been so convincingly demonstrated as to refute other hypotheses. Support for the presence of a true biologic protective effect of smoking was presented by Tanner *et al.*, who found that twin brothers of PD patients smoked more than their non-twin brothers, and the effect of smoking on PD risk was most pronounced among monozygotic twins (Tanner *et al.*, 2002). Because confounding and additional alternative explanations cannot be ruled out to account for these findings, these results merely suggest that an environmental component or set of components is responsible for the association.

Two primary biologic mechanisms for the smoking-PD risk association have been proposed: (1) that smoking decreases the activity of monoamine oxidase (MAO), a type of enzyme that catalyses the oxidation of monoamines; and (2) that nicotine provides direct neuroprotection for the development of PD. Smoking reduces the activity of both types of MAO (MAO-A and MAO-B) in human brains and blood platelets (Fowler *et al.*, 1996, 2000). MAO-A and MAO-B are found in different areas of the body (although both are found in neurons and astroglia) and each catalyses different reactions. MAO-B provides neuroprotection, at least in part, by activating the Parkinsonian-inducing neurotoxin 1-methyl-4-phenyl-1,2,3,6-tetrahydropyridine (MPTP) (Castagnoli and Murugesan, 2004; Tan *et al.*, 2003b). The MAO-B genotype may modify the association between smoking and PD. Gender-specific interactions between smoking and genetic polymorphisms of MAO B intron 13 (G or A allele), MAO A EcoRV (Yor N allele) and dopamine D2 receptor (DRD2) Taq1B (B1 or B2 allele) were examined in a case-control study. Risk of PD for ever smokers versus never smokers was 73% lower for men of genotype G, and was 26% higher for men of genotype A, and a statistical test confirmed these observations (Kelada *et al.*, 2002). In contrast, for women, PD risk was 38% lower for ever-smokers versus never-smokers for women of genotype GG/GA and was 36% lower for women of genotype AA, and a statistical test did not confirm this result among women (Kelada *et al.*, 2002). These results support the plausibility of smoking as a true biologically protective factor for PD, and suggest that there is an effect of MAO-B genotype on the association between smoking and PD among men but not among women.

As for the second proposed mechanism, two components in cigarette smoke (nicotine and hydroquinone) inhibit alpha-synuclein fibril, a small presynaptic protein abundantly distributed in the brain. The aggregated form of alpha-synuclein is a pathological hallmark of PD. Both nicotine and hydroquinone act in a concentration-dependent manner, with nicotine being the more effective inhibitor (Hong *et al.*, 2009). This inhibition of presynaptic protein by nicotine corresponds to a clear biological mechanism for protection against PD. The neuroprotective capacity of nicotine and other components of cigarette smoke should be considered in future studies. Given the studies conducted to date, results from cohort studies and inhibition of presynaptic protein by nicotine provide the best evidence that the biologic theory is the most plausible explanation for the smoking–PD risk association.

As presented in the above section, protection against PD by tobacco smoking is backed by strong epidemiological evidence. The idea that a habit known to be detrimental to human health could actually prevent the development of a neurological disease is initially hard to accept. Yet several biological mechanisms have been proposed to account for this association, including a role for MAO activity, and the direct inhibition of presynaptic protein by nicotine. Further studies of the genetic basis of MAO activation, as well as neuro-modulation by tobacco smoke components, could be key to the early diagnosis and treatment of PD.

Future challenges and questions

Can the paradoxes described above provide clues for the future prevention or treatment of these neurological diseases? For example, does the reduced risk of brain tumours among people with allergies reflect a role of the immune system in brain tumour prevention? Do the studies upon which they are based contain enough scientific information to lead us to an understanding of the possible molecular interrelationships among these disparate conditions? That is, do allergies actually reduce brain tumour risk, or does this merely appear to be the case because the tumours themselves suppress allergic responses? Additional research at the biological, molecular and epidemiologic level is needed to answer these questions, and to determine the validity of the other paradoxes briefly described in the introduction to this chapter.

References

Akdis, C. A., Joss, A., Akdis, M., & Blaser, K. (2001). Mechanism of IL-10-induced T cell inactivation in allergic inflammation and normal response to allergens. *International Archives of Allergy and Immunology*, **124**: 180–2.

Allam, M. F., Campbell, M. J., Del Castillo, A. S., & Fernandez-Crehuet Navajas, R. (2004b). Parkinson's disease protects against smoking? *Behavioural Neurology*, **15**: 65–71.

Allam, M. F., Campbell, M. J., Hofman, A., Del Castillo, A. S., & Fernandez-Crehuet Navajas, R. (2004a). Smoking and Parkinson's disease: systematic review of prospective studies. *Movement Disorders: Official Journal Of The Movement Disorder Society*, **19**: 614–21.

Baek, K., Zaslavsky, A., Lynch, R. C., *et al.* (2009). Down's syndrome suppression of tumor growth and the role of calcineurin inhibitor DSCR1. *Nature*, **459**: 1126–30.

Bahmanyar, S, Montgomery, S. M., Hillert, J., Ekbom, A., & Olsson, T. (2009). Cancer risk among patients with multiple sclerosis and their parents *Neurology*, **72**: 1170–7.

Barak, Y., Achiron, A., Mandel, A., Mirecki, I., & Aizenberg, D. (2005). Reduced cancer incidence among patients with schizophrenia. *Cancer*, **104**: 2817–21.

Barna, B. P., Estes, M. L., Pettay, J., Iwasaki, K., Zhou, P., & Barnett, G. H. (1995). Human astrocyte growth regulation: interleukin-4 sensitivity and receptor expression. *Journal of Neuroimmunology*, **60**: 75–81.

Benedetti, M. D., Bower, J. H., Maraganore, D. M., *et al.* (2000). Smoking, alcohol, and coffee consumption preceding Parkinson's disease: a case-control study. *Neurology*, **55**: 1350–8.

Burnet, N., Jeffries, S., Benson, R., Hunt, D., & Treasure, F. (2005). Years of life lost (YLL) from cancer is an important measure of population burden – and should be considered when allocating research funds. *British Journal of Cancer*, **92**: 241–5.

Castagnoli, K., & Murugesan, T. (2004). Tobacco leaf, smoke and smoking, MAO inhibitors, Parkinson's disease and neuroprotection; are there links? *Neurotoxicology*, **25**: 279–91.

Checkoway, H., Powers, K., Smith-Weller, T., Franklin, G. M., Longstreth, W. T., Jr., & Swanson, P. D. (2002). Parkinson's disease risks associated with cigarette smoking, alcohol consumption, and caffeine intake. *American Journal of Epidemiology*, **155**: 732–8.

Debanne, S. M., Bielefeld, R. A., Cheruvu, V. K., Fritsch, T., & Rowland, D. Y. (2007). Alzheimer's disease and smoking: bias in cohort studies. *Journal of Alzheimer's Disease*, **11**: 313–21.

Deleu, D. (2001). Smoking, alcohol, and coffee consumption preceding Parkinson's disease. *Neurology*, **56**: 984–5.

Dinarello, C. A. (2003). Setting the cytokine trap for autoimmunity. *Nature Medicine*, **9**: 20–2.

Dong, J. Q., Zhang, Z. X., & Zhang, K. L. (2003). Parkinson's disease and smoking: an integral part of PD's etiological study. *Biomedical and Environmental Sciences*, **16**: 173–9.

Dunn, G. P., Bruce, A. T., Ikeda, H., Old, L. J., & Schreiber, R. D. (2002). Cancer immunoediting: from immunosurveillance to tumor escape. *Nature Immunology*, 3: 991–8.

Evans, A. H., Lawrence, A. D., Potts, J., *et al.* (2006). Relationship between impulsive sensation seeking traits, smoking, alcohol and caffeine intake, and Parkinson's disease. *Journal of Neurology, Neurosurgery, and Psychiatry*, 77: 317–21.

Eysenck, H. J. (1991). Were we really wrong? *American Journal of Epidemiology*, 133: 429–33.

Eysenck, H. J. (1995). Does smoking really kill anybody? *Psychological Reports*, 77: 1243–6.

Fonarow, G. C., Abraham, W. T., Albert, N. M., *et al.* (2008). A smoker's paradox in patients hospitalized for heart failure: findings from OPTIMIZE-HF. *European Heart Journal*, 29: 1983–91.

Fowler, J. S., Volkow, N. D., Wang, G. J., *et al.* (1996). Inhibition of monoamine oxidase B in the brains of smokers. *Nature*, 379: 733–6.

Fowler, J. S., Wang, G., Volkow, N. D., *et al.* (2000). Maintenance of brain monoamine oxidase B inhibition in smokers after overnight cigarette abstinence. *American Journal of Psychiatry*, 157: 1864–6.

Fox, B. H., & Howell, M. A. (1974). Cancer risk among psychiatric patients: a hypothesis. *International Journal of Epidemiology*, 3: 207–08.

Fratiglioni, L., & Wang, H. X. (2000). Smoking and Parkinson's and Alzheimer's disease: review of the epidemiological studies. *Behavioural Brain Research*, 113: 117–20.

Fulcher, T., Griffin, M., Crowley, S., Firth, R., Acheson, R., & O'Meara, N. (1998). Diabetic retinopathy in Down's syndrome. *British Journal of Ophthalmology*, 82: 407–09.

Galanaud, J. P., Elbaz, A., Clavel, J., *et al.* (2005). Cigarette smoking and Parkinson's disease: a case-control study in a population characterized by a high prevalence of pesticide exposure. *Movement Disorders: Official Journal of the Movement Disorder Society*, 20: 181–9.

Gomez, G. G., & Kruse, C. A. (2006). Mechanisms of malignant glioma immune resistance and sources of immunosuppression. *Gene Therapy and Molecular Biology*, 10: 133–46.

Hancock, D. B., Martin, E. R., & Stajich, J. M., (2007). Smoking, caffeine, and nonsteroidal anti-inflammatory drugs in families with Parkinson disease. *Archives of Neurology*, 64: 576–80.

Hasle, H., Clemmensen, I. H., & Mikkelsen, M. (2000). Risks of leukaemia and solid tumors in individuals with Down's syndrome. *Lancet*, 355: 165–9.

Hausenloy, D. J., Mwamure, P. K., Venugopal, V., *et al.* (2007). Effect of remote ischaemic preconditioning on myocardial injury in patients undergoing coronary artery bypass graft surgery: a randomised controlled trial. *Lancet*, 370: 575–9.

Helzner, E. P., Luchsinger, J. A., Scarmeas, N., *et al.* (2009). Contribution of vascular risk factors to the progression in Alzheimer disease. *Archives of Neurology*, 66: 343–8.

Hernan, M. A., Takkouche, B., Caamao-Isorna, F., & Gestal-Otero, J. J. (2002). A meta-analysis of coffee drinking, cigarette smoking, and the risk of Parkinson's disease. *Annals of Neurology*, 52: 276–84.

Hernan, M. A., Zhang, S. M., Rueda-deCastro, A. M., Colditz, G. A., Speizer, F. E., & Ascherio, A. (2001). Cigarette smoking and the incidence of Parkinson's disease in two prospective studies. *Annals of Neurology*, 50: 780–6.

Hoffman, S., Propp, J. M., & McCarthy, B. J. (2005). Temporal trends in incidence of primary brain tumors in the United States, 1985–1999. *Neuro-Oncology [serial online]*, Doc. 05–032.

Hong, D. P., Fink, A. L., & Uversky, V. N. (2009). Smoking and Parkinson's disease: does nicotine affect alpha-synuclein fibrillation? *Biochimica et Biophysica Acta*, 1794: 282–90.

James, W. H. (2003). Coffee drinking, cigarette smoking, and Parkinson's disease. *Annals of Neurology*, 53: reply 546.

Jordan, J. T., Sun, W., Hussain, S. F., DeAngulo, G., Prabhu, S. S., & Heimberger, A. B. (2008). Preferential migration of regulatory T cells mediated by glioma-secreted chemokines can be blocked with chemotherapy. *Cancer, Immunology and Immunotherapy*, 57: 123–31.

Kandinov, B., Giladi, N., & Korczyn, A. D. (2007). The effect of cigarette smoking, tea, and coffee consumption on the progression of Parkinson's disease. *Parkinsonism & Related Disorders*, 13: 243–5.

Kandinov, B., Giladi, N., & Korczyn, A. D. (2009). Smoking and tea consumption delay onset of Parkinson's disease. *Parkinsonism & Related Disorders*, 15: 41–6.

Katayama, T., Iwasaki, Y., Sakoda, N., & Yoshioka, M. (2008). The etiology of 'smoker's paradox' in acute myocardial infarction with special emphasis on the association with inflammation. *International Heart Journal*, 49: 13–24.

Kelada, S. N., Costa-Mallen, P., Costa, L. G., et al. (2002). Gender difference in the interaction of smoking and monoamine oxidase B intron 13 genotype in Parkinson's disease. *Neurotoxicology*, 23: 515–9.

Kievit, P. C., Brouwer, M. A., Veen, G., Aengevaeren, W. R., & Verheugt, F. W. (2009). The smoker's paradox after successful fibrinolysis: reduced risk of reocclusion but no improved long-term cardiac outcome. *Journal of Thrombosis and Thrombolysis*, 27: 385–93.

Krone, B., Oeffner, F., & Grange, J. M. (2009). Is the risk of multiple sclerosis related to the biography of the immune system? *Journal of Neurology*, 256: 1052–60.

Linos, E., Raine, T., Alonso, A., & Michaud, D. (2007). Atopy and risk of brain tumors: a meta-analysis. *Journal of the National Cancer Institute*, 99: 1544–50.

Liu, H., Jacobs, B. S., Liu, J., et al. (2000b). Interleukin-13 sensitivity and receptor phenotypes of human glial cell lines: non-neoplastic glia and low-grade astrocytoma differ from malignant glioma. *Cancer, Immunology and Immunotherapy*, 49: 19–24.

Liu, H., Prayson, R. A., Estes, M. L., et al. (2000a). In vivo expression of the interleukin 4 receptor alpha by astrocytes in epilepsy cerebral cortex. *Cytokine*, 12: 1656–61.

Louis, D. N. (1997). A molecular genetic model of astrocytoma histopathology. *Brain Pathology*, 7: 755–64.

Marder, K., & Logroscino, G. (2002). The ever-stimulating association of smoking and coffee and Parkinson's disease. *Annals of Neurology*, 52: 261–2.

McGeer, P., Schultzer, M., & McGerr, E. G. (1996). Arthritis and anti-inflammatory agents as possible protective factors for Alzheimer's disease: a review of 17 epidemiologic studies. *Neurology*, 47: 425–32.

Melbye, M., Smedby, K. E., Lehtinen, T., et al. (2007). Atopy and risk of non-Hodgkin lymphoma. *Journal of the National Cancer Institute*, 99: 158–66.

Mielke, M. M., Rosenberg, P. B., Tschanz, J., et al. (2007). Vascular factors predict rate of progression in Alzheimer disease. *Neurology*, 69: 1850–8.

Mitchell, S., Elkind, V., Ramakrishnan, P., et al. (2009). Infectious burden and risk of stroke: the Northern Manhattan Study. *Archives of Neurology*, 67: doi:10.1001/achneurol.2009.271.

Moncayo, J., de Freitas, G. R., Bogousslavsky, J., Altieri, M., & van Melle, G. (2000). Do transient ischemic attacks have a neuroprotective effect? *Neurology*, 54: 2089–94.

Morozova, N., O'Reilly, E. J., & Ascherio, A. (2008). Variations in gender ratios support the connection between smoking and Parkinson's disease. *Movement Disorders: Official Journal of the Movement Disorder Society*, 23: 1414–9.

Murdoch, J. C., Rodger, J. C., Rao, S. S., Fletcher, C. D., & Dunnigan, M. G. (1977). Down's Syndrome: an atheroma-free model? *British Medical Journal*, 2: 226–8.

Nielsen, N. M., Rostgaard, K., Rasmussen, S., et al. (2006). Cancer risk among patients with multiple sclerosis: a population-based register study. *International Journal of Cancer*, 118: 979–84.

Norhashemi, F. (1999). Low Alzheimer's disease prevalence in rheumatoid arthritis patients is unrelated to ApoE genotype. *European Journal of Internal Medicine*, 10: 97–100.

O'Duffy, A. E., Bordelon, Y. M., & McLaughlin, B. (2007). Killer proteases and little strokes – how the things that do not kill you make you stronger. *Journal of Cerebral Blood Flow and Metabolism*, 27: 665–8.

Park, J. K., Lee, H. J., Kim, J. W., *et al.* (2004). Differences in p53 gene polymorphisms between Korean schizophrenia and lung cancer patients. *Schizophrenia Research*, 67: 71–4.

Patja, K., Pukkala, E., Sund, R., Iivanainen, M., & Kaski, M. (2006). Cancer incidence of persons with Down syndrome in Finland: a population-based study. *International Journal of Cancer*, 118: 1769–72.

Powers, K. M., Kay, D. M., Factor, S. A., *et al.* (2008). Combined effects of smoking, coffee, and NSAIDs on Parkinson's disease risk. *Movement Disorders: Official Journal of the Movement Disorder Society*, 23: 88–95.

Regan, C., Katona, C., Walker, Z., Hooper, J., Donovan, J., & Livingston, G. (2006). Relationship of vascular risk to the progression of Alzheimer disease. *Neurology*, 67: 1357–62.

Ritz, B., Ascherio, A., Checkoway, H., *et al.* (2007). Pooled analysis of tobacco use and risk of Parkinson disease. *Archives of Neurology*, 64: 990–7.

Sanz, C., Andrieu, S., Sinclair, A., Hanaire, H., & Vellas, B. (2009). Diabetes is associated with a slower rate of cognitive decline in Alzheimer disease. *Neurology*, 73: 1359–66.

Satge, D., Sasco, A. J, Carlsen, N. L., *et al.* (1998). A lack of neuroblastoma in Down syndrome: a study from 11European countries. *Cancer Research*, 58: 448–52.

Scheurer, M. E., El-Zein, R., Thompson, P. A., *et al.* (2008). Long-term anti-inflammatory and antihistamine medication use and adult glioma risk. *Cancer Epidemiology: Biomarkers and Prevention*, 17: 1277–81.

Schwartzbaum, J., Ahlbom, A., Malmer, B., *et al.* (2005). Polymorphisms associated with asthma are inversely related to glioblastoma multiforme. *Cancer Research*, 65: 6459–65.

Schwartzbaum, J., Xiao, Y., Liu, Y., *et al.* (2010b) Inherited variation in immune genes and pathways and glioblastoma risk. *Carcinogenesis*. Epub 2010b Aug 1.

Schwartzbaum, J. A., Ahlbom, A., Lonn, S., *et al.* (2007). An international case-control study

of glutathione transferase and functionally related polymorphisms and risk of primary adult brain tumors. *Cancer Epidemiology: Biomarkers and Prevention*, 16: 559–65.

Schwartzbaum, J. A., Huang, K., Lawler, S., Ding, B., Yu, J., & Chiocca, E. A. (2010a). Allergy and inflammatory transcriptome is predominantly negatively correlated with CD133 expression in glioblastoma. *Neuro-Oncology*, 12: 320–7.

Scott, W. K., Zhang, F., Stajich, J. M., Scott, B. L., Stacy, M. A., & Vance, J. M. (2005). Family-based case-control study of cigarette smoking and Parkinson disease. *Neurology*, 64: 442–7.

Soderberg, K. C., Jonsson, F., Winqvist, O., Hagmar, L., & Feychting, M. (2006). Autoimmune diseases, asthma and risk of haematological malignancies: a nationwide case-control study in Sweden. *European Journal of Cancer*, 42: 3028–33.

Surgeon General's Report. (2004). The health consequences of smoking: a report of the Surgeon General. Department of Health and Human Services, Centers for Disease Control and Prevention, National Center for Chronic Disease Prevention and Health Promotion, Office on Smoking and Health, Washington, DC. For sale by the Supt. of Docs., U.S. G.P.O.

Tan, E. K., Chai, A., Lum, S. Y., *et al.* (2003b). Monoamine oxidase B polymorphism, cigarette smoking and risk of Parkinson's disease: a study in an Asian population. *American Journal of Medical Genetics. Part B, Neuropsychiatric Genetics: The Official Publication of the International Society of Psychiatric Genetics*, 120B: 58–62.

Tan, E. K., Tan, C., Fook-Chong, S. M., *et al.* (2003a). Dose-dependent protective effect of coffee, tea, and smoking in Parkinson's disease: a study in ethnic Chinese. *Journal of the Neurological Sciences*, 216: 163–7.

Tanner, C. M., Goldman, S. M., Aston, D. A., *et al.* (2002). Smoking and Parkinson's disease in twins. *Neurology*, 58: 581–8.

Terabe, M., Khanna, C., Bose, S., Melchionda, F., Mendoza, A., Mackall, C. L., *et al.* (2006). CD1d-restricted natural killer T cells can down-regulate tumor immunosurveillance independent of interleukin-4 receptor-signal transducer and activator of transcription 6 or transforming growth factor-beta. *Cancer Research*, **66**: 3869–75.

Thacker, E. L., O'Reilly, E. J., Weisskopf, M. G., *et al.* (2007). Temporal relationship between cigarette smoking and risk of Parkinson disease. *Neurology* **68**: 764–8.

Umetsu, D. T., & DeKruyff, R. H. (2006). The regulation of allergy and asthma. *Immunology Review*, **212**: 238–55.

Wegener, S., Gottschalk, B., Jovanovic, V., *et al.* (2004). Transient ischemic attacks before ischemic stroke: preconditioning the human brain? A multicenter magnetic resonance imaging study. *Stroke*, **35**: 616–21.

Weisskopf, M. G., Grodstein, F., & Ascherio, A. (2007). Smoking and cognitive function in Parkinson's disease. *Movement Disorders: Official Journal of the Movement Disorder Society*, **22**: 660–5.

Wiemels, J. L., Wiencke, J. K., Patoka, J., *et al.* (2004). Reduced immunoglobulin E and allergy among adults with glioma compared with controls. *Cancer Research*, **64**: 8468–73.

Wiemels, J. L., Wilson, D., Patil, C., *et al.* (2009). IgE, allergy, and risk of glioma: update from the San Francisco Bay Area Adult Glioma Study in the Temozolomide era. *International Journal of Cancer*, **125**: 680–7.

Wigertz, A. (2008). Factors associated with brain tumor risk: with focus on female sex hormones and allergic conditions.

Dissertation, Karolinska Institutet, Stockholm, Sweden.

Wrensch, M., Lee, M., Miike, R., *et al.* (1997). Familial and personal medical history of cancer and nervous system conditions among adults with glioma and controls. *American Journal of Epidemiology*, **145**: 581–93.

Wrensch, M., Weinberg, A., Wiencke, J., Miike, R., Barger, G., & Kelsey, K. (2001). Prevalence of antibodies to four herpesviruses among adults with glioma and controls. *American Journal of Epidemiology*, **154**: 161–5.

Wrensch, M., Weinberg, A., Wiencke, J., *et al.* (2005). History of chickenpox and shingles and prevalence of antibodies to varicella-zoster virus and three other herpesviruses among adults with glioma and controls. *American Journal of Epidemiology*, **161**: 929–38.

Wrensch, M., Wiencke, J. K., Wiemels, J., *et al.* (2006). Serum IgE, tumor epidermal growth factor receptor expression, and inherited polymorphisms associated with glioma survival. *Cancer Research*, **66**: 4531–41.

Yang, Q., Rasmussen, S. A., & Friedman, J. M. (2002). Mortality associated with Down's syndrome in the USA from 1983 to 1997: a population-based study. *Lancet*, **359**: 1019–25.

Yang, Y., Xiao, Z., Chen, W., *et al.* (2004). Tumor suppressor gene TP53 is genetically associated with schizophrenia in the Chinese population. *Neuroscience Letters*, **369**: 126–31.

Chapter 15

The paradox of autism: why does disability sometimes give rise to talent?

Simon Baron-Cohen, Emma Ashwin, Chris Ashwin,
Teresa Tavassoli and Bhismadev Chakrabarti

Summary

We explore why people with autism spectrum conditions (ASC) not only show deficits but also areas of intact or even superior skill. The deficits are primarily social; the areas of intact or superior skill involve attention to detail and systemizing. Systemizing is the drive to analyse or build a system. We review the evidence related to systemizing in ASC and discuss its association with sensory hypersensitivity. We close by considering the evolution and adaptive features of systemizing and how – taken to an extreme – this can also give rise to disability.

Introduction

Paradoxes emanating from human brain functioning have long been noted – patients with amnesia who cannot *explicitly* recall information but who nevertheless reveal *implicitly* that they do recall information; patients with reported blindness who nevertheless demonstrate some 'unconscious' vision ('blindsight'); Brazilian street children who fail academic mathematics tests but who are lightening quick in performing calculations in the market place; and individuals who experience perceptions in one sensory modality when a different sensory modality is stimulated ('synaesthesia'). In some sense, paradoxes in brain functioning should perhaps not be so surprising given the number of different 'modules' and pathways in the brain, such that some functions may be impaired whilst others may simultaneously be either intact or even superior.

Whilst we are familiar with syndromes where most, if not all, cognitive functions are impaired (such as in certain forms of learning disability or dementia), this chapter focuses on what can be learnt from syndromes displaying uneven cognitive profiles. At the most general level, such syndromes may constitute evidence for neurological 'dissociations' and may reveal alternative strategies the brain can employ to solve a task. In this chapter, we focus on autism spectrum conditions (ASC) in which individuals characteristically show a mix of 'deficits' alongside 'intact' cognitive skills, and where in some individuals there are even 'islets of ability' that constitute talent – so-called 'savantism'.

Savantism describes a cognitive profile where an individual shows an area of skill that is significantly superior relative to their other skills. Savantism stands out most clearly in individuals who have a general developmental delay ('learning difficulties'), where IQ is in the below-average range, and this nicely sums up the idea of the 'paradoxical brain', since in such cases it is clear that IQ cannot explain the individual's level of functioning in all

The Paradoxical Brain, ed. Narinder Kapur. Published by Cambridge University Press. © Cambridge University Press 2011.

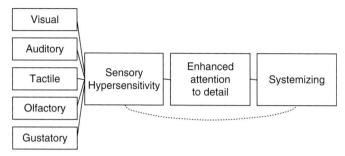

Figure 15.1 A proposed heuristic continuum suggesting how a multimodal, irregular profile of sensory hypersensitivity could lead to enhanced attention to detail. This, in turn, could lead to a drive for categorizing the external world on the basis of highly exact, perceptual details and a systemizing bias in cognition. An alternative model (dotted line) suggests that hyper-systemizing is also linked to sensory hypersensitivity, without necessarily being mediated through enhanced attention to detail (all lines represent a bidirectional flow). Current research in our lab is testing these two models. At top of first of four drawings (Figure 2) Taken from Myers *et al.* (2004).

areas. Savantism is found more commonly in ASC than in any other neurological group, and the majority of those with savantism have an ASC (Hermelin, 2002). ASC entails significant social and communication disability, alongside narrow and repetitive interests (APA, 1994). This 'co-morbidity' shows us that these two profiles are associated well above chance. This forces us to ask: why the link between talent and autism? And how is this paradox (a disability at times associated with talent) to be explained (cf. Treffert, 2010)? In this chapter we argue that whilst savantism, defined as prodigious talent, is only seen in a subgroup of people with ASC (e.g. Baron-Cohen *et al.*, 2007), a universal feature of the autistic brain is *excellent attention to detail* (Shah and Frith, 1993; Jolliffe and Baron-Cohen, 1997; O'Riordan, *et al.*, 2001). Further, we argue that excellent attention to detail exists in ASC because of evolutionary forces positively selecting brains for *strong systemizing*, a highly adaptive human ability (Baron-Cohen, 2008).

Strong systemizing requires excellent attention to detail, and in our view the latter is in the service of the former. Attention occurs at an early level of cognition, whilst systemizing is a fairly high-level aspect of cognition. Next, we argue that one can trace excellent attention to detail to its basis in *sensory hypersensitivity* in ASC (see Figure 15.1). Finally, we review our research programme exploring this in different sensory modalities. But first, what is systemizing?

Systemizing

Talent in autism comes in many forms, but a common characteristic is that the individual becomes an expert in *recognizing repeating patterns* in stimuli. We call this systemizing, defined as the drive to analyse or construct systems. These might be any kind of system. What defines a system is that it follows *rules*, and when we systemize we are trying to identify the rules that govern the system, in order to predict how that system will behave (Baron-Cohen, 2006). These are some of the major kinds of system:

- *collectible* systems (e.g. distinguishing between types of stones or wood),
- *mechanical* systems (e.g. a video-recorder or a window lock),
- *numerical* systems (e.g. a train timetable or a calendar),
- *abstract* systems (e.g. the syntax of a language, or musical notation),
- *natural* systems (e.g. the weather patterns, or tidal wave patterns),

- *social* systems (e.g. a management hierarchy, or a dance routine with a dance partner),
- *motoric* systems (e.g. throwing a Frisbee or bouncing on a trampoline).

In all these cases, you systemize by noting regularities (or structure) and rules. The rules tend to be derived by noting if p and q are *associated* in a systematic way. The general formulation of what happens during systemizing is one looks for laws of the form *'if p, then q'*. If we multiply 3 by itself, then we get 9. If we turn the switch to the down position, then the light comes on. When we think about the kinds of domains in which savants typically excel, it is those domains that can be readily systemized.

Examples might be from numbers (e.g. spotting if a number is a prime number), calendrical calculation (e.g. telling which day of a the week a given date will fall), drawing (e.g. analysing space into geometric shapes and the laws of perspective; and perfecting an artistic technique), music (e.g. analysing the sequence of notes in a melody, or the lawful regularities or structure in a piece), memory (e.g. recalling long sequences of digits or lists of information), or even learning foreign languages (e.g. learning vocabulary, or the laws of grammar). In each of these domains, there is the opportunity to repeat behaviour in order to check if one gets the very same outcome every time. Multiplying 3 by itself *always* delivers 9, the key change in this specific musical piece *always* occurs in the 13th bar, throwing the ball at this particular angle and with this particular force *always* results in it landing in the hoop.

Systemizing the Rubik's Cube

Let's take a real, cardinal example of savantism: a non-conversational child with autism who can solve the Rubik's Cube 'problem' in 1 minute and 7 seconds. This is a nice example because it illustrates several things. First, that the child's non-verbal ability with the Rubik's Cube is at a much higher level than either his communication or social skills, or indeed what one would expect of his age. Second, it prompts us to ask: what are the processes involved in solving the Rubik's Cube? At a minimum, it involves analysing or memorizing the sequence of moves to produce the correct outcome. It is a series of 'if p, then q' steps. This child with autism appeared to have 'discovered' the layer-by-layer method to solve the $3 \times 3 \times 3$ Rubik's Cube problem, which takes a minimum of 22 moves. (Note he was not as fast as the current 2008 World Champion Erik Akkersdijk who in the Czech Open championship solved the Rubik's Cube in 7.08 seconds!)

Systemizing in autism spectrum conditions

What is the evidence for intact or even unusually strong systemizing in ASC? First, such children perform above the level that one would expect on a physics test (Baron-Cohen *et al.*, 2001). Children with Asperger Syndrome (AS) as young as 8–11 years scored higher than a comparison group who were older (typical teenagers). Second, using the Systemizing Quotient (SQ), people with high functioning autism or AS score higher on the SQ compared to general population controls (Baron-Cohen *et al.*, 2003). Third, children with classic autism perform better than controls on the picture sequencing test where the stories can be sequenced using physical–causal concepts (Baron-Cohen *et al.*, 1986). They also score above average on a test of how to figure out how a Polaroid camera works, even though they have difficulties figuring out people's thoughts and feelings (Baron-Cohen *et al.*, 1985; Perner *et al.*, 1989). The Polaroid camera test was used as a mechanical equivalent to the False Belief test, since in the former all one has to do is infer what will be represented in a photograph given the 'line of sight' between the camera and an object, whereas in the latter one has to infer what belief (i.e. mental representation) a person will hold given what they saw and therefore know about. (A Polaroid camera was used because then the experimenter could state their prediction about the content of the photo, and have this verified within minutes.)

Strong systemizing is a way of explaining the non-social features of autism: the narrow interests, repetitive behaviour and resistance to change/need for sameness. This is because when you systemize, it is best to keep everything constant, and to only vary one thing at a time. That way, you can see what might be causing what, and with repetition you can verify that you get the very same pattern or sequence ('if p, then q') every time, rendering the world predictable. One issue is whether hyper-systemizing only applies to the *high*-functioning individuals with ASC. Whilst their obsessions (with computers or maths, for example) could be seen in terms of strong systemizing (Baron-Cohen *et al.*, 1999), when we think of a child with *low*-functioning autism, many of the classic behaviours can be seen as a reflection of their strong systemizing, if looked at through this theoretical framework. Some examples are listed in Box 1.

Systemizing and Weak Central Coherence

Like the Weak Central Coherence (WCC) theory (Frith, 1989), the hyper-systemizing theory is about a different cognitive style (Happe, 1996). Like that theory, it also posits *excellent attention to detail* (in perception and memory), since when you systemize you have to pay attention to the tiny details. This is because each tiny detail in a system might have a functional role leading to new information of the form 'if p, then q'. Excellent attention to detail in autism has been repeatedly demonstrated (Shah and Frith, 1983, 1993; Jolliffe and Baron-Cohen, 2001; O'Riordan *et al.*, 2001; Mottron *et al.*, 2003; Baldassi *et al.*, 2009; Joseph *et al.*, 2009).

One difference between these two theories is that the WCC theory sees people with ASC as drawn to detailed information (sometimes called a local processing bias) either for *negative* reasons (an inability to integrate was postulated in the original version of this theory), or because of stronger local processing (in the later version of this theory). In contrast, the hyper-systemizing theory sees this same quality (excellent attention to detail) as being highly purposeful; it exists in order to understand a system. Attention to detail is occurring for *positive* reasons: in the service of achieving an ultimate understanding of a system, however small and specific that system might be.

We can return to the Rubik's Cube problem to see the difference between these two theories more clearly. At one level, the Rubik's Cube is a 3D Block Design Test but where the cubes are all connected. Recall that the Block Design Test is the subtest on Weschler IQ tests on which people with autism perform at their best (Shah and Frith, 1993; Happe, 1996). The Rubik's Cube contains 21 moveable connected cubes (since the 5 central cubes do not move) with different coloured faces in the $3 \times 3 \times 3$ version. According to WCC theory, the reason why people with autism show superior perform- ance on the Block Design Test is that their good local processing enables them to 'see' each individual cube even if the design to be copied is not 'pre-segmented' (Shah and Frith, 1983). It is clear how good local processing would lead to faster 'analysis' of the whole (design) into constituent parts (the individual cubes), but to solve the Rubik's

Box 1 Systemizing in classic autism and/or Asperger Syndrome

Type of systemizing	Classic autism	Asperger Syndrome
Sensory systemizing	Tapping surfaces, or letting sand run through one's fingers	Insisting on the same foods each day
Motoric systemizing	Spinning round and round, or rocking back and forth	Learning knitting patterns or a tennis technique
Collectible systemizing	Collecting leaves or football stickers	Making lists and catalogues
Numerical systemizing	Obsessions with calendars or train timetables	Solving maths problems
Motion systemizing	Watching washing machines spin round and round	Analysing exactly when a specific event occurs in a repeating cycle
Spatial systemizing	Obsessions with routes	Developing drawing techniques
Environmental systemizing	Insisting on toy bricks being lined up in an invariant order	Insisting that nothing is moved from its usual position in the room
Social systemizing	Saying the first half of a phrase or sentence and waiting for the other person to complete it	Insisting on playing the same game whenever a child comes to play
Natural systemizing	Asking over and over again what the weather will be today	Learning the Latin names of every plant and their optimal growing conditions
Mechanical systemizing	Learning to operate the VCR	Fixing bicycles or taking apart gadgets and reassembling them
Vocal/ auditory/verbal systemizing	Echoing sounds	Collecting words and word meanings
Systemizing action sequences	Watching the same video over and over again	Analysing dance techniques

Cube (or the Block Design problem), more than just good local processing is needed. A strength in 'if p, then q' type reasoning is also required. On the classic Block Design subtest you need to *mentally or manually rotate* the cube to produce the relevant output. That is, you need to *perform an operation* on the input to produce the relevant output. The same is true (but with more cubes and therefore more complexity) in the Rubik's Cube problem: 'If the red cube with the green side is positioned on the top layer on the right side and I rotate the top layer anticlockwise by 90°, then this will complete the top layer as all one colour'.

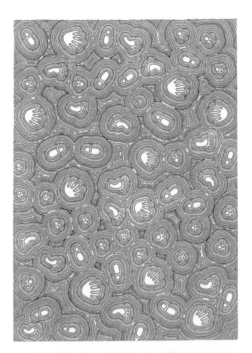

Figure 15.2 Symbolic impressions. MK-79.

Figure 15.3 Peter's Hand. MK-VII.

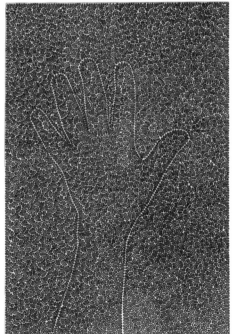

In earlier formulations of systemizing, the key cognitive process was held to be in terms of [input–operation–output] processing (Baron-Cohen, 2002, 2006). In mathematics, if the input = 3, and the operation = cubing, then the output = 27. In the Rubik's Cube notional example above, the input = [the red cube with the green side is positioned on the top

279

Figure 15.4 Untitled [Author's Note – 'A development of the well-known smiley face symbol/design'.]

Figure 15.5 Mazewandering.

layer on the right side], the operation = [rotate the top layer anticlockwise by 90°], and the output = [complete the top layer as all one colour]. Notice that WCC makes no mention of the key part of this, that is *noting the consequences of an operation*. Simply seeing the parts in greater detail would not by itself lead to *understanding the operations* (the moves) needed to solve the Rubik's Cube.

Another difference between the WCC theory and the hyper-systemizing theory is that the latter (but not the former) predicts that, over time, the person may achieve an excellent understanding of a whole system, given the opportunity to observe and control all the variables (all the 'if p, then q' rules) in that system. WCC would predict that, even given all the time in the world, the individual will be forever lost in the detail. The existence of talented mathematicians with AS like Richard Borcherds is proof that such individuals can *integrate* the details into a true understanding of the system (Baron-Cohen, 2003). In the rule 'if p, then q', the terms 'if' and 'then' are how the details become integrated, albeit one small step at a time. The idea at the neurological level that ASC involves an abundance of local short-range connectivity (Belmonte *et al.*, 2004) may explain this cognitive style of identifying one specific link between two details.

Hyper-systemizing: implications for education

Teachers, whether of children with autism or adults with AS, need to take into account that hyper-systemizing will affect not only how people with ASC learn, but also how they should be assessed. IQ test items, essays and exam questions designed for individuals who are 'neurotypical' may lead to the person with ASC scoring zero when their knowledge is actually greater, deeper and more extensive than that of most people. What can appear as a slow processing style may be because of the massively greater quantity of information that is being processed.

A man with AS reported recently: 'I see all information in terms of links. All information has a link to something and I pay attention to these links. If I am asked a question in an exam I have great difficulty in completing my answer within the allocated 45 minutes for that essay, because every fact I include has thousands of links to other facts, and I feel my answer would be incorrect if I didn't report all of the linked facts. The examiner thinks he or she has set a nice circumscribed question to answer, but for someone with autism or Asperger Syndrome, no topic is circumscribed. There is ever more detail with ever more interesting links between the details'.

When asked about the concept of apple, for example, he could not give a short summary answer such as 'an apple is a piece of fruit' (i.e. referring to the prototypical level 'apple' as linked to the superordinate level 'fruit'), but had to continue by also trying to link it to the 7500 different species of apple (the subordinate level concepts), listing many of each type and the differences in terms of the history of each species, how they are cultivated, what they taste and look like, etc. When asked about the concept of beetle, he could not just give a summary answer such as 'a beetle is an insect' but had to mention as many of the 350,000 species of beetle that he knew existed. If he was asked to be less long-winded, he could not do it, since all facts to him seemed important and it made him feel anxious to leave any out. If asked to just include the important facts and to exclude the unimportant facts, he could not decide which fell into the 'important' category.

This cognitive style is understandable in terms of the hyper-systemizing theory because a concept is a system. A concept is a way of using an 'if p, then q' rule to define what to include as members of a category (e.g. if it has scales and gills, then it is a fish). Furthermore, concepts exist within a classification system, which are rules for how categories are related to one another. So, the question 'what is a beetle?' is trivial for a neurotypical individual who simply answers in terms of a crude, imprecise and fuzzy category: 'it is an insect'. It may, however, require a very long, exhaustive answer from someone with autism: 'beetles are members of the category of animal (kingdom), arthropods (phylum), insects (class), pterygota (sub-class), neoptera (infra-class), endopterygota (super-order), coleoptera (order), and could be in one of 4 sub-orders (adephaga, archostemata, mycophaga and polyphaga), each of which has an infra-order, a super-family and a family'. Even the previous sentence would, for this man with AS, be a gross violation of the true answer to the question because so much important factual information has been left out. But for the hyper-systemizer, getting these details correct matters, because the concept – and the classification system linking concepts – is *a system for predicting* how this specific entity (this specific beetle) will behave or will differ from all other entities.

Hyper-systemizing theory vs. Executive Dysfunction theory

The Executive Dysfunction (ED) theory (Rumsey and Hamberger 1988; Ozonoff et al., 1991; Russell, 1997) is the other major theory that has attempted to explain the non-social features of ASC, and particularly the repetitive behaviour and narrow interests that characterize ASC. According to this theory, aspects of executive function (action control) involved in flexible switching of attention and planning are impaired, leading to perseveration. The ED theory, like the WCC theory, has difficulty in explaining instances of good understanding of a whole system, such as calendrical calculation, since within the well-defined system (calendar) attention can switch very flexibly. The ED theory also predicts perseveration (so-called 'obsessions'), but does not explain why in autism and AS these should centre on systems (Baron-Cohen and Wheelwright, 2004). Finally, the ED theory simply re-describes repetitive behaviour as an instance of executive dysfunction without seeing what might be positive about the behaviour.

So, when the low-functioning person with classic autism has shaken a piece of string thousands of times close to his eyes, whilst the ED theory sees this as perseveration arising from some neural dysfunction which would normally enable the individual to shift attention, the hyper-systemizing theory sees the same behaviour as a sign that the individual 'understands' the physics (i.e. recognizes the patterns) behind the movement of that piece of string. He may be able to make it move in exactly the same way every time. Or, to take another example, when he makes a long, rapid sequence of sounds, he may 'know' exactly that acoustic pattern, and get some pleasure from the confirmation that the sequence is the same every time. A mathematician might feel an ultimate sense of pleasure in the 'golden ratio' (that $(a + b)/a = a/b$ and that this *always* comes out as 1.61803399). Similarly, a child – even one with low-functioning autism – may produce the same outcome every time with their repetitive behaviour, and appear to derive some emotional pleasure at the predictability of the world. This may be what is clinically described as 'stimming' (Wing, 1997), where an individual's attention is wholly focused on their current actions or thoughts and they lapse into a trance-like state and may experience a surge of excitement that manifests as a sudden 'explosion' of movement. Autism was originally described as involving 'resistance to change' and 'need for sameness' (Kanner, 1943), and here we see that important clinical observation may be the hallmark of strong systemizing. Recent neuroimaging studies suggest that there might be aberrant processing of rewards in people with ASC (Schmitz et al., 2008; De Martino et al., 2008) and it will be important for future neuroimaging studies to test if the reward systems in the brain (e.g. the dopaminergic or cannabinoid systems) are active during such repetitive behaviour.

If we return to the Rubik's Cube example, an executive dysfunction would predict that an inability to 'plan' should make solving a Rubik's Cube impossible for a savant with autism. In contrast, as we saw earlier, the hyper-systemizing theory has no difficulty in explaining such talent.

Sensory hypersensitivity

Rather than assuming that the strong systemizing in ASC is ultimately reducible to excellent attention to detail, in this section we pursue the idea that the excellent attention to detail is itself reducible to sensory hypersensitivity. In 2001, Mottron and Burack postulated the 'enhanced perceptual functioning' (EPF) model of ASC, characterized by superior low-level perceptual processing (Mottron and Burack, 2001). To what extent is this a feature of basic sensory physiology?

Studies using questionnaires such as the Sensory Profile have revealed sensory abnormalities in over 90% of children with ASC (Leekam *et al.*, 2001; Kern *et al.*, 2006; Tomchek and Dunn, 2007). In *vision*, Bertone *et al.* found individuals with ASC are more accurate at detecting the orientation of first-order gratings (simple, luminance-defined) but less accurate at identifying second-order gratings (complex, texture-defined) (Bertone *et al.*, 2003). In the *auditory* modality, superior pitch processing has been found in ASC (Mottron *et al.*, 1999; Bonnel *et al.*, 2003; Heaton *et al.*, 2008). In a case study, Mottron *et al.* reported exceptional absolute judgement and production of pitch (Mottron *et al.*, 1999). Bonnel *et al.* found superior pitch discrimination and processing abilities in individuals with high-functioning autism (Bonnel *et al.*, 2003). O'Riordan and Passetti (2006) also reported superior auditory discrimination ability in children with ASC, and Jaevinen-Parsley *et al.* (2002) showed superior perceptual processing of speech in children with autism.

In the *tactile* modality, Blakemore *et al.* (2006) showed hypersensitivity to vibrotactile stimulation. In addition, the ASC group rated supra-threshold tactile stimulation as significantly more tickly and intense than did the control group. Tommerdahl *et al.* (2007) reported that participants with ASC outperformed controls in tactile acuity after short adaptation to a vibrotactile stimulus period of 0.5 s. (Note that this hypersensitivity is not always observed. On a tactile discrimination task, O'Riordan and Passetti (2006) found no differences in children with autism compared to controls.) Cascio *et al.* (2008) investigated tactile sensation and reported increased sensitivity to vibrations and thermal pain in ASC, while detection to light touch and warmth/cold were similar in both groups.

Only two previous studies have been reported investigating olfaction in ASC, and unlike the research into the other senses which consistently find hypersensitivity, both of these studies reported *deficits* in identifying odours despite intact odour detection (Bennetto and Kuschner, 2007; Suzuki *et al.*, 2003). Looking more closely at the two previous studies into olfaction in ASC, both required participants to explicitly identify the odour from a choice of responses, a methodology likely to involve both executive function and memory. For example, the study by Bennetto and Kuschner (2007) required participants to decide which of four possible responses an odour matched. A simpler task might provide a purer test of low-level olfactory discrimination in ASC.

An experiment from our lab examined vision in ASC in terms of basic sensory detection thresholds (acuity – Ashwin *et al.*, 2009; cf. Bach and Dakin, 2009). Ongoing studies from our lab are also testing sensory detection thresholds in other modalities (touch, audition and olfaction). Full details of these experiments are reported elsewhere (Ashwin *et al.*, 2008; Ashwin *et al.*, submitted; Tavassoli *et al.*, submitted). Results from these and other experiments demonstrated greater sensory perception in ASC across multiple modalities. In the context of the earlier discussion of hyper-systemizing and excellent attention to detail, we surmise that these sensory differences in functioning may be affecting information processing at an early stage (both in terms of sensation/cognition, and in terms of development) in ways that could both cause distress but also predispose to unusual talent. These results of hypersensitivity confirm previous findings, and mirror anecdotal reports of individuals with ASC (Grandin, 2000). For example, Temple Grandin writes that 'overly sensitive skin can be a big problem . . . Shampooing actually hurt my skin . . . To be lightly touched appeared to make my nervous system whimper, as if the nerve ends were curling up'. In terms of increased sensitivity to certain types of auditory stimuli (high frequencies), there are anecdotal reports that individuals with autism tend to avoid certain sounds. Grandin states 'I can shut out my hearing and withdraw from most noise, but certain frequencies cannot be shut out . . . High pitched, shrill noises are the worst'. Mottron et al. (1999) reported the case of a woman with autism who was hypersensitive to frequencies from 1 to 5 kHz at 13 years of age, and to 4 kHz at 18 years.

Enhanced sensitivity may be specific to certain stimuli in all modalities. In vision, Bertone et al. (2003) pointed out the importance of specific stimuli in investigating visual differences in ASC. In the case of touch, Blakemore et al. (2006) reported hypersensitivity for higher frequency (200 Hz) vibrotactile stimulation, but not for lower (30 Hz). Pinpointing the precise stimuli in which enhanced sensitivity occur in ASC will be important for future research. To our knowledge, the highest frequency that has been used to investigate hearing in ASC is 8 kHz (Bonnel et al., 2003). Our ongoing study investigates very high frequencies, up to 18 kHz (Tavassoli et al., submitted). The reported hypersensitivity through frequencies above 16 kHz is especially important since some environmental sounds operate at or above this range of frequencies. Grandin reported, 'Some of the sounds that are most disturbing to autistic children are the high-pitched, shrill noises made by electrical drills, blenders, saws and vacuum cleaners'.

Hypersensitivity could result from a processing difference at various sensory levels including the density or sensitivity of sensory receptors, inhibitory and exhibitory neurotransmitter imbalance or speed of neural processing. Belmonte et al. (2004) suggested *local range neural overconnectivity* in posterior, sensory parts of the cerebral cortex is responsible for the sensory 'magnification' in people with ASC. Whilst our lab and others have tested sensory profiles in ASC using fMRI (Gomot et al., 2006, 2008; Belmonte et al., 2010), the combination of imaging and genetic approaches to study sensory perception in fMRI may lead toward a more complete picture. We conclude that the search for the association between autism and talent should start with the sensory hypersensitivity, which gives rise to the excellent attention to detail, and which is a prerequisite for hyper-systemizing.

Finally, excellent attention to detail may exist in ASC because of evolutionary forces positively selecting brains for *strong systemizing*, a highly adaptive human ability (Baron-Cohen, 2008). Without systemizing, *Homo sapiens* would not have developed new stone tools in the Stone Age, or ornaments, metal tools weapons through smelting and the use of forges in the Iron Age. Nor would humans have developed mathematics in Greece in the sixth century BC or in China in 300 BC and India in 100 AD. Nor would we have seen the supreme achievements of suspension bridges or machines in the Industrial Revolution or computers in the Digital Revolution. There is little question that humans have dominated the planet because of their remarkable ability to transform their environment through invention, and at the heart of such fabrication of new tools is systemizing – understanding how things work. The 'paradoxical brain' is thus a phrase that neatly sums up how an ability that has been extraordinarily useful across human evolution can – when taken to extremes – also be associated with disability.

Future challenges and questions

This view outlined in this chapter nevertheless raises new questions and challenges. Why should systemizing in classic autism focus on more concrete repetitive actions whilst systemizing in Asperger Syndrome might focus on more abstract repeating patterns (such as mathematics)? Can IQ alone explain these different manifestations of strong systemizing? And why should strong systemizing give rise to social disability? Is it simply because the social world is hard if not impossible to systemize? Or is it because innate social modules are also impaired? How can the strong systemizing in ASC, and evidence of enhanced memory (Hillier *et al.*, 2007), be harnessed to facilitate education and intervention, to reduce disability? Teaching social skills via computers and in other systematic formats may be one such approach, but there is clearly an opportunity for much more in this area. Finally, what are the neural mechanisms underlying enhanced functioning in conditions such as those described in this chapter – for example, is altered connectivity between brain structures the key (Boso *et al.*, 2010), or can neuronal hypertrophy or anomalous forms of cell migration/cell structure be part of the explanation (cf. Conacher, 1990; Lee *et al.*, 2006; Casanova *et al.*, 2007; Huang, 2009)?

Acknowledgements

TT was supported by the Pinsent Darwin Trust and Autistica during the period of this work. EA, CA, BC and SBC were supported by the MRC UK. Parts of this article are reproduced from Baron-Cohen (2008), Ashwin *et al.* (2008), and Baron-Cohen *et al.* (2009) with permission.

References

APA. (1994). *DSM-IV Diagnostic and Statistical Manual of Mental Disorders, 4th Edition.* Washington, DC: American Psychiatric Association.

Ashwin, C., Ashwin, E., *et al.* (submitted). Olfactory hypersensitivity in autism spectrum conditions.

Ashwin, C., Ricciardelli, P., Baron-Cohen, S., *et al.* (2008). Positive and negative gaze perception in autism spectrum conditions. *Social Neuroscience,* 4: 153–64.

Ashwin, E., Ashwin, C., Rhydderch, D., Howells, J., & Baron-Cohen, S. (2009). Eagle-eyed visual acuity: an experimental investigation of enhanced perception in autism. *Biological Psychiatry,* 65: 17–21.

Bach, M., & Dakin, S. (2009). Regarding eagle-eyed visual acuity: an experimental investigation of enhanced perception in autism. *Biological Psychiatry,* 66: e19–20.

Baldassi, S., Pei, F., Megna, N., *et al.* (2009). Search superiority in autism within, but not outside the crowding regime. *Vision Research,* 49: 2151–6.

Baron-Cohen, S. (2002). The extreme male brain theory of autism. *Trends in Cognitive Sciences,* 6: 248–54.

Baron-Cohen, S. (2003). *The Essential Difference: Men, Women and the Extreme Male Brain.* London: Penguin.

Baron-Cohen, S. (2006). The hyper-systemizing, assortative mating theory of autism. *Progress in Neuropsychopharmacology and Biological Psychiatry,* 30: 865–72.

Baron-Cohen, S. (2008). Autism, hypersystemizing, and truth. *Quarterly Journal of Experimental Psychology,* 61: 64–75.

Baron-Cohen, S., & Wheelwright, S. (2004). The empathy quotient: an investigation of adults with Asperger Syndrome or high functioning autism, and normal sex differences. *Journal of Autism and Developmental Disorders,* 34: 163–75.

Baron-Cohen, S., Leslie, A. M., & Frith, U. (1985). Does the autistic child have a 'theory of mind'? *Cognition*, 21: 37–46.

Baron-Cohen, S., Aswhin, E., Ashwin, C., et al. (2009). Talent in autism: hyper-systemizing, hyper-attention to detail and sensory hypersensitivity. *Philosophical Transactions of the Royal Society of London B, Biological Sciences*, 364: 1377–83.

Baron-Cohen, S., Bor, D., Billington, J., Asher, J., Wheelwright, S., & Ashwin, C. (2007). Savant memory in a man with colour form-number synaesthesia and Asperger Syndrome. *Journal of Consciousness Studies*, 14: 237–51.

Baron-Cohen, S., Leslie, A. M., & Frith, U. (1986). Mechanical, behavioural and Intentional understanding of picture stories in autistic children. *British Journal of Developmental Psychology*, 4: 113–25.

Baron-Cohen, S., Richler, J., Disarya, B., et al. (2003). The Systemising Quotient (SQ): an investigation of adults with Asperger Syndrome or High Functioning Autism and normal sex differences. *Philosophical Transactions of the Royal Society*, 358: 361–74.

Baron-Cohen, S., Wheelwright, S., Spong, A., Scahill, V., & Lawson, J. (2001). Are intuitive physics and intuitive psychology independent? *Journal of Developmental and Learning Disorders*, 5: 47–78.

Baron-Cohen, S., Wheelwright, S., Stone, V., & Rutherford, M. (1999). A mathematician, a physicist, and a computer scientist with Asperger Syndrome: performance on folk psychology and folk physics test. *Neurocase*, 5: 475–83.

Belmonte, M., Gomot, K. M., Gomot, M., & Baron-Cohen, S. (2010). Visual attention in autism families; 'unaffected' sibs share delayed and prolonged fronto-cerebellar activation but not decreased functional connectivity. *Journal of Child Psychology & Psychiatry*, 51: 259–76.

Belmonte, M. K., Cook, E. H., Anderson, G. M., et al. (2004). Autism as a disorder of neural information processing: directions for research and targets for therapy. *Molecular Psychiatry*, 9: 646–63.

Bennetto, L., & Kuschner, E. S. (2007). Olfaction and taste processing in autism. *Biological Psychiatry*, 62: 1015–21.

Bertone, A., Mottron, L., Jelenic, P., & Faubert, J. (2003). Motion perception in autism: a 'complex' issue. *Journal of Cognitive Neuroscience*, 15: 218–25.

Blakemore, S. J., Tavassoli, T., Calo, S., et al. (2006). Tactile sensitivity in Asperger syndrome. *Brain and Cognition*, 61: 5–13.

Bonnel, A., Mottron, L., Peretz, I., Trudel, M., Gallun, E., & Bonnel, A. M. (2003). Enhanced pitch sensitivity in individuals with autism: a signal detection analysis. *Journal of Cognitive Neuroscience*, 15: 226–35.

Boso, M., Emanuele, E., Prestori, F., Politi, P., Barale, F., & D'Angelo, E. (2010). Autism and genius: is there a link? The involvement of central brain loops and hypotheses for functional testing. *Functional Neurology*, 25: 27–32.

Casanova, M., Switala, A., Trippe, J., & Fitzgerald, M. (2007). Comparative minicolumnar morphometry of three distinguished scientists. *Autism*, 11: 557–69.

Cascio, C., McGlone, F., Folger, S., et al. (2008). Tactile perception in adults with autism: a multidimensional psychophysical study. *Journal of Autism & Developmental Disorders*, 38: 127–37.

Conacher, G. (1990). Childhood autism as a disturbance of neuronal migration. *Psychiatric Bulletin*, 14: 744.

De Martino, B., Harrison, N., Knafo, S., Bird, G., & Dolan, R. (2008). Explaining enhanced logical consistency during decision making in autism. *Journal of Neuroscience*, 28: 10,746–50.

Frith, U. (1989). *Autism: Explaining the Enigma*. Oxford: Basil Blackwell.

Gomot, M., Belmonte, M. K., Bullmore, E. T., Bernard, F. A., & Baron-Cohen, S. (2008). Brain hyper-reactivity to auditory novel targets in children with high-functioning autism. *Brain*, 131: 2479–88.

Gomot, M., Bernard, F. A., Davis, M. H., et al. (2006). Change detection in children with autism: an auditory event-related fMRI study. *NeuroImage*, 29: 475–95.

Grandin, T. (2000). My Experiences with Visual Thinking, Sensory Problems and Communication Difficulties. The Center for the Study of Autism. www.autism.com/ind_temple_experiences.asp

Happe, F. (1996). *Autism*. London: UCL Press.

Heaton, P., Davis, R. E., & Happe, F. G. E. (2008). Research note: Exceptional absolute pitch perception for spoken words in an able adult with autism. *Neuropsychologia*, **46**: 2095–8.

Hermelin, B. (2002). *Bright Splinters of the Mind: A Personal Story of Research with Autistic Savants*. London: Jessica Kingsley.

Hillier, A., Campbell, H., Keillor, J., Phillips, N., & Beversdorf, D. (2007). Decreased false memory for visually presented shapes and symbols among adults on the autism spectrum. *Journal of Clinical and Experimental Neuropsychology*, **29**: 601–16.

Huang, Z. (2009). Molecular regulation of neuronal migration during neocortical development. *Molecular and Cellular Neuroscience*, **42**: 11–22.

Jaervinen-Pasley, A., Wallace, G. L., Ramus, F., Happe, F., & Heaton, P. (2002). Enhanced perceptual processing of speech in autism. *Developmental Science*, **11**: 109–21.

Jolliffe, T., & Baron-Cohen, S. (1997). Are people with autism or Asperger's Syndrome faster than normal on the Embedded Figures Task? *Journal of Child Psychology & Psychiatry*, **38**: 527–34.

Jolliffe, T., & Baron-Cohen, S. (2001). A test of central coherence theory: can adults with high functioning autism or Asperger Syndrome integrate fragments of an object. *Cognitive Neuropsychiatry*, **6**: 193–216.

Joseph, R., Keehn, B., Connolly, C., Wolfe, J., & Horowitz, T. (2009). Why is visual search superior in autism spectrum disorder? *Developmental Science*, **12**: 1083–96.

Kanner, L. (1943). Autistic disturbance of affective contact. *Nervous Child*, **2**: 217–50.

Kern, J. K., Trivedi, M. H., Garver, C. R., *et al.* (2006). The pattern of sensory processing abnormalities in autism. *Autism*, **10**: 480–94.

Lee, K., Choi, Y., Gray, J., *et al.* (2006). Neuronal correlates of superior intelligence: stronger recruitment of posterior parietal cortex. *Neuroimage*, **29**: 578–86.

Leekam, S. R., Neito, C., Libby, S. J., Wing., L., & Gould, J. (2001). Describing the sensory abnormalities of children and adults with autism. *Journal of Autism and Developmental Disorders*, **37**: 894–910.

Mottron, L., & Burack, J. A. (2001). *Enhanced Perceptual Functioning in the Development of Autism*. Mahwah, NJ: Erlbaum.

Mottron, L., Burack, J. A., Iarocci, G., Belleville, S., & Ennis, J. T. (2003). Locally oriented perception with intact global processing among adolescents with high-functioning autism: evidence from multiple paradigms. *Journal of Child Psychology and Psychiatry*, **44**: 904–13.

Mottron, L., Burack, J. A., Stauder, J. E., & Robaey, P. (1999). Perceptual processing among high-functioning persons with autism. *Journal of Child Psychology & Psychiatry*, **40**: 203–11.

Myers, P., Baron-Cohen, S., & Wheelwright, S. (2004). *An Exact Mind. An Artist with Asperger Syndrome*. London: Jessica Kingsley Publishers.

O'Riordan, M., & Passetti, F. (2006). Discrimination in autism within different sensory modalities. *Journal of Autism and Developmental Disorders*, **36**: 665–75.

O'Riordan, M., Plaisted, K., Driver, J., & Baron-Cohen, S. (2001). Superior visual search in autism. *Journal of Experimental Psychology: Human Perception and Performance*, **27**: 719–30.

Ozonoff, S., Pennington, B., & Rogers, S. J. (1991). Executive function deficits in high-functioning autistic children: relationship to theory of mind. *Journal of Child Psychology and Psychiatry*, **32**: 1081–106.

Perncr, J., Frith, U., Leslie, A. M., & Leekham, S. R. (1989). Exploration of the autistic child's theory of mind: knowledge, belief, and communication. *Child Development*, **60**: 689–700.

Rumsey, J., & Hamberger, S. (1988). Neuropsychological findings in high functioning men with infantile autism, residual state. *Journal of Clinical and Experimental Neuropsychology*, **10**: 201–21.

Russell, J. (1997). *How Executive Disorders can bring about an Inadequate Theory of Mind*.

Autism as an Executive Disorder. Oxford: Oxford University Press.

Sacks, O. (1995). *An Anthropologist on Mars.* London: Picador, 232.

Schmitz, N., Rubia, K., van Amelsvoort, T., Daly, E., Smith, A., & Murphy, D. (2008). Neural correlates of reward in autism. *British Journal of Psychiatry,* **192**: 19–24.

Shah, A., & Frith, U. (1983). An islet of ability in autism: a research note. *Journal of Child Psychology and Psychiatry,* 24: 613–20.

Shah, A., & Frith, U. (1993). Why do autistic individuals show superior performance on the block design test? *Journal of Child Psychology and Psychiatry,* **34**: 1351–64.

Suzuki, Y., Critchley, H. D., Rowe, A., Howlin, P., & Murphy, D. G. (2003). Impaired olfactory identification in Asperger's Syndrome. *Journal of Neuropsychiatry and Clinical Neuroscience,* **15**: 105–07.

Tavassoli, T., Ashwin, E., *et al.* (submitted). Multimodal hypersensitivity in individuals with autism spectrum conditions.

Tomchek, S. D., & Dunn, W. (2007). Sensory processing in children with and without autism: a comparative study using the short sensory profile. *American Journal of Occupational Therapy,* **61**: 190–200.

Tommerdahl, M., Tannan, V., Cascio, C. J., Baranek, G. T., & Whitsel, B. L. (2007). Vibrotactile adaptation fails to enhance spatial localization in adults with autism. *Brain Research,* **1154**: 116–23.

Treffert, D. (2010). *Islands of Genius: The Bountiful Mind of the Autistic, Acquired, and Sudden Savant.* London: Jessica Kingsley Publishers.

Wing, L. (1997). *The Autistic Spectrum.* Oxford: Pergamon.

Chapter 16

Paradoxes in creativity and psychiatric conditions

Jonathan Hurlow and James H. MacCabe

Summary

The question of whether or not mental disorder is the price humanity pays for exceptional creativity has been debated since classical times. Modern research methodologies have been adding increasingly robust empirical data to inform this debate. Studies of accomplished individuals have found that exceptionally creative writers report more affective illness. Population-based studies have found an excess of extremely high scholastic achievement amongst people with bipolar affective disorder, but not schizophrenia. These findings have been interpreted as evidence that people with affective disorders are a likely source of society's most exceptional ideas and work. Widespread stigmatization of mental health problems would be profoundly challenged by evidence that social progress relies on individuals with mental illness. However, such a romantic ideal often tempts researchers to over-interpret findings in this area. Research in this area faces many methodological difficulties, and despite decades of research, there is little that can be confidently claimed regarding putative mechanisms that could explain how mental disorder translates into creative processes, or vice versa. This chapter does not claim to put these ancient debates to rest, but it does provide an account of the current research that has explored these seemingly paradoxical associations between psychiatric disorders and creativity.

Introduction

Society throughout the ages has been drawn towards the archetype of the mad genius. Major figures from history have exemplified putative associations between exceptional creativity and mental disorder (Andreasen, 1987; Jamison, 1989, 1993; Jamison and Goodwin, 2007; MacCabe, 2010; MacCabe *et al.* 2009). Influential advocates of such links have ranged from Plato to Shakespeare. The Nobel Prize-winning mathematician, John Nash, represents one of the most widely discussed contemporary examples of people who demonstrate outstanding creative success and undergo treatment for mental illness. In this chapter we will systematically explore the current empirical basis for the paradoxical association between mental conditions characterized by suffering on the one hand, and innovative activity that conveys achievement on the other.

According to the public correspondence of researcher, Schlesinger, 'the public appetite for the doomed artist is too great' (Schlesinger, 2004). There is no doubt that the idea of an association between genius and madness is attractive. For some, the notion that great art springs from suffering and emotional torment is central to the artistic endeavour. For those

The Paradoxical Brain, ed. Narinder Kapur. Published by Cambridge University Press. © Cambridge University Press 2011.

suffering from mental disorders, the idea that there might be some positive aspects to their illness can be an important source of optimism. Another possible explanation for this appetite is that people are particularly receptive to ideas that seem counter-intuitive, selectively remembering information that is surprising or paradoxical (Boyer and Ramble, 2001). Enthusiastic but unwarranted speculation and over-interpretation of modest and often flawed empirical data have dogged this field for many years. Despite this, there could still be some robust straws in the wind that explain how and why the public and distinguished academics have argued for associations between creativity and psychiatric disorder since at least the days of Plato.

While a handful of studies (Ludwig, 1994) have found associations between panic disorder, generalized anxiety disorder, eating disorder and illicit substance misuse and creativity, the majority of research produced so far largely relates to mood and psychotic disorders (Lauronen *et al.*, 2004). In this chapter we will focus on the evidence on the association between psychotic and affective disorders, and creativity.

Challenges
Definitions

Despite thousands of years of discussion and more recent scientific enquiry, psychiatric disorder and creativity remain highly resistant to simple definition. Consequently, researchers in this field face fundamental challenges when attempting to study postulated links objectively.

Creativity

When writing about measuring creativity, the internationally renowned psychologist, Hans Eysenck, described how he found himself being 'allusive' and 'overinclusive' because 'creativity is a very complex subject' (Eysenck, 1994). One popular component is 'novelty'. Psychologist-philosopher, Boden, argues that scientists often consider this to be defined as the improbable 'combinations of old ideas' (Boden, 1994). One major challenge with this lies in how improbable a combination of ideas has to be before it can validly be called novel. Another more obscure component is characterized by the notion that rarity may be necessary, but not sufficient. Radical paradigm-shifting combinations may also have to be 'valuable in some way' (Boden, 1994). Discussion about what has sufficiently positive value to be considered creative is arguably the more complex task. Perhaps it is unwise to rely on the value judgements of experts who may be no freer from the human propensity to err. However, in the absence of an alternative system and, for the sake of brevity, we will refer to Eysenck's chosen definition provided by Vernon in one of the many Handbooks of Creativity: Creativity denotes a person's capacity to produce new or original ideas, insights, inventions, or artistic products, which are accepted by experts as being of scientific, aesthetic, social or technical value (Vernon, 1989).

Psychiatric disorders

Unsolved Cartesian debates about mind—brain relations cannot fail to generate massively varying definitions, as indicated by the psychopathologist, Sims, who broadly refers to mental disorders as 'the products of a diseased brain, the symptoms that doctors treat, or a statistical variation from the norm carrying biological disadvantage' (Sims *et al.*, 2003). Pragmatic and reliable, although not necessarily valid, solutions to these nosological dilemmas can be achieved by categorizing according to the standard psychiatric classification systems of the International Classification of Disease (World Health Organisation, 1992), administered by the World Health Organisation, and the *Diagnostic and Statistical Manual of Mental Disorders*, published by the American Psychiatric Association (APA), which is used primarily in the USA (APA, 1996).

Rarity

By definition, exceptional creativity must be rare. The mental disorders of interest here, particularly schizophrenia and bipolar disorder, are also rare. The ideal study to assess the presence and strength of any association between mental disorder and creativity would take a representative sample of the population, measure both creativity and mental disorder, and then examine the relationship between these two rare factors at the population level. However, the rarity of both creativity and mental disorder means that such a study would require very large samples, so epidemiologically rigorous research is expensive and time-consuming. Much of the literature, therefore, uses small, case-control designs, with their inherent methodological weaknesses.

Putative mechanisms linking creative thinking with mental disorder

Affective mechanisms

Jamison and Goodwin (2007) have comprehensively reviewed hypotheses regarding the psychological mechanisms that could explain how bipolar affective mental disorder could enhance creative behaviour amongst writers and visual artists. These include the increased potential for creative thinking to occur in the context of increased frequency of thoughts and a broadened range of ideas being combined. They postulate that manic patients may have more amplified perceptual processes and may thus be more likely to incorporate novel responses to their environment into their thought processes. In the same vein, enhanced negative or positive emotional responses in patients suffering from disordered mood could intensify creative expression.

Other affective mechanisms whereby mania might enhance creativity include increased energy, positivity and reduced inhibition. Thus, a person with mania may be more productive because they feel less fatigued, more hopeful and less restrained. In this case, a person might appear to be more exceptionally creative because they are more likely to produce more work. Although the bulk of work created may be worthless or mundane, simply producing more output increases the probability of producing something more memorable.

The depressed phase of bipolar disorder may also be useful in the creative process. Indeed, the duality of bipolar disorder is suggested to offer the added benefit of two creative industry employees for the price of one; both the creator and the critic. Whilst in the hypomanic or manic state a person could exhibit the above disinhibited loosely associated productivity, the same person in a depressed state could then bring enhanced realism.

Jamison's compilation of these fascinating and plausible hypotheses remains largely speculative. The evidence provided is mainly anecdotal in nature, referring to the personal experiences of literary figures and citing mid-twentieth century research literature, attempting to interpret the impact of mental disorder on visual artistic expression.

Figure 16.1 Painting of Sir Winston Churchill, British Prime Minister during World War Two (1939–1945), by British artist, Annie Kevans. This painting is taken from an exhibit of her work in 2009, with the theme description, *Ship of Fools*. The exhibit addressed her interest in the changing perception of psychiatric illness, and its relationship to examples of outstanding success and achievement. Sir Winston Churchill was well-known to suffer from bouts of severe depression, which he called his 'black dog'. Reproduced by kind permission.

Divergent thinking and heightened perception

Crossing back across the Kraeplinian divide to schizophrenia and schizotypy, there have been recurrent attempts to examine potential non-affective psychotic mechanisms of creativity. Independent of any distortions of affect, the divergent idiosyncrasy of thought associated with schizophrenia spectrum disorders could produce the necessary increased stream of novel ideas required for creative activity. A similar increased propensity to atypically perceive sensory information could also increase the likelihood of reaching radically new interpretations of our surrounding world. Before Andreasen had linked writers with bipolar disorder in 1976, Dykes and McGhie (1976) used non-vocational creativity measures to compare psychology students with inpatients suffering from non-paranoid schizophrenia. Whilst three forms of psychometric tests were applied to assess both cognitive divergence and heightened perception, the only significant commonality shared between those with schizophrenia and students with high creativity was enhanced novelty in categorizing objects.

More recently, Nettle (2005) and several other creativity researchers have found further mixed evidence for schizotypal mechanisms of creativity through psychometric survey comparisons. Nettle used a schizotypy questionnaire amongst a heterogeneous mix of professional poets, mathematicians, visual artists, mental health charity participants and members of the general population. However, he did not find an excess of schizotypal traits amongst creative professionals.

In a similar vein, Cox and Leon (1999), and Schuldberg (2001) have correlated different descriptions of schizotypy with even more measures of creativity amongst psychology students. Although different versions of schizotypy did appear to correlate with some measures of creativity, they were not consistently the same measures of creativity. Furthermore, Schuldberg (2001) found that two measures of hypomanic traits also correlated with some of the same measures of creativity. Thus, characterization of consistent links between specific components of creativity with schizotypy has not yet been possible.

Neurobiological mechanisms

Dopamine dysregulation has long been associated with the psychotic disorders character-ized by the psychological processes described above. Perhaps this neurotransmitter also represents a core of substrate for creativity. This appears to be the implication from case reports demonstrating how the provision of dopamine agonists to people with Parkinson disease led to the emergence of poetic ability (Schrag and Trimble, 2001) and artistic creativity (Walker *et al.*, 2006; Chatterjee *et al.*, 2006; Kulisevsky *et al.*, 2009). In particular, the emergence of overt manic symptoms alongside new creative abilities in one case appears to demonstrate just how closely correlated both creativity and affective psychosis can be with dopamine agonism (Schrag and Trimble, 2001).

Social mechanisms

It is possible to highlight that the social outcomes of ill health could encourage behaviour classically viewed as creative, such as painting and writing poetry. For example, a person struggling more than most to sleep at night and work during the day may theoretically favour the less-rigid working hours of a painter compared with the shift work of a repetitive factory job. It is possible to speculate about a host of different ways in which creative activity may be more likely to occur for these kinds of reasons by thinking about the broad range of ways in which we can be affected by ill health. However, there does not appear to have been significant research into these broader social mechanisms.

Disorders of accomplished individuals

Biographies and bias

Post (1994, 1996), Jamison (1993), Jamison and Goodwin (2007), Ludwig (1994) and several others have conducted research using data abstracted from published biographies as their source material. However, biographic studies of this type are beset with problems of methodological rigour including selection and information biases.

Selection bias

Research focusing on these individuals is inevitably subject to selection bias. In some studies, attempts are made to reduce selection bias through the use of independent criteria for inclusion such as membership of an institute rather than the judgement of the researcher; others have used more subjective criteria, such as enhanced skills and ability to achieve increased social status, as surrogate markers of creativity.

Information bias

The data of the narrative produced by an author of a biography is already subject to the biases of synthesizing a story from the wealth of sources that they decided to include. Their sources, such as an interview with a relative, may be subject to recall bias influenced by awareness that the information disclosed to the interviewer may appear in print. The biographer himself may favour facts that emphasize the dramatic connections between mental distress and creativity. The investigator who then approaches such information is studying information that has already gone through a minimum of two stages of distortion. As the investigators are not blind to the outcome of their subject's life as a consequence of reading the individual's biography comprehensively, there can be a significant risk of observer bias. Furthermore, all the biographical attempts have involved only one rater. Thus, experts such as Jamison have rated biographies without reporting reproducible rules for the interpretation of these complex narratives.

Louis Sass (2001) questions the reliability and validity of Jamison's finding that 'virtually all of the psychosis in creative individuals is manic–depressive rather than schizophrenic in nature' (Jamison, 1993). Prospective study designs have allowed for the possibility of living creative and mentally disordered people being assessed directly.

Iowa writers and affective disorders

In her comprehensive writings on this topic, Jamison has also catalogued the less methodologically developed early twentieth-century attempts to study mental disorder of the accomplished (Jamison and Goodwin, 2007). We will focus on the first modern research that began to use increasingly more valid and reliable methods to study mental disorder in the accomplished individuals. This era appears to have begun in the 1970s, when the Renaissance literature scholar and academic psychiatrist, Nancy Andreasen, used reproducible diagnostic tools and psychometric measures (Raven Progressive Matrices, WAIS) to study the Faculty members of the Iowa Writer's Group (Andreasen and Canter, 1974; Andreasen, 1987).[1]

The faculty group were compared with a control group matched for age, sex and educational status (Jamison, 1993; Jamison and Goodwin, 2007). The structured interviews detected that Research Diagnostic Criteria for affective disorder were met by 80% of the writers compared to 30% of the control group. The only statistically significant subcategory of affective disorder detected in this group of writers was a broadly defined bipolar affective disorder. Forty-three percent of writers fulfilled criteria for bipolar affective disorder compared with 10% of the control group.

Andreasen reports that the structured interview measure was not widely used and validated, and the very high rate of affective disorder found in the control group compared to the general population is of some concern. It is perhaps not surprising that the writers scored significantly higher on the vocabulary subtest (Andreasen and Canter, 1974). This raises the possibility that excellent verbal skills have a particularly strong association with affective disorders.

Other accomplished individuals and their problems

In 1989, Jamison overcame the biases inherent in diagnosing mental disorder through narrative-based interviews with writers by using the more objective measures of hospital-ization and use of lithium, antidepressants and psychotherapy in a heterogeneous collection of eminent British writers and artists. Her findings appear to corroborate Andreasen's study. However, there are different significant flaws regarding the sample size and potential for selection bias regarding the subject group (Jamison, 1989).

---

[1] This group describes its members as 'well-known figures in American letters', although Jamison warns us that some 'were graduates or teaching fellows not nationally or internationally renowned'. Nevertheless, she argues that meeting the criteria for entry into the faculty of this institution demonstrates sufficiently significant creativity. Candidates must have already produced 'strong work that shows evidence of talent and individuality' to reach the Masters of Fine Arts degree programme, let alone the teaching faculty.

By 1994, Ludwig had the opportunity to attempt to resolve both flaws by comparing participants in the University of Kentucky Women Writers Conference with a control group matched for educational status, father's occupational status and age. The subjects completed a battery of self-report inventories and diagnostic questionnaires which showed a statistically significant excess of affective disorders in the writers, including subcategories of depression and mania, as well as panic attacks, generalized anxiety, eating disorders and unspecified mental disorder. However, as Jamison pointed out, these inventories and questionnaires were not well validated and relied on self-report (Jamison and Goodwin, 2007). This raises the possibility of reporting bias: perhaps writers are simply more disposed to admit to or express their own emotional difficulties than non-writers?

Ludwig does, however, begin to address the problem of quantifying creativity by using a standardized creativity measure, the Lifetime Creativity Scale (Richards *et al.*, 1988), which showed significantly higher overall scores in the sample of writers than in the comparison group (Ludwig, 1994).

These three researchers have provided us with compelling attempts to measure the prevalence of mental disorder amongst small numbers of creative individuals. They have provided some indication that affective disorders are more common in creative writers. However, these studies are beset with biases and other methodological problems. Furthermore, as Ludwig (1994) points out, precisely how much more creative and disordered the subjects are than the rest of the population remains untested without a national sample for comparison.

Population studies

Nordic record keeping for their general population remains internationally renowned for its rigour amongst epidemiological researchers. It has also provided fertile soil for increasingly more robust population based attempts to determine whether the exceptionally creative are at greater risk of mental disorder than the general population.

Odegard and Noreik (1966) employed this kind of research design as early as 1966 in Norway, but it was Karlsson's first large-scale comprehensive attempt (Karlsson, 1999) that led to a research programme lasting over 30 years. He used Icelandic case registers to study associations between mental illness and a number of measures of high functioning. In the most recent study, he compared individuals with exceptionally good academic functioning at age 18 (the top two individuals in the country each year) to the remainder of the population (Karlsson, 1999). This objective level of achievement partially overcomes subjective disputes regarding just how creative the subjects are. He showed that these individuals were at increased risk of psychosis. In a later analysis, it appeared that high achievers in mathematics were at particularly high risk. There are several problems with these studies. First, psychosis is treated as a unitary category and is not precisely defined. Second, despite the large number of individuals studied, the numbers were very small in each of these comparisons, and the statistical treatment of the data appeared to be flawed. The statistical procedure is not fully described, but it seems that only one chi-square test was conducted on a group that combined index cases and several categories of relatives – thus, hypotheses about rates of illness in index cases, parents, siblings and children appear to have been tested simultaneously. Although the number of cases of psychosis observed in the top graduates was slightly greater than the number expected to occur by chance, it is hardly persuasive evidence. We should be very cautious when Karlsson then adds all the relatives of top graduates as well. Since psychosis runs in families, any excess in the relatives could simply be explained by the fact that there is a small, chance excess in the index cases.

There have been several further population attempts which even led to a resurgence of postulations regarding associations between schizophrenia and giftedness. This followed the publication of findings from the 1966 Northern Finland Birth Cohort study, in which boys with excellent school performance at age 16 were shown to have a fourfold risk of schizophrenia compared with controls. However, again, the numbers were small, and if just two fewer cases of schizophrenia had occurred in the excellent performance group, the result would not have been statistically significant. Furthermore, the effect was completely absent in girls (Isohanni *et al.*, 1999).

The school grades of individuals finishing compulsory schooling in Sweden between 1988 and 1997 have provided the most recent and largest population based study on the topic to date (MacCabe *et al.*, 2010). Isohanni's finding that there is an increased risk of schizophrenia with high school grades was not corroborated in this larger study – in fact, there was a strong negative association between school performance and schizophrenia, such that the highest performers were the least at risk. However, a small number of people scoring exceptionally well in compulsory examinations aged ~16 years old were later diagnosed with bipolar affective disorder. Statistical analysis controlling for socioeconomic, educational and demographic confounding factors showed that people achieving these excellent grades were 3.45 times more likely to develop bipolar affective disorder compared with those with more average scores. Even so, the bulk of people with bipolar disorder fell within the group whose exam scores were categorically average.

We should be cautious in assuming that the use of national hospital diagnostic records provides a diagnostically valid measure of mental disorder. The heterogeneous group of Nordic doctors making these diagnoses may not be any more accurate than the non-standardized interviews of the earlier studies. Furthermore, the relationship between scholastic achievement and creativity is far from clear.

Creativity and public health

It is very tempting to report that these population studies are getting closer to providing corroboration of Andreasen's findings on a large scale. However, such is the rarity of exceptional achievement and mental disorder that even these large-scale population-based studies find only a handful of cases of high achievement coinciding with mental disorder, so the results of these studies need to be viewed with some caution.

Louis Sass (2001) has written much on creativity in schizophrenia spectrum disorders and warns of the possible 'collateral damage' that could occur 'in the course of a vigorous pursuit of the affective–creativity connection'. These increasingly comprehensive studies are influential, but given the high stakes of drawing conclusions we should perhaps request even greater numbers of mentally disordered high achievers than the population studies have provided us with so far. Furthermore, we can more confidently argue that the absence of large numbers of highly creative people presenting with mental disorder at a population level suggests that this is not a major public health problem. Initiatives to target interventions on high achievers would therefore be unlikely to provide direct benefit for the majority of the population.

Creativity and disorder in the family
Evolutionary advantage

At this stage, we could tentatively accept the evidence that creative writers are more likely to demonstrate a cluster of symptoms that make up affective disorders and in particular bipolar disorder. Perhaps it is now worth discussing one evolutionary-psychology hypothesis that attempts to explain why an exceptionally creative person may pay the price of such psychiatric disorders. It has been proposed that creative cognitive styles may share a genetic basis with severe mental disorders, and that creativity may enhance reproductive fitness (Nettle, 2006). Thus, increased fitness in the unaffected relatives of patients with mental disorder might explain the continuing existence of psychotic disorders in the population, despite the devastating effects of psychiatric disorders on reproductive success (MacCabe et al., 2009). Thus the out-lying writer in the elite institution of Iowa could be viewed as living genetically on Dryden's 'thin partition' between the traits of enhanced function and increased vulnerability to the mental disorder (Dryden, 1973). However, are there any experimental findings that can add weight to these Darwinian hypotheses?

Many of the researchers above, including Andreasen and Ludwig, attempted to comment on the psychiatric diagnostic status of the first-degree relatives, but often through broadly defined processes based on secondary descriptions provided by the exceptionally creative subjects. Of the population-based researchers, only Karlsson appears to have explored primary evidence of creativity and psychiatric disorder in the first-degree relatives of the population. Similarly, Makikyro et al. (1997) found that the parents of those diagnosed with early-onset schizophrenia achieve enhanced socioeconomic status. This arguably provides an intriguing surrogate measure of the creative status-enhancing behaviours of first-degree relatives of Finnish people diagnosed with schizophrenia.

Before examining the most developed evidence relating to this creativity-focused hypothesis, it is worth considering the fertility of unaffected relatives. If the unaffected relatives are felt to have an enhanced cognitive style that confers increased biological fitness, then they would also be expected to have increased fertility rates. There was some research in the 1990s that suggested this may be the case amongst the relatives of people diagnosed with schizophrenia (Fananas and Bertranpetit, 1995; Srinivasan and Padmavati, 1997). However, more recently, MacCabe et al. (2009) have measured the number of offspring produced by Swedish people for over two generations. They corroborated the findings of Haukka et al. when they determined that first-degree siblings of the people with schizophrenia did not have more children than the remaining unaffected people in the study (Haukka et al., 2003). Furthermore, this was found to be the case for the relatives of the people diagnosed with an affective psychosis as well. They also reproduced the well-accepted findings that people with schizophrenia have fewer children and that people with affective disorders have a similar number of children to the unaffected population.

Danish adoptees with creative careers

In his published dissertation, McNeil (1971) examined the psychiatric diagnostic status of creative Danish adoptees, their first-degree biological relatives and their adopted relatives. From thousands of potential adoptees, very few were included and even fewer of these were described as 'highly creative'. The identification of creative adoptees and diagnostic processes faced major challenges. Highly varied groups of occupation were judged creative or non-creative according to the assessment of three judges who went on to rate individuals according to their degree of creativity. Other than reference to enhanced social status, limited objective criteria were used when rating an adoptee's creative status. Unfortunately, due to international variations in diagnostic practice during this era of research, it is impossible to be certain about the modern equivalent of these diagnoses. However, the criterion used, being registered for treatment by psychiatric services, at least minimizes the possibility of observer bias.

Although the results were not statistically significant, half of those judged highly creative had been treated, compared with none of those judged to demonstrate low creativity. There was also a general pattern of lower levels of treatment for mental disorder amongst the adoptive parents for all adoptees no matter what their level of rated creativity. Conversely, the psychiatric treatment of the biological parents of the adoptees was found to have occurred in a greater proportion and in particular a much greater proportion of the biological parents of those judged to be highly creative. McNeil proposed that this pattern proves that the causes of mental disorder in the creative are clearly genetic or else the adoptive parents would have measured a similarly increased rate. This clearly supports Nettle's postulation that heritable genetic muta-tional loads could simultaneously increase risk of creativity and mental disorder. However, we should remain cautious before accepting that these small numbers of creative adoptees were fully representative of Danish creativity.

Danish adoptees from parents with schizophrenia

Kinney *et al.* returned to Danish adoptees in the last decade, but on this occasion they looked for evidence of enhanced creativity amongst adoptees who had already been established to have a high genetic loading for schizophrenia spectrum disorders (Kinney *et al.*, 2001).

The latest method of mental disorder classification applied to this dataset benefited from the availability of DSM-III internationally operationalized criteria. The extensive transcripts of the interviews with these adoptees were reassessed blindly by both Kinney and Zimbalist with sufficient inter-rater reliability. Although the interview was not designed to ensure optimal information for analysis of creativity, the researchers used the same standardized creativity scale as Ludwig. With the Lifetime Creativity Scales they focused on the Overall Peak Creativity 'that indicates the highest qualitative level of creative accomplishment displayed in either vocational or avocational activities over a person's adult years'. Fifteen adopted offspring of parents with schizophrenia presented with schizoid personality dis-order, schizotypal disorder or multiple schizotypal signs. These 15 also had higher scores for creativity when compared with asymptomatic control adoptees. However, like McNeil's findings, these differences are not statistically significant.

Overall, the empirical basis for hypotheses postulating an evolutionary advantage of creativity accompanying genetic mutations contributing to mental disorder remains weak. This is demonstrated both by the above research focusing on the creativity of adoptees, and the research that has demonstrated no enhanced fertility amongst those with mental disorder and their relatives.

Future challenges and questions

The problems relating to definitions and measurement of creativity and mental disorders and the rarity of both have made research in this area difficult to conduct. A further problem is the zeal of some researchers to uncritically over-interpret tentative associations between creativity and mental disorder. The great majority of research that we have reviewed has significant limitations and is difficult to interpret. Arguably, the most reliable and valid findings associating enhanced creativity with psychiatric conditions are Andreasen's studies of the Iowa writers group and the more recent population studies. Both these studies find associations between creativity and high scholastic achievement with bipolar disorders and it is for that diagnosis that the strongest evidence exists of an association with creativity. However, the mechanisms for such an association, the evolutionary implications, and the extent to which other diagnoses are associated with creativity remain unclear. With this in mind, we should continue building on the current body of evidence by employing every rigorous study design available for measuring associations between all forms of creativity and psychopathology in as large a population as possible.

References

American Psychiatric Association. (1996). *DSM-IV Sourcebook*. Washington, DC: American Psychiatric Association.

Andreasen, N. C. (1987). Creativity and mental illness: prevalence rates in writers and their first-degree relatives. *American Journal of Psychiatry*, **144**: 1288–92.

Andreasen, N. C., & Canter, A. (1974). The creative writer: psychiatric symptoms and family history. *Comprehensive Psychiatry*, **15**: 123–31.

Boden, M. (1994). *What Is Creativity? Dimensions in Creativity*. London: The MIT Press.

Boyer, P., & Ramble, C. (2001). Cognitive templates for religious concepts: cross-cultural evidence for recall of counter-intuitive representations. *Cognitive Science*, **25**: 535–64.

Chatterjee, A., Hamilton, R. H., & Amorapanth, P. X. (2006). Art produced by a patient with Parkinson's disease. *Behavioural Neurolology*, **17**: 105–08.

Cox, A. J., & Leon, J. L. (1999). Negative schizotypal traits in the relation of creativity to psychopathology. *Creativity Research Journal*, **12**: 25–36.

Dryden, J. (1681). *Absalom and Achitopel*. Published by Collins, (1973). London.

Dykes, M., & McGhie, A. (1976). A comparative study of attentional strategies of schizophrenic and highly creative normal subjects. *British Journal of Psychiatry*, **128**: 50–6.

Eysenck, H. J. (1994). *The Measurement of Creativity. Dimensions of Creativity*. London: The MIT Press.

Fananas, L., & Bertranpetit, J. (1995). Reproductive rates in families of schizophrenic patients in a case-control study. *Acta Psychiatrica Scandinavica*, **91**: 202–04.

Haukka, J., Suvisaari, J., & Lonnqvist, J. (2003). Fertility of patients with schizophrenia, their siblings, and the general population: a cohort study from 1950 to 1959 in Finland. *American Journal of Psychiatry*, **160**: 460–3.

Isohanni, I., Jarvelin, M.-R., Jones, P., Jokelainen, J., & Isohanni, M. (1999). Can excellent school performance be a precursor of schizophrenia? A 28-year follow-up in the Northern Finland 1966 birth cohort. *Acta Psychiatrica Scandinavica*, **100**: 17–26.

Jamison, K. R. (1989). Mood disorders and patterns of creativity in British writers and artists. *Psychiatry*, **52**: 125–34.

Jamison, K. R. (1993). *Touched With Fire*. New York, NY: The Free Press.

Jamison, K. R., & Goodwin, F. K. (2007). *Creativity. Manic-Depressive Illness*. Oxford: Oxford University Press.

Karlsson, J. L. (1999). Relation of mathematical ability to psychosis in Iceland. *Clinical Genetics*, **56**: 447–9.

Kinney, D. K., Richards, R., Lowing, P. A., LeBlanc, D., Zimbalist, M. E., & Harlan, P. (2001). Creativity in offspring of schizophrenic and control parents: an adoption study. *Creativity Research Journal*, **13**: 17–25.

Kulisevsky, J., Pagonabarraga, J., & Martinez-Corral, M. (2009). Changes in artistic style and behaviour in Parkinson's disease: dopamine and creativity. *Journal of Neurology*, **256**: 816–9.

Lauronen, E., Veijola, J., Isohann, I., Jones, P. B., Nieminen, P., & Isohanni, M. (2004). Links between creativity and mental disorder. *Psychiatry*, **67**: 81–98.

Ludwig, A. M. (1994). Mental illness and creative activity in female writers. *The American Journal of Psychiatry*, **151**: 1650–6.

MacCabe, J. H. (2010). *The Extremes of the Bell Curve: Excellent and poor school performance and risk for severe mental disorders*. New York, NY: Psychology Press.

MacCabe, J. H., Koupil, I., & Leon, D. A. (2009). Lifetime reproductive output over two generations in patients with psychosis and their unaffected siblings: the Uppsala 1915–1929 Birth Cohort Multigenerational Study. *Psychological Medicine*, **39**: 1667–76.

MacCabe, J. H., Lambe, M. P., Cnattingius, S., *et al.* (2010). Excellent school performance at age 16 and risk of adult bipolar disorder: a national cohort study. *British Journal of Psychiatry*, **196**: 109–15.

Makikyro, T., Isohanni, M., Moring, J., *et al.* (1997). Is a child's risk of early onset schizophrenia increased in the highest social class? *Schizophrenia Research*, **23**: 245–52.

McNeil, T. F. (1971). Prebirth and postbirth influence on the relationship between creative ability and recorded mental illness. *Journal of Personality*, **39**: 391–406.

Nettle, D. (2005). Schizotypy and mental health amongst poets, visual artists, and mathematicians. *Journal of Research in Personality*, **40**: 876–90.

Nettle, D. (2006). Reconciling the mutation-selection balance model with the schizotypy-creativity connection. *Behavioural and Brain Sciences*, **29**: 418.

Odegard, O., & Noreik, K. (1966). Psychoses in Norwegians with a background of higher education. *British Journal of Psychiatry*, **112**: 43–55.

Post, F. (1994). Creativity and psychopathology. A study of 291 world-famous men. *British Journal of Psychiatry*, **165**: 22–34.

Post, F. (1996). Verbal creativity, depression and alcoholism. an investigation of one hundred american and british writers. *British Journal of Psychiatry*, **168**: 545–55.

Richards, R. L., Kinney, D. K., Benet, M., & Merzel, A. P. C. (1988). Assessing everyday creativity: characterisitcs of the Lifetime Creativity Scales and validation with three large samples. *Journal of Personality & Social Psychology*, **54**: 476–85.

Sass, L. A. (2001). Schizophrenia, modernism, and the 'creative imagination': on creativity and psychopathology. *Creativity Research Journal*, **13**: 55–74.

Schlesinger, J. (2004). Correspondence. Creativity and mental health. *British Journal of Psychiatry*, **184**: 184.

Schrag, A., & Trimble, M. (2001), Poetic talent unmasked by treatment of Parkinson's disease. *Movement Disorders*, **16**: 1175–6.

Schuldberg, D. (2001). Six subclinical spectrum traits in normal creativity. *Creativity Research Journal*, **13**: 5–16.

Sims, A., Mundt, C., Berner, P., & Barocka, A., *et al.* (2003). Descriptive phenomenology. In: Gelder, M. G., Lopez-Ibor, J. J. & Andreasen, N. C. (Eds.). *New Oxford Textbook of Psychiatry*. Oxford: Oxford University Press.

Srinivasan, T. N., & Padmavati, R. (1997). Fertility and schizophrenia: evidence for increased fertility in the relatives of schizophrenic patients. *Acta Psychiatrica Scandinavica*, **96**: 260–4.

Vernon, P. E. (1989). The nature–nuture problem in creativity. In: Glover, J. A., Ronning, R. R. & Reynolds, C. R. (Eds.). *The Handbook of Creativity*. New York, NY: Plenum Press.

Walker, R. H., Warwick, R., & Cercy, S. P. (2006). Augmentation of artistic productivity in Parkinson's disease. *Movement Disorders*, **21**: 285–6.

World Health Organisation. (1992). *International Statistical Classification of Diseases and Related Health Problems*. Geneva: World Health Organisation.

The paradox of psychosurgery to treat mental disorders

Perminder S. Sachdev

Summary

The creation of lesions in healthy brain tissue in order to treat psychiatric disorders is paradoxical in view of the frequent occurrence of psychiatric disorders after focal and diffuse brain lesions. Thus, the introduction of neurosurgery for psychiatric disorders, or psychosurgery, in the 1930s was seen as a bold, indeed desperate, attempt in the face of a therapeutic impasse. The rationale for psychosurgery was based on very modest evidence, and while the evidence base has grown in subsequent years, it remains a controversial treatment, limited in its scientific base and unable to shrug off the legacy of its early days of over-enthusiastic application. The recent introduction of neuromodulatory techniques, in particular deep brain stimulation, has altered the tone but not the nature of the debate, and better empirical evidence as well as theoretical rationale are necessary before the paradox underlying psychosurgery can be readily explained.

The history of paradoxical treatments in psychiatry

Psychiatric treatment is no stranger to paradoxes, and its history is littered with examples of counter-intuitive strategies, and bold attempts to heal the fractured mind. One ancient treatment that can be traced to prehistoric times is the practice of trepanation, or the creation of holes in the skull to treat diseases (Restak, 2000). When performed for mental illnesses or epilepsy, the rationale was to permit malevolent spirits to escape the skull. The practice of seemingly antithetical treatments continued into the twentieth century, although the scientific grounding of some of these treatments had improved. A much celebrated treatment was malarial therapy for general paralysis of the insane, which resulted in the first Nobel Prize for a psychiatric treatment being awarded to Julius Wagner von Jauregg in 1927. When it became clear that it was the fever rather than malaria that led to the improvement in these patients, other strategies such as hot baths, diathermy, infrared light bulb cabinets, electric bags, etc., were used to induce fever (Neyman, 1938). This treatment was applied to many psychiatric disorders, including schizophrenia, often with unsubstantiated claims of success.

Physicians had frequently made the observation that hormones influenced mental states, especially in women. This resulted in a spate of operations such as thyroidectomies, ovariectomies and male castration in the 1920s to treat mental illness (Freeman, 1935). Also prevalent about the same time was the notion of the restorative effects of sleep, resulting in the introduction of 'prolonged narcosis' or 'deep sleep therapy', credited in

---

Europe to Jakob Klaesi (1922). Patients were kept in a deep sleep with drugs such as barbiturates and opiates for one to two weeks, and sometimes as long as a month. In some parts of Europe, electrical brain stimulation was used to maintain the sleep state. Deep sleep therapy continued to be used until the 1970s, even though its initial claims of 70–80% improvement were no longer tenable. The theory of 'psychic stimulation' led to the introduction of carbon dioxide therapy in which a 30% mixture of CO_2 was used in extended inhalation sessions, ostensibly to stimulate the brain. An unusual approach to stimulate the brain was the use of sodium amytal or the 'truth drug'. Another prevalent theory of that time was that mental illness was caused by oxygen insufficiency, and many psychiatric patients were placed in hyperbaric chambers. Interestingly, some of the arguments for these treatments were couched in psychodynamic terms, with amytal purportedly unlocking the unconscious, while CO_2 activated the unconscious fears, leading to their eventual assimilation.

A theory also popular in the 1920s for the causation of mental illness was proposed by Henry Cotton, a prominent American psychiatrist, which implicated focal infection. Foci were identified in the teeth, tonsils, gastrointestinal tract and the cervix, and surgical procedures followed, ranging from extraction of teeth to tonsillectomies, hysterectomies and colonic resections. Cotton (1922) reported the results of more than 1400 surgical detoxifications with an impressive 70–80% improvement. The treatment was endorsed by the doyen of American psychiatry, Adolf Meyer, until a 1923 controlled investigation failed to support the claims of effectiveness (Kopeloff and Kirby, 1923), which led to its demise. Other treatments used in the 1920s, that were based on inadequate theoretical knowledge and which lacked sound empirical basis, are too numerous to detail here, and have been described elsewhere by historians (Valenstein, 1986).

A treatment that received an enthusiastic reception with its introduction in 1933 was insulin coma therapy. After his initial report on the results of this treatment, Manfred Sakel (1937) propagated it with great zeal. Insulin coma therapy was hailed as a breakthrough in biological treatments in countries around the world, and psychiatrists with a biological orientation adopted Sakel as a counterpoint to the psychoanalytical theories of another Viennese psychiatrist, Sigmund Freud. On the other hand, some analysts, including the prominent American psychiatrist Smith Ely Jelliffe, regarded the therapeutic effect of insulin comas in highly interpretative terms such as bringing the patient to the edge of the death threat (Sakel, 1937). While Sakel's enthusiasm in promoting insulin coma therapy was unmatched, his theoretical justification was vague and unconvincing, and the empirical studies that followed were not supportive. The use of this treatment waned in the 1960s, and died out in the 1970s because of the lack of empirical support. It also had no cogent theoretical basis.

The paradox of convulsive therapy

While electroconvulsive therapy is covered in detail in another chapter of this book, it is useful to discuss convulsive therapy in its historical context. The origins of convulsive therapy are usually traced back to the observation that psychosis and epilepsy are sometimes antithetical, and that psychosis may improve when the patient has a seizure (the antagonism hypothesis). The relationship between psychosis and epilepsy was, however, paradoxical, as psychosis was more common in patients with epilepsy and vice versa (the affinity hypothesis). Recently, an attempt has been made to reconcile this antagonism–affinity paradox by suggesting that the underlying mechanisms may be common for alternating psychosis, in which epilepsy and brief psychosis are antithetical, and for post-ictal psychosis which occurs in patients after a flurry of seizures. The brain's homeostatic inhibitory processes in response to seizures may play a key role in the development of the psychosis. These homeostatic mechanisms manifest as electrophysiological, cerebral blood flow, neurotransmitter and receptor changes. Both syndromes are likely to be associated with prolonged inhibition in limbic circuits, with further seizures modifying the psychosis depending upon whether it is associated with disinhibition or hypersynchrony involving enhanced inhibition (see Sachdev, 2007a for a detailed explanation).

Joseph Ladislas von Meduna, working in the 1930s in Hungary, was impressed by the antagonism and went on to carry out a neuropathological study in which he observed glial cell proliferation in epilepsy patients but not in schizophrenia (Meduna, 1935a, cited in Fink, 1984). On the basis of this, he developed the idea of inducing convulsions in schizophrenic patients. After experimenting with a number of compounds in animals, he chose camphor and later metrazol for this purpose, and published his first report in 1935 (Meduna, 1935b). Convulsive therapy was extensively applied thereafter, and in 1938 electrically induced convulsive therapy was introduced, which eventually replaced chemically induced seizures as the favoured modality. Although its mechanism of action is still poorly understood, electroconvulsive therapy is generally accepted as the most effective antidepressant treatment, but its role in the treatment of schizophrenia is less well established (Merkl et al., 2009). Understanding why inducing a seizure should relieve depression remains a challenge.

Neurosurgery for mental disorders

Brain lesions are well known to cause psychiatric disorders and there is considerable literature on mental disorders following brain trauma, stroke, brain tumours, demyelination and other types of brain lesions (Lishman, 1998). The suggestion that lesions should be created in otherwise healthy brain tissue to treat mental illness therefore seems paradoxical. One of the earliest attempts to do this are attributed to Gottlieb Burckhardt (1891), who performed brain operations on six mentally ill patients in an asylum in Switzerland. These patients suffered from intractable mental illnesses characterized by delusions, hallucinations and aggressive behaviour and were diagnosed to have 'primare Verrucktheit', which may be considered equivalent to our current concept of schizophrenia. The operations involved bilateral localized topectomies, or selective removal of cerebral cortex in the temporal, frontal and parietal lobes. Three patients were said to have improvement in symptoms (aggression and delusions), two were unchanged and one died five days post-operative from status epilepticus.

The modern era of psychosurgery began with the Portuguese neurologist Egas Moniz and his neurosurgical colleague, Almeida Lima, who commenced operating upon the frontal lobe in 1935. Moniz was apparently influenced by the work of Yale neurophysiologists, John Fulton and Carlyle Jacobsen, who had performed bilateral removal of the orbitofrontal cortex in two chimpanzees, Becky and Lucy, with a marked reduction in anxiety and emotionality in the animals (Jacobsen et al., 1935). In Jacobsen's words, the animals were described as having joined the 'happiness cult'. While Moniz's translation of this somewhat limited laboratory observation into treatment of mental disorders was bold, he did not perform a lobectomy, as the animals had undergone, but a leucotomy by initially injecting alcohol into the frontal lobes of patients, and later switching to a plunger-activated corer. In the first series of 20 cases, he reported the best improvement in agitated depression and melancholia, with only two of seven schizophrenic patients improving (Moniz, 1936). 'Psychosurgery', as Moniz referred to it, was taken up enthusiastically in the United States by the neurologist Walter Freeman and his neurosurgical colleague, James Watts, who performed thousands of operations in the next few years (Valenstein, 1986). Psychosurgery was extensively adopted around the world, with nearly 40,000 operations in the United States alone until the early 1950s.

When Dr Moniz was awarded the Nobel Prize in Physiology and Medicine in 1949, the *New England Journal of Medicine* (1949) announced in an editorial that a new era in psychiatry may be said to have been born in 1935. However, subsequent decades have not necessarily been kind to the legacy of Moniz. After its rapid acceptance in the 1940s and 1950s, psychosurgery went through a period of gradual decline. The 1970s was the period of greatest public debate on, and in opposition to, the procedure, sparked by the controversial book *Violence and the Brain* (Mark and Ervin, 1970), even though the lobotomy of earlier years had been abandoned and the frequency of psychosurgical procedures had declined markedly. The result was a spate of commissions of enquiry (Department of Health, Education and Welfare, 1977; Parliament of New South Wales Report, 1977) and regulatory legislation (Oregon Senate Bill, 1973; California Legislative Assembly, 1976; Grimm, 1980; Kiloh, 1977). At the end of the decade, Valenstein (1980) summarized the state of the procedure and concluded that the use of psychosurgery was limited to a few centres internationally. Lobotomy, or psychosurgery as practised initially, had been abandoned and all centres restricted themselves to stereotactic surgery, with fairly focal lesions guided by brain imaging.

Modern psychosurgery

In the 1980s and 1990s, four procedures were described as being used in different centres – anterior cingulotomy, subcaudate tractotomy, limbic leucotomy and anterior capsulotomy. The major indications for the procedures were chronic and treatment resistant major depression and obsessive–compulsive disorder (OCD), with severe anxiety disorder and bipolar disorder being treated less often. Intractable pain was another infrequent indication. Psychosurgery is not currently used to treat schizophrenia or aggressive and violent behaviour. There had been no direct comparison of the different procedures, each being preferred by a different centre, with data being presented to suggest that they were comparable in their outcome. The efficacy data up until 1980 were summarized by Kiloh *et al.* (1988), until 1988 by Waziri (1990), and until 1999 by the Royal College of Psychiatrists (2000) report, and are presented in Table 17.1. There are a number of limitations to these data, which will be summarized below.

There is very limited controlled evidence for the efficacy of psychosurgery. Most studies have used a retrospective control group (e.g. Marks *et al.*, 1966; Tan *et al.*, 1971; Bridges and Goktepe, 1973; Hay *et al.*, 1993; Cosyns *et al.*, 1994), and an adequately powered prospective control study has never been conducted. Some sham procedures have been reported, which generally comprised a skin lesion and a burr hole, but with no brain lesion. Four cases of sham surgery were reported by Livingstone (1953) for psychosis, one case by Cosyns and Gybels (1979) for obsessional symptoms, three cases by Balasubramanium *et al.* (1973) for

Table 17.1 Consolidated outcome of neurosurgery for psychiatric disorders according to three published reviews

Outcome rating	Depression		OCD		Non-OCD anxiety	
Kiloh et al. (1988)	Studies (n = 21)	Cases (n = 727)	Studies (n = 24)	Cases (n = 478)	Studies (n = 10)	Cases (n = 290)
	Outcome		Outcome		Outcome	
Marked improvement	63%		58%		52%	
Lesser improvement	22%		27%		25%	
No response	14%		14%		21%	
Worse	1%		1%		2%	
Waziri et al. (1990)			Studies (n = 12)	Cases (n = 300)	Studies (n = 11)	Cases (n = 225)
	Outcome		Outcome		Outcome	
Symptom-free	N/a		38%		32%	
Minor symptoms	N/a		29%		23%	
Mild/moderate symptoms	N/a		20%		22%	
Severe symptoms	N/a		10%		14%	
Worse/dead	N/a		3%		9%	
Royal College of Psychiatrists (2000)	Studies (n = 3)	Cases (n = 189)	Studies (n = 5)	Cases (n = 198)	Studies (n = 3)	Cases (n = 80)
	Outcome		Outcome		Outcome	
Symptom-free	34%		33%		20%	
Minor symptoms	23%		34%		20%	
Moderate symptoms/ some improvement	22%		23%		27%	
Unchanged	19%		8%		30%	
Worse	2%		2%		3%	

addictive behaviours, and one by Corkin *et al.* (1979) for pain. None of these cases showed anything more than a transient benefit. This evidence of the lack of a placebo effect cannot, unfortunately, be generalized because of the small number of cases reported and the fact that the indications for surgery, such as psychosis and addictive behaviours, were unusual. In addition to the ethical concern offered as a reason for the lack of sham procedures, it has been suggested that patients who come to psychosurgery have chronic psychiatric disorders that have not responded to any other treatment. Such patients are unlikely to show a placebo response (Sachdev and Sachdev, 2005), and the close temporal association between surgery and improvement is sufficient evidence for its efficacy. While some evidence for the lack of placebo response in such resistant disorders has been presented (Hay *et al.*, 1993;

(a)   (b)

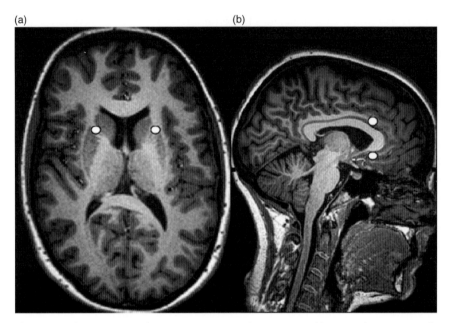

Figure 17.1 Brain sections to demonstrate target sites for neurosurgical lesions in the treatment of psychiatric disorders. (a) Axial section showing site of anterior capsulotomy lesions; (b) saggital section with site for anterior cingulotomy (upper) and subcaudate tractotomy (lower).

Poynton *et al.*, 1995), studies of other treatments, such as transcranial magnetic stimulation for resistant depression, suggest that a placebo response can confound the interpretation of treatment efficacy even in resistant cases (Loo *et al.*, 1999), in spite of the fact that the placebo response is likely to be transient.

The four commonly used procedures outlined above target different brain regions, and are differentially preferred by different groups; direct comparisons between these procedures are lacking. The anatomical sites are depicted in Figure 17.1.

Anterior cingulotomy. The target is the anterior cingulum, as originally suggested by Fulton in 1936 (Whitty *et al.*, 1952), and this procedure has been extensively used by the Boston group (Ballantine *et al.*, 1967). The anterior cingulate cortex is an important structure within the Papez circuit, which has been proposed as the anatomical substrate for anxiety (MacLean, 1949). Abnormal metabolism in the cingulate cortex has been reported in OCD, although this is not the exclusive or most consistent abnormality (Saxena *et al.*, 1998). This procedure is therefore more likely to be used for OCD or non-OCD anxiety disorders, but not mood disorders. While the target in anterior cingulotomy is the cingulate bundle, the cingulate cortex is likely to be lesioned.

Subcaudate tractotomy. The target sites are the orbitomedial quadrants of the frontal lobes bilaterally, with the intention of interrupting fibres connecting the frontal lobe with subcortical structures such as the amygdala and the thalamus (Knight, 1964). This procedure has been popular in the UK, and has been used for both mood disorders and anxiety disorders (Hodgkiss *et al.*, 1995). Knight (1964) originally performed the procedure by implanting radioactive seeds into the substantia innominata, just below the head of the caudate nucleus.

Limbic leucotomy. This is a combination of anterior cingulotomy and subcaudate tractotomy and was used extensively by Kelly and colleagues in London for both refractory depression and OCD (Kelly, 1980).

Anterior capsulotomy. This targets the anterior limb of the internal capsule between the caudate and putamen. It has been popular in Europe, particularly in Sweden, after the gamma-knife stereotaxis developed by the neurosurgeon Leksell (Leksell and Backlund, 1979). It targets frontal–thalamic fibres that form part of the frontal-subcortical circuits.

Rationale for the procedures: is there a paradox?

While psychosurgery was initiated following the observation that brain lesions can change mood state and sometimes alleviate mental illness, the supporters of this form of treatment have faced a dilemma: does one follow the Hippocratic dictum of 'first do no harm' or attempt to try any legitimate means to ameliorate the suffering of patients? No one disputes the fact that the parts of the brain that are lesioned in psychosurgery do not in themselves demonstrate any pathology. The rationale for the lesions is the interruption of presumably abnormal or possibly hypoactive/hyperactive neuronal circuits that underlie these disordered states. There have been anecdotal reports in the literature of improvement in psychiatric disorders due to incidental lesions from a variety of aetiologies (Logue *et al.*, 1968; Storey, 1970; Solyom *et al.*, 1987; Hutchinson *et al.*, 1993; Levine *et al.*, 2003; Naqvi *et al.*, 2007), but these have been too inconsistent to provide a rationale for surgery.

Considerable neuroimaging evidence has been presented to suggest abnormal activity in frontal–subcortical circuits in patients with depression and OCD. The limbic–cortical–striatal–pallidal–thalamic circuitry was originally described by Nauta (1972) and elaborated by Alexander *et al.* (1986). The ventral frontal cortex has extensive interconnections with subcortical structures, including the caudate, putamen and globus pallidum, the mediodorsal nucleus of the thalamus, amygdala and hippocampus, and lesions in any of these regions have been associated with mood disturbance (Mega and Cummings, 1994). Models have been proposed to explain the symptomatology of depression on the basis of altered activity in this circuit (Drevets *et al.*, 1992; Mayberg, 1994; Sheline, 2003). The difficulty in reconciling these models with psychosurgery is that some of these models suggest an underactivity in the frontal cortex, leading to reduced inhibition of the excitatory loop involving the mediodorsal thalamus, prefrontal cortex and amygdala (Swerdlow and Koob, 1987). Psychosurgical lesions would arguably further compromise this inhibition and worsen the depressive state. Some models have taken note of both hypo- and hypermetabolism in frontal–limbic regions, and have argued that synchronized modulation of the cortical–subcortical neuronal circuits is necessary for depression to remit (Mayberg, 2006). This suggests that the regulation of these circuits is complex and that a simple model may not suffice. Why lesions within the circuit should lead to 'correction' of an abnormality in some patients is not certain. On the other hand, worsening of depression after psychosurgery has rarely been reported (Kiloh *et al.*, 1988), which may relate to the fact that these patients are already at the nadir of their illnesses when they come to this procedure. Surgery is used for patients with extremely severe illness, and regression to the mean might explain some improvement at the group level.

The neurobiological models of OCD present a more cogent argument for the creation of surgical lesions. The models have been based on neuroimaging data which suggest increased activity in the cortico-subcortical networks (Machlin *et al.*, 1991;

Swedo *et al.*, 1989), which is further increased if patients are subjected to symptom provocation while being imaged (Mataix-Cols *et al.*, 2004; Rauch *et al.*, 1994). Treatment with drugs or cognitive-behaviour therapy attenuates these deficits (Baxter *et al.*, 1992; Rubin *et al.*, 1995; Saxena *et al.*, 1999). The most consistent finding has been hypermetabolism of the orbitofrontal cortex, which lends an argument to the creation of lesions to disconnect this hypermetabolic region from its more important connecting brain regions.

Some investigators would regard the empirical evidence of improvement in some patients as adequate support for the theoretical models. However, the limitations of the evidence are obvious.

(i) Only a proportion of patients show benefit from the lesions. It can be argued that an equally important mechanism in the therapeutic effect of surgery is possibly the brain's response to the lesions. The brain may be considered a homeostatic organ with a tendency to maintain its equipoise, and drugs, psychotherapy and surgery may all assist it in reaching that 'normal' functional state when it is locked in a psychopathological state deemed responsible for depression or OCD (Sachdev, 2009). Only a proportion of brains may be capable of mounting this homeostatic response, thereby explaining the 40% response rate in many of the studies.

(ii) Most outcome studies of psychosurgery did not carefully examine the accuracy of placement of lesions. The few studies that did attempt this provided only partial support for the specificity of the site of lesion for a positive response to occur. In a post-mortem study of two suicide cases who had received neurosurgical treatment, Evans (1971) reported that these patients with failed treatment had intact fronto-thalamic connections. In his small series, Mindus (1991) attributed about half of the failures to misplaced lesions. Sachdev and Hay (1996) determined that a minimum size of lesion was necessary, beyond which there was no additional benefit. Re-operation rates vary from 20 to 39% in different studies (Royal College of Psychiatrists, 2000), but the response rate is low in this group. In the report by Steele *et al.* (2007), patients with more anterior lesions but with smaller volumes showed greater improvement, and the authors argued that these lesions were in the region of the medial prefrontal cortex noted to be abnormal in depression. The authors used normalized images and the Montreal Neurological Institute (MNI) atlas to determine the lesion location, and proposed that a 750 mm^3 lesion centred at the MNI coordinate (−9, 19, 30) was the optimal lesion. They did not, however, perform fibre tracking to determine whether the target, i.e. the cingulum bundle, had indeed been lesioned, and they acknowledged that the lesions ablated both white matter as well as part of the anterior cingulate gyrus. A previous study from the Boston group examined the significance of targeting the cingulum (Spangler *et al.*, 1996) and found that it was not necessary – the response rate in anterior cingulotomy was no better whether the cingulum was targeted or not (33 vs. 38%, respectively).

(iii) The data do not support the view that there is specificity in terms of the type of surgery and the disorder being treated, and the choice is related to the expertise or bias of the neurosurgical team. In general, subcaudate tractotomies have been used more often for depression and anterior capsulotomies for OCD and anxiety disorders.

(iv) The data do not suggest that selection of patients has improved since the early evidence that depression and OCD patients were most likely to respond. In fact, more recent studies have reported lower rates of remission, which may reflect the characteristics of the patient population likely to receive neurosurgical treatment (Sachdev and Chen, 2009).

Current status of psychosurgery

A survey of the field in the last three decades reveals further attrition of stereotactic psychosurgery, although it continues to be performed in a few centres. In Australia and New Zealand, from an annual 10–20 operations in the early 1980s, the number went down to 1–2 operations per year in the mid 1990s (Hay and Sachdev, 1992) and, as far as I am aware, no procedures have been carried out in the 2000s. In the UK, 26 operations were performed between 1993 and 1999, and a report from the Royal College of Psychiatrists (2000) raised the possibility of the demise of the procedure. A group from Dundee, Scotland (Steele *et al.*, 2008) reported 48 patients who were operated upon between 1999 and 2004 with anterior cingulotomy for severe depression. The frequency of psychosurgery in the US is difficult to estimate, but a 2002 prospective study of 21 patients (Montoya *et al.*, 2002) attests to its ongoing use at a low rate in at least one centre in Massachusetts. A Spanish report (Barcia *et al.*, 2007) estimated that 121 operations were performed in that country during 1999 to 2003, most frequently for OCD. There have been reports from other countries such as Korea (Kim *et al.*, 2002), Taiwan (Cho *et al.*, 2008) and Mexico (del Valle *et al.*, 2006), and it is likely that these operations continue to be performed in some South American and Eastern European countries (Royal College of Psychiatrists, 2000).

New data are, however, difficult to find. The last report from the Boston group was in 2002 (Montoya *et al.*, 2002) and they reported the outcome of limbic leucotomy in 21 patients (15 OCD, 6 Major Depression) over 26 months. Using various outcome criteria, they judged 36–50% of patients to have responded to treatment. The last report from Australia was in 2005 (Sachdev and Sachdev, 2005). Patients with severe depression treated between 1973 and 1995 ($n = 76$) were followed up after a mean 14.4 years. Only 23 were interviewed and, of these, 5 (22.7%) were judged to be completely recovered and another 11 (50%) showed significant improvement, with the improvement having been noted within days or weeks of surgery. The recent report from Scotland (Steele *et al.*, 2008) comprised eight patients with severe depression who were treated with stereotactic anterior cingulotomy. At one year, two (25%) met criteria for response and three (37.5%) met criteria for remission. The report of the Flemish Advisory Board on stereotactic neurosurgery for psychiatric disorders (Gabriels *et al.*, 2008) is of interest. In the period 2000–06 (inclusive), 91 applications were submitted to the Board, with 24 (26%) being from foreign countries, 23 from other European countries and one from India. Treatment-resistant OCD was the overwhelming reason for referral. Of the 91 initiations, 65 received a positive recommendation for surgery and 50 proceeded to have it; 36 had anterior capsulotomy and 14 deep brain stimulation (DBS). Since this is the only centre in Belgium performing psychosurgery, the authors estimate a rate of 0.6 per million inhabitants, which is an increase of over 0.2 per million in the period 1971–1997. The outcome data are not presented, but the paper highlights the continuing interest in psychosurgery in Europe, but mostly as a treatment for OCD. A survey of the attitudes of psychiatrists in Belgium showed that 44% would consider referral for ablative surgery and 74% would consider DBS for their patients.

The above reports suggest that while stereotactic psychosurgery has continued at a small level in a few centres around the world, there has been a gradual decline in its use in the last 30 years. The few attitudinal surveys and the large number of articles on the ethics of the procedure attest to the ambivalence toward the procedure in the profession, and open hostility in some sections of the public. Despite the oft-repeated claims of rapid advances in neuroscience in the last three decades, the practice of psychosurgery has not seen any major advances from the time that stereotactic surgery became available. New models for the pathogenesis of major depression and OCD have not informed the ablative psychosurgical lesions. Technically, stereotactic surgery has become more widely available, and frameless stereotaxy can now be applied to this procedure with great precision using magnetic resonance imaging (MRI) (Woerdeman et al., 2006). Yet the lack of a controlled investigation, and the fact that this is unlikely to happen, remains a major drawback. Predictors of response have generally not been identified in the majority of the outcome studies, thereby making it difficult to tailor a patient to any particular procedure or to improve the response rate in the future. Detailed neuropsychological investigations have revealed subtle abnormalities following psychosurgery that would be missed by routine procedures (Ridout et al., 2007). The availability of stimulation techniques has recently challenged the survival of ablative psychosurgery. If there has been a revival in recent years in surgical techniques, it has related to brain stimulation.

Ethical considerations

The legacy of lobotomy and excessive zeal of the early proponents of psychosurgery has been a black mark on psychiatric treatments (Valenstein, 1986; Pressman, 1998). The replacement of extensive and 'free-hand' surgery with stereotactic placement under local anaesthesia creating discrete and well-localized lesions was an important advance in this regard. The use of MRI-guided stereotaxy has improved the localization of the lesions and reduced misadventure. A review (Kiloh et al., 1988) of 854 stereotactic operations reported an operative mortality of 0.1%, chronic epilepsy in 0.4%, marked personality change in 0.4% and mild personality change in 3%. It is likely that newer technological developments have further reduced adverse effects. Recent investigations have suggested that adverse personality change of the frontal lobe type is extremely unlikely to occur with stereotactic techniques (Mindus and Hyman, 1991; Sachdev and Hay, 1995). The same can be said for significant cognitive impairment (Bridges et al., 1994; Baer et al., 1995) and, in fact improvement in cognitive performance has sometimes been reported (Nyman and Mindus, 1995), presumably because of improvement in the primary psychiatric illness. Psychosurgery is also unique amongst medical treatments to be regulated by statutory bodies in many jurisdictions and banned in others (Pressman, 1998; Heller et al., 2006). Its place in modern medicine therefore remains uncertain.

Deep brain stimulation (DBS)

The last decade has seen the introduction of a number of novel brain stimulation techniques – deep brain stimulation (DBS), vagus nerve stimulation (VNS), transcranial magnetic stimulation (TMS), magnetic seizure therapy (MST) and transcranial direct current stimulation (tDCS). While two of these (DBS and VNS) can be considered as surgical, only DBS involves direct brain intervention and can be related to traditional psychosurgery. In DBS, electrodes are chronically implanted in specific brain regions and high-frequency electrical stimulation is delivered through these electrodes to stimulate the brain regions around the tips of the electrodes. An implanted, externally programmable stimulation device is used to deliver the current. It is perhaps important at the outset to state that DBS is not 'psychosurgery', even though it involves neurosurgery for the treatment of psychiatric illness (Sachdev, 2007b). This is because no brain lesion is created, except for any inadvertent damage produced by the insertion of electrodes. The precise mechanisms by which DBS produces its effect are still debated. The suggested mechanisms are: depolarization blockade, synaptic inhibition, synaptic depression and stimulation-induced modulation of pathological network activity. Using various sources of evidence, McIntyre et al. (2004) concluded that the most likely mechanism was the modulation of pathological network activity. Of course, DBS does not replace the abnormal endogenous brain activity with normal activity, as the pattern of electrical activity induced by DBS is not normal. The final result appears to be similar to ablation, but precisely how that is achieved remains to be understood.

As discussed in Chapter 10, DBS is a well-accepted treatment for end-stage Parkinson's disease and other movement disorders, including dystonia and tremor (Wichmann and Delong, 2006). The objective of the stimulation is to reduce overactivity in the basal ganglia in these disorders. In Parkinson's disease, the currently preferred target is the subthalamic nucleus, and chronic stimulation of these nuclei results in reductions in 'off time', the dose of dopaminergic drugs needed and the severity of dyskinesias often seen in late-stage Parkinson's disease (Pahwa et al., 2006).

The original use of brain direct stimulation for psychiatric disorders can be traced to Poole in 1948 (Poole, 1954). More recently, a Belgian group, well-versed in the application of psychosurgery, published in 1999 a series of patients with OCD who were treated with DBS in the anterior capsular region (Nuttin et al., 1999). Since then, there have been a number of publications on DBS in psychiatric disorders. The first report on OCD has been followed up by a series of similar reports (Nuttin et al., 2003; Anderson and Ahmed, 2003; Sturm et al., 2003; Aouizerate et al., 2004; Abelson et al., 2005; Gabriels et al., 2003). The rationale and targeting of the lesions in OCD has been based to a great extent on the ablative psychosurgery literature, even though it is acknowledged that the volume of tissue ablated in psychosurgery is greater than that targeted by DBS devices. The Belgian group targeted the anterior limb of the internal capsule, akin to anterior capsulotomy, and a subsequent multicentric study in the USA has combined this with stimulation of the ventral striatum (Greenberg et al., 2006). The nucleus accumbens has been the target in one report (Sturm et al., 2003).

DBS for treatment-resistant depression has progressed in the last few years, although it remains in its infancy. The first report of successful treatment (Mayberg et al., 2005) involved bilateral stimulation of the region of the subgenual cingulate cortex (area 25), based on previous neuroimaging studies showing abnormal blood flow and metabolism in this region which reversed with pharmacological treatment (Mayberg et al., 2000). Of the six patients treated, four had a good outcome at six months, one showed fluctuating change in level of depression and one had no change. The authors described an acute affective response to switching the stimulation on and off, which – if consistent – could serve as a useful guide in the location of the optimal site. The authors later demonstrated neuroimaging changes in the expected direction (Lozano et al., 2008). This group subsequently used tractography to examine the connectivity of the anterior cingulate cortex in healthy individuals, and identified two regions: a pregenual region strongly connecting the anterior cingulate cortex to medial prefrontal and anterior mid-cingulate cortex, and a subgenual region with strongest connections from the anterior cingulate to the nucleus accumbens, amygdala, hypothalamus and orbitofrontal cortex (Johansen-Berg et al., 2008). The latter was the target of DBS in the patients with depression, although the tracts were not defined by diffusion tensor imaging in the patients, something that the authors recommended for the future.

Other sites of stimulation for depression have been reported. The 'reward' area has been targeted by some investigators (Aouizerate et al., 2004; Schlaepfer et al., 2008). Schlaepfer et al. (2008) implanted electrodes in the shell and core of the nucleus accumbens in three patients. They manipulated stimulation parameters in a double-blind manner, and noted improvement when the stimulator was on and worsening when it was off. Imaging one week before and after implantation showed metabolic changes consistent with activation of the fronto-striatal network. The depressive symptoms did not remit in the short follow-up period, but the stimulation was well tolerated.

Velasco et al. (2005) identified the inferior thalamic peduncle, a fibre tract connecting the thalamus with the orbitofrontal cortex, as a potential target for depression treatment. Two patients, one each with major depression and OCD, were subsequently treated with this procedure by the same group (Jiménez et al., 2005), with improvement in both disorders. Other areas proposed include the rostral cingulate area 24a based on neuroimaging work (Sakas and Panourias, 2006), and the lateral habenula based on animal data (Sartorius and Henn, 2007). One patient showed an improvement in depression when the globus pallidus interna was stimulated for the treatment of tardive dyskinesia (Kosel et al., 2007). Careful examination of the results of stimulation at these sites is necessary before clear guidelines can emerge.

Since DBS is a well-accepted procedure for advanced Parkinson's disease and dystonia, there has been some focus on any neuropsychiatric consequences of this application, which include the unmasking of depression, precipitation of mania and higher rates of suicide after subthalamic nucleus DBS for PD (Bejjani et al., 1999; Kulisevsky et al., 2002; Berney et al., 2002; Soulas et al., 2008; Lilleeng and Dietrichs, 2008). A meta-analysis of 10 years' experience showed that most side-effects of DBS were procedure- or device-related. The prevalence of depression (2–4%), mania (0.9–1.7%) and emotional changes (0.1–0.2%) was considerably low, and suicidal ideation/attempts were as high as 0.3–0.7%, warranting intensive evaluation of suicidal risk in these patients before they undergo DBS procedures (Appleby et al., 2007). In an animal model, it was shown that high-frequency stimulation DBS of the subthalamic nucleus (STN) was associated with a decrease in the activity of neighbouring 5-HT (serotonin) neurons, which related to the depressive-like behaviour observed in the rat. Interestingly, this effect was corrected by administering a selective 5-HT enhancing antidepressant, suggesting a link between post-DBS depression and the 5-HT neural circuit (Temel et al., 2007). More recent large-scale studies have not supported an increased risk of depression, other psychiatric disorder or cognitive deficits with DBS for PD (Witt et al., 2008; Mueller et al., 2008; McNeely et al., 2008; Fraraccio et al., 2008; Zibetti et al., 2007; Kiss et al., 2007). However, the increased risk of depression after STN stimulation cannot be dismissed, and strategies to stimulate only the 'motor' part of the STN must be discovered.

The preliminary nature of the DBS studies in psychiatric disorders is compounded by the fact that the exact mechanism of action of DBS is not known. Stimulation may result in both excitation and inhibition, depending upon the target. Inhibition may be produced by depolarization blockade, synaptic inhibition or synaptic depression, and excitatory axonal response may occur with high-frequency stimulation (McIntyre *et al.*, 2004). The effects on glia might further complicate the issue. It appears to be emerging, however, that DBS is not producing a lesion akin to ablation of tissue, and may work by altering the complex firing patterns of the neurons in the region, thereby altering the activity in the neuronal circuits. What is encouraging is that the effect is reversible, and the ability to switch the stimulator on and off permits controlled investigation, since most patients do not report an acute effect of switching the stimulation on and can therefore be blinded to the stimulation status. However, the results of such investigations in large series of patients are awaited. Some recent reviews of this field are worthy of note (Hardesty and Sackeim, 2007; Hauptman *et al.*, 2008), and another review discussed the issues in the translation of basic neuroscience relating DBS to clinical practice (Kringelbach *et al.*, 2007). It is interesting that in a recent paper, a patient was noted to improve from DBS of the Cg25 region after having failed anterior cingulotomy (Neimat *et al.*, 2008).

DBS is not without adverse effects. Intracranial complications do occur; bleeding is reported in 2–2.5% of cases, and while infection is rare, its occurrence necessitates explanation. Lead fracture and dislocation may occur, and limited battery life means that surgical replacement must occur every few years. The devices are very expensive and consideration needs to be given to ethical issues related to monopolist manufacturers.

Conclusions, future challenges and questions

The continuation of psychosurgery into modern times, albeit to a minimal extent and in a controlled fashion, and its transformation into neuromodulatory brain techniques, suggests that the notion of direct brain intervention to alter activity in neuronal circuits remains an accepted form of intervention. Professional and public attitudes to it range from reluctant acceptance to ambivalence to open hostility. There have been no major advances in the techniques of ablative surgery, the target brain regions or predictors of outcome. The introduction of DBS in the last few years offers reversibility, at least in principle, for a procedure in which the choice of surgical targets is based on tentative neurophysiological models in the absence of valid animal models. It also permits the examination of outcome in a controlled investigation, within the constraints of a surgical procedure. It does not, however, resolve the paradox of creating lesions in a brain not judged to be diseased by the conventional standards. Multicentre trials of DBS in OCD and mood disorders are underway and the final results are keenly awaited. The mechanisms of DBS also must be better understood to help resolve the surgical paradox of psychiatric therapy. This requires a combination of neuroimaging, neuronal recording, microdialysis and computer modelling. Modern imaging techniques permit the examination of both structural and functional brain networks which are ostensibly being manipulated by these techniques. Neural network studies before and after DBS will inform the functional changes in the brain that underlie treatment response, and remain a challenge for the future. It is also necessary, through large-scale studies, to identify the patient and illness characteristics that predict the best response.

Acknowledgements

The author thanks Angie Russell for assistance in manuscript preparation, and Dr Wei Wen for the figure.

References

Abelson, J. L., Curtis, G. C., & Sagher, O. (2005). Deep brain stimulation for refractory obsessive-compulsive disorder. *Biological Psychiatry*, **57**: 510–16.

Alexander, G. E., Delong, M. R., & Strick, P. L. (1986). Parallel organization of functionally segregated circuits linking basal ganglia and cortex. *Annual Review of Neuroscience*, **9**: 357–81.

Anderson, D., & Ahmed, A. (2003). Treatment of patients with intractable obsessive-compulsive disorder with anteriorcapsular stimulation. Case report. *Journal of Neurosurgery*, **98**: 1104–08.

Aouizerate, B., Cuny, E., Martin-Guehl, C., et al. (2004). Deep brain stimulation of the ventral caudate nucleus in the treatment of obsessive–compulsive disorder and major depression. Case report. *Journal of Neurosurgery*, **101**: 682–6.

Appleby, B. S., Duggan, P. S., Regenberg, A., & Rabins, P. V. (2007). Psychiatric and neuropsychiatric adverse events associated with deep brain stimulation: a meta-analysis of ten years' experience. *Movement Disorders*, **22**: 1722–8.

Assembly Bill (AB) No. 1032 (1976). California legislation on psychosurgery and electroconvulsive therapy. Los Angeles: California Legislative Assembly. Reprints as Chapter 1109 of California Welfare Institutional Code.

Baer, L., Rauch, S. L., Ballantine, H. T. Jr., et al. (1995). Cingulotomy for intractable obsessive–compulsive disorder. Prospective long-term follow-up of 18 patients. *Archives of General Psychiatry*, **52**: 384–92.

Balasubramanium, V., Kanaka, T. S., & Ramanujam, P. B. (1973). Stereotactic cingulotomy for drug addiction. *Neurology India*, **21**: 63–6.

Ballantine, H. T. Jr., Cassidy, W. L, Flanagan, N. B., & Marino, R. Jr. (1967). Stereotaxic anterior cingulotomy for neuropsychiatric illness and intractable pain. *Journal of Neurosurgery*, **26**: 488–95.

Barcia, J. A., Bertolin-Guillen, J. M., Barcia-Gonzalez, J., Campos, J., &

Hernandez, M. E. (2007). Present status of psychosurgery in Spain. *Neurocirugia (Astur)*, **18**: 301–11.

Baxter, L. R. Jr., Schwartz, J. M., & Bergman, K. S., et al. (1992). Caudate glucose metabolic rate changes with both drug and behavior therapy for obsessive compulsive disorder. *Archives of General Psychiatry*, **49**: 681–9.

Bejjani, B. P., Damier, P., Arnulf, I., et al. (1999). Transient acute depression induced by high-frequency deep-brain stimulation. *New England Journal of Medicine*, **340**: 1476–80.

Berney, A., Vingerhoets, F., Perrin, A., et al. (2002). Effect on mood of subthalamic DBS for Parkinson's disease: a consecutive series of 24 patients. *Neurology*, **59**: 1427–9.

Bridges, P. K., & Goktepe, E. O. (1973). A review of patients with obsessional symptoms treated by psychosurgery. In: Laitinen, L. V., & Livingstone, K. E. (Eds). *Surgical Approaches in Psychiatry*. Baltimore, MA: University Park Press, 96–100.

Bridges, P. K., Bartlett, J. R., Hale, A. S., Poynton, A. M., Malizin, A. L., & Hodgkiss, A. D. (1994). Psychosurgery: stereotactic subcaudate tractotomy. An indispensable treatment. *British Journal of Psychiatry*, **165**: 599–611.

Burckhardt, G. (1891). Über Rindenexcisionen als Beitrag zur Operativen therapie der Psychosen. *Allegemaine Zeitschrift für psychiatrie*, **47**: 463–548.

Cho, D. Y., Lee, W. Y., & Chen, C. C. (2008). Limbic leukotomy for intractable major affective disorders: a 7-year follow-up study using nine comprehensive psychiatric test evaluations. *Journal of Clinical Neuroscience*, **15**: 138–42.

Corkin, S., Twitchell, T., & Sullivan, E. (1979). Safety and efficacy of cingulotomy for pain and psychiatric disorder. In: Hitchcock, E. R., Ballantine, H. T., & Meyerson, B. A. (Eds). *Modern Concepts in Psychiatric Surgery*. Amsterdam: Elsevier/North Holland Biomedical Press, 253–71.

Cosyns, P., & Gybels, J. (1979). Psychiatric process analysis of obsessive compulsive behaviour modification by psychiatric surgery. In: Hitchcock, E. R., Ballantine, H. T., & Meyerson, B. A. (Eds). *Modern*

Concepts in Psychiatric Surgery. Amsterdam: Elsevier/North Holland Biomedical Press, 225–33.

Cosyns, P., Caemaert, J., Haaijman, W., *et al.* (1994). Functional stereotactic neurosurgery for psychiatric disorders: an experience in Belgium and the Netherlands. *Advances and Technical Standards in Neurosurgery*, **21**: 239–79.

Cotton, H. (1922). The etiology and treatment of the so-called functional psychoses. Summary of the results based on the experience of four years. *American Journal of Psychiatry*, **2**: 157–210.

del Valle, R., de Anda, S., Garnica, R., *et al.* (2006). Radiocirugía psiquiátrica con gamma knife. *Salud Mental*, **29**: 18–27.

Drevets, W. C., Videen, T. O., Price, J. L., Preskorn, S. H., Carmichael, S. T., & Raichle, M. E. (1992). A functional anatomical study of unipolar depression. *Journal of Neuroscience*, **12**: 3628–41.

Editorial (1949). The Nobel Prize in Medicine. *New England Journal of Medicine*, **241**: 1025–6.

Evans, P. (1971). Failed leucotomy with misplaced cuts: a clinico-anatomical study of two cases. *British Journal of Psychiatry*, **118**: 165–70.

Fraraccio, M., Ptito, A., Sadikot, A., Panisset, M., & Dagher, A. (2008). Absence of cognitive deficits following deep brain stimulation of the subthalamic nucleus for the treatment of Parkinson's disease. *Archives of Clinical Neuropsychology*, **23**: 399–408.

Freeman, W. (1935). Personality and the endocrines: a study based upon 1400 quantitative necropsies. *Annals of Internal Medicine*, **9**: 444–50.

Gabriels, L., Cosyns, P., Nuttin, B., Demeulemeester, H., & Gybels, J. (2003). Deep brain stimulation for treatment of refractory obsessive–compulsive disorder: psychopathological and neuropsychological outcome in three cases. *Neurosurgery Clinics of North America*, **107**: 275–82.

Gabriels, L., Nuttin, B., & Cosyns, P. (2008). Applicants for stereotactic neurosurgery for psychiatric disorders: role of the Flemish advisory board. *Acta Psychiatrica Scandinavica*, **117**: 381–9.

Greenberg, B. D., Malone, D. A., Friehs, G. M., *et al.* (2006). Three-year outcomes in deep brain stimulation for highly resistant obsessive-compulsive disorder. *Neuropsychopharmacology*, **31**: 2384–93.

Grimm, R. J. (1980). Regulation of psychosurgery. In: Valenstein, E. S. (Ed.). *The Psychosurgery Debate: Scientific, Legal and Ethical Perspectives*. San Francisco, CA: WH Freeman, 421–38.

Hardesty, D. E., & Sackeim, H. A. (2007). Deep brain stimulation in movement and psychiatric disorders. *Biological Psychiatry*, **61**: 831–5.

Hauptman, J. S., DeSalles, A. A., Espinoza, R., Sedrak, M., & Ishida, W. (2008). Potential surgical targets for deep brain stimulation in treatment-resistant depression. *Neurosurgical Focus*, **25**: E3.

Hay, P., Sachdev, P. S., Cumming, *et al.* (1993). Treatment of obsessive–compulsive disorder by psychosurgery. *Acta Psychiatrica Scandinavica*, **87**: 197–207.

Hay, P. J., & Sachdev, P. S. (1992). The present status of psychosurgery in Australia and New Zealand. *Medical Journal of Australia*, **157**: 17–9.

Heller, A. C., Amar, A. P., Liu, C. Y., & Apuzzo, M. L. (2006). Surgery of the mind and mood: a mosaic of issues in time and evolution. *Neurosurgery*, **59**: 720–39.

Hodgkiss, A. D., Malizia, A. L., Bartlett, J. R., & Bridges, P. K. (1995). Outcomes after the psychosurgical operation of stereotactic subcaudate tractotomy, *Journal of Neuropsychiatry and Clinical Neurosciences*, **7**: 230–4.

Hutchinson, M., Stack, J., & Buckley, P. (1993). Bipolar affective disorder prior to the onset of multiple sclerosis. *Acta Neurologica Scandinavica*, **88**: 388–93.

Jacobsen, C. F., Wolfe, J. B., & Jackson, T. A. (1935). An experimental analysis of the functions of the frontal association areas in primates. *Journal of Nervous and Mental Disease*, **82**: 1–14.

Jiménez, F., Velasco, F., Salin-Pascual, R., *et al.* (2005). A patient with a resistant major depression disorder treated with deep brain stimulation in the inferior thalamic peduncle. *Neurosurgery*, **5**: 585–93.

Johansen-Berg, H., Gutman, D. A., Behrens, T. E., *et al.* (2008). Anatomical connectivity of the subgenual cingulate region targeted with deep brain stimulation for treatment-resistant depression. *Cerebral Cortex*, **18**: 1374–83.

Kelly, D. (1980). *Anxiety and Emotions. Physiological Basis and Treatment.* Springfield, IL: Charles Thomas.

Kiloh, L. G. (1977). Commentary on the report of the committee of inquiry into psychosurgery. *Medical Journal of Australia*, **2**: 296–301.

Kiloh, L. G., Smith, J. S., & Johnson, G. F. (1988). *Physical Treatments in Psychiatry.* Melbourne: Blackwell Scientific Publications.

Kim, M. C., Lee, T. K., & Choi, C. R. (2002). Review of long-term results of stereotactic psychosurgery. *Neurologia Medico-Chirurgica*, **42**: 365–71.

Kiss, Z. H., Doig-Beyaert, K., Eliasziw, M., Tsui, J., Haffenden, A., & Suchowersky, O. (2007). The Canadian multicentre study of deep brain stimulation for cervical dystonia. *Brain*, **130**: 2879–86.

Klaesi, J., (1922). Uber die therapeutische Andwendung des Daverschafes mittles Sonifen bei Schizophrenen. *Ztschr f. d. ges Neurol u Psychiatry*, **74**: 557–63.

Knight, G. C. (1964). The orbital cortex as an objective in the surgical treatment of mental illness: the development of the stereotactic approach. *British Journal of Surgery*, **53**: 114–24.

Kopeloff, N., & Kirby, G. H. (1923). Focal infection and mental disease. *American Journal of Psychiatry*, **3**: 149–97.

Kosel, M., Sturm, V., Frick, C., *et al.* (2007). Mood improvement after deep brain stimulation of the internal globus pallidus for tardive dyskinesia in a patient suffering from major depression. *Journal of Psychiatric Research*, **41**: 801–03. Epub 2006 Sep 8. *PMID:* 16962613.

Kringelbach, M. L., Jenkinson, N., Owen, S. L., & Aziz, T. Z. (2007). Translational principles of deep brain stimulation. *Nature Reviews Neuroscience*, **8**: 623–35.

Kulisevsky, J., Berthier, M. L., Gironell, A., Pascual-Sedano, B., Molet, S., & Pares, P. (2002). Mania following deep brain stimulation for Parkinson's disease. *Neurology*, **59**: 1421–4.

Leksell, L., & Backlund, E. O. (1979). Stereotactic gamma capsulotomy. In: Hitchcock, E. R., Ballantine, H. T., & Meyerson, B. A. (Eds). *Modern Concepts in Psychiatric Surgery.* Amsterdam: Elsevier/North Holland Biomedical Press, 213–6.

Levine, R., Lipson, S., & Devinsky, O. (2003). Resolution of easting disorders after right temporal lesions. *Epilepsy Behaviour*, **4**: 781–3.

Lilleeng, B., & Dietrichs, E. (2008). Unmasking psychiatric symptoms after STN deep brain stimulation in Parkinson's disease. *Acta Neurologica Scandinavica*, **S188**: 41–5.

Lishman, A. W. (1998). *Organic Psychiatry: The Psychological Consequences of Cerebral Disorder.* Oxford: Blackwell Science Ltd.

Livingstone, K. E. (1953). Cingulate cortex isolation for the treatment of psychoses and psychoneurosis. In: *Psychiatric Treatment.* London: Williams & Wilkins.

Logue, V., Durward, M., Pratt, R., Piercy, M., & Nixon, W. (1968). The quality of survival after rupture of an anterior cerebral aneurysm. *British Journal of Psychiatry*, **114**: 137–60.

Loo, C., Mitchell, P., Sachdev, P., McDarmont, B., Parker, G., & Gandevia, S. (1999). Double-blind controlled investigation of transcranial magnetic stimulation for the treatment of resistant major depression. *American Journal of Psychiatry*, **156**: 946–8.

Lozano, A. M., Mayberg, H. S., Giacobbe, P., Hamani, C., Craddock, R. C., & Kennedy, S. H. (2008). Subcallosal cingulate gyrus deep brain stimulation for treatment-resistant depression. *Biological Psychiatry*, **64**: 461–7.

Machlin, S. R., Harris, G. J., Pearlson, G. D., Hoehn-Saric, R., Jeffery, P., & Camargo, E. E. (1991). Elevated medial-frontal cerebral blood flow in obsessive–compulsive patients: a SPECT study. *American Journal of Psychiatry*, **148**: 1240–2.

MacLean, P. D. (1949). Psychosomatic disease and the visceral brain: recent developments bearing on the Papez theory of emotion. *Psychosomatic Medicine*, **11**: 338–53.

Mark, V. H., & Ervin, F. R. (1970). *Violence and the Brain*. New York, NY: Harper and Row.

Marks, I. M., Birley, J. L., & Gelder, M. G. (1966). Modified leucotomy in severed agarophobia: a controlled serial inquiry. *British Journal of Psychiatry*, **122**: 757–69.

Mataix-Cols, D., Wooderson, S., Lawrence, N., Brammer, M. J., Speckens, A., & Phillips, M. L. (2004). Distinct neural correlates of washing, checking, and hoarding symptom dimensions in obsessive compulsive disorder. *Archives of General Psychiatry*, **61**: 64–76.

Mayberg, H. S. (1994). Frontal lobe dysfunction in secondary depression. *Journal of Neuropsychiatry and Clinical Neurosciences*, **6**: 428–42.

Mayberg, H. S. (2006). Defining neurocircuits. *Depression Psychiatric Annals*, **36**: 259–68.

Mayberg, H. S., Brannan, S. K., Tekell, J. L., *et al.* (2000). Regional metabolic effects of fluoxetine in major depression: serial changes and relationship to clinical response. *Biological Psychiatry*, **48**: 830–43.

Mayberg, H. S., Lozano, A. M., Voon, V., *et al.* (2005). Deep brain stimulation for treatment-resistant depression. *Neuron*, **45**: 651–60.

McIntyre, C. C., Savasta, M., Kerkerian-Le Goff, L., & Vitek, J. L. (2004). Uncovering the mechanism(s) of action of deep brain stimulation: activation, inhibition, or both. *Clinical Neurophysiology*, **115**: 1239–48.

McNeely, H. E., Mayberg, H. S., Lozano, A. M., & Kennedy, S. H. (2008). Neuropsychological impact of Cg25 deep brain stimulation for treatment-resistant depression: preliminary results over 12 months. *Journal of Nervous and Mental Disease*, **196**: 405–10.

Meduna, L. (1935a), cited in Fink, M. (1984). Meduna and the origins of convulsive therapy. *American Journal of Psychiatry*, **141**: 1034–41.

Meduna, L. (1935b). Versuche über die biologische Beeinflussung des Abaufbaues der Schizophrenia. I. Camphor und Cardiazol Krampfe. *Neurologie und Psychiatrie*, **152**: 235–62.

Mega, M. S., & Cummings, J. L. (1994). Frontal–subcortical circuits and neuropsychiatric disorders. *Journal of Neuropsychiatry and Clinical Neurosciences*, **6**: 358–70.

Merkl, A., Heuser, I., & Najbouj, M. (2009). Antidepressant anticonvulsive therapy: mechanisms of action, recent advances and limitations. *Experimental Neurology*, **219**: 20–6.

Mindus, P. (1991). Capsulotomy in Anxiety Disorders: A Multidisciplinary Study. Thesis. Stockholm: Karolinska Institute.

Mindus, P., & Hyman, H. (1991). Normalization of personality characteristics in patients with incapacitating anxiety disorders after capsulotomy. *Acta Psychiatrica Scandinavica*, **83**: 238–91.

Moniz, E. (1936). Essai d'un traitement chirurgical de certaines psychoses. *Bulletin de l'Academie de Medecine (Paris)*, **115**: 385–92.

Montoya, A., Weiss, A. P., Price, B. H., *et al.* (2002). Magnetic resonance imaging-guided stereotactic limbic leukotomy for treatment of intractable psychiatric disease. *Neurosurgery*, **50**: 1043–9.

Mueller, J., Skogseid, I. M., Benecke, R., *et al.* (2008). Pallidal deep brain stimulation improves quality of life in segmental and generalized dystonia: results from a prospective, randomized sham-controlled trial. *Movement Disorders*, **23**: 131–4.

Naqvi, N. H., Rudrauf, D., Damasio, H., *et al.* (2007). Damage to the insula disrupts addiction to cigarette smoking. *Science*, **315**: 531–2.

National commission for the protection of human subjects of biomedical and behavioral research. Report and Recommendations: Psychosurgery. (1977). Department of Health, Education and Welfare. Washington DC: US Government Printing Office, Pub No. (OS) 77–0002.

Nauta, W. J. (1972): Neural associations of the frontal cortex. *Acta neurobiologiae experimentalis (Warsz)*, **32**: 125–40.

Neimat, J. S., Hamani, C., Giacobbe, P., *et al.* (2008). Neural stimulation successfully treats depression in patients with prior ablative cingulotomy. *American Journal of Psychiatry*, **165**: 687–93.

Neyman, C. A. (1938). *Artificial Fever.* Springfield, IL: Charles C Thomas.

Nuttin, B., Cosyns, P., Demeulemeester, H., Gybels, J., & Meyerson, B. (1999). Electrical stimulation in anterior limbs of internal capsules in patients with obsessive–compulsive disorder. *Lancet*, **354**: 1526.

Nuttin, B. J., Gabriels, L., van Kuyck, K., & Cosyns, P. (2003). Electrical stimulation of the anterior limbs of the internal capsules in patients with severe obsessive–compulsive disorder: anecdotal reports. *Neurosurgery Clinics of North America*, **14**: 267–74.

Nyman, H., & Mindus, P. (1995). Neuropsychological correlates of intractable anxiety disorder before and after capsulotomy. *Acta Psychiatrica Scandinavica*, **91**, 23–31.

Oregon Senate Bill (SB) 298 (1973). *Oregon Psychosurgery Bill.* Portland, OR: Oregon Legislative Assembly.

Pahwa, R., Factor, S. A., Lyons, K., *et al.* (2006). Practice parameter: treatment of Parkinson disease with motor fluctuations and dyskinesia (an evidence-based review). Report of the Quality Standards Subcommittee of the American Academy of Neurology. *Neurology*, **66**: 983–95.

Parliament of New South Wales report of the committee of inquiry into psychosurgery (1977). Sydney: NSW Government Printer.

Poole, J. L. (1954). Psychosurgery of older people. *The Journal of the American Geriatric Society*, **2**: 456–65.

Poynton, A. M., Kartsounis, L. D., & Bridges, P. K. (1995). A prospective clinical study of stereotactic subcaudate tractotomy. *Psychological Medicine*, **25**: 763–70.

Pressman, J. (1998). *Last Resort: Psychosurgery and the Limits of Medicine.* New York, NY: Cambridge University Press.

Rauch, S. L., Jenike, M. A., Alpert N., *et al.* (1994). Regional cerebral blood flow measured during symptom provocation in obsessive–compulsive disorder using oxygen 15-labeled carbon dioxide and positron emission tomography. *Archives of General Psychiatry*, **51**: 62–70.

Restak, R. (2000). 'Fixing the brain'. *Mysteries of the Mind.* Washington, DC: National Geographic Society, 206–17.

Ridout, N., O'Carroll, R. E., Dritschel, B., Christmas, D., Eljamel, M., & Matthews, K. (2007). Emotion recognition from dynamic emotional displays following anterior cingulotomy and anterior capsulotomy for chronic depression. *Neuropsychologia*, **45**: 1735–43.

Royal College of Psychiatrists (2000). *Neurosurgery for mental disorders. Report from the Neurosurgery Working group of the Royal College of Psychiatrists (Council Report CR89).* London: Royal College of Psychiatrists.

Rubin, R. T., Ananth, J., Villanueva-Meyer, J., Trajmar, P. G., & Mena, I. (1995). Regional 133-xenon cerebral blood flow and cerebral 99mTc-HMPAO uptake in patients with obsessive–compulsive disorder before and during treatment. *Biological Psychiatry*, **38**: 429–37.

Sachdev, P. (2007b). Is deep brain stimulation a form of psychosurgery? *Australasian Psychiatry*, **15**: 97–9.

Sachdev, P. (2009). *The Yipping Tiger and Other Tales from the Neuropsychiatric Clinic.* Sydney: UNSW Press; and Baltimore, MD: Johns Hopkins University Press.

Sachdev, P., & Hay, P. (1995). Does neurosurgery for obsessive–compulsive disorder produce personality change? *Journal of Nervous and Mental Disease*, **183**: 408–13.

Sachdev, P., & Hay, P. (1996). Site and size of lesion and psychological outcome on obsessive compulsive disorder: a magnetic resonance imaging study. *Biological Psychiatry*, **39**: 739–42.

Sachdev, P. S. (2007a). Alternating and postictal psychoses: review and a unifying hypothesis. *Schizophrenia Bulletin*, **33**: 1029–37.

Sachdev, P. S., & Chen, X. (2009). Neurosurgical treatment of mood disorders: traditional psychosurgery and the advent of deep brain stimulation. *Current Opinion in Psychiatry*, **22**: 25–31.

Sachdev, P. S., & Sachdev, J. (2005). Long-term outcome of neurosurgery for the treatment of resistant depression. *Journal of Neuropsychiatry and Clinical Neurosciences*, **17**: 478–85.

Sakas, D. E., & Panourias, I. G. (2006). Rostral cingulate gyrus: a putative target for deep brain stimulation in treatment-refractory depression. *Medical Hypotheses*, **66**: 491–4.

Sakel, M, (1937). Origin and nature of hypoglycemic therapy of the psychoses, and sicussion. *Archives of Neurology and Psychiatry*, **38**: 188–203.

Sartorius, A., & Henn, F. A. (2007). Deep brain stimulation of the lateral habenula in treatment resistant major depression. *Medical Hypotheses*, **69**: 1305–08.

Saxena, S., Brody, A. L., Maidment, K. M., *et al.* (1999). Localized orbitofrontal and subcortical metabolic changes and predictors of response to paroxetine treatment in obsessive–compulsive disorder. *Neuropsychopharmacology*, **21**: 683–93.

Saxena, S., Brody, A. L., Schwartz, J. M., & Baxter, L. R. (1998). Neuroimaging and frontal–subcortical circuitry in obsessive–compulsive disorder. *British Journal of Psychiatry*, **S35**: 26–37.

Schlaepfer, T. E., Cohen, M. X., Frick, C., *et al.* (2008). Deep brain stimulation to reward circuitry alleviates anhedonia in refractory major depression. *Neuropsychopharmacology*, **33**: 368–77.

Sheline, Y. I. (2003). Neuroimaging studies of mood disorder effects on the brain. *Biological Psychiatry*, **5**: 338–52.

Solyom, L., Turnbull, I. M., & Wilensky, M. (1987). A case of self-inflicted leucotomy. *British Journal of Psychiatry*, **151**: 855–7.

Soulas, T., Gurruchaga, J. M., Palfi, S., Cesaro, P., Nguyen, J. P., & Fenelon, G. (2008). Attempted and completed suicides after subthalamic nucleus stimulation for Parkinson's disease. *Journal of Neurology, Neurosurgery and Psychiatry*, **79**: 952–4.

Spangler, W. J., Cosgrove, G. R., Ballantine, H. T. Jr., *et al.* (1996). Magnetic resonance image-guided stereotactic cingulotomy for intractable psychiatric disease. *Neurosurgery*, **38**: 1071–6; discussion 1076–8.

Steele, J. D., Christmas, D., Eljamel, M. S., & Matthews, K. (2008). Anterior cingulotomy for major depression: clinical outcome and relationship to lesion characteristics. *Biological Psychiatry*, **63**: 670–7.

Steele, J. D., Currie, J., Lawrie, S. M., & Reid, I. (2007). Prefrontal cortical functional abnormality in major depressive disorder: a stereotactic meta-analysis. *Journal of Affective Disorders*, **101**: 1–11.

Storey, P. (1970). Brain damage and personality change after subarachnoid haemorrhage. *British Journal of Psychiatry*, **117**: 129–42.

Sturm, V., Lenartz, D., Koulousakis, A., *et al.* (2003). The nucleus accumbens: a target for deep brain stimulation in obsessive compulsive and anxiety disorders. *Journal of Chemical Neuroanatomy*, **26**: 293–9.

Swedo, S. E., Schapiro, M. B., Grady, C. L., *et al.* (1989). Cerebral glucose metabolism in childhood-onset obsessive–compulsive disorder. *Archives of General Psychiatry*, **46**: 518–23.

Swerdlow, N. R., & Koob, G. F. (1987). Dopamine, schizophrenia, mania and depression: toward a unified hypothesis of cortico-striato-pallido-thalamic function. *Behavioral and Brain Sciences*, **10**: 197–245.

Tan, E., Marks, I. M., & Marset, P. (1971). Bimedial leucotomy in obsessive–compulsive neurosis: a controlled serial enquiry. *British Journal of Psychiatry*, **118**: 155–64.

Temel, Y., Boothman, L. J., Blokland, A., *et al.* (2007). Inhibition of 5-HT neuron activity and induction of depressive-like behavior by high-frequency stimulation of the subthalamic nucleus. *Proceedings of the National Academy of Sciences USA*, **104**: 17,087–92.

Valenstein, E. S. (1980). *The Psychosurgery Debate: Scientific, Legal and Ethical Perspectives*. San Francisco, CA: WH Freeman.

Valenstein, E. S. (1986). *Great and Desperate Cures: The Rise and Decline of Psychosurgery and Other Radical Treatments for Mental Illness*. New York, NY: Basic Books.

Velasco, F., Velasco, M., Jiménez, F., Velasco, A. L., & Salin-Pascual, R. (2005). Neurobiological background for performing

surgical intervention in the inferior thalamic
peduncle for treatment of major depression
disorders. *Neurosurgery*, **57**: 439–48.

Waziri, R. (1990). Psychosurgery for anxiety and
obsessive compulsive disorders. In: Noyes,
R., Roth, M., & Burrows, G. D. (Eds.).
Handbook of Anxiety, Volume 4. Amsterdam:
Elsevier Science Publications.

Whitty, C. W., Duffield, J. E., Tow, P. M., &
Cairns, H. (1952). Anterior cingulectomy in
the treatment of mental disease. *Lancet*, **1**:
475–81.

Wichmann, T., & Delong, M. R. (2006).
Deep brain stimulation for neurologic
and neuropsychiatric disorders. *Neuron*, **52**:
197–204.

Witt, K., Daniels, C., Reiff, J., *et al.* (2008).
Neuropsychological and psychiatric changes
after deep brain stimulation for Parkinson's
disease: a randomised, multicentre study.
Lancet Neurology, **7**: 605–14.

Woerdeman, P. A., Willems, P. W., Noordmans,
H. J., Berkelbach van der Sprenkel, J. W., &
van Rijen, P. C. (2006). Frameless stereotactic
subcaudate tractotomy for intractable
obsessive–compulsive disorder. *Acta
Neurochir (Wien)*, **148**: 633–7.

Zibetti, M., Torre, E., Cinquepalmi, A., *et al.*
(2007). Motor and nonmotor symptom
follow-up in Parkinsonian patients after deep
brain stimulation of the subthalamic nucleus.
European Neurology, **58**: 218–23.

Chapter 18

The paradox of electroconvulsive therapy

Angela Merkl and Malek Bajbouj

Summary

One of the most dramatic paradoxes in psychiatry is the mechanism of action and efficacy of electroconvulsive therapy (ECT), in which people are anaesthesized and given an electric shock sufficient to produce an epileptic seizure. Although known for over 70 years, many of the hypothesized underlying mechanisms still remain unresolved and under debate. The practice of ECT has evolved into a complex procedure and its application worldwide has had extensive clinical impact in the field of neuropsychiatric disorders. Within this background, we report on current neurophysiological models of ECT, its efficacy and further questions and directions of its use. The chapter reports how the paradox that an epileptic seizure has a beneficial effect on mood has influenced our understanding of brain pathologies.

Introduction

There is arguably no treatment more negatively judged, no treatment more controversially discussed and no treatment more effective in psychiatry than electroconvulsive therapy (ECT). This treatment raises a number of different paradoxes: first, why is a highly effective treatment perceived so negatively at the same time? Second, why can this treatment work at the same time in conditions with increased dopaminergic neurotransmission (like psychosis) and in diseases with decreased dopaminergic neurotransmission (like Parkinson's disease)? Third, why does this therapy work at the same time as an intervention against depression and against mania? And fourth, the main paradox: why does a treatment based on the repetitive induction of generalized seizure activity not lead to considerable brain damage but – on the contrary – have beneficial effects?

Historical background

Describing the history of ECT and the concept of 'forced normalization' may help to address the question why ECT works in such different conditions as described above. ECT and its application today in psychiatric and neurological diseases has been well established since the first ideas from Meduna's early theory of antagonism between epilepsy and schizophrenia. Ladislas Joseph von Meduna was born in Budapest, Hungary, in 1896. As Max Fink wrote in 1984, 'the origin of convulsive therapy is often attributed to Sakel, who introduced insulin shock therapy, or to Cerletti and Bini, who demonstrated that seizures could be induced more easily with electric currents. But it

The Paradoxical Brain, ed. Narinder Kapur. Published by Cambridge University Press. © Cambridge University Press 2011.

was Meduna who tested a theory of biological antagonism between epilepsy and schizo-phrenia and developed this novel treatment' (Fink, 1984).

Meduna studied medicine in Budapest from 1914 to 1921, his studies being interrupted by military service in the Italian front from 1915 to 1918 during the First World War. At the Department of Psychiatry in Budapest, he reported two patients with dementia praecox who developed epileptic attacks during the acute phase of their disorder and were subsequently relieved of their symptoms. Meduna postulated that schizophrenia and seizures were 'antagon-istic', and that therefore, seizures could be used to treat schizophrenia (Fink, 2001). While this idea no longer currently holds as the basis for the use of ECT, the antagonism between seizures and behavioural disorders is a prominent paradox akin to a similar antagonism such as the concept of 'forced normalization' in epilepsy (Krishnamoorthy and Trimble, 1999).

What is the basis of forced normalization? In 1953, Heinrich Landolt, described two groups of epileptic patients with acute psychoses (Landolt, 1953): in one group, the electroencephalo-gram (EEG) changed during the psychosis toward increased epileptiform activity, which was intuitively easy to understand. However, in the second group, a previously abnormal EEG 'normalized' during the psychosis. Landolt chose the term 'forcierte Normalisierung' to describe this EEG change. So far, there is no certainty as to underlying mechanisms that fully describe such a phenomenon, one of several suggestions being that amygdaloid and limbic kindling may play a role in its development (Krishnamoorthy and Trimble, 1999).

Possible mechanisms may include the neurochemical changes that may accompany forced normalization, such as changes in neurotransmission of dopamine, glutamate and GABA. The potential for dopamine agonists to precipitate psychosis is well known, as is the antipsychotic effect of dopamine antagonists. Additionally, enhanced glutaminergic excita-tion is considered to be a potential epileptogenic mechanism, particularly with respect to the role of the N-methyl-D-aspartate (NMDA) glutamate receptor.

Meduna investigated several substances which could produce epileptic attacks and tried several pharmacological agents to safely induce convulsions, such as the alkaloids strych-nine, thebaine, coramin, caffeine and brucin (Fink, 2001). Finally, he discovered that camphor dissolved in oil was effective in animals as well as in humans. On 23 January 1934, he tried the injection of camphor oil in a severe 33-year-old catatonic patient. After just five treatments, catatonia and psychotic symptoms were abolished. Increasing his case series to 26 patients, Meduna achieved recovery in 10 of them and improvement in 3 more, which was an improvement of 50%. Afterwards, Meduna discovered pentylenetetrazol, or metrazol, a powerful convulsant agent, as being more effective and faster-acting than camphor, and started using it in intramuscular and intravenous injections.

He published his results in 1935 and his observations quickly released a movement in the psychiatry community around the world, because schizophrenia was then considered a hereditary and incurable condition. In 1939, he published in German a monograph titled 'Die Konvulsionstherapie der Schizophrenie' (Meduna, 1935), describing his results with 110 patients. He reported an astounding 95% remission rate in acute schizophrenic patients, and of 80% in patients with less than one year duration of the disease. Longer durations of disease had increasingly reduced effectiveness of metrazol therapy. Due to the discovery by Meduna, a new therapeutic era in treating psychiatric disorders had begun. His results were reproduced in many other centres around the world and this form of therapy became commonplace, despite its harsh adverse effects.

Meduna's work was notable in influencing the discovery of a more stable, less detri-mental and more effective form of convulsive therapy, by means of electroshock. This was

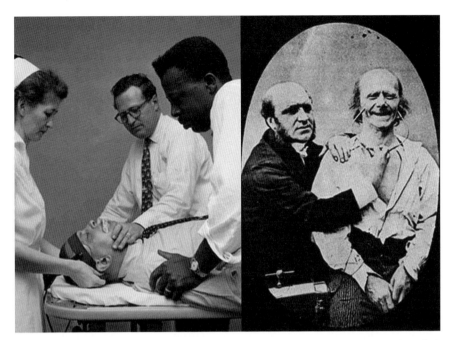

Figure 18.1 *Left*: Electroconvulsive therapy is often misunderstood. This patient was treated at Hillside Mental Hospital *circa* 1955. Carl Purcell/Three Lions/Getty Images. *Right*: Expression des passions G. B. Duchenne de Boulogne. Paris: 1852–1856. Epreuve sur papier. 110–130 mm. Extrait de G. B. Duchene de Boulogne. Mécanismes de la physionomie humaine, ou analyse électro-physiologique de l'expression des passions Paris, Baillière 1862. Duchenne maintained a longstanding interest in electricity (faradism) as a means of stimulating the skeletal muscles. He was especially interested in the facial muscles of expression. In 1850, he began his work on faradic stimulation of these muscles with an induction coil. In 1860, Jean-Martin Charcot, Duchenne's close personal friend, established the first clinical photography department in a hospital. This was at the Salpêtrière, where Duchenne spent many hours pursuing his science. (http://commons.wikimedia.org/wiki/File: Duchenne_de_Boulogne_1.jpg)

discovered in 1938 by Italian researchers Ugo Cerletti and Lucio Bini (Abrams, 2002). Metrazol convulsive therapy was abandoned afterwards. Thus, the idea of using electricity applied to the cranium for patients would re-emerge with Cerletti and Bini (Cerletti and Bini, 1938). The first patient to receive ECT was a 39-year-old man who was diagnosed as having schizophrenia. His affect was flat and he was passive in behaviour (Fink, 1984). He was successfully treated, with full recovery after a course of 11 ECTs. At follow-up one year later, he could work in his former job (Abrams, 2002). An important statement at this time was made by Cerletti: 'I have always maintained that in the therapeutic mechanism of electroshock the electricity itself is of little importance: it is only the epileptogenic stimulus, while the important and fundamental factor is the epileptic-like seizure, no matter how it is obtained' (Cerletti, 1956).

ECT was then introduced at a time when no effective treatment for the severely mentally ill was known. It was thus received enthusiastically and promoted as effective in depression, mania, bipolar disease and schizophrenia.

One of the pioneers in the history of ECT was Max Fink, who was one of the first to introduce a scientific approach to ECT research (Abrams, 2002). He published on the relationship between ECT-induced EEG delta activity and treatment response in ECT, and he recognized the importance of EEG as a tool for analysing ECT (Abrams, 2002).

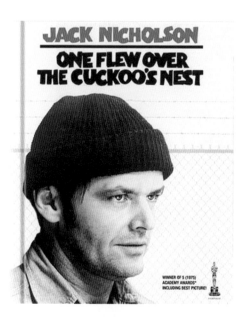

Figure 18.2 In the 1970s, strong movements against institutionalized psychiatry began in Europe and particularly in the USA. Together with psychosurgery, ECT was denounced, and the most famous libel was a 1962 novel written by Ken Kesey, based on his experiences in an Oregon mental hospital. Entitled 'One Flew Over the Cuckoo's Nest', it was later made into a highly successful movie by Czech director Milos Forman, starring Jack Nicholson. (http://www.filmsite.org/onef.html)

Additionally, in the late 1950s, he was conducting controlled studies on clinical, electro-physiological and pharmacological aspects of ECT, and was one of the first to publish on the relationship between the clinical efficiency of ECT and its effects on memory and learning (Fink *et al.*, 1956). ECT remains widely used to this day, with improvements in efficacy, safety of use and ease of administration. Advanced muscle relaxation and anaesthesia procedures have been introduced in recent years.

Effects and adverse effects of electroconvulsive therapy

The question and paradox remains unresolved as to how ECT improves mood symptoms by producing an epileptic seizure. How can this intervention, which seems to be 'pathological' at first glance, normalize brain function at a behavioural level?

ECT has been reported to result in major improvements in the symptoms of depression in the majority of depressed patients treated. The Consortium for Research in ECT (CORE) observed a 75% remission rate among 217 patients who completed a short acute course of ECT during an acute episode of depression, with 65% of patients having remission by the fourth week of therapy (Husain *et al.*, 2004). In 2003, another review of 6 trials involving 256 patients by the UK ECT Review Group (2003) showed that the effect size (a measure of improvement) for ECT was 0.91 and significantly more effective than sham ECT. A review of 18 trials involving 1144 patients showed that the effect size for ECT was 0.80, which was more effective than pharmacotherapy. In a study involving 253 patients, the CORE group reported that, in particular, patients with the psychotic subtype of depression showed a response that was significantly higher than in patients without psychotic features (Petrides *et al.*, 2001). The CORE group also found that response rates were higher among elderly patients (O'Connor *et al.*, 2001).

Patients with a catatonic form of schizophrenia – a subtype with prominent movement symptoms – respond well to ECT. However, the results for paranoid forms of schizophrenia

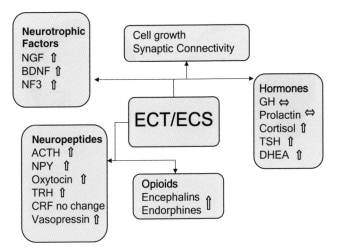

Figure 18.3 Effects of ECT or electroshocks (ECS) on various biological variables. Arrows indicate increase, decrease or inconsistent data. (For an overview, see Wahlund and van Rosen, 2003.)

are heterogeneous (Fink and Taylor, 2003). For those catatonic patients with very high temperature, in delirium, or at physiologic risk, or who do not quickly respond to lorazepam, bilateral ECT is recommended for daily treatments for 2–5 days and is reported to be most effective (Fink and Taylor, 2009). Additionally, cycloid psychoses are reported to respond very well to ECT (Little *et al.*, 2000; Neuhaus *et al.*, 2007). There may be a more favourable response to ECT when symptoms such as overt delusions and hallucinations, and motor hyperactivity, are dominating in schizophrenia (Fink, 1979), although there is currently a lack of carefully controlled ECT studies in large study samples in schizophrenia.

Retrograde amnesia and anterograde amnesia are the most common adverse effects of ECT (UK ECT Review Group, 2003) However, no study contrasting ECT patients with controls has observed anterograde amnesia to persist more than four weeks (Nobler and Sackeim, 2008). There is no evidence in longitudinal studies that ECT-induced cognitive deficits are persistent (UK ECT Review Group, 2003) and long-term or irreversible cognitive deficits in ECT-treated patients are anecdotal. If there is loss of recall in single cases, then memory of autobiographical information is less affected by ECT than the memory of events of an impersonal nature (Lisanby *et al.*, 2000). Cognitive impairment which was already pre-existing is considered to be a predictor of amnesia after ECT, and amnesia is also more likely in the elderly (Donahue, 2000; Mulsant *et al.*, 1991). Furthermore, the different electrode applications of the ECT technique itself can reduce the incidence and severity of retrograde amnesia substantially, as studies have shown that right unilateral electrode placement and ultrabrief pulse width diminish cognitive adverse effects (Sackeim *et al.*, 1993). Right unilateral ECT at high dosage was shown as effective as bilateral ECT at a lower fixed dosage and was reported to produce less severe and persistent cognitive side-effects (Sackeim *et al.*, 2000).

Mode of action of electroconvulsive therapy

While the efficacy of ECT is clear and its adverse effect profile has been well described, the mode of action remains unclear. Of the various possible accounts, two key ones revolve around neuroplasticity and the GABAergic mode-of-action hypothesis.

In the case of neuroplasticity, the observation that electroconvulsive shock (ECS), the animal model version of ECT, is known to facilitate plasticity in itself constitutes another

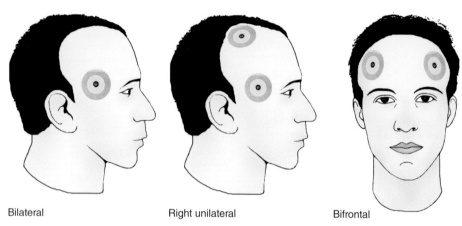

Bilateral   Right unilateral   Bifrontal

Figure 18.4 The three standard electrode placements are bifrontotemporal (commonly referred to as 'bilateral'), right unilateral, and bifrontal. In bilateral placement, there is one electrode on each side of the head. In right unilateral placement, one electrode is in the right frontotemporal position, and the second electrode is placed to the right of the vertex. In bifrontal placement, there is one electrode on each side of the head, but the placement is more frontal than it is in standard bilateral placement. Unilateral ECT is used first to minimize side-effects (memory loss).

paradox. Molecular studies have revealed that brain-derived neurotrophic factor (BDNF) is upregulated by ECT (Bocchio-Chiavetto *et al.*, 2006). BDNF has been shown to facilitate cellular proliferation and differentiation during normal development or after insult-induced restructuring of the brain (Vicario-Abejon *et al.*, 1998). Hence, according to the neuroplasticity hypothesis of Manji and Duman (Manji and Duman, 2001), the pathogenesis of affective disorders is due to morphological deficits such as a poor dendritic arborization or a reduced neuron number in the cerebral cortex and the hippocampus. These deficits can make the brain more vulnerable to stress. Therefore, it has been suggested that growth factors such as BDNF are responsible for counteracting stress-induced neural insult by promoting neurogenesis and axonal sprouting as well as preventing cell death. ECT and ECS have been suggested to induce BDNF and to trigger neuronal proliferation in the dentate gyrus and sprouting of mossy fibers (Bocchio-Chiavetto *et al.*, 2006; Chen *et al.*, 2001). At least in animal models, ECS-induced transcription factors are described (Sun *et al.*, 2007). Additionally, in rats, proliferation of blood vessels by ECT, which might supply newly generated neurons, has been observed (Newton *et al.*, 2006). Although not all studies have demonstrated these findings (e.g. Fernandes *et al.*, 2009), it would seem at the very least that ECT does not promote destructive neuronal processes. However, it remains doubtful that neuroplasticity is the main factor explaining the mode of action of ECT.

Another suggestion for the mode of action of ECT is modulation of the GABAergic system, since there is a view that the pathogenesis of major depression is related to GABAergic dysfunction. Converging evidence for involvement of central nervous inhibitory circuits has been provided by clinical observations, in-vivo studies using magnetic resonance spectroscopy (Sanacora *et al.*, 2004) and single photon emission tomography (Mervaala *et al.*, 2001), as well as post-mortem data and animal studies. Clinically, it is a regular observation that seizure threshold increases in the course of treatment. In-vivo studies investigating cortical excitability using transcranial magnetic stimulation of the motor cortex as a surrogate marker have indicated altered motor cortical inhibition in

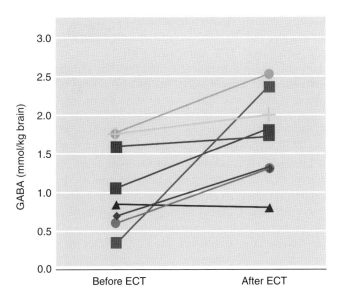

Figure 18.5 Occipital cortex GABA concentrations in eight depressed subjects before and after a course of ECT. Post-ECT GABA concentrations were significantly higher compared with pre-ECT concentrations. Mean GABA concentrations rose from 0.85 to 1.51 mmol/kg brain tissue. Seven of the eight subjects demonstrated an increase in cortical GABA concentrations at the time of the post-ECT study, and four showed increases of greater than 85% over their pre-ECT levels (see Sanacora et al., 2003).

healthy volunteers and increased intracortical inhibition after a single session and series of ECT sessions (Bajbouj et al., 2005a, 2005b, 2006a, 2006b). Additionally, in line with these observations, a decrease in number of GABAergic neurons has been reported in post-mortem brains obtained from depressed patients (Rajkowska et al., 1999). Finally, it has been shown in animal models that repeated application of ECS increases GABA release in the cerebral cortex and striatum (Green and Vincent, 1987). If an enhancement of inhibition has antidepressant effects, this might be another clue that addresses the paradoxical relationship between the antidepressant and epileptogenic effects of treatment. Sackeim has postulated that ECT may in fact raise the seizure threshold and therefore may be therapeutic in cases of epilepsy (Sackeim, 1999). This topic is discussed more fully in Chapter 11.

Future challenges and questions

One of the major challenges will be to fully understand the mechanisms of ECT, in the context of a better understanding of the pathophysiology of mood disorders and schizophrenia on a neurobiological basis. ECT is probably the most efficacious acute antidepressant therapy that also appears to have profound effects on the mechanisms of neuroplasticity (Malberg et al., 2000). Animal studies have shown increases in neurotrophic factors and cell proliferation (Perera et al., 2007), and in particular, electroconvulsive shock (ECS) robustly increased precursor cell proliferation in the subgranular zone (SGZ) of the dentate gyrus in the monkey hippocampus (Perera et al., 2007). However, adverse effects such as subtle memory impairment, although largely reversible, can occur and the challenge will be to improve stimulation settings and parameters, e.g. stimulus wave forms, stimulus frequency, pulse width, electrode placements (bifrontal, bitemporal or right unilateral) and subsequently trigger a more focal brain stimulation. For example, the findings of Sackeim and colleagues (Sackeim et al., 2008) on stimulus pulse width have generated considerable debate about the optimal algorithm in the use of ECT in mood disorders. In a double-blind study, 90 depressed patients were randomly assigned to right unilateral ECT at 6 times seizure threshold or bilateral ECT at 2.5 times seizure threshold, using either a traditional brief pulse (1.5 ms) or an ultra-brief pulse (0.3 ms). The authors observed a final remission rate for ultra-brief bilateral ECT which was 35%, compared with 73% for ultra-brief unilateral ECT, 65% for standard pulse width bilateral ECT, and 59% for standard pulse width unilateral ECT. Their results strongly support initial use of high-dosage ultra-brief right-unilateral ECT. However, some patients will show poor or slow response to this. So far, there is insufficient information to decide at this point whether subsequent treatment should involve an increase of dosage of the ultra-brief right-unilateral stimulus, a switch to a traditional pulse (i.e. 0.5–1.5 ms) width with high-dosage right-unilateral ECT or a switch to bilateral ECT (bitemporal of bifrontal). It is worth noting that long-term differences between bilateral and right-unilateral ECT in the extent of retrograde amnesia have been observed (Sackeim et al., 2007, 2008). Hence, a challenge for the future is to study short- and long-term cognitive differences between different stimulus width of right-unilateral ECT and bilateral ECT in depression as well as in other conditions.

Another challenge will be to find suitable predictors for ECT efficacy in different neuropsychiatric disorders. Which subtypes of depressive patients will respond better to ECT? The second edition of the guidelines of the American Psychiatric Association (APA) Task Force on Electroconvulsive Therapy, which was published in 2001, includes a complete description of the current clinical use of ECT (Task Force on Electroconvulsive Therapy, 2001). One of the primary indications for ECT among patients with depression is lack of a response to, or intolerance of, antidepressant medication, a good response to previous ECT and the need for a rapid response (e.g. because of psychosis or a risk of suicide). ECT is used in both unipolar and bipolar disorders as well as in mania. The decision to apply ECT depends on several factors, including the severity and chronicity of the patient's depression, the likelihood that alternative treatments would be effective and the patient's preference and choice. Although ECT has been shown to be more effective than antidepressant medication in acute therapy, and at least as effective during continuation therapy (Sackeim et al., 2001), it is typically reserved for use after several failed medication trials because of its relatively higher risk of side-effects. To date, factors that have been associated with reduced efficacy in ECT in depression include a prolonged episode of depression, lack of response to medication and co-existing psychiatric diagnoses such as personality disorder (Prudic et al., 2004). Patients with unstable cardiac disease such as ischemia, or arrhythmias, cerebrovascular disease such as recent cerebral haemorrhage or stroke, or raised intracranial pressure may be at increased risk for complications (Lisanby, 2007). Before starting an ECT treatment, the workup should comprise a comprehensive medical and neurological evaluation to manage such conditions and decide upon a potential contraindication in these cases. ECT can be used safely in elderly patients and in persons with cardiac pacemakers or implantable cardioverter–defibrillators (Dolenc et al., 2004). ECT can also be a treatment of last resort during pregnancy, with proper precautions and in consultation with an obstetrician (Lisanby, 2007). Hence, it will be important to further investigate in large controlled studies the predictors for response to ECT in order to strengthen recommendation for individual patients. A key question that remains is how we can manage to minimize side-effects of ECT while sustaining its efficacy.

A recent innovation has been the introduction of magnetic seizure therapy (MST) devices. MST is a more powerful type of magnetic stimulation than repetitive transcranial magnetic stimulation (rTMS) method, using rapidly alternating magnetic fields to induce generalized seizures (Lisanby et al., 2003). It is currently under debate if the same benefits will occur with MST as with the treatment of depression by ECT. MST is presumed to stimulate more localized regions of the cerebral cortex than conventional ECT, due to magnetic fields that pass through tissue without impedance (Lisanby, 2002). Therefore, it has been argued that minimizing disturbances of the medial temporal regions of the brain would reduce cognitive side-effects such as retrograde amnesia. MST is applied with higher intensity, greater frequency, and longer durations of stimulation than rTMS. Hence, this larger dose of magnetic stimulation can produce generalized tonic-clonic seizures resembling ECT (Lisanby et al., 2001). Preliminary controlled studies and case studies involving a small number of patients have suggested that MST is an effective antidepressant, with minimal cognitive side-effects (Kayser et al., 2009; Lisanby et al., 2001).

References

Abrams, R. 2002. *Electroconvulsive Therapy*, 4th Edition. Oxford: Oxford University Press.

Bajbouj, M., Brakemeier, E. L., Schubert, F., et al. (2005a). Repetitive transcranial magnetic stimulation of the dorsolateral prefrontal cortex and cortical excitability in patients with major depressive disorder. *Experimental Neurology*, **196**: 332–8.

Bajbouj, M., Lang, U. E., Neu, P., & Heuser, I. (2005b). Therapeutic brain stimulation and cortical excitability in depressed patients. *American Journal of Psychiatry*, **162**: 2192–3.

Bajbouj, M., Lang, U. E., Niehaus, L., Hellen, F. E., Heuser, I., & Neu, P. (2006a). Effects of right unilateral electroconvulsive therapy on motor cortical excitability in depressive patients. *Journal of Psychiatric Research*, **40**: 322–7.

Bajbouj, M., Lisanby, S. H., Lang, U. E., Danker-Hopfe, H., Heuser, I., & Neu, P. (2006b). Evidence for impaired cortical inhibition in patients with unipolar major depression. *Biological Psychiatry*, **59**: 395–400.

Bocchio-Chiavetto, L., Zanardini, R., Bortolomasi, M., et al. (2006). Electroconvulsive therapy (ECT) increases serum brain derived neurotrophic factor (BDNF) in drug-resistant depressed patients. *European Neuropsychopharmacology*, **16**: 620–4.

Cerletti, U. (1956). Electroshock therapy. In: Sackler, A., Sackler, M., & Sackler, R. (Eds.). *The Great Physiodynamic Therapies in Psychiatry*. New York, NY: Hoeber-Harper.

Cerletti, U., & Bini, L. (1938). Un nuevo metodo di shockterapie 'L'elettroshock'. *Bolletino Accademia Medica Roma*, **64**: 136–8.

Chen, A. C., Shin, K. H., Duman, R. S., & Sanacora, G. (2001). ECS-induced mossy fiber sprouting and BDNF expression are attenuated by ketamine pretreatment. *Journal of ECT*, **17**: 27–32.

Dolenc, T. J., Barnes, R. D., Hayes, D. L., & Rasmussen, K. G. (2004). Electroconvulsive therapy in patients with cardiac pacemakers and implantable cardioverter defibrillators. *Pacing and Clinical Electrophysiology*, **27**: 1257–63.

Donahue, A. B. (2000). Electroconvulsive therapy and memory loss: a personal journey. *Journal of ECT*, **16**: 133–43.

Fernandes, B., Gama, C. S., Massuda, R., et al. (2009). Serum brain-derived neurotrophic factor (BDNF) is not associated with response to electroconvulsive therapy (ECT): a pilot study in drug resistant depressed patients. *Neuroscience Letters*, **453**: 195–8.

Fink, M. (1979). *Convulsive Therapy: Theory and Practice*. New York, NY: Raven Press.

Fink, M. (1984). Meduna and the origins of convulsive therapy. *American Journal of Psychiatry*, **141**: 1034–41.

Fink, M. (2001). Convulsive therapy: a review of the first 55 years. *Journal of Affective Disorders*, **63**: 1–15.

Fink, M., & Taylor, M. A. (2003). *Catatonia: A Clinician's Guide to Diagnosis and Treatment*. Cambridge: Cambridge University Press.

Fink, M., & Taylor, M. A. (2009). The catatonia syndrome: forgotten but not gone. *Archives of General Psychiatry*, **66**: 1173–7.

Fink, M., Korin, H., & Kwalwasser, S. (1956). Relation of changes in memory and learning to improvement in electroshock. *Confinia Neurologica*, **16**: 88–96.

Green, A. R., & Vincent, N. D. (1987). The effect of repeated electroconvulsive shock on GABA synthesis and release in regions of rat brain. *British Journal of Pharmacology*, **92**: 19–24.

Husain, M. M., Rush, A. J., Fink, M., *et al.* (2004). Speed of response and remission in major depressive disorder with acute electroconvulsive therapy (ECT): a Consortium for Research in ECT (CORE) report. *Journal of Clinical Psychiatry*, **65**: 485–91.

Kayser, S., Bewernick, B., Axmacher, N., & Schlaepfer, T. E. (2009). Magnetic seizure therapy of treatment-resistant depression in a patient with bipolar disorder. *Journal of ECT*, **25**: 137–40.

Krishnamoorthy, E. S., & Trimble, M. R. (1999). Forced normalization: clinical and therapeutic relevance. *Epilepsia*, **40**: S57–64.

Landolt, H. (1953). Some clinical EEG correlations in epileptic psychoses (twilight states). *EEG and Clinical Neurophysiology*, **5**: 121.

Lisanby, S. H. (2002). Update on magnetic seizure therapy: a novel form of convulsive therapy. *Journal of ECT*, **18**: 182–8.

Lisanby, S. H. (2007). Electroconvulsive therapy for depression. *New England Journal of Medicine*, **357**: 1939–45.

Lisanby, S. H., Luber, B., Schlaepfer, T. E., & Sackeim, H. A. (2003). Safety and feasibility of magnetic seizure therapy (MST) in major depression: randomized within-subject comparison with electroconvulsive therapy. *Neuropsychopharmacology*, **28**: 1852–65.

Lisanby, S. H., Maddox, J. H., Prudic, J., Devanand, D. P., & Sackeim, H. A. (2000). The effects of electroconvulsive therapy on memory of autobiographical and public events. *Archives of General Psychiatry*, **57**: 581–90.

Lisanby, S. H., Schlaepfer, T. E., Fisch, H. U., & Sackeim, H. A. (2001). Magnetic seizure therapy of major depression. *Archives of General Psychiatry*, **58**: 303–05.

Little, J. D., Ungvari, G. S., & McFarlane, J. (2000). Successful ECT in a case of Leonhard's cycloid psychosis. *Journal of ECT*, **16**: 62–7.

Malberg, J. E., Eisch, A. J., Nestler, E. J., & Duman, R. S. (2000). Chronic antidepressant treatment increases neurogenesis in adult rat hippocampus. *Journal of Neuroscience*, **20**: 9104–10.

Manji, H. K., & Duman, R. S. (2001). Impairments of neuroplasticity and cellular resilience in severe mood disorders: implications for the development of novel therapeutics. *Psychopharmacology Bulletin*, **35**: 5–49.

Meduna, L. J. (1935). Die Konvulsionstherapie der Schizophrenie. *Psychiatrisch-neurologische Wochenschrift*, **37**: 317–9.

Mervaala, E., Kononen, M., Fohr, J., *et al.* (2001). SPECT and neuropsychological performance in severe depression treated with ECT. *Journal of Affecticve Disorders*, **66**: 47–58.

Mulsant, B. H., Rosen, J., Thornton, J. E., & Zubenko, G. S. (1991). A prospective naturalistic study of electroconvulsive therapy in late-life depression. *Journal of Geriatric Psychiatry and Neurology*, **4**: 3–13.

Neuhaus, A. H., Luborzewski, A., Opgen-Rhein, C., Jockers-Scherubl, M. C., & Neu, P. (2007). Electroconvulsive monotherapy in confusion psychosis: a potential standard regimen? *Pharmacopsychiatry*, **40**: 170–1.

Newton, S. S., Girgenti, M. J., Collier, E. F., & Duman, R. S. (2006). Electroconvulsive seizure increases adult hippocampal angiogenesis in rats. *European Journal of Neuroscience*, **24**: 819–28.

Nobler, M. S., & Sackeim, H. A. (2008). Neurobiological correlates of the cognitive side effects of electroconvulsive therapy. *Journal of ECT*, **24**: 40–5.

O'Connor, M. K., Knapp, R., Husain, M., *et al.* (2001). The influence of age on the response of major depression to electroconvulsive therapy: a C.O.R.E. Report. *American Journal of Geriatric Psychiatry*, **9**: 382–90.

Perera, T. D., Coplan, J. D., Lisanby, S. H., *et al.* (2007). Antidepressant-induced neurogenesis in the hippocampus of adult nonhuman primates. *Journal of Neuroscience*, **27**: 4894–901.

Petrides, G., Fink, M., Husain, M. M., *et al.* (2001). ECT remission rates in psychotic versus nonpsychotic depressed patients: a report from CORE. *Journal of ECT*, **17**: 244–53.

Prudic, J., Olfson, M., Marcus, S. C., Fuller, R. B., & Sackeim, H. A. (2004). Effectiveness of electroconvulsive therapy in community settings. *Biological Psychiatry*, **55**: 301–12.

Rajkowska, G., Miguel-Hidalgo, J. J., Wei, J., *et al.* (1999). Morphometric evidence for neuronal and glial prefrontal cell pathology in major depression. *Biological Psychiatry*, **45**: 1085–98.

Sackeim, H. A. (1999). The anticonvulsant hypothesis of the mechanisms of action of ECT: current status. *Journal of ECT*, **15**: 5–26.

Sackeim, H. A., Haskett, R. F., Mulsant, B. H., *et al.* (2001). Continuation pharmacotherapy in the prevention of relapse following electroconvulsive therapy: a randomized controlled trial. *Journal of the American Medical Association*, **285**: 1299–307.

Sackeim, H. A., Prudic, J., Devanand, D. P., *et al.* (1993). Effects of stimulus intensity and electrode placement on the efficacy and cognitive effects of electroconvulsive therapy. *New England Journal of Medicine*, **328**: 839–46.

Sackeim, H. A., Prudic, J., Devanand, D. P., *et al.* (2000). A prospective, randomized, double-blind comparison of bilateral and right unilateral electroconvulsive therapy at different stimulus intensities. *Archives of General Psychiatry*, **57**: 425–34.

Sackeim, H. A., Prudic, J., Fuller, R., Keilp, J., Lavori, P. W., & Olfson, M. (2007). The cognitive effects of electroconvulsive therapy in community settings. *Neuropsychopharmacology*, **32**: 244–54.

Sackeim, H. A., Prudic, J., Nobler, M. S., *et al.* (2008). Effects of pulse width and electrode placement on the efficacy and cognitive effects of electroconvulsive therapy. *Brain Stimulation*, **1**: 71–83.

Sanacora, G., Gueorguieva, R., Epperson, C. N., *et al.* (2004). Subtype-specific alterations of gamma-aminobutyric acid and glutamate in patients with major depression. *Archives of General Psychiatry*, **61**: 705–13.

Sanacora, G., Mason, G. F., Rothman, D. L., *et al.* (2003). Increased cortical GABA concentrations in depressed patients receiving ECT. *American Journal of Psychiatry*, **160**: 577–9.

Sun, W., Choi, S. H., Park, S. K., *et al.* (2007). Identification and characterization of novel activity-dependent transcription factors in rat cortical neurons. *Journal of Neurochemistry*, **100**: 269–78.

Task Force on Electroconvulsive Therapy. (2001). *Recommendations for Treatment, Training, and Privileging*. Washington, DC: American Psychiatric Publishing.

UK ECT Review Group (2003). Efficacy and safety of electroconvulsive therapy in depressive disorders: a systematic review and meta-analysis. *Lancet*, **361**: 799–808.

Vicario-Abejón, C., Collin, C., McKay, R. D., & Segal, M. (1998). Neurotrophins induce formation of functional excitatory and inhibitory synapses between cultured hippocampal neurons. *Journal of Neuroscience*, **18**: 7256–71.

Wahlund, B., & von Rosen, D. (2003). ECT of major depressed patients in relation to biological and clinical variables: a brief overview. *Neuropsychopharmacology*, **28** (Suppl 1): S21–6.

Chapter 19

Paradoxes of comparative cognition

Howard C. Hughes

Summary

The *scala naturae* (latin for 'natural ladder') is a concept of the order of natural forms that is often referred to as the great chain of being. It dates from medieval Christianity, and applies a rigid hierarchical organization to all matter and life. At the bottom of this hierarchy is earth, while God occupies the pinnacle. When applied to various forms of life, the hierarchy takes a very intuitive form, beginning with simple organisms which are followed by invertebrates, and then the vertebrates are placed in a relatively intuitive 'evolutionary' sequence (amphibians, reptiles, 'lower' mammals, 'intermediate' mammals and 'higher' mammals, e.g. primates). Perhaps not surprisingly, humans placed themselves at the pinnacle of this 'tree of life' (see Figure 19.1).

The earliest versions of the *scala naturae* predate Charles Darwin by several centuries, and despite the fact that over 150 years have passed since the original publication of *The Origin of Species* (1859), current notions of evolution are often imbued with elements of the *scala naturae*. While such hierarchical conceptualizations are apparently quite seductive, these intrusions of the *scala* do not serve theories of comparative cognition (Hodos and Campbell, 1969).

This chapter explores several cases in which the visual cognition of animals appears to surpass that of humans. These cases are quite naturally considered paradoxical, but the reader is encouraged to consider why any instance of superiority of non-human visual cognition is so readily regarded as paradoxical.

Introduction

On 9 June 2008, IBM issued a press release announcing that it had successfully built a supercomputer that had set a new world record for processing speed. Aptly named the Roadrunner (see Figure 19.2), this machine broke the storied pentaflop barrier. The pentaflop is a measure of processing speed – it means the Roadrunner can execute one thousand trillion (1,000,000,000,000,000) floating point operations per second. That is an amazing rate of calculation by any standard. Achieving this magnitude of computing power takes over 18,000 state-of-the-art microchips (over 12,000 of which are the newest generation of the chips used in Sony Playstation® 3s), 98 terabytes (98,000,000,000,000 bytes) of memory and 5200 square feet of space (a footprint of 22×22 m). According to IBM, this machine is the equivalent of 100,000 of today's fastest laptop computers; if those laptops were stacked atop one another they would be 1.5 miles tall.

The Paradoxical Brain, ed. Narinder Kapur. Published by Cambridge University Press. © Cambridge University Press 2011.

PEDIGREE OF MAN.

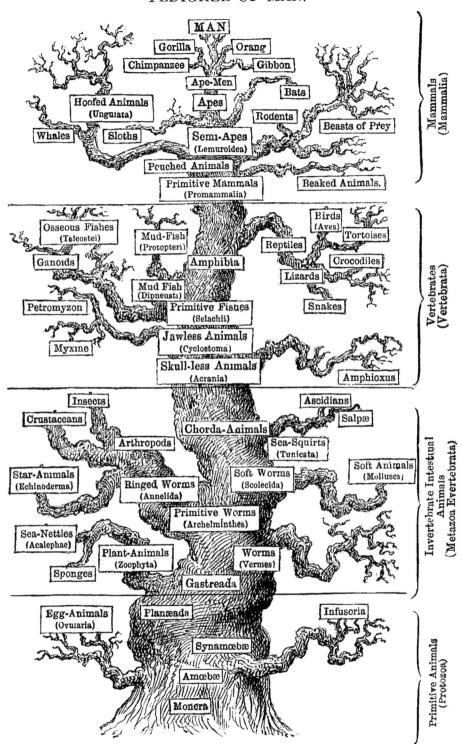

Figure 19.1 A post-Darwinian version of the *scala naturae*. Reprinted from Ernst Haeckel, *The Evolution of Man* (1866; New York, 1896), p. 189.

How does this prodigious computing power compare to that of a human brain, or for that matter, the brain of a bat, a moth or a honey bee? I confess to having no idea, and suspect that no one else does either. In competitions between supercomputers, the standard test is called the Linpack benchmark, which measures the time it takes to solve an $N \times N$ system of linear equations. It is not difficult to see how the Linpack benchmark can measure the relative computational power of different computers using the same criterion. Each computer gets the same system of linear equations and solves the problem using the same algorithm and the same language (Fortran). Thus, the machines are being compared using exactly the same metrics. If we try to compare digital computers with the computational power of nervous systems, however, we no longer have equivalent metrics of performance, and that makes any comparisons very tenuous and difficult. The same difficulty is often encountered if we try to compare the computational or cognitive abilities of different species. It is often difficult to find a single metric that can be equally applied to very different creatures.

Imagine, for example that you have been studying the foraging behaviour of honey bees, and you notice and carefully document a very strong preference the bees demonstrate for one flower over another. There is, however, one very puzzling thing about the bees' preferences – they much prefer a very drab little blue flower over a spectacular large and elaborately shaped red one. You wonder how they could find the dusty little blue petals more alluring than the brilliant red ones. As you pursue the question further, you discover that although the eye of a honey bee is much different from our own, the bees do see in colour. In fact, bees have three different wavelength-sensitive photoreceptors that support their colour vision just as humans do. However, the bee's photoreceptors have peak sensitivities to the green, blue and ultraviolet (UV) portions of the electromagnetic spectrum. In comparison, the photoreceptors responsible for human colour vision have peak sensitivities in the red, green and blue portions of the electromagnetic spectrum. Because of this very fundamental difference between honey bee and human colour vision, bees cannot really distinguish red from green, so the red flowers that look so conspicuous to us do not look nearly as impressive to a honey bee. In contrast, the flowers that bees find most alluring often have 'nectar markers' that are only visible in the UV part of the spectrum, and so they are invisible to humans (e.g. Hughes, 1999; see Figure 19.3). These UV markers do not appear very impressive to us, but they are very alluring to the bees.

Many flowers that depend on bees for their pollination have evolved ultraviolet nectar markers that are very effective at attracting bees. Flowering plants that depend on other vehicles for their pollination tend not to be so reflective of UV light, suggesting that different plants have adapted to be most attractive to the species they depend on for pollination. We see, then, how easily one may misunderstand the behaviour of another species and mistake it for some type of inferiority relative to our own biased (and imperfect) perception of the environment.

When exploring comparative cognition, we are on the firmest footing when we compare two different species performing exactly the same task. This is not often possible, but when it is the results can be quite startling. Consider the recent report by Inoue and Matsuzawa (2008) comparing the immediate memory span for visually presented digits in chimpanzees and humans. The subjects were six chimpanzees – three mothers and three of their offspring. Each of the chimpanzees was first taught to associate the Arabic numerals 1–9 with collections of objects of the corresponding number (e.g. six bananas with 6, eight

Figure 19.2 The Roadrunner, IBM's new supercomputer.

Glechoma hederacea L. (A) (B)

Arnica angustifolia Vahl (C) (D)

http://www.naturfotograf.com/UV_flowers_list.html

Figure 19.3 Two varieties of flowers as seen under normal illumination (A and C) and under ultra-violet illumination (B and D). Panels A and C illustrate how these flowers look to humans. Since panels B and D emphasize reflectance of ultra-violet light, it is a simulation of how they might look to a honey bee. Photography by Bjørn Rørslett, downloaded from http://www.naturfotograf. com/UV_flowers_list.html and used with permission.

grapes with 8, etc.). The chimpanzees were then taught to tap out the correct sequence of the Arabic numerals (1 to 9 in succession) presented in random locations on a computer-controlled touch screen. The chimps thus demonstrated a concept of ordinal numbers, and also spontaneously generalized that concept to subsets of the originally learned digits. That is, they could correctly tap out the sequence illustrated in Figure 19.4, even though 2 and 5 are missing from the array. Inoue and Matsusawa (2008) do not say how long their chimps took to master these tasks, but they do state that training of the younger chimps did not begin until they were 3–4 years old. By way of comparison, most human children can count to 10 by the time they are two years old. As far as math ability goes, there is no real paradox

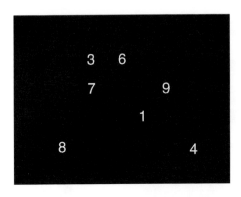

Figure 19.4 A randomly distributed array of numerals in which the 2 and 5 are missing from the sequence. Chimpanzees can touch these numerals in sequence much more quickly than humans.

here. However, a very startling paradox arose when Inoue and Matsuzawa introduced the chimps to a small variation in the number tapping task.

This new task also involved visual presentations of arrays of Arabic numerals in random positions, but with one important modification: the exposure duration of the numerals was limited by replacing them with white squares as soon as the chimps touched the first digit in the sequence. The chimps were then required to tap out the remaining locations based on their *memory* of the array. The arrangement for this modified experiment, which is a test of visual working memory, is illustrated in Figure 19.5. Remarkably, all the chimpanzees learned to master this memory task, indicating they could encode the locations of nine different numbers in a fraction of a second *and* hold them in memory long enough to touch each location in the correct sequence. Human subjects could not perform the sequence of touches as quickly as the three younger chimps and, more importantly, their latencies to start the tapping sequence were longer than those of the chimps. Since the white square masks did not appear until the first numeral was tapped and the reaction times of the chimps and humans were not the same, the actual exposure time for the numerals was not exactly the same (the humans had more time). Inoue and Matsuzawa therefore modified the memory task in order to compare performance of the chimpanzee and human subjects using exactly the same conditions. This 'limited-hold memory task' produced a very surprising result.

In this last variation of the test, the numerals appeared for a specific duration and were then immediately replaced by the white square masks. The exposure durations ranged from 210 to 650 ms (0.21–0.65 s). The shortest of these durations is very close to the latency of saccadic eye movements, which means that the identity and locations of all presented digits must be encoded in a single glance, i.e. without the aid of any scanning eye movements. The astonishing finding is that the performance of the best chimps far exceeds human performance on the same test. Video clips of chimps outperforming humans in this test of the span of apprehension (what can be 'seen' in a single glance) are available at http://www.current-biology.com/cgi/content/full/17/23/R1004/DC1. At the shortest exposure duration of 210 ms, the best chimpanzee's performance was twice that of the human observers.

It is a disconcerting experience to watch a video of a chimpanzee doing something with great facility that you know you simply cannot do at all. The state of affairs would be much less troublesome if the tasks involved something that might be *expected* to favour the chimpanzees' performance over that of humans, such as recognizing food items in dense vegetation or knowing which leaves have medicinal value. However, this visual memory span task lies squarely in the human domain. We invented the numbers, the computers and the touch

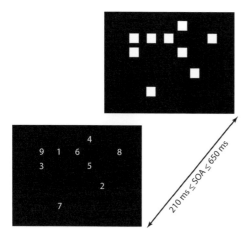

Figure 19.5 A schematic illustration of a test of visual working memory that both humans and chimpanzees can perform, although not necessarily with equal facility. The white squares mask the numbers, so their positions must be encoded very rapidly and held in visual working memory as the subjects tap out the squares in the proper sequence. 'SOA' is an acronym for 'stimulus onset asynchrony', which specifies the temporal interval between the onset of the numerals and the onset of the masking squares.

screens! This is more than a little embarrassing. It would be different if we could attribute the superior performance of the chimps to extra motivation or practice, but such explanations are not likely to hold up to empirical scrutiny. Which human college student would be indifferent to being outperformed by a chimpanzee on a memory task? In order to fully appreciate the extent to which these chimps exceed human performance, it will be helpful to consider some classic experiments on the *span of apprehension* that were performed independently by Sperling (1960) and by Averbach and Coriell (1961). The span of apprehension is the number of visual items that can be correctly identified and reported in a single brief presentation.

Let us now turn to a description of the method used to measure how many items can be simultaneously 'apprehended'. The description that follows is the one used by Sperling (1960). The basic task has many similarities to the ones used by Inoue and Matsuzawa (2008). An array of letters is briefly presented and the (human) subjects try to report as many of the letters as they can. The key experimental variable in such experiments is the number of letters that are present in the display. This number typically varies randomly from trial to trial. The main measure of performance is the average number of correctly reported letters as a function of the number of letters presented in the display.

A typical outcome is illustrated in Figure 19.6, along with some samples of the displays. It must be remembered, however, that these displays would only appear for a very brief duration, often around 50 ms (0.05 s). This display duration is much too short for the subject to scan the display with any eye movements, so all the letters that are reported must be encoded in a single glance. The data illustrated in Figure 19.6 show that there is a very distinct limit on the number of items that can be correctly reported, and that limit is surprisingly low (about 4.5 items, on average). Of course, if you presented a 12-item display for 50 ms and asked an observer how many items were presented, they would be able to estimate the number with reasonable accuracy. They might say that there were 11 or 12 letters presented, but they can only tell you the identity of 4 of those letters. Observers realize there were more items than the four they identified, but they did not *see* what they were. In this case, a person might use the word 'seeing' to mean 'identifying'. The letters that weren't identified were of course, in some sense, 'seen' because our observer knows that there were many more letters in the display than the four they were able to report. This particular measure of the span of apprehension is called the 'full report procedure' because the observer's task is to report as many letters as they can.

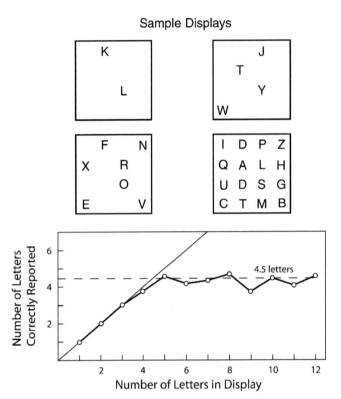

Sample Displays

Figure 19.6 Examples of the letter displays used to measure the span of apprehension, which is the number of items that can be correctly reported in a very brief display. Typical results are shown in the lower panel, where it is seen that no matter how many letters are presented, human observers can only identify 4 or 5 of them.

In 1960, George Sperling introduced a second test of the span of visual apprehension, and this second measure made his experiment one of the most famous in all of cognitive science. It was called the partial report procedure. The partial report paradigm is illustrated in Figure 19.6. There is one small but important difference between the full report and partial report procedures. In the partial report, the observer only has to name the letters in one row of the display. As indicated in Figure 19.7, which row the observer must report is cued by the frequency of a tone which is presented *after* the letters have disappeared. A high-frequency tone means report the top row, an intermediate frequency means report the middle row and a low-frequency the cue to report the bottom row. Sperling discovered that subjects can accurately report all 4 letters in any one of the 3 rows of a 12-letter array. What makes this finding remarkable is the fact that the subject does *not know which row* they will have to report until *after* the array has been removed. Thus, it must be the case that the identity of all 12 letters are available to the observer in some form for a period of time after the display is removed, but that only 4 or so of these available letters can be reported. If the tone that indicates which row is to be reported is delayed more than about 500 ms, then performance is equivalent to the full report procedure (the subject can only name about four items, and the ones they can report come from any of the three rows).

The very important difference in reporting accuracy that Sperling discovered by comparing the full report and partial report procedures implies that there is a representation of the full 12-letter display that persists for several tenths of a second after the display has disappeared. This representation is considered to be visual in nature – a rapidly fading literal 'copy' of the display that has been called *iconic memory*. The idea is that when the tone cue closely follows the offset of the multi-letter display, the observers can 'read' the letters in the cued row from their fading icon. One important factor that influences the duration of the icon is the contents of the screen after the multi-letter array disappears. The icon will last longer if the post-exposure screen is dark, and any visual items like the white square masks used by Inoue and Matsuzawa will overwrite the icon.

To be fair, the experiments by Inoue and Matsuzawa (2008) have had some detractors (Silberberg and Kearns, 2009; Cook and Wilson, 2010). The central criticism has been that the chimps had much more extensive practise than the human subjects with whom they were compared. Silberberg and Kearns (2009) reported that they were able to approximate the level of performance achieved by one of the chimps (Ayumu) after extensive practise, a finding which may represent a particularly impressive demonstration of *perceptual learning*. However, since 1960 many human subjects have received a great deal of experience in performing span of apprehension tasks, and I am unaware of any other report in which human subjects have come close to the performance that Inoue and Matsuzawa's chimps demonstrate in their videos. Like many surprising paradoxes, this one needs further investigation. For now these chimps appear to present a vexing puzzle for perceptual psychologists: they seem to have a span of apprehension that exceeds that of typical humans by a great deal. Perhaps they can learn this ability, but, at least until recently, there was no evidence that humans can learn to increase their visual memory span so dramatically. Not only do the chimps *identify* more digits than a human could ever do in a single glance, but they also *remember the locations* of each digit since they can touch them in the correct order. Inoue and Matsuzawa suggest that perhaps their chimps have 'photographic memories'. There have been reports of eidetic imagery (the formal term for photographic memories) in humans, but the topic has not been investigated as much as you might think. Although eidetic imagery is exceedingly rare in adults, reports early in the twentieth century claimed that eidetic imagery was quite commonplace in children (cf. Haber and Haber, 1964). Later work could not confirm high rates of eidetic imagery in children, but did find that 8% of a sample of children aged 8–12 had an ability to report on the fine details of images after they had been removed (Haber and Haber, 1964). The duration of these eidetic images could last 40 s or more after a 10-s exposure. Eidetic imagery is distinguished from both afterimages and iconic memory in that an eidetic image can be scanned with eye movements, whereas afterimages and iconic memories are fixed on the retina and therefore move in concert with movements of the eyes. Moreover, eidetic images are seen in the same colours as the original scene, while afterimages are usually seen in colours that are the complements of the original colours. Figure 19.8 can be used as a test of eidetic imagery. Ask someone to study the picture for 10 s. Then turn the page and see if they can answer the following question: 'How many black stripes are on the Cheshire cat's tail'? Anyone who can answer that question correctly almost surely has eidetic imagery.

The world-record holder of eidetic imagery was a woman, 'Elizabeth', who was extensively studied by C.S. Stromeyer (1982). Elizabeth was not her real name, but she gained a great deal of notoriety when Stromeyer discovered that Elizabeth could view one half of a 10,000-element random dot stereogram using one eye on one day, and view the other half of the stereogram with her other eye the next day, and 'fuse' the seen image with an eidetic image from the previous day into a stereoscopic 3D percept (see Figure 19.9)! It is only fair to point out that no one with comparable talents had been studied before or has been discovered since. Perhaps eidetic imagery is simply much more commonplace in chimps than humans, but

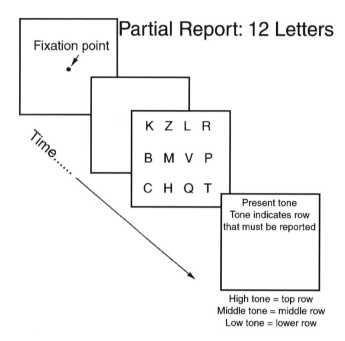

Partial Report: 12 Letters

Fixation point

K Z L R

B M V P

C H Q T

Present tone
Tone indicates row
that must be reported

Time......

High tone = top row
Middle tone = middle row
Low tone = lower row

Figure 19.7 The partial report procedure is a modified method for measuring the span of apprehension. In this variant, 12 items appear in the display, but the observer never needs to report more than 4 of them. Which 4 is determined by a tone which occurs after the display has disappeared. The classic finding is that observers can report all 4 items in any row, even though they do not know which row will be cued until after the display has been removed. Thus, all 12 items are 'available' for a brief period of time. This very short visual memory is called iconic memory.

that suggestion really does little to explain the paradoxical superiority of the chimp's performance over our own, since the addition of the masking squares would 'overwrite' any traces of a long-lasting form of iconic memory. The mechanism that enables the memory span of these chimpanzees seems to be a great deal less fragile than what we typically think of as iconic memory, and there has never been a report of eidetic images being formed with exposure durations of only 200 ms.

We are left with a puzzle with no known solution. Humans can only encode about four items simultaneously. This appears to be a limitation in the resources of attention. Identification of individual items when more than four are presented is thought to require attention to each item, and the act of attending to the items is a serial process. You attend to one item, encode its identity and store it in short-term memory. Then you attend to another item and its identity is also put into short-term memory. Attention and memory are very closely related. Attended items are remembered, and unattended ones are not. Viewed in this context, it would appear that chimps have more attentional resources than humans, but something about that conclusion does not seem quite right either. Perhaps the chimps simply perform the task differently than we do. One difference might relate to language. When humans are confronted with the task of identifying an array of numerals or letters, we *recode* them from their visual form to their verbal form. We name them. Chimps don't speak, so they don't name things either. Perhaps the mental operation of recoding the items from a visual, nonverbal to a verbal code takes time, and the chimps avoid this time-consuming process to their benefit.

One particularly vexing aspect of this mystery of chimp superiority over human perceptual processing is that it may not be the only instance. To see what may be another, let us return to our earlier consideration of differences between human vision

Figure 19.8 An image that could have been used by Haber and Haber (1964) to study eidetic imagery in children. See text for further details. From *Alice in Wonderland* by Lewis Carroll, illustrated by Marjovie Torney, © 1955, reviewed 1983 by Random House, Inc. used by permission of Random House Children's Books, a division of Random House, Inc.

and that of insects, bearing in mind that any comparisons we make here must be made with extreme caution, since there is no way to compare honey bees and humans using exactly the same task.

Entomologists have long been fascinated with what are often truly astonishing navigational abilities of foraging insects. Many species of wasps and ants readily find their nests after extensive foraging journeys, even though the nest may be little more than an inconspicuous hole in an otherwise uniform expanse of sand. Moreover, they can also unerringly return to a rich food source after only one visit, a journey which often requires traversing long distances over what seems to us a completely featureless landscape. In contrast, we are all familiar with stories recounting the ineptitude of human navigation; the instances in which some unfortunate group of travellers has car trouble in the middle of a desert. They may know they were headed east when the car broke down, and decide to continue in that direction to seek help. Hours later, they are horrified to discover they were walking in one big circle when they discover their abandoned car is just ahead. The navigational senses of humans often seem unimpressive when compared to those of other species, a fact that has been highlighted in a recent book by experimental psychologist, Colin Ellard (2009) entitled *You Are Here: Why We Can Find Our Way to the Moon but Get Lost in the Mall*. Ellard maintains that we have become far too dependent on our GPS devices, and should practise navigating, including finding our own way home after getting lost, without them! If we practise finding our way without technological aids, maybe our own abilities would improve.

One reason for the apparent superiority of insect navigation over human navigation appears to relate to the way insects encode their visual surroundings. As unlikely as it may seem, insect navigation seems to depend on a type of insect eidetic imagery (e.g. Collett and Cartwright, 1983; Wehner, 1981). Tinbergen (1974) provided early evidence that wasps use visual landmarks to help locate their nests. He placed pinecones around the nest opening,

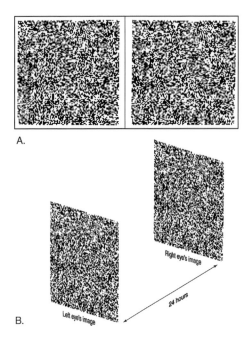

A.

B.

Figure 19.9 A random dot stereogram. If the left image is viewed by the left eye, and the right image is viewed by the right eye, then stereo-sighted observers can 'fuse' the two images into a single percept, which in this case is that of a central square that is floating above the background texture. Readers that can cross their eyes in the manner used to see forms in the 'magic eye' books may be able to do the same trick (called 'free-fusing') and perceive the two different depth planes portrayed in this stereogram. Note that no square is perceived if each member of the pair is viewed alone – the depth planes are only appreciated when the brain is able to compare the left and right eye images. Thus, we can appreciate the excitement caused when C.S. Stromeyer reported that Elizabeth could view the left member of the pair with her left eye, and view the right member of the pair with her right eye the next day, and 'perceive' a square floating in depth.

and found that if he displaced the pinecones to a new location, the wasps would search the new location for their nest. They were obviously using the pinecones as a visual landmark.

The fact that foraging insects use visual landmarks is not in itself that surprising. All these insects can see, even though their visual acuity is quite poor (about 100 times lower than ours, e.g. Hecht and Wolf, 1929; Macuda *et al.*, 2001). What *is* surprising is the way they *encode* their landmarks. There is good evidence that many foraging insects maintain a literal, retinotopic memory for the appearance of their nesting site – what many researchers refer to as an *iconic image* or *visual snapshot*. Let us consider the evidence for iconic memory in arthropods because, as you might imagine, it takes a great deal of ingenuity and creativity to find out that insects use such a literal representation of their visual environment.

Imagine that a foraging insect (it could be one of a variety of species of bee) has learned to use a cylindrical landmark to find its nest, as is schematically illustrated in Figure 19.10. On the first several outgoing flights, the bee would emerge from the nest, hover for a moment or two by the opening while looking at the nesting site, and then fly off in search of food. This behaviour is no longer observed after the first few flights.

Now, we introduce a critical test: while the bee is off in search of nectar, we replace the cylinder with one that is identical except for the fact that it is twice as large. This new landmark is placed at the exact same location as the original landmark, as illustrated in the lower portion of Figure 19.10. The question is, when the bee returns and approaches the landmark, where does it look for the nest? If the insect encodes the location of the nest in terms of a distance and direction from the cylinder, then it should look at location A. If, however, it encodes the location of the nest in terms of a 'snapshot' of the visual scene, it should look at a location that is twice as far from the landmark as the actual location. That is exactly what has been reported repeatedly (e.g. Collett and Cartwright, 1983; Hölldobler, 1980; Wehner, 1981).

It is as if what the bee remembers is not the distance of the landmark from the nest, but the exact *retinal* size and *retinal* location of the landmark when it approaches the nest from a fixed direction. So as the insect returns from foraging, it does so in a fixed direction and it approaches the landmark until its retinal image matches a stored template. Humans (or most vertebrates, for that matter) would not do that. They would have encoded the scene around the nest in real-world spatial coordinates (what are often called 'allocentric coordinates'). However, many insects appear to be unable (or uninterested) in deriving an allocentric frame of reference. Instead, they appear to rely on a system that stores a largely unprocessed version (a 'snap shot') of the environment. In an especially dramatic demonstration of 'iconic imagery' in insects, Hölldobler (1980) has shown that the African stink ant (*Paltothyreus tarsatus*), a phylogenetically ancient species of foraging ant that lives in heavily forested areas of sub-Saharan Africa, does not use the sun or complex patterns of polarized skylight that many more advanced foragers have evolved as navigational aids. Perhaps the density of the forest canopy precludes these more elaborate mechanisms (see Hughes, 1999 for a discussion). Rather, Hölldobler (1980) discovered that the stink ant takes a much more direct approach to navigation in the African forest: it memorizes the pattern of the forest canopy directly! He showed this in an elegant series of experiments in which ants learned to navigate in a large open arena, which was located within a building and thus provided the level of environmental control typical of a laboratory experiment (as opposed to field studies). The stink ants learned to forage in a certain location within this area, and return to their nest without difficulty. The ceiling of the environment where they learned the route consisted of a large photographic reproduction of a forest canopy. On test trials, however, while the ants had entered a small enclosure that contained their food source, Hölldobler rotated the canopy photograph. When the ants emerged, they headed home in the wrong direction. Their errors matched the angle through which the canopy had been rotated, demonstrating that stink ant navigation relies on a stored representation of the visual pattern of the forest canopy.

These are the sorts of findings that have led to the generally accepted view that many of the remarkable navigational abilities of foraging arthropods appear to be based on a surprisingly simple system that in some ways appears like a photographic memory of critical locations in their environments. I hasten to note that the resolution of this photographic memory is necessarily quite coarse – remember, the visual acuity of these animals is 100 times less than our own. Even so, it seems astonishing that insects utilize cues (like the pattern of the forest canopy) that completely escape our notice without extensive and elegant experimentation. In one sense, the paradox is that these simple organisms with their very simple eyes and nervous systems encode 'snapshots' of significant parts of their world, while the vast majority of humans with their sophisticated visual systems do not and really cannot. Rather, humans encode scenes in terms of their primary characteristics – our recognition is based on rapid acquisition of the 'gist' of the scene. Is this a forest scene or a city scene? Are there people in it? What appears to be going on in the scene? What is likely to happen next?

This emphasis on acquiring the gist of a scene has the advantage of extremely rapid processing, but it may come with a cost. Many perceptual psychologists think that 'gist processing' renders the human visual system vulnerable to a phenomenon called *change blindness* (e.g. Rensick *et al.*, 1997; Simons and Levin, 1997). Change blindness refers to a surprising inability of human observers to notice changes in a scene that are very conspicuous once they are recognized. Figure 19.11 illustrates one reliable method for producing

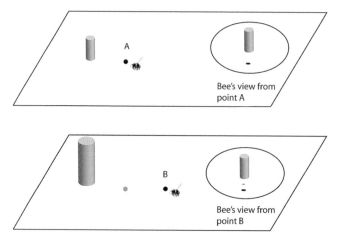

Figure 19.10 A schematic illustration of 'eidetic imagery' in honey bees. The bee learns the location of the nest in relation to a cylindrical marker. On the critical test, the marker is replaced with one that is twice the original size. The bee searches twice as far from this oversized marker as usual, indicating that it has encoded the marker in terms of the size of the proximal stimulus rather than the real world distance between the landmark and the nest. See text for further details.

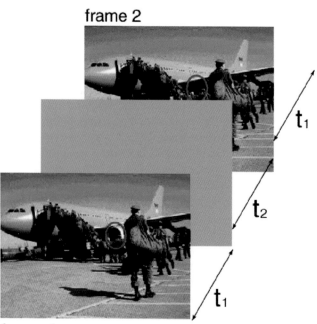

Figure 19.11 The 'flicker technique' for producing change blindness. The subject's task is to identify how the two images differ (without the aid of the red ovals). Adapted from Caplovitz *et al.*, 2008. See text for details.

change blindness. This demonstration is available on the internet at http://www.usd.edu/ psyc301/Rensink.htm. The paradigm is called the flicker technique, because the two images are presented successively, with a blank screen interleaved between each frame (i.e. after frame 2, the grey screen would be presented again, followed by frame 1 again, etc.). Frame 1 and frame 2 are images of the same scene, but they are not identical: the jet engine in frame 1 is missing in frame 2. In a typical change blindness experiment, subjects view alternate presentations of 2 such images (always interleaved with the grey screen) searching for the (often quite conspicuous) difference between them. They know that there is in fact a difference, and they are usually free to scan the images, scrutinizing them however they like. The surprising finding is how poor we can be at detecting the difference between the images. Often it takes many cycles of the alternating stimulus frames, which can result in a great deal of frustration on the part of the participants. Indeed, increasingly frantic observers who know that a change is present somewhere in the alternating images often do not detect changes even when they are looking directly at them (Caplovitz *et al.*, 2008).

It is important to recognize that the blindness to change is heavily dependent on the presence of the intervening grey screen. If the grey screen was eliminated, and onset of frame 2 occurred immediately after the offset of frame 1, then no change blindness would occur. Indeed, the appearance and disappearance of the engine would be immediately obvious and would capture your attention instead of escaping your notice. No extensive searching for the change would be needed – it would 'pop out' at you.

Change blindness has often been interpreted as illustrating how very little of the literal information from a scene enters our short-term visual memory. From Sperling's experiments we know that we can only 'see' 4 or 5 letters in a single glance, but from other experiments we know that we apprehend the gist of a scene within small fractions of a second. For instance, while viewing a rapid sequence of natural scenes, we can report whether a horse was presented at any point within the sequence with very great accuracy (e.g. Potter and Fox, 2009). Yet experiments on change blindness tell us that ultra-rapid encoding of the gist is not good enough to detect that some salient object disappears and reappears when the gist does not change. Surely, we would have great difficulty if we had to memorize the pattern of the forest canopy in order to find our way home, but stink ants routinely do just that.

Foraging insects are apparently very facile at storing literal representations of a biologically significant retinal image, but are poor at representing the real-world objects that produced that image. On the other hand, we are very poor at remembering the retinal image, but are very good at extracting and remembering the general properties of objects that produced the retinal image. To some extent, these two types of representation relate to the age-old distinction made in the perceptual literature between proximal and distal stimuli (Berkeley, 1709; Koffka, 1935; Gibson, 1960). The distal stimulus is the real-world object. The proximal stimulus is the image of that object that is formed on the retina by the optics of the eye. Human perception is a process whereby information about the distal stimulus is gained by processing information available in the proximal stimulus. When we look at a scene, our experience is one of seeing visible objects in our environment – that is, our subjective visual experience is of distal stimuli. However, that is just an illusion, created by the fact that our perceptual systems are so good at extracting information about distal stimuli from the more impoverished proximal stimuli. For instance, objects in the environment have three dimensions, but the retinal image of those objects has only two dimensions. Since the goal of the human perceptual system is to create representations of the world around us, human vision transcends proximal stimuli. Apparently, arthropods find it sufficient to base their visually guided behaviour on relatively raw versions of proximal stimuli.

It is important to recognize that storing a relatively unprocessed, low-resolution version of a scene does not require any specific conception about the nature of the scene or the real-world objects that occupy it. A camera takes pictures but does not posses anything we would wish to call cognition. During the first half of the twentieth century, the very concept of concepts was essentially banished from psychological theory, especially in the United States (e.g. Hothersall, 2004). Behaviourism reigned and behaviourists eschewed all 'mentalistic' notions, arguing instead that associations between stimuli (S–S associations) in combination with associations between stimuli and responses (S–R associations) were both necessary and sufficient to explain observable behaviour. During the 1950s, however, behaviourism began to lose its pre-eminent position in psychological theorizing. There were, of course, many contributing factors to the decline of strict behaviourism and the rise of cognitive psychology. One was a very influential symposium held at the California Institute of Technology in 1950 called the Hixon Symposium. A number of prominent psychologists at the Hixon Symposium presented papers that introduced the field to a variety of new concepts, including hierarchically organized motor programs (Lashley, 1951) and an early conceptualization of artificial intelligence (Von Neumann, 1951). Another important empirical and theoretical contribution was provided by Harlow (1949), who introduced a method for demonstrating the formation of concepts in animals. Harlow called his method 'learning sets', and his influential paper described the formation of learning sets in primates. The method works as follows. The subject is taught a series of visual discrimination problems. Each problem involves presentations of two stimuli. The animal must learn that choosing one of the items leads to a reward and choosing the other one does not. The rewarded item is determined randomly, so on the first trial of each problem, the subject must guess which of the two items will be designated correct for that problem. The probability of choosing the correct object on the first trial is therefore 0.5. However, Harlow was not interested in performance on the first trial. His interest was focused on the second trial, because the first trial provides all the information needed to solve the problem. If the object chosen on the first trial is rewarded, then the subject should simply choose that item for all remaining trials. If the first trial is not rewarded, the subject should pick the other object on the remaining trials. Harlow trained Rhesus monkeys on many repetitions of the two-object discrimination task, using novel objects in each repetition. Each problem lasted only six trials. The goal was to determine whether the monkeys could improve their performance on the critical second trial. He found that after working on several hundred unique problems, the animals did indeed learn to choose the correct item on the second trial. Harlow reasoned that the animals had learned more than a simple association between stimuli and responses – he suggested they had learned an abstract concept, one that is often called the 'win stay, loose shift' strategy.

Perhaps not surprisingly, there were many subsequent attempts to compare the formation of learning sets in different primate species (cf. Tomasello and Call, 1997). The hypothesis was that great apes could acquire the concept most rapidly, followed by old world monkeys, and followed perhaps by new world monkeys and then prosimians. Any differences in the acquisition rates would presumably reflect the relative 'intelligence' of the various members of the primate order. However, it became clear that there was no obvious order in the acquisition of learning sets (see review by Tomasello and Call, 1997). Moreover, the formation of learning sets is not even restricted to the primate order, as many mammals and even pigeons are capable of acquiring the concept (e.g. Fobes and King, 1982). Although evidence of concept formation in a pigeon may seem surprising, it seems quite pedestrian in comparison to recent work indicating the concept learning in insects. Consider, for example, the report by Giurfa and colleagues (Giurfa et al., 2001) that honey bees acquire the concepts of 'same' and 'different'. This is what they did. Honey bees were trained to navigate through a Y-maze. Upon entering the maze, they passed a visual stimulus. In one version of the problem the stimulus was a striped pattern (grating) that was either horizontally or vertically oriented. In another version of the problem, the stimulus was a colour (either yellow or blue). This single visual stimulus was the 'sample', and after passing the sample, the insect entered a decision chamber. Within this chamber the insect could see a stimulus at the end of each arm of the Y maze. One arm of the maze contained a stimulus that matched the sample and the other arm contained the other, non-matching stimulus. The bees were taught two different tasks. The first is called a 'delayed match-to-sample'. In this task, the insect is rewarded (with a sucrose solution) for approaching the stimulus that is the same as the sample. In the 'delayed non-match-to sample', the rewarded stimulus is the one that is different than the sample. Bees can learn both the matching and non-matching versions of the task, but it takes them over 300 trials to achieve 75% accuracy. Note, however, that the initial task could be learned by simple associations between stimuli and responses. There is no need to invoke any notion of a concept to explain this initial learning.

The remarkable finding reported by Giurfa *et al.* (2001) was that the bees readily transferred their matching or non-matching behaviour to a new set of stimuli (either from the colours to the gratings or from the gratings to the colours). Although it took over 300 trials to reach a criterion of 75% correct choices in initial training, the bees averaged 75% accuracy over the first 70–90 trials on the transfer tests. In fact, they even demonstrated good transfer *between* sensory modalities! That is, if they learned a delayed match-to-sample using odour cues, they transferred that learning to visual stimuli (and also successfully transferred visual learning to the olfactory modality). The authors contend that this demonstrates that bees possess the concepts of 'sameness' and 'difference'. The logic is equivalent to that used by Harlow to demonstrate concept formation in primates over 60 years ago. It seems clear that, at least as far as these particular demonstrations of concept formation in animals are concerned, brain size is a not a particularly good predictor of conceptual ability.

The fundamental goal of comparative perception and cognition is not to determine whether one system is superior to another. All animals have evolved exquisite sensory systems that admirably fulfill their particular needs. Our real goal should be to understand how these very different systems are optimized to perform the different perceptual tasks required by each species given the diversity of constraints imposed by interrelated properties such as body size, neural complexity, lifestyle and biological niche.

Future challenges and questions

A future challenge is to see how the findings reported in this chapter fit in with related findings, observations and hypotheses in other areas of comparative cognition. In a classic study of memory for sequences of stimuli in pigeons, monkeys and humans, Wright *et al.* (1985) found similar patterns of performance were apparent in all three species when the opportunity for humans to deploy verbal labels was eliminated through the use of kaleido-scopic images as the to-be-remembered stimuli (cf. Scarf and Colombo, 2008). Humphrey (2002) has argued in evolutionary terms that the advent of language has resulted in restrictions in cognitive processing in the human species, in particular reduced visual memory capacity, and that this may help to explain some of the limitations in aspects of nonverbal human memory compared to non-human species. Some authors (e.g. Vallortigara *et al.*, 2008) have suggested a possible link between fine perceptual skills in autism and superior nonverbal performance on some tasks in animal species. This may complement related studies in comparative social cognition (Emery and Clayton, 2009). A major challenge for the future is to couch fascinating behavioural observations related to enhanced species-specific functioning in terms of neural structures and pathways (Kanwal and Rauschecker, 2007; Oelschläger, 2008; Kaas, 2008; Chittka and Niven, 2009). Another challenge is to carefully document and validate clinical observations, such as the phenomenon of dogs who can warn epileptic owners before the onset of seizures (e.g. Di Vito *et al.*, 2010). In terms of methodological challenges, in the case of human versus non-human comparisons it will be important to devise tasks that have both similar behavioural demands and tap similar cognitive processes (cf. Boesch, 2007; Cantlon and Brannon, 2007). Paradoxes in comparative cognition have tended to derive from taking human-based tasks, and seeing the extent to which non-human species can be trained to perform these tasks at a similar or enhanced level. It remains to be seen whether the reverse strategy may be fruitful, e.g. exploring whether magnetoreception, which is so uniquely beneficial in some non-human species (Gould, 2010), can be found and trained in human subjects (cf. Carrubba *et al.*, 2007). Finally, paradoxes in comparative cognition may well have implications for evolutionary theory, and these should also be explored (cf. Patton, 2008).

References

Averbach, E., & Coriell, A. S. (1961). Short-term memory in vision. *Bell Systems Technical Journal*, **40**: 309–28.

Berkeley, G. (1709). *An Essay Towards a New Theory of Vision*. Gloucester: Dodo Press. [Republished in 2007.]

Boesch, C. (2007). What makes us human (Homo-sapiens)? The challenge of cognitive cross-species comparison. *Journal of Comparative Psychology*, **121**: 227–40.

Cantlon, J. F., & Brannon, E. M. (2007). Basic math in monkeys and college students. *PLoS Biology*, **5**: 2912.

Caplovitz, G. P., Fendrich, R., & Hughes, H. C. (2008). Failure to see: attentive blank stares revealed by change blindness. *Consciousness and Cognition*, **17**: 877–86.

Carrubba, S., Frilot II, C., Chesson, Jr A., & Marino, A. (2007). Evidence of a nonlinear human magnetic sense. *Neuroscience*, **144**: 356–67.

Chittka, L., & Niven, J. (2009). Are bigger brains better? *Current Biology*, **19**: R995–1008.

Collett, T. S., & Cartwright, B. A. (1983). Eidetic images in insects: their role in navigation. *Trends in Neuroscience*, **6**: 101–05.

Cook, P., & Wilson, M. (2010). In practice, Chimp memory study flawed. *Science*, **328**: 1228.

Darwin, C. (1859). *The Origin of Species by Means of Natural Selection*. London: John Murrray Albemarle Street.

Di Vito, L., Naldi, I., Mostacci, B., Licchetta, L., Bisulli, F., & Tinuper, P. (2010). A seizure response dog: video recording of reacting behaviour during repetitive prolonged seizures. *Epileptic Disorders*, May 17 [Epub ahead of print].

Ellard, C. (2009). *You Are Here: Why We Can Find Our Way to the Moon but get Lost in the Mall*. New York, NY: Knopf/Doubleday publishing.

Emery, N., & Clayton, N. S. (2009). Comparative social cognition. *Annual Review of Psychology*, **60**: 87–113.

Fobes, J. L., & King, J. E. (1982). Measuring primate learning abilities. In: Fobes, J. L. & King, J. E. (Eds.). *Primate Behaviour*. New York, NY: Academic Press, pp. 289–326.

Gibson, J. J. (1960). The concept of the stimulus in Psychology. *American Psychologist*, **15**: 694–703.

Giurfa, M., Zhang, S., Jenett, A., Menzel, R., & Srinivasan, M. V. (2001). The concepts of 'sameness' and 'difference' in an insect. *Nature*, **410**: 930–3.

Gould, J. (2010). Magnetoreception. *Current Biology*, **25**: R431–5.

Haber, R. N., & Haber, R. B. (1964). Eidetic imagery: I. Frequency. *Perceptual and Motor Skills*, **19**: 131–8.

Harlow, H. F. (1949). The formation of learning sets. *Psychological Review*, **56**: 51–65.

Hecht, S., & Wolf, E. (1929). The visual acuity of the honey bee. *The Journal of General Physiology*, **12**: 727–60.

Hodos, W., & Campbell, C. B. G. (1969). *Scala naturae*: why there is no theory in comparative psychology? *Psychological Review*, **76**: 337–50.

Hölldobler, B. (1980). Canopy orientation: a new kind of orientation in ants. *Science*, **210**: 86–8.

Hothersall, D. (2004). *History of Psychology*, 4th Edition. Boston, MA: McGraw Hill.

Hughes, H. C. (1999). *Sensory Exotica: A World Beyond Human Experience*. Cambridge, MA: MIT Press.

Humphrey, N. (2002). *Chapter 14 – The Deformed Transformed in The Mind Made Flesh*. Oxford: Oxford University Press, pp. 165–99.

Inoue, S., & Matsuzawa, T. (2008). Working memory of numerals in chimpanzees. *Current Biology*, **17**: R1004.

Kaas, J. H. (2008). The evolution of the complex sensory and motor systems of the human brain. *Brain Research Bulletin*, **75**: 384–90.

Kanwal, J., & Rauschecker, J. (2007). Auditory cortex of bats and primates: managing species-specific calls for social communication. *Frontiers in Bioscience*, **12**: 4621–40.

Koffka, H. (1935). *Principles of Gestalt Psychology*. New York, NY: Harcourt Brace.

Lashley, K. S. (1951). The problem of serial order in behavior. In: Jeffress, L. A. (Ed.). *Cerebral Mechanisms in Behavior. The Hixon Symposium*.New York, NY: John Wiley & Sons, pp. 112–36.

Macuda, T., Gegear, R. J., Laverty, T. M., & Timney, B. (2001). Behavioural assessment of visual acuity in bumblebees (*Bombus impatiens*). *The Journal of Experimental Biology*, **204**: 559–64.

Oelschläger, H. H. (2008). The dolphin brain – a challenge for synthetic neurobiology. *Brain Research Bulletin*, **75**: 450–9.

Patton, P. (2008). One world, many minds. *Scientific American Mind*, December issue, 72–9.

Potter, M. C., & Fox, L. F. (2009). Detecting and remembering simultaneous pictures in a rapid serial visual presentation. *Journal of Experimental Psychology: Human Perception and Performance*, **35**: 28–38.

Rensink, R. A., O'Regan, J. K., & Clark, J. J. (1997). To see or not to see: the need for attention to perceive changes in scenes. *Psychological Science*, **8**: 368–73.

Scarf, D., & Colombo, M. (2008). Representation of serial order: a comparative analysis of humans, monkeys, and pigeons. *Brain Research Bulletin*, **76**: 307–12.

Silberberg, A., & Kearns, D. (2009). Memory for the order of briefly presented numerals in humans as a function of practice. *Animal Cognition*, **12**: 405–07.

Simons, D. J., & Levin, D. T. (1997). Change blindness. *Trends in Cognitive Science*, **1**: 261–7.

Sperling, G. (1960). The information available in brief visual presentations. *Psychological Monographs*, **74**.

Stromeyer, C. F. (1982). An adult eidetiker. In: Neisser, U. (Ed.), *Memory Observed: Remembering in Natural Contexts*. New York, NY: W.H. Freeman and Co, Chapter 40, pp. 399–404.

Tinbergen, N. (1974). *Curious Naturalists*. Harmondsworth: Penguin Education.

Tomasello, M., & Call, J. (1997). *Primate Cognition*. New York, NY: Oxford University Press.

Vallortigara, G., Snyder, A., Kaplan, G., Bateson, P., Clayton, N., & Rogers, L. (2008). Are animals autistic savants? *PLoS Biology*, **6**: 0208–14.

Von Neumann, J. (1951). The general and logical theory of automata. In: Jeffress, L. A. (Ed.). *Cerebral Mechanisms in Behavior. The Hixon Symposium*. New York, NY: John Wiley & Sons, pp. 1–32.

Wehner, R. (1981). Spatial vision in Arthropods. In: *The Handbook of Sensory Physiology, Vol. VII/6C Vision in Invertebrates*. Berlin: Springer-Verlag, Chapter 4, pp. 287–616.

Wright, A. A., Santiago, H. C., Sands, S. F., Kendrick, D. F., & Cook, R. G. (1985). Memory processing of serial lists by pigeons, monkeys, and people. *Science*, **229**: 287–9.

Chapter 20

Paradoxical phenomena in brain plasticity

Bryan Kolb and G. Campbell Teskey

Summary

Brain plasticity refers to the potential for the brain to change physically, chemically or physiologically to adapt to environmental change and to compensate for brain perturbations such as injury. Although there is a tendency to perceive plasticity as a singular change in which synapses are added or subtracted, experience-dependent change in the nervous system is much more complex and it is clear that experience modulates plasticity in unpredictable ways. Thus, the same experience can have different effects at different ages, in the two sexes, in the two hemispheres and in different cortical layers and regions. Many of these differential changes present a paradox in that they are not predictable a priori. The challenge is to understand how plastic changes occur, which ultimately will be at the level of gene expression, so that the rules governing brain plasticity can be written.

Introduction

Behavioural neuroscience has been guided throughout the twentieth century by the principle of localization of function. One underlying assumption has been that there are continuously adaptive responses to the experiences that challenge the cerebral cortex – processes referred to as *plasticity*. For example, if we learn a motor skill such as playing the piano, there are correlated changes in the organization of the motor representations of the fingers in the cerebral cortex. Indeed, it is likely that the increasing dexterity of the fingers as the piano-playing skill improves occurs because of the changed motor representation. The effects of experience are profound and often very large and can be seen at a fairly gross level with noninvasive imaging techniques, all the way down to molecular levels as changes in gene expression. Over the past 25 years, there has been a tendency to think of any experience as having a singular effect on the brain. It is becoming clear, however, that this idea is quite wrong. For instance, experience can have multiple effects that vary with age, sex, cerebral region, cortical layer and cerebral hemisphere. Experience may differentially select different plastic processes in different brain regions, or each region may be specialized with respect to its plastic response to experience. Whichever possibility is correct, many of the plastic changes are paradoxical and still poorly understood. For example, when laboratory rats are trained on a visual learning task, there is an increase in synaptic number in the visual cortex – a result that appears quite predictable (Kolb *et al.*, 2008). In contrast, however, when the animals are trained to respond to an auditory cue, there is a decrease in synaptic number in the auditory cortex – a result that is just the opposite of the visual

The Paradoxical Brain, ed. Narinder Kapur. Published by Cambridge University Press. © Cambridge University Press 2011.

Table 20.1 Factors affecting the synaptic organization of the normal brain

Factor	Basic reference
1. Sensory and motor experience	Greenough and Chang, 1988
2. Task learning	Greenough and Chang, 1988
3. Gonadal hormones	Stewart and Kolb, 1994
4. Psychoactive drugs (e.g. stimulants, THC)	Robinson and Kolb, 2004
5. Neurotrophic factors (e.g. NGF, bFGF)	Kolb *et al.*, 1997
6. Natural rewards (e.g. social interaction, sex)	Fiorino and Kolb, 2003
7. Ageing	Kramer *et al.*, 2004
8. Stress	McEwen, 2005
9. Anti-inflammatories (e.g. COX-2 inhibitors)	Silasi and Kolb, 2007
10. Diet (e.g. choline)	Meck and Williams, 2003
11. Electrical stimulation: kindling	Teskey *et al.*, 2006
12. Long-term potentiation	Monfils & Teskey, 2004
13. Long-term depression	Teskey *et al.*, 2007

task (Brown *et al.*, 2010). In both cases, the animals learned the task, but the memory trace of the task was produced by very different, and seemingly opposite, changes in cerebral neurons.

We have chosen to focus on four different types of experience-dependent brain plasticity because they provide compelling examples, but they are most certainly not going to be the only examples of plasticity that appear counter-intuitive. In short, a simple view that adding synapses underlies positive changes in behaviour will not suffice and, as noted in the Introductory chapter to the book, understanding paradoxes will play a key role in developing principles of brain functioning.

Experience modulates brain plasticity in unpredictable ways

Virtually every experience has the potential to alter the brain, at least briefly. It has now been shown that enduring changes can be produced by a wide variety of experiences, ranging from general sensory-motor experience to psychoactive drugs to electrical brain stimulation (see Table 20.1). The bulk of these studies have used morphological techniques such as electron microscopy or Golgi-like stains and have shown that experience-dependent changes can be seen in every species of animal tested, ranging from fruit flies and bees to rats, cats, monkeys and humans (for a review see Kolb and Whishaw, 1998). The general gist of all these studies is that experience leads to the generation of new synapses in brain regions that are activated by the experiences. The 'gold standard' example from the nonhuman animal literature is complex ('enriched') housing.

When animals are placed in complex environments rather than simple laboratory cages, within 30 days there is about a 5% increase in brain weight and cortical thickness, an increase in synaptic space (longer dendrites and more spines), an increase in cortical acetylcholine and neurotrophic factors, as well as changes in physiological properties of neurons such as those measured in studies of long-term potentiation (LTP); for a review, see Kolb and Whishaw (1998). Although most studies have focused on neocortical changes, similar changes can also be seen in the hippocampus and striatum. The anatomical and physiological changes are associated with improved performance on tests of both motor and cognitive behaviours and, although the data are correlational, it is generally assumed that the morphological changes are responsible for the facilitation in behaviour.

Given that the developing brain is usually more plastic than the adult brain, it is reasonable to expect that placing animals in complex environments as soon as they are weaned would produce even larger effects on the brain. To our surprise, however, placing animals in complex environments as juveniles does not produce larger effects, but rather *different* effects. Specifically, when young adult, middle-aged and senescent rats are placed in complex environments, there is an increase in spine density in comparison to age-matched rats living in social groups in standard laboratory cages. In contrast, juvenile rats placed in the complex environments show a *decrease* in spine density across the cerebral cortex in adulthood when compared to age-matched animals in standard laboratory cages (Kolb et al., 2003a). This decrease is present after only 4 days of complex housing and persists into adulthood. A decrease in spine density implies that there is a decrease in total number of synapses, which is the opposite of what happens in adults. Yet, in spite of this, there is an enhancement of behaviour. It seems paradoxical that both an increase and a decrease in synaptic space are correlated with enhanced behaviour. A subsequent set of studies looked at stimulation in infant rats (Kolb and Gibb, 2010). In these studies, infant rats were tactilely stimulated with a soft blush brush for 15 min, 3 times a day for the first 14 days of life. Again, when the brains were examined in adulthood, there was a general *decrease* in spine density and this was correlated with enhanced motor and cognitive behaviours. Any simple view that experience increases the number of synapses, which provides a behavioural advantage, is obviously not correct.

However, things get yet more complex when we look beyond the sensory and motor regions and peer into the prefrontal cortex. The prefrontal cortex (PFC) is typically characterized as a 'higher-level' or 'executive' region of the brain. Dynamic imaging studies have shown in human subjects that the PFC is activated in a wide range of complex cognitive tasks and damage to the PFC produces disturbances in motor, attentional, mnemonic, emotional and social behaviours (e.g. Kolb and Whishaw, 2009). It is thus generally assumed that the PFC should be among the most plastic regions of the brain in response to experience, but until recently, nobody had actually looked. When we investigated, we were surprised to discover that neurons in the PFC show virtually no chronic change (Kolb et al., 2003b), even though every other cerebral area we examined did change. We wondered if it was possible that the PFC might show transient changes to complex housing and indeed that is the case: there is an acute synaptic *increase* in one region of the rat PFC (the medial PFC or mPFC), and a corresponding acute *decrease* in another nearby PFC region (the orbital frontal cortex or OFC) over the first 2–4 days. These changes then reverse back to baseline by 7–10 days (Comeau et al., 2010). In contrast, the adjacent motor and parietal cortex show no obvious synaptic change in the first few days, but later show a synaptic increase as the PFC reverts to baseline (Comeau et al., 2010). Thus, there are three surprising findings. First, two adjacent regions of the PFC show opposite changes in response to the same experience. Second, the PFC and the rest of the cortex show completely different timelines for change. Third, in contrast to the general idea that plastic changes persist as long as the enhanced behaviours persist, there are clearly, currently unspecified, dynamic interactions among cortical regions that underlie the reorganization of neural networks.

The unexpected complementary changes in the subregions of the PFC are not confined to studies of the effects of complex housing. For example, Bell *et al.* (2010) have shown that play behaviour in juvenile rats differentially alters the structure of mPFC and OFC neurons: the complexity of OFC neurons is directly related to the number of playmates, whereas the complexity of mPFC neurons is directly related to the amount of play. Similarly, male rats allowed the opportunity to mate daily for 14 days show reduced synaptic space in mPFC whereas OFC shows increased space (Fiorino and Kolb, 2003). Psychoactive drugs also induce the unexpected complementary changes. Thus, whereas mPFC neurons show a 20% *increase* in dendritic length and spine density in response to sensitizing doses of amphetamine or nicotine, OFC neurons show exactly the *reverse* effect (Robinson and Kolb, 2004) – see Figure 20.1. Finally, when animals are trained in neuropsychological tests known to be sensitive to PFC injury, once again there are opposite changes in the mPFC and OFC, the details varying with different tasks (Comeau *et al.*, 2010; Kolb *et al.*, 2008).

The consistency in complementary plastic responses in the two PFC subfields is not predicted by previous work and remains puzzling. The two regions receive parallel inputs from the medial dorsal nucleus of the thalamus, ventral tegmental area and amygdala. They both receive extensive inputs from posterior sensory regions and send outputs to the basal ganglia and other subcortical targets (Uylings *et al.*, 2003). In view of the similar patterns of connectivity, it was reasonable to expect changes that, if not equivalent in size, were in the same direction. There are extensive connections between the two PFC regions, which is likely part of the reason for the complementary changes. In addition, it is possible that the same inputs somehow produce different patterns of gene expression in the two regions, although this is complete speculation at this point. In any event, the results imply some type of dynamic balance between the two prefrontal regions.

Studies of the effects of brain stimulation have also revealed paradoxical results. Kindling refers to the phenomena whereby epileptiform after-discharges become progressively more severe as they are repeatedly elicited (for a review see Teskey, 2001). The resulting persistent state of heightened seizure susceptibility is correlated with long-lasting increases in synaptic efficacy and unit activity, which are measures of neuronal plasticity. Indeed, kindling is an extremely robust example of plasticity and would be expected to be associated with neuronal morphological correlates. Studies of both hippocampus and amygdala have shown such synaptic changes, so we anticipated that the neocortex would as well. It does. What is unexpected, however, is that different layers of the cortex change differently, as shown in Figure 20.2. Thus, kindling results in an initial dendritic hypertrophy in layer V but a hypotrophy in layer III. With time, layer V basilar dendrites reverse their changes and become hypotrophic, whereas the layer III dendrites return to baseline levels (Teskey *et al.*, 2006). Given that cortical columns have long been thought to act as a unit (Mountcastle, 1997), it was generally assumed that there would be a singular change in synaptic space across the column, but

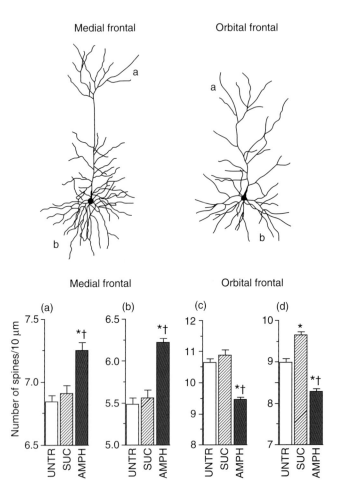

Figure 20.1 Top. Representative neurons from the medial and orbital frontal regions. a, apical field; b, basilar field. Bottom. Mean (± SEM) spine density on apical (a,c) and basilar (b,d) dendrites of pyramidal neurons in the mPFC and OFC in the amphetamine self-administration (grey bars), sucrose-reward training (hatched bars) or in untreated control groups (open bars). The asterisk and daggers indicate a significant difference from the untrained and sucrose conditions, respectively ($P < 0.05$). Note that the drug effects are opposite in the two prefrontal regions. (After Crombag et al., 2005.)

this is not the case. However, such layer-specific changes are not unique to brain stimulation studies. We have found parallel paradoxical findings in studies of the brains of rats learning various neuropsychological tasks (Comeau et al., 2010; Kolb et al., 2008). We interpret these data as evidence that layers III and V have different and perhaps opposing roles in at least some forms of plasticity.

Plasticity and timing of early cerebral injury does not follow simple rules

One of the most influential findings in neuropsychology in the past 150 years was the demonstration by Broca, and later many others, that injury to specific regions of the left hemisphere of right-handed people produced chronic deficits in various aspects of language functions (see Kolb and Whishaw, 2009). It was not long, however, before it was noted by Broca and others that children rarely had persistent language deficits from left hemisphere injuries, even if those injuries were very extensive. About 100 years later,

Dendritic Length

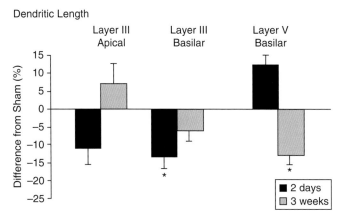

Figure 20.2 Quantification (mean±SEM) of the effect of 25 sessions of kindled seizures at either 2 days (black), or 3 weeks (grey) following the last seizure on layer III apical, layer III basilar, and layer V basilar dendritic length in pyramidal cells in frontal cortex (area Fr1). Kindling induction was associated with significant decreases in dendritic length in both apical and basilar fields in layer III, but significant increases in layer V following the last seizure. At 3 weeks kindling was associated with a significant increase in layer III and a decrease in layer V. * indicates a significant difference from implanted controls, $p < 0.05$. (After Teskey *et al.*, 2006.)

Rasmussen and Milner (1977) showed, using brain stimulation in conscious patients, that early injuries that invade either the anterior or posterior speech zone in human infants cause the language maps to move either to the opposite hemisphere or to other regions of the left hemisphere. Importantly, the authors found that the extent (and efficacy) of language reorganization was better in the first few years of infancy and had pretty much disappeared by about 10 years. Rasmussen and Milner's findings account for the absence of language deficits in children but it runs counter to the idea that language regions of the brain are specified very early in prenatal development (Wada *et al.*, 1975).

The first systematic laboratory studies of the effects of early brain injury were carried out by Margaret Kennard in the 1930s and 1940s. She made unilateral motor cortex lesions in infant and adult monkeys and confirmed the general idea that 'earlier is better'. The behavioural impairments in the infant monkeys were milder than those in the adults, which led Kennard to hypothesize that there had been a change in cortical organization in the infants and that these changes supported the behavioural recovery. In particular, she hypothesized that if some synapses were removed as a consequence of brain injury, 'others would be formed in less usual combinations' and that 'it is possible that factors which facilitate cortical organization in the normal young are the same by which reorganization is accomplished in the imperfect cortex after injury' (Kennard, 1942, p. 239). Although intuitively appealing, Donald Hebb's studies of children with early brain injury in the 1940s led to a different conclusion (Hebb, 1947, 1949). Hebb noticed that children with frontal lobe injuries often had worse outcomes than adults with similar injuries and proposed that the early injuries prevented a normal initial organization of the brain, thus making it difficult for the child to develop many behaviours, especially socio-affective behaviours. Thus, whereas Kennard hypothesized that recovery from early brain damage was associated with reorganization into novel neural networks that supported functional recovery, Hebb postulated that the failure to recover was correlated with a failure of initial

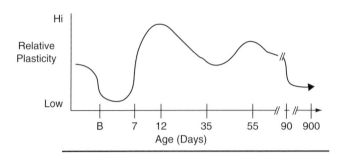

Figure 20.3 Relative recovery from cortical injury varies with age. The best outcomes are prenatal, the second week of infancy, and peri-adolescence.

organization that prevented the normal development of many behaviours. Extensive studies of both cats and rats with cortical injuries have shown that both views are partially correct (e.g. Kolb, 1995; Gramsburgen, 2007; Schmanke and Villablanca, 2001; Villablanca et al., 1993). It is the precise developmental age at injury and the behaviour being examined that predicts the Kennard or Hebb outcome.

The behavioural and anatomical effects of *focal cortical injury* in the rat are tightly tied to the precise time of injury, allowing investigators to identify times that we can loosely refer to as 'critical periods' for early injury. The timing of these periods is consistent across neocortical areas, but quite unexpected. Thus, there appear to be at least three windows of resilience from early injury: (1) during the third (and last) prenatal week; (2) during the second postnatal week; (3) during the peri-adolescent period (about 50–60 days). In contrast, injury between the first and second critical periods is an exceptionally bad, and likely the *worst*, time to have a cortical injury (Kolb and Gibb, 2007; Nemati and Kolb, 2010). Morphological studies of the effects of injuries at the different time points find a consistent result: whenever there is good functional outcome there is a correlated increase in synaptic space in residual cortex, whereas a poor outcome is correlated with a reduction in synaptic space (Figure 20.3). These results do not lend themselves to a simple 'earlier is better' interpretation and appear to be inconsistent with the findings in children with left hemisphere injuries, but more recent studies of children provide some insight into the apparent contradiction. Specifically, although children with early left hemisphere lesions invading the language regions are virtually never aphasic, careful studies of language development in such children has shown that they do have persistent language deficits. Again, paradoxically, it does not matter whether the injuries are in the language zones or beyond them – they always have language impairments (Bates et al., 1997; Reilly et al., 1998). In addition, these children virtually always pay a price in general intelligence (e.g. Duval et al., 2008), but as in the lab animals with early injuries, the effect on intelligence is not linear. Earlier-onset injuries are associated with a greater loss in IQ than later-onset lesions (Anderson et al., 2009, 2010). The worst outcomes are observed when injuries occur before two years of age, and the best outcomes are observed when injuries occur around eight years of age.

There is some evidence in support of the 'earlier is better' idea, however, and that evidence comes from studies of large or diffuse cerebral injuries, such as in hemispherectomy (or hemidecortication) or certain forms of hypoxia/ischaemia. One of the most publicized findings was in the report by Lewin (1980) that documented several cases of severe hydrocephalus in which people had apparently normal cognitive functions. Although these cases were dramatic they represented an unusual sample, as most children with such hydrocephalus have significant intellectual deficits (e.g. Dennis *et al.*, 1981). Nonetheless, the fact that some people have such good outcomes remains puzzling. There is, however, a precedent for laboratory animals with large early injuries showing remarkable functional outcomes. For example, rats with hemidecortications at different ages in development show a consistent linear relationship between age and functional outcome (Kolb and Tomie, 1988). Once again, level of function is directly correlated with dendritic hypertrophy, but this time in the intact hemisphere. Similarly, when infant rats are given episodes of unilateral hypoxia/ ischemia, which leads to an extensive, but diffuse, cortical injury, we see the best functional outcome in the youngest animals and the worst outcome in adults (Williams, 2010). Although these results are consistent with the studies of language functions in children, it is difficult to explain what is different between the multiple critical period findings in animals with focal lesions versus the findings after large lesions. The different injuries clearly are stimulating different plastic processes, but we currently have no idea why or what the differences might be.

Finally, we noted earlier that Kennard and Hebb reached very different conclusions about the effects of early brain injuries in monkeys and children. One critical difference is that they were measuring very different behaviours. Kennard was impressed with motor recovery, whereas Hebb was impressed by impairments in more complex behaviours such as social behaviour. Studies in both rats and monkeys are consistent with the idea that there is differential sparing of different behaviours. For example, Kolb and Whishaw (1981, 1983) compared the recovery of cognitive, motor and species-typical behaviours (nest building, food hoarding, maternal behaviour) in rats with restricted medial frontal injuries on postnatal day seven. When the rats were tested in adulthood, the authors found virtually completely normal cognitive behaviour, mildly impaired motor behaviour and severely impaired species-typical behaviour. These results are curious because later studies showed that the day seven lesions led to dendritic hypertrophy in cortical neurons. Evidently, the neuronal plasticity provides differential support for different types of behaviour. This again is counter-intuitive and to date there is no compelling evidence explaining why the behaviourally dependent benefits of the cerebral plasticity should be task-dependent. Nonetheless, these findings are reminiscent of the effects of early injuries in children: it is rare to see aphasia after early injury but social behaviours are especially sensitive to early injury.

Drugs and experience modulate brain plasticity in counter-intuitive ways

As animals travel through life, they have an almost infinite number of experiences that could alter brain organization. There are virtually no experimental studies attempting to determine how a lifetime's experiences might interact. We attempted to address this question in a series of studies in which animals received psychoactive drugs before placement in complex environments (Hamilton and Kolb, 2005; Kolb *et al.*, 2003c). We hypothesized that, because structures such as the nucleus accumbens (NAcc) were so profoundly altered by the drugs, they might show less (or no) change in response to the housing experience. To our surprise, not only did the NAcc show no response to the experience, neither did any other cortical regions (Figure 20.4). For example, pyramidal neurons in the parietal cortex, which normally show large experience-dependent change but little drug-dependent change, showed no response to the complex housing after prior experience with amphetamine, cocaine or nicotine. An obvious question was whether prior

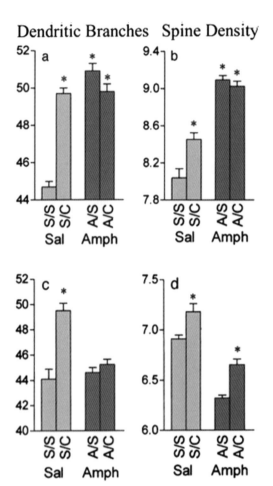

Figure 20.4 Effects of amphetamine and housing in a complex environment on dendritic branches and spine density in Nucleus Accumbens (a,b) and layer III parietal cortex (c,d). Complex housing (C) increased both dendritic branching and spine density in nucleus accumbens and parietal cortex in saline-treated (S) rats. Amphetamine (A) increased both measures in Nucleus Accumbens but not parietal cortex. Complex housing after amphetamine administration failed to alter neuronal morphology, even in the parietal cortex neurons that did not show a change in response to amphetamine. * indicates a significant difference from controls, $p<0.05$. (After Kolb et al., 2003c.)

experience with complex housing would interfere with drug-dependent changes. It does. Animals given complex housing experience prior to repeated doses of nicotine show a much-attenuated response to the drug, although they still showed some drug-induced change. We are not certain if psychoactive drugs are more potent in changing cortical neurons or if the environment versus drug difference simply reflects a difference in the 'dose' of each experience. This is a difficult question to address without extensive investigations.

The drug–behaviour interactions in cerebral plasticity are not just found in studies of the effects of drug and complex housing combinations. Prior exposure of adult rats to nicotine, or of juvenile rats to methylphenidate, interferes with later motor and cognitive learning respectively (Comeau and Kolb, 2011; Gonzalez et al., 2005). In both cases, the drugs changed the cortical neurons, but there was no evidence of a subsequent experience-dependent change in those neurons.

Plasticity can be maladaptive

As the concept of neural plasticity emerged and flourished in the 1980s, there was a natural bias to see plasticity as a good thing that accounted for behavioural changes such as enhanced sensory and motor capacities related to training. However, there is a dark side to plasticity too.

Consider the example of the syndrome of dystonia, which is the loss of fine motor movements often seen in professional musicians. It is well known that string players in a symphony, for example, are susceptible to career-ending loss of flexibility in their fingers. Although historically there were many explanations offered, it now appears that the villain is cerebral plasticity. Merzenich and his colleagues have shown in an extensive series of studies that if monkeys have two fingers sewn together, the brain comes to treat the two fingers as one (e.g. Blake *et al.*, 2002). When the fingers are separated, there is a severe deficit both in localizing stimuli to a single finger or in moving the fingers individually. The treatment to return the functions is to repeatedly stimulate the fingers separately, with a distinct temporal separation. Now consider the string players. As they become highly proficient, they make finger movements that become very fast and in pathological cases the brain begins to treat the fingers as a single finger, much like in the case of the experimental monkeys. As this begins to happen, the player cannot make independent finger movements. The treatment is simple: just like in the experimental monkeys, the dystonic players are given training distinguishing the fingers and they recover (Byl *et al.*, 2003). Plasticity caused the syndrome and plasticity reverses it.

Parallel findings of pathological plasticity can be seen in people with severe writer's cramp. Baumer *et al.* (2006) hypothesized that the writer's cramp was related to hypersensitivity in neurons in the somatosensory cortex of these individuals. They used low-frequency stimulation of the cortex with transcranial magnetic stimulation and found that, whereas the stimulation failed to affect any response in control subjects, the individuals with writer's cramp showed an abnormal response in the finger muscles. It is possible that a reversal of this abnormal plastic response would alleviate the writer's cramp, just as it did in the dystonia patients.

Another example can be seen in the effects of stroke. When people or laboratory animals have a stroke in the motor cortex they lose the capacity to make fine movements, such as those required to pick up a grain of rice by the thumb and index finger with the affected hand. One obvious solution to the problem is to use the other hand. The effect of this is that the affected limb becomes progressively worse (e.g. Nudo *et al.*, 1996), even as the non-affected limb may become more proficient. The former phenomenon is often referred to as learned non-use. Here we have maladaptive and adaptive plasticity occurring in concert. Again, the treatment is to force the subject to use the affected limb by putting the good limb in a sling (e.g. Gauthier *et al.*, 2008) – see Chapter 4. This acts to reverse the learned nonuse and often facilitates some modest recovery beyond the learned nonuse.

There is also a paradoxical relationship between seizures and behaviour (see also Chapter 11). Sustained hypersynchronous and hyperexcitable brain activity is known as a seizure. During seizures, both pre- and post-synaptically coupled neurons obey the Hebb plasticity rule; as they fire together, they consequently wire together. They also obey the corollary and once they are wired together they fire together, often leading to kindling as we saw earlier. Repeatedly imposed seizures cause a variety of plastic changes in the brain that are expressed at the molecular, synaptic, cellular and network levels. These plastic changes result in altered behaviours such as increased anxiety, poorer spatial ability, sexual dysfunction and reduced motor skilled learning, all of which are considered maladaptive. Moreover, these maladaptive behaviours in rats mirror those observed in people with epilepsy that have 'spontaneous' or easily provoked seizures (Teskey and Corcoran, 2009). Thus, it is easy to conclude that the consequences of seizures in humans and non-humans are bad. In fact neurologists, with good reason, view seizures as so problematic that they prescribe anticonvulsant medications with known side-effects and negative developmental consequences because the costs associated with these treatments are outweighed by the benefits of reduced seizure frequency. And yet, electroconvulsive therapy, the repeated application of electrical stimulation that elicits seizures, effectively relieves severe and chronic depression (see Chapter 18). The electroconvulsive seizures must also be resulting in some plastic change that results in improved mood. Thus, the plastic changes mediated by seizures can be both maladaptive and adaptive, and yet no theory accounts for why this is so.

Our examples of unexpected changes in experience-dependent brain organization illustrate the challenge in writing the rules of brain plasticity and behaviour. The same experiences, such as complex housing or drugs, differentially alter neural networks at different ages. Similarly, although the subregions of the prefrontal cortex receive very similar inputs, experiences frequently have opposite effects on brain plasticity in the two regions. Additionally, not all plasticity is good. Plastic changes can be maladaptive and produce serious behavioural or psychological consequences. Understanding the rules governing plastic changes in the nervous system are fundamental to our understanding of how the brain functions.

Future challenges and questions

Neuronal plasticity is a highly conserved phenomenon that can be seen in the simplest of organisms, such as the nematode worm *Caenorhabditis elegans* (e.g. Ardiel and Rankin, 2010) and the sea slug, *Aplysia* (Roberts and Glanzman, 2003). There has been a pretty ubiquitous tendency to see plasticity as a singular phenomenon in which synapses are added, and sometimes subtracted, to reorganize neuronal networks. As we have learned more about the principles of plasticity, we have encountered many puzzling findings that are forcing the field to rethink the nature of plasticity.

One developing idea is being referred to as *metaplasticity*, which can be thought of as plasticity of plasticity: metaplasticity is induced by neuronal activity, but it is not necessarily expressed as a change in the efficacy of normal synaptic transmission. Rather, it is observed as a change in the ability to induce subsequent synaptic plasticity (e.g. Abraham and Bear, 1996). Our earlier example of exposure to psychomotor stimulants blocking later effects of complex housing provides an example. Thus, although we found no obvious effect of the drugs on neurons in the parietal cortex, these neurons failed to change in response to later complex housing. This was unexpected and has important implications for understanding inconsistencies in brain plasticity. Thus, although we can at least partly control the experience that laboratory animals receive, our lives are more complex. We travel through life being exposed to a myriad of experiences that must interact with one another. For example, perinatal experiences such as prenatal stress are known to change the brain and may account for later predispositions to behavioural pathologies such as addiction or severe depression. We have shown, for example, that if infant rats are given tactile stimulation with a soft brush for 15 min, 3 times daily, for 14 days beginning the day after birth, their behavioural and anatomical response to psychomotor stimulants in adulthood is dramatically attenuated (Muhammad *et al.*, 2011). We hypothesize that negative stimuli such as prenatal stress will have the opposite effect.

The idea of metaplasticity may begin to explain some of the puzzling findings such as those described above. The question for future research is why and by what mechanism. One likely explanation is that experiences alter the way that genes are expressed. Although our DNA does not change during our lifetime, not all genes are active: some are on and some are off. The newly emerging field of *epigenetics* focuses on the changes in gene activity and what switches the genes on and off. The simple answer is experience. For example, it is now known that lifespan can be influenced by the diet of one's grandparents between the ages of 8 and 12 years (Kaati *et al.*, 2007). Our genes can be 'set' by the experiences of our ancestors as well as ourselves. The future of neuroplasticity research will lead to an explosion of information about how epigenetic changes modify plastic changes in the brain. An example will serve to illustrate. Mychasiuk *et al.* (2009) found that if a pregnant rat dam is housed with a female that is given mild daily stress, the brains and the behaviour of the offspring of the pregnant dam were different than if she was housed with an unstressed female. Specifically, there were changes in the patterns of expression in the brain, and the animals showed slower behavioural development. We can now ask how such animals would respond to complex housing, drugs, brain injury and so on.

The inconsistencies and puzzles in earlier studies of brain plasticity may be understood once we begin to understand how changes in gene expression relate to changes in brain organization and function. Furthermore, once genes are identified that are associated with specific brain changes, it should eventually be possible to manipulate epigenetic changes. For example, Weaver *et al.* (2006) have shown that early life experiences can alter gene expression and brain function, and that this can be reversed chemically in adults.

In sum, understanding the role of gene expression in brain plasticity will help resolve many of the apparent paradoxes and will play a key role in developing principles of brain functioning.

References

Abraham, W. C., & Bear, M. F. (1996). Metaplasticity: the plasticity of synaptic plasticity. *Trends in Neuroscience*, **19**: 126–30.

Anderson, V., Jacobs, R., Spencer-Smith, M., *et al.* (2010). Does age at brain insult predict worse outcome? Neuropsychological implications. *Journal of Pediatriac Psychology*, **24**: 612–22.

Anderson, V., Spencer-Smith, M., Leventer, R., *et al.* (2009). Childhood brain insult: can age at insult help us predict outcome? *Brain*, **132**: 45–56.

Ardiel, E. L., & Rankin, C. H. (2010). An elegant mind: learning and memory in *Caenorhabditis elegans*. *Learning and Memory*, **17**: 191–201.

Bates, E., Thal, D., Trauner, D., *et al.* (1997). From first words to grammar in children with focal brain injury. *Developmental Neuropsychology*, **13**: 275–343.

Baumer, T., Demiralay, C., Hidding, U., *et al.* (2006). Abnormal plasticity of the sensorimotor cortex to slow repetitive transcranial magnetic stimulation in patients with writer's cramp. *Movement Disorders*, **22**: 81–90.

Bell, H., Pellis, S., & Kolb, B. (2010). Juvenile peer play experience and the development of the orbitofrontal and medial prefrontal cortex. *Behavioural Brain Research*, **207**: 7–13.

Blake, D. T., Byl, N. N., Cheung, S., *et al.* (2002). Sensory representation abnormalities that parallel focal hand dystonia in a primate model. *Somatosensory and Motor Research*, **19**: 347–57.

Brown, A. R., Hu, B., Kolb, B., & Teskey, G. C. (2010). Acoustic tone or medial geniculate stimulation cue training in the rat is associated with neocortical neuroplasticity and reduced akinesia under haloperidol challenge. *Behavioural Brain Research*, **214**: 85–90.

Byl, N. N., Nagajaran, S., & McKenzie, A. L. (2003). Effect of sensory discrimination training on structure and function in patients with focal hand dystonia: a case series. *Archives of Physical Medicine and Rehabilitation*, **84**: 1505–14.

Comeau, W., & Kolb, B. (2011). Administration of methylphenidate to juvenile rats blocks later experience-dependent plasticity. Manuscript in submission.

Comeau, W., McDonald, R., & Kolb, B. (2010). Learning-induced alterations in prefrontal cortical dendritic morphology. *Behavioural Brain Research*, **214**: 91–101.

Crombag, H. S., Gorny, G., Li, Y., Kolb, B., & Robinson, T. E. (2005) Opposite effects of amphetamine self-administration experience on dendritic spines in the medial and orbital prefrontal cortex. *Cerebral Cortex*, **15**: 341–8.

Dennis, M., Fitz, C. R., Netley, C. T., *et al.* (1981). The intelligence of hydrocephalic children. *Archives of Neurology*, **38**: 607–15.

Duval, J., Braun, C. M., Montour-Proulx, I., Daigneault, S., Rouleau, I., & Begin, J. (2008). Brain lesions and IQ: recovery versus decline depends on age of onset. *Journal of Child Neurology*, **23**: 663–8.

Fiorino, D., & Kolb, B. (2003). Sexual experience leads to long-lasting morphological changes in male rat prefrontal cortex, parietal cortex, and nucleus accumbens neurons. *Society for Neuroscience Abstracts*, **29**: 402.3.

Gauthier, L. V., Taub, E., Perkins, C., Ortmann, M., Mark, V. W., & Uswatte, G. (2008). Remodeling the brain: plastic structural brain changes produced by different motor therapies after stroke. *Stroke*, **39**: 1520–5.

Gonzalez, C. L., Gharbawie, O. A., & Kolb, B. (2005). Nicotine alters learning and dendritic structure. *Synapse*, **55**: 183–91.

Gramsbergen, A. (2007). Neural compensation after early lesions: a clinical view of animal experiments. *Neuroscience and Biobehavioural Reviews*, **31**: 1088–94.

Greenough, W. T., & Chang, F. F. (1988). Plasticity of synapse structure and pattern in the cerebral cortex. In: Peters, A., & Jones, E. G. (Eds.). *Cerebral Cortex, Volume 7*. New York, NY: Plenum Press, pp. 391–440.

Hamilton, D., & Kolb, B. (2005). Nicotine, experience, and brain plasticity. *Behavioral Neuroscience*, **119**: 355–65.

Hebb, D. O. (1947). The effects of early experience on problem solving at maturity. *American Psychologist*, **2**: 737–45.

Hebb, D. O. (1949). *The Organization of Behavior*. New York, NY: Wiley.

Kaati, G., Bygren, L. O., Pambrey, M., & Sjostrom, M. (2007). Transgenerational response to nutrition, early life circumstances and longevity. *European Journal of Human Genetics*, **15**: 784–90.

Kennard, M. (1942). Cortical reorganization of motor function. *Archives of Neurology*, **48**: 227–40.

Kolb, B. (1995). *Brain Plasticity and Behavior*. Mahwah, NJ: Erlbaum.

Kolb, B., & Gibb, R. (2007). Brain plasticity and recovery from early cortical injury. *Developmental Psychobiology*, **49**: 107–18.

Kolb, B., & Gibb, R. (2010). Tactile stimulation after frontal or parietal cortical injury in infant rats facilitates functional recovery and stimulates synaptic changes. *Behavioural Brain Research*, **214**: 115–20.

Kolb, B., & Tomie, J. (1988). Recovery from early cortical damage in rats. IV. Effects of hemidecortication at 1, 5, or 10 days of age. *Behavioural Brain Research*, **28**: 259–74.

Kolb, B., & Whishaw, I. Q. (1981). Neonatal frontal lesions in the rat: sparing of learned but not species-typical behavior in the presence of reduced brain weight and cortical thickness. *Journal of Comparative and Physiological Psychology*, **95**: 863–79.

Kolb, B., & Whishaw, I. Q. (1983). Generalizing in neuropsychology: problems and principles underlying cross-species comparisons. In: Robinson, T. E. (Ed.). *Behavioral Contributions to Brain Research*. New York, NY: Oxford University Press.

Kolb, B., & Whishaw, I. Q. (1998). Brain plasticity and behavior. *Annual Review of Psychology*, **49**: 43–64.

Kolb, B., & Whishaw, I. Q. (2009). *Fundamentals of Human Neuropsychology*, 6th Ed. New York, NY: Worth.

Kolb, B., Cioe, J., & Comeau, W. (2008). Contrasting effects of motor and visual learning tasks on dendritic arborization and spine density in rats. *Neurobiology of Learning and Memory*, **90**: 295–300.

Kolb, B., Cioe, J., & Muirhead, D. (1998). Cerebral morphology and functional sparing after prenatal frontal cortex lesions in rats. *Behavioural Brain Research*, **91**: 143–55.

Kolb, B., Gibb, R., & Gorny, G. (2003a). Experience-dependent changes in dendritic arbor and spine density in neocortex vary with age and sex. *Neurobiology of Learning and Memory*, **79**: 1–10.

Kolb, B., Gorny, G., Cote, S., Ribeiro-da-Silva, A., & Cuello, A. C. (1997). Nerve growth factor stimulates growth of cortical pyramidal neurons in young adult rats. *Brain Research*, **751**: 289–94.

Kolb, B., Gorny, G., Li, Y., Samaha, A. N., & Robinson, T. E. (2003c). Amphetamine or cocaine limits the ability of later experience to promote structural plasticity in the neocortex and nucleus accumbens. *Proceedings of the National Academy of Sciences USA*, **100**: 10,523–8.

Kolb, B., Gorny, G., Sonderpalm, A., & Robinson, T. E. (2003b). Environmental complexity has different effects on the structure of neurons in the prefrontal cortex versus the parietal cortex or nucleus accumbens. *Synapse*, **48**: 149–53.

Kramer, A. F., Bherer, L., Colcombe, S. J., Dong, W., & Greenough, W. T. (2004). Environmental influences on cognitive and brain plasticity during aging. *Journals of Gerontology, Series A*, **59**: M940–57.

Lewin, R. (1980). Is your brain really necessary? *Science*, **210**: 1232–4.

McEwen, B. S. (2005). Glucocorticoids, depression, and mood disorders: structural remodeling in the brain. *Metabolism*, **54**(5 Suppl 1): 20–3.

Meck, W. H., & Williams, C. L. (2003). Metabolic imprinting of choline by its availability during gestation: implications for memory and attentional processing across the lifespan. *Neuroscience and Biobehavioral Reviews*, **27**: 385–99.

Monfils, M.-H., & Teskey, G. C. (2004). Induction of long-term depression is associated with decreased dendritic length and spine density in layers III and V of sensorimotor neocortex *Synapse*, **53**: 114–21.

Mountcastle, V. B. (1997). The columnar organization of the neocortex. *Brain*, **120**: 701–22.

Muhammad, A., Hossain, S., Pellis, S. M., & Kolb, B. (2011). Tactile stimulation during development attenuates amphetamine sensitization and structurally reorganizes prefrontal cortex and striatum in a sex-dependent manner. *Behavioral Neuroscience*, in press.

Mychasiuk, R. M., Kolb, B., & Gibb, R. (2009). Prenatal stress (bystander or direct) results in dose-dependent epigenetic and behavioral changes for offspring. *Society for Neuroscience Abstracts*, **468**: 25.

Nemati, F., & Kolb, B. (2010). The effects of juvenile motor cortex injuries vary with age. *Behavioral Neuroscience*, **24**: 612–22.

Nudo, R. J., Wise, B. M., SiFuentes, F., & Milliken, G. W. (1996). Neural substrates for the effects of rehabilitative training on motor recovery after ischemic infarct. *Science*, **272**: 1791–4.

Rasmussen, T., & Milner, B., (1977). The role of early left-brain injury in determining lateralization of cerebral speech functions. *Annals of the New York Academy of Sciences*, **299**: 355–67.

Reilly, J. S., Bates, E., & Marchman, V. (1998). Narrative discourse in children with early focal brain injury. *Brain and Language*, **61**: 335–75.

Roberts, A. C., & Glanzman, D. L. (2003). Learning in *Aplysia*: looking at synaptic plasticity from both sides. *Trends in Neuroscience*, **26**: 662–70.

Robinson, T. E., & Kolb, B. (2004). Structural plasticity associated with drugs of abuse. *Neuropharmacology*, **47**: 33–46.

Schmanke, T. D., & Villablanca, J. R. (2001). A critical maturational period of reduced brain vulnerability to injury. A study of cerebral glucose metabolism in cats. *Developmental Brain Research*, **26**: 127–41.

Silasi, G., & Kolb, B. (2007). Chronic inhibition of cyclooxygenase-2 induces dendritic hypertrophy and limited functional improvement following motor cortex stroke. *Neuroscience*, **144**: 1160–8.

Stewart, J., & Kolb, B. (1994). Dendritic branching in cortical pyramidal cells in response to ovariectomy in adult female rats: suppression by neonatal exposure to testosterone. *Brain Research*, **654**: 149–54.

Teskey, G. C. (2001). Using kindling to model the neuroplastic changes associated with learning and memory, neuropsychiatric disorders, and epilepsy. In: Shaw, C. A., &

McEachern, J. C. (Eds). *Toward a Theory of Neuroplasticity*. Philadelphia, PA: Taylor and Francis, pp. 347–58.

Teskey, G. C., & Corcoran, M. E. (2009). Interictal behavioural comorbidities in a model of epilepsy. In: Schwartzkroin, P. (Ed.). *Encyclopedia of Basic Epilepsy Research.* Oxford. Elsevier, Vol. 3, pp. 1254–60.

Teskey, G. C., Monfils, M. H., Silasi, G., & Kolb, B. (2006). Neocortical kindling is associated with opposing alterations in dendritic morphology in neocortical layer V and striatum from neocortical layer III. *Synapse,* **59**: 1–9.

Teskey, G. C., Young, N. A., van Rooyen, F., *et al.* (2007). Induction of long-term depression results in smaller movement representations, fewer excitatory perforated synapses, and more inhibitory synapses. *Cerebral Cortex,* **17**: 434–42.

Uylings, H., Groenewegen, H., & Kolb, B. (2003). Does the rat have a prefrontal cortex? *Behavioural Brain Research,* **146**: 3–17.

Villablanca, J. R., Hovda, D. A., Jackson, G. F., & Infante, C. (1993). Neurological and behavioral effects of a unilateral frontal cortical lesion in fetal kittens: II. Visual system tests, and proposing a 'critical period' for lesion effects. *Behavioural Brain Research,* **57**: 79–92.

Wada, J. A., Clarke, R., & Hamm, A. (1975). Cerebral hemispheric asymmetry in humans. Cortical speech zones in 100 adults and 100 infant brains. *Archives of Neurology,* **32**: 239–46.

Weaver, I. C., Meaney, M. J., & Szyf, M. (2006). Maternal care effects on the hippocampal transcriptome and anxiety-mediated behaviors in the offspring that are reversible in adulthood. *Proceedings of the National Academy of Sciences (USA),* **103**: 3480–5.

Williams, P. (2010). Factors influencing recovery from neonatal hypoxia/ischemia. Unpublished PhD thesis, University of Lethbridge.

Chapter 21

Immature neurons in the adult brain. Breaking all the rules

J. Martin Wojtowicz

Summary

Paradoxes in the field of adult neurogenesis are many. This may be partly due to the fact that this field of research is relatively new and that ideas outpace hard facts. Moreover, evidence originating from different laboratories is often inconsistent due to varied experimental conditions. We will not concern ourselves with such trivial controversies, but instead try to point out the perceived inconsistencies that may represent true exceptions to the rule. Such paradoxes make one pause and wonder about accepted theories, and importantly, may point us in new and creative directions.

The chapter begins with an explanation of neurogenesis in the context of brain anatomy. Description of neuronal 'assembly line' is followed by explanation of what new neurons look like and how they function. At the end of this chapter the reader will realize that the very existence of adult neurogenesis is still denied by some, and that most debates are yet to be settled.

Glossary

Apoptosis – a type of cell death resulting from a sequence of chemical reactions within the cell. It can be triggered 'on purpose' to eliminate excessive cell numbers during brain growth.

Contextual learning – a type of learning depending strongly on the context in which the learning took place. Often associated with specific brain structures such as the hippocampus.

Entorhinal cortex – part of the cortex immediately adjacent to the hippocampus. It contains neurons that send information to and receive information from the hippocampus.

Hippocampal formation – includes three main brain components constituting neuronal circuitry responsible for learning. Dentate gyrus, Cornus Ammonis – CA3 and Cornus Ammonis – CA1.

Mitosis – mechanism of cell division where DNA is replicated so that each daughter cell will receive an exact DNA copy.

Progenitor cells – specialized cells descending from stem cells and giving rise to either neurons (neuroprogenitors) or other supporting cell types such as glia.

BrdU – Bromodeoxyuridine. A molecule that can be injected into the animals in order to label dividing cells. BrdU acts by inserting itself into the DNA of the dividing cells.

The Paradoxical Brain, ed. Narinder Kapur. Published by Cambridge University Press. © Cambridge University Press 2011.

Neurogenesis in a nutshell

The theory that the adult brain can produce new neurons and incorporate them into a functional circuitry had a difficult birth. As Gross (2000) pointed out, pioneering evidence for the existence of the mitotically dividing cells in the adult brain obtained by Joseph Altman and colleagues (Altman and Das, 1965) was dismissed in the face of the dominant dogma that the adult brain is essentially post-mitotic. Thus, until around 1990, in textbooks and in common knowledge, we were taught that in the course of adult life we can only lose nerve cells and never gain any new ones. There were of course exceptions, most notably in research on birds which showed that certain species of song birds seasonally generate neurons to produce a new set of cells every spring (Wilbrecht et al., 2002). However, the case for birds was considered not to be applicable to mammals and certainly not to primates.

Twenty years later, it has been universally accepted that there are at least two brain regions in most mammals capable of producing de novo neurons from undifferentiated progenitor cells. Both neurogenic regions originate from a single source, the primordial neuroepithelium, which gives rise to the subventricular layer surrounding the brain ventricles, and separately, to the dentate gyrus (DG) in a strictly choreographed sequence of cell migrations (Altman and Bayer, 1990). The transition from embryonic migration and neurogenesis to adult neurogenesis is gradual. In mice and rats, neurogenesis assumes its adult pattern at around one month after birth, i.e. at the time of puberty. Neurogenesis in the subventricular zone (SVZ) is entirely different from neurogenesis in DG in that it involves a long migratory pathway from the ventricles to the olfactory bulb. Neurogenesis in the DG is more localized, with cells migrating for short distances only. Thus, the two neurogenic regions appear to be quite distinct, but may interact, since physiology of olfactory perception is closely linked with the hippocampus (Cohen and Eichenbaum, 1993). Memories of olfactory stimuli are strongly represented in the hippocampus. They are carried via a direct route, lateral olfactory tract, from the olfactory bulb to the entorhinal cortex, and subsequently into the dentate gyrus (de Castro, 2009). For the sake of simplicity, this chapter will be mostly concerned with DG, but will also point out some of the contrasting features of the two regions.

According to a widely accepted view, the hippocampal formation, including the dentate gyrus, plays a crucial role in learning and memory. The learning process includes several steps: stimulus detection, initial association with pre-existing memory traces, association with the context in which learning takes place and short-term encoding of a memory trace. This sequence is usually followed by repetition of a task, strengthening of the memory trace, and finally long-term storage. In addition to the hippocampus, this learning also involves surrounding cortical regions with which the hippocampus communicates via reciprocal synaptic connections, and perhaps also other structures in the limbic–diencephalic–forebrain system. The question of interest here is: How does neurogenesis fit into this scheme?

Within the hippocampal formation, one can distinguish the dentate gyrus, CA3 and CA1, three functionally distinct regions that are serially connected to each other in the so-called tri-synaptic circuit. All three regions also receive parallel connections from the entorhinal cortex. Adult hippocampal neurogenesis should be presented in the context of hippocampal circuitry, recognizing that it is limited to only one of its regions, the dentate gyrus (Figure 21.1).

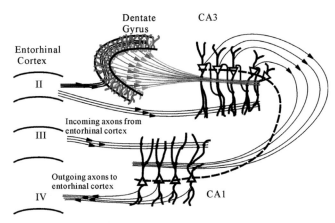

Dentate Gyrus

CA3

Entorhinal Cortex

II

Incoming axons from entorhinal cortex

III

Outgoing axons to entorhinal cortex

IV

CA1

Figure 21.1 Neuronal circuit involving neurogenesis. Thin lines show axons carrying electrical signals from one region to another. Arrows indicate direction of information flow through the circuit. Dentate gyrus is one of the major hubs of adult neurogenesis. Dentate gyrus is also the gateway to the hippocampus, the major part of the brain involved in learning and memory. The axons originating from the entorhinal cortex enter the dentate gyrus and form synaptic connections on mature (red) and immature (green) neurons residing in the dentate gyrus. These neurons in turn project to area CA3, composed of large pyramidal neurons. The CA3 pyramids in turn project to area CA1. Together, the dentate gyrus, CA3 and CA1 form the tri-synaptic circuit critical for normal functions of the whole hippocampus in learning and memory. Additional projections from the entorhinal cortex project directly to CA3 and CA1, providing alternate (direct) pathways complementing the tri-synaptic path. Adult neurogenesis is found only in dentate gyrus where it is responsible for continuous replacement and recruitment of neurons, providing a unique resource in plasticity and ultimately learning and memory.

Within the DG there exists a neurogenic niche where neurons are born and develop. Adult neurogenesis in DG is a progression of developmental steps, feeding off each other and taking several weeks to complete (Figure 21.2). Week 1 is a period of increasing the numbers of neurons by repeated mitotic divisions. The first division is asymmetric, i.e. it is a division of quiescent, rarely dividing, neuroprogenitor cells into two unequal halves. The original quiescent cell acts as a neural 'mother cell' and its morphology is plant-like, with leafy projections on top and a bulbous root-like base at the bottom (Figure 21.2). The bottom half gives rise to proliferating neural progenitor cells by secondary divisions. These cells can replicate themselves several times by repeated mitosis while leaving the original mother cell essentially intact and ready to produce more amplifying cells at some later time point.

This replication of amplifying progenitors during the first week can be demonstrated indirectly in a population of cells labelled with the mitotic marker bromodeoxyuridine (BrdU), which is an analogue of a naturally occurring component of DNA and gets substituted for that component when injected into the body. In one such experiment, BrdU was injected into animals in sufficiently large doses to label all dividing cells over the course of 12 h, and the numbers of surviving cells were estimated by sampling the brain tissue from different groups of animals at 1, 3, 7, 14, 28 and 60 days following the injections (McDonald and Wojtowicz, 2005). The results show an increase in the number of BrdU-tagged cells during the first 7 days, indicating proliferation of the amplifying cells (Figure 21.2).

The second phase of neurogenesis begins at 7 days and ends at approximately 14 days. In this period, some of the proliferating cells die off. This is a similar process to natural cell death occurring during embryonic brain development when neuronal overproduction

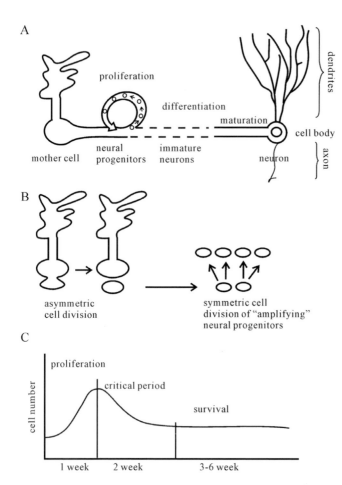

A

proliferation

differentiation

maturation

cell body

dendrites

axon

neuron

mother cell   neural   immature
               progenitors   neurons

B

asymmetric   symmetric cell
cell division   division of "amplifying"
                    neural progenitors

C

cell number

proliferation

critical period

survival

1 week   2 week   3-6 week

Figure 21.2 (A) 'Assembly line' for adult-born neurons. A stem mother cell gives rise to proliferating progenitor cells that replicate themselves and differentiate into immature neurons. Maturation is complete when neurons form a typical dendritic tree and an axon. (B) The mother cell divides asymmetrically to retain its core but also to produce offspring in the form of proliferating cells. The amplifying cells divide symmetrically several times prior to the beginning of differentiation and maturation. (C) Timeline of adult neurogenesis with proliferation taking approximately 7 days and ending with the beginning of a critical period (also 7 days) when the cell number declines but the surviving cells differentiate and progress towards maturation.

is followed by elimination of unused cells. During this process, the unnecessary neurons self-destruct via a process called apoptosis (Kuhn, 2008; Sun *et al.*, 2004). However, the most dramatic is the growth of the cells once they finish replicating. Within a few days the amorphous, migrating amoeba-like cells are transformed into bona fide neurons that are anchored in place with branching dendrites extending in one direction from a well-defined cell body and a single axon searching out the target neurons in the opposite direction (Figure 21.3). This week is also called a critical period, since cells at this stage are very sensitive to physiologically relevant stimuli that determine whether a cell lives or dies. Numerous stimuli may be involved at this stage. Among those that have been identified are the hippocampus-dependent learning processes, exposures to rich environmental conditions and, perhaps, physical exercise such as running (Shors, 2009). The neurons in their critical period of development are still very primitive and lack complete structural and functional features such as synaptic connections. They migrate from the site of their birth to the ultimate location within the granule cell layer. During this migration the cells are not yet 'wired' into the synaptic circuit and their dendrites are disorganized and devoid of dendritic spines, which are the normal sites of the excitatory synaptic contacts. These cells cannot be active in the usual, neuronal sense,

Day 7   Day 14   Day 28

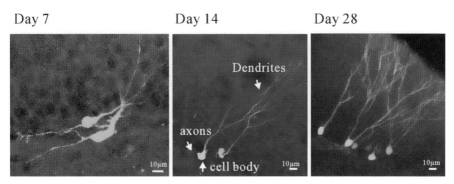

Figure 21.3 Images of typical cells observed during developmental stages. Day 7, day 14 and day 28 show progression from undifferentiated progenitors to immature and mature neurons. Cells are labelled with green fluorescent protein for identification.

but they could receive external stimuli, neurotransmitters and neurotrophins by their non-synaptic receptors. Potentially, these partially developed cells could also emit signals via axons, which appear to project quite far from the cell bodies while still growing towards their intended targets.

The third phase lasts 3–6 weeks, during which new cells look like neurons and could act like neurons but may not be completely mature in all aspects. We are only beginning to learn about the possible roles of these neurons at this 'utilization' phase. There are two schools of thought in this regard. One view is that the new cells are essentially indistinguishable from the pre-existing cohort of neurons and seamlessly merge with the old population to perform their functions (van Praag *et al.*, 2002). According to this view, the role of neurogenesis is to recruit mature neurons without assigning them any particular functions. Another view is that the young neurons act as a separate population and perform specialized functions. This young subpopulation of cells is characterized initially by having pliable synapses that can easily be strengthened or weakened. This is in contrast to the mature synapses of mature neurons, which are often quite strong but inflexible (Atwood and Wojtowicz, 1999). Another important characteristic feature of the immature neurons is their transient presence. Once these cells make the transition into a more mature state they may become functionally altered to make them less plastic but perhaps more stable and are succeeded by the next generation of the immature recruits. Such waves of transiently hyperplastic neurons present a unique feature to the adult brain.

Paradox 1: a contradiction of an expected result

A paradox frequently arises when a carefully planned experiment fails to produce an expected result but instead yields results exactly opposite to what was anticipated. Such an experiment took place in the author's laboratory in the late 1990s, when we began to study functional consequences of adult neurogenesis. Our approach was to use standard electrophysiological methods to probe properties of young vs. mature granule neurons in the dentate gyrus. For this we utilized a tried and true hippocampal slice preparation where one can readily visualize the granule cell layer in the DG (Figure 21.4). This layer is 5–10 cells thick, and although it is difficult to distinguish individual cell bodies one can readily attach a recording electrode to either the inner or outer edge of the layer. The former is packed with immature neurons because this area borders the subgranular zone where the neurons are born. During their growth, the neurons must pass through the inner layer before moving on to the middle or outer

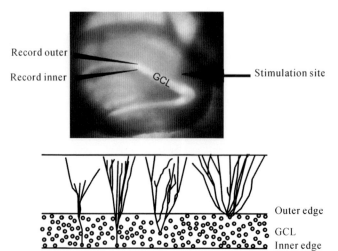

Record outer

Record inner

GCL

Stimulation site

Outer edge

GCL

Inner edge

Figure 21.4 Hippocampal slice for electrophysiological experiments with the recording electrodes placed in the inner and outer edges of the granule cell layer (GCL). The inner edge contains predominantly newly born neurons, while the outer edge contains only mature neurons, as shown in the lower diagram. Recording electrode is placed for stimulation of the incoming axons from the entorhinal cortex, an area outlined in Figure 21.1.

layers. This configuration results in a convenient layout of neurons as though they were placed on an amphitheatre stage, with the youngest cells at the bottom and the most senior ones on top (Figure 21.4). The anticipated result in the electrophysiological experiment was that young neurons would receive predominantly GABAergic synapses producing inhibition. This was based on the general developmental sequence worked out for various types of brain neurons, in which the initial establishment of GABAergic synapses is followed later by glutamatergic synapses (Ben-Ari et al., 1997). Thus, in the inner layer we expected strong inhibition but no effective excitation in response to the afferent perforant path stimulation. In contrast, the most mature neurons positioned in the upper echelons of the granule cell layer were expected to be well endowed with excitatory synapses and perhaps show predominantly excitation. Paradoxically, the results turned out differently. The young neurons showed complete lack of inhibition and strong excitation while the mature neurons were almost completely inhibited (Wang et al., 2000). These results led us to propose that the young neurons within adult brains are more plastic because they lack inhibition (Snyder et al., 2001); more strictly, they can react more strongly to incoming excitation. Further studies elaborated this concept by showing that GABA, that is inhibitory in mature neurons, can produce excitation in the young neurons (Ge et al., 2007). This immature GABAergic input is at first non-synaptic, presumably via ambient GABA surrounding the cells, but later synaptic and consistent with depolarizing GABA responses in the dendrites. The transition from excitatory to inhibitory GABAergic transmission, along with the delayed formation of glutamatergic synapses, creates a very dynamic and flexible state when young neurons can react in unpredictable fashion. Electrophysiological studies show that, in general, the excitatory responses dominate and impart hyperplastic properties onto young granule neurons, although reduced inhibition may make their 'handling' of information less selective. This concept appears to support the notion of immature neurons as a separate, specialized population rather than just a transient population of neurons 'in waiting'.

The moral of this story is that the most revealing experimental outcome can occur when the hypothesis is not confirmed and instead yields results that contradict those expected. These types of results become a clear beacon for an alternative way of thinking and ultimately a revised understanding of a problem.

Paradox 2: neurogenesis can be harmful

The development of neuronal circuits is a tumultuous process consisting of cell proliferation, migration, dendritic and axonal growth, pruning of excessive neurites and even elimination of cells. Having this sort of upheaval while the rest of the brain is performing its regular duties is like inviting a group of teenagers to a mundane tea party for seniors – certainly one of the reasons why adult neurogenesis was originally dismissed as too disruptive for the perceived requirement of the adult brain to retain memories (Rakic, 1985).

In fact, under certain circumstances neurogenesis does appear to be disruptive and counterproductive. Pathological seizures in the brain induce neurogenesis accompanied by increased proliferation and abnormally rapid cell development, producing an unwanted cohort of new cells that do not 'fit in'. This phenomenon can initiate a cascade of pathological events that degrade the performance of the brain more than the initial seizure (Wojtowicz, 2008). Another example of unsustainable cell production is observed in genetically engineered mice lacking the ability to eliminate cells via apoptosis (Sun *et al.*, 2004). These mice show not only abnormal neuronal plasticity but also impaired learning behaviours, presumably because of too many neurons attempting to integrate into the limited space and creating 'interference' effect. Paradoxically, structural abnormalities are seen mostly in mature cells and not in the growing cells, as though the young intruders were overwhelming pre-existing mature neurons and upsetting their normal functions.

Paradox 3: cell birth needs to be accompanied by cell death

Many experiments show that thousands of new neurons are generated in the rat brain every day (Cameron and McKay, 2001; McDonald and Wojtowicz, 2005; Snyder *et al.*, 2009). This begs the question: where exactly are these neurons located and is there enough space for them to grow? Five thousand neurons produced every day over the course of a year will amount to almost two million new units that have to be properly placed and connected. Is there enough space in the hippocampus to accommodate such growth? In reality there is not, and there is no evidence that the hippocampus grows to any significant extent in adulthood, at least not in the species examined thus far. It would appear then that many neurons are born but vanish. This would be a futile process. An even more extreme situation exists in the subventricular zone where up to 50,000 cells are produced daily, and yet there is no evidence at all that the olfactory bulb, the main recipient of these new neurons, grows with age. The answer to this dilemma lies partly in the age-dependent decay of neurogenesis. Adult neurogenesis should perhaps be renamed juvenile neurogenesis because of the tremendous rate of neurogenesis during this stage of life. In rats, the decline of neurogenesis corresponds roughly to the onset of sexual maturity. Thus, a one-month-old animal has about 10 times more new cells in comparison to a one-year-old adult. The other factor that brings the cell number down is cell death. Convincing, albeit indirect, evidence comes from genetically modified mice lacking the cell death-inducing gene *bax* (Sun *et al.*, 2004). Such *bax*-knockout mice produce almost double the number of granule neurons during the first year of the animal's life, confirming the idea that there is a large creative potential in adult neurogenesis. Alas, releasing of this potential without due control comes at the cost of numerous morphological and functional abnormalities.

The moral of the story is that cell birth needs to be balanced with a roughly equivalent and controlled cell death in order to maintain a sustainable cell population.

Paradox 4: neuronal rescue is different from neuronal function

There is a common misconception about functions of new neurons. This is especially evident when scientists attempt to popularize complex phenomena to make them understandable to the general public. One can imagine a scenario in which adult neurogenesis is strictly and purposefully regulated to make new neurons only when and where they are needed. This kind of regulation by specific behaviours has been proposed and has received experimental support (Shors, 2009). The idea in turn has been linked with a popular notion that mental activity is good for the brain. The difficulty is that the idea is not compatible with the timeline of neurogenesis as outlined at the beginning of this chapter. Without an understanding of this timeline a person reading a popular book, advocating the idea that mental exercises improve so called 'Brain Fitness', is left with the impression that the cells that are being rescued by exercises are the same cells that currently participate in mental processes such as learning. The concept is reminiscent of a situation with atrophied muscle that can be rebuilt by exercise, but in the brain this is almost certainly not the case. As explained in the Introduction, the cells that are being saved are very immature and not capable of doing anything as specific as the processing of learned information. Yet, the reader is led along this erroneous path by statements such as 'use it or lose it' or 'the tasks that rescue the most neurons are the ones that are hardest to learn', etc. However, upon further reading one discovers that we still do not know what exactly the new neurons do, and that their participation in learning is probably delayed until a much later stage in their development beyond the rescuing stage. This delay may correspond to the maturation stage (Figure 21.2), providing that they survive that long. Thus, the 'use it lose it' rule applies to neurogenesis only in most general terms, where 'use it' applies to the brain as a whole and 'lose it' applies to a particular cohort of cells. The paradox arises due to the subtle difference between neuronal rescuing and neuronal function. The two phenomena occur at different times, and yet they get mixed up in translation from the scientific to popular literature.

A possible explanation of this paradox needs further research, and may lie in yet undiscovered feedback mechanisms, which regulate neuronal production of very young cells, by activity of more mature neurons. In this scenario, 3–6-week-old neurons are put to work in a learning task and, while performing this task, send a positive signal back to the upcoming 1–2-week-old group to stimulate its differentiation and inhibit its rate of death. Possible schemes are described in another article (Wojtowicz, 2008).

Paradox 5: neurogenesis appears to be more important for long-term retention than for learning

It is generally accepted among neuroscientists that learning is not the same as remembering. The scientific literature is quite definite that spatial learning, i.e. learning locations, requires the hippocampus. Yet, most components of long-term storage of spatial memories likely take place in various brain regions outside the hippocampus, probably within the cerebral cortex (Squire, 1992). One of the first tasks employed to 'save' new neurons in their critical period was a spatial learning task (Gould *et al.*, 1999). This type of learning is tested in laboratory animals using a water maze task, where an animal has to locate the hidden platform in a circular tank filled with water by swimming around and orienting itself according to external cues placed around the tank. Although the first series of experiments did show results in agreement with the idea that specialized learning rescues young neurons, subsequent findings in other laboratories did not (Snyder *et al.*, 2005). Looking at the other side of the neurogenesis coin, Snyder *et al.* deleted new neurons by destroying the progenitor cells with high-energy radiation, and found that rats learned just fine without these neurons. Why would certain behaviours rescue neurons if they were not needed? The story gets more complicated because tests of irradiated rats several weeks after the initial learning showed lack of spatial memory. The experiments clearly showed that this deficit in long-term spatial memory is not due to a delayed side-effect of irradiation, but rather to a true deficit in remembering where the platform is (Abrous and Wojtowicz, 2008). Hence, new neurons are essential for long-term memory but not for the initial learning. The explanation of this confounding result will presumably be found in detailed analysis of the hippocampal circuitry and in different functions performed by young and mature neurons. Last but not least, studies utilizing different species should be evaluated separately since it appears that large differences exist among the species (Snyder *et al.*, 2009). This is an example of a paradoxical result that leads to further studies and ultimately to a better understanding of the phenomena that were previously thought to be well understood.

Paradox 6: a real-life paradox

Although laboratory rodents are indispensable for scientific research, they give us a distorted view of the biology that may not be applicable to wild animals living in the natural environment. Laboratory rats and mice are usually highly inbred and selected for characteristics that facilitate laboratory research. Even though the breeding practices over the last 150 years may not produce large genetic differences to distinguish these animals from naturally evolved animals that were subject to natural selection over millions of years, there is evidence that the laboratory animals are different in significant ways. For example, some strains of laboratory rats lack aggression and are less susceptible to stress in comparison to wild animals (Amrein *et al.*, 2008). Life histories of the animals kept in 'shoe box' containers are very uniform and limited to monotonous procedures in the sterile and artificial environment of animal facilities. One wonders if their brain activity, and hence activity-dependent plasticity, is anything like the brain activity of animals living in their natural environment. In fact, it is well established that laboratory animals taken from their impoverished environment and exposed to an 'enriched environment' benefit by producing more synapses in the cortex and more neurons in the hippocampus (Nithianantharajah and Hannan, 2006). These structural changes in turn bring improvements in brain plasticity. Consequently, it has been proposed that environmental enrichment would be optimal in free-living animals because their natural environment provides normal natural stimulation of various brain regions. Experimental testing of this prediction yielded unexpected results and yet another paradox. Comparative measurements of rates of neurogenesis in several strains of inbred rats, as opposed to wild rats, showed very similar numbers of proliferating and differentiating neurons in all animals, inbred and wild (Epp *et al.*, 2009). This paradoxical result indicates that predictions based on laboratory experiments do not always hold for the real world and calls for more widely based studies, outside of the laboratory, taking natural living conditions into account.

Another case in point is lack of adult neurogenesis in certain species. A study on bats, mammals relying heavily on spatial navigation for their survival, shows only minimal adult neurogenesis in the hippocampus (Amrein *et al.*, 2007). Such studies remind us that neurogenesis may be species-specific and results from one species cannot be readily applied to all others.

Another look at paradoxes in neurogenesis

What's paradoxical to one person may seem obvious to another. It is likely that paradoxical phenomena that puzzle us today will have perfectly rational explanations in the future. On the other hand, the phenomena that appear straightforward to a specialist may seem puzzling and hence paradoxical to a novice. Let's look at some examples from this perspective.

Is the presence of young neurons in the adult brain really a contradiction?

I am reminded of a student in my undergraduate physiology course who lacked a science background but had a strong desire to learn physiology in order to qualify for admission to a professional programme in speech pathology. For someone who had been trained in humanities such as history, theology and music it was a big challenge to interpret intricate cellular mechanisms that he had never studied. His peers, students with a biology background, were familiar with such mechanisms, but also recognized that stable biological systems frequently depend on a balance of at least two opposing mechanisms, such as chemical synthesis vs. breakdown of a substance, repulsion vs. attraction of electrically charged molecules or equilibrium between influx and efflux from a cell. Another common example of a system depending on several opposing mechanisms is the concept of homeostasis. Homeostasis, as introduced in introductory physiology courses, is a set of mechanisms that maintain a constant internal environment for the brain and other parts of the body. On the other hand, in more advanced courses we teach the concept of plasticity, i.e. mechanisms that allow the brain to learn and adapt and therefore depart from homeostasis, at least temporarily. Plasticity and homeostasis seem to oppose each other, yet they obviously co-exist. This apparent friction relates to a fundamental brain paradox between change and stability, both of which are required in certain contexts. Similarly, neurogenesis seems to be able to co-exist with established neuronal circuitry. Neurogenesis is a type of plasticity in which neurons are added and replaced, but in a fashion that spares pre-existing brain structures. It is no longer a contradiction. How did a humanities student come to grips with such apparent contradictions? Ingeniously, he used the metaphor of Good and Evil. In this context, it was easier for him to understand that a stable state can indeed occur as a result of the friction of two opposing forces.

Effects of neurogenesis on learning or vice versa?

The idea that new neurons are rescued by purposeful learning activity in the hippocampal circuit has led to considerable controversy in the field. One source of confusion is the observation that learning a spatial task in the water maze rescues neurons very specifically, while a similar activity, aimless swimming does not. However, what would be the purpose of rescuing neurons in this way if these neurons do not participate in spatial learning? In fact, subsequent studies have shown that neuronal rescue is not a specific result of spatial learning. Studies have shown that training rats in a water maze activates new neurons, preferentially in the ventral part of the hippocampus (Snyder *et al.*, 2008). Because the ventral hippocampus is specialized for non-spatial tasks, such activation is more consistent with the stress or anxiety-related aspect of the training process and not with learning per se. These results further suggest that neuronal survival is not necessarily equivalent to neuronal involvement in the learning task. Hence, rescuing of cells may be specific for the task but not for learning.

There is also evidence for increased proliferation of neurons following a task rather than rescuing during a critical period. Thus, the specificity of neuronal rescue may not hold for spatial learning (Dupret *et al.*, 2007). This way of thinking is in line with experiments showing no change in spatial learning in animals whose neurogenesis has been blocked at the proliferative stage. All other effects of impaired neurogenesis on spatial learning are very weak and apply only to limited trials or specific phases of learning (Dupret *et al.*, 2007; Abrous and Wojtowicz, 2008).

Are we reading too much into things?

Some paradoxes arise because of incorrect preconceptions. For example, researchers assumed that the task most often used to test for spatial learning in the water maze would somehow involve neurogenesis. This assumption turned out to be incorrect. Experiments suggest that either mature neurons in DG can adequately perform spatial learning functions with the new neurons being present, or perhaps spatial learning can occur without participation of DG. As described in the Introductory section, DG is only a small part of the overall hippocampal circuit, with alternative cortico-hippocampal pathways possibly playing a large role (Figure 21.1). Contextual learning, which also has been known for some time to depend on the hippocampus, seems to depend strongly on neurogenesis, and the best described example of such dependence involves remembering a location in which a memorable stimulus takes place. This type of learning is often demonstrated in animals exposed to a painful stimulus in a cage, where the surrounding landmarks serve as context. Animals with reduced neurogenesis are impaired in learning and remembering the predictive significance of the cage (Winocur *et al.*, 2006). Thus, contextual rather than spatial learning has emerged as the most neurogenesis-dependent behaviour.

Are we looking for a needle in the haystack?

Some observations may seem out of place because of undue focus on detail, without taking the bigger picture into account. For example, most studies of neurogenesis tend to focus on the numbers of new cells and not on their functions. The problem with the present methodology is that researchers use 'snapshot' measures of neurogenesis by counting cells at a single time-point, or at most at a few time-points. This type of measurement may be misleading if a particular experiment creates a 'bottleneck' for neuronal development. The observed increase in the number of new cells at a certain age may represent their inability to progress onto the next stage of differentiation. The opposite scenario is also feasible and indeed has been shown experimentally; treatment with fluoxetine, a drug that blocks reuptake of serotonin into the cells, has been shown to decrease the number of immature neurons (Wang *et al.*, 2008). Such a decrease is not due to decreased neuronal production but rather to enhanced rate of differentiation. According to the evidence, the new immature neurons 'disappear' because they mature more quickly than in normal circumstances, and not because fewer are arriving from the proliferative phase (Figure 21.2).

Are we looking under the lamppost?

Paradoxes in science remind me of a story about a drunk who was found to stubbornly look for his door keys under a lamppost in front of his house while ignoring the possibility that he may have dropped them somewhere on the way from the bar. When asked by a passerby why he was looking in this one place only, he replied: 'This is the only place where there is light!' This metaphor applies to science more often than one would care to admit. Projects are often tailored to the easiest and most convenient methodologies and not to the most direct studies of the most likely possibilities. For example, most research on neurogenesis has so far focused on acute effects of newly produced neurons. An alternative view is that neurogenesis should be looked at as a life-long phenomenon and in the context of lifestyle. The idea stems from studies of human populations which show that individuals who experienced higher levels of mental activity in their youth showed better cognitive performance, learning and memory in old age (Nithianantharajah and Hannan, 2006). Although this well-documented phenomenon may have numerous explanations, accumulation of neurons early in the animal's life and a gradual buildup of a more robust circuitry to be used later in life fits the idea nicely. In this context, one can think of neurogenesis as analogous to charging the battery to be utilized later in life. In the end, we may be looking at a mix of certain mechanisms that rely on acute functions of adult-born neurons and others that rely on their recruitment for the long haul.

Future challenges and questions

Inconsistencies and differences among results generated by laboratories around the world add both excitement and promise to neuroscience and the field of neurogenesis in particular. By its very nature, adult neurogenesis creates controversies and paradoxes because it tries to reconcile the phenomena that used to be considered as separate – presence of young, developing and mature neurons in the same place, neurons that are plastic on one day but static on the next day, neurons that are excited by an inhibitory transmitter and neurons that can store short-term information but also act as a potential reservoir of life-long plasticity. These are all characteristics of adult neurogenesis that truly 'break the rules' of traditional neuroscience. Many questions remain and most of them are quite contentious.

One of the most fundamental remaining questions is why adult neurogenesis exists in the first place and why is it restricted to specific brain niches? The answer to this question may be found in future considerations of neurogenesis as an evolved, adaptive trait. Thus, hippocampal neurogenesis may be seen as adaptive because it facilitates an animal's survival. However, depending on the species, staying out of trouble or allowing time for regeneration may be two alternative ways of ensuring survival. Another concept that may explain the prominence of neurogenesis at a young age is the concept of neurogenic reserve. As proposed by Kempermann (2008), hippocampal neurons can be produced and accumulated for later use. Changes in the rate of production at a young age would have lasting consequences for an individual later in life because neurons could be kept in reserve until needed. The phenomenon would be reminiscent of cognitive reserve seen in human populations. Studies have shown that rich educational experience early in life contributes to improved cognitive state and resistance to degenerative diseases in old age (Nithianantharajah and Hannan, 2006; Valenzuela and Sachdev, 2006). Thus, adult neurogenesis may hold the secret not only to learning by young individuals but also to their healthy ageing. Before we arrive at answers to so many outstanding questions, the only certainty appears to be that there will be more uncertainty.

Acknowledgements

Professor Harold Atwood generously edited the manuscript and offered helpful suggestions. Ms Yao-Fang Tan was instrumental in research activities and prepared the figures. The author was supported by grants from CIHR and NSERC, Canada.

References

Abrous, D. N., & Wojtowicz, J. M. (2008). Neurogenesis and the hippocampal memory system. In: Gage, F. H., Kempermann, G., & Song, H.-J. (Eds.). *Adult Neurogenesis*. New York, NY: Cold Spring Harbor Laboratory Press, pp. 445–62.

Altman, J., & Bayer, S. A. (1990). Mosaic organization of the hippocampal neuroepithelium and the multiple germinal sources of dentate granule cells. *Journal of Comparative Neurology*, **301**: 325–42.

Altman, J., & Das, G. D. (1965). Autoradiographic and histological evidence of postnatal hippocampal neurogenesis in rats. *Journal of Comparative Neurology*, **124**: 319–36.

Amrein, I., Boonstra, R., Lipp, H.-P., & Wojtowicz, J. M. (2008). Adult hippocampal neurogenesis in natural populations of mammals. In: Gage, F. H., Kempermann, G., & Song, H.-J. (Eds.). *Adult Neurogenesis*. New York, NY: Cold Spring Harbor Laboratory Press, pp. 645–59.

Amrein, I., Dechmann, D. K., Winter, Y., & Lipp, H.-P. (2007). Absent or low rate of adult neurogenesis in the hippocampus of bats (chiroptera). *PLoS ONE*, **2**: e455.

Atwood, H. L., & Wojtowicz, J. M. (1999). Silent synapse in neural plasticity: current evidence. *Learning & Memory*, **6**: 542–71.

Ben-Ari, Y., Khazipov, R., Leinekugel, X., Caillard, O., & Gaiarasa, J.-L. (1997). GABAA, NMDA and AMPA receptors: a developmentally regulated 'menage a trois'. *Trends in Neuroscience*, **20**: 523–9.

Cameron, H. A., & McKay, R. D. G. (2001). Adult neurogenesis produces a large pool of new granule cells in the dentate gyrus. *Journal of Comparative Neurology*, **435**: 406–17.

Cohen, N. J., & Eichenbaum, H. (1993). *Memory, Amnesia and the Hippocampal System*, 1st ed. Cambridge, MA: The MIT Press.

De Castro, F. (2009). Wiring olfaction: the cellular and molecular mechanisms that guide the development of synaptic connections from the nose to the cortex. *Frontiers in Neurogenesis*, **1**: 4. doi:10.3389/neuro.

Dupret, D., Fabre, A., Dobrossy, M. D., *et al.* (2007). Spatial learning depends on both the addition and removal of new hippocampal neurons. *PLoS biology*, **5**: 1683–94.

Epp, J. R., Barker, J. M., & Galea, L. A. M. (2009). Running wild: neurogenesis in the hippocampus across the lifespan in wild and laboratory-bred norway rats. *Hippocampus*, **19**: 1040–9.

Ge, S., Pradhan, D. A., Ming, G.-I., & Song, H. (2007). GABA sets the tempo for activity-dependent adult neurogenesis. *Trends in Neuroscience*, **30**: 1–8.

Gould, E., Beylin, A., Tanapat, P., Reeves, A. J., & Shors, T. J. (1999). Learning enhances adult neurogenesis in the hippocampal formation. *Nature Neuroscience*, **2**: 260–5.

Gross, C. G. (2000). Neurogenesis in the adult brain: death of a dogma. *Nature Reviews*, **1**: 67–73.

Kempermann, G. (2008). The neurogenic reserve hypothesis: what is adult hippocampal neurogenesis good for? *Trends in Neuroscience*, **31**: 163–214.

Kuhn, H. G. (2008). The balance of trophic support and cell death in adult neurogenesis. In: Gage, F. H., Kempermann, G., & Song, H.-J. (Eds.). *Adult Neurogenesis*. New York, NY: Cold Spring Harbor Laboratory Press.

McDonald, H. Y., & Wojtowicz, J. M. (2005). Dynamics of neurogenesis in the dentate gyrus of adult rats. *Neuroscience Letters*, **385**: 70–5.

Nithianantharajah, J., & Hannan, A. J. (2006). Enriched environments, experience-dependent plasticity and disorders of the nervous system. *National Review of Neuroscience*, **7**: 697–709.

Rakic, P. (1985). Limits of neurogenesis in primates. *Science*, **227**: 1054–8.

Shors, T. J. (2009). Saving new brain cells. *Scientific American*, **3**: 47–54.

Snyder, J. S., Choe, J., Clifford, M., *et al.* (2009). Adult-born hippocampal neurons are more numerous, faster maturing and more involved in behavior in rats than in mice. *Journal of Neuroscience*, **29**: 14,484–95.

Snyder, J. S., Hong, N., McDonald, R. J., & Wojtowicz, J. M. (2005). A role for adult hippocampal neurogenesis in spatial long-term memory. *Neuroscience*, **130**: 843–52.

Snyder, J. S., Kee, N., & Wojtowicz, J. M. (2001). Effects of adult neurogenesis on synaptic plasticity in the rat dentate gyrus. *Journal of Neurophysiology*, **85**: 2423–31.

Snyder, J. S., Radik, R., Wojtowicz, J. M., & Cameron, H. A. (2008). Anatomical gradients of neurogenesis and activity: young neurons in the ventral dentate gyrus are activated by water maze training. *Hippocampus*, **19**: 360–70.

Squire, L. R. (1992). Memory and the hippocampus: a synthesis from findings with rats, monkeys and humans. *Psychology Review*, **99**: 195–231.

Sun, W., Winseck, A., Vinsant, S., Park, O., Kim, H., & Oppenheim, R. W. (2004). Programmed cell death of adult-generated hippocampal neurons is mediated by the preapoptotic gene *Bax*. *Journal of Neuroscience*, **24**: 11,205–13.

Valenzuela, M. J., & Sachdev, P. (2006). Brain reserve and dementia: a systematic review. *Psychological Medicine*, **36**: 441–54.

van Praag, H., Schinder, A. F., Christie, B. R., Toni, N., Palmer, T. D., & Gage, F. H. (2002). Functional neurogenesis in the adult hippocampus. *Nature*, **415**: 1030–4.

Wang, J.-W., David, D. J., Monckton, J. E., Battaglia, F., & Hen, R. (2008). Chronic fluoxetine stimulates maturation and synaptic plasticity of adult born hippocampal granule cells. *Journal of Neuroscience*, **28**: 1374–84.

Wang, S., Scott, B. W., & Wojtowicz, J. M. (2000). Heterogenous properties of dentate gyrus granule neurons in the adult rat. *Journal of Neurobiology*, **42**: 248–57.

Wilbrecht, L., Crionas, A., & Nottebohm, F. (2002). Experience affects recrutiment of new neurons but not adult neuron number. *Journal of Neuroscience*, **22**: 825–31.

Winocur, G., Wojtowicz, J. M., Sekers, M., Snyder, J. S., & Wang, S. (2006). Inhibition of neurogenesis interferes with hippocampal-dependent memory function. *Hippocampus*, **16**: 296–304.

Wojtowicz, J. M. (2008). Potential consequences of altered neurogenesis on learning and memory in the epileptic brain. *Epilepsia*, **49**(Suppl. 5): 42–9.

Chapter 22

The paradoxical hippocampus: when forgetting helps learning

Howard Eichenbaum

Summary

It is well established that the hippocampal region is critical to declarative and relational memory. Therefore, it is reasonable to expect that damage to the hippocampal region would cause impairment on any test that requires some feature of declarative/relational memory, and that on any other test, hippocampal damage is expected to have no effect. However, there have been several reports of paradoxical facilitation of learning and memory following hippocampal damage. Here, several examples in the study of animal learning and memory are discussed. In some experiments, hippocampal region damage results in the facilitation of learning simple stimulus–reward–response associations. In other experiments, the 'flexibility' of memory, exhibited in reversal learning and in learning multiple partially contradictory choice problems, is also facilitated following hippocampal damage. In yet other experiments, recognition based on the familiarity of stimulus combinations is improved following hippocampal damage. Each of these cases of paradoxical facilitation of learning and memory informs us about the distinctions between hippocampal-dependent memory processing and memory processes supported by other brain areas or systems. Furthermore, these findings show that competition between these systems can result in slower learning when the hippocampus is engaged, compared to when its contribution is removed.

Introduction

In the field of human memory research, our understanding of how the brain supports memory began with neuropsychological studies of patients with pervasive, 'global' amnesia. An initial breakthrough came with the report by Scoville and Milner (1957) of one of the most famous neurological patients in the literature, the man known by his initials, H.M. In this patient, the hippocampal region was removed to alleviate his severe epileptic attacks, but H.M. consequently suffered a nearly complete loss of the ability to form new long-term memories. His impairment, tested over more than 50 years, extended to verbal and nonverbal memory, spatial and nonspatial memory, and indeed cut across all categories of learning materials. Yet, there was a spared domain of learning capacity reflected in a few exceptions to an otherwise pervasive deficit. H.M. was able to learn new motor skills, and he showed a facilitation of perceptual identification resulting from prior exposure to objects or words (Corkin, 1984).

The second breakthrough in our understanding of the function of the hippocampal region came in 1980 when Cohen and Squire proposed that the 'exceptions' to amnesia were indicative of a large domain of preserved learning capacities. Their conclusion was based

---

The Paradoxical Brain, ed. Narinder Kapur. Published by Cambridge University Press. © Cambridge University Press 2011.

on the observation of complete preservation of a perceptual skill (reading mirror-reversed words) in amnesic patients. These patients showed fully intact skilled performance, yet were markedly impaired both in recognizing the particular words on which they trained and in recollecting their training experiences. Cohen and Squire (1980) were struck by the dissociation between the intact ability to have performance shaped by a series of training experiences, and a marked impairment in the capacity to explicitly remember the contents of the training experiences. Cohen and Squire attributed the observed dissociation, together with the earlier findings of spared memory capacities in amnesia, to the operation of distinct forms of memory. These forms of memory were seen as functionally distinct memory systems, one dedicated to the tuning and modification of networks that support skilled performance, and the other to the encoding, storage and retrieval on demand of memories for specific facts and events. Furthermore, these functionally distinct memory systems were tied to separate brain systems, with declarative memory critically dependent on the hippocampal system damaged in various amnesias. Procedural memory is mediated by various brain systems, such as the basal ganglia, specialized for particular types of skilled performance.

The initial results on H.M. and other amnesic patients inspired a large number of experimental analyses showing that damage to the hippocampus in animals also results in impairments in a broad variety of learning and memory tasks, but not others. Of particular relevance to this chapter, several theorists pursued the idea that there are multiple memory systems in animals, and that the hippocampal region supports just one of them. Thus, O'Keefe and Nadel (1978) summarized a large literature showing that animals with hippocampal damage are impaired on most spatial learning and memory tasks, but are unimpaired on most non-spatial learning and memory tasks. Olton and colleagues (1979) argued that animals with hippocampal damage are impaired when they must remember experiences as distinctly unique episodes, but are unimpaired when they can accrue appropriate responses over multiple repeated experiences. Hirsh (1974) argued that animals with hippocampal damage are impaired in learning that is dependent on the context of experience, but are unimpaired in learning that involves modifications of performance that are context-independent. While the specifics on the fundamental role of the hippocampus differ among these proposals, each proposal involves a domain of hippocampal memory contrasted with a domain of hippocampal-independent memory, similar to the declarative-procedural distinction.

The observation of distinct hippocampal-dependent and -independent learning and memory domains has been verified and extended by many studies on humans and animals that have followed (see Eichenbaum and Cohen, 2001, for review). Furthermore, the succeeding work has largely confirmed the importance of spatial, episodic and contextual aspects of memory in animals, and these features of memory are also hallmarks of declarative memory in humans (Figure 22.1). At the same time, this literature has provided increasing detail about the characteristics of memory domains supported by non-hippocampal systems. These studies have shown that one of the main alternative systems involves learning characterized by the adoption of reinforced behavioural responses to specific stimuli, that is, the acquisition of habits. This kind of learning is mediated by a brain system that involves the neostriatum (caudate and putamen). The other major alternative system involves learning characterized by the adoption of appetitive or aversive values to otherwise neutral stimuli, that is, reward learning. This type of learning is mediated by a brain system that involves the amygdala.

The combined work on all these memory systems leads to the reasonable prediction that damage to the hippocampal region would result in impairments in tasks that demand

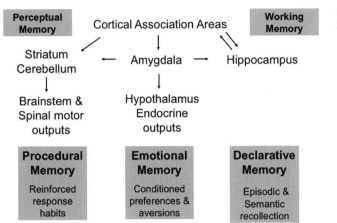

Figure 22.1 Three major memory systems of the brain.

features of declarative memory, but not learning that can be supported by the acquisition of habits or reward values of stimuli. However, there have also been several observations where hippocampal damage results in a *facilitation* of learning and memory, and many of these cases have been observed in animals. These observations go against the otherwise well-established expectation that a compromise of the functions of a memory system can result only in diminished memory function, and are therefore examples of a paradoxical phenomenon wherein the observed effects of brain damage are opposite of the norm. Here we will consider how these paradoxical findings, which seem to show an enhancement of learning resulting from hippocampal region damage, are actually some of the most compelling evidence that the hippocampus supports one type of memory whereas other areas and systems support different kinds.

There are a large number of paradoxical findings on the effects of brain manipulations in animals, often with a focus on paradoxical functional facilitation (Glick and Greenstein, 1972; Mumby *et al.*, 1996; Ayalon *et al.*, 2004; Rawashdeh *et al.*, 2007; Saxe *et al.*, 2007; Stalnaker *et al.*, 2007; Plamondon *et al.*, 2008; Raber *et al.*, 2009; Zhou *et al.*, 2009). In this chapter, I will focus on examples that involve damage to the hippocampal region resulting in unexpected, paradoxical enhancement of some form or aspect of learning and memory. I will first compare conditions in which hippocampal region damage impairs nonspatial sensory discrimination learning and contrast them with other conditions in which hippocampal region damage facilitates the same sensory discriminations. Second, I will compare the ability of animals with hippocampal damage to alter their responses corresponding to changes in stimulus reward contingencies both for nonspatial stimuli and in the spatial domain, and explore what aspects of learning are enhanced by hippocampal damage. Third, I will examine animal models of episodic memory, and compare conditions where memory performance is impaired or enhanced by hippocampal damage.

The nature of hippocampal memory representations that support stimulus discrimination learning

Our investigations of nonspatial sensory discrimination learning exploited the excellent learning and memory capacities of rats in odour discrimination learning (Eichenbaum *et al.*, 1986, 1988, 1989). In these studies, the learning performance of intact rats was

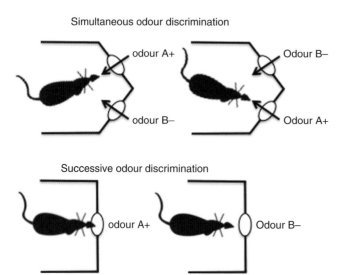

Simultaneous odour discrimination

Figure 22.2 Two variations of odour discrimination learning. In the simultaneous odour discrimination, rats can sample the two odours at the same time and chose between them by poking its nose into the port that presents the rewarded odour (A+) and not the port that presents the non-rewarded odour (B−). In the successive odour discrimination, rats sample each odour on different trials and either nose pokes for odour A+ or withholds the response to odour B− independently.

compared with that of rats in which we had transected the fornix, a fibre bundle supporting critical connections between the hippocampus and subcortical structures. We evaluated learning performance using two variations of a simple odour discrimination-learning paradigm: one version where two odours are presented simultaneously and the other version where the same odours were presented successively (Figure 22.2; Eichenbaum *et al.*, 1988). In the simultaneous discrimination task, two odour cues were presented at the same time and in close spatial juxtaposition; the discriminative response required selecting the odour that was arbitrarily associated with reward regardless of whether it appeared on the left or right. Under these training conditions, rats with fornix lesions were severely and persistently impaired on a series of odour discrimination problems.

The other task involved training on a successive discrimination task where, in each problem, the two odours were presented separately across trials and the response required only completing or discontinuing the stimulus sampling behaviour. In striking contrast to the preceding results, under these training conditions rats with fornix lesions were *superior* to normal rats in acquiring the same series of discrimination problems that they had failed to learn under other task demands (see also Otto *et al.*, 1991; Staubli *et al.*, 1984)! How could damage to the fornix/hippocampal system enhance learning of the same odour discriminations in which impairment had been observed using a different protocol?

Our interpretation of these findings is that severe impairment or facilitation may be observed under different task demands, even with identical stimulus materials. Moreover, the differences in performance by rats with hippocampal system damage can be associated with differences in the demand for relating the different stimuli to each other, to the different locations of their appearance and to the outcomes of responses made to each. Thus, in the simultaneous discrimination task, the odours were presented at the same time and side-by-side, and appeared in both left–right configurations. Furthermore, the rat had to explicitly select one of the odours and reject the other. These conditions encourage comparisons between the distinct odour stimuli independent of their positions, and encourage learning how the different experiences related to one another. In contrast, in the successive discrimination task, the odours were presented individually, hindering comparison among items, and responding to each stimulus was rewarded or unrewarded, thus eliminating the response choice requirement. These conditions encourage rats to develop a distinct reward association, and the appropriate response, for each object individually. How could hippocampal system lesions improve performance on the successive discrimination task? We concluded that intact rats employ their hippocampal system to remember and compare the different stimuli that occur across trials. This processing, which is not advantageous in that task, might lead to more errors than if they simply associated a specific value and response to each independent stimulus, which can be accomplished readily by the habit and reward association systems and the operations of the neostriatum and amygdala (Figure 22.1; for other similar findings, see Wirth *et al.*, 1998; Laurent-Demir and Jaffard, 2000; Wingard and Packard, 2008; Bernabeau *et al.*, 2006).

Further investigation explored another surprising finding in these studies, specifically in the results from the simultaneous discrimination training condition (Eichenbaum *et al.*, 1989). Although rats were generally impaired on this version of the task, they succeeded in learning some of the discrimination problems at least as rapidly as normal animals. We hypothesized that normal animals represent each of the two odours in each problem as the same independent stimulus regardless whether it appears on the left or right position. In contrast, we suspected that rats with fornix lesions might not separate the stimulus elements of each type of stimulus presentation, but instead learn specific left and right responses to each left–right stimulus configuration, e.g. if the two odours are A-rewarded and B-not rewarded, they learned to "go left" for A−B and "go right" for B−A. On just those problems where the rats with hippocampal damage could distinguish A−B from B−A, they might succeed in learning.

To understand why the rats with fornix lesions occasionally succeeded and to explore the nature of memory representation when they did succeed, we trained yoked pairs of normal rats and rats with fornix lesions on a series of simultaneous odour discrimination problems until the rat with the fornix lesion in each pair had acquired two problems within the normal range of scores. Then we challenged them with probe trials composed of familiar odours 'mispaired' in combinations not previously experienced. Thus, having succeeded on A + B− and C + D−, we tested them on A + D− and C + B−. Note that each mispairing contains a rewarded and an unrewarded stimulus, so if animals learned the reward association of each stimulus, they should have no difficulty with the novel pairings. However, if animals formed configural representations for stimulus combinations, then the mispairings would be unfamiliar. Both normal rats and rats with fornix lesions continued to perform well on the trials composed of the odour pairings used on instruction trials. Normal rats also performed accurately on the novel probe trials, but, in striking contrast, rats with fornix lesions performed at chance levels on the probe trials when they were introduced, as if presented with novel stimuli!

A further analysis focusing on the response latencies of animals performing the simultaneous discrimination provided additional evidence that the nature of learned odour representations was abnormal in rats with hippocampal system damage. This analysis also provided insight into how they succeeded in learning some simultaneous discrimination problems. We determined that each rat with a fornix lesion had quantitatively shorter average response latencies than each normal rat, even though all rats performed consistently at high accuracy. Furthermore, rats with fornix lesions also had an abnormal pattern of latencies to respond to the stimuli. Each normal rat had a bimodal distribution of response latencies, and each of the two modes was associated with one of the positions where the rewarded odour was presented and response executed. This pattern of findings suggests that the rat consistently approached and sampled one odour port first, then either performed a nose-poke there, or approached and sampled the other odour port. In contrast, rats with fornix lesions had a unimodal distribution of response latencies, and the pattern of their response latencies was the same regardless of odour and response positions.

Our interpretation of these results was that rats with hippocampal system damage sample the entire stimulus compound at once, requiring less time to complete the trial. On just those problems where different left–right combinations of the odours were distinguishable, they succeeded in learning an individual association for each odour compound and the appropriate response. Indeed, this account of representational strategies suggests that the performance of rats with hippocampal damage did not support correct choices on the probe tests because novel mispairings of odours were perceived as unfamiliar odour compounds.

A more recent study that confirms and extends this view about hippocampal representations examined the performance of monkeys learning the transverse patterning problem. This task involves concurrent training on a series of three stimulus discrimination problems where all the stimuli are equally often rewarded or not. In this particular experiment, on each trial the monkeys viewed two stimulus patterns on a touch screen display and had to select the correct one to receive a reward (Saksida et al., 2007; see also Bussey et al., 1998). In one discrimination problem, stimulus A was rewarded and B not rewarded; in another problem, B was rewarded and C not rewarded; and in the third problem, C was rewarded and A not rewarded. Normal control animals gradually learned this combination of concurrently presented problems over many blocks of trials. One main finding was that damage to the perirhinal cortex retarded learning. The other main, and paradoxical, finding was that damage to the hippocampus facilitated learning! How could hippocampal lesions improve performance on transverse pattern learning? Similar to the findings on rats learning simultaneous odour discriminations with closely juxtaposed stimuli, monkeys with hippocampus damage may have configured simultaneously presented visual patterns and learned a specific 'go-left' response to one configuration and a 'go-right' response to the complementary configuration of the same stimulus elements. In the case of this very difficult learning problem, the latter strategy may have been more productive than learning the independent stimuli and the relations among them. Interestingly, the results of this study also suggest that perirhinal lesions may be critical to configuring the stimulus pairs. Notably, this area is a critical input and output of the hippocampus, such that perirhinal lesions would be expected to impair both configural learning and learning the relations among the items, as observed.

In interpreting these findings, it is useful to consider two ways in which multiple stimuli or events can be linked. One way is by configuring (also called 'unitizing') elements of stimuli or events into a single compound representation. Perhaps the most prominent example of a configural stimulus is a face, where all the features of the face are fused into a single configuration that is not separable into its parts. The second way to link stimuli and events is by association, where the elements are considered as perceptually and conceptually distinct, but related. I will refer to such associations as involving a relational representation. Following this distinction, an interpretation that accounts for all these findings is that the hippocampus represents relations among experiences with all the stimuli, and that these relational representations can be used to compare and contrast all variations of pairings, including novel pairings of the stimuli. Without the hippocampus, other brain areas learn a specific rewarded response, or learn not to respond, to each stimulus or stimulus configuration. In most situations, a relational representation is advantageous, as observed in simultaneous odour discrimination in rats, but not always, as in concurrent visual discrimination in monkeys. However, under conditions where learning about each stimulus alone is possible, as in successive odour discrimination in rats, or each stimulus configuration alone, as in transverse patterning in monkeys, the hippocampus is an impediment because other brain systems can acquire reinforced responses to those stimuli more readily than the hippocampus can relate a large number of experiences with different stimuli. In simpler terms, relational representation is 'overthinking' the problem in some situations. Later, we will return to the distinction within the hippocampal system between perirhinal cortex supporting the configuration of multiple stimulus elements and the hippocampus separating and learning relevant relations among experiences with those elements.

The flexibility of hippocampal-dependent memories

Another fundamental feature of memory that is dependent on the hippocampal region is representational flexibility, the capacity to employ established memories to solve novel problems. A classic example of flexibility in memory is the capacity to rapidly reverse a learned association. To understand why rapid reversal is a form of representational flexibility and how 'rapid' reversal is measured, it is important to consider how reversal learning is accomplished by non-hippocampal brain systems. When the original learning is accomplished by acquisition of a reinforced behavioural response, or by adopting a reward value to a stimulus, reversal initially involves extinction of the initially acquired response or reward association, then acquisition of the newly relevant reinforced response or reward association. Therefore, it might be expected that reversal will require a number of trials that equals the sum of that required for the extinction phase, plus that required for the re-acquisition phase. If we assume that each of these phases requires approximately as many trials as that required for the original learning, a first-level approximation of the requirement for reversal is to double the number of trials required for the original acquisition. Rapid reversal learning, then, is reflected in learning to alter behavioural responses within fewer trials than double that required for original learning. A review of experiments on the role of the hippocampus in reversal learning using nonspatial stimuli indicated that, in most cases where reversal learning was accomplished in less than twice the number of trials required for learning the original sensory discrimination, a deficit in animals with hippocampal damage was observed (see Eichenbaum et al., 1986). In each of these cases, the number of trials required for reversal in animals with hippocampal region damage was at least double that required for initial learning, consistent with the view that reversal learning without the hippocampus involves a combination of extinction and re-acquisition.

However, there are also a few exceptions to this rule. One involved monkeys that were initially highly trained on a series of visual discrimination problems, such that the newer problems were learned very rapidly (Zola and Mahut, 1973). In this situation, fornix transection resulted in a paradoxical facilitation of reversal learning. Here I will also consider in greater detail another exception to the reversal rule, one that involved odour discrimination learning and reversal in rats (Eichenbaum et al., 1986). In this study, rats were initially trained on a series of three odour discrimination problems. The first problem required 200–300 trials, but subsequent problems were learned in many fewer trials, typically around 50. On the reversal learning task, there were two surprising findings. First, normal animals required many more trials to reverse than they had taken to learn discrimination of the same odours. Indeed, they required approximately as many trials as required to learn the initial discrimination problem. It was as if they had acquired a 'rule' for assigning odour values, including the 'rule' that, once assigned, values are consistent; it appears that the reversal had sufficiently violated the consistency rule that the rats began anew, requiring as many trials to learn the reversal as for the first discrimination problem. The second surprise and apparent paradox was that animals with fornix transections *outperformed* normal animals on the reversal. How could damage to the hippocampal system result in an enhancement in reversal learning, especially in the context of several other studies describing impairment in sensory discrimination reversal following hippo-campal damage? Of note, the number of trials required for rats with fornix transections to learn the reversal was about twice that required to learn the discrimination of the same odours. Our explanation was that, without an intact hippocampal system, learning pro-ceeded in the usual extinction followed by re-acquisition stages. It was the normal rats that had behaved paradoxically – the representational format supported by the hippocampus had engaged a framework that could not tolerate alteration of reward assignments and this made learning the reversal particularly difficult for normal rats.

Other situations that require highly flexible memory representations involve tasks that demand switching responses on a trial-to-trial basis. This property of hippocampal-dependent learning and memory, contrasted with other systems that support the acquisition of consistent responses to and value associations of stimuli, is best illustrated by the work of White and his colleagues (Packard *et al.*, 1989; White and McDonald, 1993). These distinctions were impressively drawn in 'double dissociations' of performance on variations of the radial maze test – studies compared the effects of damage to the hippocampal system *versus* damage to the neostriatum and amygdala systems (Figure 22.3A). In one experiment, rats were tested on two variations of the radial maze task, called 'win-shift' and 'win-stay' (Packard *et al.*, 1989). In the conventional win-shift version of the radial maze task, an eight-arm maze was placed in the midst of a variety of extra-maze stimuli in the testing room, providing animals with the opportunity to encode the spatial relations among these stimuli as spatial cues. On every daily trial, a food reward was placed at the end of each of the eight maze arms, and the animal was released from the centre and was allowed to retrieve the rewards. Optimal performance would entail entering each arm only once, and subsequently avoiding already-visited arms in favour of the remaining unvisited arms. The central memory demand of this task, the 'win-shift' rule, emphasizes memory for each particular daily episode with specific maze arms. Also, the task requires 'flexible' use of memory by using the approach into previously rewarded locations to guide the selection of other new arms to visit. Under these conditions, rats with fornix transections made more errors by entering previously visited maze arms. Even after extended training, fornix-damaged rats continued to make substantially more errors than controls. By contrast, neostriatum lesions had no effect on task performance.

The second test involved the 'win-stay' variant of the same radial maze task (Figure 22.3B). In this version, the maze was again surrounded by a curtain, and lamps were used to cue particular maze arms. On the first trial of each daily training session, four arbitrarily selected arms were illuminated and baited with food, and the other arms were not baited. After the first occasion a lit arm was entered, that arm was re-baited, so that the animal could return to the arm for a second reward. Subsequently, the lamp in that particular arm

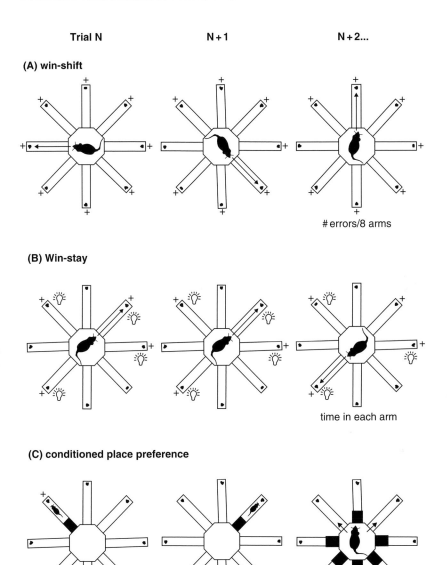

Trial N   N + 1   N + 2...

(A) win-shift

\# errors/8 arms

(B) Win-stay

time in each arm

(C) conditioned place preference

% correct choices

Figure 22.3 Three variations of the radial maze task. Each involves the same maze, but the task demands differ as described in the text.

was turned off and no more food was provided at that arm. Thus, the task here was characterized by a 'win-stay' rule in which animals could approach any cued arm at any time and could even re-execute the approach to a particular arm for reward one time in each daily trial. This version of the task emphasized reinforced responses to arms that were cued, independent of their spatial locations and recent history of rewards at particular locations. Also, the win-stay task did not require flexible expression of memory. Under these conditions, normal control subjects learned the appropriate behavioural responses to the lit arms gradually over several training sessions. Animals with neostriatal damage were impaired, barely exceeding chance performance even with extended training. By contrast, animals with fornix transections succeeded in learning and, indeed *outperformed* the control subjects in learning rate. How could hippocampal system damage produce a paradoxical facilitation of learning? Our conclusion is that the declarative system would have encouraged animals to switch responses to repeated arm presentations, which is counterproductive to learning this task, and that removing the hippocampal system allows the habit system to learn more rapidly.

Another experiment by the same group involved yet another variant of the radial maze task in which animals were separately conditioned to a strong reward value for one maze arm and not another arm (Figure 22.3C; White and McDonald, 1993). In this version, rats initially explored the maze to learn about the surrounding spatial cues. Then conditioning proceeded with daily exposures to one of two arms. On each trial, one arm was associated with food by confining the animal in that arm for 30 min with a large amount of food and, on the next day, the rat was placed on a different arm with no food for the same amount of time. Different groups of animals were trained for one to four pairs of rewarded and non-rewarded arm exposures. In a final test session, no food was placed on the maze and the access to both arms was allowed. The amount of time spent in each arm was recorded to measure the preference for each of the two arms. This version of the radial maze task emphasized the strong and separate associations between a location and food reward and a different location with absence of reward, and rats were not required to approach an arm to obtain rewards. Also, because the same arms used during training were re-presented in testing, the task did not require flexible expression of memory under conditions substantially different than original conditioning. Normal animals trained for one or two paired trials showed no spatial preference, but animals trained for three or four trials showed a significant preference for the arm associated with food. These findings indicate that at least three exposures to rewarded and non-rewarded arms are needed to acquire the consistent spatial preference for arms that have food. Rats with amygdala damage showed no conditioned place preference even by the end of training. In contrast, rats with fornix transections showed robust place preferences even after a single exposure to the rewarded and non-rewarded arms. In another apparently paradoxical finding, hippocampal system damage *facilitated* the learning of place preferences! How could hippocampal damage facilitate reward learning? Our conclusion is that the declarative and reward learning systems compete for control of this task as well, and that removing the hippocampal system allows the reward system to learn more rapidly.

Episodic recollection and the roles of distinct components of the hippocampal system

Recent studies have exploited findings from cognitive science and neuroscience to develop a rodent model of episodic memory. These studies are based on the widely held view that recognition can be supported by either of two processes – recollection of previous study events, or a sense of familiarity for recently experienced stimuli. The experiments employ signal detection analyses of recognition memory, using features of Receiver Operating Characteristics (ROC) functions to distinguish the contributions of episodic recollection and familiarity to memory performance. In a typical ROC experiment on item recognition, human subjects study a list of stimuli, then are tested with a longer list that includes both the old items (the items on the study list) and an equal number of new items, and must distinguish each item as 'old' or 'new'. ROC curves then relate the proportion of 'hits' (correct identifications of old items) to false alarms (incorrect identifications of new items as "old") across a range of response criteria that vary from liberal (accepting an item as 'old' based on a low threshold) to conservative (accepting items as 'old' based on a high criterion). The probability of hits [P(hits)] is plotted against the probability of false alarms [P(false alarms)]. In normal human subjects, the ROC function is typically characterized by two features: the curve is asymmetrical, involving an above-zero Y-intercept, and the shape is curvilinear, such that it bows (Figure 22.4, top). According to one interpretation, called the Dual Process Signal Detection (DPSD) model, the magnitude of the asymmetry reflects recollection and that of the curvilinearity reflects familiarity (Yonelinas, 2001). Confirming this view, under conditions where recollection is favoured, the ROC function remains asymmetrical, but becomes linear. Conversely, under conditions where familiarity is favoured, the ROC function remains curvilinear but becomes symmetrical.

We have developed a procedure that is similar to that used in humans (Fortin et al., 2004). We used stimuli composed of ordinary household odours (e.g. lemon, thyme, cumin) mixed in sand within small plastic cups. Initially, every day, rats studied a series of 10 stimuli, each baited with a bit of sweetened cereal buried in the sand of each cup. After a 30-min delay, a series of stimuli composed of a random ordering of 10 old odours and 10 new odours is presented, with the contingency that only new odour cups are baited. To manipulate the animal's bias for responding or not responding to target cups, we varied both the ratio of rewards in the target cup versus that in the alternate cup and the height of the target cup. Under these conditions for this non-match contingency, rats were less inclined to dig in a target cup for which they could obtain only a small reward or had to apply more effort (equivalent to a liberal threshold for 'old' responses in humans) and were more inclined to dig in a target cup in which they could obtain a greater reward or with less effort (equivalent to a conservative threshold in humans).

In the item recognition task, the ROC curve of intact rats was asymmetric, containing both an asymmetrical component (above-zero Y-intercept) and a strong curvilinear component (Figure 22.4, bottom). This pattern is remarkably similar to the ROC of humans in verbal recognition performance, consistent with a combination of recollection-like and familiarity-based components of recognition in animals. We have subsequently pursued this model by developing an associative recognition version of the task. In humans, a requirement to remember associations among stimulus elements cannot be supported by mere familiarity of the elements. Thus, when humans are required to remember pairings of distinct stimuli, the ROC curve remains asymmetrical, but becomes linear (Yonelinas, 2001; Parks and Yonelinas, 2007). However, recent studies with humans have shown that, alternatively, when the elements of a stimulus pairing are readily 'unitized' into a single configuration, such as when the elements are features of a face or parts of a compound word, familiarity can support memory for stimulus pairings just as it does for single stimuli (Quamme et al., 2007).

We developed a version of the associative recognition paradigm for rats, using stimulus pairs composed of combinations of an odour mixed into one of several digging media (e.g. wood chips, beads, sand) contained in a cup (Sauvage et al., 2008). Rats can readily learn to separately attend to odours and media as distinct stimulus dimensions (Birrell and Brown, 2000), so we expected the rats to distinguish these elements and rely on recollection

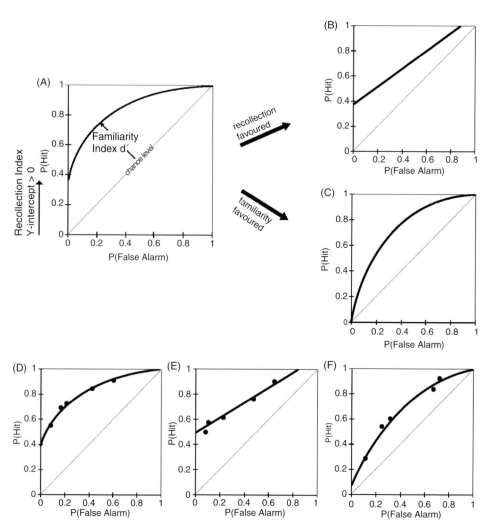

Figure 22.4 Receiver Operating Characteristics (ROC) functions. Top: the standard ROC function and ideal ROC functions under different task demands in humans. Bottom: ROC functions of normal rats on item recognition (left) and on associative recognition (middle), and the ROC function of rats with hippocampal damage on associative recognition (right).

of their associations (e.g. lemon is associated with wood chips). Each day the animals would initially sample a series of 10 odour–medium pairings, then following a 30-min delay, they had to distinguish re-presentations of the 10 original (old) pairs from 10 rearranged (new) pairings of the same odours and media, using the same 'non-matching' rule and manipulations of bias as in our study on item recognition described above. The resulting ROC function was highly asymmetric, indicating the presence of a strong recollection component, and linear, indicating the absence of a familiarity component (Figure 22.4, bottom). This pattern is similar to the ROC function of human subjects when they rely selectively on recollection in associative recognition and source memory studies.

To the extent that associative recognition depends on recollection, and if hippocampal damage eliminates recollection, one might expect that rats with hippocampal damage would perform poorly on associative recognition. However, we found that rats with hippocampal damage were only modestly, and not significantly, impaired on overall recognition performance (sham $68 \pm 2\%$, hippocampal $62 \pm 1\%$). Nevertheless, hippocampal damage substantially and significantly reduced performance based on recollection, reflected in a decrease in the Y-intercept of the ROC function. In addition, rats with hippocampal damage paradoxically had an *increased* contribution of familiarity, reflected in a significant curvilinearity of the ROC function, unlike normal rats (Figure 22.4, bottom). These findings provide strong evidence in favour of the DPSD model of recognition memory, and are inconsistent with other prominent models that suggest recognition is based on a single process (Wixted, 2007).

How could hippocampal damage improve familiarity-based recognition memory? These findings show that rats with hippocampal damage can perform as well as normal animals on an associative recognition task, using different strategies. The control subjects relied solely on recollection whereas rats with hippocampal damage relied principally on familiarity. The present findings do not directly show that the observed decrease in recollection and increase in familiarity in rats with hippocampal damage is due to an enhanced tendency to unitize the stimulus elements. However, other studies described above have shown that hippocampal damage increases the tendency to unitize stimulus elements into configural stimuli. For example, rats with hippocampal damage tend to unitize pairs of odour stimuli presented in close juxtaposition in simultaneous discrimination problems, such that they subsequently perform poorly when required to identify individual stimuli selected from different pairs (Eichenbaum *et al.*, 1989). Also, in monkeys, the explicit learning of visual stimulus configurations is facilitated over that of normal animals by damage limited to the hippocampus, whereas configural representation is severely impaired following damage to the perirhinal cortex (Saksida *et al.*, 2007). Consistent with these findings, it appears that rats with hippocampal damage and preserved perirhinal function have an increased tendency to unitize the elements of stimulus pairs, allowing them to employ familiarity as a compensatory strategy for distinguishing new and old pairs (see Bowles *et al.*, 2007; Winters *et al.*, 2007a,b).

Another study used a different popular model where episodic memory is defined as the ability to remember what happened where and when for unique experiences. In an experiment designed to explore whether the hippocampus is critical in memory for integrating what–where–when information, we trained rats on a task that assesses memory for events from single episodes involving a combination of odours ('what') presented in unique places ('where') in a specific order ('when' – Ergorul and Eichenbaum, 2004). On each trial, rats sequentially sampled a unique series of four rewarded odour stimulus cups, each in a different place along the periphery of a large open field (Figure 22.5). Then, memory for the order of those events was tested by presenting a choice between an arbitrarily selected pair of the odour cups in their original locations. Because rats could employ memory for the locations of the cups ('where') without using odour information ('what'), we also measured responses based purely on location information in two ways. First, we recorded the initial stimulus the animal approached; we separately determined that rats cannot tell which odour is inside until they approach the odour cup. Second, we presented probe memory tests in which the odours were omitted and the rats had to use the locations only to identify which odour was presented earlier.

Normal animals performed well in the standard what–where–when tests. Furthermore, they performed above-chance but less well than on the standard test in first

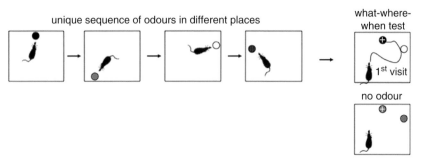

Figure 22.5 The 'what', 'where' and 'when' task. In the study phase, rats approach a unique sequence of four odours presented at different locations on a platform. Rats are then tested on a choice of two of those odours, and must choose the earlier presented one to obtain reward. On the test trial, both the first odour visited and the final choice are recorded. In addition, probe test trials are presented occasionally wherein cups with no odour are presented in two of the study locations.

approaching the correct cup. Therefore, it appears that normal rats make an initial good guess about which item occurred first ('when') based on location information ('where') and then they confirmed or disconfirmed their choice based on the odour in the cup ('what'). Furthermore, normal rats fall to chance performance in the probe tests that omitted the odours, providing strong evidence that normal rats form strongly integrated representations of what happened when and where, such that they considered items that lacked the correct 'what' component distinct from either correct item. Rats with hippocampal damage were severely impaired on the standard what–where–when memory judgements, performing no better than chance. Interestingly, animals with hippocampal damage had, paradoxically, *below chance* performance in first visits, that is, they tended to first approach the most recently reinforced cup in opposition to their training to approach the earlier presented cup. This finding suggests that the performance of rats with hippocampal damage was driven by an intact system that guides the rat to the place associated with the most recent reinforcement, consistent with the operation of the habit system. These observations indicate that normal rats can remember single episodes of what happened, where and when, and that this ability is based on highly integrated what–where–when representations that are supported by the hippocampus. One would expect that hippocampal damage would merely reduce performance to chance in all tests of memory. However, in the absence of hippocampal function, we observed that other brain systems can alter performance in a paradoxical way, in this case, to result in below-chance performance.

Conclusions

Here I have considered several experiments in which damage to the hippocampal region results in a paradoxical facilitation of learning and memory. I considered experiments in which hippocampal region damage resulted in the facilitation of learning simple stimulus–reward–response associations. In other experiments that involved reversal learning or learning multiple partially contradictory choices, hippocampal damage sometimes resulted in superior 'flexibility' in memory. In experiments on recognition, memory performance based on familiarity of stimulus combinations was also improved following hippocampal damage.

Each of the examples of paradoxical enhancement described here is consistent with the idea that there are multiple memory systems supported by different brain areas and pathways. In some circumstances, these systems operate independently and, in these situations, damage to the hippocampal system either produces a deficit or has no effect, depending on whether or not the form of learning is predominantly supported by that system. However, there are also several exceptions to this finding. Thus, in some situations described above, damage to the hippocampal system enhances the acquisition of habits or the adoption of reward values, or enhances the learning of stimulus configurations. These findings go beyond the idea of multiple parallel systems and suggest that memory systems sometimes compete, and that declarative memory sometimes may be less efficient than other systems. Under these circumstances, learning proceeds more rapidly when the influence of declarative memory is eliminated by hippocampal damage. These considerations suggest that the multiple memory systems outlined in Figure 22.1, and distinct components of the medial temporal lobe system (hippocampus and perirhinal cortex), can compete and cooperate with each other. In many cases they may each contribute to the same goal of learning and memory, but sometimes damaging one system or structure can reveal some degree of competition (Gaskin and White, 2006; Poldrack and Packard, 2003; Wingard and Packard, 2008), interference (Han *et al.*, 1998; Winters *et al.*, 2007a,b) or mutual inhibition (Schroeder *et al.*, 2002; Packard and McGaugh, 1996) that is revealed when one system is eliminated (see also Poldrack and Rodriguez, 2004; White and McDonald, 2002; Bussey *et al.*, 1999).

Future challenges and questions

There still remain many questions to be resolved about precisely what circumstances result in facilitation versus impairment following hippocampal damage. Under what circumstances is habit or emotional learning slowed by an intact hippocampal system? How is it determined whether multiple stimuli are learned as distinct representations and when are they unitized into configural representations? What are the interactions between the memory systems that underlie a competition that slows learning? Studies aimed directly at these mechanistic questions can be pursued using paradigms where slight changes in the testing protocols, several of which have been considered here, determine whether hippocampal function is critical or detrimental.

References

Ayalon, L., Doron, L., Weiner, I., & Joel, D. (2004). Amelioration of behavioural deficits in a rat model of Huntington's Disease by an excitotoxic lesion to the globus pallidus. *Experimental Neurology*, **186**: 46–58.

Bernabeau, R., Thiriet, N., Zwiller, J., & DiScala, G. (2006). Lesions of the lateral entorhinal cortex amplifies odour induced expression of c-fos, junB, and zif268 mRNA in rat brain. *Synapse*, **59**: 135–43.

Birrell, J. M., & Brown, V. J. (2000). Medial prefrontal cortex mediates perceptual attentional set shifting in the rat. *Journal of Neuroscience*, **20**: 4320–4.

Bowles, B., Crupi, C., Mirsattari, S. M., *et al.* (2007). Impaired familiarity with preserved recollection after anterior temporal lobe resection that spares the hippocampus. *Proceedings of the National Academy of Sciences USA*, **104**: 16,382–7.

Bussey, T. J., Muir, J. L., & Aggleton, J. P. (1999). Functionally dissociating aspects of event memory: the effects of combined perirhinal and postrhinal cortex lesions on object and place memory in the rat. *Journal of Neuroscience*, **19**: 495–502.

Bussey, T. J., Warburton, E., Aggleton, J. P., & Muir, J. L. (1998). Fornix lesions can facilitate acquisition of the transverse patterning task: and challenge for 'configural' theories of hippocampal function. *Journal of Neuroscience*, **18**: 1622–31.

Cohen, N. J., & Squire, L. R. (1980). Preserved learning and retention of a pattern-analyzing skill in amnesia: dissociation of knowing how and knowing that. *Science*, **210**: 207–10.

Corkin, S. (1984). Lasting consequences of bilateral medial temporal lobectomy: clinical course and experimental findings in H.M. *Seminars in Neurology*, **4**: 249–59.

Eichenbaum, H., & Cohen, N. J. (2001). *From Conditioning to Conscious Recollection: Memory Systems of the Brain*. New York, NY: Oxford University Press.

Eichenbaum, H., Fagan, A., & Cohen, N. J. (1986). Normal olfactory discrimination learning set and facilitation of reversal learning after medial temporal damage in rats: implications for preserved learning in amnesia. *Journal of Neuroscience*, **6**: 1876–84.

Eichenbaum, H., Fagan, A., Mathews, P., & Cohen, N. J. (1988). Hippocampal system dysfunction and odour discrimination learning in rats: mpairment or facilitation depending on representational demands. *Behavioral Neuroscience*, **102**: 331–9.

Eichenbaum, H., Matthews, P., & Cohen, N. J. (1989). Further studies of hippocampal representation during odour discrimination learning. *Behavioral Neuroscience*, **103**: 1207–16.

Ergorul, C., & Eichenbaum, H. (2004). The hippocampus and memory for 'What', 'When', and 'Where'. *Learning and Memory*, **11**: 397–405.

Fortin, N. J., Wright, S. P., & Eichenbaum, H. (2004). Recollection-like memory retrieval in rats is dependent on the hippocampus. *Nature*, **431**: 188–91.

Gaskin, S., & White, N. (2006). Coopertion and competition between the dorsal hippocampus and lateral amygdala in spatial discrimination learning. *Hippocampus*, **16**: 577–85.

Glick, S., & Greenstein, S. (1972). Facilitation of recovery after lateral hypothalamic damage by prior ablation of frontal cortex. *Nature New Biology*, **239**: 187–8.

Han, J. S., Gallagher, M., & Holland, P. (1998). Hippocampal lesions enhance configural learning by reducing proactive interference. *Hippocampus*, **8**: 138–46.

Hirsh, R. (1974). The hippocampus and contextual retrieval of information from memory: a theory. *Behavioral Biology*, **12**: 421–44.

Laurent-Demir, C., & Jaffard, R. (2000). Paradoxical facilitatory effect of fornix lesions on acquisition of contextual fear conditioning in mice. *Behavioural Brain Research*, **107**: 85–91.

Mumby, D., Wood, E., Duva, C., Kornecook, T., Pinel, J., & Phillips, A. (1996). Ischemia-induced object-recognition deficits in rats are attenuated by hippocampal ablation before or soon after ischemia. *Behavioral Neuroscience*, **110**: 266–81.

O'Keefe, J., & Nadel, L. (1978). *The Hippocampus as a Cognitive Map*. New York, NY: Oxford University Press.

Olton, D. S., Becker, J. T., & Handlemann, G. E. (1979). Hippocampus, space, and memory. *Brain and Behavioral Sciences*, **2**: 313–65.

Otto, T., Schottler, F., Staubli, U., Eichenbaum, H., & Lynch, G. (1991). Hippocampus and olfactory discrimination learning: effects of entorhinal cortex lesions on olfactory learning and memory in a successive-cue, go/no-go task. *Behavioral Neuroscience*, **105**: 111–19.

Packard, M. G., & McGaugh, J. L. (1996). Inactivation of hippocampus or caudate nucleus with lidocaine differentially affects expression of place and response learning. *Neurobiology of Learning and Memory*, **65**: 65–72.

Packard, M. G., Hirsh, R., & White, N. M. (1989). Differential effects of fornix and caudate nucleus lesions on two radial maze tasks: Evidence for multiple memory systems. *The Journal of Neuroscience*, **9**: 1465–72.

Parks, C. M., & Yonelinas, A. P. (2007). Moving beyond pure signal-detection models: comment on Wixted (2007). *Psychological Reviews*, **114**: 188–202.

Plamondon, H., Davignon, G., Khan, S., & Charron, C. (2008). Cerebral ischemic preconditioning induces lasting effects on CA1 neuronal survival, prevents memory impairments but not ischemia-induced hyperactivity. *Behavioral Brain Research*, **189**: 145–51.

Poldrack, R., & Packard, M. (2003). Competition among multiple memory systems: converging evidence from animal and human brain studies. *Neuropsychologia*, **41**: 245–51.

Poldrack, R., & Rodreiguez, P. (2004). How do memory systems interact? Evidence from human classification learning. *Neurobiology of Learning and Memory*, **82**: 324–32.

Quamme, J. R., Yonelinas, A. P., & Norman, K. A. (2007). The effect of unitization on associative recognition in amnesia. *Hippocampus*, **17**: 192–200.

Raber, J., Villasana, L., Rosenberg, J., Zou, Y., Huang, T., & Fike, J. (2009). Irradiation enhances hippocampus-dependent cognition in mice deficient in extracellular superoxide dismutase. *Hippocampus*, [Epub ahead of print].

Rawashdeh, P., de Borsetti, N., Roman, G., & Cahill, G. (2007). Melatonin suppresses nighttime memory formation in zebrafish. *Science*, **318**: 1144–6.

Saksida, L. M., Bussey, T. J., Buckmaster, C. A., & Murray, E. A. (2007). Impairment and facilitation of transverse patterning after lesions of the perirhinal cortex and hippocampus, respectively. *Cerebral Cortex*, **17**: 108–15.

Saxe, M. D., Malleret, G., Vronskaya, S., *et al.* (2007). Paradoxical influence of hippocampal neurogenesis on working memory. *Proceedings of the National Academy of Sciences*, **104**: 4642–6.

Stalnaker, T., Franz, T., Singh, T., & Schoenbaum, G. (2007). Basolateral amygdala lesions abolish orbitofrontal-dependent reversal impairments. *Neuron*, **54**: 51–8.

Sauvage, M. M., Fortin, N. J., Owens, C. B., Yonelinas, A. P., & Eichenbaum, H. (2008). Recognition memory: opposite effects of hippocampal damage on recollection and familiarity. *Nature Neuroscience*, **11**: 16–18.

Schroeder, J., Wingard, J. C., & Packard, M. G. (2002). Post-training reversible inactivation of hippocampus reveals interference between memory systems. *Hippocampus*, **12**: 280–4.

Scoville, W. B., & Milner, B. (1957). Loss of recent memory after bilateral hippocampal lesions. *Journal of Neurology, Neurosurgery and Psychiatry*, **20**: 11–12.

Staubli, U., Ivy, G., & Lynch, G. (1984). Hippocampal denervation causes rapid forgetting of olfactory information in rats. *Proceedings of the National Academy of Science*, **81**: 5885–7.

White, N. M., & McDonald, R. J. (1993). Acquisition of a spatial conditioned place preference is impaired by amygdala lesions and improved by hippocampal lesions. *Behavioural Brain Research*, **55**: 269–81.

White, N. M., & McDonald, R. J. (2002). Multiple parallel memory systems in the brain of the rat. *Neurobiology of Learning and Memory*, **77**: 125–84.

Wingard, J., & Packard, M. (2008). The amygdala and emotional modulation of competition between cognitive and habit memory. *Behavioural Brain Research*, **193**: 126–31.

Winters, B. D., Bartko, S. J., Saksida, L. M., & Bussey, T. J. (2007a). Scopolamine infused into perirhinal cortex improves object recognition memory by blocking the acquisition of interfering object recognition. *Learning and Memory*, **14**: 590–6.

Winters, B. D., Saksida, L. M., & Bussey, T. J. (2007b). Paradoxical facilitation of object recognition memory after infusion of scopolamine into perirhinal cortex: implications of cholinergic system function. *Journal of Neuroscience*, **26**: 9520–6.

Wirth, S., Ferry, B., & DiScala, G. (1998). Facilitation of olfactory recognition by lateral entorhinal cortex lesions in rats. *Behavioural Brain Research*, **91**: 49–59.

Wixted, J. T. (2007). Dual process theory and signal detection theory of recognition memory. *Psychological Review*, **114**: 152–76.

Yonelinas, A. P. (2001). Components of episodic memory: the contribution of recollection and familiarity. *Philosophical Transactions of the Royal Society of London, Series B: Biological Sciences*, **356**: 1363–74.

Zhou, S., Zhu, M., Shu, D., *et al.* (2009). Preferential enhancement of working memory in mice lacking adenosine A_{2A} receptors. *Brain Research*, **1303**: 74–83.

Zola, S. M., & Mahut, H. (1973). Paradoxical facilitation of object reversal learning after transection of the fornix in monkeys. *Neuropsychologia*, **11**: 271–84.

Chapter 23

Paradoxical effects of drugs on cognitive function: the neuropsychopharmacology of the dopamine and other neurotransmitter systems

Roshan Cools, Esther Aarts and Mitul A. Mehta

Summary

Neurotransmitters are the means by which one neuron influences the action of another. Abnormalities in neurotransmitter function are implicated in a variety of neurological and neuropsychiatric disorders and drugs that influence the neurotransmitter systems are often used in treating the symptoms of such disorders. The effects of these drugs can be paradoxical. A small dose of a pharmacological agent might have entirely the opposite effect to a large dose, a drug may improve one ability whilst impairing another, a drug may have opposite effects in different populations or opposite effects in the same individual at different times. In this chapter, we illustrate these effects using clinical data and data from healthy volunteers in experimental studies. With one of the best studied neuromodulators – dopamine – as our focus, we introduce key principles that can help to explain these apparent paradoxes. First, the effect of a drug depends on baseline levels of the neurotransmitter already in the system. When baseline levels are low, a given pharmacological dose can increase function closer to an optimal level. When baseline levels are high, the *same* dose can over-stimulate the system and trigger compensatory mechanisms that reduce performance on a given task. Second, a drug could have quite different effects in different brain regions. Accordingly, a function that is predominantly influenced by one region may be enhanced, whilst another function, more dependent on another region, may be impaired. In the final section of the chapter, we turn to attention deficit hyperactivity disorder (ADHD). ADHD symptoms are very commonly targeted using neurotransmitter-influencing drugs. We discuss the implications of baseline-dependent effects and region-specific effects for understanding this disorder and its treatment.

Introduction

In her adventures in Wonderland, Alice drinks from a bottle labelled 'DRINK ME' and becomes tiny. Following a piece of 'EAT ME' cake, she becomes extremely tall. Curious enough, but how much more curious if one sip of the drink had caused her to shrink whilst two sips caused her to grow; or if the drink made her shorter if she was tall or taller if she was short. As we shall see in this chapter, drugs have exactly this

The Paradoxical Brain, ed. Narinder Kapur. Published by Cambridge University Press. © Cambridge University Press 2011.

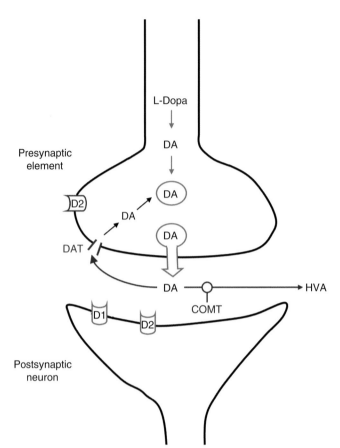

Figure 23.1 Neurotransmitter messages across the synapse between two neurons (schematic of dopaminergic neurotransmission). Neurotransmission is controlled by electrical impulses, which are transmitted between neurons by one 'hurling' a chemical messenger across its synapse to a receptor on the other. This occurs primarily in one direction, from the pre-synaptic axon terminal to a post-synaptic neuron. In addition, neurotransmitters can spill over by diffusion to sites distant from its own synapse, acting wherever there are relevant receptors, via so-called volume transmission (see Stahl, 2008 for further details). In the specific case of dopamine, this is synthesized from a precursor called L-Dopa. It is released from the presynaptic neuron into the gap (synaptic cleft) and subsequently stimulates dopamine receptors (called D1 and D2). This receptor binding can be mimicked by dopamine agonists or blocked by dopamine receptor antagonists. Dopamine transmission is controlled by a protein called DAT, a re-uptake pump, and by catechol-O-methyltransferase (COMT), an enzyme that ultimately degrades dopamine into homovanillic acid. For further details, see Cooper and others (2003).

sort of paradoxical effect on cognition – our ability to think, remember and concentrate. The study of drugs that influence cognition, mood and other, 'higher-level' brain processes is called neuropsychopharmacology.

Individual neurons carry electrical signals. Communication between neurons, however, involves an intricate exchange of chemicals across junctions (synapses; see Figure 23.1). Some of these chemicals, the ascending neurotransmitters, are secreted by a small group of cells in the brainstem and diffuse through large (overlapping) areas of the brain (Figure 23.2). When an ascending neurotransmitter projects to a certain brain region, it modulates the function associated with that region (Stahl, 2008). For this reason, the term 'neuromodulation' is sometimes used to describe the action of neurotransmitters in the brain.

One very important reason to study neurotransmitters is the devastating effect that abnormalities in these systems can produce. Parkinson's disease, for example, affects between 100 and 200 people per 100,000. Sufferers are progressively handicapped by movement tremor, muscular rigidity, difficulty initiating actions and changes in posture. The underlying biochemical changes in the brain leading to the condition were first identified in the 1950s; in particular degeneration of cells in the midbrain that produce

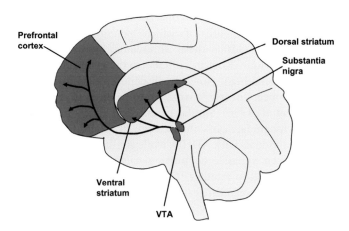

Figure 23.2 Schematic medial view of the brain showing dopamine projections from dopamine-containing cells in midbrain areas to striatum (caudate and putamen) and prefrontal cortex (PFC).

a neurotransmitter called dopamine. Additional changes associated with Parkinson's disease, such as reduced flexibility of thought, fuelled interest in the effects of different transmitters and different transmitter concentrations on cognitive function. Other conditions in which cognitive problems and abnormalities of neurotransmitter pathways occur include schizophrenia, drug addiction, Alzheimer's disease, Lewy Body Dementia, stroke, depression and attention deficit hyperactivity disorder (ADHD). We devote the concluding section of this chapter to ADHD.

Understanding paradoxical effects of alterations in neurotransmitter function is vital because drugs that target these systems are widely used. ADHD, for example, is commonly treated with methylphenidate (e.g. Ritalin), which increases dopamine, while Parkinson's disease is commonly treated with L-Dopa, the precursor of dopamine, or dopamine receptor agonists, which simulate the effect of naturally produced – 'endogenous' – dopamine. Similarly, chemical interventions used to modulate the neurotransmitters serotonin and GABA are sometimes used in therapy for depression and during recovery from stroke, respectively. The same drug has quite different, even opposite, effects depending on the individual in question, their clinical condition, the dose, duration of administration or the type of activity used to measure its effect. Clearly a better understanding of these paradoxical effects provide important clinical information, while also having the potential to tell us something about the underlying brain systems.[1]

Paradoxical neuropsychopharmacological effects

In the context of this chapter, paradoxical drug effects are defined as occurring when the same or similar drugs have diametrically opposite or at least highly variable effects in

---

[1] Paradoxical effects in pharmacology are not limited to those influencing neurotransmitter function in the brain. In a seminal paper, Bond (2001) reviews a number of these phenomena. He notes, for example, that beta-blockers should in theory be contraindicated for certain heart conditions in that they 'block' receptors that trigger healthy heart contractions. It turns out, however, they can be paradoxically beneficial, perhaps because they counter desensitization of these receptors from the body's natural response to the disorder (see also Yun *et al.*, 2005, 2007).

different populations or contexts. A well-known example concerns drugs such as methylphenidate (e.g. Ritalin) and amphetamine, both of which potentiate dopamine and noradrenaline transmission. In healthy adults these 'stimulants' increase activity (Rapoport *et al.*, 1980) and energize behaviour (Koelega, 1993) – to the extent that some individuals use them to create a recreational high. However, in children diagnosed with ADHD, whose behaviour sometimes appears overly 'energized' to begin with, they can have a calming influence (Castellanos *et al.*, 1996). Similar paradoxical effects have been observed on cognitive function. Methylphenidate can enhance cognitive stability (i.e. help people to keep focused on a task) in individuals with ADHD, while similar drugs that also raise dopamine levels (like L-Dopa) can enhance cognitive *flexibility* in Parkinson's disease, i.e. help in switching from one task to another (Cools *et al.*, 2001). Increasing dopamine receptor stimulation with receptor agonists can have quite different effects on people with relatively low and high working memory ability – working memory is the capacity to maintain and update information 'in mind' during a short delay, for example, holding a phone number in mind between reading it and dialing (Baddeley, 1986). Where people are relatively poor at these tasks, working memory performance (both in terms of manipulating and retrieving information) and the efficiency with which they can switch between different cognitive tasks can all be enhanced with increased dopamine concentrations (Mehta *et al.*, 2000; Frank and O'Reilly, 2006; Gibbs and D'Esposito, 2005). Strikingly, the same drugs have the reverse effect on people with initially relatively high working memory capacity, now impairing their performance on such tasks compared with pre-drug levels (e.g. Kimberg *et al.*, 1997; Cools *et al.*, 2007a; Frank and O'Reilly, 2006).

Diversity in response to neurotransmitter modulation occurs within, as well as between, different individuals. For example, dopamine increases due to L-Dopa and dopamine receptor agonists can both remediate the physical and mental rigidity of Parkinson's disease whilst, at least in a minority of patients, triggering pathological gambling and other forms of addiction and impulsivity. Administration of a GABA agonist (or an *N*-methyl-D-asparate (NMDA) receptor blocker) can have favourable long-term effects if administered in the early hours after stroke, but be deleterious if given days later (Cramer, 2008a) – indeed, this 'beneficial' agent can cause re-emergence of symptoms apparently long-since vanished after the stroke (Cramer, 2008b). The use of antidepressants that target the serotonin neurotransmitter (selective serotonin reuptake inhibitors (SSRIs) such as fluoxetine – 'Prozac') can have quite different effects in a single acute dose compared with repeated administrations over time (Burghardt *et al.*, 2004; Harmer *et al.*, 2003).

Mechanisms that can give rise to paradoxical drug effects

In beginning to explain these apparently paradoxical responses to neurotransmitter targeting drugs, and thereby thinking about the nature of the neurotransmitter systems, four concepts are critical. The first is the idea of homeostatic regulation. One of the most simple and elegant mechanical devices, used in windmills since the seventeenth century and later in steam engines, is the centrifugal governor. It consists of two weighted arms rotating around a central spindle. If the wheel on which it sits is turning slowly, the arms of the centrifugal governor drop allowing more water, steam, etc., to flow and turn the wheel more quickly. As the wheel speeds up, centrifugal force raises the arms, shutting

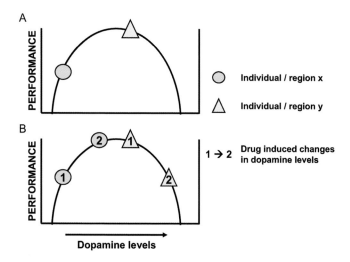

Figure 23.3 Schematic representation of the 'inverted U'-shaped dose–response curve. (A) Individual or brain region *x* (circle) has lower baseline dopamine levels relative to individual or brain region *y* (triangle) with optimal baseline dopamine levels. (B) Dopaminergic drugs that enhance dopamine transmission might be beneficial for performance in individual *x* or performance related to processing in region *x* (circle), while it would be detrimental for performance in individual *y* or performance related to processing in brain region *y* with already optimized baseline dopamine levels (triangle).

down the input. For as long as there is power, and without the requirement for any supervision, the centrifugal governor thus maintains the speed of the engine around the optimum. Self-regulation or homeostasis is crucial to many biological and other systems (e.g. body temperature, predator–prey balance, economic supply and demand, home central heating) and, depending on the precise nature of the system, a degree of oscillation may occur as it 'strives' to achieve its optimal level. In other words, in correcting for a very low value, a regulatory system might 'overshoot' and produce a high value, and vice versa.

The second, somewhat related, construct is that of an 'inverted U-shaped function'. Yerkes and Dodson, in the early twentieth century, observed that a certain level of environmental stress improved performance on an easy task, but impaired performance on a more difficult version. They suggested that, for any given task, there was an optimal level of arousal below which, or above which, performance would decline (the 'Yerkes–Dodson law', Yerkes and Dodson, 1908). When plotted as a graph (see Figure 23.3) this relationship forms a curve (the inverted U-shaped function). The effects of increasing someone's arousal level on performance will depend crucially on where they start on the graph. If they are over to the left side, it will improve performance, if they are at the summit or to its right, it will impair their performance. Inverted U-shaped functions are not limited to the relationship between arousal and performance and pertain to many systems, including, as we shall see, neurotransmitter levels and cognitive function.

The third concept is that of 'hormesis'. This refers to the observation that low doses of some drugs or agents can have beneficial effects whilst high doses prove harmful. Radiation is a classic example – in a high dose, it can cause death, in a low dose it can treat cancer. Calabrese (2008) discusses the 150-year history of such observations and the debate as to whether these effects reflect a stressor (e.g. radiation, poison) disrupting homeostasis and causing beneficial overcompensation by the body (in effect, varieties of the overshoot self-regulation idea outlined above) or whether low doses can directly stimulate beneficial processes. Hormesis also encompasses the general principle that a system responds differently to an administered pharmacological intervention over time ('*temporal hormesis*';

Bond, 2001). It should be noted that although practitioners may sometimes use the term, hormesis is not the same as *homeopathy*.[2]

The fourth important idea is that of regional specificity in the brain. This means that one area of the brain may respond differently to changes in neurotransmission from another (function A, largely determined by activity in region X, may show relative improvement, while function B, largely determined by region Y, may be compromised). Thus there might be different optimal levels of neurotransmission for different brain regions (see Figure 23.3). Homeostatic self-regulation, inverted U-shaped responses, other causes of hormesis, and regional specificity are potential mechanisms underlying apparently paradoxical effects – as we will illustrate in the following.

Self-regulation and inverted U-shaped responses in neuropsychopharmacology

Let us start with one of the best documented neuromodulators, dopamine. Dopamine pathways originate in the midbrain and project heavily to a set of subcortical brain structures, including the striatum (composed of the caudate nucleus and the putamen), and the prefrontal cortex, which is strongly connected to the striatum (Alexander *et al.*, 1986; see Figure 23.2). Like other neuromodulatory systems, the dopamine system is highly dynamic and constantly regulates itself in order to maintain equilibrium, both at the molecular and at the systems level. As discussed, because of this self-regulation, responses to pharmacological agents that change dopamine transmission are unlikely to be linear. Instead, low and high doses may have opposite effects and, if oscillations of self-regulation are slow, these may change with time. There is certainly evidence consistent with this model. Indeed, high-dose dopamine receptor agonists might induce impairment to the same degree as do dopamine receptor antagonists that block dopamine transmission. Some have suggested that this impairing effect of high-dose agonists might reflect a blocking of postsynaptic activity with supra-optimal levels of D1 receptor stimulation (Zahrt *et al.*, 1997) – much as turnstiles might break down under heavy crowd pressure and end up letting no one through. Furthermore, DA receptor agonists can also have opposite effects depending on the time of measurement, with initial suppression of motor activity and subsequent potentiation of motor activity (Pizzolato *et al.*, 1985). The mechanism underlying this effect may be that, initially, detectors on the cell that is transmitting dopamine (presynaptic receptors, Figure 23.1) are triggered. These presynaptic receptors inhibit firing, dopamine release and/or synthesis, leading to an 'undershoot' dip in production. Whether or not a given boost of dopamine will trigger these suppressing mechanisms will likely depend on the starting levels of dopamine in the system (Torstenson *et al.*, 1998). Following an inverted U-shaped function, if dopamine levels are initially low, increased levels may lead to

---

[2] Homeopathy is the eighteenth-century idea that a substance that causes certain symptoms in people can, in a highly diluted form, benefit people who have similar symptoms. The problem that the dilutions used are so great that there is unlikely to be any of the active substance in a dose led to theories such as that the water might contain a 'memory' of the substance. There is no convincing evidence of the efficacy of these preparations when compared with placebos in randomized trials (e.g. Altunç *et al.*, 2007). Protestors complaining that the UK National Health Service spends £4m annually on this 'unscientific, absurd pseudoscience' recently staged a 'mass homeopathic overdose' in various cities around the country (http://news.bbc.co.uk/1/hi/scotland/glasgow_and_west/8488286.stm).

performance improvements. If levels are initially high, additional dopamine may block the system and/or trigger self-regulatory systems thus leading to a reduction in performance.[3]

If this is true of aspects of movement, is it also true of cognitive performance? We have already discussed how people who performed relatively poorly on working memory tests showed gains from drugs that increased dopamine levels, while their initially more able peers (in this respect) became worse following the same intervention (Mehta *et al.*, 2000; Frank and O'Reilly, 2006; Gibbs and D'Esposito, 2005; Kimberg *et al.*, 1997; Cools *et al.*, 2007a; see also Williams and Goldman-Rakic, 1995; Zahrt *et al.*, 1997; Arnsten, 1998; Phillips *et al.*, 2004; Vijayraghavan *et al.*, 2007). Such results invite speculation that one of the reasons that some people do poorly on working memory tasks is that they have relatively low baseline levels of dopamine. They are to the left of the inverted U-shaped function and the drug-induced boost brings them nearer to the optimal middle (Figure 23.3). People with good working memory, in contrast, have naturally high baseline levels of dopamine. Increasing this level pushes them from the summit down the right-hand slope of the inverted U-shaped function. Is there any direct evidence of this inverted U-shaped response hypothesis?

Inverted U-shaped functions and genetic variations

One source of such evidence comes from genetic differences between individuals. Catechol-O-methyltransferase (COMT) is an enzyme that breaks down dopamine released into the synaptic gap between two neurons (Figure 23.1). If there is relatively little COMT activity, there is more dopamine in the synapse. Where COMT is more active, there is less dopamine in the synapse. It turns out that in the general population there are two common variants

---

[3] In this chapter, we will be talking about differential effects of the same drug on people who perform relatively well or poorly in cognitive tasks and discussing this primarily in terms of inverted U-shaped functions. An important confound to deal with in this respect is 'regression to the mean'. Let us take an everyday example. Suppose your journey to work takes, *on average*, 40 min. The actual time it takes you each day will vary according to road conditions, train stoppages, whether it is a school holiday, etc. If we measured your journey time on one day and found that it had taken you 4 h, the next time that we measured it, it is *very likely* to be substantially less – much closer to the average or mean because this is, by definition, much more common. Similarly, if we measured your journey and you had completed it in just 5 min (perhaps you forgot it was a national holiday), the *next* time that we measure it is very likely to be longer – closer to the average. The same is true of cognitive tests. Suppose the average number of digits that people can remember in order is seven. If a person (say, female volunteer) remembers just one digit, all else being equal, she is likely to perform better if she has another try (perhaps she was distracted or could not hear properly the first time). Similarly, if she remembered 14 digits on one go (maybe the digits happened to come in the order 1 2 3 4 5 6 7 1 2 3 4 5 6 7), the next time she is likely to do worse. The problem of hypothesizing *different* effects of drugs on people who perform at different levels on tests becomes clear. If we take people who perform *very* poorly at a test and people who perform *very* well and do nothing at all, on re-test the former will tend to improve and the latter will tend to get worse. How can we tell if our drug produces this pattern over and above the effect of regression to the mean? The answer is to make multiple observations (i.e. find the true mean for each participant) before administration of the drug and/or, at a group level, to compare the drug with a sugar pill designed to have no effect (in addition to dealing with regression to the mean, such placebos have the well-known advantage of separating potential effects of the real drug from effects that stem from participants' expectations about the drug). For more detailed discussion of regression to the mean in relation to psychoactive medication see (Robbins and Sahakian, 1979; Robbins and Everitt, 1987; Teicher *et al.*, 2003; Arnsten, 1998; Granon *et al.*, 2000).

(allele polymorphisms) of the gene determining COMT levels. People with what is called the Val-allele are thought to have relatively high COMT activity/low baseline dopamine levels. People with the Met-allele are thought to have relatively low COMT activity/high baseline dopamine levels. There is good evidence that those amongst us with the Met-allele (high dopamine) do indeed tend to perform significantly better on working memory tasks than those of us with the Val variant (Egan et al., 2001; Diamond et al., 2004). In support of this, consistent differences in activity in the dorsolateral prefrontal cortex during working memory tasks have been reported between Val and Met participants – specifically, the high-dopamine Met volunteers show lower activity levels, suggestive of more efficient processing (Mier et al., 2010; Mattay et al., 2003). Critically, the prefrontal cortical activity of Val volunteers during working memory tasks can be reduced to more closely resemble that of their Met peers with dextroamphetamine, a stimulant that increases dopamine levels. In line with the U-shaped function hypothesis, exactly the same stimulant *increased* frontal activity in Met participants (Mattay et al., 2003).

Imaging and neuropsychopharmacology

Direct evidence for the hypothesis that differential effects of drugs on working memory capacity might reflect differences in baseline dopamine levels came from a recent neuro-chemical positron emission tomography (PET) study (Cools et al., 2008). Readers may be familiar with PET studies of cognitive function in which the uptake of radioactive labelled glucose is monitored in three-dimensional space to examine which parts of the brain are working harder during a particular task (a type of study now more routinely performed using functional magnetic resonance imaging (fMRI) techniques). In PET scanning, other chemicals can also be radioactively labelled to monitor changes in their concentrations. Cools et al. (2008) used a radiotracer (6-[^{18}F]fluoro-L-*m*-tyrosine, FMT) to monitor dopamine synthesis capacity in the striatum. They found that healthy volunteers with relatively low working memory capacity indeed showed significantly lower dopamine synthesis than did those with greater working memory capacity.

This method also enabled a direct test of whether the effects of dopamine-altering drugs in healthy volunteers vary as a function of baseline levels of dopamine (Cools et al., 2009). Volunteers who underwent a PET scan were also tested after taking an oral dose of 1.25 mg bromocriptine, a dopamine receptor agonist (i.e. which increases dopamine receptor stimulation) that is used in the treatment of Parkinson's disease. On another occasion, they were tested after taking a placebo pill. Performance was measured using a reversal learning task. In this test, participants first learn that a certain stimulus leads to a reward whilst another does not. Once learned, however, the rules governing which stimuli trigger rewards are switched. The crucial measure is how quickly participants adapt to the change so that they continue to predict accurately which stimuli are associated with reward. Cools et al. found a highly significant correlation between performance and baseline dopamine synthesis capacity in the striatum in the placebo condition – participants with higher dopamine synthesis capacity were better at reversal learning (Cools et al., 2009). Bromocriptine improved the performance of volunteers with relatively low baseline levels of dopamine but *reduced* performance in those with high baseline levels. This study was particularly important because it extended evidence of an inverted U-shaped response beyond standard working memory paradigms and showed that dopamine-enhancing drugs have contrasting effects on reversal learning in healthy volunteers as a function of baseline levels of dopamine function.

This conclusion is further substantiated by another study examining the effects of the drug widely used in the management of ADHD, methylphenidate, on reversal learning. Clatworthy *et al.* (2009) used PET imaging to look at the levels of dopamine that were released in healthy volunteers after taking this drug. They found that, when methylphenidate caused relatively small changes in dopamine levels, this tended to be associated with improved reversal learning performance. In participants who showed relatively large changes in dopamine levels, the drug tended to worsen performance on the task. Although this was not a clinical group, the participants completed questionnaires including a question that documented how impulsive they were in everyday situations. It turned out that the more impulsive among the volunteers tended to show smaller changes in dopamine levels with methylphenidate, and tended to benefit more in their reversal learning performance. This is particularly interesting given indications that people who meet diagnostic criteria for ADHD also tend to show relatively small changes in dopamine after methylphenidate (see further below; Volkow *et al.*, 2007b).

So far we have discussed apparent paradoxes in response to drugs that target the dopamine system. There is evidence that the same self-regulation/inverted U-shaped function patterns may apply to other neurotransmitter systems. As discussed, the symptoms of depression are sometimes treated with SSRIs such as Prozac that increase levels of the neurotransmitter serotonin by inhibiting its 'reuptake'. There is evidence that the increase in serotonin (also called 5-hydroxytryptamine or 5-HT) produced by acute administration of SSRIs not only stimulates postsynaptic receptors, but also floods (5-HT1A) autoreceptors (Blier and de Montigny, 1999; Artigas, 1993). Autoreceptors are located on the dendrites and soma of the transmitting neuron and normally inhibit release of neurotransmitter (see Figure 23.1 for an example in the case of dopamine). This self-regulation leads to a short-term undershoot in production and a net reduction of activity in the serotonin system. Over the longer term, however, these autoreceptors appear to become desensitized, allowing higher levels of serotonin (Blier and de Montigny, 1999; Artigas, 1993). This helps to explain why these drugs need to be taken for some time before therapeutic effects develop.

The above-reviewed studies have suggested that the large variability in drug effects can be explained partly by variation in basal levels of dopamine between different individuals. However, dopaminergic drug effects vary not only between individuals, but also between different tasks within the same individuals. The cognitive demands of the task might be the critical determinant of where the optimal dopamine level is set for the task under study.

Differential drug effects on distinct tasks

We have already seen that naturally occurring genetic variations (e.g. those of us carrying Val allele of the COMT gene) are associated with working memory deficits. It turns out that these variations may also confer benefits. For example, Nolan *et al.* (2004) observed that Val-allele carriers were impaired in terms of sticking to task, but in fact exhibited improved mental flexibility. Two recent studies of mental flexibility, one of reversal learning (Krugel *et al.*, 2009) and one of repeated task-switching (Colzato *et al.*, 2010) have substantiated this observation and have also shown improved cognitive flexibility in Val compared with Met participants. Intriguingly, reductions of dopamine levels in the prefrontal cortex of marmosets (non-human primates) have indeed been found to be associated with, on the one hand, increased distractibility, but on the other hand greater mental flexibility (Roberts *et al.*, 1994; Crofts *et al.*, 2001). Taken together, these findings suggest that high dopamine levels in the prefrontal cortex favour stable, well-maintained representations/task (or, expressed negatively, mental 'rigidity'), whilst relatively low dopamine levels in the prefrontal cortex favour flexibility and task switching (or, expressed negatively, distractibility and difficulty keeping focused). Thus different optimum levels of dopamine might exist for different forms of cognitive processing, even if this processing reflects the output of a single brain region, here the prefrontal cortex.

Differential drug effects on distinct brain regions

Another important factor to consider when interpreting the mechanism of dopaminergic drug effects is its locus of action. Cognitive neuropsychology involves drawing inferences about what different parts of the brain do by looking at the effects of localized brain damage. The pioneering case studies of Paul Broca and Carl Wernicke in the nineteenth century, for example, separated regions implicated in the production of speech (in the frontal cortex) and comprehension of speech (in the temporal lobe), respectively. The debate continues about regional specialization, relatively self-contained cognitive 'modules' and perspectives that take into account the influence of multiple, widely distributed systems on a given capacity. However, it is clear that some regions are disproportionately involved in certain cognitive or perceptual operations. If baseline levels of dopamine or other neurotransmitters are different in different parts of the brain, then this gives the potential for apparently paradoxical effects – a drug that helps one ability may hinder another by acting simultaneously at different brain regions. An additional complexity is where changes in neurotransmitter function in one region induce changes in another (Akil et al., 2003; Meyer-Lindenberg et al., 2002, 2005; Pycock et al., 1980).

An example of the potential importance of regional specialization is illustrated by a hypothesis developed by us and by others that, in Parkinson's disease, the different effects of dopaminergic therapy might reflect differential dopamine depletion in different parts of the striatum (Gotham et al., 1988; Swainson et al., 2000; Cools et al., 2001, 2003, 2007b). In early Parkinson's disease, dopamine depletion is relatively restricted to the more dorsal (upper) parts of the striatum, areas associated with cognition and movement control. At this early disease stage, the ventral (lower) part of the striatum – associated with reward and motivation – is still relatively intact (Kish et al., 1988). Medication doses that are necessary to restore the severe dopamine depletion in the dorsal striatum might thus detrimentally overdose the relatively intact ventral striatum, in some individuals leading to problems such as gambling and disinhibition (Cools et al., 2001). Indeed, we have observed that the same dopaminergic medication can remediate cognitive function as measured with a task associated with the dorsal striatum, while at the same time impairing cognitive function associated with the ventral striatum (Cools et al., 2001). Thus an important factor to consider when interpreting the mechanism of dopaminergic drug effects is its locus of action.

Further evidence for regional specificity of the effects of dopaminergic drugs comes from a range of studies with experimental animals and human volunteers. For example, in contrast to the increased distractibility and the improved flexibility observed following dopamine lesions of the prefrontal cortex (see above), dopamine lesions of the striatum in marmosets induced reduced distractibility and impaired flexibility within the same paradigm (Crofts et al., 2001). Animals with dopamine lesions in the striatum were significantly less distractible and less flexible than control monkeys. Together this raises the possibility that the prefrontal cortex and the striatum mediate different effects of dopamine. This hypothesis was recently strengthened by an event-related fMRI study with healthy volunteers (Cools *et al.*, 2007a). In this study, subjects performed a working memory (delayed response) paradigm, which enabled the separate investigation of attentional switching during encoding and resistance to distraction during the delay. Subjects were scanned on two occasions, once after intake of an oral dose (1.25 mg) of bromocriptine and once after placebo (in a double-blind, cross-over design). Critically, bromocriptine modulated distinct brain regions, the striatum and the prefrontal cortex, during switching and distractor-resistance, respectively. It potentiated neural activity in the striatum during switching between aspects of encoding stimuli, while potentiating neural activity in the prefrontal cortex during a distractor presented during the delay. Interestingly, these effects depended on individual differences in trait impulsivity, so that the greatest potentiating effects were seen in high-impulsive individuals. In contrast, the same drug attenuated, albeit non-significantly, neural activity in low-impulsive individuals. These impulsivity-dependent effects on task-switching are reminiscent of those on reversal learning obtained by Clatworthy *et al.* (2009), described earlier, and confirm that dopamine has different functional consequences depending on individual differences in impulsivity and on the site of modulation. The results suggest one mechanism by which drugs that raise dopamine can enhance cognitive stability in some individuals (e.g. with ADHD), while enhancing cognitive flexibility in others, e.g. with Parkinson's disease. Specifically, anti-parkinson drugs such as L-Dopa might act to increase dopamine at the level of the striatum to potentiate cognitive flexibility, while stimulants like methylphenidate might act to increase dopamine at the level of the prefrontal cortex to potentiate cognitive stability (i.e. reducing distractibility).

What can neuropsychopharmacological studies tell us about ADHD and its treatment?

In this chapter, we have discussed Parkinson's disease, the insights it offers into the dopamine system and some of the insights that other dopamine research can bring to this condition. We have also mentioned ADHD. In this final section, we consider what the results of the studies reviewed so far may reveal about the treatment of this condition – one that, if you live in the US, may be diagnosed in up to one fifth of the boys in your state (Rader *et al.*, 2009).

ADHD is a psychiatric diagnosis made on the basis of observation of behaviour, and parent and teacher reports. It used to be called hyperkinetism (i.e. showing excessive movement), but, with revisions to diagnostic criteria, emphasis has broadened to include cognitive function. There are no established biomarkers or performance-based cognitive assessments that formally contribute to this diagnosis. To meet the criteria, you have to exhibit some (but not all: 12/18) of a list of characteristics, such as fidgeting or talking excessively, appearing 'on the go', having difficulty waiting your turn, being disorganized, disliking activities that require sustained mental effort and so on. In addition, you must have shown such traits before the age of 7 and in more than one context (e.g. school and home; American Psychiatric Association, 1994). This diagnosis is between two and four times more likely to be made in boys than girls – whether this reflects referral bias rather that real incidence remains controversial (Sciutto *et al.*, 2004). Although the diagnostic criteria have been lampooned (the satirical publication *The Onion* ran an exposé on 'Youthful Tendency Disorder' affecting an estimated 20 million US children with symptoms including running, jumping, twirling, dancing and entering states of make-believe (http://www.theonion.com/articles/more-us-children-being-diagnosed-with-youthful-ten, 248/), the diagnosis is nevertheless reliable – in the sense that two independent clinicians will agree – and there is surprisingly strong evidence of a high level of heritability (Khan and Farone, 2007).

The reason to discuss ADHD here is that differences in neurotransmitter function, particularly dopamine function, are widely viewed as contributory 'risk' factors (Acosta *et al.*, 2004) and treatment with dopamine-targeting agents such as methylphenidate is extremely common. Such treatments have been used since the 1930s and, whilst many have deep concerns about the administration of psychoactive medication to such large numbers of children, there are many trials attesting to their efficacy in calming behaviour and facilitating concentration. Remarkably, perhaps, the precise *mechanisms* whereby these effects are achieved are far from conclusively established. It is to these that we now turn. Not surprisingly, given what we have already covered, it is a complicated area. Those hoping for a complete and simple account are likely to be disappointed.

ADHD is increasingly recognized to be accompanied by deficits in inhibitory control, working memory and incentive motivation (Nigg and Casey, 2005). One type of hypothesis about how stimulant medication can possibly help people who are already 'on the go' stems from observations that dopamine in the ventral striatum is implicated in the relationship between salient or rewarding stimuli and behaviour. Such salient or rewarding stimuli are known to lead to a sudden high-amplitude ('phasic') burst of dopamine activity in the ventral striatum. One possibility is that these dopamine bursts are abnormal in ADHD, thereby leading to enhanced incentive motivation (i.e. the capacity of a reward to elicit (approach) behaviour) and impulsive behaviour. Various researchers have proposed that long-term treatment with methylphenidate might help to reduce impulsive behaviour by paradoxically attenuating reward-related phasic dopamine activity. Therefore, sustained increases in dopamine might reduce phasic bursting of dopamine neurons, thus reducing behaviour that is more determined by immediate reinforcement and less by careful consideration of cost: shall I complete my homework or the next level of this exciting computer game? How could such reward-based dopamine phasic release be reduced? Paradoxically, it seems by increasing the overall level of extracellular dopamine with a stimulant. Once again, self-regulatory mechanisms may be useful in explaining this – namely, that the induced high levels of dopamine trigger inhibitory processes in autoreceptors that damp down the short-term ('phasic') dopamine responses to rewarding stimuli and thereby reduce their influence over behaviour (see Figure 23.4; Grace, 2000, 2001; Seeman and Madras, 2002).

Is there any empirical support for this suggestion? Relevant evidence comes from studies examining baseline cerebrospinal fluid (CSF) in relation to stimulant drug responses (Shetty and Chase, 1976). Castellanos *et al.* (1994, 1996) found significant positive correlations between CSF levels of homovanillic acid (HVA, a metabolite of dopamine, see Figure 23.1) and teachers' ratings of hyperactivity in two subgroups of boys with ADHD. Critically, correlations between CSF HVA and stimulant drug responses were also positive, with the best drug response in subjects with the highest baseline HVA levels. Therefore, these findings are at least consistent with the idea that stimulants decrease hyperactivity by decreasing dopamine turnover in the striatum, with activation of inhibitory presynaptic autoreceptors being one possible mechanism.

Another way to study dopamine levels before and after methylphenidate medication is to use PET to monitor the concentration of radioactively labelled chemicals in the brain. This method can be used to track dopamine synthesis and release, dopamine transporter (DAT) density, the degree to which DAT is blocked by medication (called 'DAT occupancy') and dopamine receptor (D1, D2) densities. For technical reasons, these scans tend to tell us most

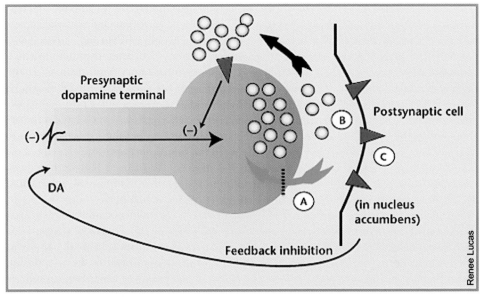

Figure 23.4 Schematic representation of the cellular actions of methylphenidate (MPH) in the ventral striatum (nucleus accumbens). MPH blocks the dopamine transporter (the green arrow, A), resulting in accumulation of dopamine (circles, B) in the synaptic cleft. Initially, this accumulation of dopamine could lead to increased postsynaptic receptor stimulation (triangles, C). However, in the long term, down-regulation of dopamine release takes place via a number of processes illustrated here (–), including the stimulation of presynaptic autoreceptors (see triangle on top). This down-regulation might underlie the, at first sight paradoxical, therapeutic effect of MPH in ADHD (Grace, 2001). Reprinted with permission from *Nature Medicine* (Robbins, 2002), copyright 2002.

about dopamine in the striatum (the signals from this region are stronger). Most recent results suggest that dopamine transporter density is reduced in adults with ADHD (Volkow *et al.*, 2007a; Hesse *et al.*, 2009), possibly leading to increased dopamine in the synapse (Figure 23.1), and that participants who show the greatest reductions also tend to have the highest ratings of inattention (Volkow *et al.*, 2009). A study has also indicated that stimulant medication causes *smaller, blunted* increases in dopamine release in people with ADHD compared with non-ADHD participants (Volkow *et al.*, 2007b). Together with observations that reduced dopamine release after methylphenidate in ADHD (Rosa-Neto *et al.*, 2005) and healthy volunteers (Clatworthy *et al.*, 2009) correlated with better performance, these observations can be reconciled with the hypothesis that improved performance after methylphenidate is associated paradoxically with a relative reduction in dopamine release. Finally, functional neuroimaging evidence supports the hypothesis that methylphenidate can have effects on striatal function in ADHD that are opposite to that seen in healthy volunteers (Vaidya *et al.*, 1998).

As we have seen, however, it is important not to take a single cognitive task and use this as the exclusive measure of function. Thus while some improvements might be mediated by relative reductions in phasic dopamine release in the striatum, other types of improvements might be mediated by more sustained increases in dopamine in other brain regions. Indeed, Clatworthy and colleagues (2009) have shown that a negative correlation between performance and methylphenidate-induced dopamine release was present only for reward-based reversal learning. It can be argued that improvements in reversal learning (adapting your responses along with changes to the rules governing what is rewarded) might particularly benefit from the damping down of striatal phasic dopamine responses. Conversely, the same study revealed a *positive* correlation between dopamine release and spatial working memory performance. Thus improvements in spatial working memory were associated with *greater* rather than smaller increases in dopamine after methylphenidate. It is indeed possible that drug-induced changes in cognitive functions such as working memory, distractor-resistance, sustained attention and response inhibition (Tannock *et al.*, 1989; Aron *et al.*, 2003; DeVito *et al.*, 2009) operate via different mechanisms than those proposed for reward-based learning. For example, methylphenidate is known to increase dopamine (and noradrenaline) levels also in the prefrontal cortex. Self-regulatory mechanisms are less abundant in the prefrontal cortex than in the striatum and accordingly, methylphenidate might not augment sustained levels of dopamine in the prefrontal cortex, while at the same time dampening phasic dopamine activity in the striatum. Working memory, distractor-resistance, sustained attention and response inhibition might benefit from amplification of dopamine transmission in the prefrontal cortex (Robbins, 2007; Engert and Pruessner, 2008). Instead of a single mechanism of stimulant effects, different models may be needed in accounting for diverse effects, most notably in the striatum and prefrontal cortex.

Baseline-dependency could also offer an explanation of the different uses and effects of psychostimulants in people without ADHD. Whereas some people without ADHD use (a high dose of) methylphenidate to party, others use it (in a low dose) to study. The short-term effects of a high dose of the immediate-release methylphenidate might activate the striatum, such that it increases hyperactivity and euphoria in healthy adults. This is in accordance with the finding that the psychostimulant D-amphetamine increased movement activity in normal adult men, but reduced it in boys with ADHD and, to a lesser degree, boys without this diagnosis (Rapoport *et al.*, 1980). Adults generally show lower activity levels than children and therefore, by inference, have greater scope for the activating effects of the stimulants. As we have seen in the arguments concerning reward processing, children – particularly those with ADHD – may be nearer to ceiling levels, such that the addition of more stimulation triggers self-regulation and reduces activity. However, it seems that self-regulatory processes may not always be enough (or fast enough). Even in adults with ADHD who generally show a calming influence from prescribed stimulants, a very high dose of the immediate-release version of methylphenidate or D-amphetamine can lead to reinforcement, reward and euphoria as the dopamine transporter is saturated, leaving greater concentrations of dopamine in the synaptic cleft (Stahl, 2008). The risk of this is greatly reduced when long-acting controlled-release methylphenidate (such as Concerta) is used. Such slow release may help to enhance sustained ('tonic'), extracellular dopamine levels in prefrontal cortex and striatum.

We have seen how common variants of genes in the normal population influence response to stimulants. As discussed earlier, while some of these effects are reminiscent of ADHD, it is important to stress that ADHD is not, for example, synonymous with having the Val variant of the COMT gene. Rather ADHD (or varieties of ADHD) are thought to arise from a complex interplay of genetic and environmental influences. However, data from recent work highlights how genetic variables may further complicate response to stimulants in ADHD diagnosed individuals. For example, in one study, ADHD participants with the Val allele showed greater benefits from increased prefrontal levels of dopamine than those with the Met variety (Kereszturi *et al.*, 2008). However, studies addressing the possible involvement of the variants in the dopamine transporter gene in ADHD have produced ambiguous results. Some have reported an association between better responses to methylphenidate and possession of a certain variant of a gene influencing the amount of dopamine transporters (the catchily entitled 10-repeat allele of the 40bp VNTR in the 3'untranslated region of the *DAT1*,

SLC6A3 (Kirley *et al.*, 2003; Joober *et al.*, 2007; Lott *et al.*, 2005; Stein *et al.*, 2005). Other studies have reported the opposite association (Winsberg and Comings, 1999; Roman *et al.*, 2002; Cheon *et al.*, 2005) or no association (Langley *et al.*, 2005; Mick *et al.*, 2006; van der Meulen *et al.*, 2005; Zeni *et al.*, 2007). However, these clinical studies have not taken into account the functional specificity of dopamine's effects, which, as reviewed above, will depend on task demands and associated neural systems. Future pharmaco-genetic work should recognize the multi-componential nature of impulsivity (Evenden, 1999) and combine sophisticated neurocognitive measurements with functional neuroimaging to enable assessment of task-specificity and the neural locus of the drug's action.

Conclusions

Accumulating evidence from work with healthy volunteers indicates that drugs that influence the dopamine system can have diametrically opposite effects. Contrasting effects are observed in different individuals and as a function of different task demands. These differences may be attributed, at least in part, to individual differences in baseline dopamine function and reflect the existence of distinct optimal dopamine levels for different functions mediated by different brain regions. These factors also likely play a role in the paradoxical effects of psychostimulants in ADHD. Specifically, methylphenidate might reduce hyperactivity and impulsivity by attenuating dopamine release in the striatum in response to salient events such as rewards, while also enhancing working memory and distractor-resistance by potentiating more sustained extracellular dopamine levels in the prefrontal cortex. Baseline-dependency can explain why the same dopaminergic drugs can have activating effects in individuals without ADHD and, at the same time, calming effects in individuals with ADHD. It can also account for the cognitive-enhancing versus cognitively impairing effects of dopaminergic medication in Parkinson's disease on functions associated with the depleted dorsal and intact ventral striatum respectively. Overall this work demonstrates how advances in cognitive neuroscience contribute to resolving apparent paradoxes in neuropsychopharmacology and also illustrates the complexity of the experimental work needed to draw inferences about underlying function.

Future challenges and questions

Assessments of the relationships between brain, cognition and behaviour have greatly increased our knowledge of the neurocognitive effects of pharmacological manipulations. However, there are still paradoxes left unexplained. For example, in the domain of ADHD, the exact underlying mechanism of the therapeutic action of stimulants is still debated. This debate might in future be resolved by taking into account the different (fast phasic vs. more sustained tonic) modes and functional specificity in different brain regions (e.g. striatum versus prefrontal cortex) of catecholamine action.

In human research, advances in our understanding of the phasic and tonic modes of catecholamine action currently relies heavily on computational modelling with a relative lack of experimental data. Techniques that can measure changes in dopamine activity and/ or release in vivo over a time-frame of milliseconds[4] will be necessary to inform the development of more precise models.

---

[4] For example, single cell recording, electrochemical voltammetry and optogenetic methods.

The study of common genetic variations in the general population and the in-vivo tracking of neurochemistry using positron emission tomography (PET) have offered early insights into baseline-dependency and the neurochemical specificity of drug effects. However, such studies have often used broad, non-specific measures such as clinical symptom ratings as the primary dependent measures. In future work, it will be important to recognize the multi-faceted nature of constructs such as 'impulsivity' (Evenden, 1999). It will also be important to combine sophisticated cognitive measurements with functional neuroimaging to enable assessment of task-specificity and the neural locus of a drug's action. Combining psychopharmaco-genetics with PET imaging might be able to further explain, for example, why some individuals with Parkinson's disease become addicted to their medication, whilst others using the same medication do not. A multimodal approach that is able to capture both genetic and adaptive variations in baseline neurotransmitter levels – in different brain regions associated with different task demands – will elucidate further why drug responses differ across individuals and contexts.

References

Acosta, M. T., Arcos-Burgos, M., & Muenke, M. (2004). Attention deficit/hyperactivity disorder (ADHD): complex phenotype, simple genotype? *Genetics in Medicine*, **6**: 1–15.

Akil, M., Kolachana, B. S., Rothmond, D. A., Hyde, T. M., Weinberger, D. R., Kleinman, J. E. (2003). Catechol-*O*-methyltransferase genotype and dopamine regulation in the human brain. *Journal of Neuroscience*, **23**: 2008–13.

Alexander, G., DeLong, M., & Stuck, P. (1986). Parallel organisation of functionally segregated circuits linking basal ganglia and cortex. *Annual Review of Neuroscience*, **9**: 357–81.

Altunç, U., Pittler, M. H., & Ernst, E. (2007). Homeopathy for childhood and adolescence ailments: systematic review of randomized clinical trials. *Mayo Clinic Proceedings*, **82**: 69–75.

American Psychiatric Association. (1994). *Diagnostic and Statistical Manual of Mental Disorders*, 4th Edition. Washington, DC: American Psychiatric Association.

Arnsten, A. F. (1998). Catecholamine modulation of prefrontal cortical cognitive function. *Trends in Cognitive Science*, **2**: 436–46.

Aron, A., Dowson, J., Sahakian, B., & Robbins, T. (2003). Methylphenidate improves response inhibition in adults with attention-deficit/hyperactivity disorder. *Biological Psychiatry*, **54**: 1465–8.

Artigas, F. (1993). 5-HT and antidepressants: new views from microdialysis studies. *Trends in Pharmacological Science*, **14**: 262.

Baddeley, A. D. (1986). *Working Memory*. Oxford: Clarendon Press.

Blier, P., & de Montigny, C. (1999). Serotonin and drug-induced therapeutic responses in major depression, obsessive-compulsive and panic disorders. *Neuropsychopharmacology*, **21**: 91S–98S.

Bond, R. A. (2001). Is paradoxical pharmacology a strategy worth pursuing? *Trends in Pharmacological Science*, **22**: 273–6.

Burghardt, N., Sullivan, G., McEwen, B., Gorman, J., & LeDoux, J. E. (2004). The selective serotonin reuptake inhibitor citalopram increases fear after acute treatment but reduces fear with chronic treatment: a comparison with tianeptine. *Biological Psychiatry*, **55**: 1171–8.

Calabrese, E. J. (2008). Converging concepts: adaptive response, preconditioning, and the Yerkes–Dodson Law are manifestations of hormesis. *Ageing Research Reviews*, **7**: 8–20.

Castellanos, F. X., Elia, J., Kruesi, M. J., *et al.* (1994). Cerebrospinal fluid monoamine metabolites in boys with attention-deficit hyperactivity disorder. *Psychiatry Research*, **52**: 305–16.

Castellanos, F. X., Elia, J., Kruesi, M. J., *et al.* (1996). Cerebrospinal fluid homovanillic acid predicts behavioral response to stimulants in 45 boys with attention deficit/hyperactivity disorder. *Neuropsychopharmacology*, **14**: 125–37.

Cheon, K. A., Ryu, Y. H., Kim, J. W., & Cho, D. Y. (2005). The homozygosity for 10-repeat allele at dopamine transporter gene and dopamine transporter density in Korean children with attention deficit hyperactivity disorder: relating to treatment response to methylphenidate. *European Neuropsychopharmacology*, **15**: 95–101.

Clatworthy, P. L., Lewis, S. J., Brichard, L., *et al.* (2009). Dopamine release in dissociable striatal subregions predicts the different effects of oral methylphenidate on reversal learning and spatial working memory. *Journal of Neuroscience*, **29**: 4690–6.

Colzato, L. S., Waszak, F., Nieuwenhuis, S., Posthuma, D., & Hommel, B. (2010). The flexible mind is associated with the catechol-*O*-methyltransferase (COMT) Val158Met polymorphism: evidence for a role of dopamine in the control of task-switching. *Neuropsychologia*, **48**: 2764–8.

Cools, R., Barker, R. A., Sahakian, B. J., & Robbins, T. W. (2001). Enhanced or impaired cognitive function in Parkinson's disease as a function of dopaminergic medication and task demands. *Cerebral Cortex*, **11**: 1136–43.

Cools, R., Barker, R. A., Sahakian, B. J., & Robbins, T. W. (2003). L-Dopa medication remediates cognitive inflexibility, but increases impulsivity in patients with Parkinson's disease. *Neuropsychologia*, **41**: 1431–41.

Cools, R., Frank, M., Gibbs, S., Miyakawa, A., Jagust, W., & D'Esposito, M. (2009). Striatal dopamine synthesis capacity predicts dopaminergic drug effects on flexible outcome learning. *Journal of Neuroscience*, **29**: 1538–43.

Cools, R., Gibbs, S., Miyakawa, A., Jagust, W., & D'Esposito, M. (2008). Working memory capacity predicts dopamine synthesis capacity in the human striatum. *Journal of Neuroscience*, **28**: 1208–12.

Cools, R., Lewis, S., Clark, L., Barker, R., & Robbins, T. W. (2007b). L-DOPA disrupts activity in the nucleus accumbens during reversal learning in Parkinson's disease. *Neuropsychopharmacology*, **32**: 180–9.

Cools, R., Sheridan, M., Jacobs, E., & D'Esposito, M. (2007a). Impulsive personality predicts dopamine-dependent changes in frontostriatal activity during component processes of working memory. *Journal of Neuroscience*, **27**: 5506–14.

Cooper, J., Bloom, F., & Roth, R. (2003). *The Biochemical Basis of Neuropharmacology*, 8th Edition. Oxford: Oxford University Press.

Cramer, S. C. (2008a). Repairing the human brain after stroke. II. Restorative therapies. *Annals of Neurology*, **63**: 549–60.

Cramer, S. C. (2008b). Repairing the human brain after stroke: I. Mechanisms of spontaneous recovery. *Annals of Neurology*, **63**: 272–87.

Crofts, H. S., Dalley, J. W., Van Denderen, J. C., Everitt, B. J., Robbins, T. W., & Roberts, A. C. (2001). Differential effects of 6-OHDA lesions of the frontal cortex and caudate nucleus on the ability to acquire an attentional set. *Cerebral Cortex*, **11**: 1015–26.

DeVito, E. E., Blackwell, A. D., Clark, L., *et al.* (2009). Methylphenidate improves response inhibition but not reflection-impulsivity in children with attention deficit hyperactivity disorder (ADHD). *Psychopharmacology (Berlin)*, **202**: 531–9.

Diamond, A., Briand, L., Fossella, J., & Gehlbach, L. (2004). Genetic and neurochemical modulation of prefrontal cognitive functions in children. *Archives of General Psychiatry*, **161**: 125–32.

Egan, M. F., Goldberg, T. E., Kolachana, B. S., *et al.* (2001). Effect of COMT Val108/158 Met genotype on frontal lobe function and risk for schizophrenia. *Proceedings of the National Academy of Sciences of the USA*, **98**: 6917–22.

Engert, V., & Pruessner, J. C. (2008). Dopaminergic and noradrenergic contributions to functionality in ADHD: the role of methylphenidate. *Current Neuropharmacology*, **6**: 322–8.

Evenden, J. (1999). Varieties of impulsivity. *Psychopharmacology*, **146**: 348–61.

Frank, M. J., & O'Reilly, R. C. (2006). A mechanistic account of striatal dopamine function in human cognition: psychopharmacological studies with cabergoline and haloperidol. *Behavioral Neuroscience*, **120**: 497–517.

Gibbs, S. E., & D'Esposito, M. (2005). A functional MRI study of the effects of bromocriptine, a dopamine receptor agonist, on component processes of working memory. *Psychopharmacology (Berlin)*, **180**: 644–53.

Gotham, A. M., Brown, R. G., & Marsden, C. D. (1988). 'Frontal' cognitive function in patients with Parkinson's disease 'on' and 'off' levodopa. *Brain*, **111**: 299–321.

Grace, A. (2000). The tonic/phasic model of dopamine system regulation and its implications for understanding alcohol and psychostimulant craving. *Addiction*, **95**: S119–28.

Grace, A. (2001). Psychostimulant actions on dopamine and limbic system function: relevance to the pathophysiology and treatment of ADHD. In: Solanto, M., Arnsten, A., & Castellanos, F. (Eds.). *Stimulant Drugs and ADHD. Basic and Clinical Neuroscience* . Oxford: Oxford University Press, pp. 134–57.

Granon, S., Passetti, F., Thomas, K. L., Dalley, J. W., Everitt, B. J., & Robbins, T. (2000). Enhanced and impaired attentional performance after infusion of D1 dopaminergic receptor agents into rat prefrontal cortex. *Journal of Neuroscience*, **20**: 1208–15.

Harmer, C. J., Bhagwagar, Z., Perrett, D. I., Vollm, B. A., Cowen, P. J., & Goodwin, G. M. (2003). Acute SSRI administration affects the processing of social cues in healthy volunteers. *Neuropsychopharmacology*, **28**: 148–52.

Hesse, S., Ballaschke, O., Barthel, H., & Sabri, O. (2009). Dopamine transporter imaging in adult patients with attention-deficit/hyperactivity disorder. *Psychiatry Research*, **171**: 120–8.

Joober, R., Grizenko, N., Sengupta, S., *et al.* (2007). Dopamine transporter 3'UTR VNTR genotype and ADHD: a pharmaco-behavioural genetic study with methylphenidate. *Neuropsychopharmacology*, **32**: 1370–6.

Kereszturi, E., Tarnok, Z., Bognar, E., *et al.* (2008). Catechol-O-methyltransferase Val158Met polymorphism is associated with methylphenidate response in ADHD children. *American Journal of Medical Genetics. Part B, Neuropsychiatric Genetics*, **147B**: 1431–5.

Khan, S. A., & Faraone, S. V. (2007). The genetics of ADHD: a literature review of 2005. *Current Psychiatry Reports*, **8**: 393–7.

Kimberg, D. Y., D'Esposito, M., & Farah, M. J. (1997). Effects of bromocriptine on human subjects depend on working memory capacity. *Neuroreport*, **8**: 3581–5.

Kirley, A., Lowe, N., Hawi, Z., *et al.* (2003). Association of the 480 bp DAT1 allele with methylphenidate response in a sample of Irish children with ADHD. *American Journal of Medical Genetics. Part B, Neuropsychiatric Genetics*, **121B**: 50–4.

Kish, S. J., Shannak, K., & Hornykiewicz, O. (1988). Uneven patterns of dopamine loss in the striatum of patients with idiopathic Parkinson's disease. *New England Journal of Medicine*, **318**: 876–80.

Koelega, H. S. (1993). Stimulant drugs and vigilance performance: a review. *Psychopharmacology*, **111**: 1–16.

Krugel, L. K., Biele, G., Mohr, P. N., Li, S. C., & Heekeren, H. R. (2009). Genetic variation in dopaminergic neuromodulation influences the ability to rapidly and flexibly adapt decisions. *Proceedings of the National Academy of Sciences of the USA*, **106**: 17,951–6.

Langley, K., Turic, D., Peirce, T. R., *et al.* (2005). No support for association between the dopamine transporter (DAT1) gene and ADHD. *American Journal of Medical Genetics. Part B, Neuropsychiatric Genetics*, **139B**: 7–10.

Lott, D. C., Kim, S. J., Cook, E. H., Jr., & de Wit, H. (2005). Dopamine transporter gene associated with diminished subjective response to amphetamine. *Neuropsychopharmacology*, **30**: 602–09.

Mattay, V., Goldberg, T., Fera, F., *et al.* (2003). Catechol *O*-methyltransferase *Val*[158]-*met* genotype and individual variation in the brain response to amphetamine. *Proceedings of the National Academy of Sciences USA*, **100**: 6186–91.

Mehta, M., Owen, A. M., Sahakian, B. J., Mavaddat, N., Pickard, J. D., & Robbins, T. W. (2000). Methylphenidate enhances working memory by modulating discrete frontal and parietal lobe regions in the human brain. *Journal of Neuroscience*, **20**: RC65.

Meyer-Lindenberg, A., Kohn, P. D., Kolachana, B., *et al.* (2005). Midbrain dopamine and prefrontal function in humans: interaction and modulation by COMT genotype. *Nature Neuroscience*, **8**: 594–6.

Meyer-Lindenberg, A., Miletich, R. S., Kohn, P. D., *et al.* (2002). Reduced prefrontal activity predicts exaggerated striatal dopaminergic function in schizophrenia. *Nature Neuroscience*, **5**: 267–71.

Mick, E., Biederman, J., Spencer, T., Faraone, S. V., & Sklar, P. (2006). Absence of association with DAT1 polymorphism and response to methylphenidate in a sample of adults with ADHD. *American Journal of Medical Genetics. Part B Neuropsychiatric Genetics*, **141B**: 890–4.

Mier, D., Kirsch, P., & Meyer-Lindenberg, A. (2010). Neural substrates of pleiotropic action of genetic variation in COMT: a meta-analysis. *Molecular Psychiatry*, **15**: 918–27.

Nigg, J., & Casey, B. (2005). An integrative theory of attention-deficit/hyperactivity disorder based on the cognitive and affective neurosciences. *Developmental Psychopathology*, **17**: 785–806.

Nolan, K., Bilder, R., Lachman, H., & Volavka, K. (2004). Catechol *O*-Methyltransferase Val158Met polymorphism in schizophrenia: differential effects of Val and Met alleles on cognitive stability and flexibility. *American Journal of Psychiatry*, **161**: 359–61.

Phillips, A., Ahn, S., & Floresco, S. (2004). Magnitude of dopamine release in medial prefrontal cortex predicts accuracy of memory on a delayed response task. *Journal of Neuroscience*, **14**: 547–53.

Pizzolato, G., Soncrant, T. T., & Rapoport, S. I. (1985). Time-course and regional distribution of the metabolic effects of bromocriptine in the rat brain. *Brain Research*, **341**: 303–12.

Pycock, C. J., Kerwin, R. W., & Carter, C. J. (1980). Effect of lesion of cortical dopamine terminals on subcortical dopamine receptors in rats. *Nature*, **286**: 74–7.

Rader, R., McCauley, L., & Callen, E. C. (2009). Current strategies in the diagnosis and treatment of childhood attention-deficit/hyperactivity disorder. *American Family Physician*, **79**: 657–65.

Rapoport, J., Buchsbaum, M., Weingartner, H., Zahn, T., Ludlow, C., & Mikkelsen, E. (1980). Dextroamphetamine. Its cognitive and behavioral effects in normal and hyperactive boys and normal men. *Archives of General Psychiatry*, **37**: 933–43.

Robbins, T. (2007). Shifting and stopping: fronto-striatal substrates, neurochemical modulation and clinical implications. *Philosophical Transactions of the Royal Society B: Biological Sciences*, **362**: 917–32.

Robbins, T. W. (2002). ADHD and addiction. *Nature Medicine*, **8**: 24–5.

Robbins, T. W., & Everitt, B. J. (1987). Psychopharmacological studies of arousal and attention. In: Stahl, S., Iversen, S., & Goodman, E. (Eds.). *Cognitive Neurochemistry*. Oxford: Oxford University Press.

Robbins, T. W., & Sahakian, B. J. (1979). 'Paradoxical' effects of psychomotor stimulant drugs in hyperactive children from the standpoint fo behavioural pharmacology. *Neuropharmacology*, **18**: 931–50.

Roberts, A. C., De Salvia, M. A., Wilkinson, L. S., *et al.* (1994). 6-Hydroxydopamine lesions of the prefrontal cortex in monkeys enhance performance on an analog of the Wisconsin card sort test: possible interactions with subcortical dopamine. *Journal of Neuroscience*, **14**: 2531–44.

Roman, T., Szobot, C., Martins, S., Biederman, J., Rohde, L. A., & Hutz, M. H. (2002). Dopamine transporter gene and response to methylphenidate in attention-deficit/

hyperactivity disorder. *Pharmacogenetics*, 12: 497–9.

Rosa-Neto, P., Lou, H. C., Cumming, P., et al. (2005). Methylphenidate-evoked changes in striatal dopamine correlate with inattention and impulsivity in adolescents with attention deficit hyperactivity disorder. *Neuroimage*, 25: 868–76.

Sciutto, M. J., Nolfi, C. J., & Bluhm, C. (2004). Effects of child gender and symptom type on referrals for ADHD by elementary school teachers. *Journal of Emotional and Behavioural Disorders*, 12: 247–53.

Seeman, P., & Madras, B. (2002). Methylphenidate elevates resting dopamine which lowers the impulse-triggered release of dopamine: a hypothesis. *Behavior and Brain Research*, 130: 79–83.

Shetty, T., & Chase, T. N. (1976). Central monoamines and hyperkinase of childhood. *Neurology*, 26: 1000–02.

Stahl, S. (2008). *Stahl's Essential Psychopharmacology. Neuroscientific Basis and Clinical Applications*, 3rd Edition. Cambridge: Cambridge University Press.

Stein, M. A., Waldman, I. D., Sarampote, C. S., et al. (2005). Dopamine transporter genotype and methylphenidate dose response in children with ADHD. *Neuropsychopharmacology*, 30: 1374–82.

Swainson, R., Rogers, R. D., Sahakian, B. J., Summers, B. A., Polkey, C. E., & Robbins, T. W. (2000). Probabilistic learning and reversal deficits in patients with Parkinson's disease or frontal or temporal lobe lesions: possible adverse effects of dopaminergic medication. *Neuropsychologia*, 38: 596–612.

Tannock, R., Schachar, R. J., Carr, R. P., Chajczyk, D., & Logan, G. D. (1989). Effects of methylphenidate on inhibitory control in hyperactive children. *Journal of Abnormal Child Psychology*, 17: 473–91.

Teicher, M., Polcari, A., Anderson, C., Anderson, S., Lowen, S., & Navalta, C. (2003). Rate dependency revisited: understanding the effects of methylphenidate in children with attention hyperactivity disorder. *Journal of Child and Adolescent Psychopharmacology*, 13: 41–51.

Torstenson, R., Hartvig, P., Langstrom, B., Bastami, S., Antoni, G., & Tedroff, J. (1998). Effect of apomorphine infusion on dopamine synthesis rate relates to dopaminergic tone. *Neuropharmacology*, 37: 989–95.

Vaidya, D., Austin, G., Kirkorian, G., et al. (1998). Selective effects of methylphenidate in attention deficit hyperactivity disorder: a functional magnetic study. *Proceedings of the National Academy of Sciences*, 95: 14,494–9.

van der Meulen, E. M., Bakker, S. C., Pauls, D. L., et al. (2005). High sibling correlation on methylphenidate response but no association with DAT1–10R homozygosity in Dutch sibpairs with ADHD. *Journal of Child Psychology and Psychiatry*, 46: 1074–80.

Vijayraghavan, S., Wang, M., Birnbaum, S., Williams, G., & Arnsten, A. (2007). Inverted-U dopamine D1 receptor actions on prefrontal neurons engaged in working memory. *Nature Neuroscience*, 10: 176–84.

Volkow, N. D., Wang, G. J., Kollins, S. H., et al. (2009). Evaluating dopamine reward pathway in ADHD: clinical implications. *Journal of the American Medical Association*, 302: 1084–91.

Volkow, N. D., Wang, G. J., Newcorn, J., et al. (2007a). Brain dopamine transporter levels in treatment and drug naive adults with ADHD. *Neuroimage*, 34: 1182–90.

Volkow, N. D., Wang, G. J., Newcorn, J., et al. (2007b). Depressed dopamine activity in caudate and preliminary evidence of limbic involvement in adults with attention-deficit/ hyperactivity disorder. *Archives of General Psychiatry*, 64: 932–40.

Williams, G. V., & Goldman-Rakic, P. S. (1995). Modulation of memory fields by dopamine D1 receptors in prefrontal cortex. *Nature*, 376: 572–5.

Winsberg, B. G., & Comings, D. E. (1999). Association of the dopamine transporter gene (DAT1) with poor methylphenidate response. *Journal of the American Academy of Child and Adolescent Psychiatry*, 38: 1474–7.

Yerkes, R. M., & Dodson, J. D. (1908). The relation of the strength of stimulus to the rapidity of habit formation. *Journal of*

Comparative Neurology and Psychology, **18**: 459–82.

Yun, A. J., Doux, J., Daniel, S., *et al.* (2007). Brewing controversies: Darwinian perspective on the adaptive and maladaptive effects of caffeine and ethanol as dietary autonomic modulators. *Medical Hypotheses,* **68**: 31–6.

Yun, A. J., Lee, P., Bazarm, K., *et al.* (2005). Paradoxical strategy for treating chronic diseases where therapeutic effect is derived from compensatory response rather than drug effect. *Medical Hypotheses,* **64**: 1050–9.

Zahrt, J., Taylor, J. R., Mathew, R. G., & Arnsten, A. F. (1997). Supranormal stimulation of D1 dopamine receptors in the rodent prefrontal cortex impairs spatial working memory performance. *Journal of Neurosciecnce,* **17**: 8528–35.

Zeni, C. P., Guimaraes, A. P., Polanczyk, G. V., *et al.* (2007). No significant association between response to methylphenidate and genes of the dopaminergic and serotonergic systems in a sample of Brazilian children with attention-deficit/hyperactivity disorder. *American Journal of Medical Genetics. Part B Neuropsychiatric Genetics,* **144B**: 391–4.

The paradoxical brain – so what?

Narinder Kapur, Tom Manly, Jonathan Cole
and Alvaro Pascual-Leone

Summary

Paradoxical findings relating to the human brain have implications for our understanding of the workings of the normal brain, and for how normal functioning may be enhanced. Paradoxical findings may also have implications for how we can prevent and detect brain disease, and how we may best repair and rehabilitate the damaged brain. The brain may best be modelled as a nonlinear device, which relies on dynamic synchrony and balance between neural systems. Damage to the brain may upset this dynamic state, and repair may often entail interventions that restore a degree of synchrony and balance. In this final chapter, we propose 10 principles of brain function that can help accommodate paradoxical phenomena, and we also speculate on paradoxical therapeutic interventions that may be beneficial to human brain functioning.

Figure 24.1 'Paradoxemeter' by Pablo Bernasconi, reproduced with permission.

Introduction

If we can be forgiven a degree of owner's pride, the human brain is quite extraordinary. A three-pound mass of jelly-like material is the only entity in the universe (that we know of) which can form and test theories about that universe. It can also speculate about structures much smaller or larger than it can possibly see. It might be thought that, when it comes to studying itself, the brain would have a number of inherent advantages, being on home turf, as it were. It is certainly true that we are very familiar with what the brain can achieve. How it does this, how this electrochemical mass of 86 billion cells (Herculano-Houzel, 2009), with reportedly 1000 trillion synaptic connections, gives rise to syntax, self-consciousness, sonnets, symphonies, schizophrenia, self-destructive urges and science, is a mystery and a challenge to match those of the 'big bang', DNA and the quark.

In attempting to understand the brain, we are essentially being asked to reverse-engineer a supercomputer that we did not build and for which we have no manual. There are many ways to do this – from examining the biochemistry of the synapse, to in-vivo brain imaging, to examination of the effects of perturbations of the brain on function. The latter may include electrical stimulation, pharmacological intervention and lesions. At each level of analysis, the paradox – the finding that is contrary to existing principles – is a locked door. If we can find the key to that door, if we can see how that paradox comes about, better understanding will generally follow.

When we started this book, we had a general idea as to what we meant by paradoxes relating to brain function. There were a number of 'established principles' which, in the context of discrepant observations, led to the occurrence of paradoxical findings. These established principles have included (this list is not meant to be exhaustive!):

- sensory loss invariably results in deficits in performance;
- a damaged brain is a cognitively suboptimal brain;
- more damage to the brain leads to more impairment;
- lesions to an already damaged brain makes an existing condition worse;
- psychiatric disorder is always associated with below-normal cognitive functioning;
- distraction results in impaired cognition;
- infants do not function better than adults;
- the elderly are cognitively impaired compared to their younger counterparts;
- distortions to reality impede function;
- experts have superior cognitive functioning across the board; and
- non-human species perform at suboptimal levels compared to human beings.

Principles such as these are generally concordant with evidence that has been assembled over the years, and they are often well-founded. However, it is the unexpected and counter-intuitive exceptions to these principles which lead to phenomena that are labelled 'paradoxical', and to the search for new sets of principles which may accommodate evidence that deviates from the expected. Thus, for example, at the epidemiological level, we have learned that one disease may sometimes prevent another. At the developmental level, we have seen that there may be a nonlinear correspondence between the age of the brain and level of performance. At the biochemical and biological level, we have learned that benefits come with costs, and that to produce benefit may require an intervention that initially may be detrimental.

Many apparently paradoxical phenomena occur because our understanding of how the brain works is incomplete. Explanations of such paradoxes present a picture of the brain as a highly plastic, dynamic, nonlinear, network-based biological system. Such phenomena point to a system where functional trade-offs emanate from the operation of brain networks, and where these trade-offs may sometimes be associated with deficits occurring in parallel with evidence of superior functioning. The system appears to rely on delicate balances and synchronies, such as those between inhibitory and excitatory systems. Lesions, and forms of direct or indirect brain stimulation may, on occasions, help restore a degree of balance or synchrony, and thus generate seemingly paradoxical treatments for particular neurological and psychiatric conditions.

The optimization pressures of Darwinian natural selection have shaped the human brain. This is not to suggest that its function in any given context or task is optimal. Rather, that from a given starting point, more optimal trade-offs between competing factors such as computational efficiency, weight, energy consumption, etc., have accumulated, through the failure of less-optimal solutions to thrive. It is not, therefore, a 'perfect' machine designed *de novo* by an engineer (Krubitzer, 2007). Indeed, if it were such a machine, we are not sure of the single purpose, or purposes, for which it might have been designed. Evolved structures can be good for some tasks, but not so good for others, and the resultant evolutionary compromises may make for paradoxes in behaviour. This scenario may also promote competing activities across brain networks, in turn encouraging paradoxical phenomena to occur.

Just as natural selection can be viewed as an optimization mechanism, the brain can itself be considered as an optimization machine. Its business is to optimize neuronal processing and (implicitly) adaptive fitness – fitness in differentiating and attending to relevant stimuli, fitness in making predictions and sensible decisions, fitness in everything we do. An optimization perspective is useful because complex systems 'searching' for good solutions will have to traverse valleys of (apparently paradoxical) suboptimality to get there.

In this final chapter, we consider more general implications of paradoxical brain phenomena. This chapter will of necessity be somewhat speculative, and we ask for tolerance where we stray too far from an empirical path.

1. The paradoxical brain – what sort of brain may produce paradoxical phenomena?

Paradoxical phenomena in neuroscience represent a theoretical challenge to models of brain function (Young *et al.*, 1999). Karl Pribram, whose 1971 book included references to several paradoxes in brain research, commented, 'My courses [on the brain] centred on the puzzles and paradoxes uncovered by experiment. What was lacking was some overall structure, some coherent set of principles with which to approach these paradoxes' (Pribram, 1971, p. 391). To an extent we still lack such principles, but we suggest that paradoxical phenomena can best be accommodated within a framework that incorporates at least some of the following 10 'principles' of brain function. Our classification is inevitably somewhat arbitrary – one principle might arise as a consequence of another – and we imply no hierarchy (principle 1 is no more important than principle 10).

(1) *Hierarchical representation.* In the case of language, for example, representations will range from early visual or auditory perception of letters and sounds through to high-level processing of meaning. Distinct but related representations within the brain can include those with contrasting, even opposing, features (cf. Botvinick, 2008). This can lead to

paradoxes in which particular facility at one level may impede use or access at another level. In Chapter 3, for example, we saw how in the healthy population memory for gist can lead to false memories for the precise words presented in an experiment and how patients with memory impairments may be less vulnerable to this cognitive illusion. Similarly, enhanced attention to visual detail may, in some patients, be at the cost of seeing the overall picture – essentially being unable to see the wood for the trees (see Halligan and Marshall, 1994, and also Chapters 3 and 15 in this book). There is an emerging view of the brain as a statistical learning device that tests predictions (prior beliefs) and updates them on the basis of sometimes scant available information. This view dates back to Helmholtz (1866), and has been articulated in psychology by researchers such as Gregory (1980), who regarded perception as a form of statistical inference. Others have formulated hierarchical inference in the brain within a Bayesian framework that is closely linked to cortical neuroanatomy (Mumford, 1992; Friston, 2008; George and Hawkins, 2009). Hierarchical models lend themselves to top-down and bottom-up interactions that help to regulate activity in certain brain systems. Such reciprocal interactions may be evident, for example, in the interaction between frontal/anterior temporal lobe systems and more posterior, sensory systems (e.g. Beck and Kastner, 2009), and also between subcortical and cortical systems (e.g. Varga et al., 2009).

(2) *Network organization.* It is now recognized that one of the key features of the human brain is not its size, nor the number of neurons it contains, but the connectivity between networks of specialized modules (Chittka and Niven, 2009). The functions of the brain sometimes appear surprisingly robust to the effects of damage. The representation of information across multiple brain areas is one factor that may underpin this resilience (Finger, 2009). Varied organization of interconnected networks may render them more or less vulnerable to damage. Thus, networks in which nodes are randomly interconnected, which feature many long-scale connections, or which have significant information bottlenecks, appear more susceptible to disruption. By contrast, networks characterized by dense, locally highly interconnected clusters, with relatively few long-scale connections between these clusters (so-called 'small world models'), appear robust. While the necessary in-vivo imaging of functional connectivity in the human brain remains at an early stage, there are suggestions that the organization of the brain may correspond more to this latter class of networks (Young et al., 2000; Kaiser et al., 2007; Bullmore et al., 2009; Barabasi, 2007, 2009). Much remains to be learned about the impact of such organization on, for example, recovery from brain injury. Such observations provide a basis, however, for the apparent paradox of why large lesions may sometimes produce only minor disruption to cognition or behaviour, whilst small lesions can sometimes have devastating effects (see Chapter 3). Analysis of connectivity between networks in conditions such as autism may also yield evidence for the paradoxical occurrence of greater order in some forms of brain 'abnormality' (de Haan et al., 2009). Background intrinsic neural activity may also be a major factor when considering functional connectivity between networks and the patterns of activations in response to task demands (Zhang and Raichle, 2010).

(3) *Fine-grained temporal synchrony.* In addition to spatial representation, neural function is also about timing – ranging from the firing rate of individual cells to oscillations across networks. Temporal synchrony in the activity of brain networks, and the coding of that synchrony, are important (Uhlhaas et al., 2009). This allows for representation of

temporally distributed and temporally aligned forms of neural codes (cf. Zufall, 2005; Gregoriou *et al.*, 2009). Synchronous activity may also have a cost or risk, as in the hypersynchrony that is often associated with epileptic activity (e.g. Dauwels *et al.*, 2009). Some forms of creativity in neurological conditions and psychiatric disorders might also be framed in terms of hypersynchronous activity, where divergent ideas are pulled together into a meaningful original whole (cf. Chapters 12 and 16). Once again, we see how changes in the balance of mechanisms necessary for normal functioning may lead to impairment and also paradoxical advantage in certain individuals or contexts.

(4) *Multifunctionality.* The concept of multifunctionality is common to a number of biological systems, and is akin to the concepts of pluripotency in stem cell research and pleiotropy in genetics. Specific neural structures may be capable of performing several distinct, discrete functions, thus enabling flexibility in domains such as encoding, storage and retrieval (cf. Briggman and Kristan, 2008). Multifunctionality can, in principle, give rise to paradoxical phenomena. For example, if activity in a region facilitates function A, but if the same activity impedes function B, in which it is also involved, then individual differences in this activity may lead to groups whose excellence in some tasks is inevitably tinged by disadvantage in others. Damage to such a region might also lead to apparently paradoxical 'superfunctioning' in B. Similarly, if a region is involved in multiple processes and these interfere or compete under normal circumstances, damage that disproportionately compromises one function may lead to enhancement of the other.

(5) *Degeneracy (diverse routes to function).* Just as part of the brain may be involved in multiple and diverse functions (point 4), a given function may be achieved in a number of ways. The notion that structurally or computationally different elements may perform the same function or generate the same output is a feature found in a number of biological systems, ranging from genetics to immune systems. The term 'degeneracy' has been applied to describe such properties (Edelman and Gally, 2001), although, unhelpfully, the word has a number of rather different technical meanings in different fields. Recent years have seen the application of this concept to human brain functioning (Noppeney *et al.*, 2004; Edelman, 2006; Green *et al.*, 2006). Under normal circumstances, one route or means for performing a given brain function may predominate. However, if that route is damaged, function may be possible via the alternative route, albeit in a modified or less-efficient form. For example, it has been argued (Jang, 2009) that recovery of motor function following stroke may be achieved at least in part by an increased use of ipsilateral motor pathways. It is possible that apparently paradoxical rehabilitation interventions, such as preventing people from using their intact limbs to achieve everyday tasks ('constraint-induced therapy' – see Chapter 4), may help to develop such relatively latent pathways that are capable of supporting lost function.

(6) *Plasticity.* Plasticity is a ubiquitous feature of brain systems, including elementary visual processing (Wandell and Smirnakis, 2009). Plasticity underpins the brain's response to adverse lesion consequences. Plasticity endows the brain with a flexibility in learning and development, and it harnesses compensatory mechanisms when systems are damaged, stressed or subject to processes such as ageing. Plasticity itself can be seen as being related, in part, to the number and diversity of cognitive modules that an organism has available and to the brain's capacity to flexibly customize and reconfigure

neural networks relating to these modules (Mercado, 2008). However, plasticity is not a panacea for all adaptive brain function; plasticity is itself subject to the same optimization and selective pressures (at many scales) that shape all aspects of dynamics and connectivity in the brain. In this book, we have seen (Chapter 6) how neural plasticity in infants may result in enhanced perceptual functioning compared to more mature neural systems in older individuals. We have also seen how in the area of recovery of function after a brain insult plasticity may give rise to paradoxical phenomena (Chapter 20).

(7) *Homeostasis and stability.* Unstable entities are not around for very long. Most organisms that endure for a while, including ourselves, have internal mechanisms that correct for instability (homeostasis) and form part of a broader system (e.g. biosphere) which has stabilizing properties. Indeed, we could regard homeostasis as yet another example of optimization – optimizing the status quo. In the brain, homeostasis is relevant at a number of levels, including neurotransmitters and hormones. In terms of neural activity, homeostasis may operate both at a cellular and network level (Davis and Bezprozvanny, 2001; Marder and Goaillard, 2006; Maffei and Fontanini, 2009). We saw in Chapter 23 how many of the apparently paradoxical effects in stimulant neuropharmacology, when a given drug helps cognitive function in one person but hinders it in another, can be understood through homeostatic neurotransmitter system responses. At a very different level, it can be argued that some of the examples outlined in Chapter 5 are consistent with the idea that human rationality seeks a form of homeostasis in model(s) of the world and of itself. Information that is strongly discrepant with these models can be ignored (e.g. apparent unawareness of paralysis) or the models themselves can become bizarrely distorted to reduce aversive discrepancy (e.g. Cotard's Syndrome, when a person may conclude that he or she has died). When some brain abnormalities, acquired or developmental, result in maladaptive alterations in homeostasis, these may also lend themselves to seemingly paradoxical interventions such as intracranial or extracranial brain stimulation, as reviewed in Chapters 10 and 13.

(8) *Competitive dynamics.* Whilst a unifying feature of brain activity may be that it ultimately serves the survival goals of its phenotype/genotype, the mechanisms that produce those ends may be internally competitive. Influential accounts posit attention essentially as an adaptive competitive process in which the effects of goal-irrelevant information are dampened (see Chapter 4). The integration of this competition across sensory modalities and levels of processing may account for some surprising and paradoxical rehabilitation effects, e.g. why induced distortions in a patient's spatial systems may lead to improved perception and awareness (see Chapter 4). This view also promotes accounts of biased competition, that have in part been inspired by electrical recordings from the brain (Desimone, 1996). Rivalry between the two cerebral hemispheres has been linked to paradoxical lesion effects (Hilgetag *et al.*, 1999), such as improvements in function following a second lesion (see Chapter 3). Disruption to normal within-hemisphere competition has also been linked to paradoxical speeding of responses in patients with spatial neglect (Coulthard *et al.*, 2008). Similarly, competitive interactions between multiple neural sites may account for paradoxical effects in binocular rivalry (Tong *et al.*, 2006). In the domain of memory, there may be cases where more conscious 'declarative' learning unhelpfully competes/interferes with less conscious 'habit' learning and where distraction may then produce paradoxical

benefits (Foerde *et al.*, 2006). Competitive harmony helps to maintain a balance between influences which may achieve similar goals, but which do so by differing mechanisms (Poldrack and Packard, 2003; Martel *et al.*, 2007).

(9) *Nonlinearity.* Nonlinearity is the characteristic of systems like the brain that show great context-sensitivity and a fundamental indeterminacy in their dynamics; in other words, systems whose end states are not predictable, given their starting state (cf. Chen *et al.*, 2010; Liu *et al.*, 2010). The weather is nonlinear in that tiny differences in some initial parameter can, through the complexities of subsequent interactions, produce radically different outcomes that are apparently paradoxical from a linear perspective – 'The flapping of a single butterfly's wings today produces a tiny change in the state of the atmosphere. Over a period of time, what the atmosphere actually does diverges from what it would have done' (Stewart, 1997, p. 129). Evolution through natural selection is a nonlinear system par excellence in which the emergence of some feature through random mutation can have cascading unpredictable effects over subsequent generations on all players in the biosphere. Nonlinearity is a cornerstone of optimization and selection; if a given system always responded in exactly the same way to a given input, that system would be static, incapable of change. The brain, sometimes to its cost, is not like that! Nonlinearity is the basis for a number of the principles outlined here, for example, the self-organizing behaviours that such systems can display (see below), the inherent selection of stable configurations (see homeostasis) and itinerant dynamics, to which we now turn.

(10) *Itinerant dynamics.* Just as itinerant teachers travel from location to location, nonlinear systems may travel between distinct, relatively stable states. One benefit that arises from the generation of random but stable states is that it affords adaptive selection – those states which work best in the context of a given environment and in the context of the activity of other systems will tend to persist. Less-optimal or compatible states will not. As already discussed, this form of optimization has been argued to be relevant in evolution, in brain development, in long-term adaptive changes made by the brain to the environment, and in moment-to-moment alterations in neural function. Friston *et al.* (2006) consider this optimization in terms of free energy – a measure of adaptive fitness from statistical dynamics. Itinerancy (searching or wandering behaviour) allows the brain to explore different hypotheses and furnishes an essential source of variation, upon which selection can act, at a neuronal or evolutionary timescale. An important source of itinerancy is *self-organized criticality*. This is a property of complex biological systems (and some non-biological systems) that compels them to approach critical states in which things remain stable – but only just (De Arcangelis *et al.*, 2006). Self-organization is closely related to the notion of the edge of chaos and may be mandated in systems that aspire to stability and homeostasis, while at the same time exploring their options. Clearly, in this exploration, suboptimal options will be entertained and paradoxical behaviour is inevitable.

Stochastic features, that is a non-deterministic, random quality to the behaviour of a system, may be an important component in the optimization of function. Beneficial effects can sometimes accrue from the introduction of noise to a system (McDonnell and Abbott, 2009; MacDonald *et al.*, 2009; Rolls and Deco, 2010). In the case of paradoxical phenomena, the closest findings would appear to be those outlined in Chapter 4, where 'random noise' in the form of nonspecific alerting cues, may promote attention in certain cognitive task settings.

2. The paradoxical brain – implications for how we may enhance normal brain functioning

While many of the chapters in this book have dealt with brain abnormalities and their effects on the human condition, several authors have focused on cognitive function in healthy individuals. Thus, Dror (Chapter 9) has pointed to the interface between expertise and human error, and Roediger and Butler (Chapter 8) have discussed paradoxes in normal human memory. What are the implications of these chapters for the reduction of human error, and for the enhancement of cognitive functioning?

In some situations, it may help simply to have increased awareness of the fallibility of human reasoning, and of the 'certainty of uncertainty' in our knowledge of the world (Burton, 2008). Errors in cognitive functioning often consist of lapses in retrieval of knowledge from semantic memory, and failure to apply rules in particular settings due to internal factors (e.g. fatigue) or external factors (e.g. distracting environment). Simple strategies, such as the use of checklists, may be useful to minimize such errors (Gawande, 2010). In Chapter 8, Roediger and Butler have pointed to (sometimes counter-intuitive) variables that should enhance human memory in educational and other settings – e.g. increased use of retention test trials as a means to improve long-term memory consolidation.

Knowledge may sometimes be a handicap, as best exemplified in the 'curse of knowledge' effect, also discussed by Roediger and Butler. One simple example of this effect is leaving your front door unlocked overnight – you have that knowledge, but no-one passing by your home has that knowledge; yet you still do not sleep well because you fear someone may enter, even though the probability of this happening is extremely low. Attempts to limit the significance of such knowledge may therefore be beneficial in some settings. Language may also sometimes appear to interfere with efficient task performance, as suggested by some of the findings reviewed by Hughes (Chapter 19) in his review of enhanced cognitive functioning in non-human primates. In certain nonverbal settings that primarily tap perceptual-motor knowledge and skills, such as in airline cockpits, operating theatres and driving a car, it may be useful to monitor the use of language, especially where it seems to interfere with task performance. Explicit declaration of knowledge may interfere with expert performance (e.g. Flegal and Anderson, 2008): experts in certain domains, such as some sports or certain areas of medicine, may do best to occasionally follow their instincts/habits rather than try to comply with explicit (conscious) rules.

The remarkable plasticity of infants in the broad spectrum of their perceptual capacities, as discussed by Lewkowitz in Chapter 6, lends support to the value of exposing infants to several languages even at an early stage, since this may help to make it easier for them to learn these languages formally at a lager stage. Young infants might be said to 'absorb' language early, whereas in later years they have to 'learn' it (cf. Ojima et al., 2011). This is supported by evidence that different brain processes appear to be involved for early and late language acquisition (Isel et al., 2010).

Adjustment and well-being in healthy individuals is now a focus of a number of initiatives (Beddington et al., 2008). Perhaps we can learn from instances of 'post-traumatic growth' in patients with psychiatric disorders or neurological conditions (see Chapter 3), and perhaps we should more actively promote strategies used in cognitive behavioural therapy, such as 'cognitive reframing', to encourage healthy adjustment in the general population.

The clinical and experimental benefits of transcranial and direct current stimulation were reviewed by Pascual-Leone and his colleagues in Chapter 13. Recent studies

(Snyder, 2009; Gallate *et al.*, 2009) raise the prospect of transcranial magnetic stimulation being used to enhance creativity or reduce false memories in healthy individuals. However, this remains speculative, and the possibility of adverse side-effects in the short term and long term needs to be monitored carefully.

Amnestic agents, such as drugs with sedative effects, usually cause anterograde amnesia, but the paradoxical finding of retrograde facilitation when certain drugs are administered after a learning event (Reder *et al.*, 2007) raises the possibility that this may be one avenue for research in the area of cognitive enhancement. Such cognitive enhancement is relevant for situations such as student learning, and it will be important to discover whether the use of drugs to improve academic performance over the short term has any longer-term deleterious effects. If such cognitive enhancement is effective, then 'clean' students may be at a disadvantage, just like 'clean' athletes; these and other ethical issues will need to be addressed (Sahakian and Morein-Zamir, 2011).

3. The paradoxical brain – implications for prevention, detection and understanding of brain disease and brain disorder

Advances in environmental epidemiology, in particular for neurodegenerative conditions such as Parkinson's disease, may have implications for the prevention of such conditions (cf. Tanner, 2010). In certain conditions with a possible genetic predisposition, might some forms of prophylactic intervention be worth considering? Thus, following findings of a paradoxical relationship between smoking and Parkinson's disease reviewed by Schwartzbaum *et al.* in Chapter 14, individuals with a Parkin gene that predisposes to Parkinson's disease might benefit from benign forms of nicotine therapy, e.g. nicotine patches to help prevent or delay onset of the disease. However, it should be noted that this has not, as yet, helped those with established Parkinson's disease (Vieregge *et al.*, 2001).

In patients with Alzheimer's disease, there is some preliminary evidence that 'positive' interventions in the form of mental, social and physical stimulation may, in some cases, help to delay onset of the disease (Mowszowski *et al.*, 2010; Radak *et al.*, 2010), but definitive evidence has yet to be gathered. On the other hand, some individuals with reduced cognitive function may carry significant Alzheimer pathology which remains subclinical due to implicit or explicit compensatory strategies that is related to factors such as past cognitive activity – this may result in slower decline before dementia onset, but paradoxically faster decline thereafter (Wilson *et al.*, 2010). In this group of patients, more sensitive neuropsychological tests for the diagnosis of Alzheimer's disease may need to be developed to tease apart normal and abnormal memory decline (not least to inform patients and their carers about what they can expect over time). It remains uncertain whether individuals with a genetic predisposition to a neurological condition may be helped by immunotherapy, as seems to be a possibility in the case of Alzheimer's disease (Lemere and Masliah, 2010).

A number of neurological conditions, such as focal cortical dysplasia, are associated with abnormal cell migration (Guerrini and Parrini, 2010). With a better understanding of brain disease and brain disorder, it is possible we may find evidence that more subtle forms of abnormal or idiosyncratic cell migration (Métin *et al.*, 2008) play a part in at least some cases of neurodevelopmental disorders, such as autism spectrum syndrome (Wegiel *et al.*, 2010), as well as other conditions such as some types of epilepsy (Chang *et al.*, 2005). Similarly, the adult brain response to insults may sometimes include abnormalities of cell migration (Golan *et al.*, 2009; Huang, 2009). How such cell migration, if it were shown to be relevant, contributes to instances of paradoxical functional facilitation remains a matter of conjecture. Possible mechanisms might include the following.

- Greater cell concentration in certain parts of the brain, sometimes to the detriment of other parts, e.g. more cells in the parietal lobe and less in the frontal lobe (cf. Conacher, 1990).
- Similar levels of cell concentration, but distinctive and enhancing forms of cell organization within certain regions.
- Stronger pathways linking certain structures to the detriment of other pathway connections – e.g. dorsolateral frontal-to-parietal connections may be enhanced to the detriment of dorsolateral frontal-to-orbitofrontal connections (cf. Lee *et al.*, 2006; Jung and Haier, 2007).

It is intriguing to consider whether cases of creativity or genius in the healthy population might be governed by similar mechanisms to those seen in some forms of brain dysfunction. For example, there is the apparently unique structural features of the parietal lobe of Albert Einstein's brain (Witelson *et al.*, 1999; Falk, 2009). In addition, enhanced concentration of mini-columns has been reported in the brains of three outstanding scientists (Casanova *et al.*, 2007), a pattern that is associated with some features of autism, such as greatly focused attention. Brain imaging and post-mortem studies of such cases, and also cases of idiot savant syndrome, may yield clues to the neural mechanisms underlying superior cognitive functioning/individuals classified as 'genius'. Such studies may also shed light on whether observations relating to autistic brains, such as small neuronal cell size and increased cell packing density (Bauman and Kemper, 2005), generalize to other cases of idiosyncratic cognition and, if so, whether they have any significance.

4. The paradoxical brain – implications for repair of the damaged brain and the disordered brain

If, as seems evident from a number of the chapters in this book, brain disease and brain disorder result in a disturbance in neural synchrony, harmony or balance, then it would seem that interventions which help to reduce such disturbance may be worth exploring. It is for this reason that interventions such as selective tissue ablation, deep brain stimulation, transcranial magnetic stimulation and transcranial direct current stimulation may be worth exploring in both brain disease and brain disorder. In episodic brain disturbances, such as epilepsy, implantable brain stimulators which activate seconds, minutes or hours before the occurrence of clinical seizure activity may help prevent or minimize seizure occurrence (Jobst *et al.*, 2010).

There may of course be individual differences in response to these interventions, reflecting differences at a genetic level, at the level of past experience and 'cognitive reserve', etc., or reflecting a combination of such factors. The most effective use of stimulation technologies may incorporate a particular mix that also includes certain rehabilitation procedures or pharmacological interventions. The temporal features of such a 'mix' may be critical – whether one form of intervention occurs at the same time as the other or at a critical time before or after. As ever in recovery from brain impairments, motivation and compliance of individual patients is also important in such settings.

Chapter 21 noted that there seem to be, paradoxically, both adaptive and maladaptive forms of neurogenesis. Harnessing knowledge from neurogenesis and stem cell research to promote brain plasticity and brain recovery remains one of the major challenges in translational brain research. In the case of autologous cell transplantation, a preliminary clinical trial has shown the benefits of bone marrow-derived mesenchymal stromal cells in promoting recovery from brain injury (Zhang *et al.*, 2008). In the case of neurogenesis, some initial results are also encouraging (Xiong *et al.*, 2010; Im *et al.*, 2010). Similar paradoxes occur in initial immune and inflammatory responses to brain trauma, with these sometimes being protective and sometimes being harmful – a better understanding of the nature of these paradoxes may help in the formulation of effective treatments (Xiong *et al.*, 2009). Plasticity after a brain insult may also show paradoxical adaptive and maladaptive features, as outlined in Chapter 20, and a better understanding of such differences may similarly lead to novel treatment possibilities (Johnston, 2009).

We have known for generations that drugs may sometimes help and sometimes harm, but recent advances in neuropharmacology hold promise for translating specific paradoxical phenomena into treatments. The nonlinear, modulating effects of certain agents were found to occur across a range of compounds (Chapter 23), and this nonlinearity may relate not only to the dose level of the drug in question, but also to other factors such as the stage of the injury or illness when the drug is administered, concurrent drug or other interventions (cf. Myslobodsky, 2009), age of the patient, etc. A further possible application of paradoxical findings in neuropharmacology is in the use of amnestic agents shortly after an event, or at the time of re-consolidation, to reduce the likelihood of long-term post-traumatic stress disorder. As in many fields, more evidence clearly needs to be gathered, since some findings have been negative (McGhee *et al.*, 2009), and there are also ethical issues relating to this application (Donovan, 2009).

5. The paradoxical brain – implications for rehabilitation of the brain-damaged and brain-disordered person

An unanticipated paradox lies in the way in which some people with neurological impairment and brain damage respond to their impairment. Remembering his response to a severe, clinically complete cervical spinal cord injury which rendered him tetraplegic, one man said:

> You can't imagine how devastating this was when you've just turned 20. And that they can't do anything about it. Absolutely nothing. You cannot imagine the anger, the grief, and the devastation . . . I could not do anything. Even now 30 years later, I cannot come to terms with it. I never come to terms. I just had too much of a life, too much to live for that no amount of counselling or patronising could help. (Cole, 2004, p. 41)

In contrast, another man who became tetraplegic said:

> I didn't lie there thinking all the time 'Oh My God what have I done, what's this going to mean?' I never burst into tears because, from the early stages of living with the injury, I have seen the whole thing as a challenge. How do I overcome so and so? How do I deal with this? How do I come to terms with that? I never thought, 'I can't do that'. (Cole, 2004, p. 49)

These responses may reflect pre-existing disposition and personality, sociability, the effects of rehabilitation, as well as family and social support, etc. However, with time another phenomenon can occur. A man who, as the result of a spinal injury, had been tetraplegic and insentient from the shoulders down for two decades remarked:

> I can almost kid myself that I can feel something when I sit in a chair, even though I know I cannot. It feels exactly the same sitting in a chair now to before I was injured. It can't but it does. My mind tells me so. My mind makes me think I am like you over there. It learns what is the norm for this body. It tells me there is nothing wrong, so I feel comfortable and correct. (Cole, 2004, p. 276)

So well-adjusted to his new body and new way of living was the person that he was uncertain, if offered a cure, whether he would take it.

Researchers who have investigated patients' experience of Locked-in-Syndrome have found a significant number of patients who maintain a good quality of life and one which is often in the same range as age-matched healthy individuals (Lulé *et al.*, 2009). Similarly, in that study, depression was not predicted by the physical state of the patients. Rather, having a successful psychological adjustment to the disease was related to problem-oriented coping strategies, such as seeking information, and emotional coping strategies. The strongest predictor of psychosocial adjustment was, in turn, perceived social support. Interestingly, Lulé *et al.* (2009) also found evidence that significant others, like primary caregivers or spouses, rated Locked-in-Syndrome patients' quality of life significantly lower than the patients themselves rated their quality of life.

These examples echo the work of the German neurologist Kurt Goldstein, based on his observations on soldiers with brain injury after World War I (Goldstein, 1935). He described how some people have a capacity to actively adapt and adjust to catastrophic losses. He suggested that this involved, amongst other things, withdrawal to a more limited range of functioning and expectations which could in turn be managed by a redistribution of reduced energies, thus reclaiming as much wholeness and 'meaning' as their new circumstances allow. This often involved a transformation of identity and a willingness to accept change, to become 'all that one can become'. He described how, using this mental framework, success arose through a focus on residual strengths rather than on any negative consequences of pathology.

The emerging fields of 'positive neurology' and 'positive neuropsychology' in the rehabilitation of the brain-damaged individual draw on similar ideas. These fields suggest that we concentrate on intact skills, on past strengths and interests, and on how both rehabilitation efforts and domestic, social and work environments can be modified to take these skills and talents into account. Such an approach can learn from neurodevelopmental disorders, such as the autism spectrum syndrome, where enhanced abilities can sometimes result in talent (see Chapter 15). The work on post-traumatic growth that was briefly reviewed in Chapter 3 also points to an approach that regards an acute adverse event as, in part, a form of learning experience, one from which the individual has the potential to become stronger in terms of mental attitude and ability to cope with stress. Why some patients are able to adapt better than others, and how best to help each person remains uncertain, but what is clear is that these approaches are tailored to individuals' needs and abilities and that they place the patient in their social setting rather than in a purely clinical one.

In addition to the brain stimulation procedures that were discussed above, other more general stimulation approaches, such as caloric stimulation, music and non-specific arousal, hold promise as adjuvant therapies to more standard rehabilitation interventions. These were discussed in Chapter 4, which also pointed to the potential value of constraint-induced therapy, and its possible extension to cognitive domains (cf. Kirmess and Maher, 2010). There will clearly be boundary factors and other issues to be aware of in these novel therapeutic approaches. That chapter also pointed to situations where illusions may be helpful in therapeutic settings, with benefits emerging in conditions such as phantom limb pain. These tie in with the broad message emerging from Chapter 5 that illusions can sometimes be adaptive, and that we may in fact sometimes be applying nature's remedies, but in a more formal clinical setting.

6. Conclusions

Lilienfeld and O'Donohue (2007) identified five criteria for ideas making major contributions in the psychological sciences, criteria which appear relevant to other disciplines such as neuroscience. These criteria are: the ideas should (i) influence our perception of human nature; (ii) have an applied impact; (iii) stimulate research; (iv) stand the test of time; and (v) promote consilience across diverse domains of knowledge. We hope that the pursuit of paradoxical phenomena of the type described in the chapters of this book meets at least some of these criteria. Moreover, we hope that by looking at apparently paradoxical phenomena we can understand brain function and dysfunction better. The challenges offered by paradoxical phenomena may encourage novel conceptual frameworks that may, in turn, guide innovative empirical studies and innovative therapeutic interventions. As alluded to in the Introduction, we hope that some of the observations in this book will help to usher in new fields of inquiry that subsume 'positive neurology' and 'positive neuropsychology', and encourage researchers and clinicians to view neurological differences not solely in terms of pathology, but also sometimes as other ways of living.

We would like to end with a quote from one of the great neurologists of the twentieth century, who effectively created the field of behavioural neurology, the Harvard neurologist Norman Geschwind (1926–1984). In a thought-provoking lecture which he delivered a couple of years before his tragic, early death, he described a number of paradoxes, including talent in dyslexia:

> One of the most important lessons to be learned from the genetic study of many diseases in recent years has been that the paradoxically high frequency of certain conditions is explained by the fact that the important advantages conferred on those who carry the predisposition to these conditions may outweigh the obvious dramatic disadvantages. (Geschwind, 1982, p. 20)

References

Barabasi, A-L. (2007). Network medicine – from obesity to the 'diseasome'. *New England Journal of Medicine*, 357: 404–07.

Barabasi, A-L. (2009). Scale-free networks: a decade and beyond. *Science*, 325: 412–3.

Bauman, M., & Kemper, T. (2005). Neuroanatomic observations of the brain in autism: a review and future directions. *International Journal of Developmental Neuroscience*, 23: 183–7.

Beck, D., & Kastner, S. (2009). Top-down and bottom-up mechanisms in biasing competition in the human brain. *Vision Research*, 49: 1154–65.

Beddington, J., Cooper, C., Field, J., et al. (2008). The mental wealth of nations. *Nature*, 455: 1057–60.

Botvinick, M. M. (2008). Hierarchical models of behavior and prefrontal function. *Trends in Cognitive Sciences*, 12: 201–08.

Briggman, K. L., & Kristan, W. B. (2008). Multifunctional pattern-generating circuits. *Annual Review of Neuroscience*, **31**: 271–94.

Bullmore, E., Barnes, A., Bassett, D. S., *et al.* (2009). Generic aspects of complexity in brain imaging data and other biological systems. *NeuroImage*, **47**: 1125–34.

Burton, R. (2008). *On Being Certain*. New York, NY: St Martin's Press.

Casanova, M. F., Switala, A. E., Trippe, J., & Fitzgerald, M. (2007). Comparative minicolumnar morphometry of three distinguished scientists. *Autism*, **11**: 557–69.

Chang, B. S., Ly, J., Appignani, B., *et al.* (2005). Reading impairment in the neuronal migration disorder of periventricular nodular heterotopia. *Neurology*, **64**: 799–803.

Chen, C., Kilner, J., Friston, K., Kiebel, S., Jolly, R., & Ward, N. (2010). Nonlinear coupling in the human motor system. *Journal of Neuroscience*, **30**: 8393–9.

Chittka, L., & Niven, J. (2009). Are bigger brains better? *Current Biology*, **19**: R995–1008.

Cole, J. (2004). *Still Lives*. London and Cambridge, MA: The MIT Press.

Conacher, G. N. (1990). Childhood autism as a disturbance of neuronal migration. *Psychiatric Bulletin*, **14**: 744.

Coulthard, E., Nachev, P., & Husain, M. (2008). Control over conflict during movement preparation: role of posterior parietal cortex. *Neuron*, **58**: 144–57.

Dauwels, J., Eskandar, E., & Cash, S. (2009). Localisation of seizure onset area from intracranial non-seizure EEG by exploiting locally enhanced synchrony. *Conference Proceedings IEEE Engineering in Medicine and Biology Society*, 2180–3.

Davis, G. W., & Bezprozvanny, I. (2001). Maintaining the stability of neural function: a homeostatic hypothesis. *Annual Review of Physiology*, **63**: 847–69.

De Arcangelis, L., Perrone-Capano, C., & Herrmann, H. (2006). Self-organized criticality model for brain plasticity. *Physics Review Letters*, **96**: 1–4.

Desimone, R. (1996). Neural mechanisms for visual memory and their role in attention. *Proceedings of the National Academy of Sciences*, **93**: 13,494–9.

Donovan, E. (2009). Propranolol use in the prevention and treatment of post-traumatic stress disorder in military veterans: forgetting therapy revisited. *Perspectives in Biology and Medicine*, **53**: 61–74.

Edelman, G. (2006). *Second Nature. Brain Science and Human Knowledge*. New Haven, CT: Yale University Press.

Edelman, G., & Gally, J. (2001). Degeneracy and complexity in biological systems. *Proceedings of the National Academy of Sciences*, **98**: 13,763–8.

Falk, D. (2009). New information about Albert Einstein's brain. *Frontiers in Evolutionary Neuroscience*, **1**: 1–6.

Finger, S. (2009). Recovery of function. Redundancy and vicariation theories. *Handbook of Clinical Neurology*, **95**: 833–41.

Flegal, K., & Anderson, M. (2008). Overthinking skilled motor performance: or why those who teach can't do. *Psychonomic Bulletin and Review*, **15**: 927–32.

Foerde, K., Knowlton, B., & Poldrack, R. (2006). Modulation of competing memory systems by distraction. *Proceedings of the National Academy of Sciences*, **103**: 11,778–83.

Friston, K. (2008). Hierarchical models in the brain. *PLoS Computational Biology*, **4**: e1000211, 1–24.

Friston, K., Kilner, J., & Harrison, L. (2006). A free energy principle for the brain. *Journal of Physiology Paris*, **100**: 70–87.

Gallate, J., Chi, R., Ellwood, S., & Snyder, A. (2009). Reducing false memories by magnetic pulse stimulation. *Neuroscience Letters*, **449**: 151–4.

Gawande, A. (2010). *The Checklist Manifesto: How to get things right*. New York, NY: Profile Books.

George, D., & Hawkins, J. (2009). Towards a mathematical theory of cortical micro-circuits. *PLOS Computational Biology*, **5**: 1–26.

Geschwind, N. (1982). Why Orton was right. *Annals of Dyslexia*, **32**: 13–30.

Golan, M. H., Mane, R., Molczadzki, G., *et al.* (2009). Impaired migration signalling in the hippocampus following prenatal hypoxia. *Neuropharmacology*, **57**: 511–22.

Goldstein, K. (1935). *The Organism.* Cambridge, MA and London: The MIT Press. [Republished in 1995.]

Green, D., Crinion, J., & Price, C. (2006). Convergence, degeneracy and control. *Language and Learning,* **56**: 99–125.

Gregoriou, G. G., Gotts, S. J., Zhou, H., & Desimone, R. (2009). High-frequency, long-range coupling between prefrontal and visual cortex during attention. *Science,* **324**: 1207–10.

Gregory, R. L. (1980). Perceptions as hypotheses. *Philosophical Transactions of the Royal Society London B,* **290**: 181–97.

Guerrini, R., & Parrini, E. (2010). Neuronal migration disorders. *Neurobiological Disorders,* **38**: 154–66.

de Haan, W., Pijnenburg, Y. A., Strijers, R. L., *et al.* (2009). Functional neural network analysis in frontotemporal dementia and Alzheimer's disease using EEG and graph theory. *BMC Neuroscience,* **10**: 101 (pp. 1–12).

Halligan, P., & Marshall, J. (1994). Focal and global attention modulate the expression of visuo-spatial neglect: a case study. *Neuropsychologia,* **32**: 13–21.

Helmholtz, H. von, (1866). Concerning the perceptions in general. In: *Treatise on Physiological Optics,* volume **III**, 3rd edition (translated by J. P. C. Southall, 1925, Opt. Soc. Am. Section 26, reprinted New York, NY: Dover, 1962).

Herculano-Houzel, S. (2009). The human brain in numbers: a linearly scaled-up primate brain. *Frontiers in Human Neuroscience,* **3**: 1–11.

Hilgetag, C., Kötter, R., & Young, M. (1999). Inter-hemispheric competition of sub-cortical structures is a crucial mechanism in paradoxical lesion effects and spatial neglect. *Progress in Brain Research,* **121**: 121–41.

Huang, Z. (2009). Molecular regulation of neuronal migration during neocortical development. *Molecular and Cellular Neuroscience,* **42**: 11–22.

Im, S., Yu, J., Park, E., *et al.* (2010). Induction of striatal neurogenesis enhances functional recovery in an adult animal model of neonatal hypoxic–ischemic brain injury. *Neuroscience,* **169**: 259–68.

Isel, F., Baumgaertner, A., Thrän, J., Miesel, J., & Büchel, C. (2010). Neural circuitry of the bilingual mental lexicon: effect of age of second language acquisition. *Brain and Cognition,* **72**: 169–80.

Jang, S. (2009). A review of the ipsilateral motor pathway as a recovery mechanism in patients with stroke. *NeuroRehabilitation,* **24**: 315–20.

Jobst, B., Darcey, T., Thadani, V., & Roberts, D. (2010). Brain stimulation for the treatment of epilepsy. *Epilepsia,* **51**: 88–92.

Johnston, M. V. (2009). Plasticity in the developing brain: implications for rehabilitation. *Developmental Disabilities Research Reviews,* **15**: 94–101.

Jung, R. E., & Haier, R. J. (2007). The parieto-frontal integration theory (P-FIT) of intelligence: converging neuroimaging evidence. *Behavioural and Brain Sciences,* **30**: 135–54.

Kaiser, M., Martin, R., Andras, P., & Young, M. P. (2007). Simulation of robustness against lesions of cortical networks. *European Journal of Neuroscience,* **25**: 3185–92.

Kirmess, M., & Maher, L. (2010). Constraint induced language therapy in early aphasia rehabilitation. *Aphasiology,* **24**: 725–36.

Krubitzer, L. (2007). The magnificent compromise: cortical field evolution in mammals. *Neuron,* **56**: 201–08.

Lee, K. H., Choi, Y. Y., Gray, J. R., *et al.* (2006). Neural correlates of superior intelligence: stronger recruitment of posterior parietal cortex. *Neuroimage,* **29**: 578–86.

Lemere, C., & Masliah, E. (2010). Can Alzheimer disease be prevented by amyloid-β immunotherapy? *Nature Reviews Neurology,* **6**: 109–19.

Lilienfeld, S., & O'Donohue, W. (2007). What are the great ideas of clinical science and why do we need them? In: Lilienfeld, S., & O'Donohue, W. (Eds.). *The Great Ideas of Clinical Science.* New York, NY: Routledge.

Liu, Z., Rios, C., Zhang, N., Yang, L., Chen, W., & He, B. (2010). Linear and nonlinear relationships between visual stimuli, EEG and BOLD fMRI signals. *Neuroimage*, **50**: 1054–66.

Lulé, D., Zickler, C., Häcker, S., *et al.* (2009). Life can be worth living in locked-in syndrome. *Progress in Brain Research*, **177**: 339–51.

MacDonald, S., Li, S., & Bäckman, L. (2009). Neural underpinnings of within-person variability in cognitive functioning. *Psychology and Aging*, **24**: 792–808.

Maffei, A., & Fontanini, A. (2009). Network homeostasis: a matter of coordination. *Current Opinion in Neurobiology*, **19**: 168–73.

Marder, E., & Goaillard, J. M. (2006). Variability, compensation and homeostasis in neuron and network function. *Nature Reviews Neuroscience*, **7**: 563–74.

Martel, G., Blanchard, J., Mons, N., Gastambide, F., Micheau, J., & Guillou, J. L. (2007). Dynamic interplays between memory systems depend on practice: the hippocampus is not always the first to provide solution. *Neuroscience*, **50**: 743–53.

McDonnell, M., & Abbott, D. (2009). What is stochastic resonance. Definitions, misconceptions, debates, and its relevance to biology. *PLoS Computational Biology*, **5**: epub May 29, 2009.

McGhee, L., Maani, C., Garza, T., Desocio, P., Gaylord, K., & Black, I. (2009). The effect of propanalol on post-traumatic stress disorder in burned service members. *Journal of Burn Care and Research*, **30**: 92–7.

Mercado, E. (2008). Neural and cognitive plasticity: from maps to minds. *Psychological Bulletin*, **134**: 109–37.

Métin, C., Vallee, R. B., Rakic, P., & Bhide, P. G. (2008). Modes and mishaps of neuronal migration in the mammalian brain. *The Journal of Neuroscience*, **28**: 11,746–52.

Mowszowski, L., Batchelor, J., & Naismith, S. (2010). Early intervention for cognitive decline: can cognitive training be used as a selective prevention technique? *International Psychogeriatrics*, **22**: 1–12.

Mumford, D. (1992). On the computational architecture of the neocortex. II. The role of cortico-cortical loops. *Biological Cybernetics*, **66**: 241–51.

Myslobodsky, M. (2009). The paradox of caffeine–zolpidem interaction: a network analysis. *Current Drug Targets*, **10**: 1009–20.

Noppeney, U., Friston, K., & Price, C. (2004). Degenerate neuronal systems sustaining cognitive functions. *Journal of Anatomy*, **205**: 433–42.

Ojima, S., Nakamura, N., Matsuba-Kurita, H., Hoshino, T., & Hagiwara, H. (2011). Neural correlates of foreign-language learning in childhood: a 3-year longitudinal ERP study. *Journal of Cognitive Neuroscience*, **23**: 183–99.

Poldrack, R. A., & Packard, M. G. (2003). Competition amongst multiple memory systems: converging evidence from animal and human brain studies. *Neuropsychologia*, **41**: 245–51.

Pribram, K. (1971). *Languages of the Brain: Experimental Paradoxes and Principles in Neuropsychology*. New York, NY: Prentice-Hall.

Radak, Z., Hart, N., Sarga, L., *et al.* (2010). Exercise plays a preventive role against Alzheimer's Disease. *Journal of Alzheimer's Disease*, Feb 24 (Epub ahead of print).

Reder, L. M., Oates, J. M., Dickison, D., *et al.* (2007). Retrograde facilitation under midazolam: the role of general and specific interference. *Psychonomic Bulletin and Review*, **14**: 261–9.

Rolls, E., & Deco, G. (2010). *The Noisy Brain. Stochastic Dynamics as a Principle of Brain Function*. Oxford: Oxford University Press.

Sahakian, B., & Morein-Zamir, S. (2011). Neuroethical issues in cognitive enhancement. *Journal of Psychopharmacology*, **25**: 197–204.

Snyder, A. (2009). Explaining and inducing savant skills: privileged access to lower-level, less processed information. *Philosophical Transactions of the Royal Society of London B, Biological Sciences*, **364**: 1399–405.

Stewart, I. (1997). *Does God Play Dice? The New Mathematics of Chaos*. Second Edition. London: Penguin.

Tanner, C. (2010). Advances in environmental epidemiology. *Movement Disorders*, **25**: S58–62.

Tong, M., Meng, M., & Blake, R. (2006). Neural bases of binocular rivalry. *Trends in Cognitive Sciences*, **10**: 502–11.

Uhlhaas, P., Pipa, G., Lima, B., *et al.* (2009). Neuronal synchrony in cortical networks: history, concept and current status. *Frontiers in Integrative Neuroscience*, **3**: 1–19.

Varga, V., Losonczy, A., Zemelman, B. V., *et al.* (2009). Fast synaptic subcortical control of hippocampal circuits. *Science*, **326**: 449–53.

Vieregge, A., Sieberer, M., Jacobs, H., Hagenah, J., & Vieregge, P. (2001). Transdermal nicotine in PD: a randomized, double-blind, placebo-controlled study. *Neurology*, **57**: 1032–5.

Wandell, B., & Smirnakis, S. (2009). Plasticity and stability of visual field maps in adult primary visual cortex. *Nature Reviews Neuroscience*, **10**: 873–84.

Wegiel, J., Kuchna, I., Nowicki, K., *et al.* (2010). The neuropathology of autism: defects of neurogenesis and neuronal migration, and dysplastic changes. *Acta Neuropathologica* [epub ahead of print].

Wilson, R., Barnes, L., Aggarwal, N., *et al.* (2010). Cognitive activity and the cognitive morbidity of Alzheimer disease. *Neurology*, **75**: 990–6.

Witelson, S. F., Kigar, D. L., & Harvey, T. (1999). The exceptional brain of Albert Einstein. *Lancet*, **353**: 2149–53.

Xiong, Y., Mahmood, A., & Chopp, M. (2009). Emerging treatments for traumatic brain injury. *Expert Opinion on Emerging Drugs*, **14**: 67–84.

Xiong, Y., Mahmood, A., & Chopp, M. (2010). Angiogenesis, neurogenesis and brain recovery of function following injury. *Current Opinion in Investigational Drugs*, **11**: 298–308.

Young, M. P., Hilgetag, C., & Scannell, J. (1999). Models of paradoxical lesion effects and rules of inference for inputing function to structure in the brain. *Neurocomputing*, **26–27**: 933–8.

Young, M. P., Hilgetag, C. C., & Scannell, J. W. (2000). On imputing function to structure from the behavioural effects of brain lesions. *Philosophical Transactions of the Royal Society B, Biological Sciences*, **355**: 147–61.

Zhang, D., & Raichle, M. (2010). Disease and the brain's dark energy. *Nature Reviews Neurology*, **6**: 15–28.

Zhang, Z. X., Guan, L. X., Zhang, K., Zhang, Q., & Dai, L. J. (2008). A combined procedure to deliver autologous mesenchymal stromal cells to patients with traumatic brain injury. *Cytotherapy*, **10**: 134–9.

Zufall, F. (2005). Connexins and olfactory synchronicity: toward the olfactory code. *Neuron*, **46**: 693–4.

Index